Maid-sama!

Volumes 3-4

CONTENTS

WELCOME BACK, MASTER!

Allow me to introduce the characters from the last volume. ♥

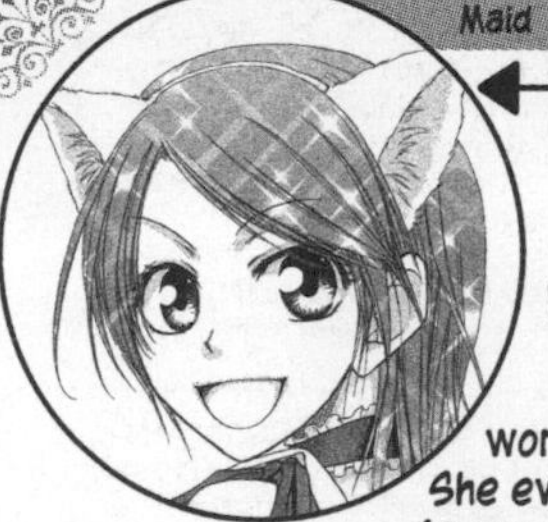

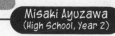

Maid

Misaki Ayuzawa
(High School, Year 2)

Student Council President

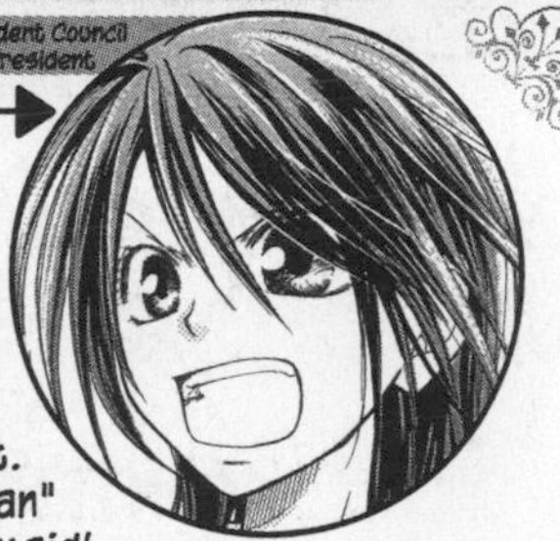

Misaki is the tough-as-nails student council president, but after school she works part time at a maid café! She's a hard worker and excellent student. She even knows aikido! "Misa-chan" is our coolest, most intellectual maid!

Takumi Usui
(High School, Year 2)

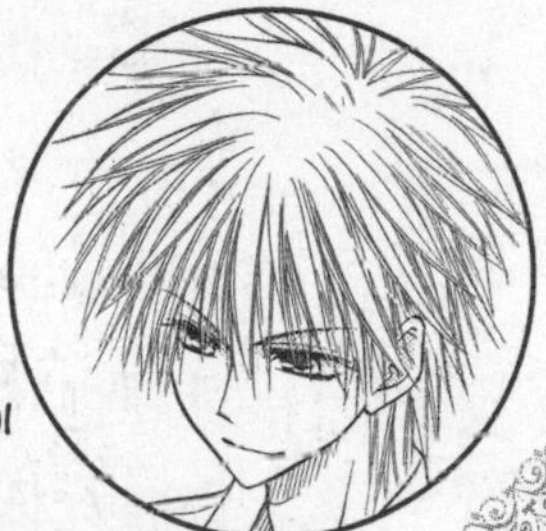

The most popular boy at school. He learns about Misaki's secret job by accident and becomes intrigued, so he starts following her around. To most girls he's the perfect guy: he has top grades, is great at sports, is handsome and is a good fighter! But to Misaki, he's that awful boy who harasses her. He's recently become a regular at Café Maid Latte.

Seika High School

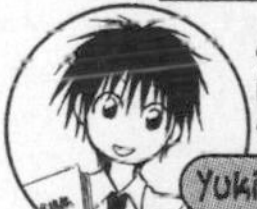

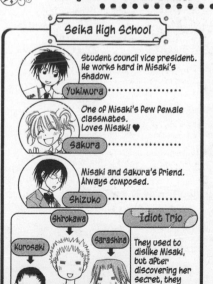

Student council vice president. He works hard in Misaki's shadow.

Yukimura

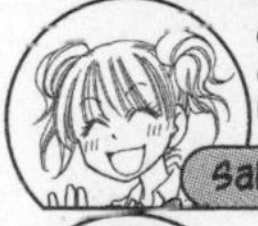

One of Misaki's few female classmates. Loves Misaki! ♥

Sakura

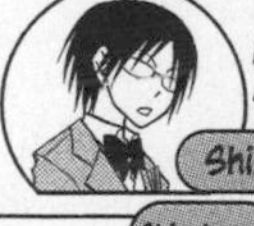

Misaki and Sakura's friend. Always composed.

Shizuko

Idiot Trio

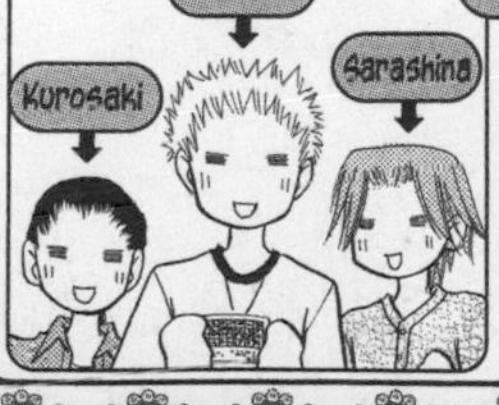
Shirokawa
Kurosaki
Sarashina

They used to dislike Misaki, but after discovering her secret, they became huge fans!

Café Maid Latte

This is where Misaki works part time. We're all just waiting for our master to arrive! ♥

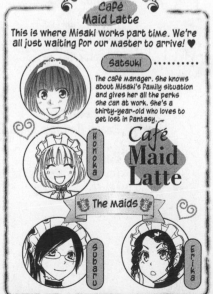

Satsuki

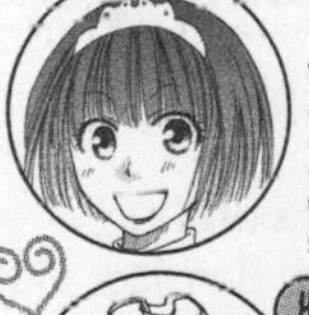

The café manager. She knows about Misaki's family situation and gives her all the perks she can at work. She's a thirty-year-old who loves to get lost in fantasy...

Café Maid Latte

The Maids

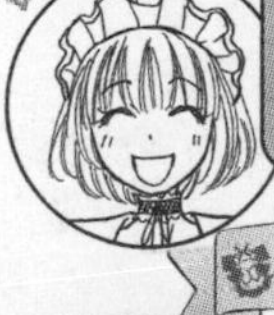

Honoka

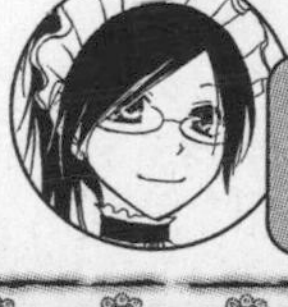

Subaru

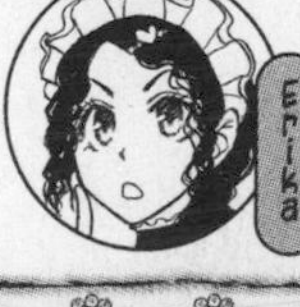

Erika

Allow me to refresh your memory on what happened last time. ♥

Misaki is the student council president of Seika High School, once an all-boys school. She spends her days fighting to protect the girls and discourage the boys' outrageous behavior. But Misaki has a secret: she works at a maid café! When her secret is discovered by Usui, the most popular boy in school, he starts following her around. Her double life as a student council president and maid is full of drama! ♥

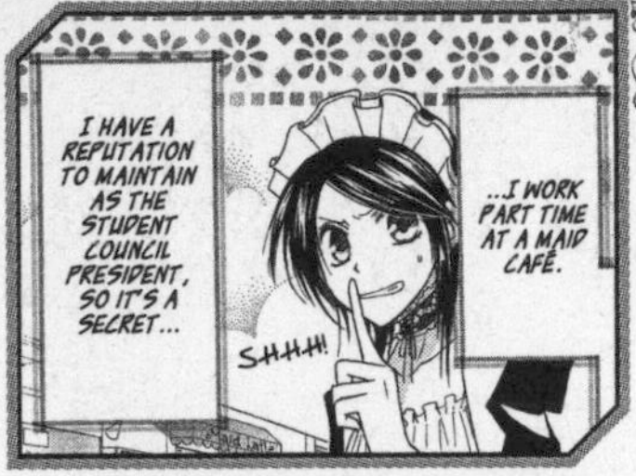
...I WORK PART TIME AT A MAID CAFÉ.
I HAVE A REPUTATION TO MAINTAIN AS THE STUDENT COUNCIL PRESIDENT, SO IT'S A SECRET...
SHHH!

Things get much worse when Tora Igarashi, the conceited student council president at Miyabigaoka—an elite private school—also learns Misaki's secret!

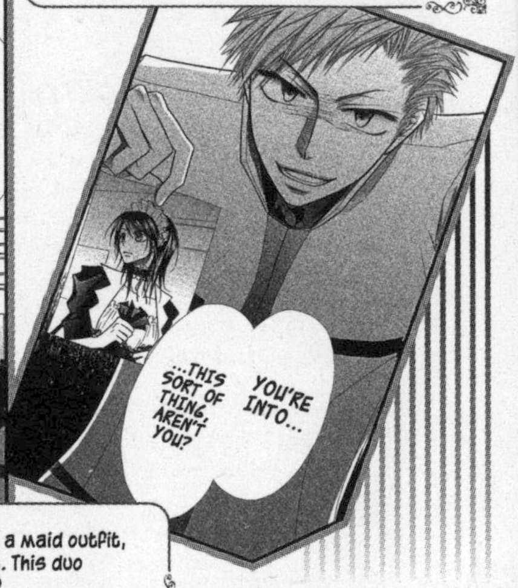
YOU'RE INTO...
...THIS SORT OF THING, AREN'T YOU?

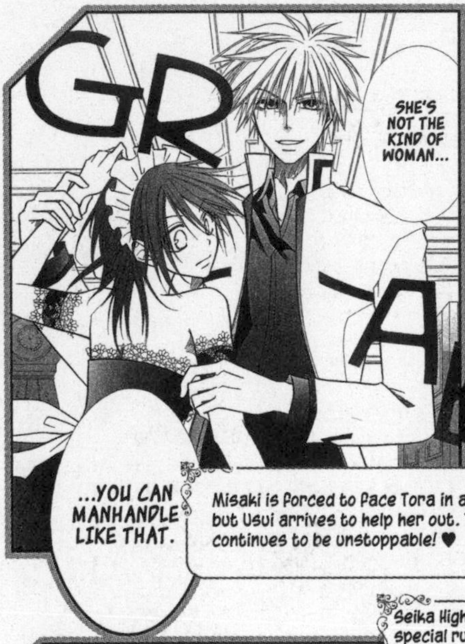
GR
A
SHE'S NOT THE KIND OF WOMAN...
...YOU CAN MANHANDLE LIKE THAT.

Misaki is forced to face Tora in a maid outfit, but Usui arrives to help her out. This duo continues to be unstoppable! ♥

Seika High School's sports festival kicks off! It has one special rule: the winner of each event will receive an extra prize! Misaki works hard to win every event and protect the female students, and Usui competes to protect (?) Misaki. The first half of the festival wraps up!

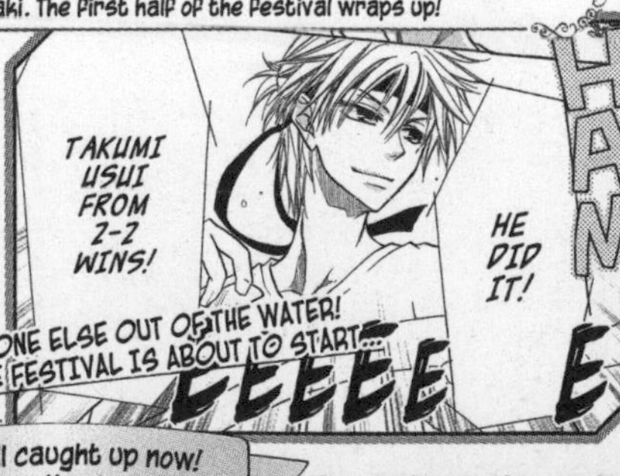
HAM
E
EEEEE
HE DID IT!
TAKUMI USUI FROM 2-2 WINS!

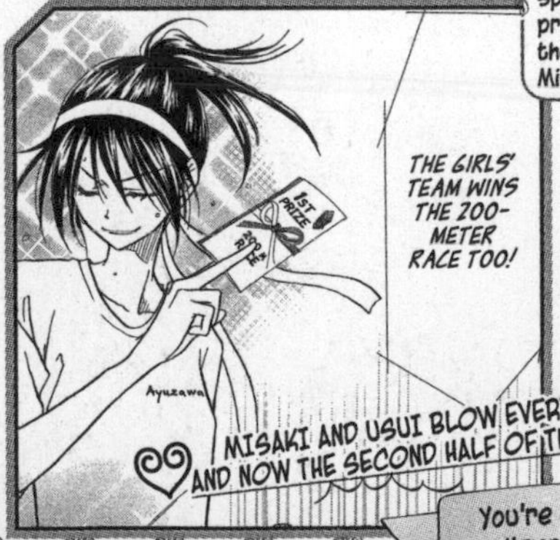
THE GIRLS' TEAM WINS THE 200-METER RACE TOO!
1ST PRIZE
Ayuzawa

MISAKI AND USUI BLOW EVERYONE ELSE OUT OF THE WATER! AND NOW THE SECOND HALF OF THE FESTIVAL IS ABOUT TO START...

You're all caught up now! Have fun, Master! ♥

Shojo Beat

Maid-sama!

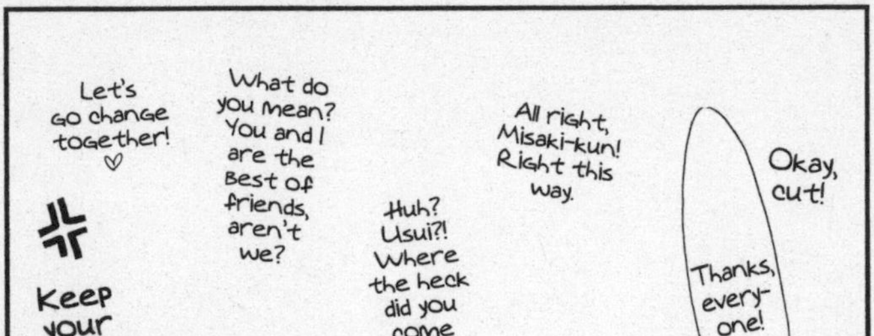
Okay, cut!
Thanks, everyone!
Break it down.
We finally did it! We're gonna be on the cover!
All right, Misaki-kun! Right this way.
Huh? Usui?! Where the heck did you come from?
What do you mean? You and I are the best of friends, aren't we?
Let's go change together!
Keep your paws to yourself, you pervert!!!

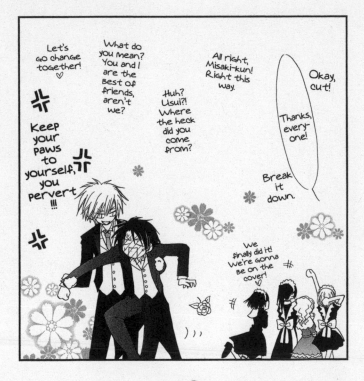

Vol. 3

Story & Art by

Hiro Fujiwara

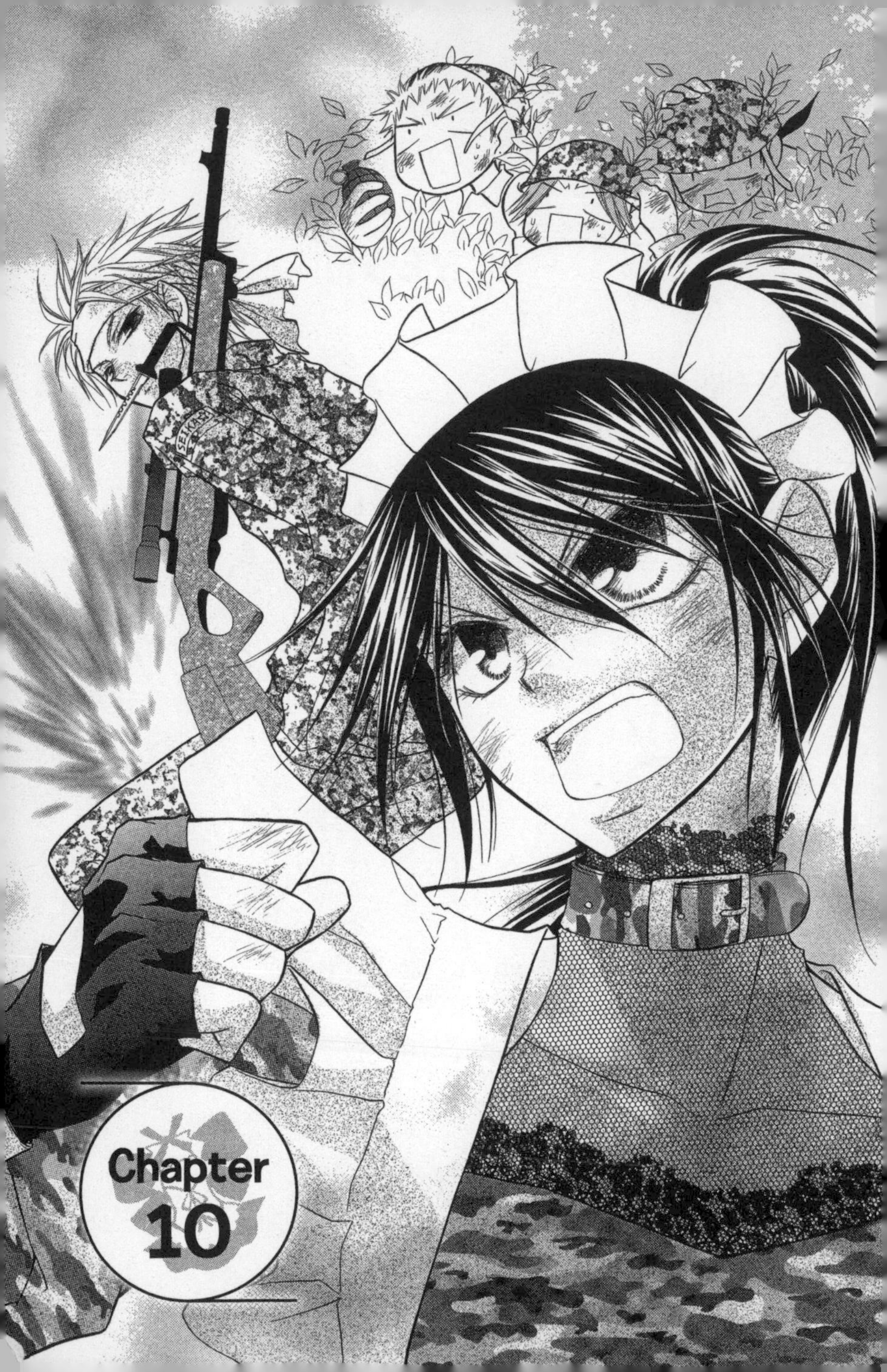
Chapter
10

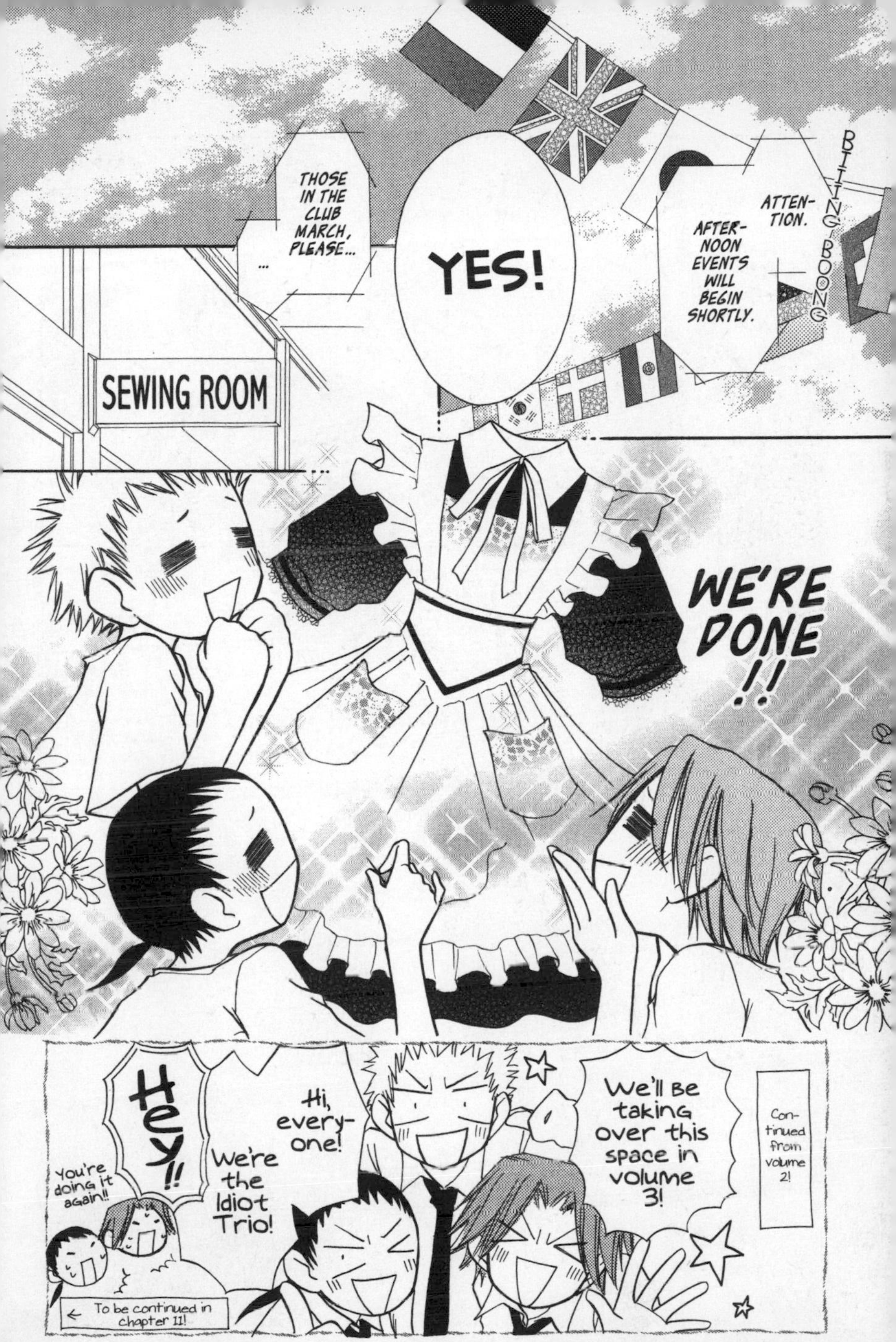
BIIING-BOONG
ATTEN-TION.
AFTER-NOON EVENTS WILL BEGIN SHORTLY.
YES!
THOSE IN THE CLUB MARCH, PLEASE...
...
SEWING ROOM
WE'RE DONE!!
Con-tinued from volume 2!
We'll be taking over this space in volume 3!
Hi, every-one!
We're the Idiot Trio!
Hey!!
You're doing it again!!
To be continued in chapter 11!

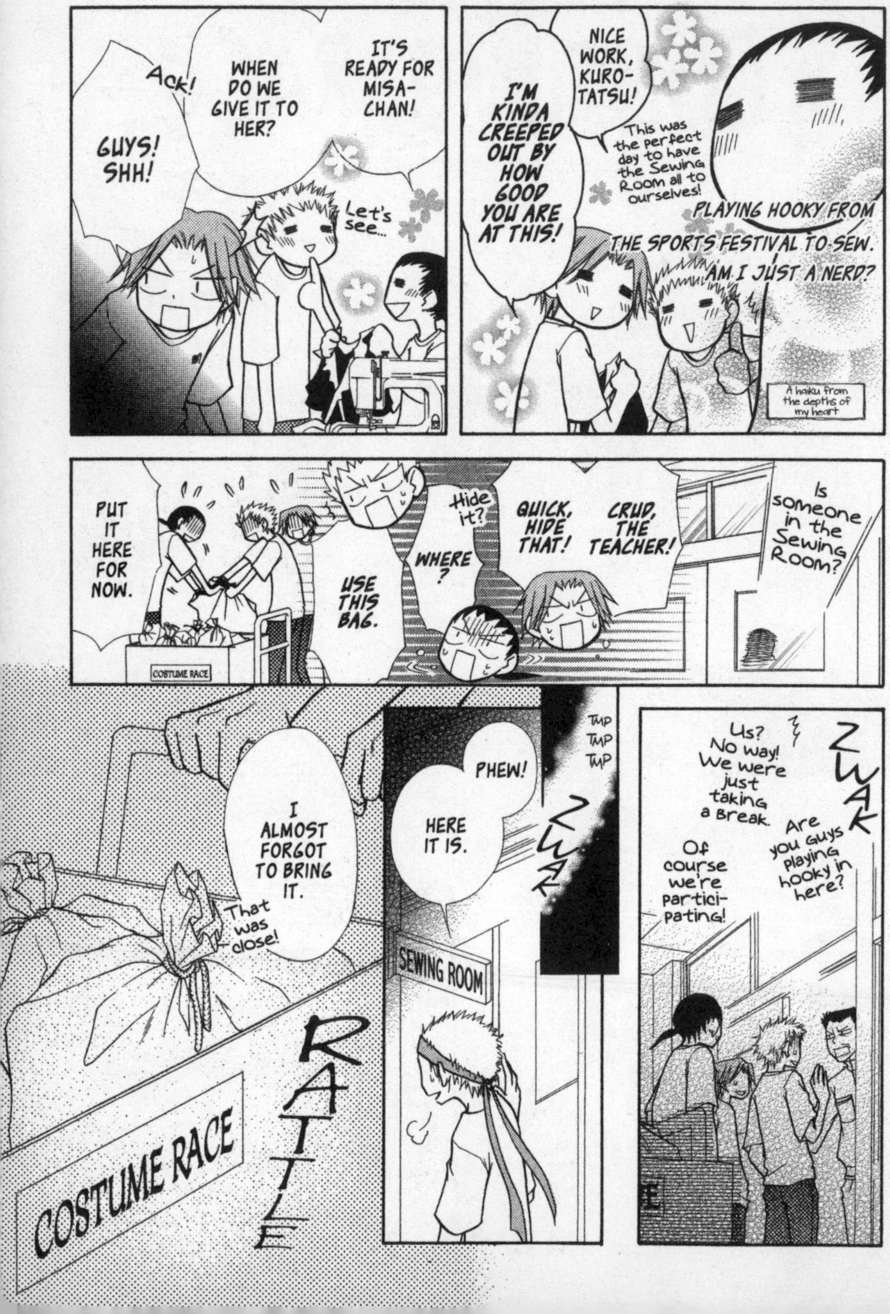
NICE WORK, KURO-TATSU!
This was the perfect day to have the Sewing Room all to ourselves!
I'M KINDA CREEPED OUT BY HOW GOOD YOU ARE AT THIS!
PLAYING HOOKY FROM THE SPORTS FESTIVAL TO SEW. AM I JUST A NERD?
A haiku from the depths of my heart
IT'S READY FOR MISA-CHAN!
WHEN DO WE GIVE IT TO HER?
Ack!
Let's see...
GUYS! SHH!
Is someone in the Sewing Room?
CRUD, THE TEACHER!
QUICK, HIDE THAT!
Hide it?
WHERE?
USE THIS BAG.
PUT IT HERE FOR NOW.
COSTUME RACE
ZWAK
Us? No way! We were just taking a break.
Are you guys playing hooky in here?
Of course we're partici-pating!
TMP TMP TMP
ZWAK
PHEW!
HERE IT IS.
SEWING ROOM
I ALMOST FORGOT TO BRING IT.
That was close!
RATTLE
COSTUME RACE

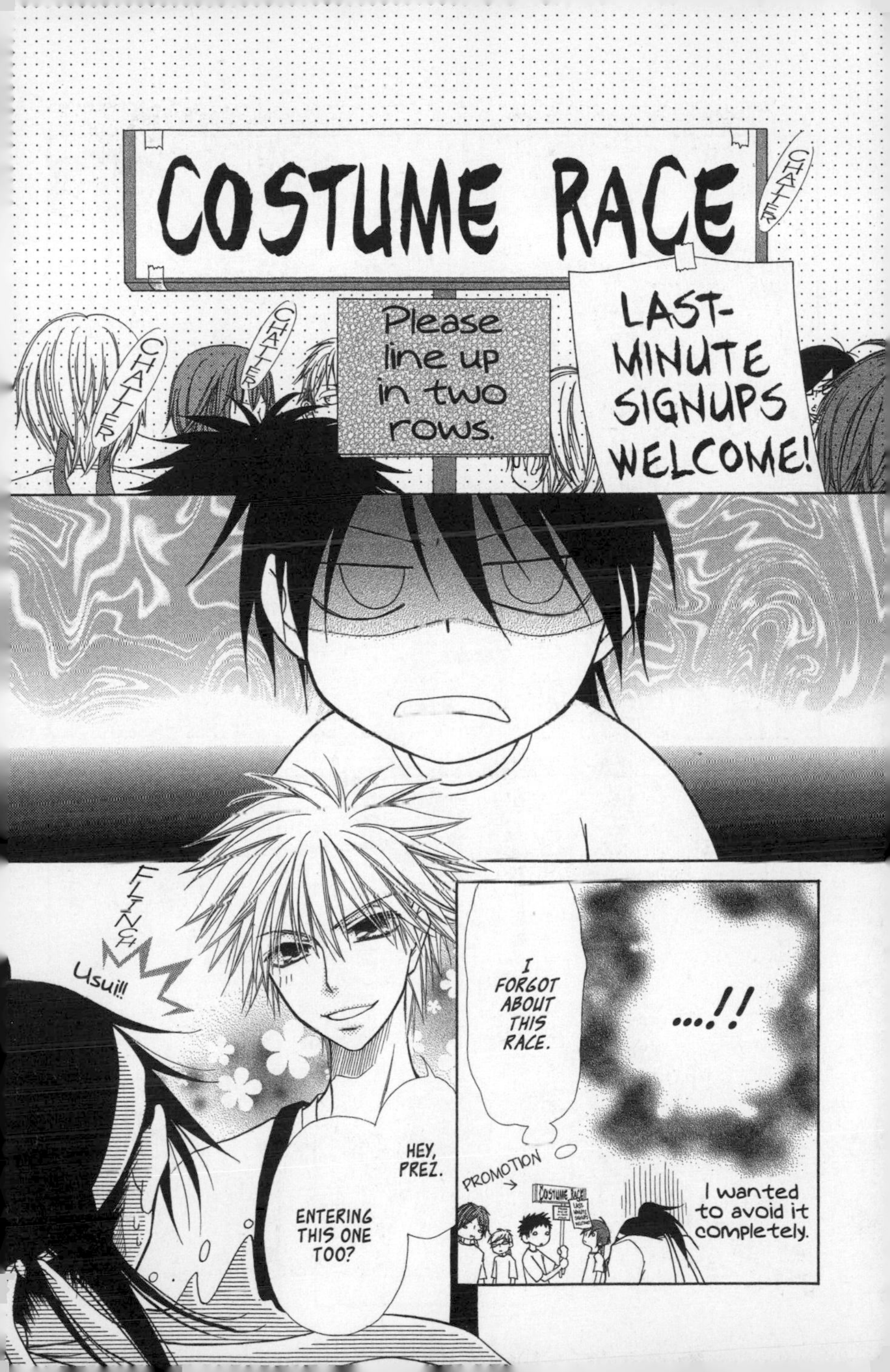
CHATTER
COSTUME RACE
LAST-MINUTE SIGNUPS WELCOME!
Please line up in two rows.
CHATTER
CHATTER
I FORGOT ABOUT THIS RACE.
...!!
PROMOTION →
I wanted to avoid it completely.
FLING
Usui!!
HEY, PREZ.
ENTERING THIS ONE TOO?

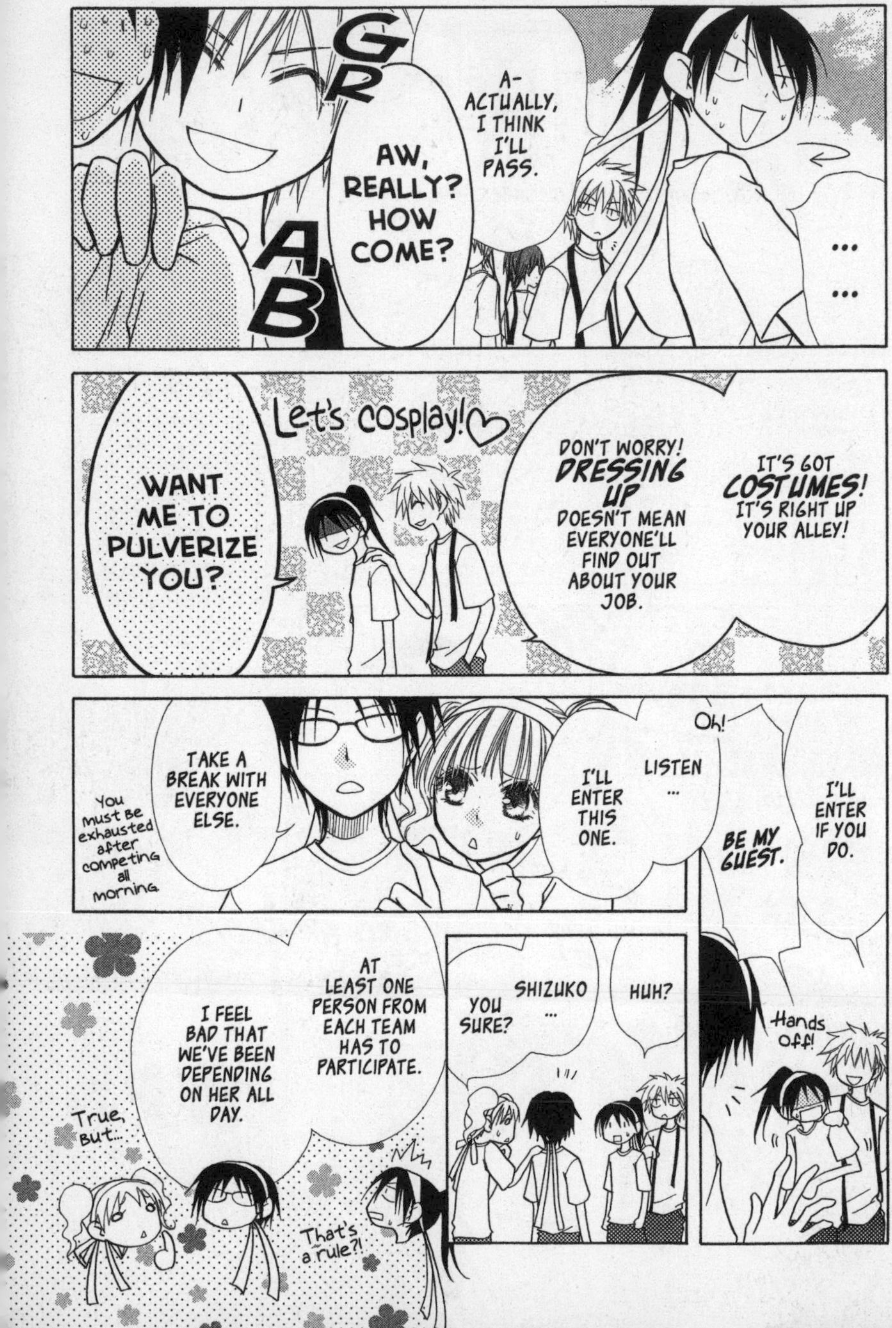

A-ACTUALLY, I THINK I'LL PASS.
...
...
AW, REALLY? HOW COME?
GRAB
IT'S GOT COSTUMES! IT'S RIGHT UP YOUR ALLEY!
DON'T WORRY! DRESSING UP DOESN'T MEAN EVERYONE'LL FIND OUT ABOUT YOUR JOB.
Let's cosplay!♡
WANT ME TO PULVERIZE YOU?
I'LL ENTER IF YOU DO.
BE MY GUEST.
Hands off!
Oh!
LISTEN ...
I'LL ENTER THIS ONE.
TAKE A BREAK WITH EVERYONE ELSE.
You must be exhausted after competing all morning.
HUH?
SHIZUKO ...
YOU SURE?
AT LEAST ONE PERSON FROM EACH TEAM HAS TO PARTICIPATE.
I FEEL BAD THAT WE'VE BEEN DEPENDING ON HER ALL DAY.
That's a rule?!
True, but...

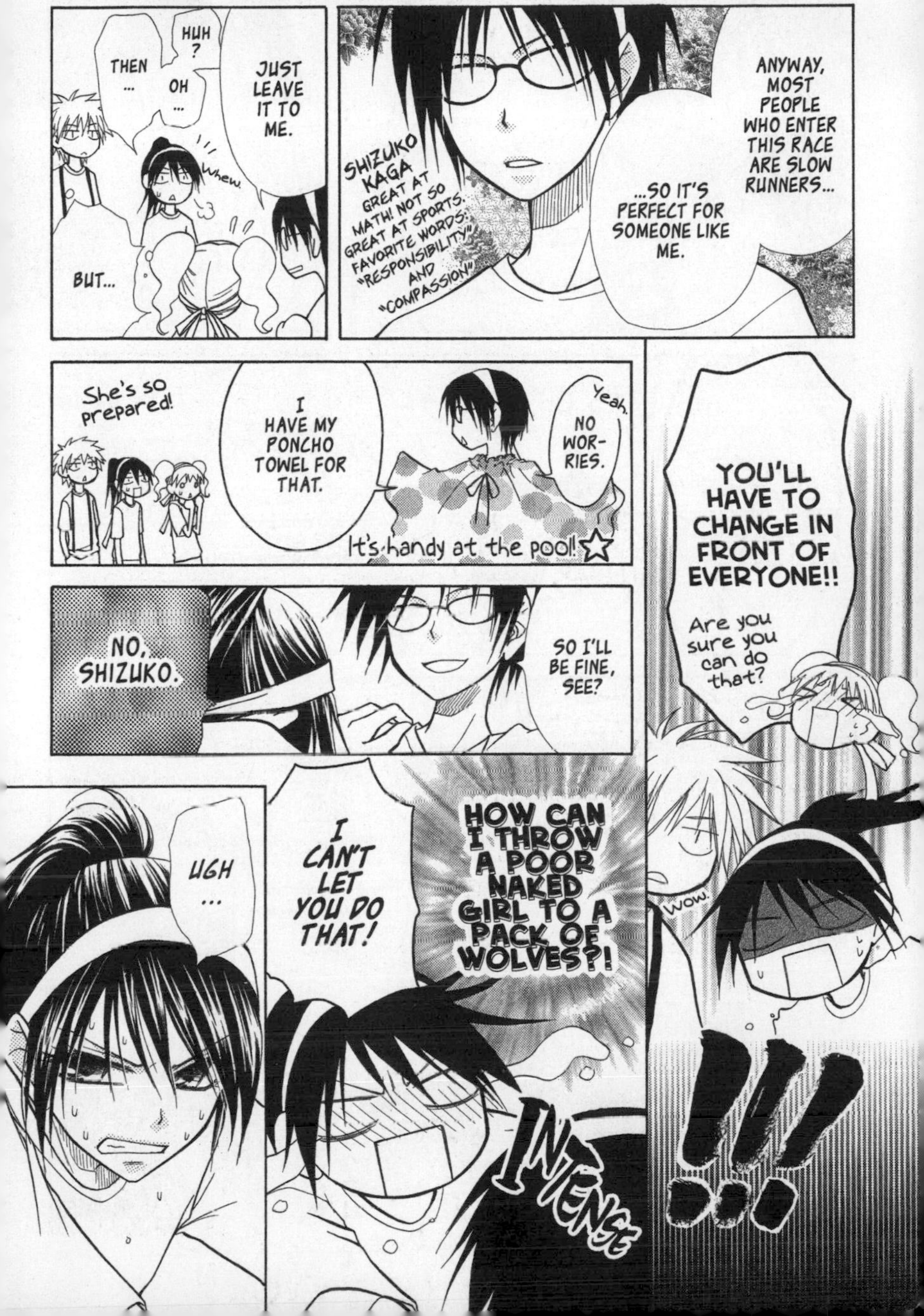
ANYWAY, MOST PEOPLE WHO ENTER THIS RACE ARE SLOW RUNNERS...
...SO IT'S PERFECT FOR SOMEONE LIKE ME.
SHIZUKO KAGA GREAT AT MATH! NOT SO GREAT AT SPORTS. FAVORITE WORDS: "RESPONSIBILITY" AND "COMPASSION"
JUST LEAVE IT TO ME.
HUH?
OH...
THEN...
Whew.
BUT...
YOU'LL HAVE TO CHANGE IN FRONT OF EVERYONE!!
Are you sure you can do that?
Yeah.
NO WORRIES.
I HAVE MY PONCHO TOWEL FOR THAT.
She's so prepared!
It's handy at the pool! ☆
SO I'LL BE FINE, SEE?
NO, SHIZUKO.
Wow.
!!!
HOW CAN I THROW A POOR NAKED GIRL TO A PACK OF WOLVES?!
I CAN'T LET YOU DO THAT!
INTENSE
UGH...

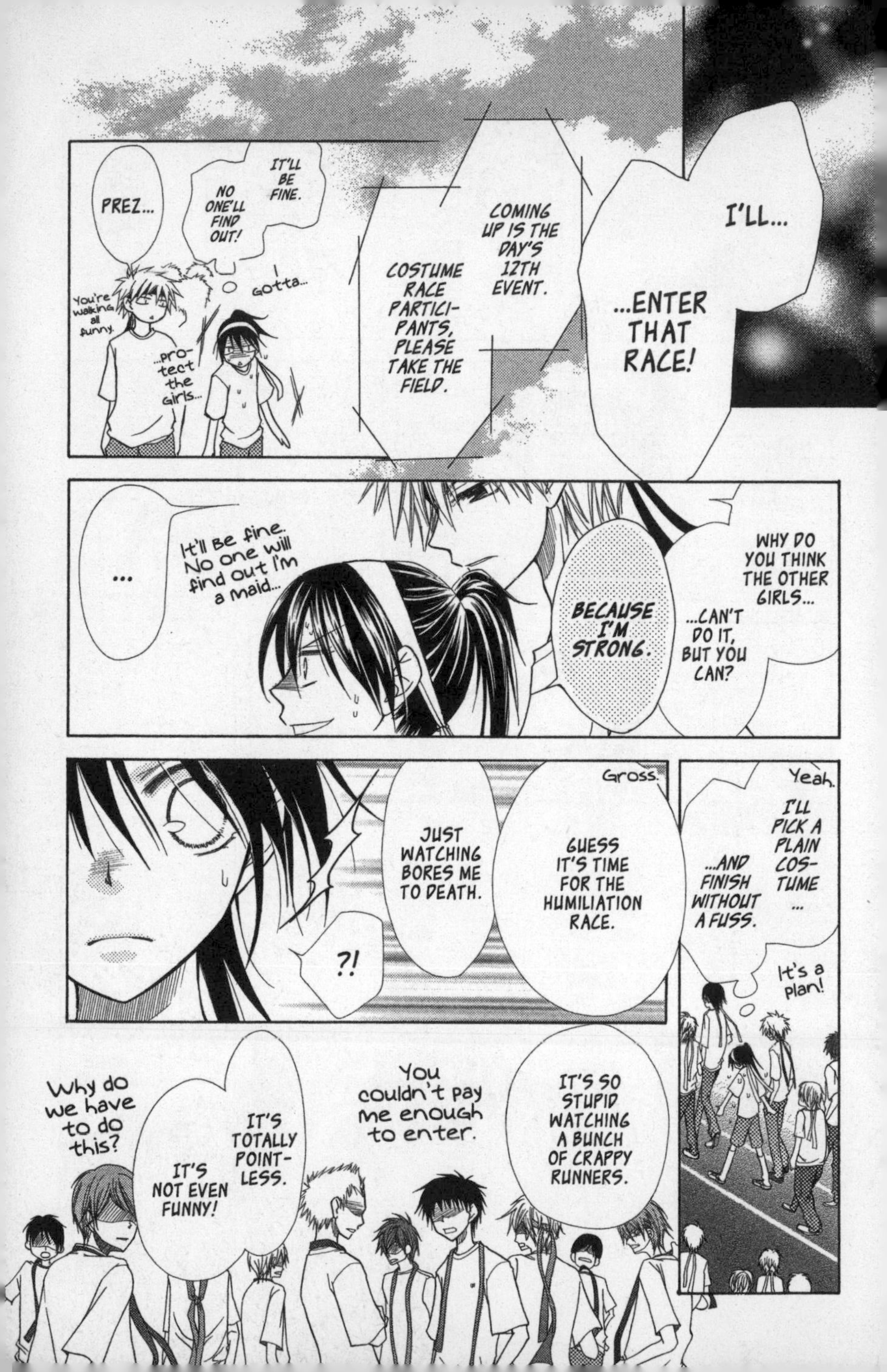
I'LL...
...ENTER THAT RACE!
COMING UP IS THE DAY'S 12TH EVENT.
COSTUME RACE PARTICIPANTS, PLEASE TAKE THE FIELD.
IT'LL BE FINE.
NO ONE'LL FIND OUT!
PREZ...
I gotta...
...protect the girls...
You're walking all funny.
WHY DO YOU THINK THE OTHER GIRLS...
...CAN'T DO IT, BUT YOU CAN?
BECAUSE I'M STRONG.
It'll be fine. No one will find out I'm a maid...
...
Yeah.
I'LL PICK A PLAIN COSTUME...
...AND FINISH WITHOUT A FUSS.
It's a plan!
Gross.
GUESS IT'S TIME FOR THE HUMILIATION RACE.
JUST WATCHING BORES ME TO DEATH.
?!
IT'S SO STUPID WATCHING A BUNCH OF CRAPPY RUNNERS.
You couldn't pay me enough to enter.
IT'S TOTALLY POINTLESS.
IT'S NOT EVEN FUNNY!
Why do we have to do this?

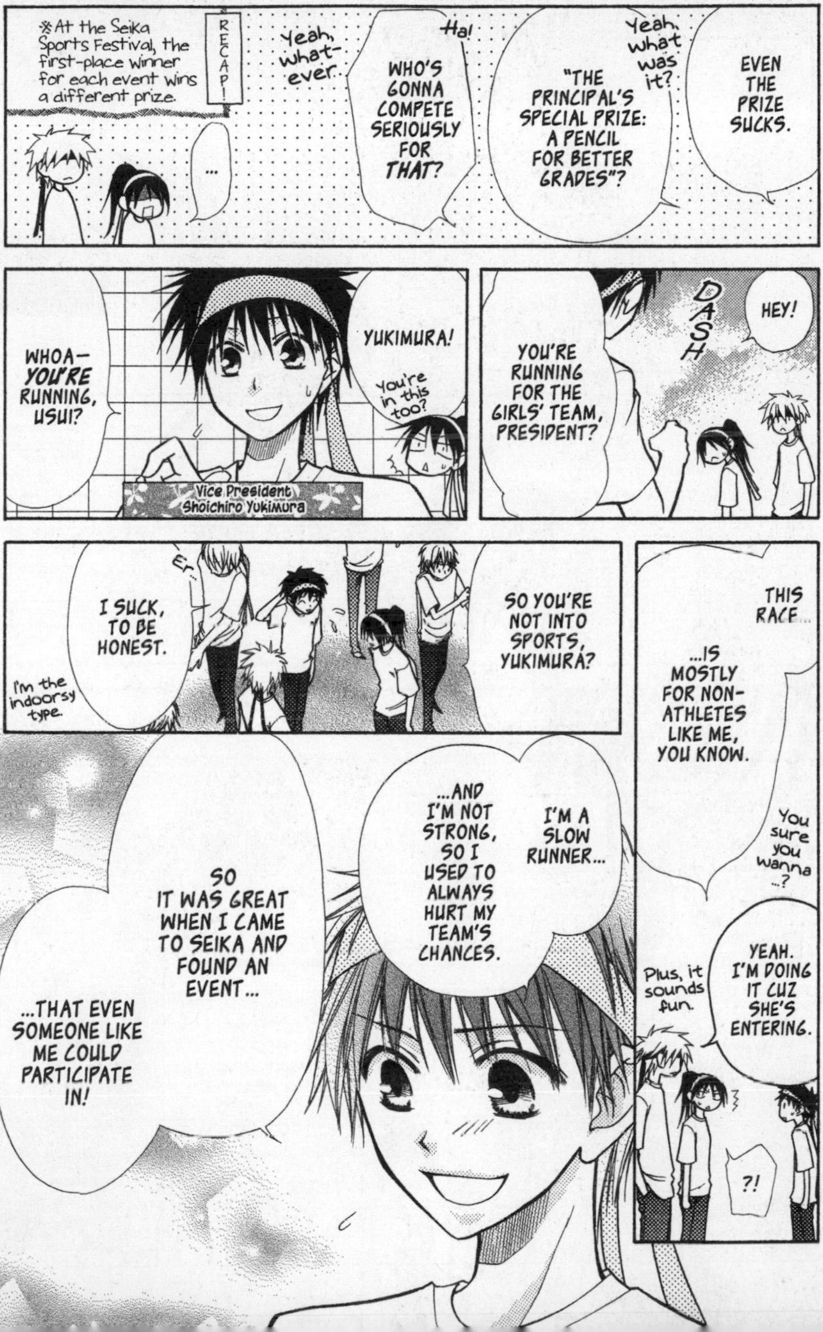

EVEN THE PRIZE SUCKS.
Yeah, what was it?
"THE PRINCIPAL'S SPECIAL PRIZE: A PENCIL FOR BETTER GRADES"?
Ha!
WHO'S GONNA COMPETE SERIOUSLY FOR THAT?
Yeah, whatever.
RECAP!
※At the Seika Sports Festival, the first-place winner for each event wins a different prize.
...
HEY!
DASH
YOU'RE RUNNING FOR THE GIRLS' TEAM, PRESIDENT?
YUKIMURA!
You're in this too?
WHOA—YOU'RE RUNNING, USUI?
Vice President Shoichiro Yukimura
THIS RACE...
...IS MOSTLY FOR NON-ATHLETES LIKE ME, YOU KNOW.
You sure you wanna...?
YEAH. I'M DOING IT CUZ SHE'S ENTERING.
Plus, it sounds fun.
?!
SO YOU'RE NOT INTO SPORTS, YUKIMURA?
Er...
I SUCK, TO BE HONEST.
I'm the indoorsy type.
I'M A SLOW RUNNER...
...AND I'M NOT STRONG, SO I USED TO ALWAYS HURT MY TEAM'S CHANCES.
SO IT WAS GREAT WHEN I CAME TO SEIKA AND FOUND AN EVENT...
...THAT EVEN SOMEONE LIKE ME COULD PARTICIPATE IN!

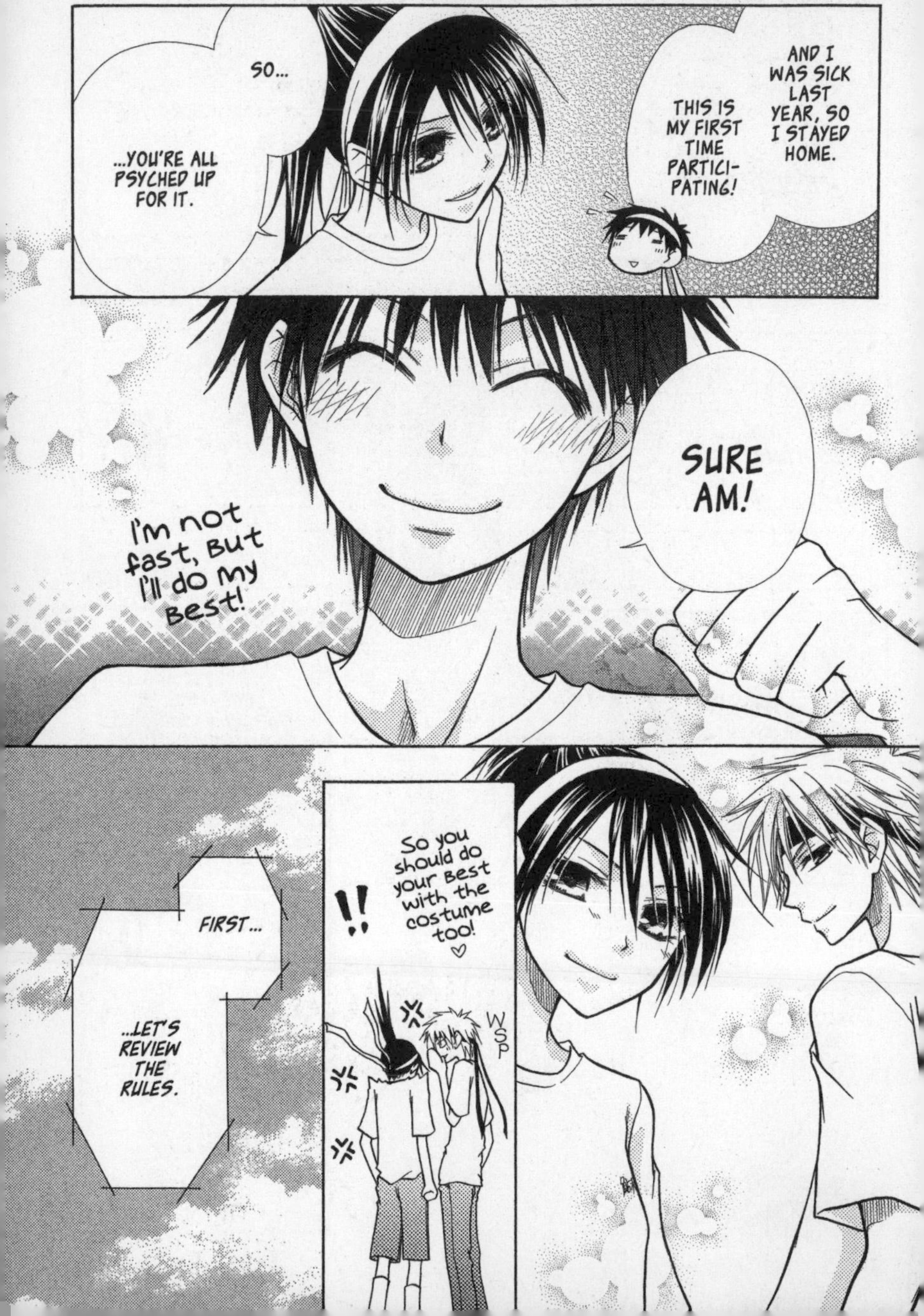
AND I WAS SICK LAST YEAR, SO I STAYED HOME.
THIS IS MY FIRST TIME PARTICIPATING!
SO...
...YOU'RE ALL PSYCHED UP FOR IT.
SURE AM!
I'm not fast, but I'll do my best!
So you should do your best with the costume too! ♡
!!
WSP
FIRST...
...LET'S REVIEW THE RULES.

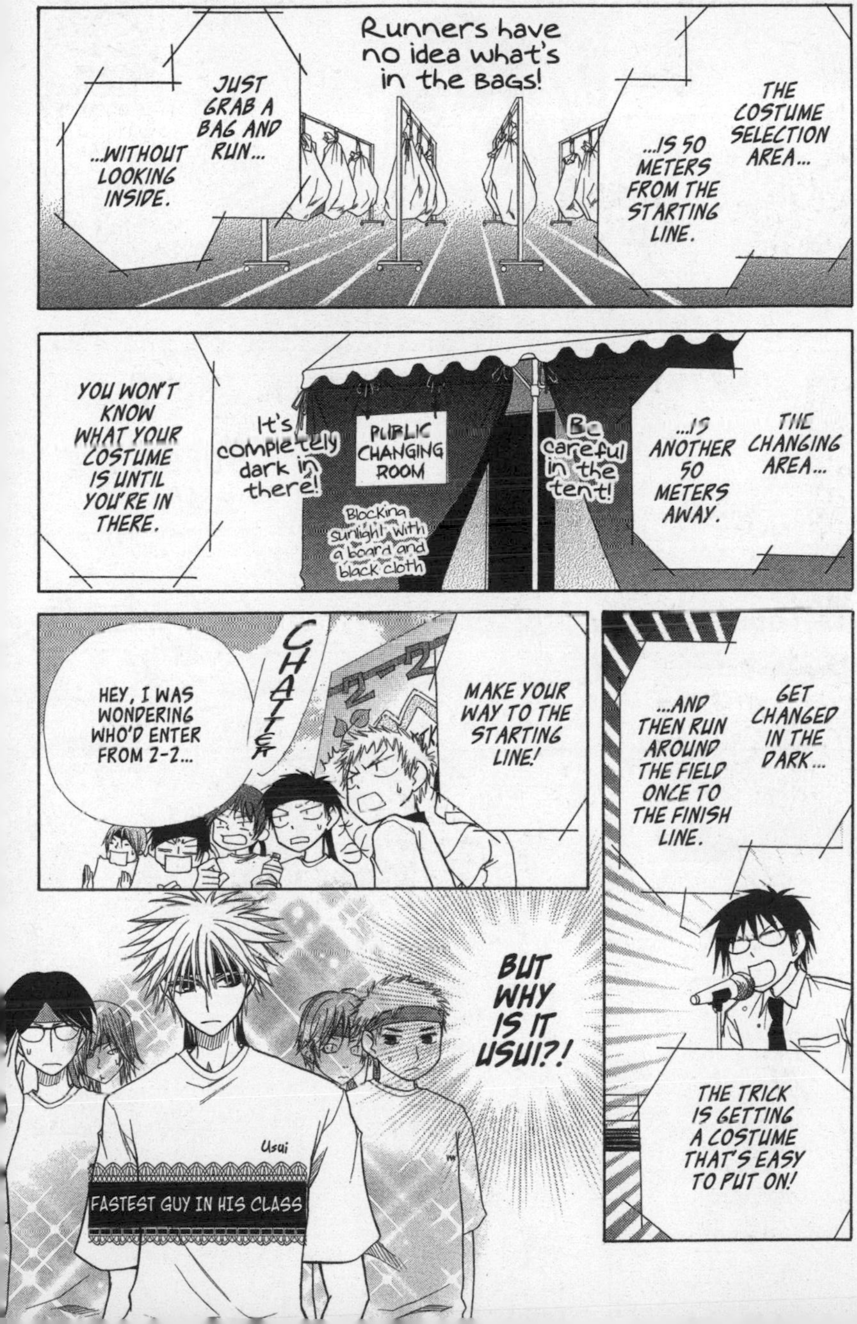
THE COSTUME SELECTION AREA...
...IS 50 METERS FROM THE STARTING LINE.
Runners have no idea what's in the bags!
JUST GRAB A BAG AND RUN...
...WITHOUT LOOKING INSIDE.
THE CHANGING AREA...
...IS ANOTHER 50 METERS AWAY.
Be careful in the tent!
PUBLIC CHANGING ROOM
It's completely dark in there!
Blocking sunlight with a board and black cloth
YOU WON'T KNOW WHAT YOUR COSTUME IS UNTIL YOU'RE IN THERE.
GET CHANGED IN THE DARK...
...AND THEN RUN AROUND THE FIELD ONCE TO THE FINISH LINE.
THE TRICK IS GETTING A COSTUME THAT'S EASY TO PUT ON!
MAKE YOUR WAY TO THE STARTING LINE!
CHATTER
HEY, I WAS WONDERING WHO'D ENTER FROM 2-2...
BUT WHY IS IT USUI?!
Usui
FASTEST GUY IN HIS CLASS

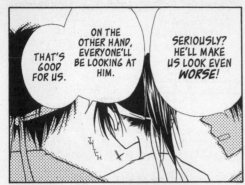

THERE ARE SO MANY OTHER EVENTS WE WANT HIM TO ENTER!
WHY?
WHY?
WHY?
SERIOUSLY? HE'LL MAKE US LOOK EVEN WORSE!
ON THE OTHER HAND, EVERYONE'LL BE LOOKING AT HIM.
THAT'S GOOD FOR US.
TWITCH
IF NO ONE NOTICES US...
...WE WON'T GET LAUGHED AT.
That's true.
...
ALL RIGHT!
ON YOUR MARK...
GET SET...
BANG
GO!
DART
HM?
Three seconds into the race

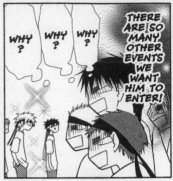

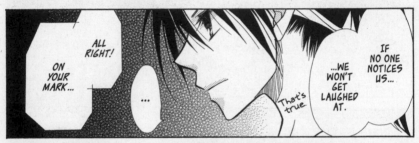

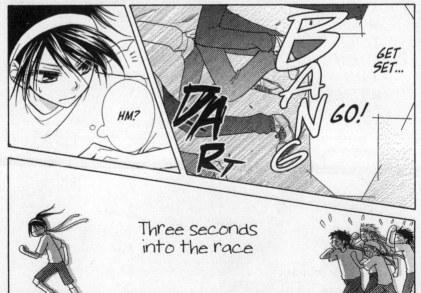

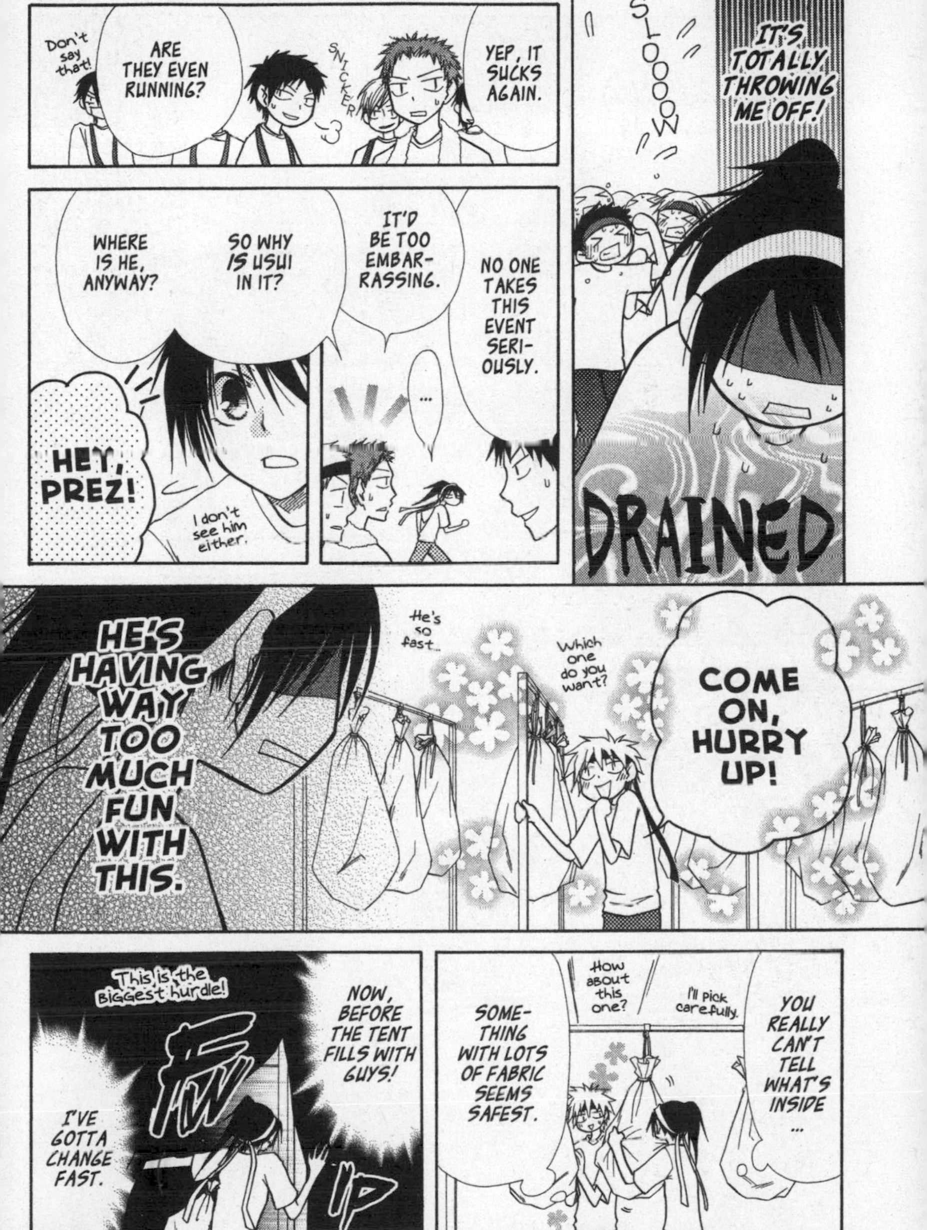
SLOOOOW
IT'S TOTALLY THROWING ME OFF!
DRAINED
YEP, IT SUCKS AGAIN.
SNICKER
ARE THEY EVEN RUNNING?
Don't say that!
NO ONE TAKES THIS EVENT SERIOUSLY.
IT'D BE TOO EMBARRASSING.
...
SO WHY IS USUI IN IT?
WHERE IS HE, ANYWAY?
HEY, PREZ!
I don't see him either.
COME ON, HURRY UP!
Which one do you want?
He's so fast...
HE'S HAVING WAY TOO MUCH FUN WITH THIS.
YOU REALLY CAN'T TELL WHAT'S INSIDE...
I'll pick carefully.
How about this one?
SOMETHING WITH LOTS OF FABRIC SEEMS SAFEST.
NOW, BEFORE THE TENT FILLS WITH GUYS!
This is the biggest hurdle!
FWIP
I'VE GOTTA CHANGE FAST.

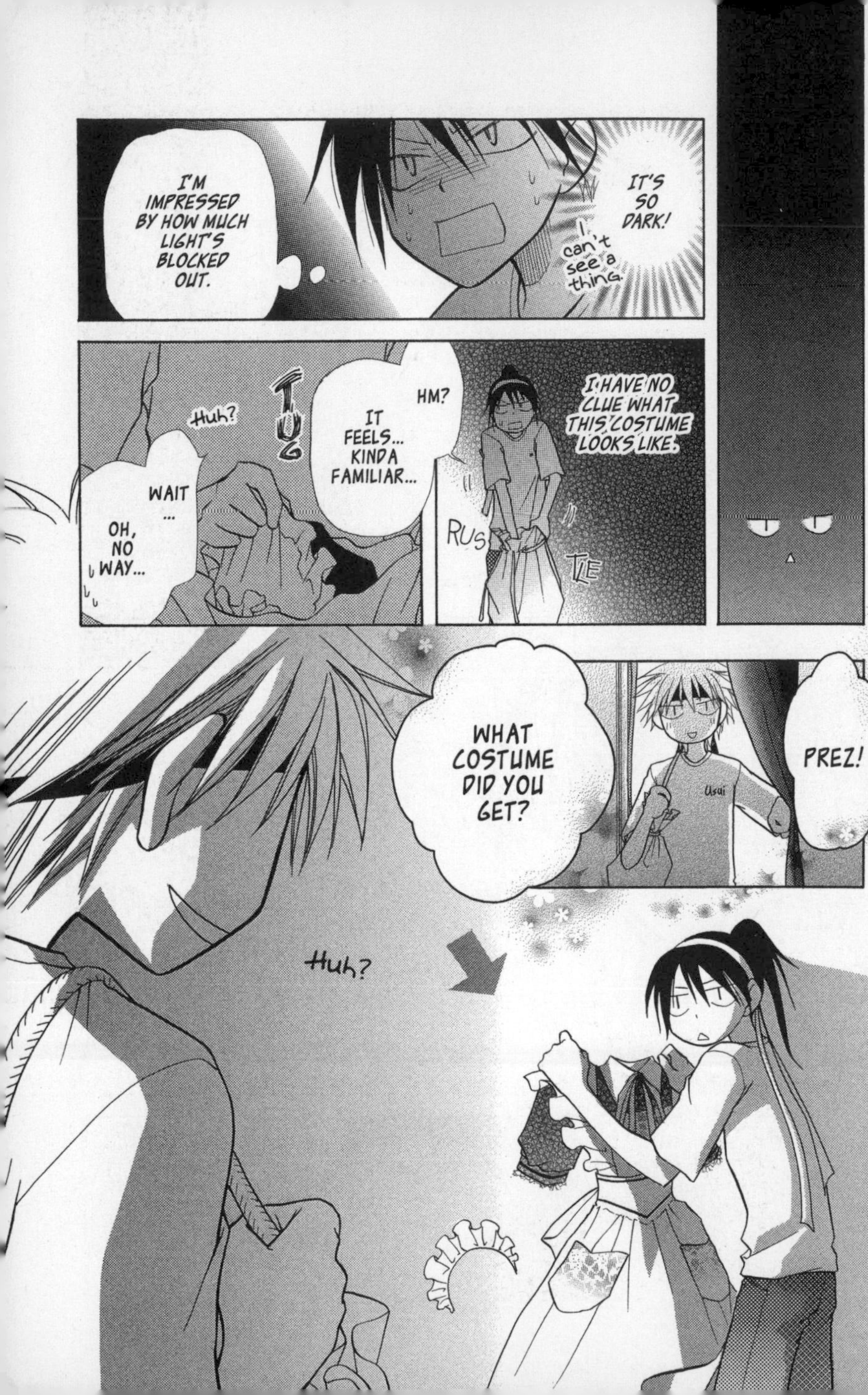
IT'S SO DARK!
I can't see a thing.
I'M IMPRESSED BY HOW MUCH LIGHT'S BLOCKED OUT.
I HAVE NO CLUE WHAT THIS COSTUME LOOKS LIKE.
RUSTLE
HM?
IT FEELS... KINDA FAMILIAR...
TUG
Huh?
WAIT...
OH, NO WAY...
PREZ!
WHAT COSTUME DID YOU GET?
Usui
Huh?

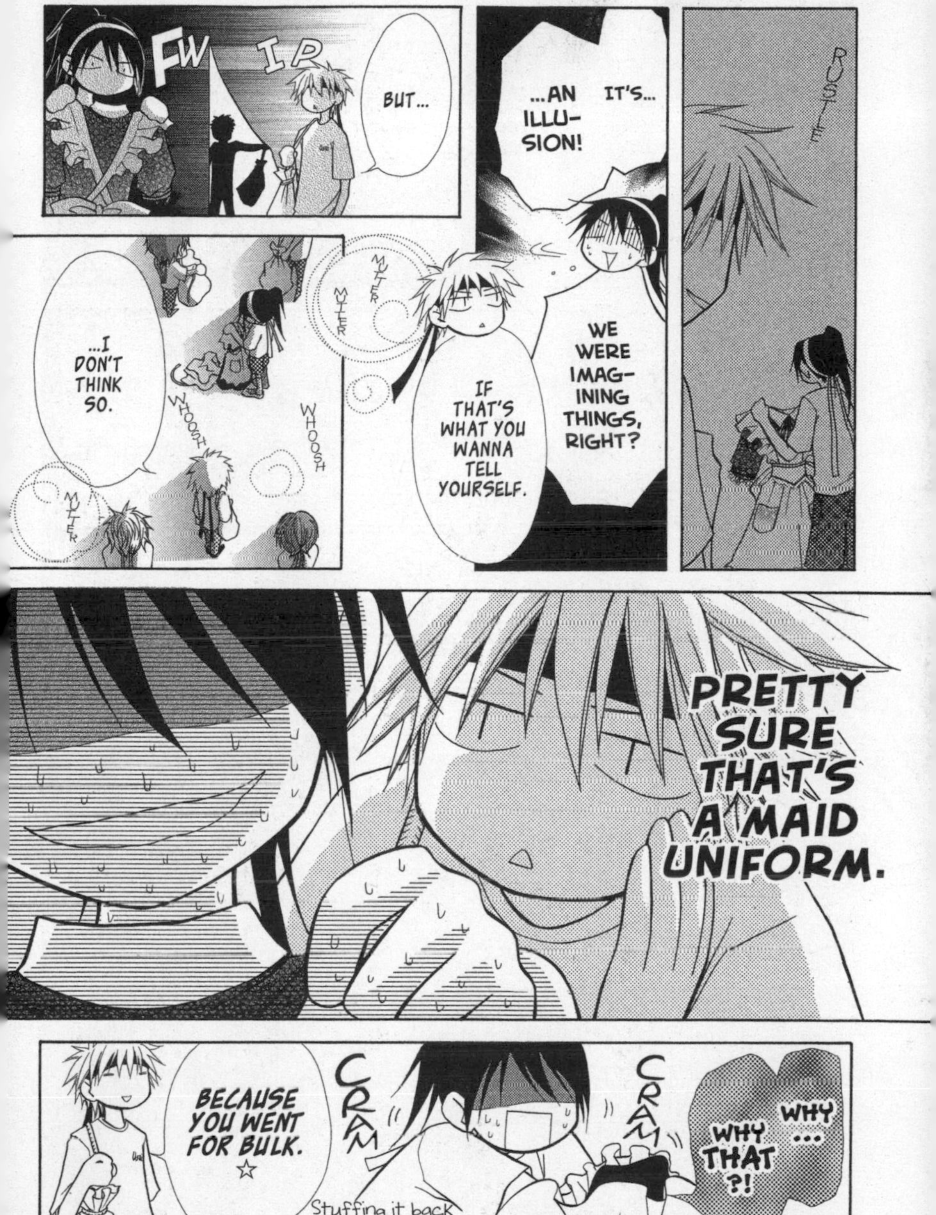
RUSTLE
IT'S...
...AN ILLUSION!
WE WERE IMAGING THINGS, RIGHT?
IF THAT'S WHAT YOU WANNA TELL YOURSELF.
FWIP
BUT...
MUTTER
MUTTER
WHOOSH
WHOOSH
...I DON'T THINK SO.
PRETTY SURE THAT'S A MAID UNIFORM.
WHY...
WHY THAT?!
CRAM
CRAM
Stuffing it back in the bag
BECAUSE YOU WENT FOR BULK. ☆

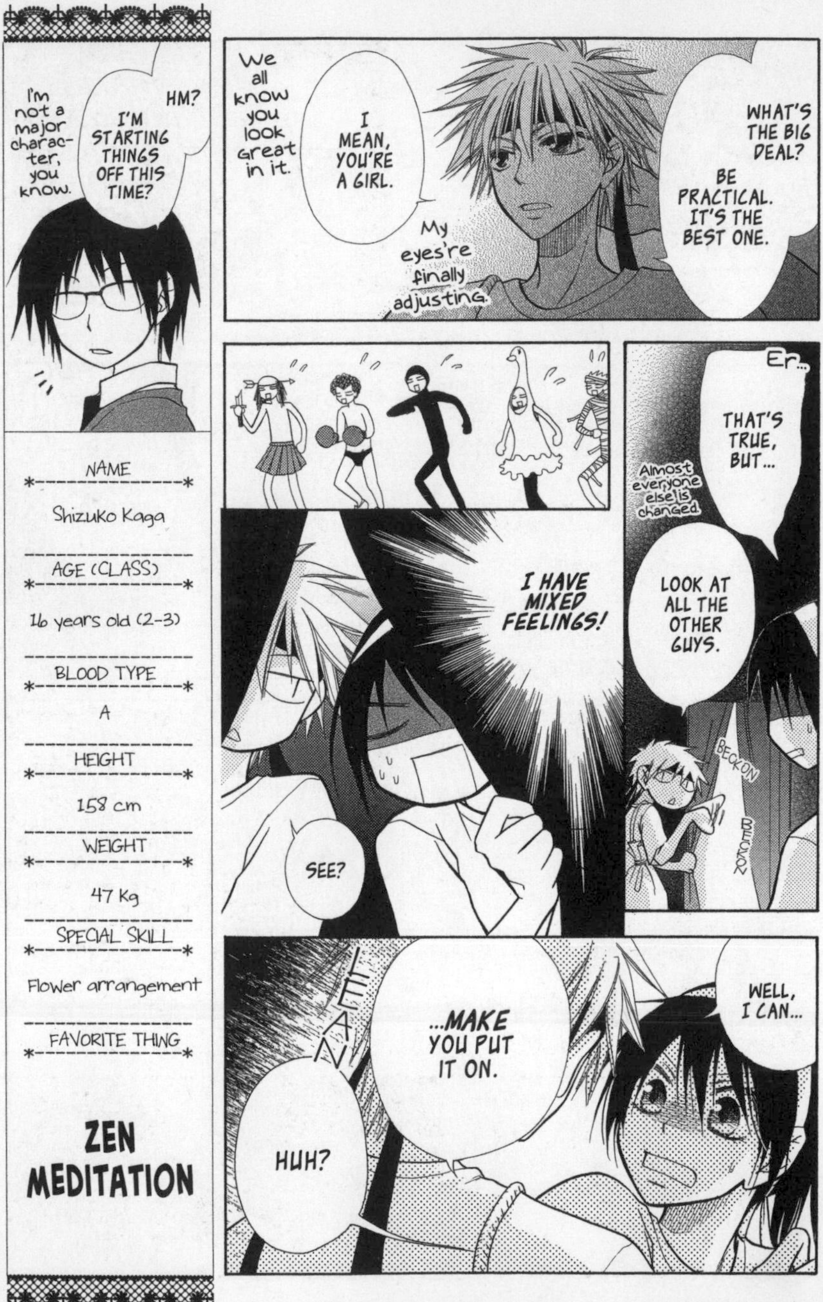
WHAT'S THE BIG DEAL?
BE PRACTICAL. IT'S THE BEST ONE.
My eyes're finally adjusting.
I MEAN, YOU'RE A GIRL.
We all know you look great in it.
Er...
THAT'S TRUE, BUT...
Almost everyone else is changed.
LOOK AT ALL THE OTHER GUYS.
BECKON
BECKON
I HAVE MIXED FEELINGS!
SEE?
WELL, I CAN...
...MAKE YOU PUT IT ON.
LEAN
HUH?
HM?
I'M STARTING THINGS OFF THIS TIME?
I'm not a major charac-ter, you know.
NAME
Shizuko Kaga
AGE (CLASS)
16 years old (2-3)
BLOOD TYPE
A
HEIGHT
158 cm
WEIGHT
47 Kg
SPECIAL SKILL
Flower arrangement
FAVORITE THING
ZEN MEDITATION

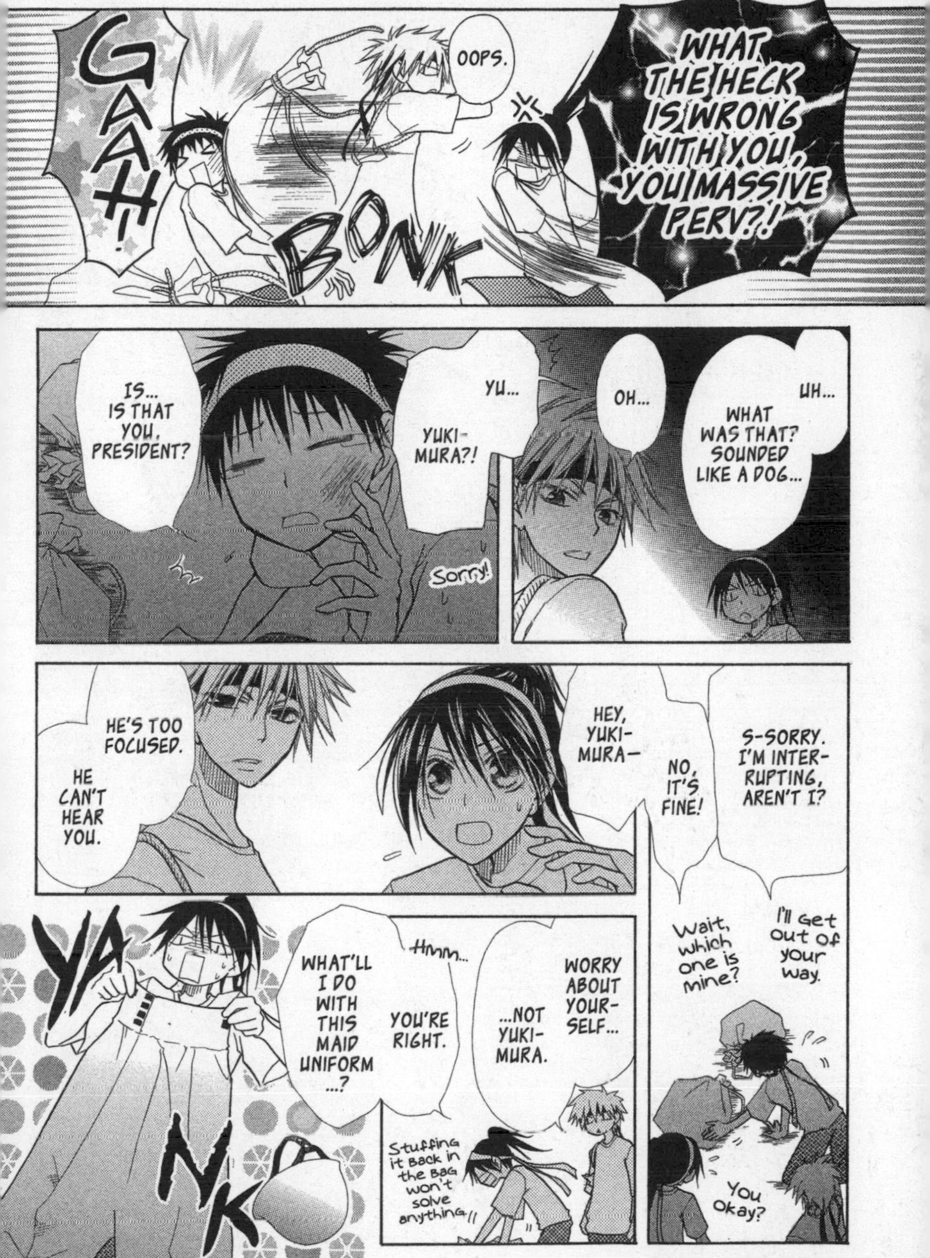
WHAT THE HECK IS WRONG WITH YOU, YOU MASSIVE PERV?!
OOPS.
BONK
GAAH!
UH...
WHAT WAS THAT? SOUNDED LIKE A DOG...
OH...
YU...
YUKI-MURA?!
IS... IS THAT YOU, PRESIDENT?
Sorry!
S-SORRY. I'M INTER-RUPTING, AREN'T I?
NO, IT'S FINE!
I'll Get out of your way.
Wait, which one is mine?
You Okay?
HEY, YUKI-MURA—
HE'S TOO FOCUSED.
HE CAN'T HEAR YOU.
WORRY ABOUT YOUR-SELF...
...NOT YUKI-MURA.
Hmm...
YOU'RE RIGHT.
WHAT'LL I DO WITH THIS MAID UNIFORM ...?
Stuffing it back in the BAG won't solve anything.
YANK

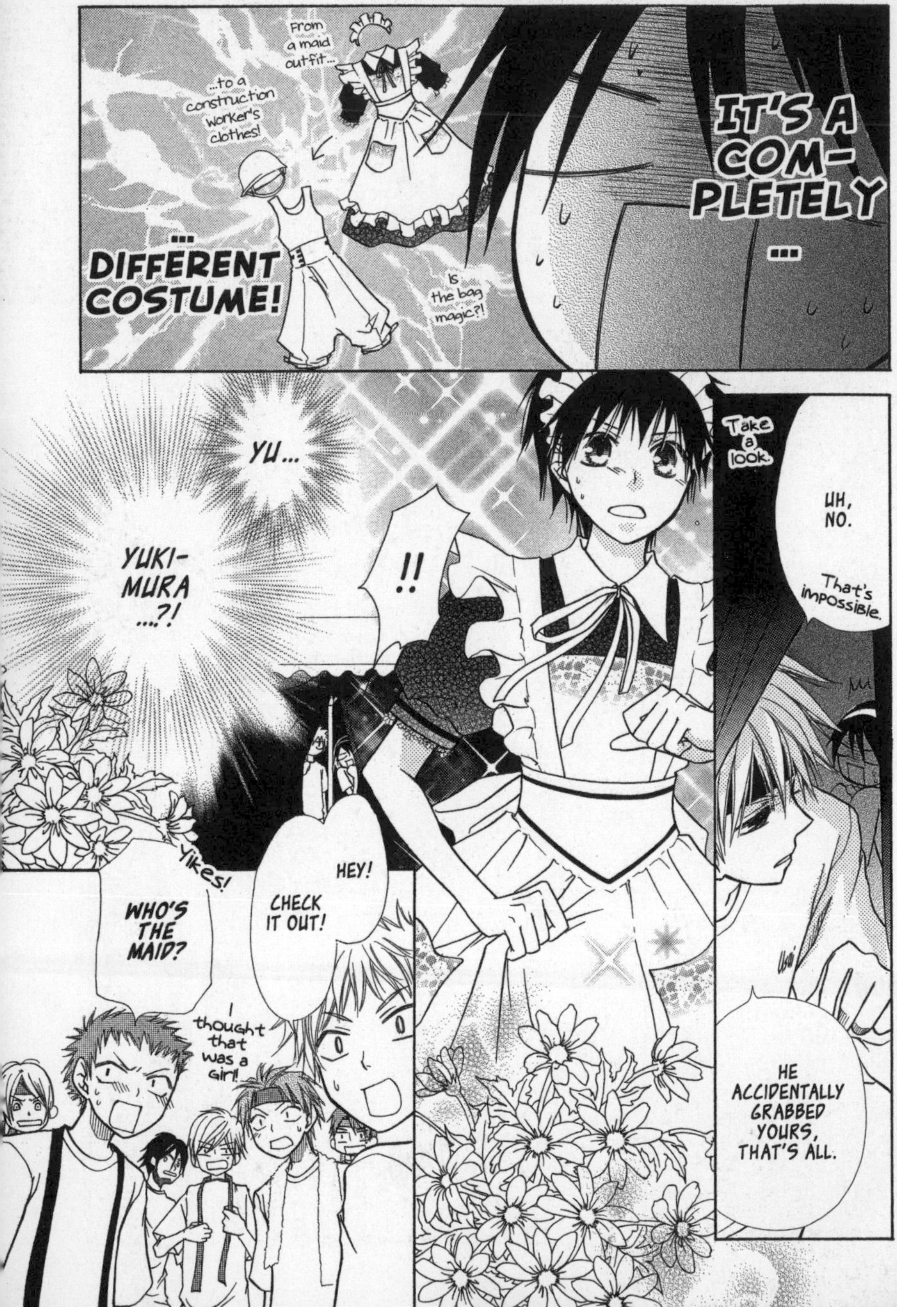
IT'S A COM-PLETELY ...
From a maid outfit...
...to a construction worker's clothes!
... DIFFERENT COSTUME!
Is the bag magic?!
Take a look.
UH, NO.
That's impossible.
HE ACCIDENTALLY GRABBED YOURS, THAT'S ALL.
!!
YU...
YUKI-MURA ...?!
HEY!
CHECK IT OUT!
Yikes!
WHO'S THE MAID?
I thought that was a girl!

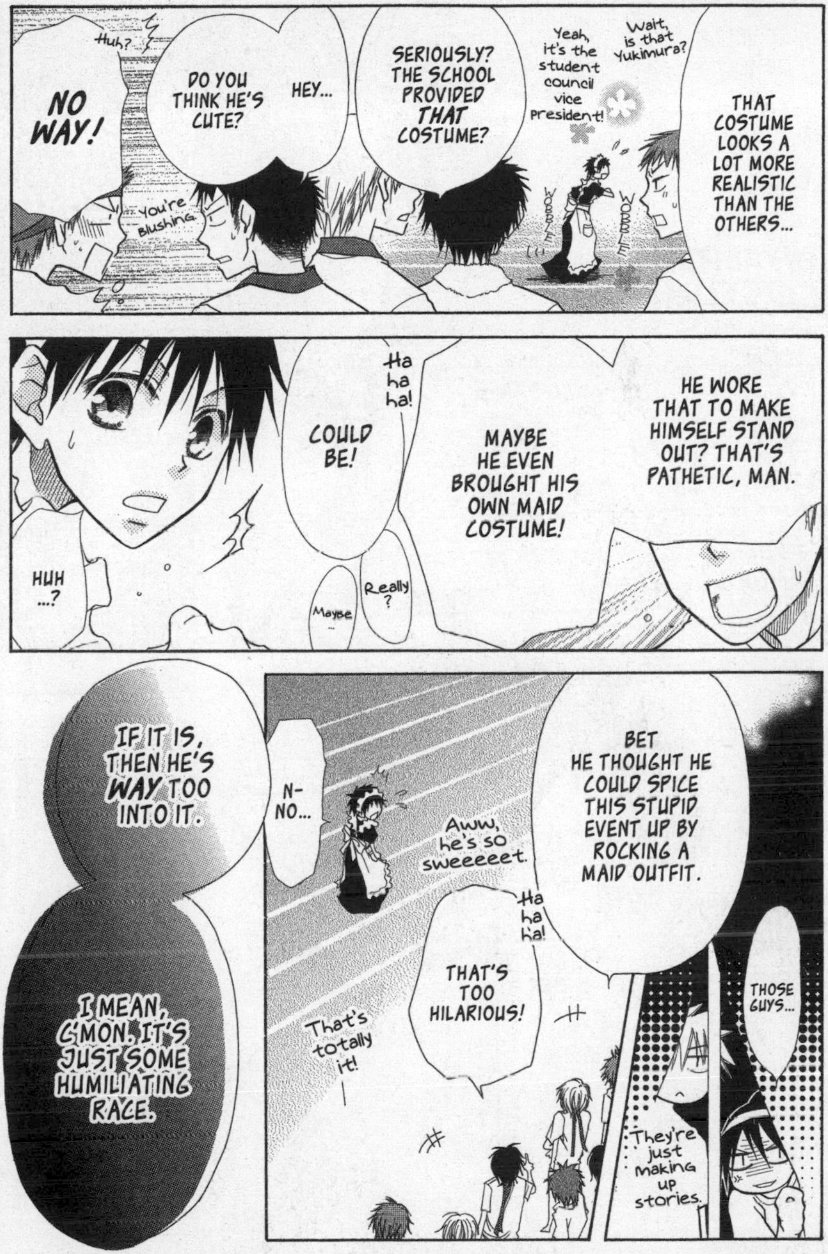
THAT COSTUME LOOKS A LOT MORE REALISTIC THAN THE OTHERS...
Wait, is that Yukimura?
Yeah, it's the student council vice president!
WOBBLE
WOBBLE
SERIOUSLY? THE SCHOOL PROVIDED THAT COSTUME?
HEY...
DO YOU THINK HE'S CUTE?
Huh?
NO WAY!
You're blushing.
HE WORE THAT TO MAKE HIMSELF STAND OUT? THAT'S PATHETIC, MAN.
MAYBE HE EVEN BROUGHT HIS OWN MAID COSTUME!
Ha ha ha!
COULD BE!
Really?
Maybe...
HUH...?
BET HE THOUGHT HE COULD SPICE THIS STUPID EVENT UP BY ROCKING A MAID OUTFIT.
THOSE GUYS...
Aww, he's so sweeeeet.
N-NO...
Ha ha ha!
THAT'S TOO HILARIOUS!
They're just making up stories.
That's totally it!
IF IT IS, THEN HE'S WAY TOO INTO IT.
I MEAN, C'MON. IT'S JUST SOME HUMILIATING RACE.

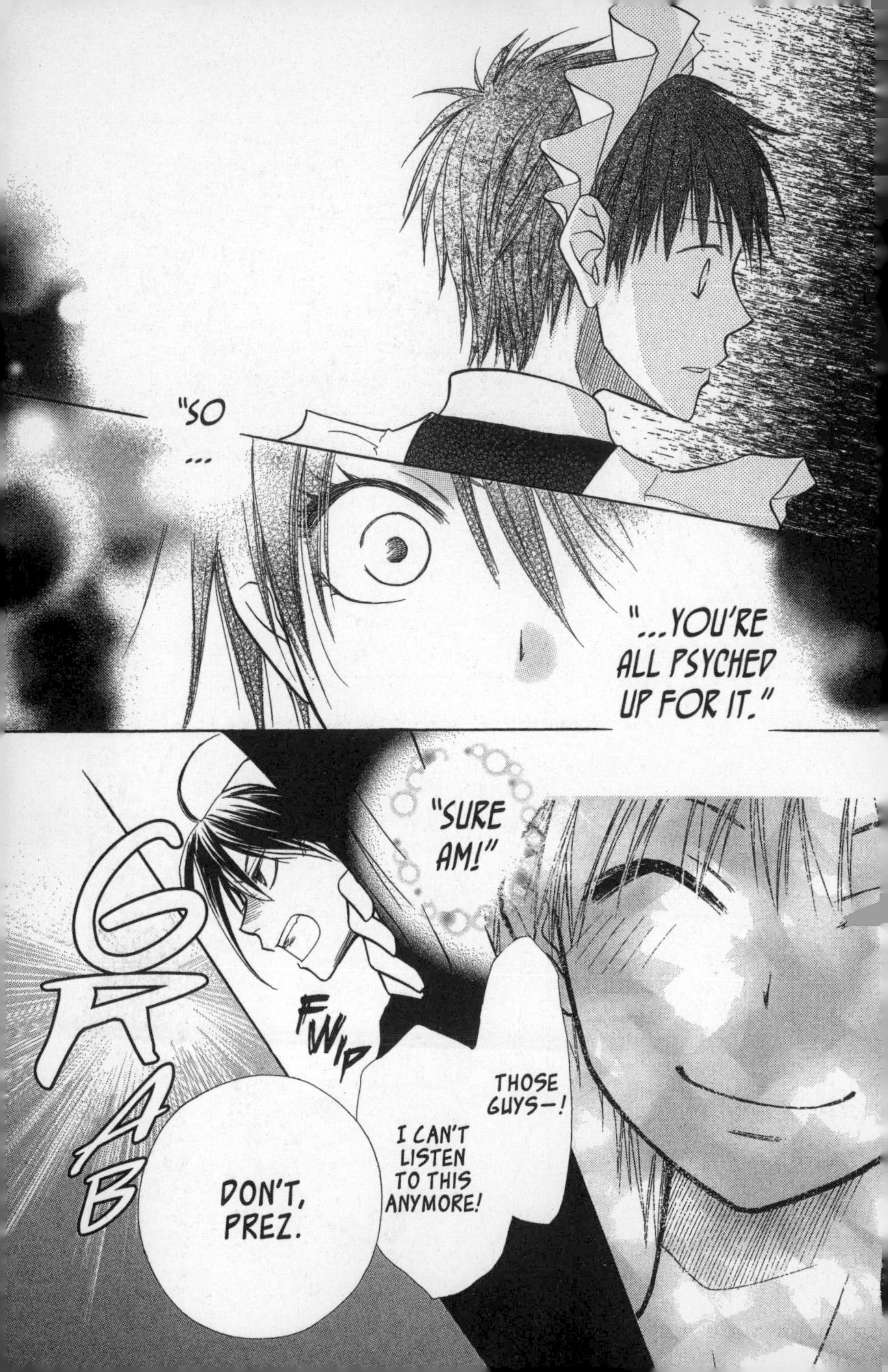
"SO ...
"...YOU'RE ALL PSYCHED UP FOR IT."
"SURE AM!"
THOSE GUYS—!
I CAN'T LISTEN TO THIS ANYMORE!
FWIP
GRAB
DON'T, PREZ.

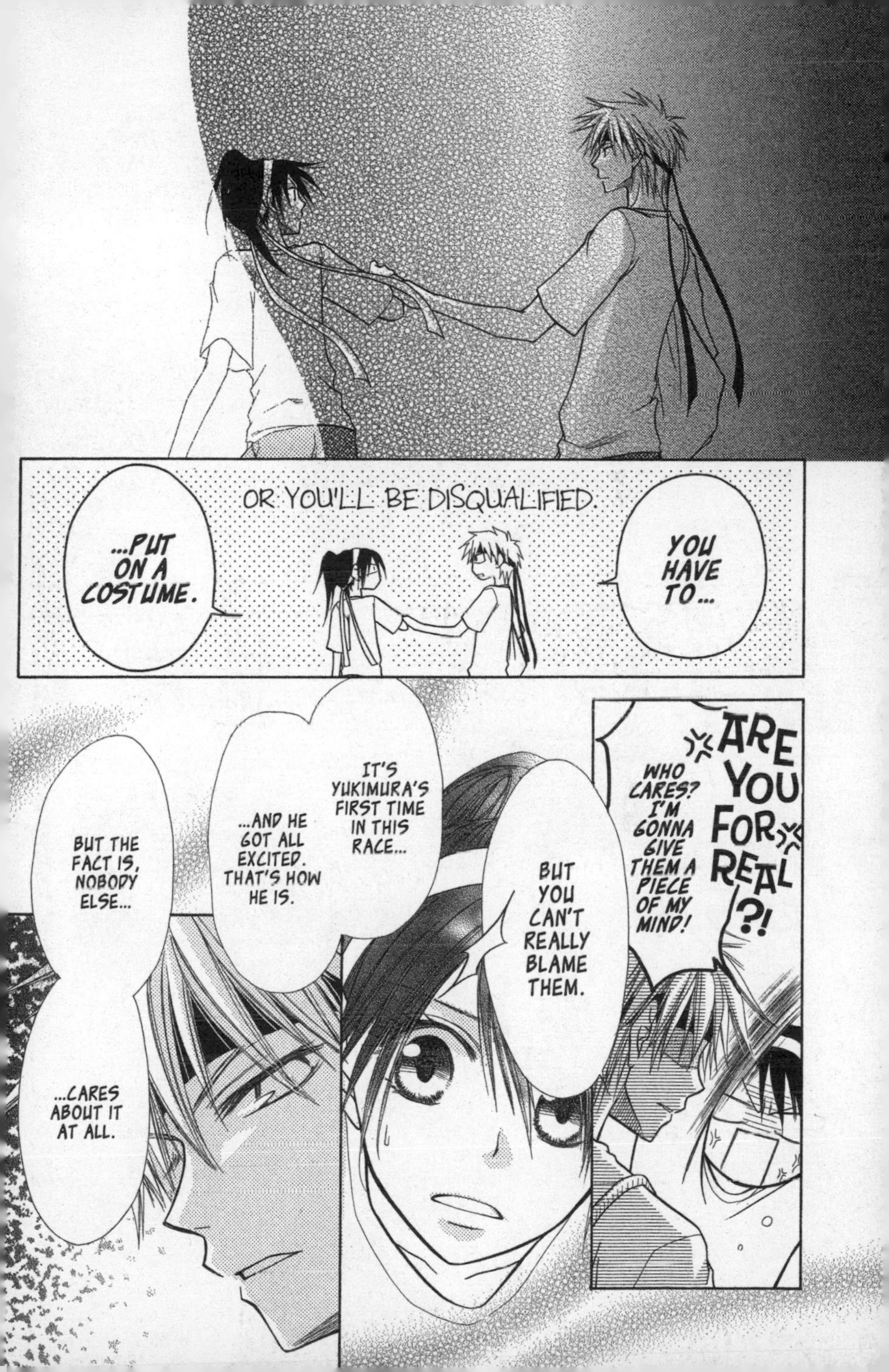
YOU HAVE TO...
...PUT ON A COSTUME.
OR YOU'LL BE DISQUALIFIED.
ARE YOU FOR REAL?!
WHO CARES? I'M GONNA GIVE THEM A PIECE OF MY MIND!
BUT YOU CAN'T REALLY BLAME THEM.
IT'S YUKIMURA'S FIRST TIME IN THIS RACE...
...AND HE GOT ALL EXCITED. THAT'S HOW HE IS.
BUT THE FACT IS, NOBODY ELSE...
...CARES ABOUT IT AT ALL.

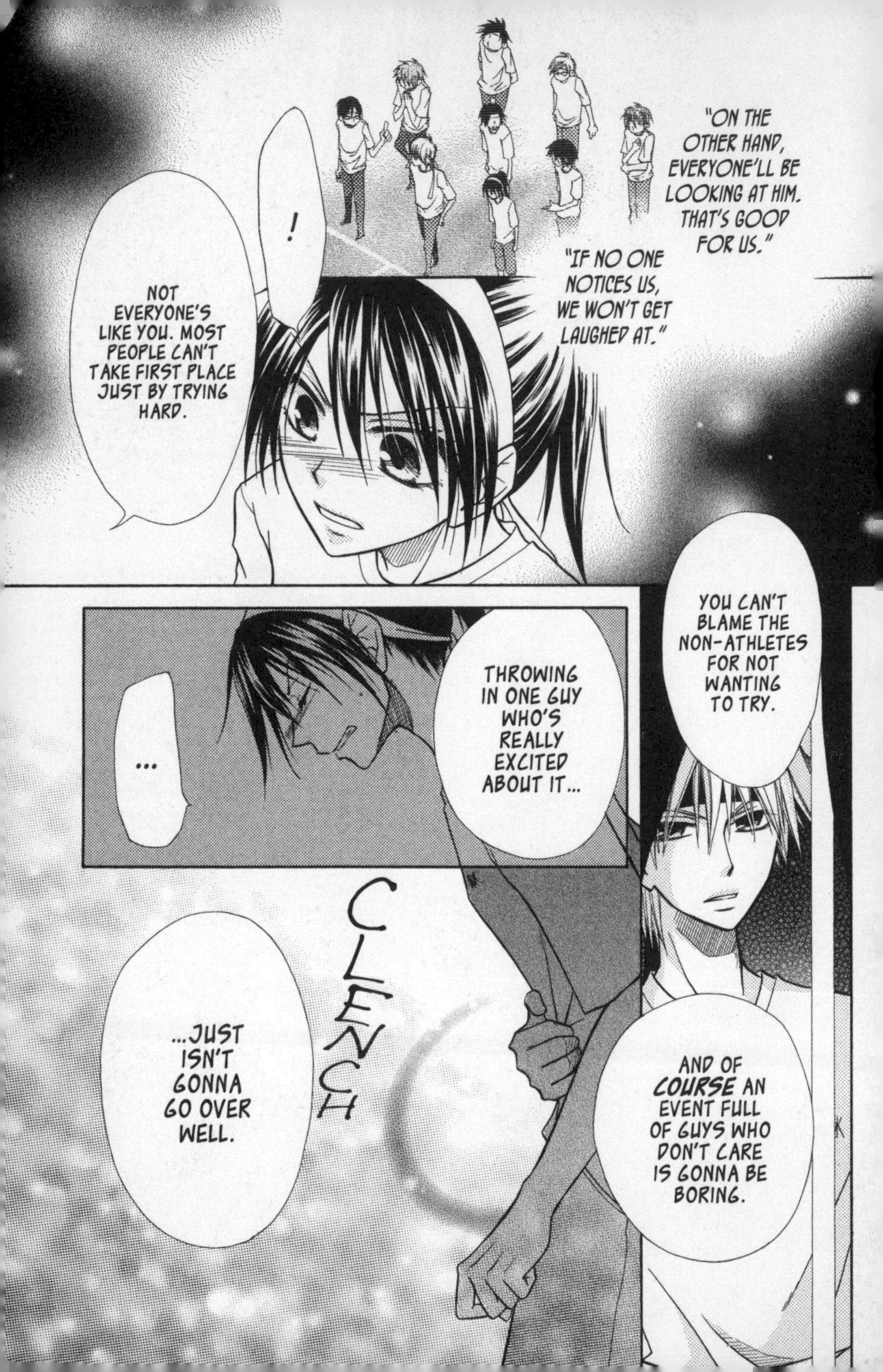
"ON THE OTHER HAND, EVERYONE'LL BE LOOKING AT HIM. THAT'S GOOD FOR US."
"IF NO ONE NOTICES US, WE WON'T GET LAUGHED AT."
!
NOT EVERYONE'S LIKE YOU. MOST PEOPLE CAN'T TAKE FIRST PLACE JUST BY TRYING HARD.
YOU CAN'T BLAME THE NON-ATHLETES FOR NOT WANTING TO TRY.
THROWING IN ONE GUY WHO'S REALLY EXCITED ABOUT IT...
...
...JUST ISN'T GONNA GO OVER WELL.
CLENCH
AND OF COURSE AN EVENT FULL OF GUYS WHO DON'T CARE IS GONNA BE BORING.

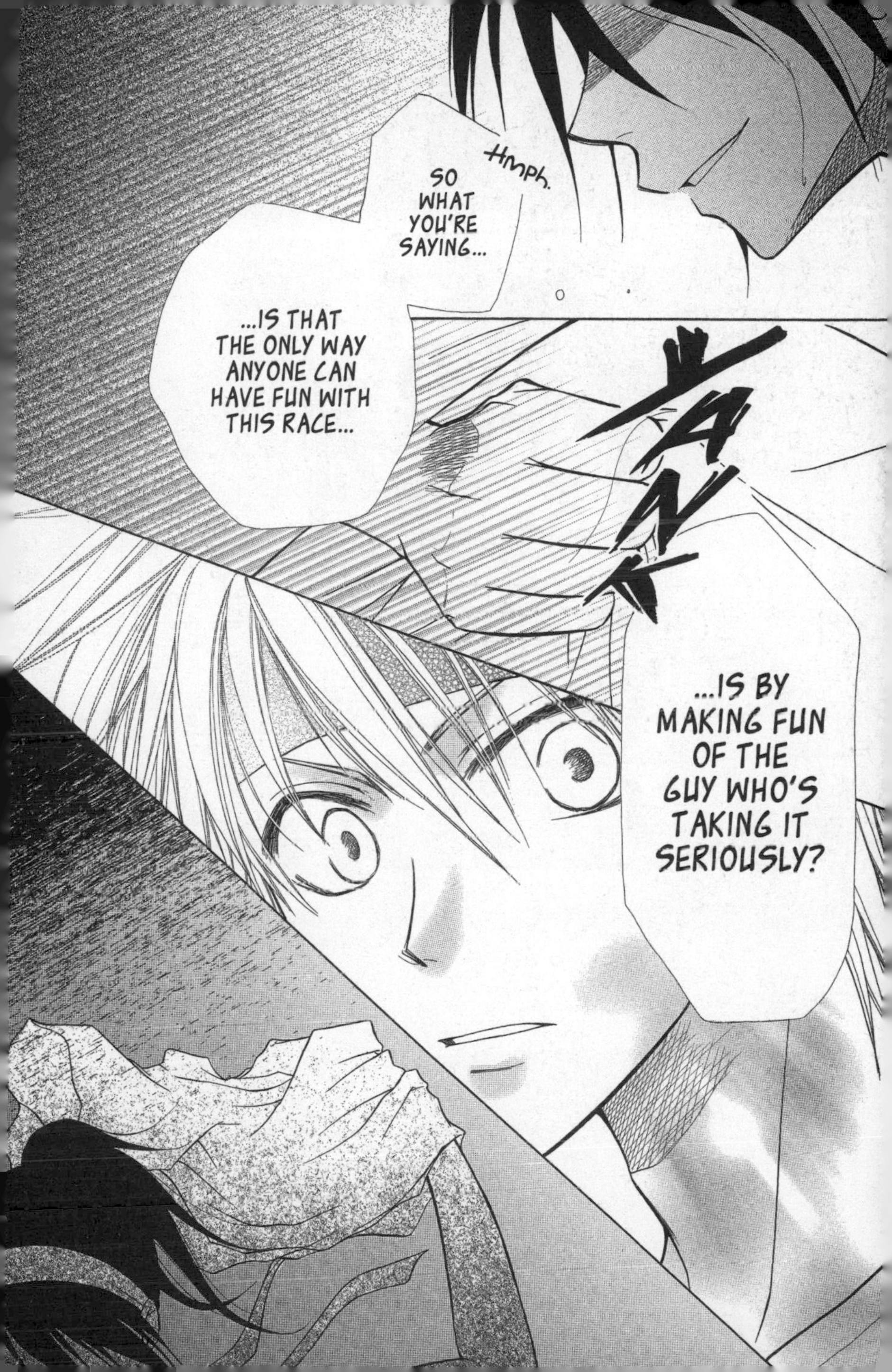
Hmph.
SO WHAT YOU'RE SAYING...
...IS THAT THE ONLY WAY ANYONE CAN HAVE FUN WITH THIS RACE...
YANK
...IS BY MAKING FUN OF THE GUY WHO'S TAKING IT SERIOUSLY?

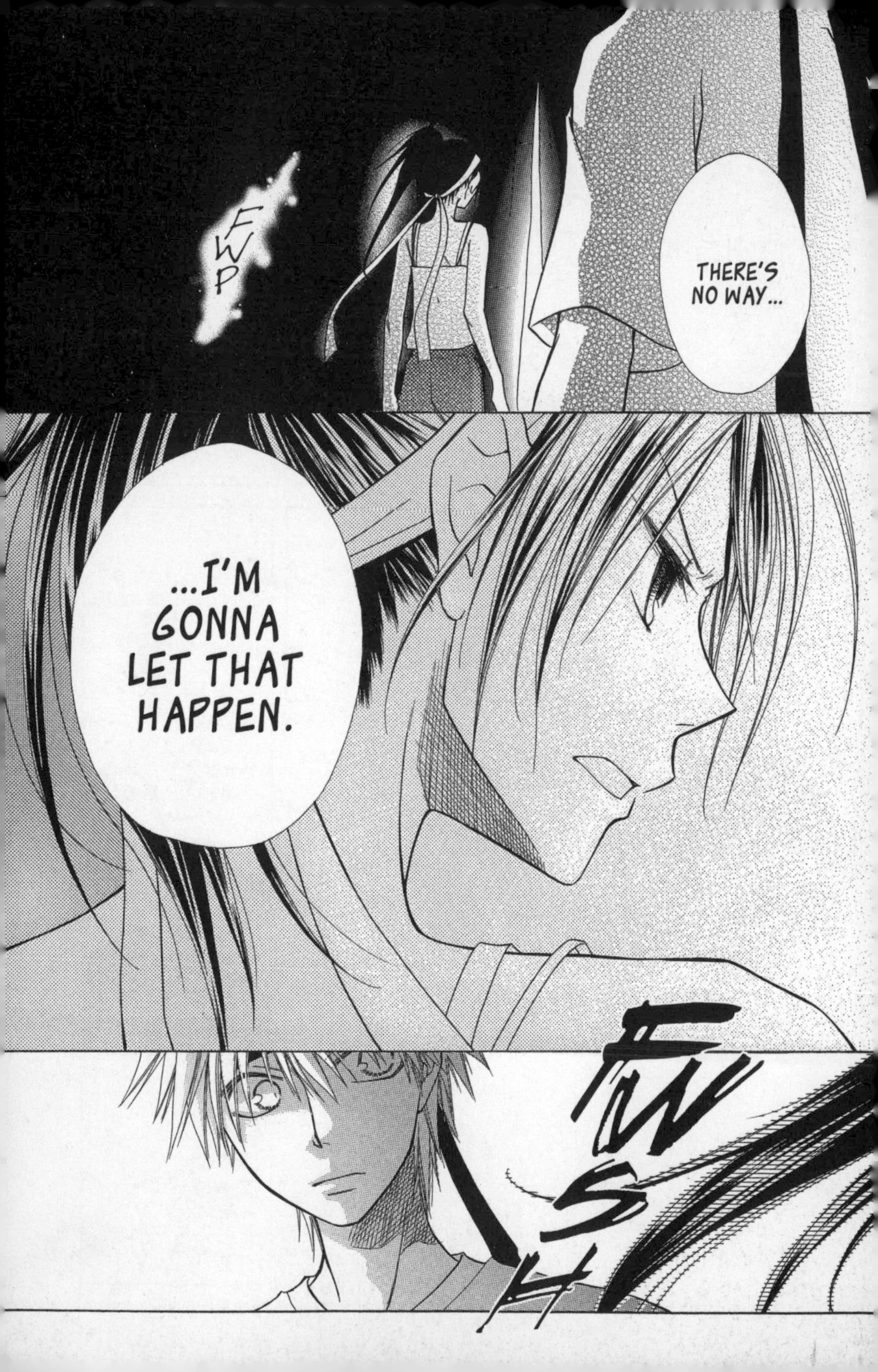
THERE'S NO WAY...
FWP
...I'M GONNA LET THAT HAPPEN.
FWSH

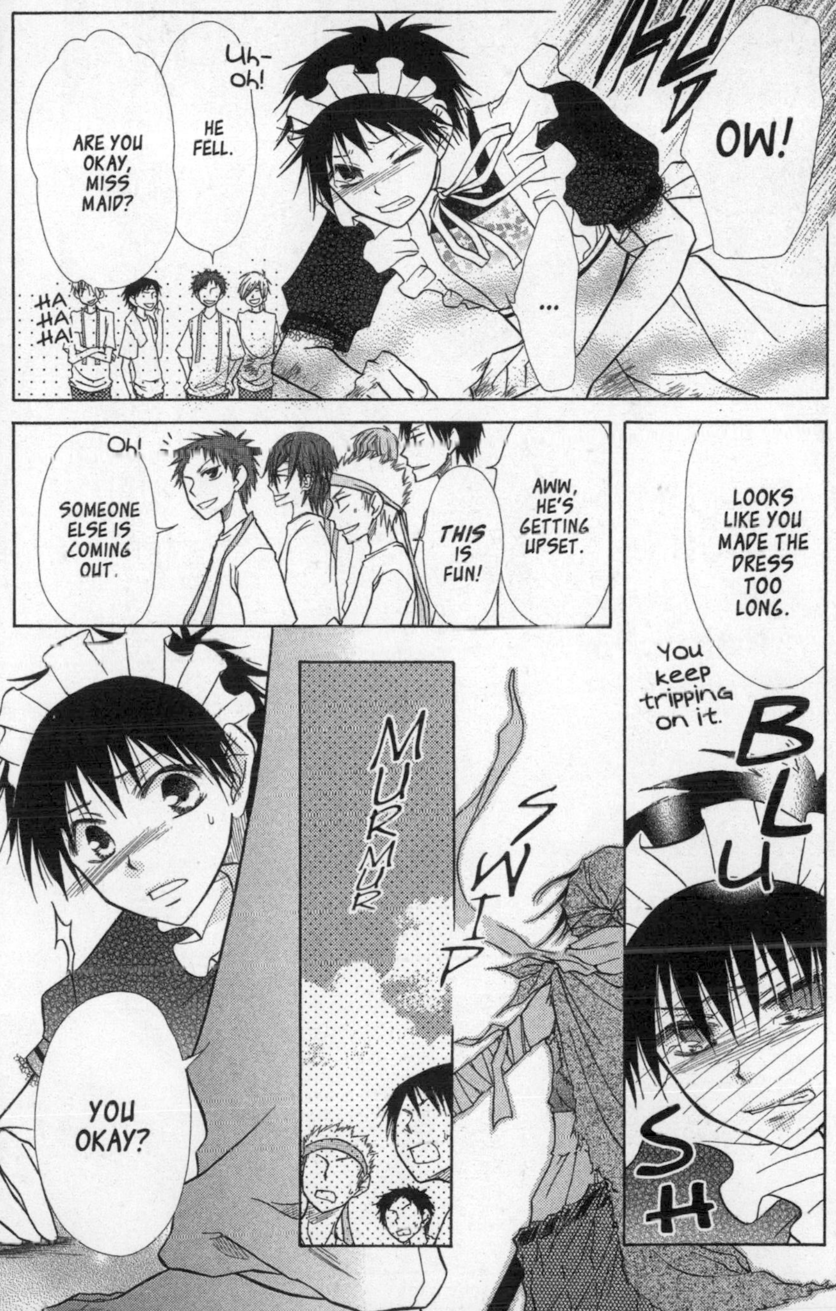
THUD
OW!
...
Uh-oh!
HE FELL.
ARE YOU OKAY, MISS MAID?
HA HA HA!
LOOKS LIKE YOU MADE THE DRESS TOO LONG.
You keep tripping on it.
AWW, HE'S GETTING UPSET.
THIS IS FUN!
Oh!
SOMEONE ELSE IS COMING OUT.
BLUSH
SWIP
MURMUR
YOU OKAY?

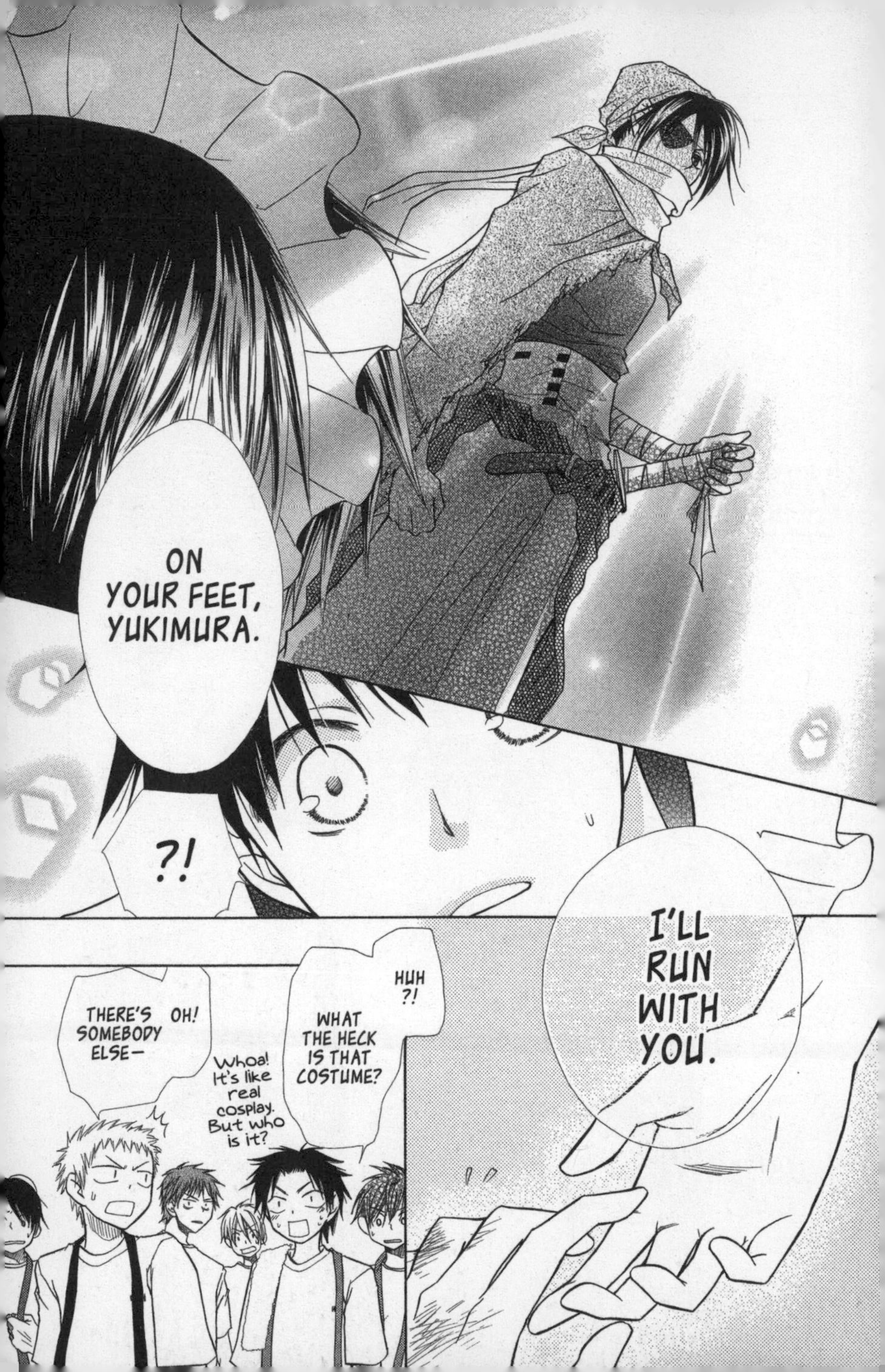
ON YOUR FEET, YUKIMURA.
?!
I'LL RUN WITH YOU.
HUH ?!
WHAT THE HECK IS THAT COSTUME?
Whoa! It's like real cosplay. But who is it?
OH!
THERE'S SOMEBODY ELSE—

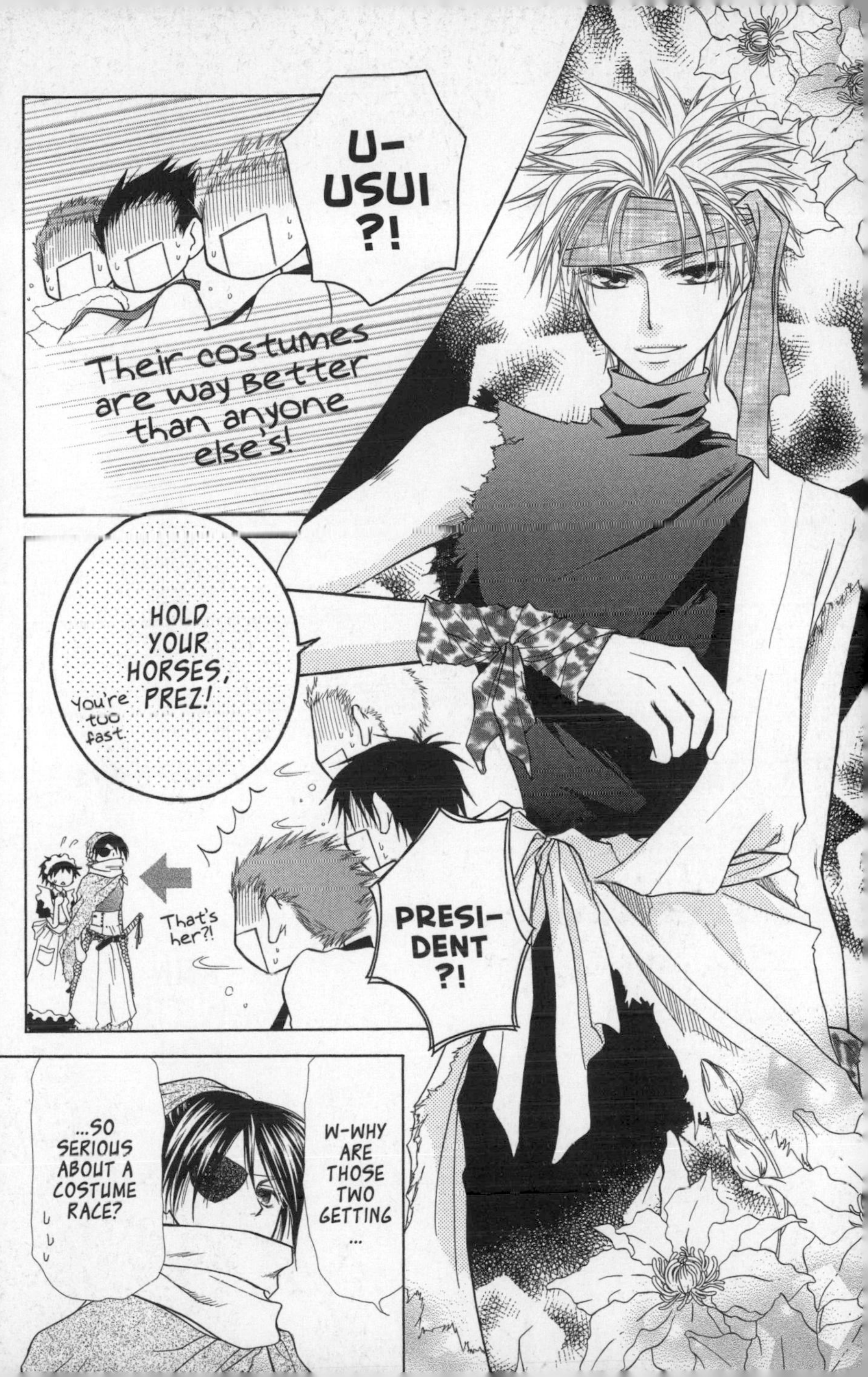
U-USUI?!
Their costumes are way better than anyone else's!
PRESIDENT?!
That's her?!
HOLD YOUR HORSES, PREZ!
You're too fast.
W-WHY ARE THOSE TWO GETTING...
...SO SERIOUS ABOUT A COSTUME RACE?

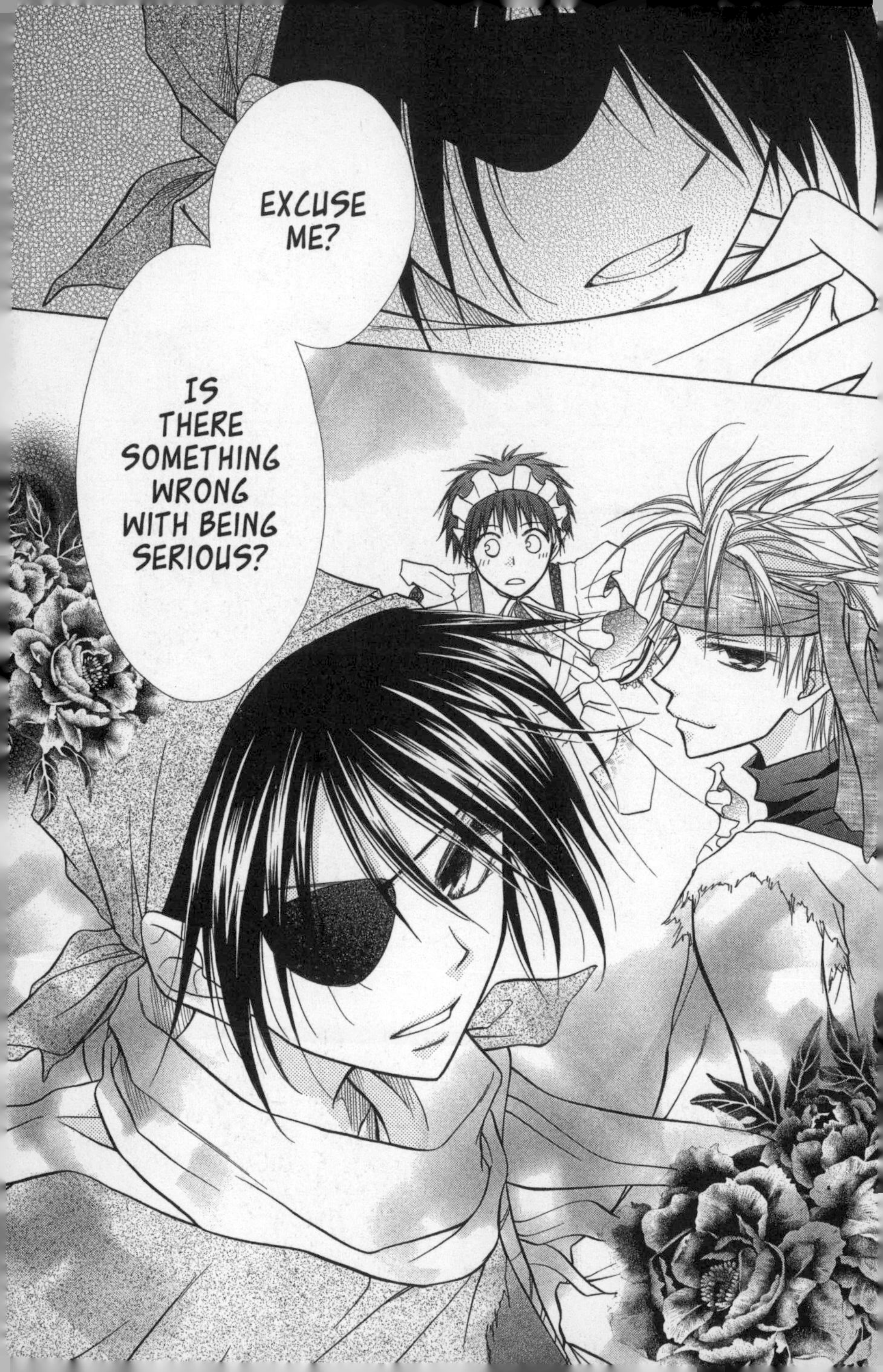
EXCUSE ME?
IS THERE SOMETHING WRONG WITH BEING SERIOUS?

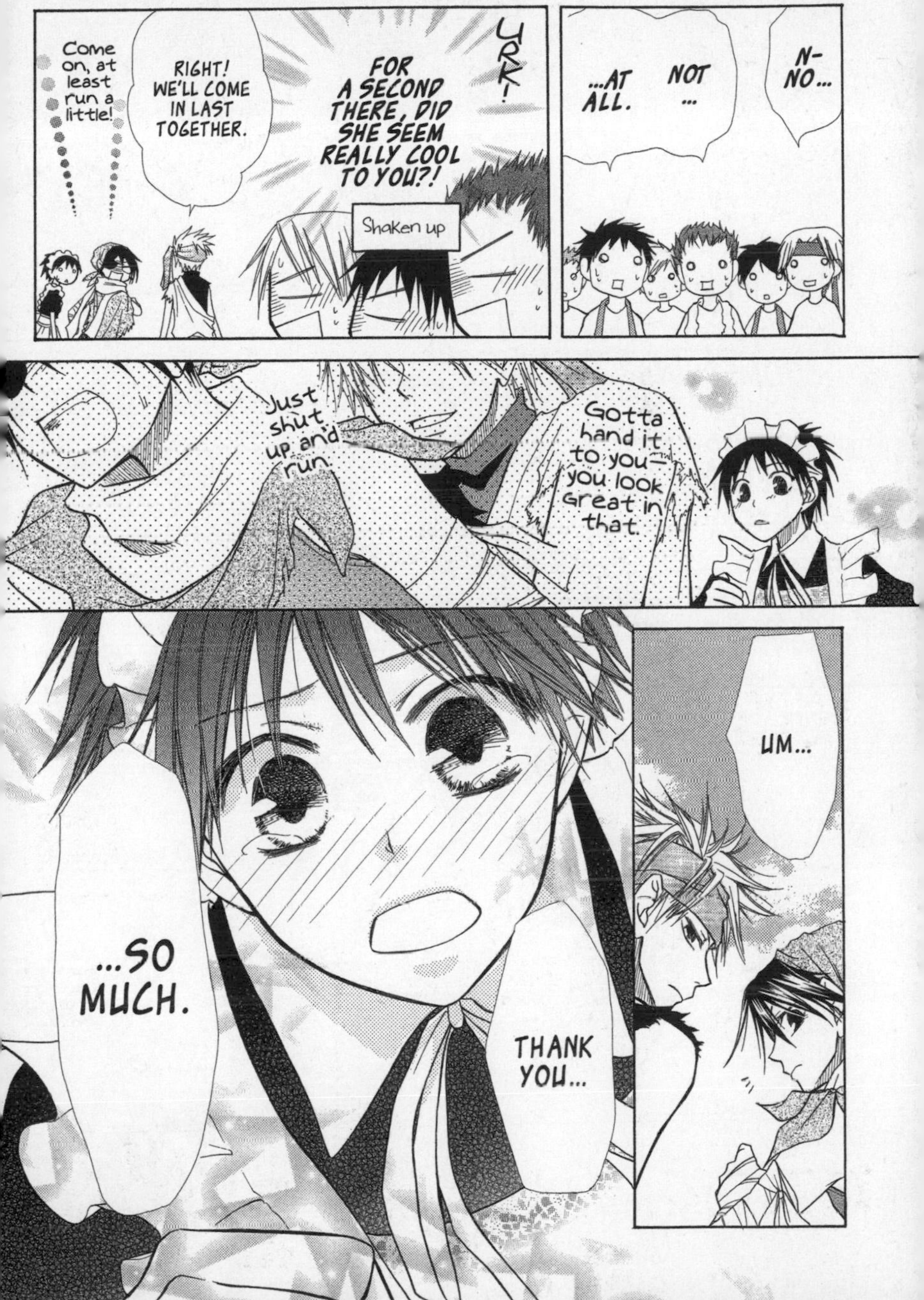
N-NO...
NOT ...
...AT ALL.
URK!
FOR A SECOND THERE, DID SHE SEEM REALLY COOL TO YOU?!
Shaken up
RIGHT! WE'LL COME IN LAST TOGETHER.
Come on, at least run a little!
Gotta hand it to you—you look great in that.
Just shut up and run.
UM...
THANK YOU...
...SO MUCH.

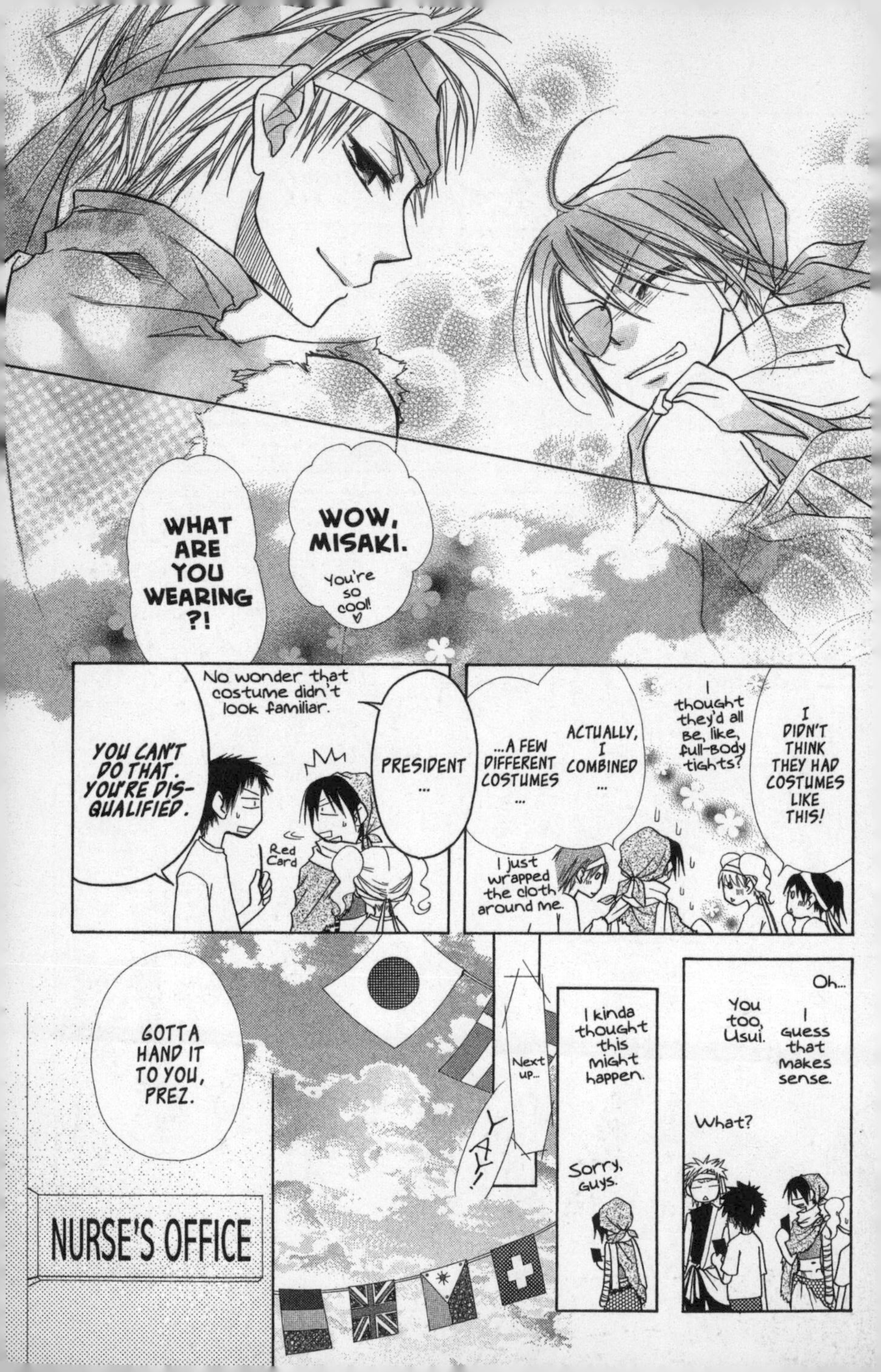
WOW, MISAKI.
You're so cool! ♡
WHAT ARE YOU WEARING?!
I DIDN'T THINK THEY HAD COSTUMES LIKE THIS!
I thought they'd all be, like, full-body tights?
ACTUALLY, I COMBINED...
...A FEW DIFFERENT COSTUMES...
I just wrapped the cloth around me.
PRESIDENT...
No wonder that costume didn't look familiar.
YOU CAN'T DO THAT. YOU'RE DISQUALIFIED.
Red Card
Oh... I guess that makes sense.
You too, Usui.
What?
I kinda thought this might happen.
Sorry, guys.
Next up...
YAY!
GOTTA HAND IT TO YOU, PREZ.
NURSE'S OFFICE

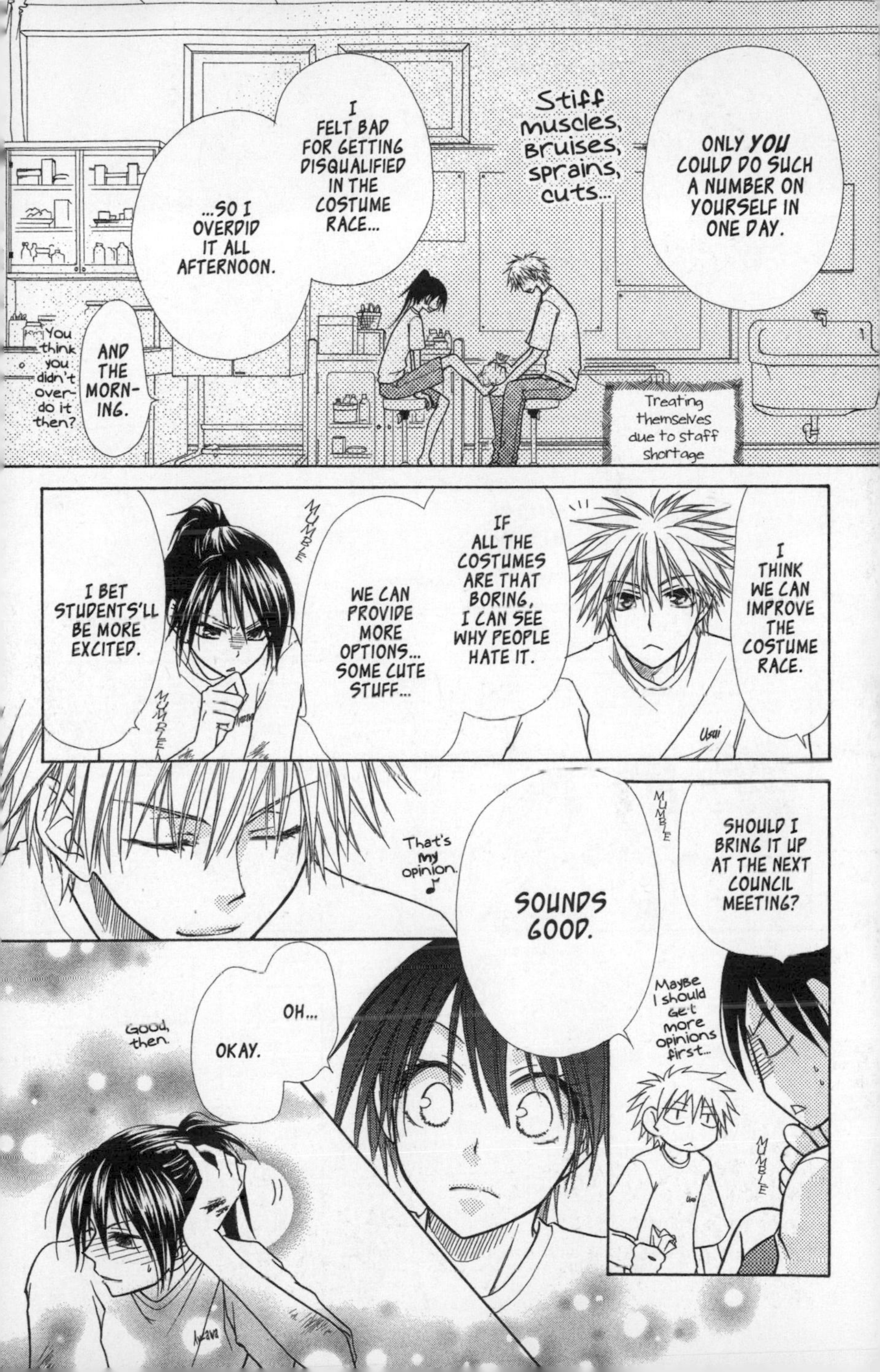
ONLY YOU COULD DO SUCH A NUMBER ON YOURSELF IN ONE DAY.
Stiff muscles, bruises, sprains, cuts...
I FELT BAD FOR GETTING DISQUALIFIED IN THE COSTUME RACE...
...SO I OVERDID IT ALL AFTERNOON.
AND THE MORNING.
You think you didn't over-do it then?
Treating themselves due to staff shortage
I THINK WE CAN IMPROVE THE COSTUME RACE.
IF ALL THE COSTUMES ARE THAT BORING, I CAN SEE WHY PEOPLE HATE IT.
MUMBLE
WE CAN PROVIDE MORE OPTIONS... SOME CUTE STUFF...
I BET STUDENTS'LL BE MORE EXCITED.
MUMBLE
SHOULD I BRING IT UP AT THE NEXT COUNCIL MEETING?
MUMBLE
SOUNDS GOOD.
That's my opinion.
Maybe I should get more opinions first...
MUMBLE
OH...
OKAY.
Good, then.

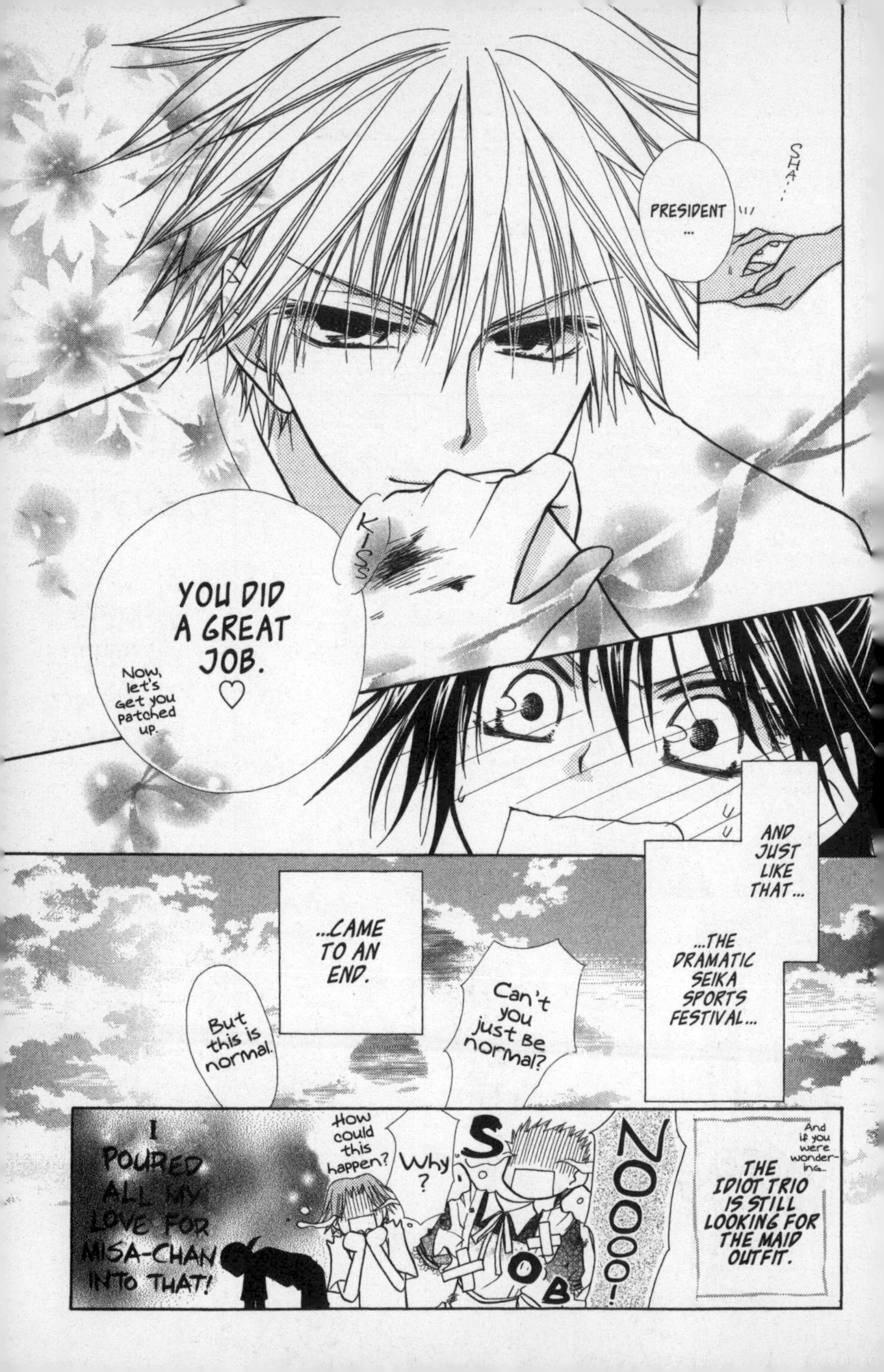
SHA...
PRESIDENT ...
KISS
YOU DID A GREAT JOB. ♡
Now, let's get you patched up.
UU
AND JUST LIKE THAT...
...THE DRAMATIC SEIKA SPORTS FESTIVAL...
...CAME TO AN END.
Can't you just be normal?
But this is normal.
And if you were wondering...
THE IDIOT TRIO IS STILL LOOKING FOR THE MAID OUTFIT.
NOOOO!
SOB
Why?
How could this happen?
I POURED ALL MY LOVE FOR MISA-CHAN INTO THAT!

Tea break...

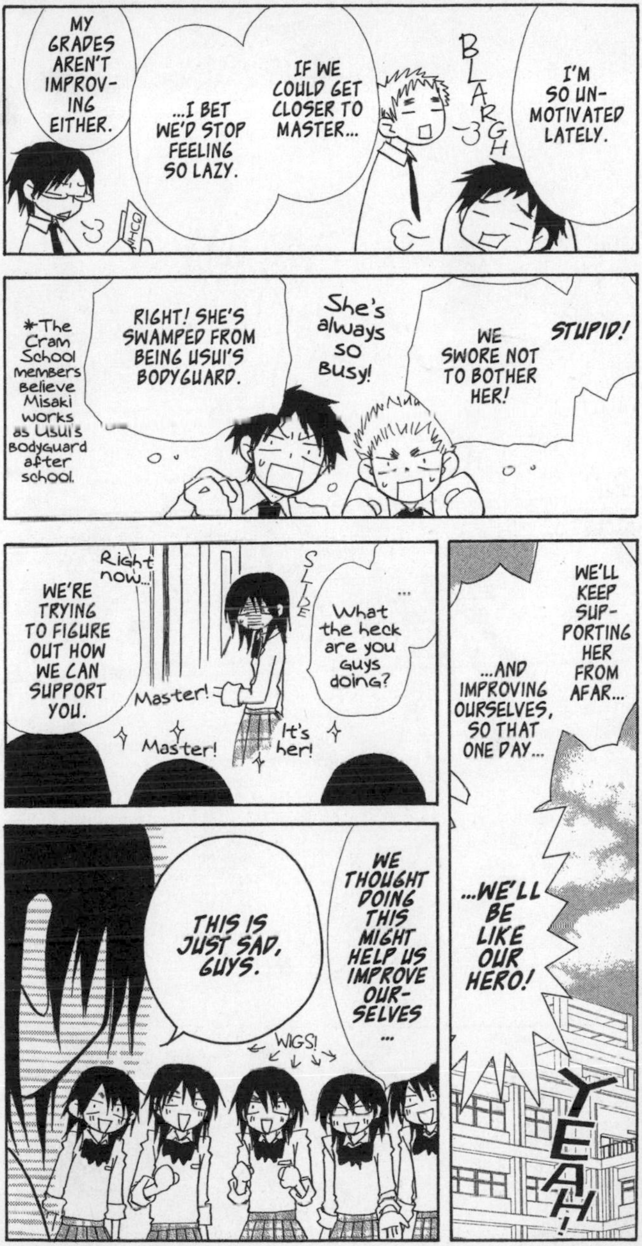
I'M SO UN-MOTIVATED LATELY.
BLARGH
IF WE COULD GET CLOSER TO MASTER...
...I BET WE'D STOP FEELING SO LAZY.
MY GRADES AREN'T IMPROVING EITHER.
STUPID!
WE SWORE NOT TO BOTHER HER!
She's always so Busy!
RIGHT! SHE'S SWAMPED FROM BEING USUI'S BODYGUARD.
*The Cram School members Believe Misaki works as Usui's Bodyguard after school.
WE'LL KEEP SUP-PORTING HER FROM AFAR...
...AND IMPROVING OURSELVES, SO THAT ONE DAY...
...WE'LL BE LIKE OUR HERO!
YEAH!
SLIDE
...
What the heck are you guys doing?
It's her!
Master!
Master!
Right now...!
WE'RE TRYING TO FIGURE OUT HOW WE CAN SUPPORT YOU.
WE THOUGHT DOING THIS MIGHT HELP US IMPROVE OUR-SELVES...
WIGS!
THIS IS JUST SAD, GUYS.

WHERE ARE THEY NOW?

- MEMBERS OF THE AYUZAWA CRAM SCHOOL -

What is the Ayuzawa Cram School?

The Cram School made its first appearance in volume 1, chapter 4. It's a group of five overenthusiastic boys who unexpectedly asked Misaki, whom they admire deeply and call "Master," to mentor them.

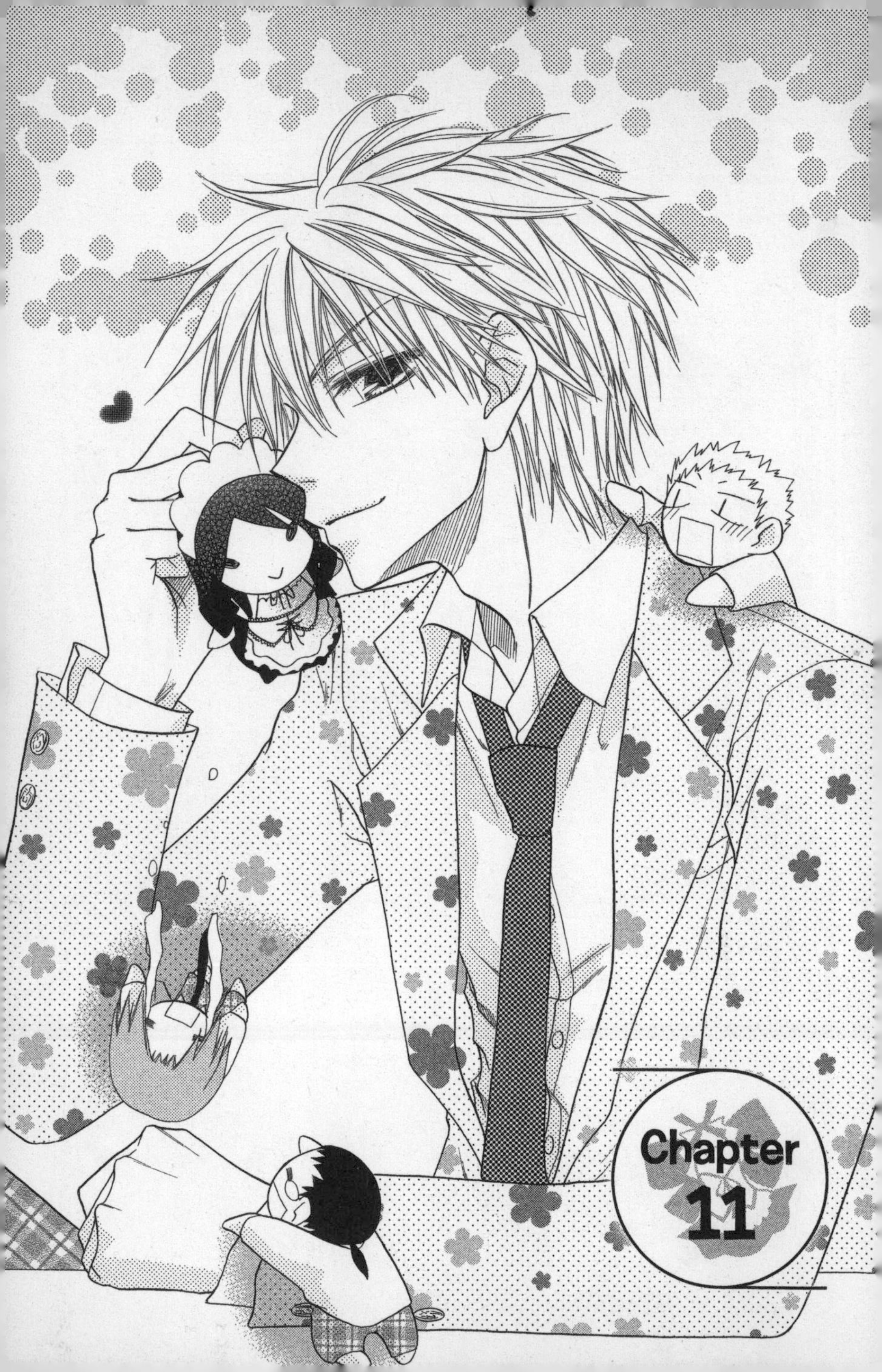
Chapter
11

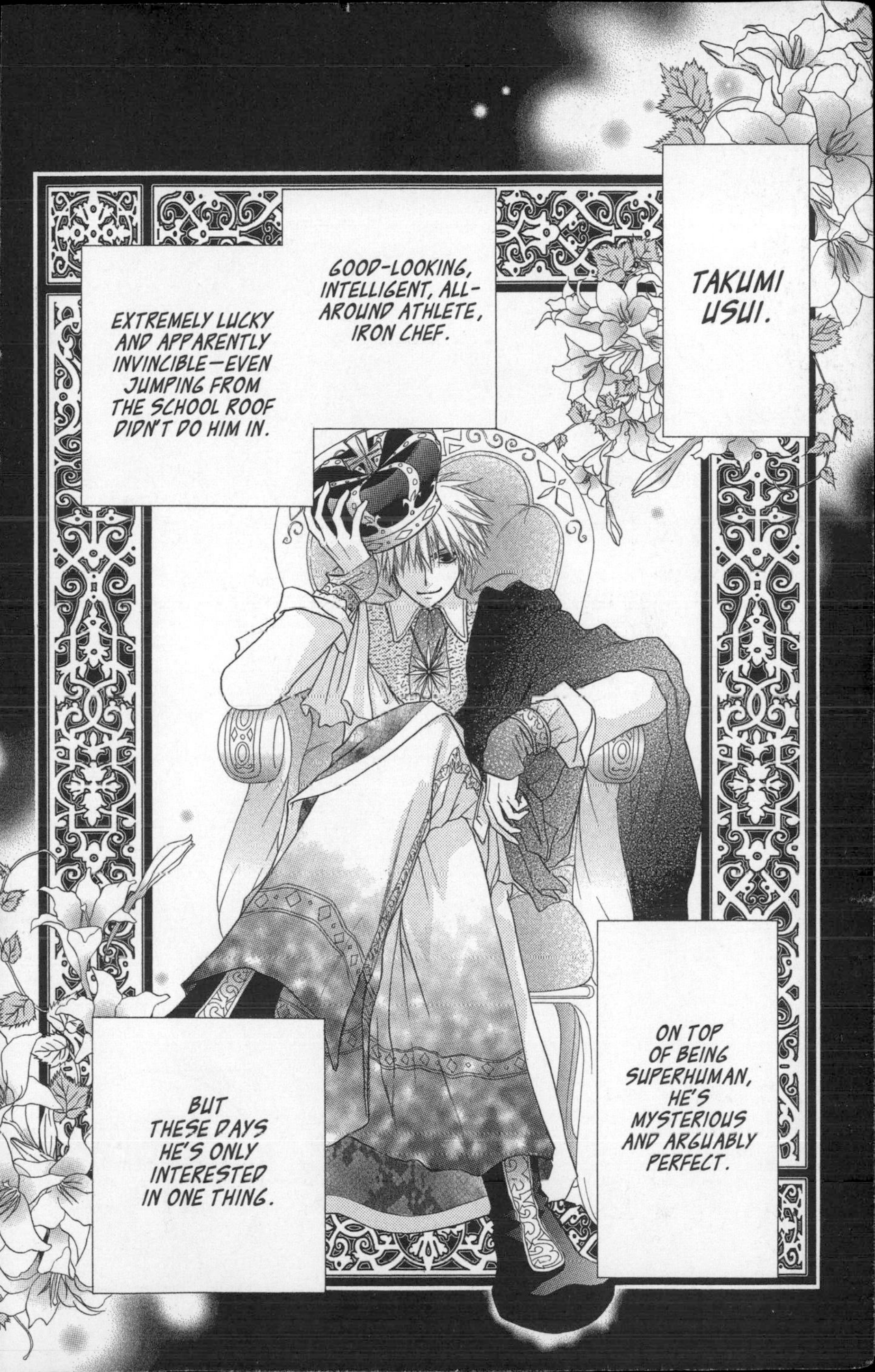
TAKUMI USUI.
GOOD-LOOKING, INTELLIGENT, ALL-AROUND ATHLETE, IRON CHEF.
EXTREMELY LUCKY AND APPARENTLY INVINCIBLE—EVEN JUMPING FROM THE SCHOOL ROOF DIDN'T DO HIM IN.
ON TOP OF BEING SUPERHUMAN, HE'S MYSTERIOUS AND ARGUABLY PERFECT.
BUT THESE DAYS HE'S ONLY INTERESTED IN ONE THING.

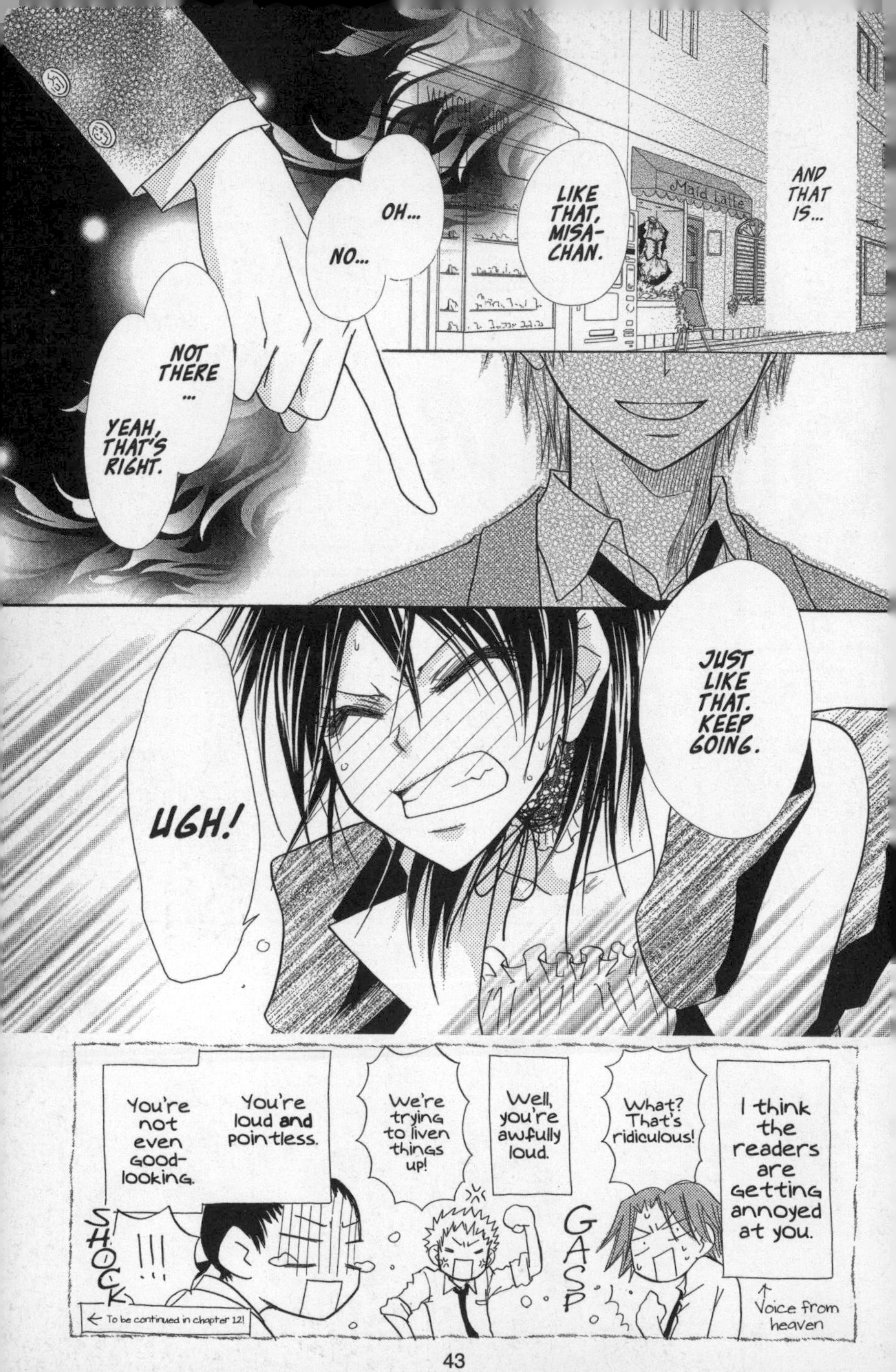
AND THAT IS...
LIKE THAT, MISA-CHAN.
Maid Latte
OH... NO...
NOT THERE ... YEAH, THAT'S RIGHT.
JUST LIKE THAT. KEEP GOING.
UGH!
I think the readers are getting annoyed at you.
↑ Voice from heaven
What? That's ridiculous!
GASP
Well, you're awfully loud.
We're trying to liven things up!
You're loud and pointless.
You're not even good-looking.
SHOCK
!!!
← To be continued in chapter 12!

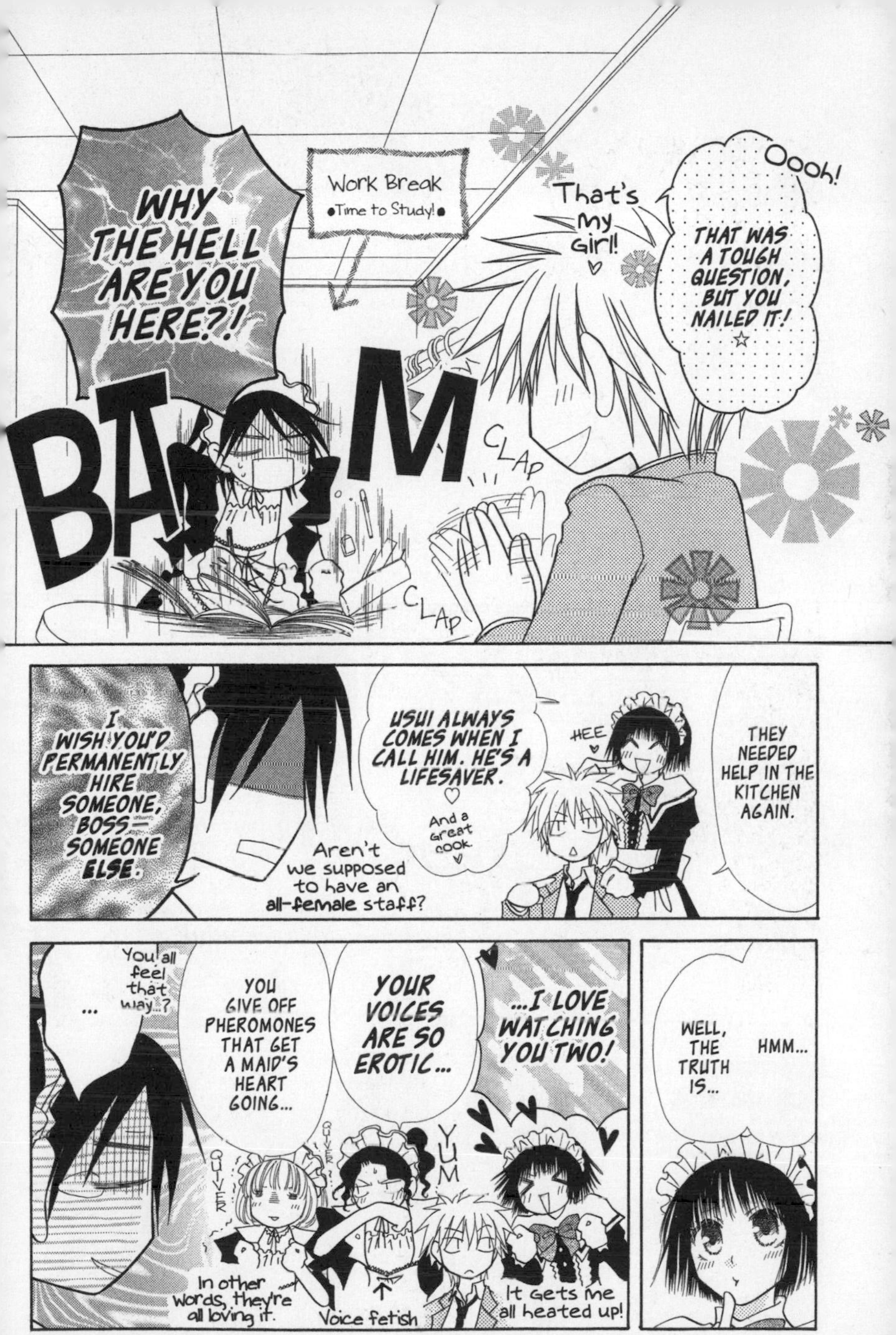
Oooh!
THAT WAS A TOUGH QUESTION, BUT YOU NAILED IT! ☆
That's my girl! ♡
Work Break
•Time to Study!•
WHY THE HELL ARE YOU HERE?!
BAM
CLAP
CLAP
THEY NEEDED HELP IN THE KITCHEN AGAIN.
HEE ♡
USUI ALWAYS COMES WHEN I CALL HIM. HE'S A LIFESAVER. ♡
And a great cook. ♡
Aren't we supposed to have an all-female staff?
I WISH YOU'D PERMANENTLY HIRE SOMEONE, BOSS—SOMEONE ELSE.
HMM...
WELL, THE TRUTH IS...
...I LOVE WATCHING YOU TWO!
YOUR VOICES ARE SO EROTIC...
YOU GIVE OFF PHEROMONES THAT GET A MAID'S HEART GOING...
You all feel that way...?
...
YUM
QUIVER
QUIVER
It gets me all heated up!
Voice fetish
In other words, they're all loving it.

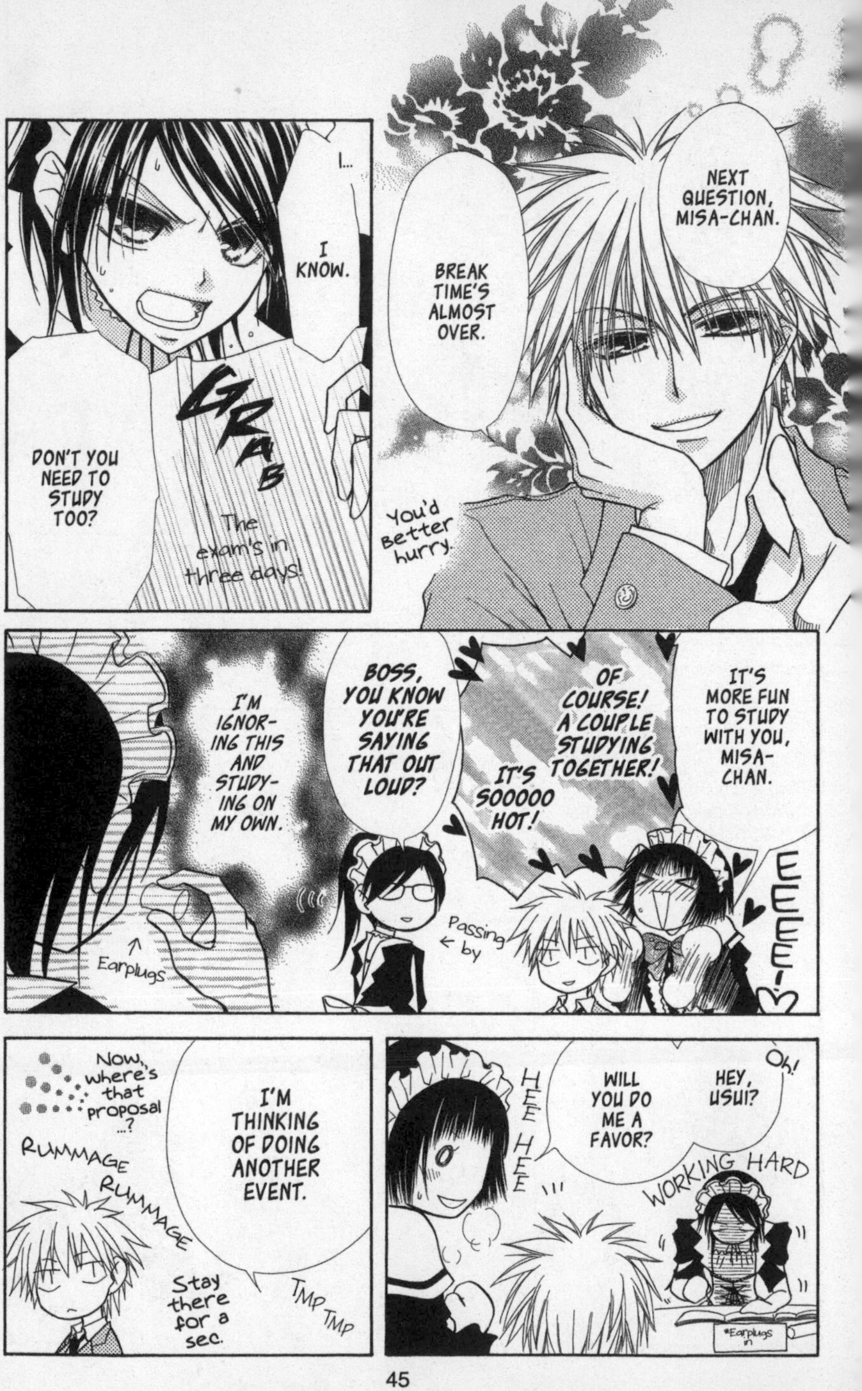
NEXT QUESTION, MISA-CHAN.
BREAK TIME'S ALMOST OVER.
You'd better hurry.
I...
I KNOW.
GRAB
The exam's in three days!
DON'T YOU NEED TO STUDY TOO?
IT'S MORE FUN TO STUDY WITH YOU, MISA-CHAN.
EEEEE!
OF COURSE! A COUPLE STUDYING TOGETHER!
IT'S SOOOOO HOT!
BOSS, YOU KNOW YOU'RE SAYING THAT OUT LOUD?
Passing by
I'M IGNORING THIS AND STUDYING ON MY OWN.
Earplugs
Oh!
HEY, USUI?
WILL YOU DO ME A FAVOR?
HEE HEE
WORKING HARD
*Earplugs in
I'M THINKING OF DOING ANOTHER EVENT.
Now, where's that proposal...?
RUMMAGE
RUMMAGE
Stay there for a sec.
TMP TMP

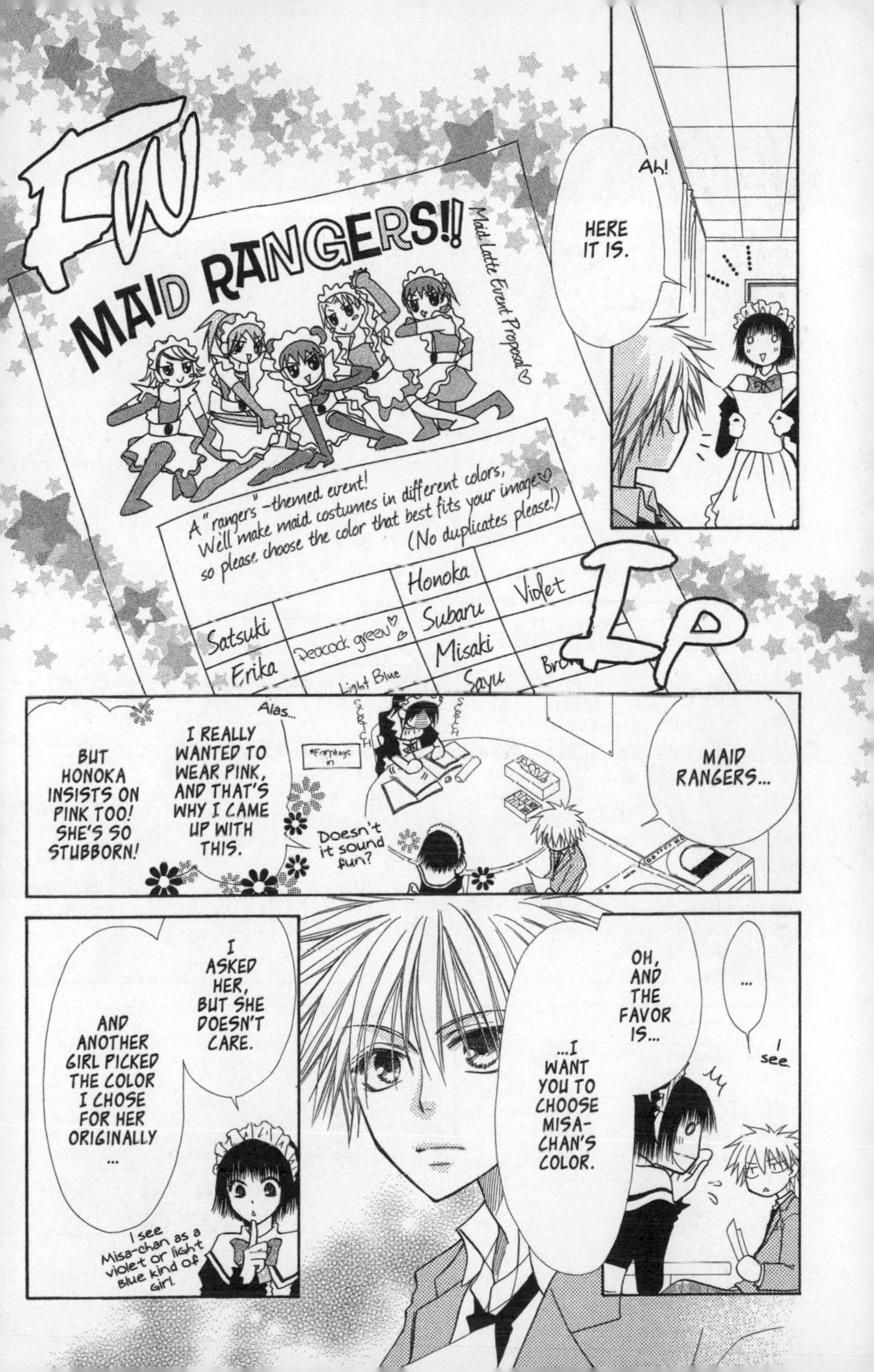

Ah!
HERE IT IS.
FW
IP
MAID RANGERS!!
Maid Latte Event Proposal♡
A "rangers"-themed event!
We'll make maid costumes in different colors,
so please choose the color that best fits your image♡
(No duplicates please!)
Honoka
Violet
Subaru
Satsuki
Peacock green♡
Misaki
Erika
Light Blue
Sayu
MAID RANGERS...
SCRTCH
SCRTCH
*Earplugs in
Alas...
I REALLY WANTED TO WEAR PINK, AND THAT'S WHY I CAME UP WITH THIS.
BUT HONOKA INSISTS ON PINK TOO! SHE'S SO STUBBORN!
Doesn't it sound fun?
...
I see.
OH, AND THE FAVOR IS...
...I WANT YOU TO CHOOSE MISA-CHAN'S COLOR.
I ASKED HER, BUT SHE DOESN'T CARE.
AND ANOTHER GIRL PICKED THE COLOR I CHOSE FOR HER ORIGINALLY ...
I see Misa-chan as a violet or light blue kind of girl.

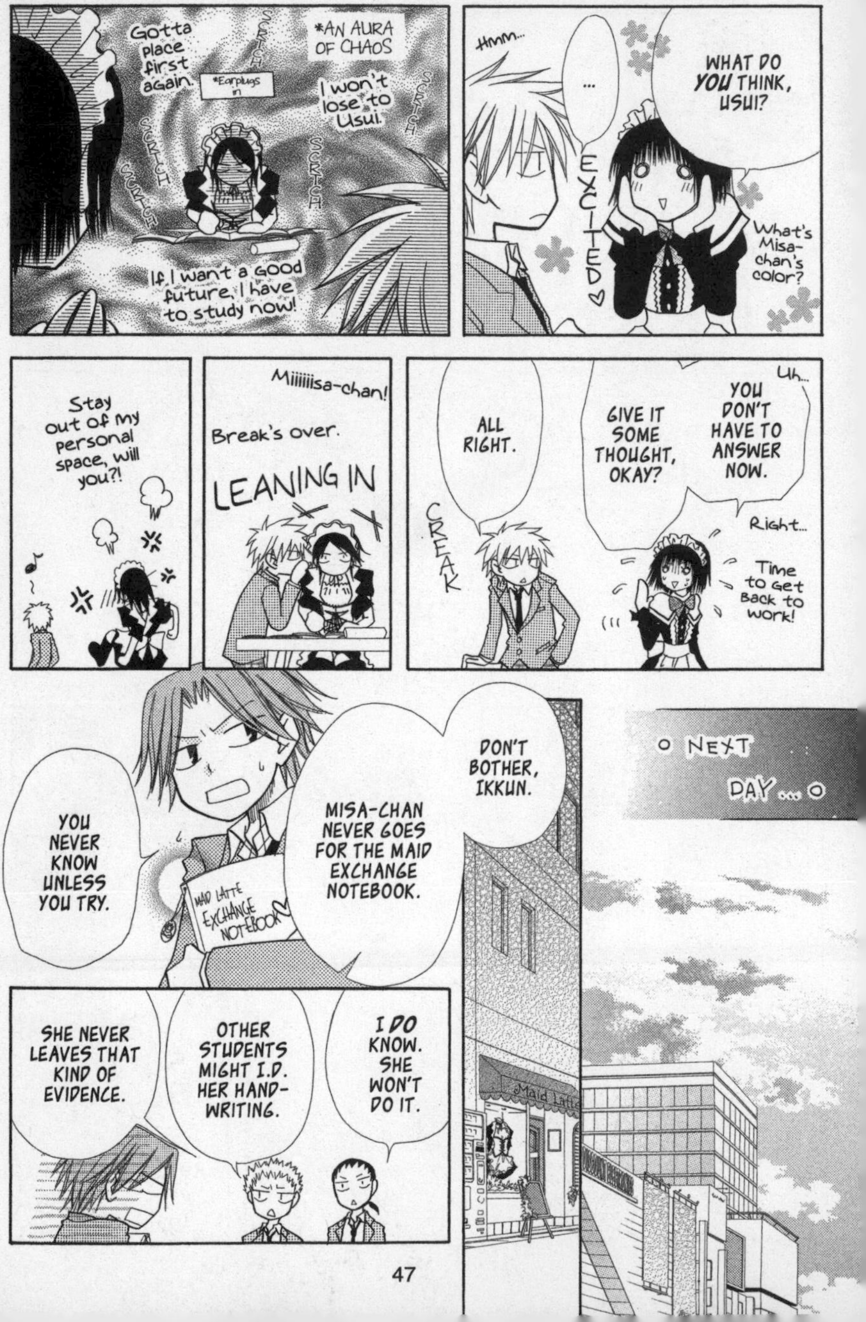
WHAT DO YOU THINK, USUI?
What's Misa-chan's color?
EXCITED ♥
...
Hmm...
*AN AURA OF CHAOS
SCRTCH
I won't lose to Usui.
Gotta place first again.
*Earplugs in
If I want a good future, I have to study now!
Uh...
YOU DON'T HAVE TO ANSWER NOW.
GIVE IT SOME THOUGHT, OKAY?
ALL RIGHT.
Right...
Time to get back to work!
CREAK
Miiiiiisa-chan!
Break's over.
LEANING IN
Stay out of my personal space, will you?!
NEXT DAY...
Maid Latte
DON'T BOTHER, IKKUN.
MISA-CHAN NEVER GOES FOR THE MAID EXCHANGE NOTEBOOK.
YOU NEVER KNOW UNLESS YOU TRY.
MAID LATTE EXCHANGE NOTEBOOK
I DO KNOW. SHE WON'T DO IT.
OTHER STUDENTS MIGHT I.D. HER HAND-WRITING.
SHE NEVER LEAVES THAT KIND OF EVIDENCE.

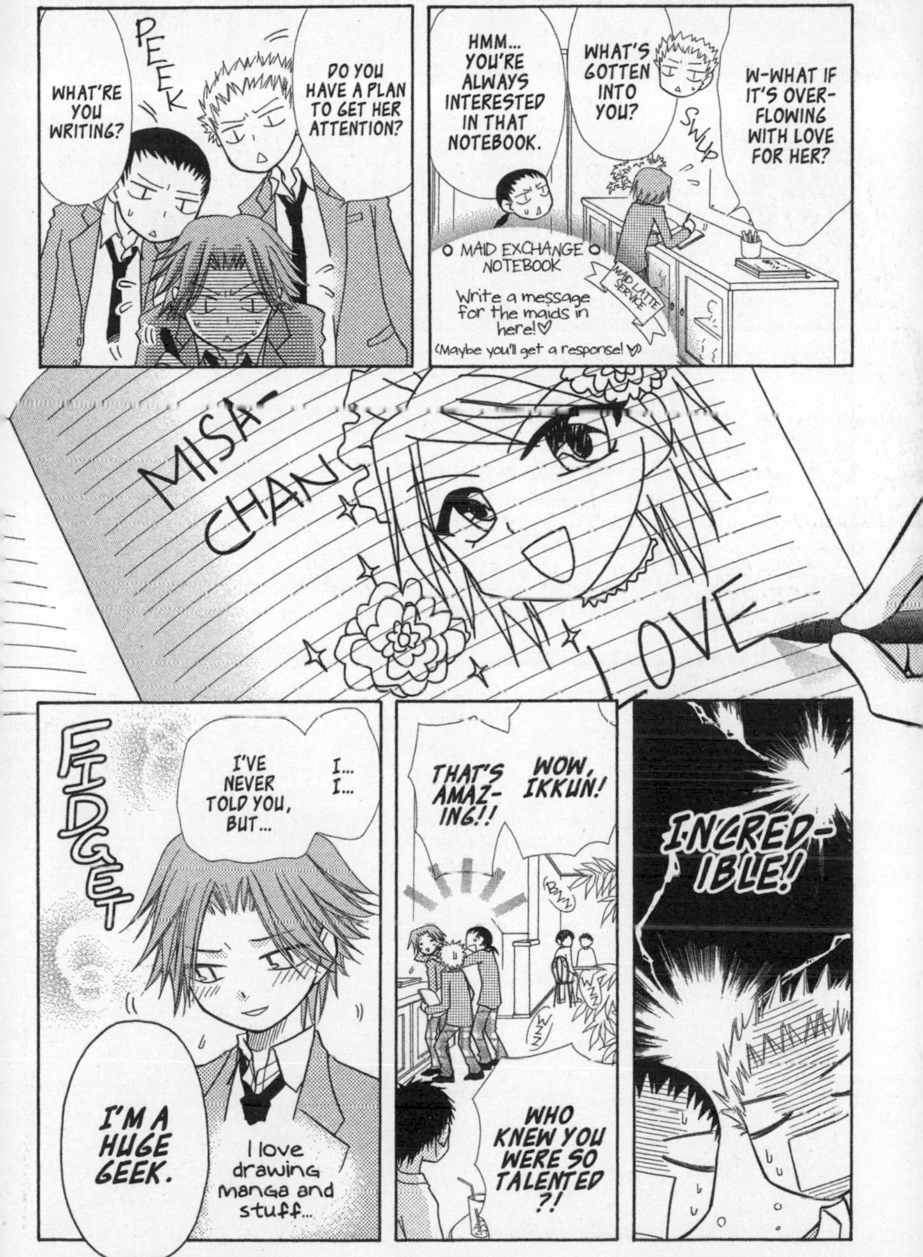
W-WHAT IF IT'S OVER-FLOWING WITH LOVE FOR HER?
WHAT'S GOTTEN INTO YOU?
HMM... YOU'RE ALWAYS INTERESTED IN THAT NOTEBOOK.
SWUP
MAID LATTE SERVICE
MAID EXCHANGE NOTEBOOK
Write a message for the maids in here!♡
(Maybe you'll get a response!♡)
DO YOU HAVE A PLAN TO GET HER ATTENTION?
PEEK
WHAT'RE YOU WRITING?
MISA-CHAN
LOVE
INCRED-IBLE!
WOW, IKKUN!
THAT'S AMAZ-ING!!
WHO KNEW YOU WERE SO TALENTED?!
I... I...
I'VE NEVER TOLD YOU, BUT...
FIDGET
I'M A HUGE GEEK.
I love drawing manga and stuff...

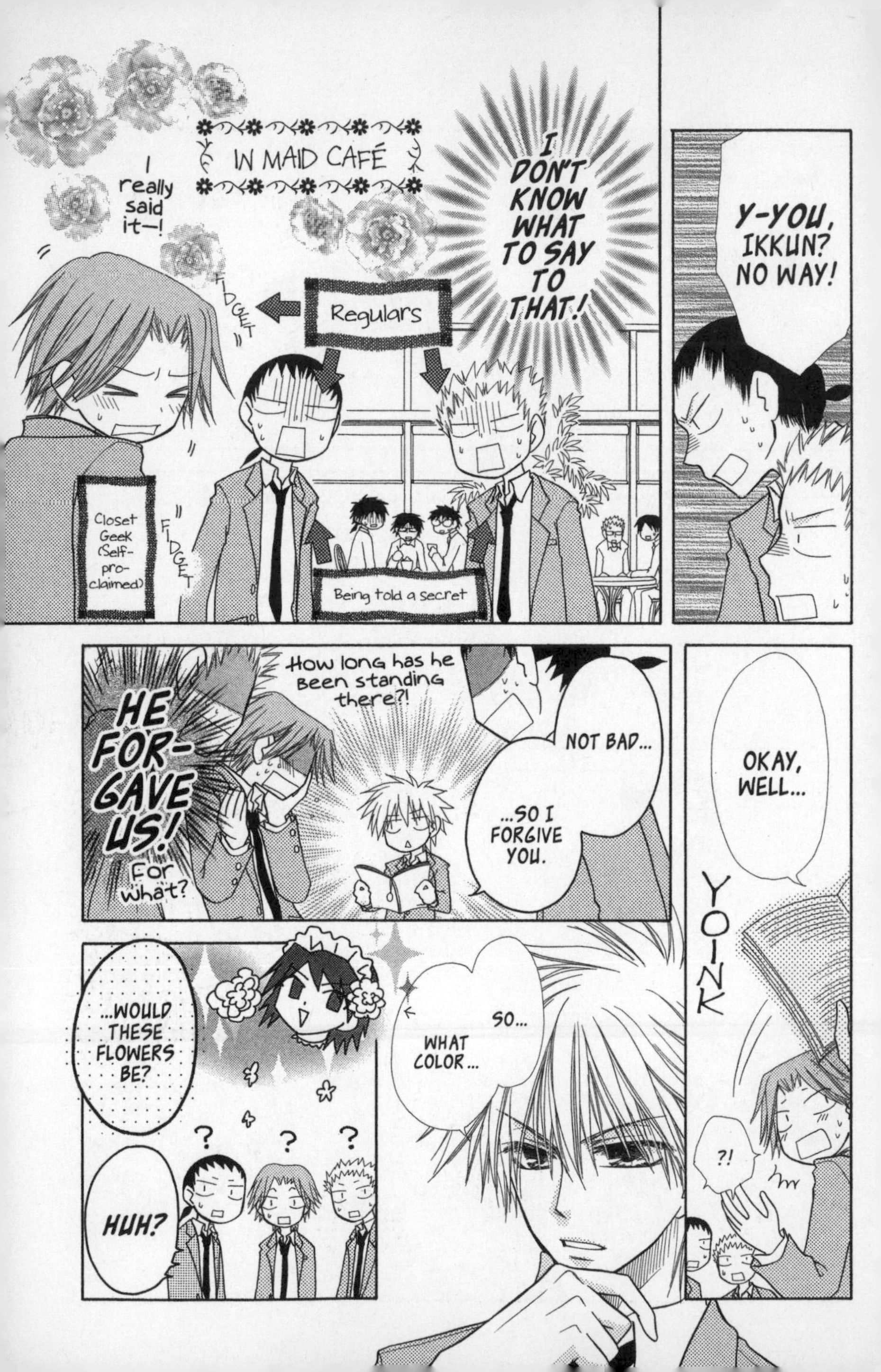
Y-YOU, IKKUN? NO WAY!
I DON'T KNOW WHAT TO SAY TO THAT!
IN MAID CAFÉ
I really said it—!
Regulars
FIDGET
FIDGET
Closet Geek (Self-proclaimed)
Being told a secret
OKAY, WELL...
YOINK
?!
NOT BAD...
...SO I FORGIVE YOU.
How long has he been standing there?!
HE FOR-GAVE US!
For what?
SO...
WHAT COLOR...
...WOULD THESE FLOWERS BE?
HUH?

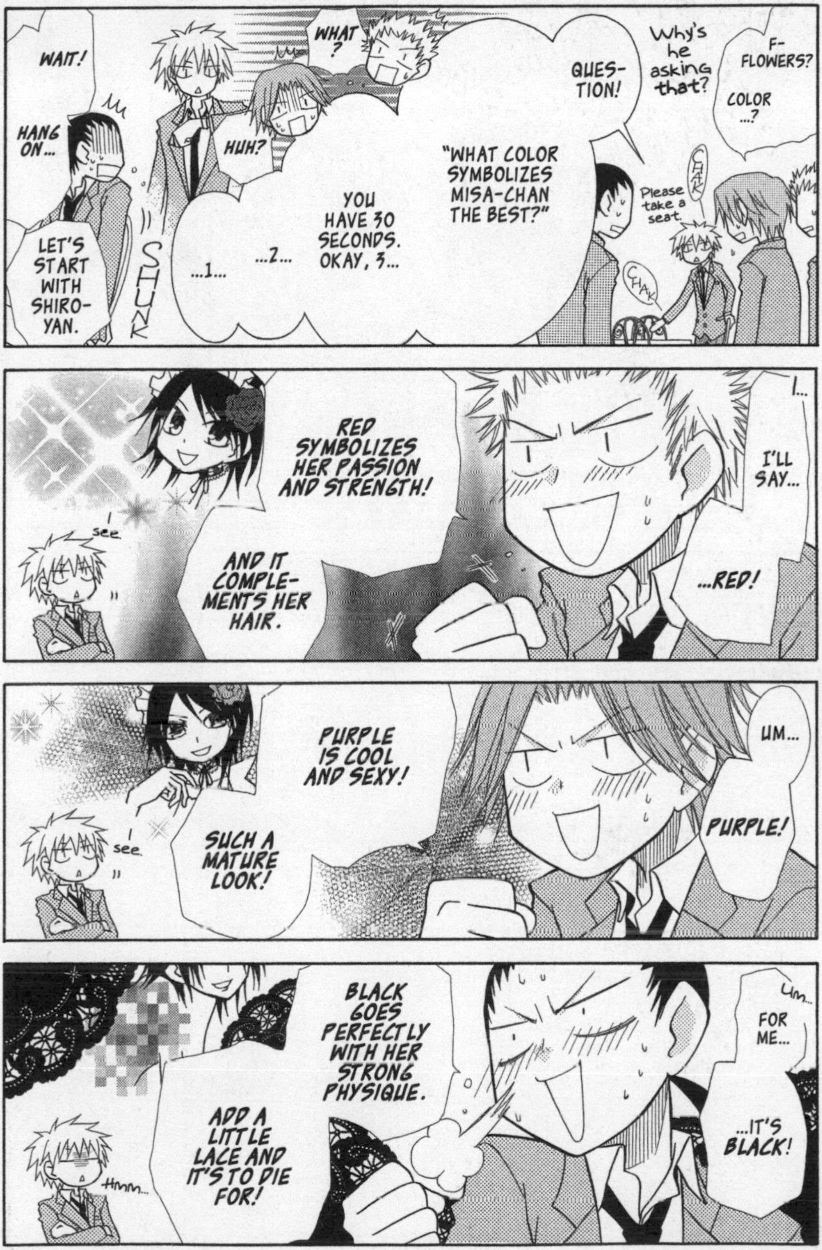
F-FLOWERS?
COLOR ...?
Why's he asking that?
CHAK
Please take a seat.
CHAK
QUES-TION!
"WHAT COLOR SYMBOLIZES MISA-CHAN THE BEST?"
YOU HAVE 30 SECONDS. OKAY, 3...
...2...
...1...
WHAT?
HUH?
WAIT!
HANG ON...
SHUNK
LET'S START WITH SHIRO-YAN.
I...
I'LL SAY...
...RED!
RED SYMBOLIZES HER PASSION AND STRENGTH!
AND IT COMPLEMENTS HER HAIR.
I see.
UM...
PURPLE!
PURPLE IS COOL AND SEXY!
SUCH A MATURE LOOK!
I see.
Um...
FOR ME...
...IT'S BLACK!
BLACK GOES PERFECTLY WITH HER STRONG PHYSIQUE.
ADD A LITTLE LACE AND IT'S TO DIE FOR!
Hmm...

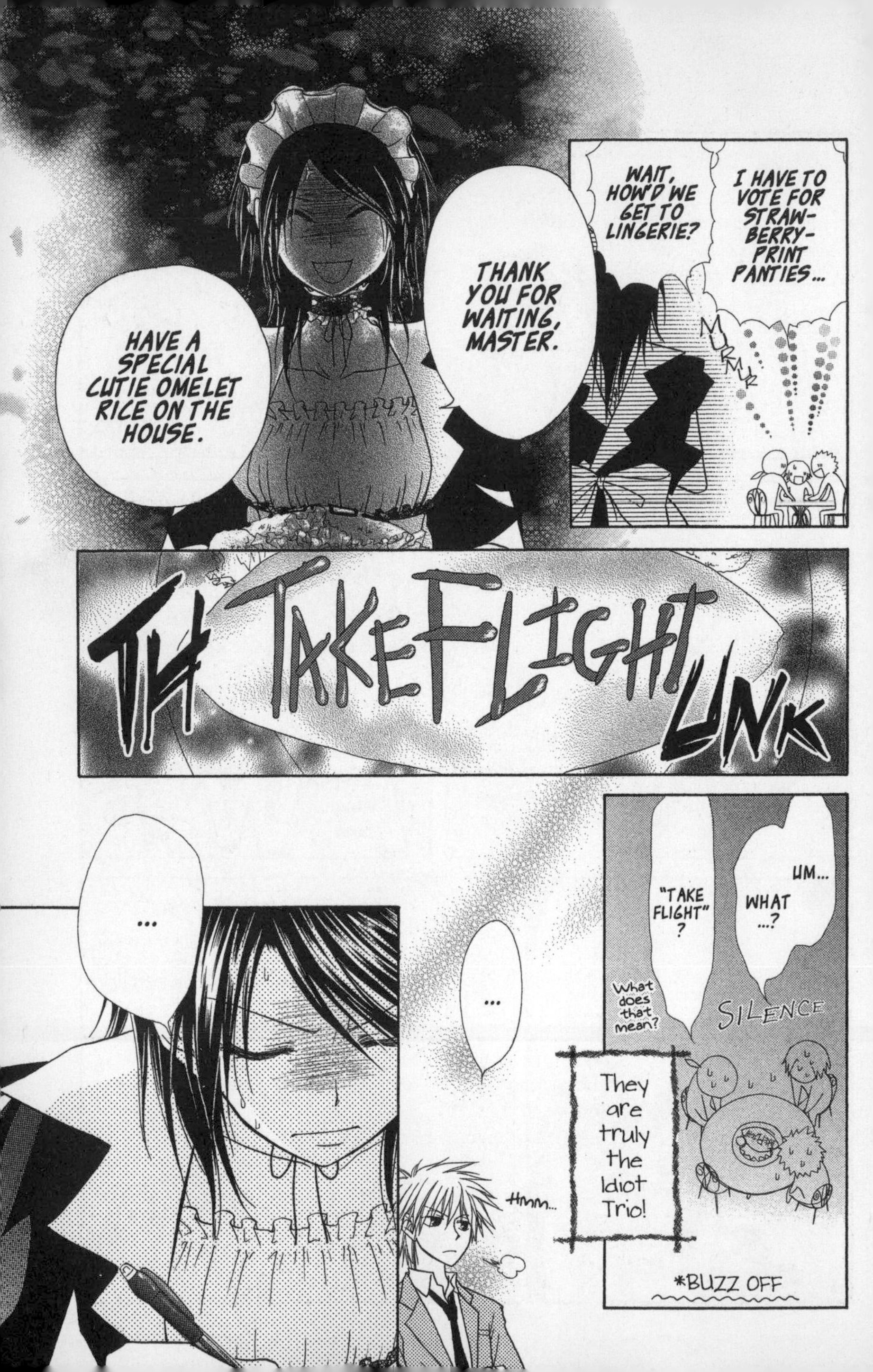
I HAVE TO VOTE FOR STRAW-BERRY-PRINT PANTIES...
WAIT, HOW'D WE GET TO LINGERIE?
MURMUR
THANK YOU FOR WAITING, MASTER.
HAVE A SPECIAL CUTIE OMELET RICE ON THE HOUSE.
TH
TAKE FLIGHT
UNK
UM... WHAT ...?
"TAKE FLIGHT" ?
What does that mean?
SILENCE
They are truly the Idiot Trio!
*BUZZ OFF
...
...
Hmm...

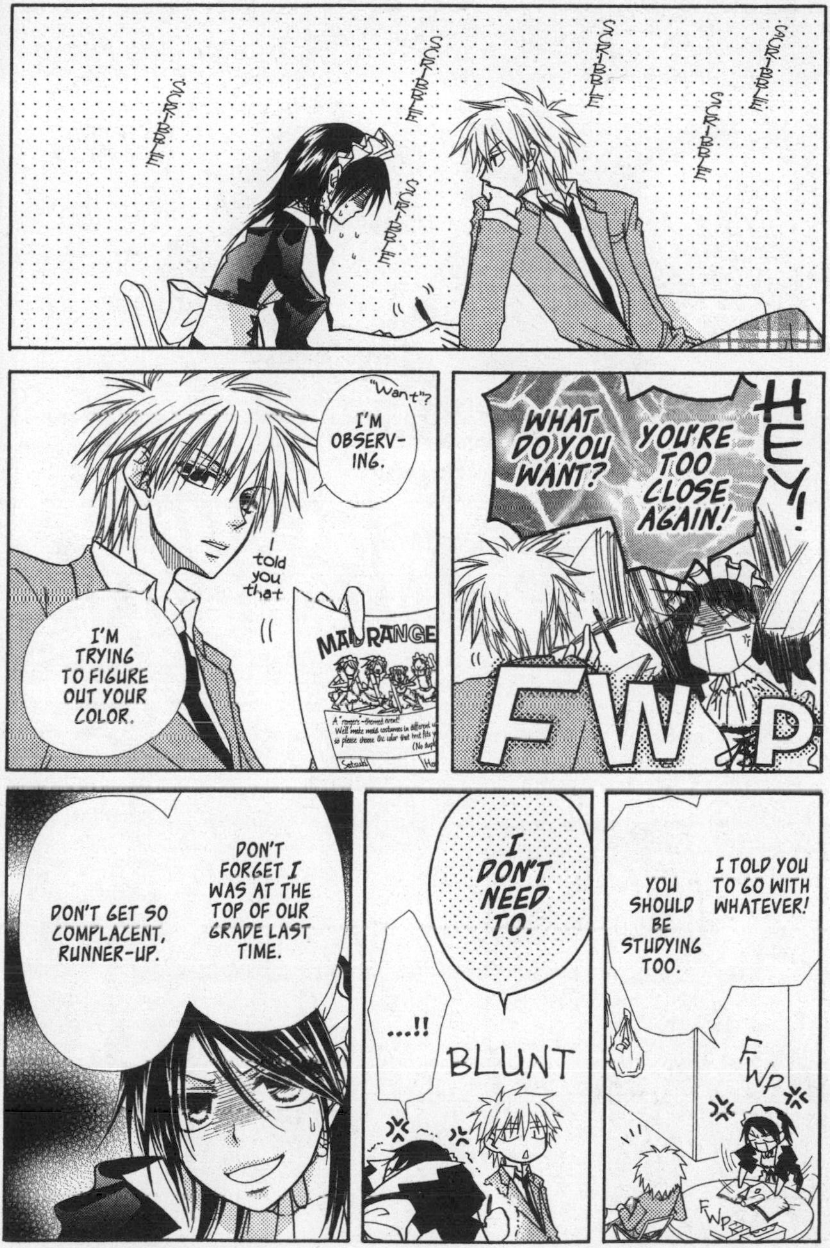
SCRIBBLE
SCRIBBLE
SCRIBBLE
SCRIBBLE
SCRIBBLE
SCRIBBLE
HEY!
YOU'RE TOO CLOSE AGAIN!
WHAT DO YOU WANT?
FWP
"Want"? I'M OBSERVING.
I told you that
I'M TRYING TO FIGURE OUT YOUR COLOR.
I TOLD YOU TO GO WITH WHATEVER!
YOU SHOULD BE STUDYING TOO.
FWP
FWP
I DON'T NEED TO.
...!!
BLUNT
DON'T FORGET I WAS AT THE TOP OF OUR GRADE LAST TIME.
DON'T GET SO COMPLACENT, RUNNER-UP.

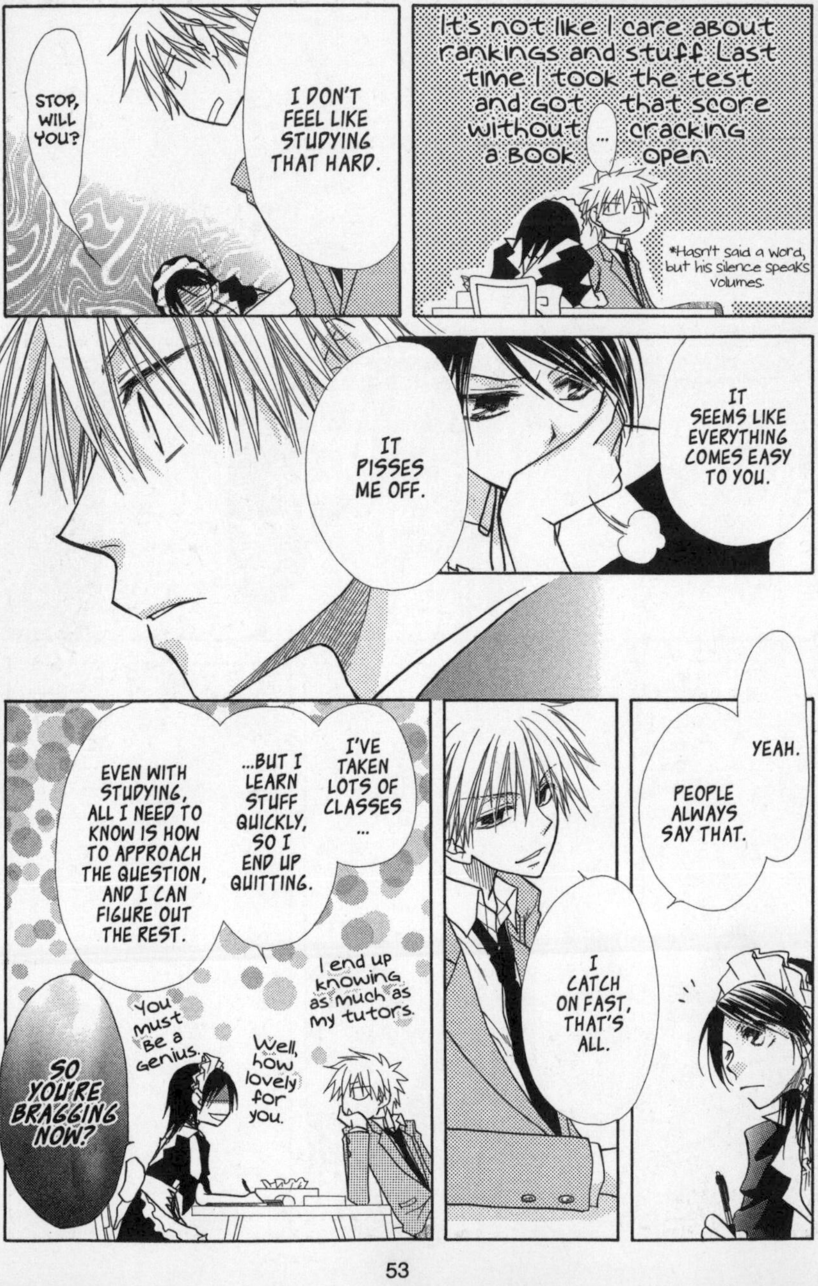
It's not like I care about rankings and stuff. Last time I took the test and got that score without cracking a book open.
...
*Hasn't said a word, but his silence speaks volumes.
I DON'T FEEL LIKE STUDYING THAT HARD.
STOP, WILL YOU?
IT SEEMS LIKE EVERYTHING COMES EASY TO YOU.
IT PISSES ME OFF.
YEAH.
PEOPLE ALWAYS SAY THAT.
I CATCH ON FAST, THAT'S ALL.
I'VE TAKEN LOTS OF CLASSES ...
...BUT I LEARN STUFF QUICKLY, SO I END UP QUITTING.
EVEN WITH STUDYING, ALL I NEED TO KNOW IS HOW TO APPROACH THE QUESTION, AND I CAN FIGURE OUT THE REST.
I end up knowing as much as my tutors.
Well, how lovely for you.
You must be a genius.
SO YOU'RE BRAGGING NOW?

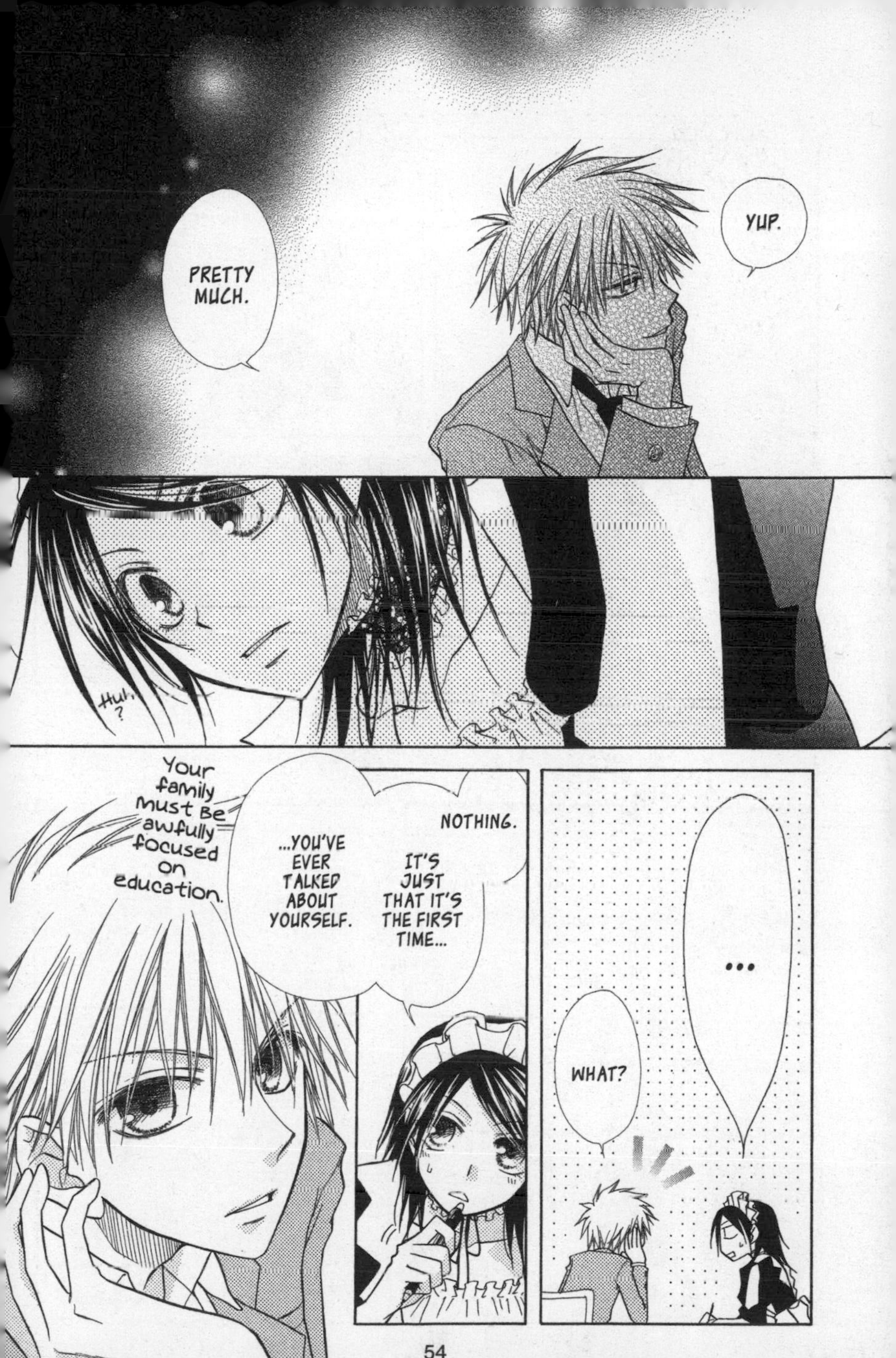
YUP.
PRETTY MUCH.
Huh?
...
WHAT?
NOTHING.
IT'S JUST THAT IT'S THE FIRST TIME...
...YOU'VE EVER TALKED ABOUT YOURSELF.
Your family must be awfully focused on education.

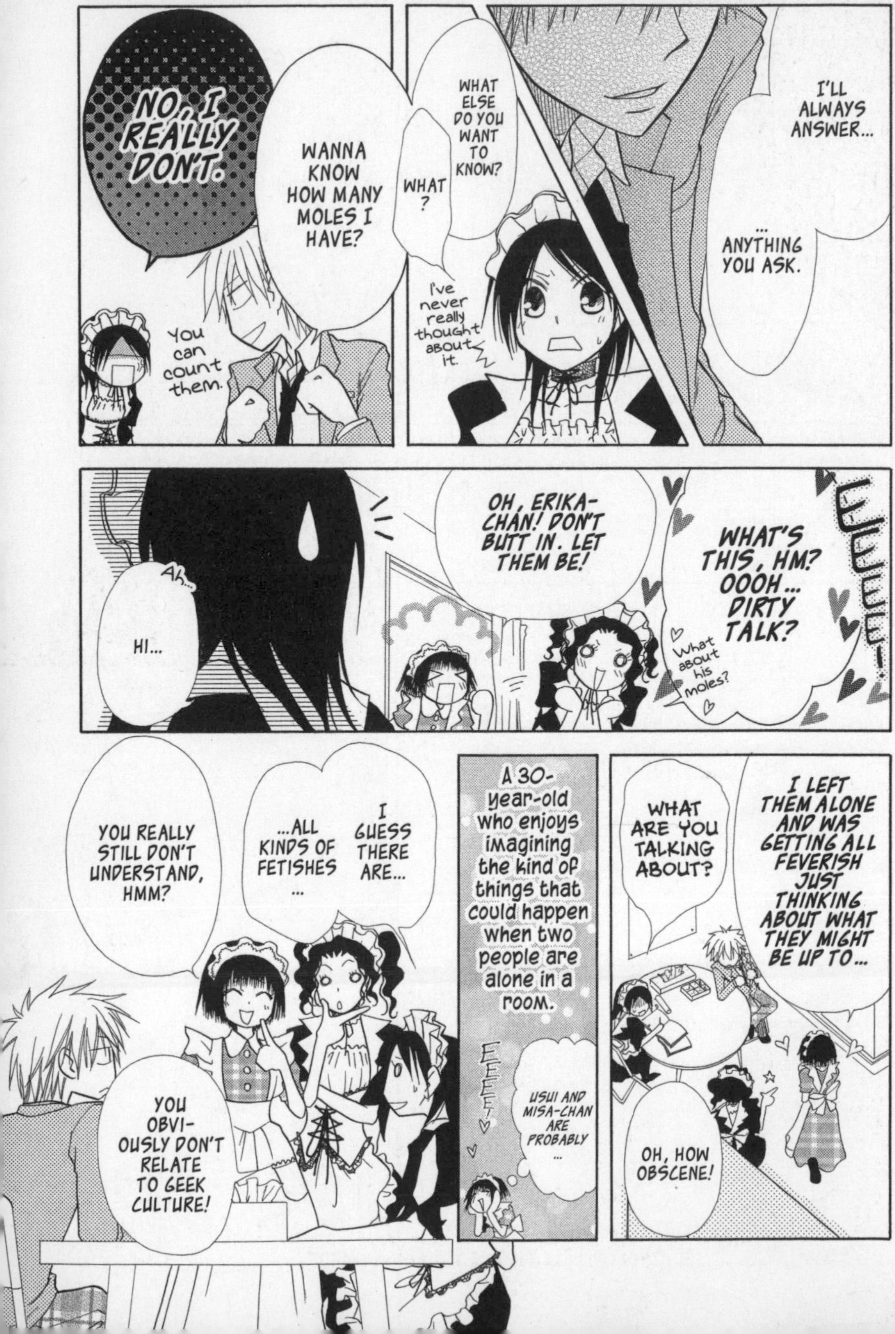
I'LL ALWAYS ANSWER...
... ANYTHING YOU ASK.
WHAT ELSE DO YOU WANT TO KNOW?
WHAT?
I've never really thought about it.
WANNA KNOW HOW MANY MOLES I HAVE?
NO, I REALLY DON'T.
You can count them.
EEEE!
WHAT'S THIS, HM? OOOH... DIRTY TALK?
What about his moles?
OH, ERIKA-CHAN! DON'T BUTT IN. LET THEM BE!
Ah...
HI...
I LEFT THEM ALONE AND WAS GETTING ALL FEVERISH JUST THINKING ABOUT WHAT THEY MIGHT BE UP TO...
WHAT ARE YOU TALKING ABOUT?
OH, HOW OBSCENE!
A 30-year-old who enjoys imagining the kind of things that could happen when two people are alone in a room.
EEEE!
USUI AND MISA-CHAN ARE PROBABLY ...
I GUESS THERE ARE...
...ALL KINDS OF FETISHES ...
YOU REALLY STILL DON'T UNDERSTAND, HMM?
YOU OBVIOUSLY DON'T RELATE TO GEEK CULTURE!

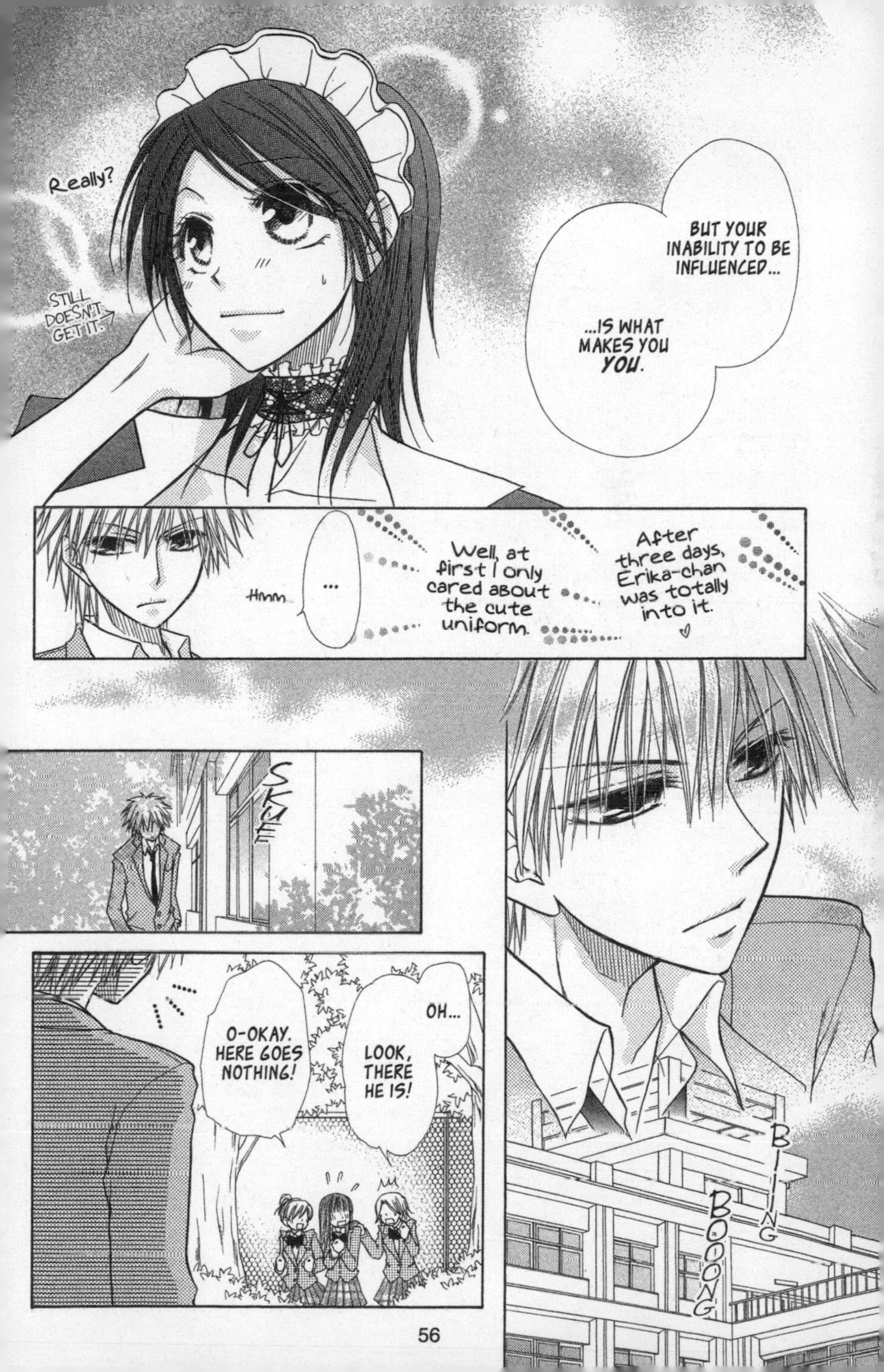
BUT YOUR INABILITY TO BE INFLUENCED...
...IS WHAT MAKES YOU YOU.
Really?
STILL DOESN'T GET IT.
After three days, Erika-chan was totally into it.
Well, at first I only cared about the cute uniform.
...
Hmm...
BIIING
BOOONG
SKUE
OH...
LOOK, THERE HE IS!
O-OKAY. HERE GOES NOTHING!
.....

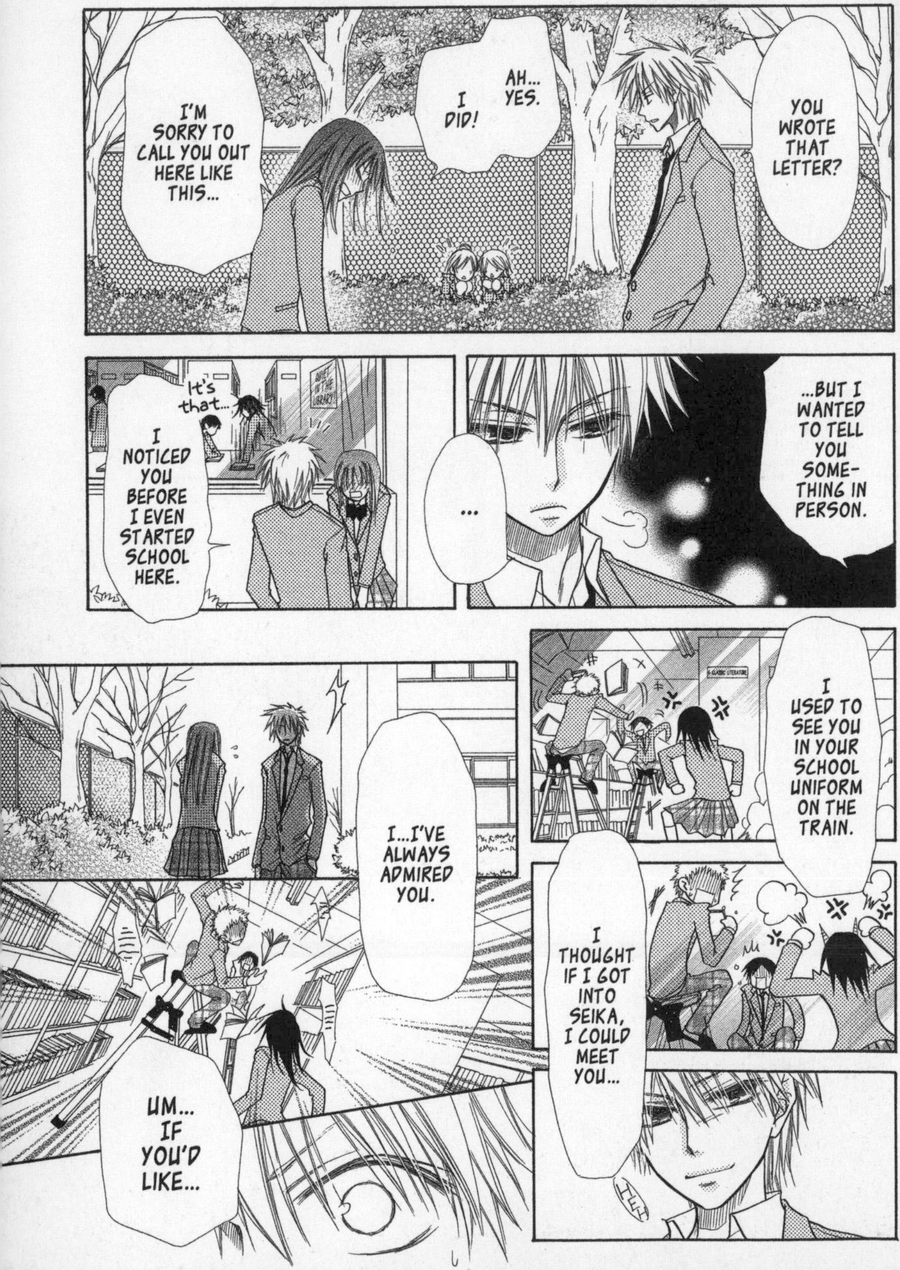
YOU WROTE THAT LETTER?
AH... YES.
I DID!
I'M SORRY TO CALL YOU OUT HERE LIKE THIS...
...BUT I WANTED TO TELL YOU SOMETHING IN PERSON.
...
It's that...
I NOTICED YOU BEFORE I EVEN STARTED SCHOOL HERE.
I USED TO SEE YOU IN YOUR SCHOOL UNIFORM ON THE TRAIN.
I THOUGHT IF I GOT INTO SEIKA, I COULD MEET YOU...
HEH
I...I'VE ALWAYS ADMIRED YOU.
UM... IF YOU'D LIKE...

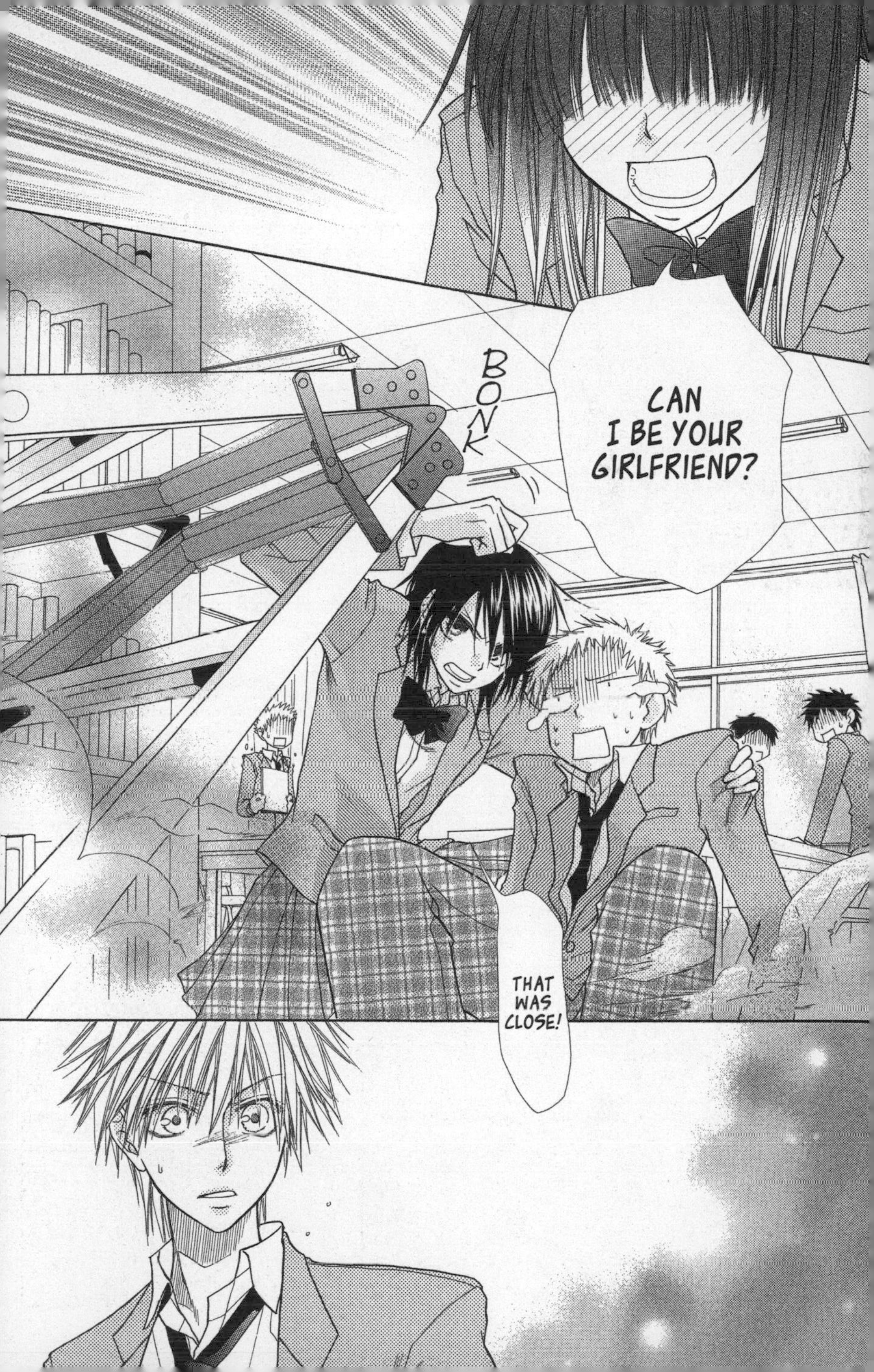
CAN I BE YOUR GIRLFRIEND?
BONK
THAT WAS CLOSE!

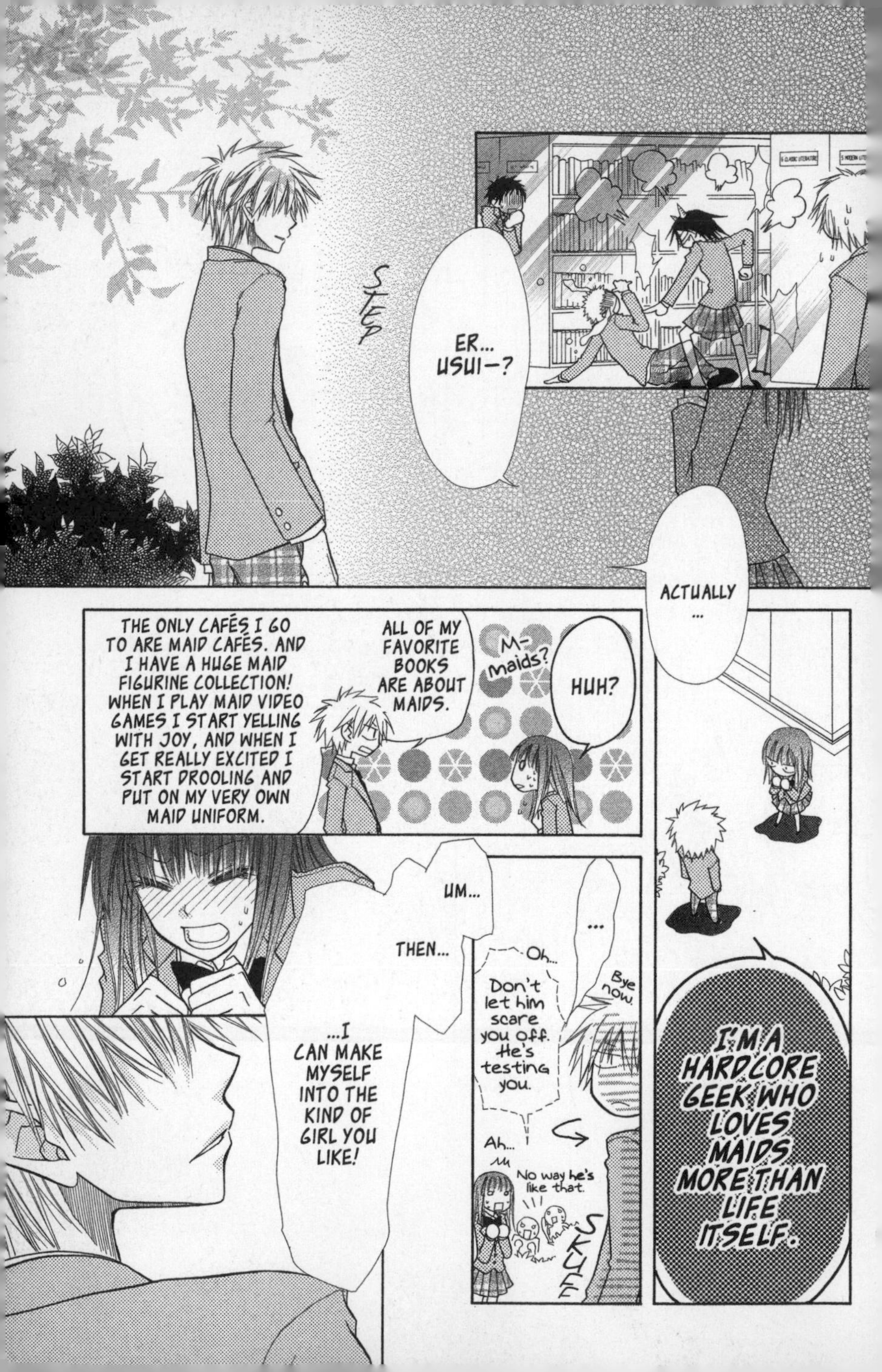
ER... USUI—?
STEP
ACTUALLY...
I'M A HARDCORE GEEK WHO LOVES MAIDS MORE THAN LIFE ITSELF.
HUH?
M-maids?
ALL OF MY FAVORITE BOOKS ARE ABOUT MAIDS.
THE ONLY CAFÉS I GO TO ARE MAID CAFÉS. AND I HAVE A HUGE MAID FIGURINE COLLECTION! WHEN I PLAY MAID VIDEO GAMES I START YELLING WITH JOY, AND WHEN I GET REALLY EXCITED I START DROOLING AND PUT ON MY VERY OWN MAID UNIFORM.
...
Bye now.
Oh... Don't let him scare you off. He's testing you.
Ah...
No way he's like that.
SKUEE
UM...
THEN...
...I CAN MAKE MYSELF INTO THE KIND OF GIRL YOU LIKE!

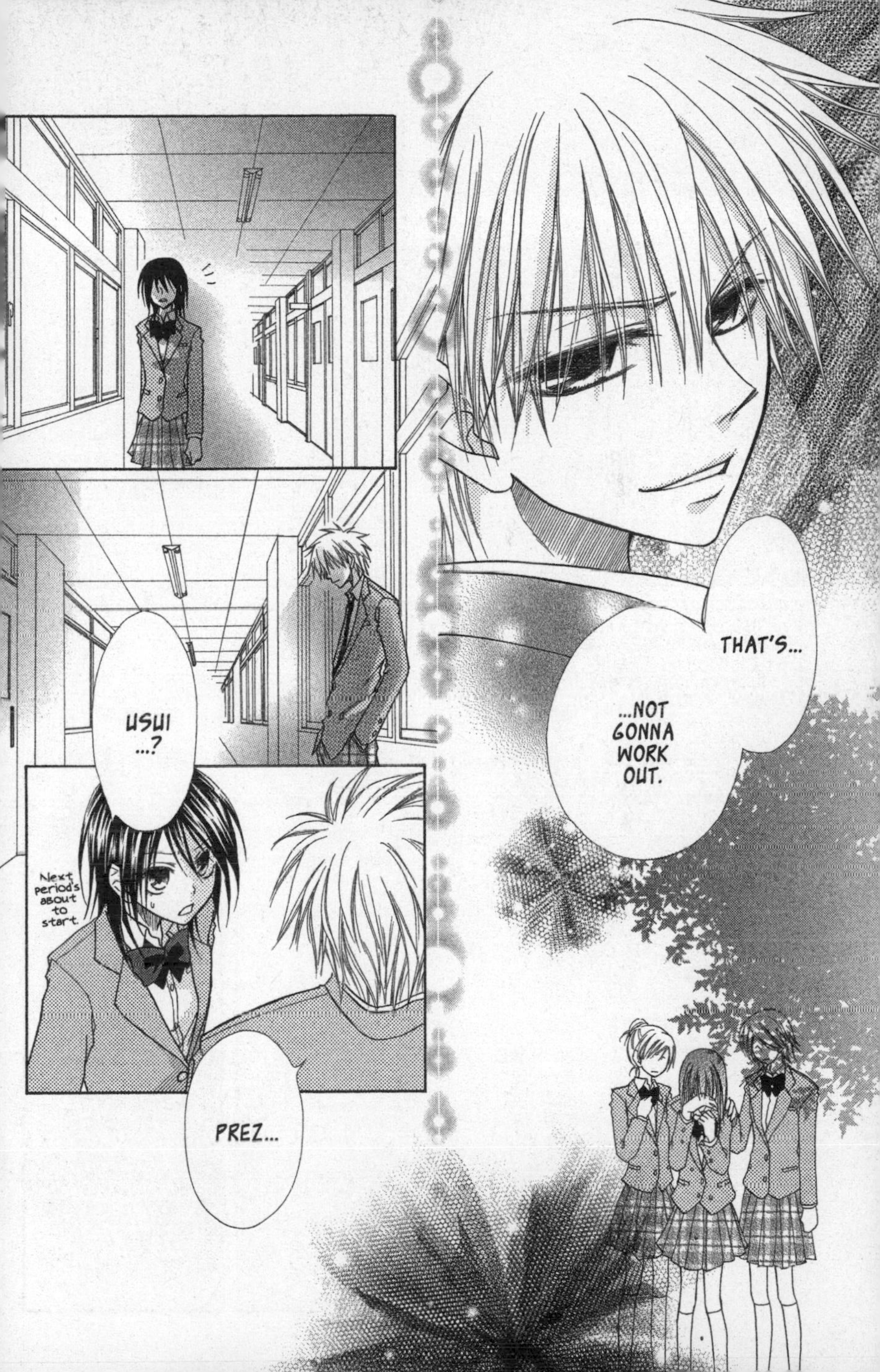
THAT'S...
...NOT GONNA WORK OUT.
USUI ...?
Next period's about to start.
PREZ...

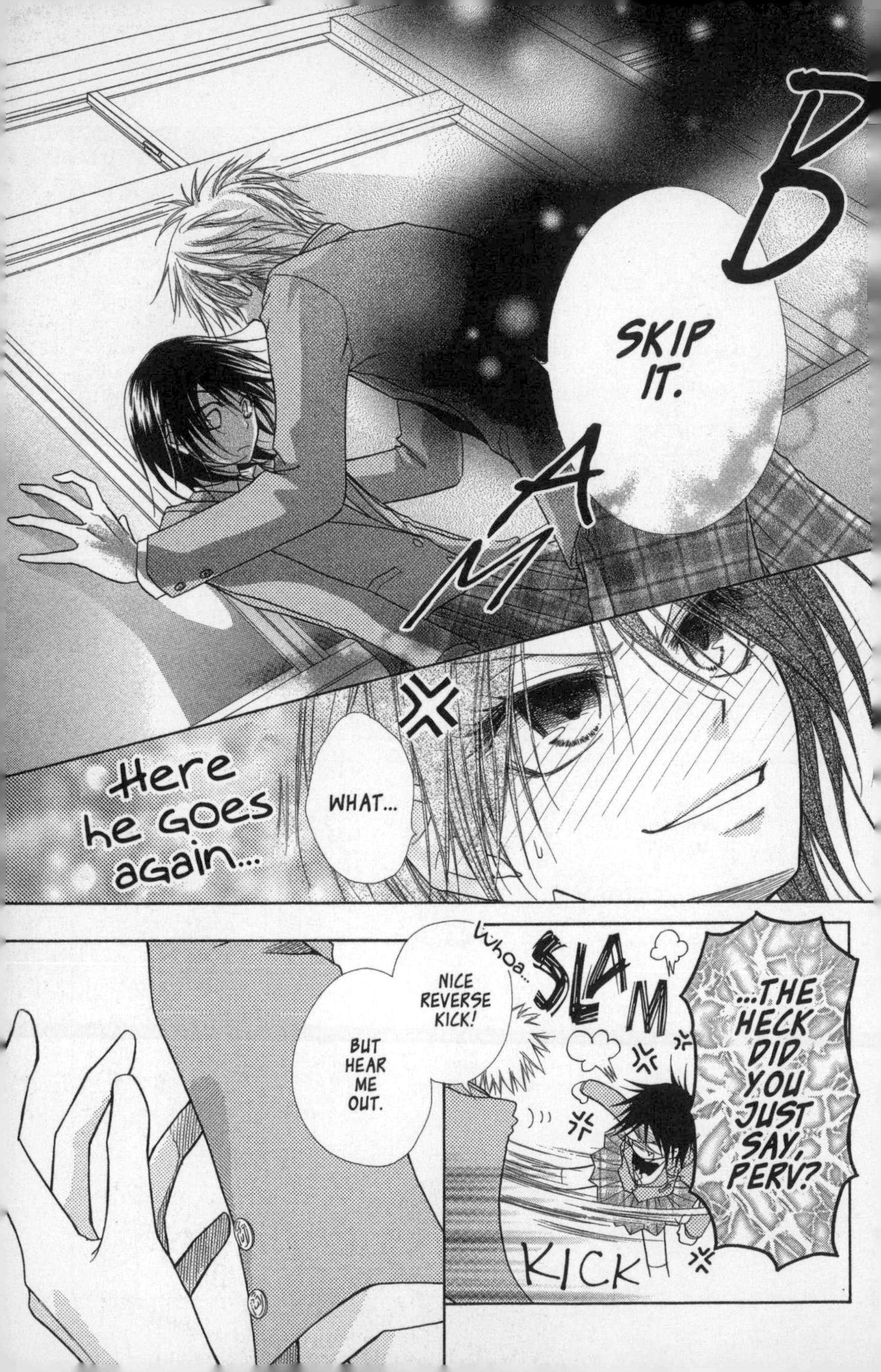
SKIP IT.
BAM
WHAT...
Here he goes again...
...THE HECK DID YOU JUST SAY, PERV?
SLAM
KICK
Whoa...
NICE REVERSE KICK!
BUT HEAR ME OUT.

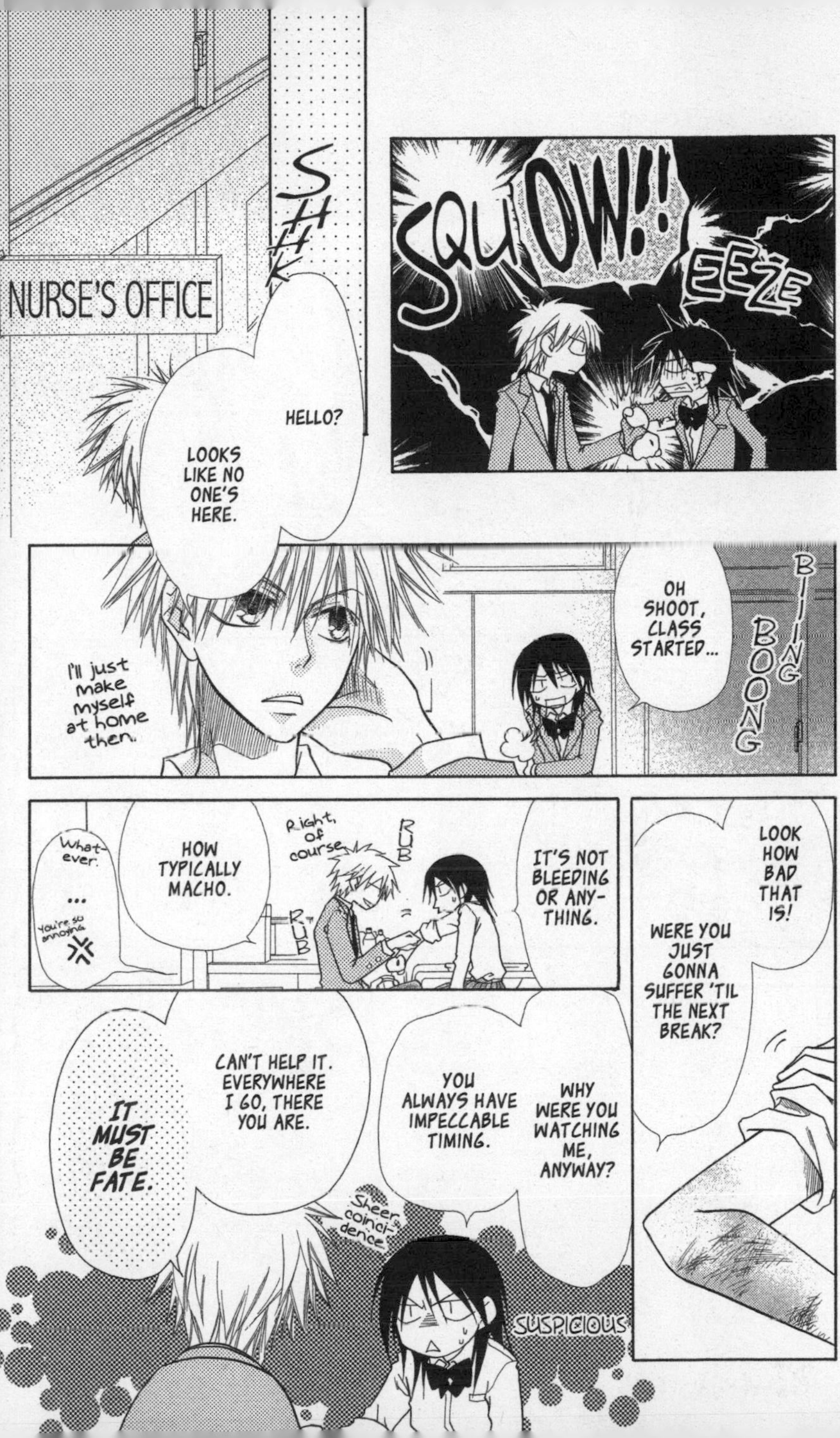
SQUOW!!
EEZE
NURSE'S OFFICE
SHHK
HELLO?
LOOKS LIKE NO ONE'S HERE.
OH SHOOT, CLASS STARTED...
BIING
BOONG
I'll just make myself at home then.
LOOK HOW BAD THAT IS!
WERE YOU JUST GONNA SUFFER 'TIL THE NEXT BREAK?
IT'S NOT BLEEDING OR ANYTHING.
RUB
RUB
Right, of course
HOW TYPICALLY MACHO.
Whatever.
...
You're so annoying
WHY WERE YOU WATCHING ME, ANYWAY?
YOU ALWAYS HAVE IMPECCABLE TIMING.
CAN'T HELP IT. EVERYWHERE I GO, THERE YOU ARE.
IT MUST BE FATE.
Sheer coincidence
SUSPICIOUS

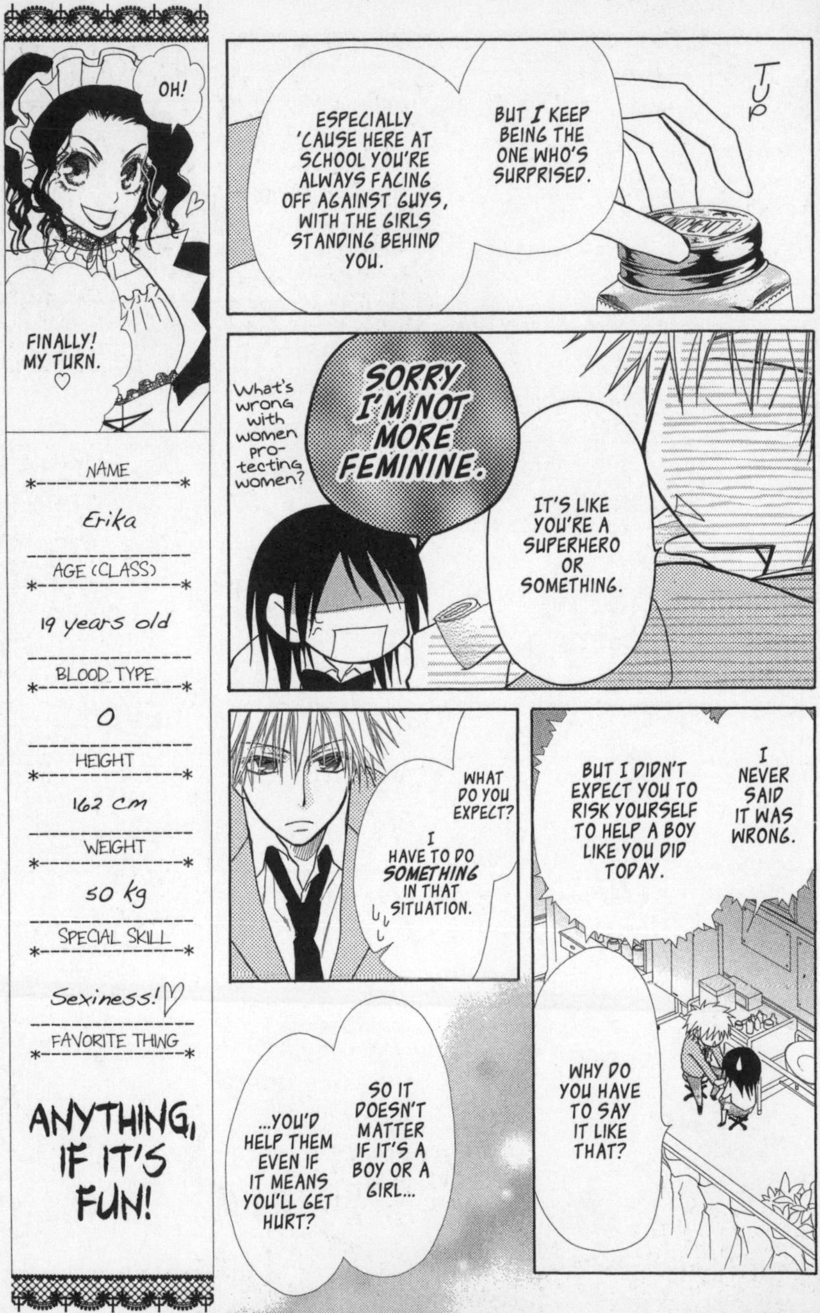
TUP
BUT I KEEP BEING THE ONE WHO'S SURPRISED.
ESPECIALLY 'CAUSE HERE AT SCHOOL YOU'RE ALWAYS FACING OFF AGAINST GUYS, WITH THE GIRLS STANDING BEHIND YOU.
IT'S LIKE YOU'RE A SUPERHERO OR SOMETHING.
SORRY I'M NOT MORE FEMININE.
What's wrong with women protecting women?
I NEVER SAID IT WAS WRONG.
BUT I DIDN'T EXPECT YOU TO RISK YOURSELF TO HELP A BOY LIKE YOU DID TODAY.
WHAT DO YOU EXPECT?
I HAVE TO DO SOMETHING IN THAT SITUATION.
WHY DO YOU HAVE TO SAY IT LIKE THAT?
SO IT DOESN'T MATTER IF IT'S A BOY OR A GIRL...
...YOU'D HELP THEM EVEN IF IT MEANS YOU'LL GET HURT?
OH!
FINALLY! MY TURN. ♡
NAME
Erika
AGE (CLASS)
19 years old
BLOOD TYPE
O
HEIGHT
162 cm
WEIGHT
50 kg
SPECIAL SKILL
Sexiness! ♡
FAVORITE THING
ANYTHING, IF IT'S FUN!

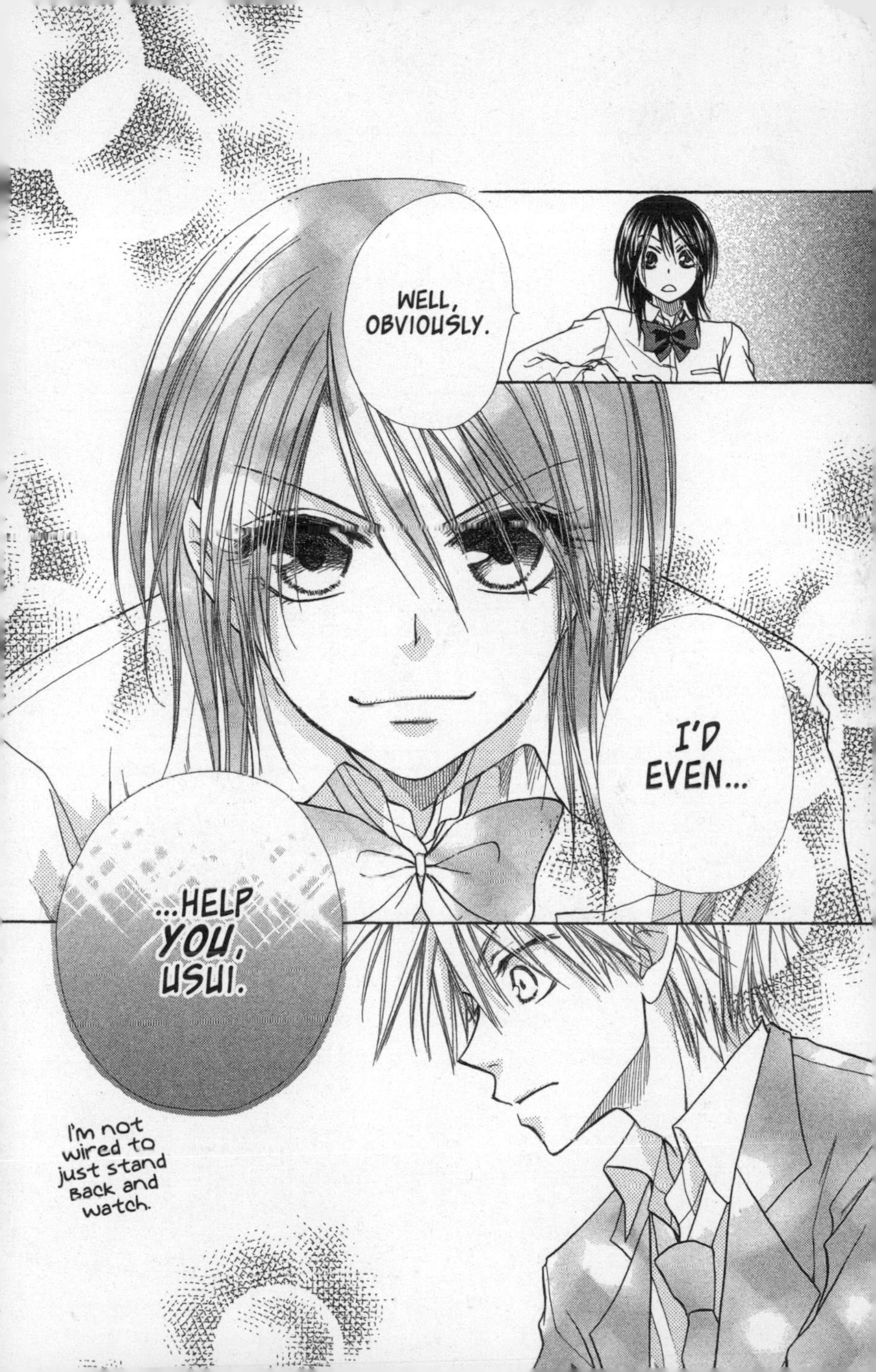
WELL, OBVIOUSLY.
I'D EVEN...
...HELP YOU, USUI.
I'm not wired to just stand back and watch.

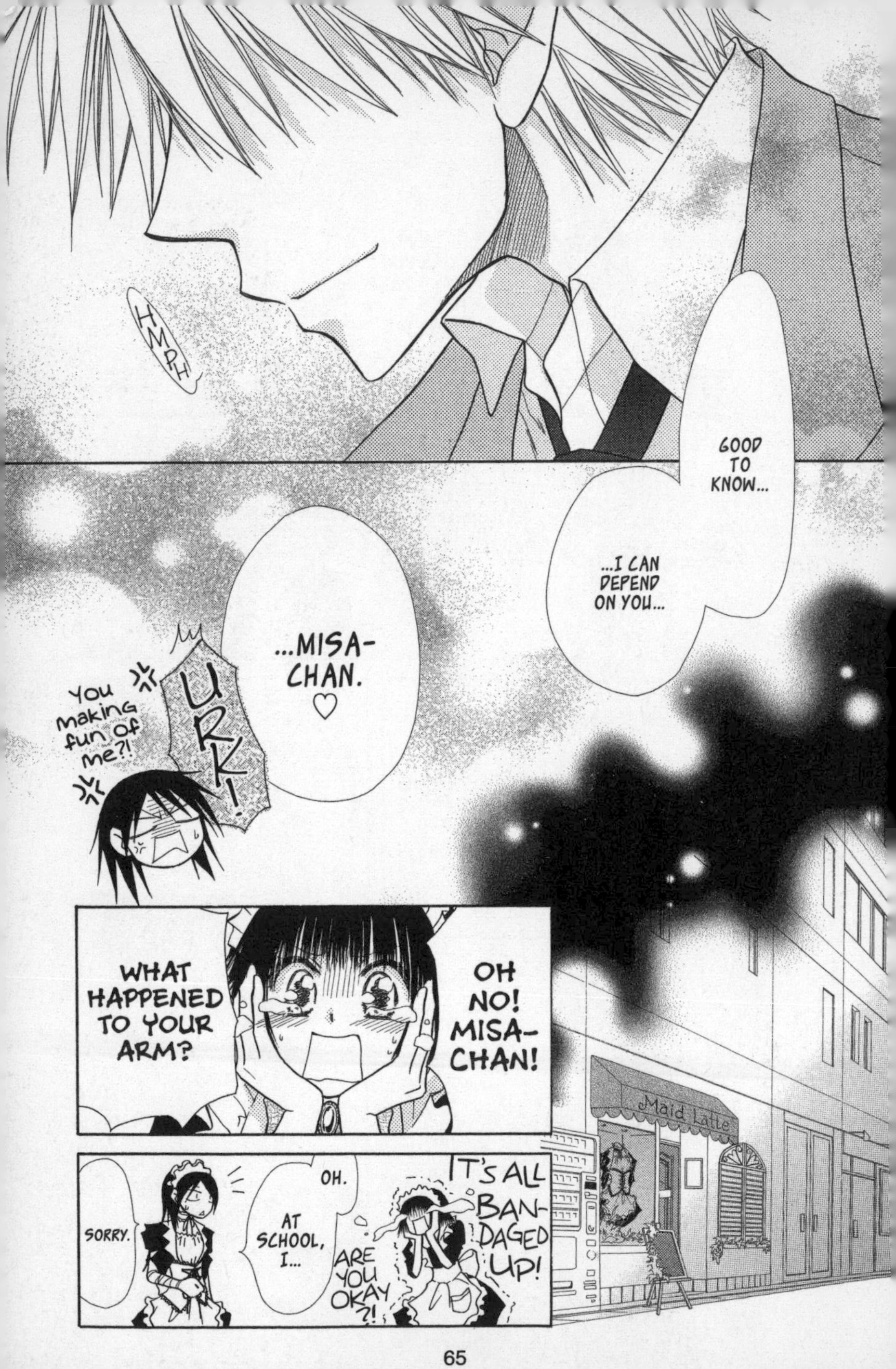
HMPH
GOOD TO KNOW...
...I CAN DEPEND ON YOU...
...MISA-CHAN. ♡
URK!
You making fun of me?!
OH NO! MISA-CHAN!
WHAT HAPPENED TO YOUR ARM?
Maid Latte
IT'S ALL BAN-DAGED UP!
ARE YOU OKAY?!
OH.
AT SCHOOL, I...
SORRY.

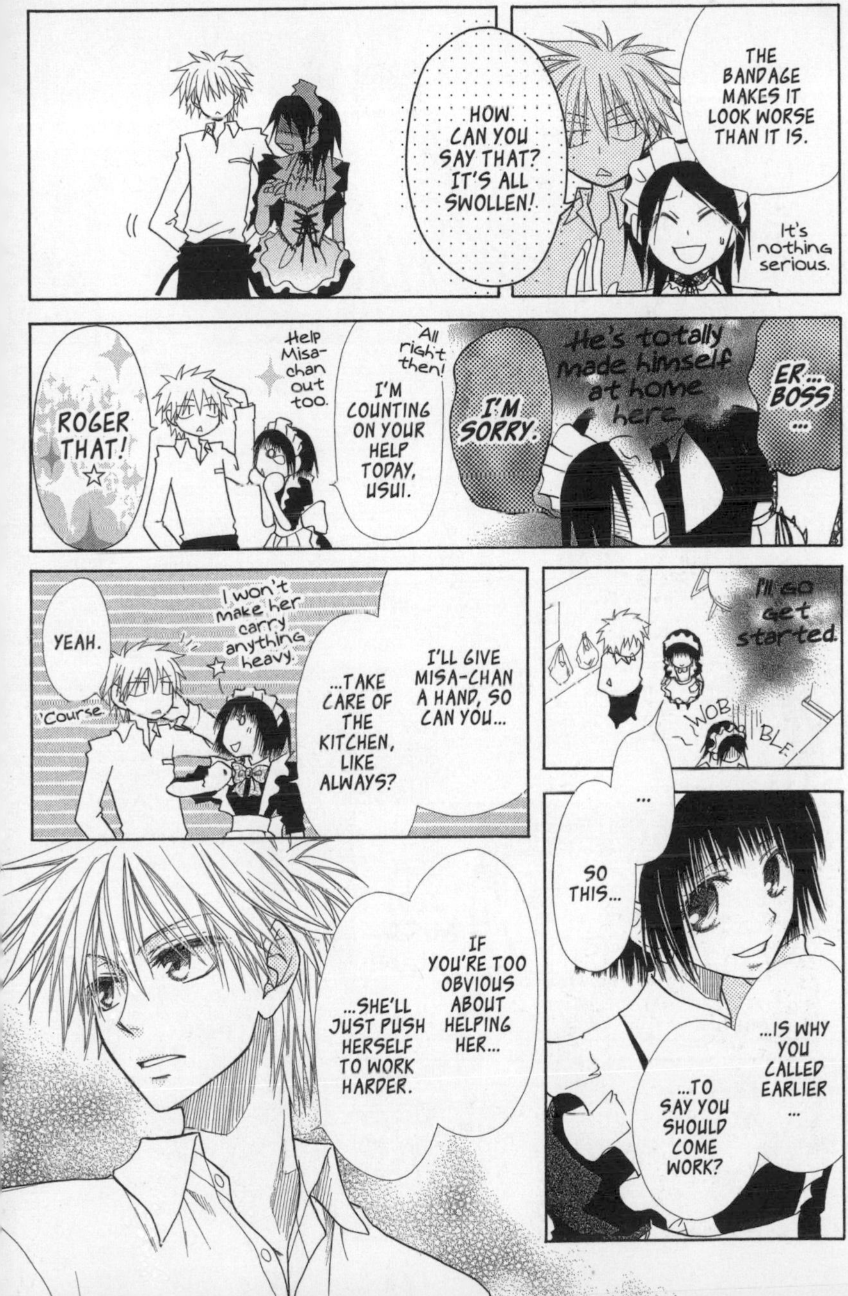
THE BANDAGE MAKES IT LOOK WORSE THAN IT IS.
It's nothing serious.
HOW CAN YOU SAY THAT? IT'S ALL SWOLLEN!
ER... BOSS ...
He's totally made himself at home here.
I'M SORRY.
All right then!
I'M COUNTING ON YOUR HELP TODAY, USUI.
Help Misa-chan out too.
ROGER THAT! ☆
I'll go get started.
WOBBLE
I'LL GIVE MISA-CHAN A HAND, SO CAN YOU...
...TAKE CARE OF THE KITCHEN, LIKE ALWAYS?
I won't make her carry anything heavy.
YEAH.
'Course.
...
SO THIS...
...IS WHY YOU CALLED EARLIER ...
...TO SAY YOU SHOULD COME WORK?
IF YOU'RE TOO OBVIOUS ABOUT HELPING HER...
...SHE'LL JUST PUSH HERSELF TO WORK HARDER.

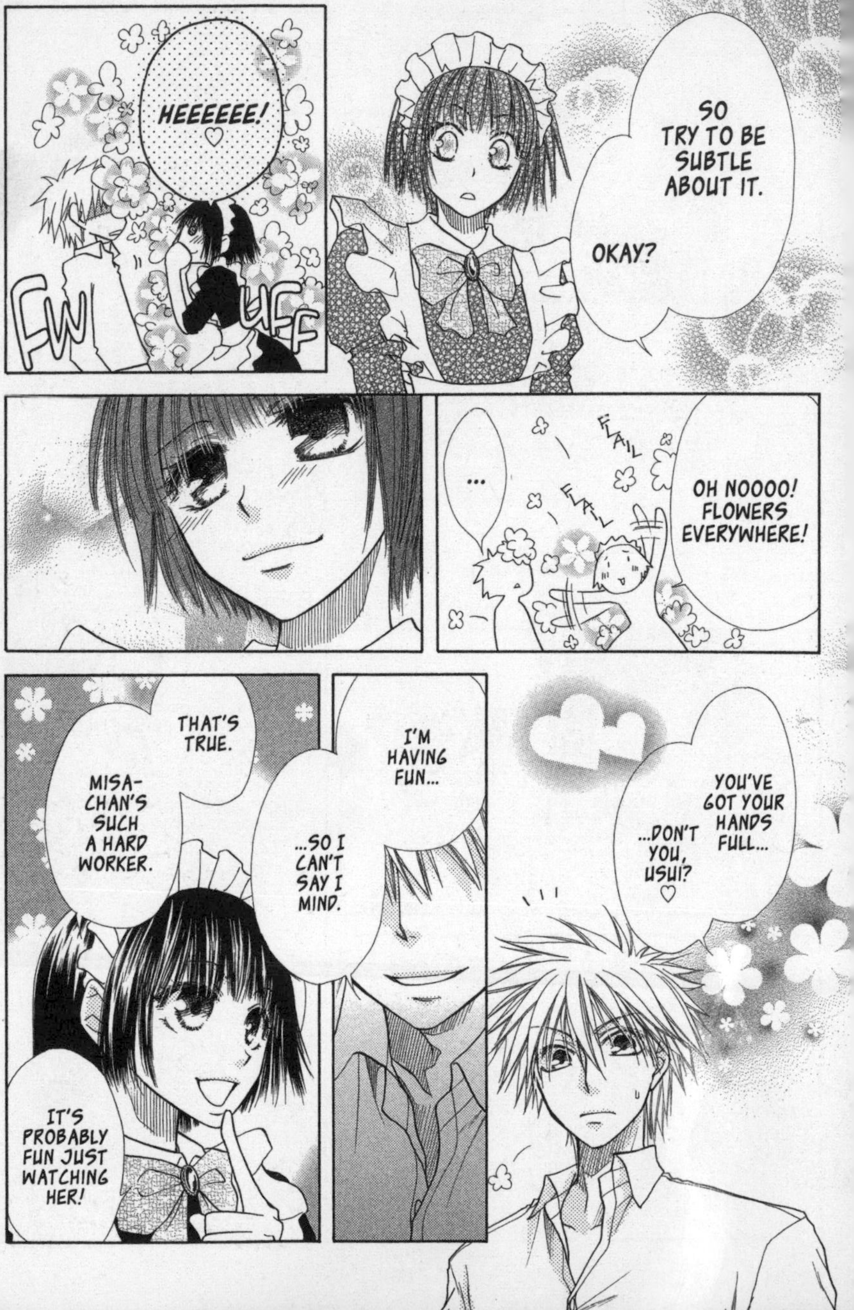
SO TRY TO BE SUBTLE ABOUT IT.
OKAY?
HEEEEEE! ♡
FWUFF
OH NOOOO! FLOWERS EVERYWHERE!
FLAIL
FLAIL
...
YOU'VE GOT YOUR HANDS FULL...
...DON'T YOU, USUI? ♡
I'M HAVING FUN...
...SO I CAN'T SAY I MIND.
THAT'S TRUE.
MISA-CHAN'S SUCH A HARD WORKER.
IT'S PROBABLY FUN JUST WATCHING HER!

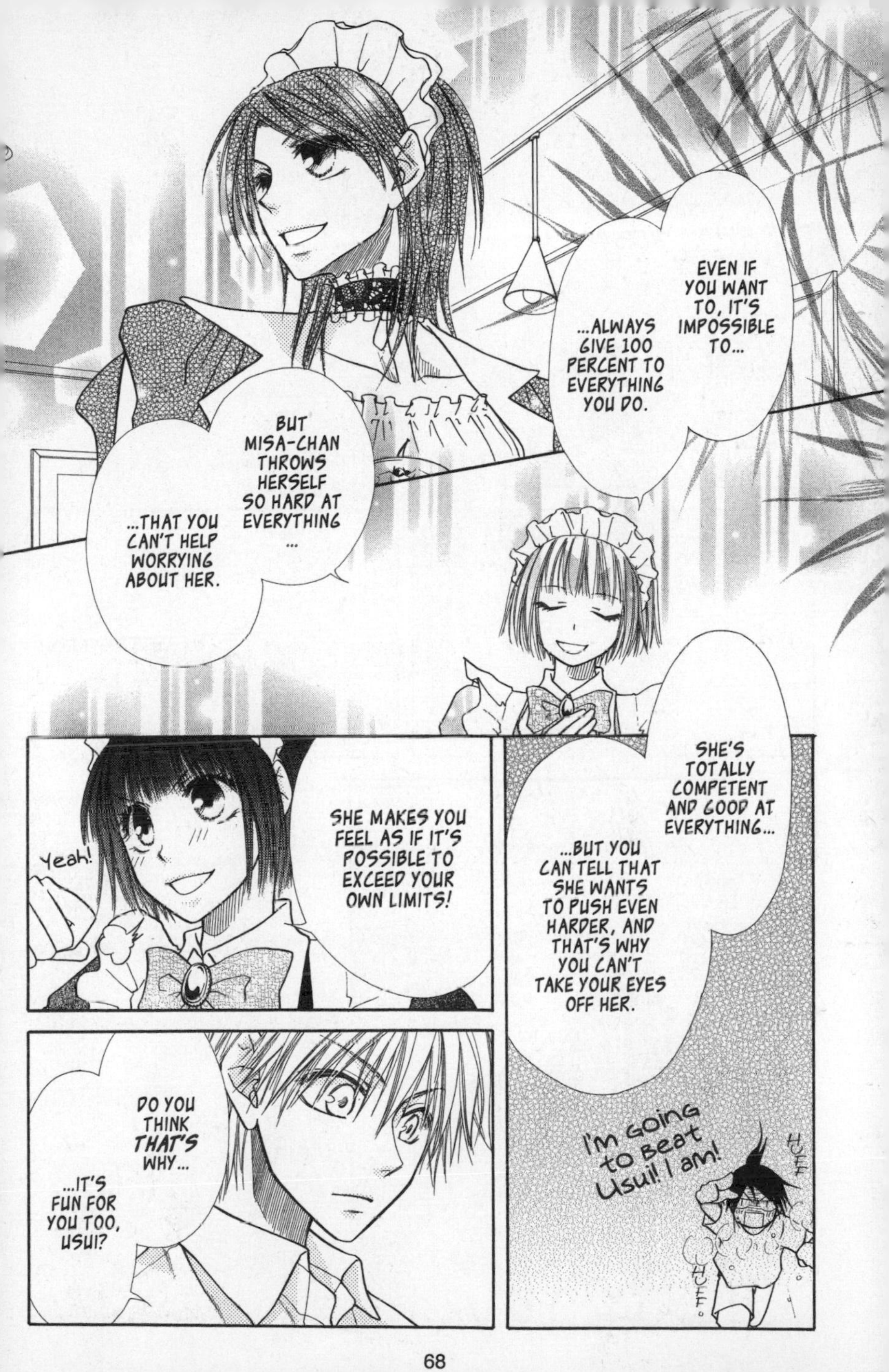
EVEN IF YOU WANT TO, IT'S IMPOSSIBLE TO...
...ALWAYS GIVE 100 PERCENT TO EVERYTHING YOU DO.
BUT MISA-CHAN THROWS HERSELF SO HARD AT EVERYTHING ...
...THAT YOU CAN'T HELP WORRYING ABOUT HER.
SHE'S TOTALLY COMPETENT AND GOOD AT EVERYTHING...
...BUT YOU CAN TELL THAT SHE WANTS TO PUSH EVEN HARDER, AND THAT'S WHY YOU CAN'T TAKE YOUR EYES OFF HER.
I'm going to beat Usui! I am!
HUFF
HUFF
SHE MAKES YOU FEEL AS IF IT'S POSSIBLE TO EXCEED YOUR OWN LIMITS!
Yeah!
DO YOU THINK *THAT'S* WHY...
...IT'S FUN FOR YOU TOO, USUI?

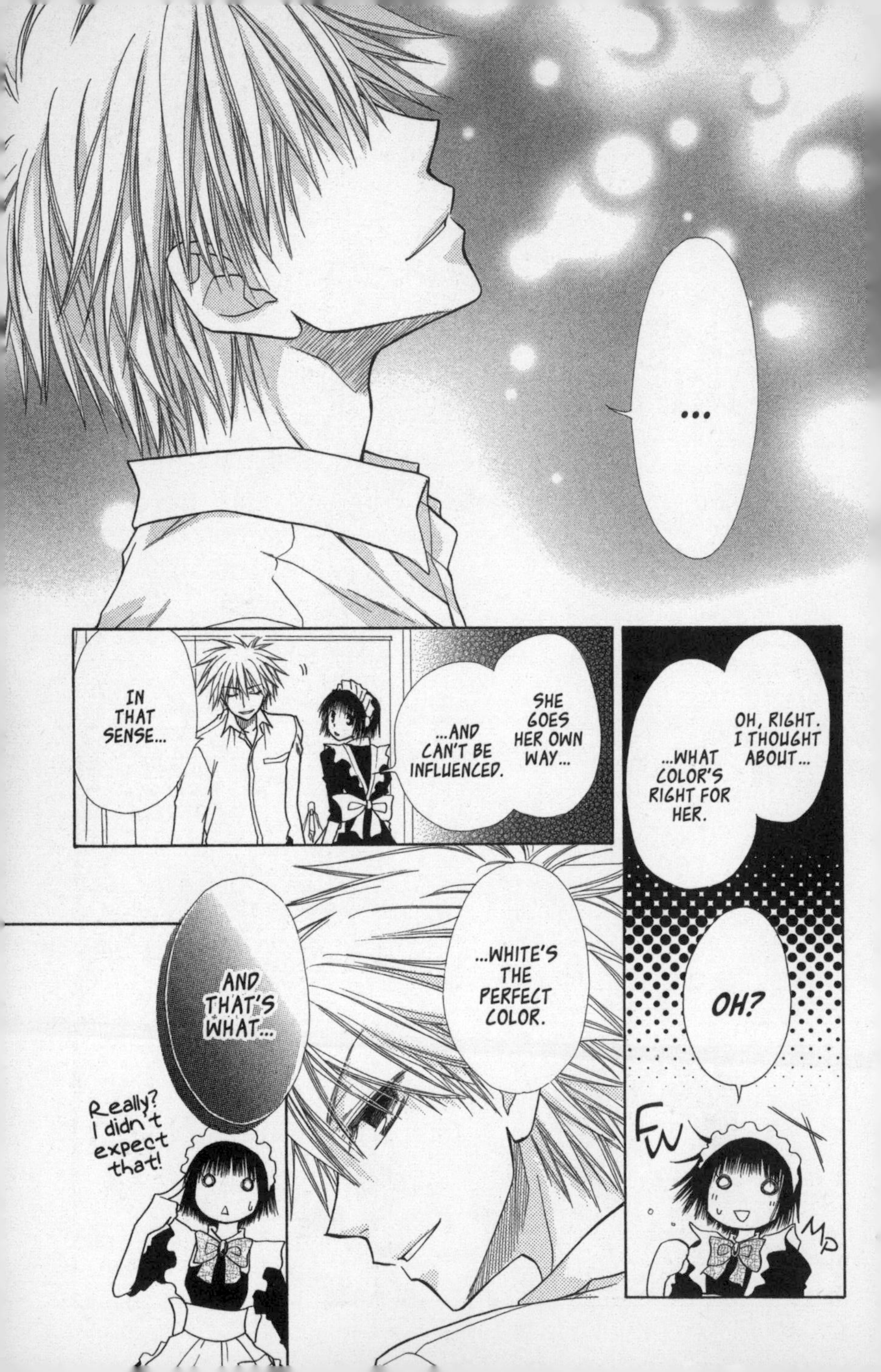
...
OH, RIGHT. I THOUGHT ABOUT...
...WHAT COLOR'S RIGHT FOR HER.
OH?
FW
MP
SHE GOES HER OWN WAY...
...AND CAN'T BE INFLUENCED.
IN THAT SENSE...
...WHITE'S THE PERFECT COLOR.
AND THAT'S WHAT...
Really? I didn't expect that!

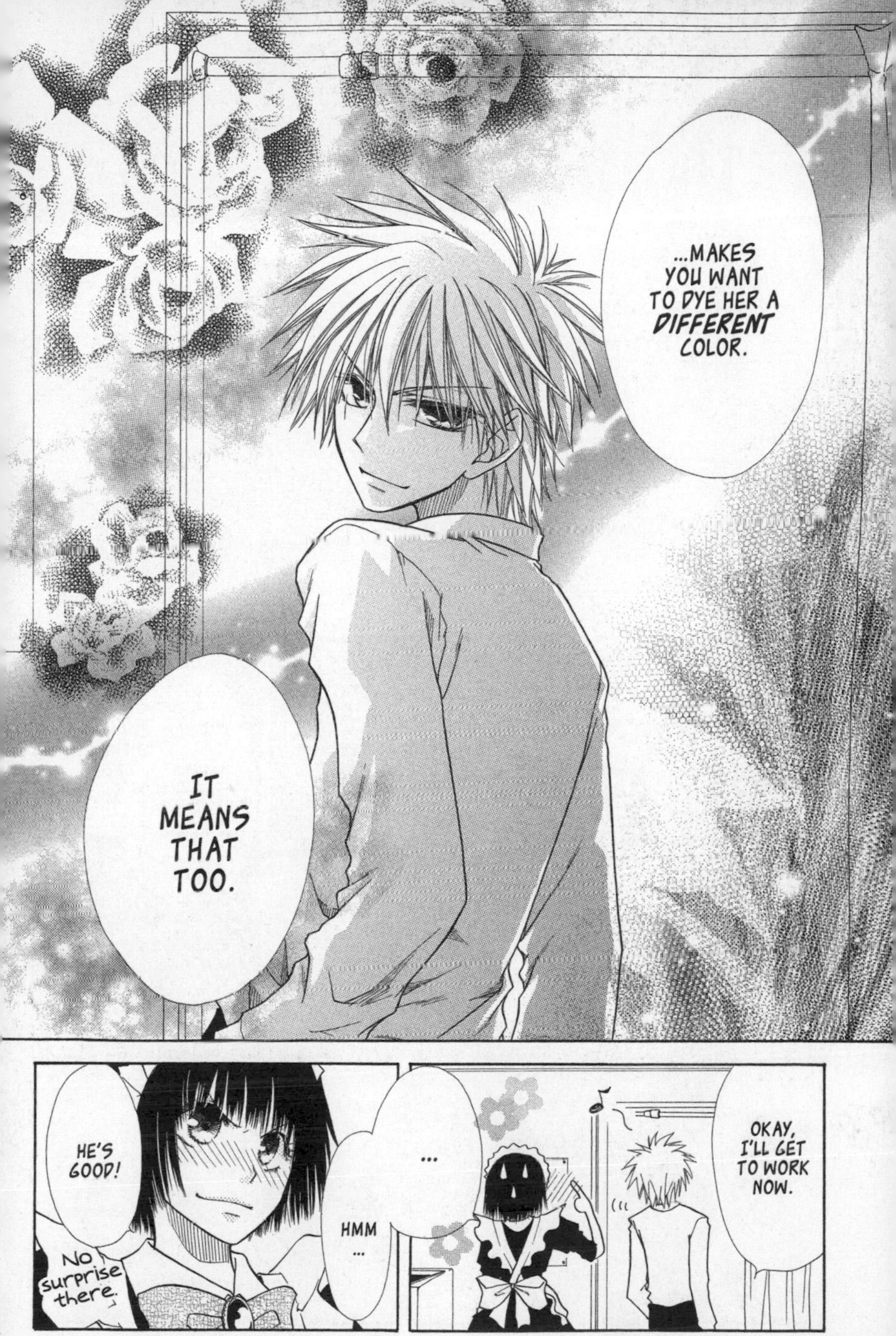
...MAKES YOU WANT TO DYE HER A DIFFERENT COLOR.
IT MEANS THAT TOO.
OKAY, I'LL GET TO WORK NOW.
...
HMM ...
HE'S GOOD!
No surprise there.

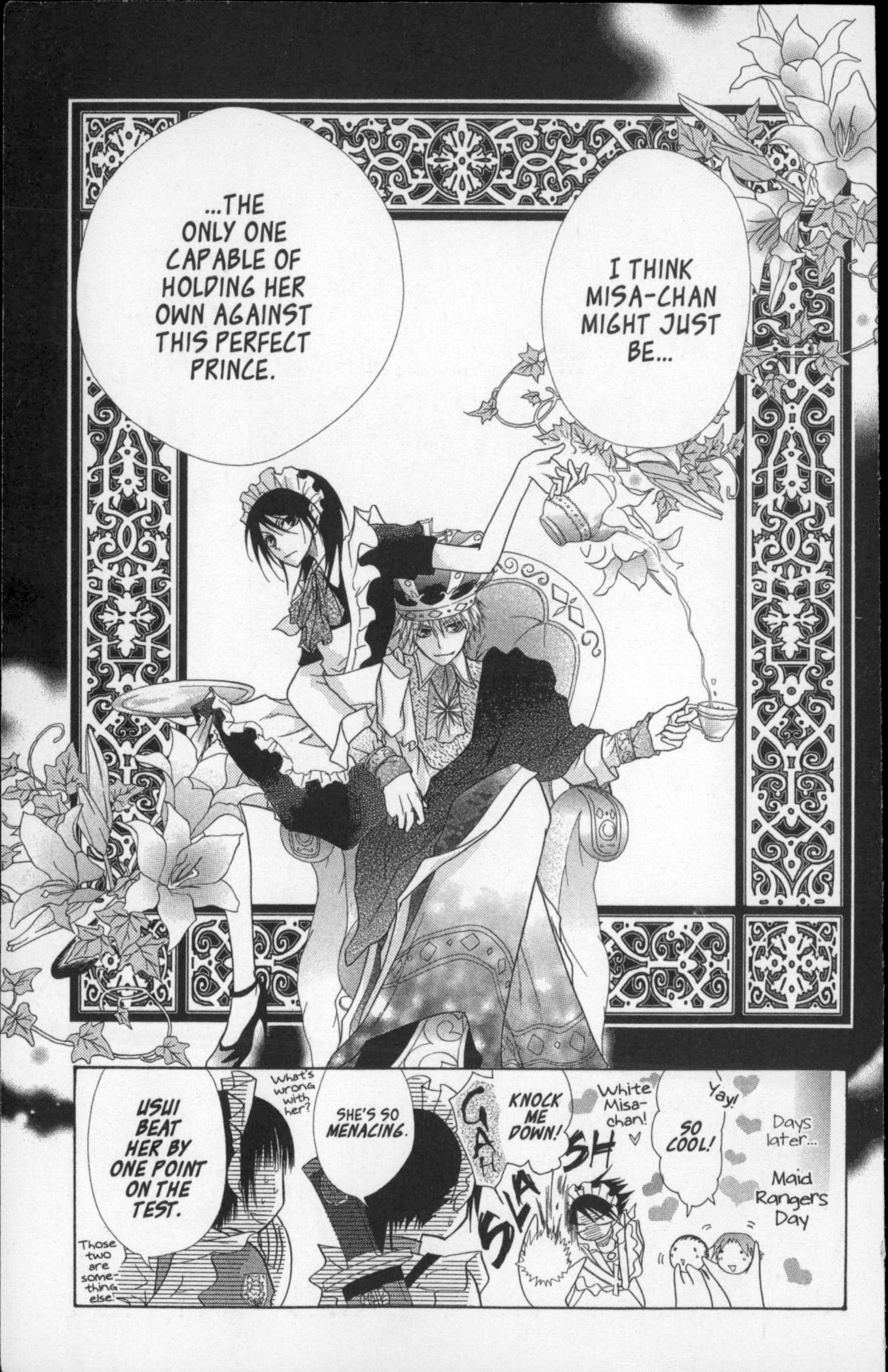
I THINK MISA-CHAN MIGHT JUST BE...
...THE ONLY ONE CAPABLE OF HOLDING HER OWN AGAINST THIS PERFECT PRINCE.
Days later... Maid Rangers Day
Yay!
SO COOL!
White Misa-chan!
KNOCK ME DOWN!
GAH
SLASH
SHE'S SO MENACING.
What's wrong with her?
USUI BEAT HER BY ONE POINT ON THE TEST.
Those two are something else!

WHERE ARE THEY NOW?

- A SINGLE-MINDED MAN -

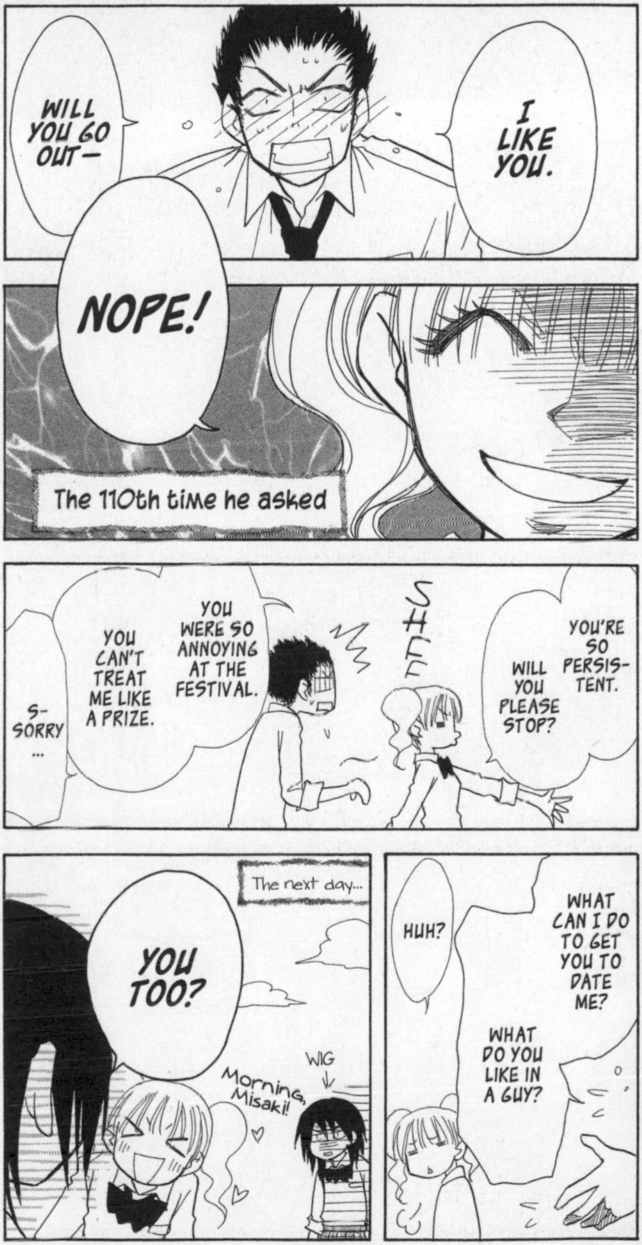
I LIKE YOU.
WILL YOU GO OUT—
NOPE!
The 110th time he asked
SHFF
YOU'RE SO PERSISTENT.
WILL YOU PLEASE STOP?
YOU WERE SO ANNOYING AT THE FESTIVAL.
YOU CAN'T TREAT ME LIKE A PRIZE.
S-SORRY ...
WHAT CAN I DO TO GET YOU TO DATE ME?
HUH?
WHAT DO YOU LIKE IN A GUY?
The next day...
YOU TOO?
WIG
Morning, Misaki!

Masaru Gouda

Appeared in volume 2, chapter 9. He's in love with Sakura Hanazono and refused to give up even though she turned him down a hundred times. He's the former captain of the rugby club.

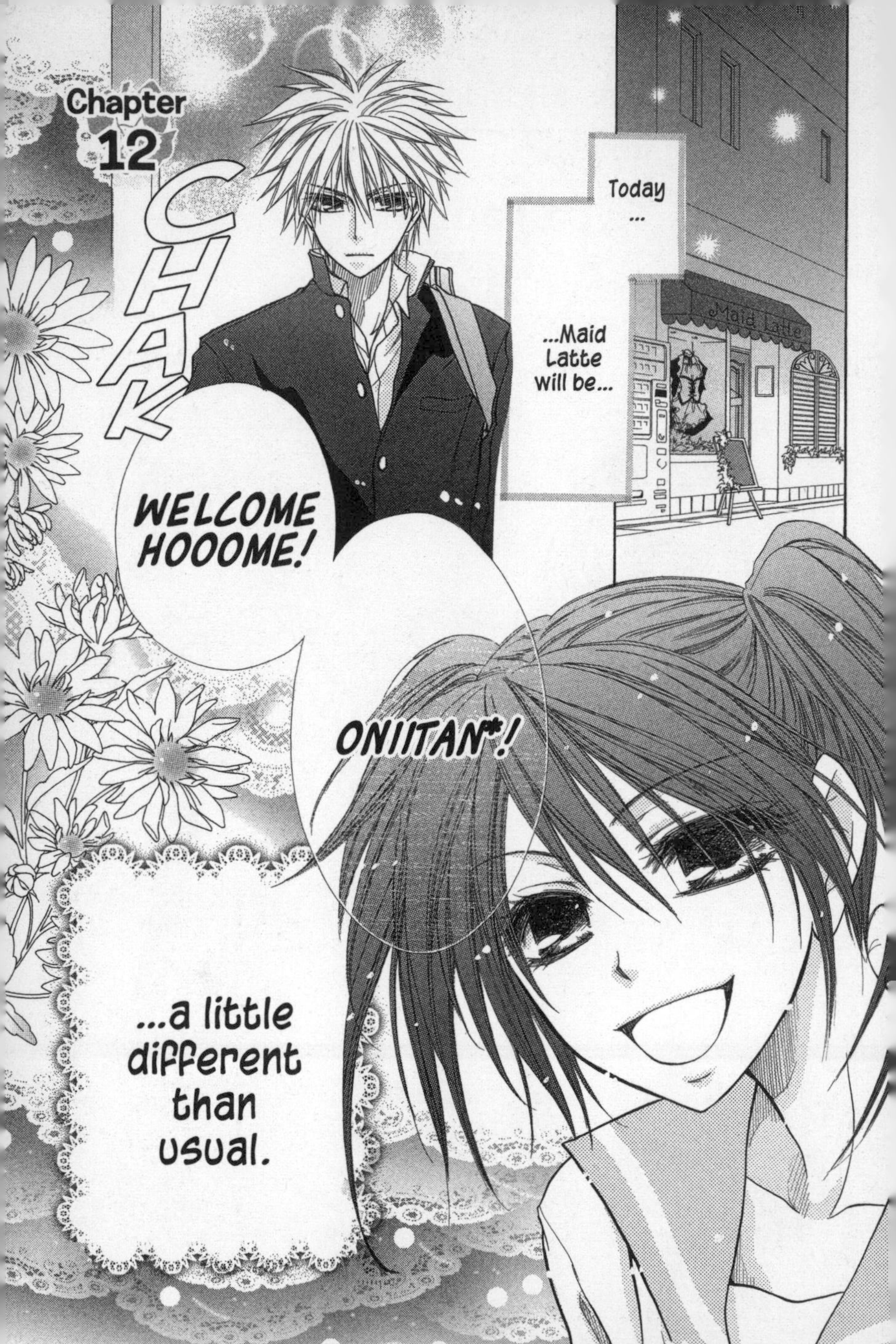
Today ...
...Maid Latte will be...
Maid Latte
Chapter 12
CHAK
WELCOME HOOOME!
ONIITAN*!
...a little different than usual.

*A CUTESY WAY OF SAYING "OLDER BROTHER" IN JAPANESE

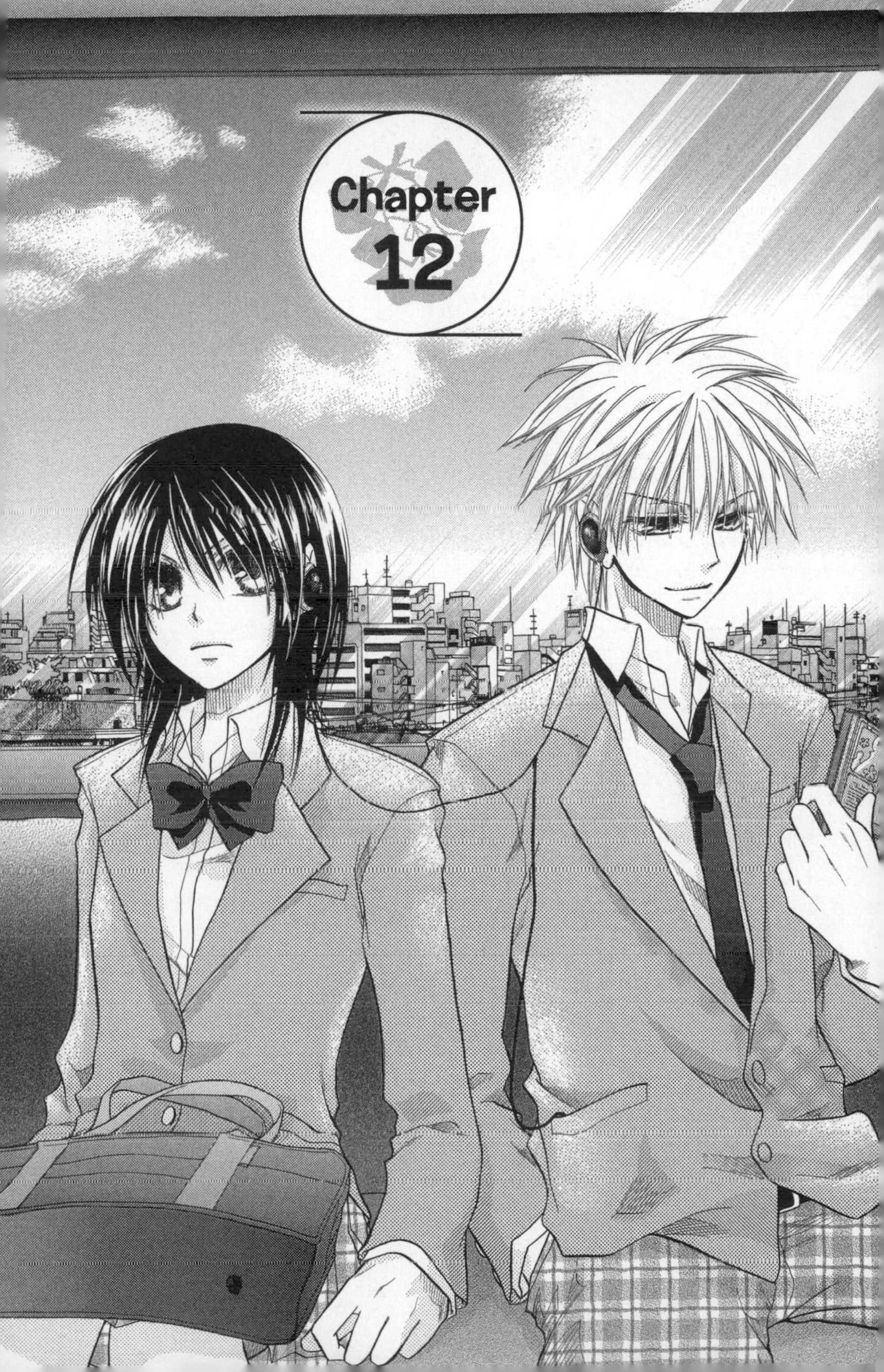
Chapter
12

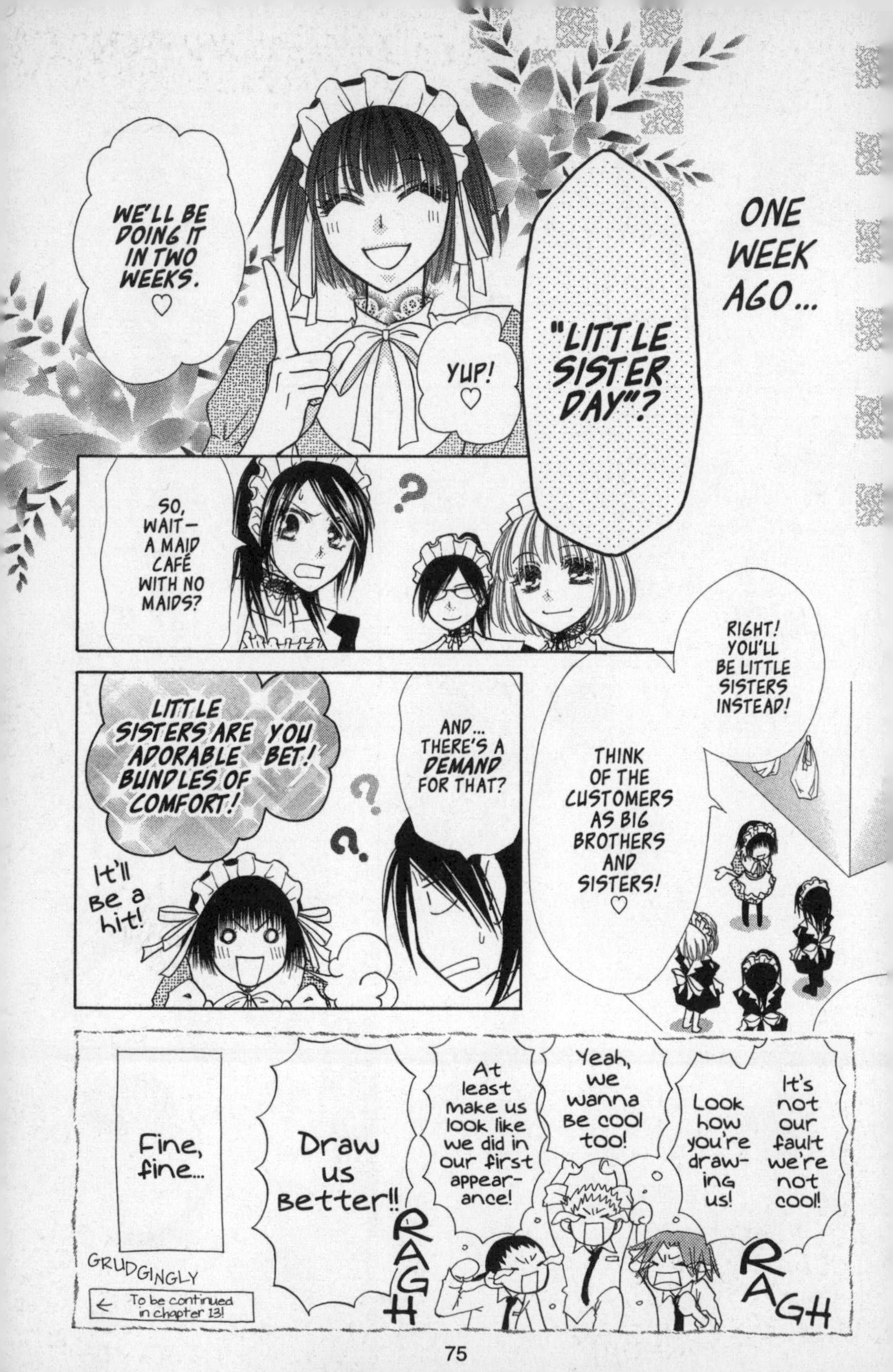
ONE WEEK AGO...
"LITTLE SISTER DAY"?
YUP! ♡
WE'LL BE DOING IT IN TWO WEEKS. ♡
SO, WAIT— A MAID CAFÉ WITH NO MAIDS?
RIGHT! YOU'LL BE LITTLE SISTERS INSTEAD!
THINK OF THE CUSTOMERS AS BIG BROTHERS AND SISTERS! ♡
AND... THERE'S A DEMAND FOR THAT?
YOU BET!
LITTLE SISTERS ARE ADORABLE BUNDLES OF COMFORT!
It'll be a hit!
It's not our fault we're not cool!
Look how you're drawing us!
RAGH
Yeah, we wanna be cool too!
At least make us look like we did in our first appearance!
Draw us better!!
RAGH
Fine, fine...
GRUDGINGLY
← To be continued in chapter 13!

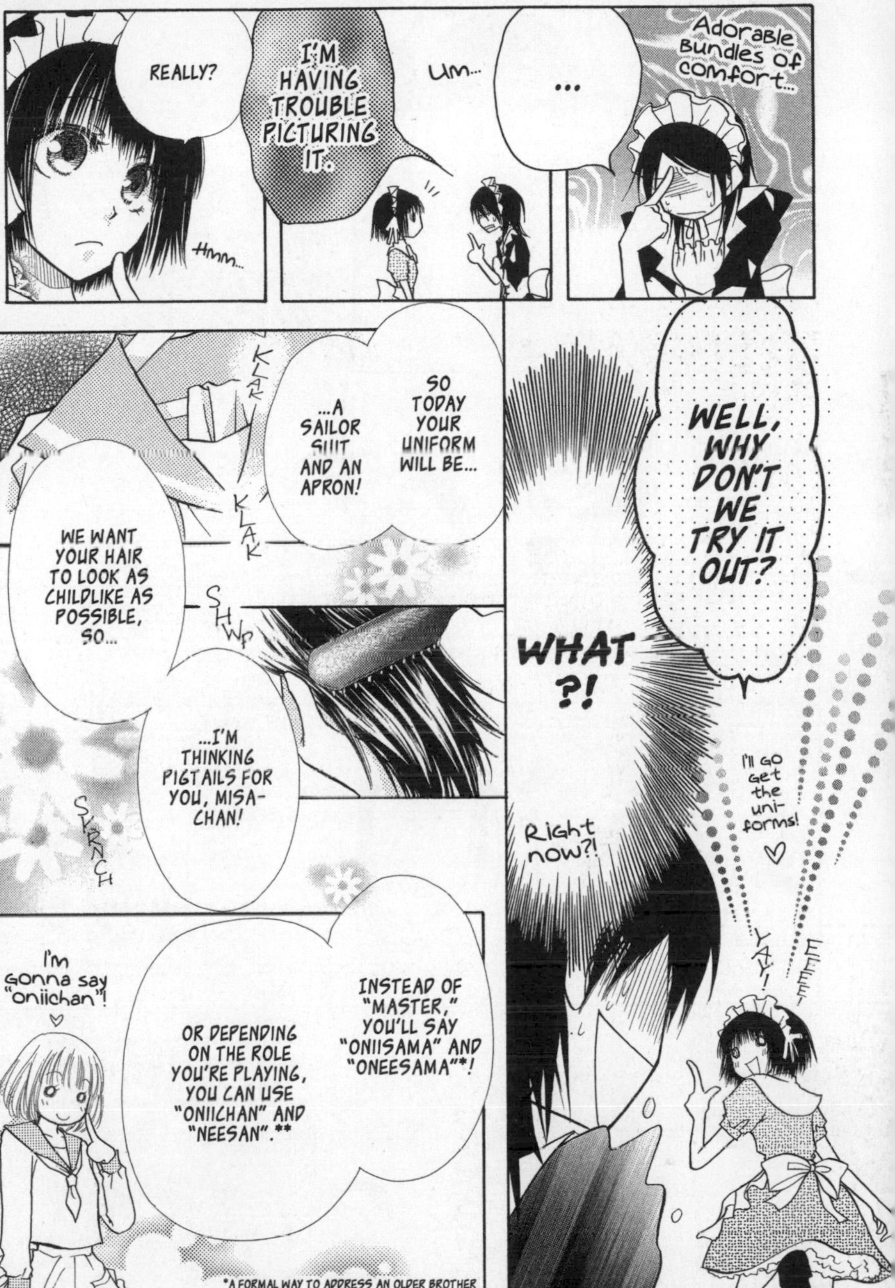

Adorable Bundles of comfort...
...
Um...
I'M HAVING TROUBLE PICTURING IT.
REALLY?
Hmm...
WELL, WHY DON'T WE TRY IT OUT?
WHAT ?!
I'll go get the uni-forms! ♥
Right now?!
YAY!
EEEE!
KLAK
KLAK
KLAK
SO TODAY YOUR UNIFORM WILL BE...
...A SAILOR SUIT AND AN APRON!
WE WANT YOUR HAIR TO LOOK AS CHILDLIKE AS POSSIBLE, SO...
SHWP
...I'M THINKING PIGTAILS FOR YOU, MISA-CHAN!
SKRNCH
INSTEAD OF "MASTER," YOU'LL SAY "ONIISAMA" AND "ONEESAMA"*!
OR DEPENDING ON THE ROLE YOU'RE PLAYING, YOU CAN USE "ONIICHAN" AND "NEESAN".**
I'm gonna say "oniichan"! ♥

*A FORMAL WAY TO ADDRESS AN OLDER BROTHER AND OLDER SISTER, RESPECTIVELY

**A MORE CASUAL WAY TO ADDRESS AN OLDER BROTHER AND OLDER SISTER, RESPECTIVELY

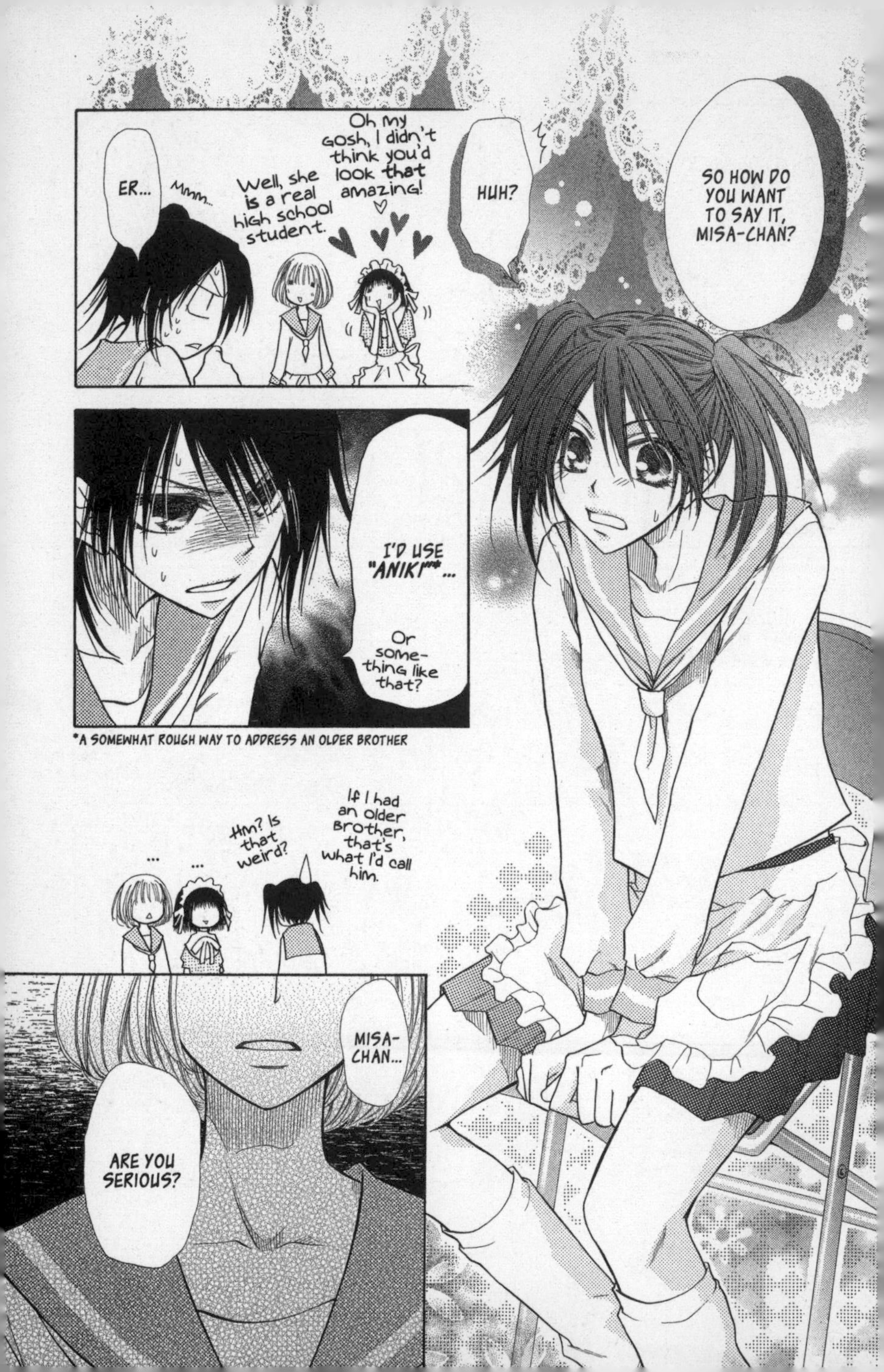
SO HOW DO YOU WANT TO SAY IT, MISA-CHAN?
HUH?
Oh my gosh, I didn't think you'd look that amazing!
Well, she is a real high school student.
ER...
Mmm...
I'D USE "ANIKI"*...
Or some-thing like that?
If I had an older brother, that's what I'd call him.
Hm? Is that weird?
...
...
MISA-CHAN...
ARE YOU SERIOUS?
*A SOMEWHAT ROUGH WAY TO ADDRESS AN OLDER BROTHER

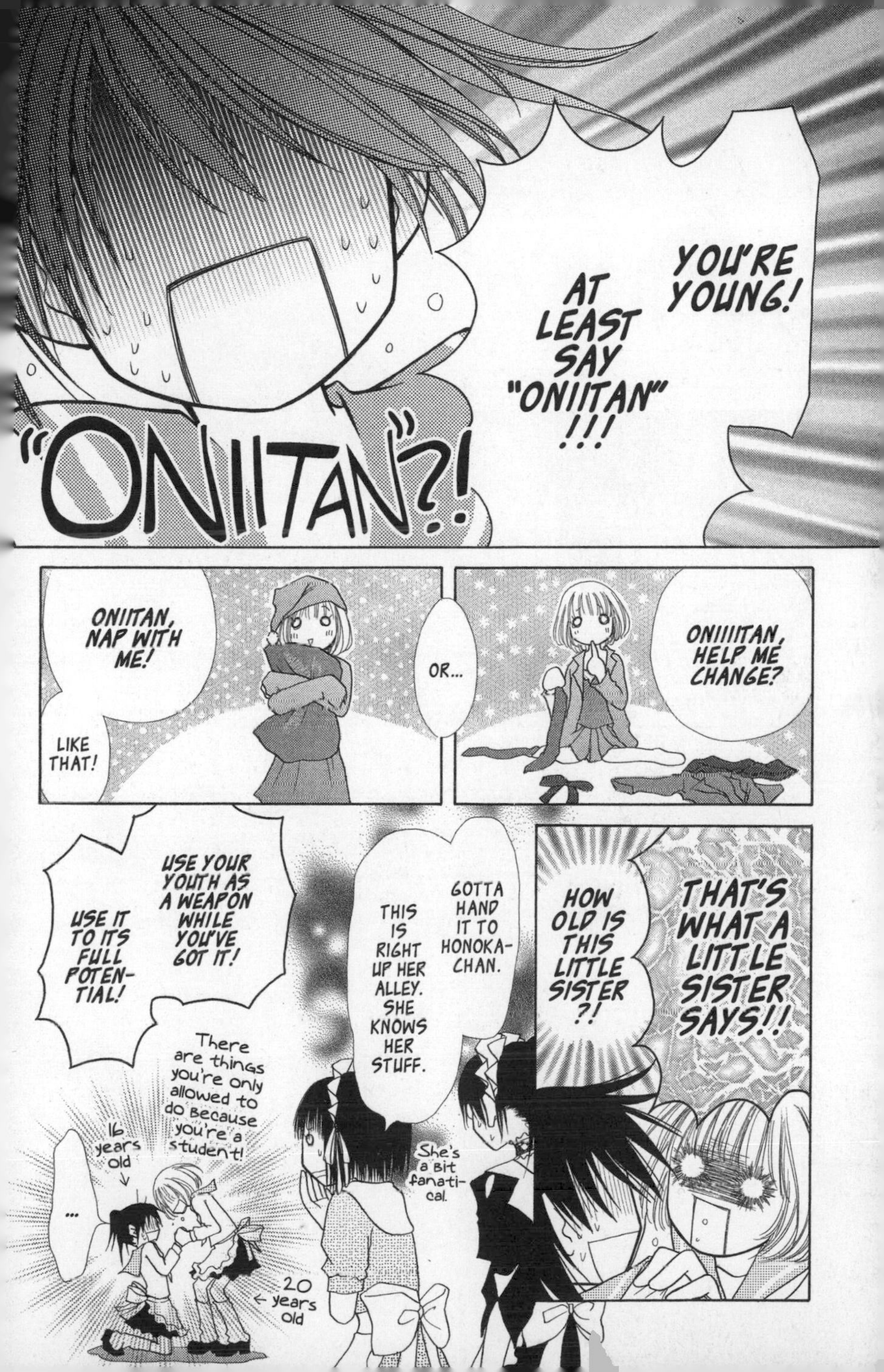
YOU'RE YOUNG!
AT LEAST SAY "ONIITAN"!!!
"ONIITAN"?!
ONIIIITAN, HELP ME CHANGE?
OR...
ONIITAN, NAP WITH ME!
LIKE THAT!
THAT'S WHAT A LITTLE SISTER SAYS!!
HOW OLD IS THIS LITTLE SISTER?!
GOTTA HAND IT TO HONOKA-CHAN.
THIS IS RIGHT UP HER ALLEY. SHE KNOWS HER STUFF.
She's a bit fanati-cal.
USE YOUR YOUTH AS A WEAPON WHILE YOU'VE GOT IT!
USE IT TO ITS FULL POTEN-TIAL!
There are things you're only allowed to do because you're a student!
16 years old
20 years old
...

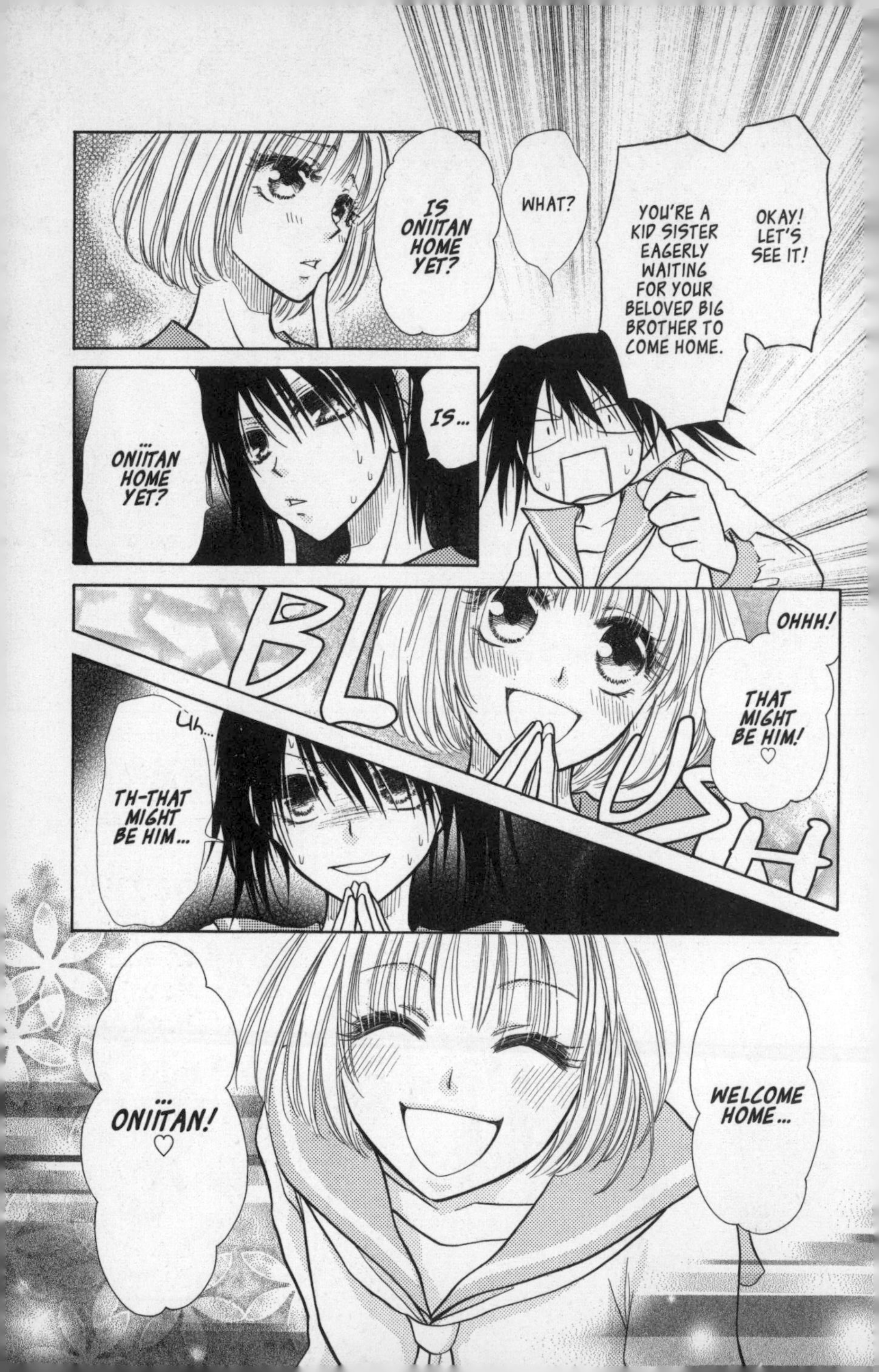
OKAY! LET'S SEE IT!
YOU'RE A KID SISTER EAGERLY WAITING FOR YOUR BELOVED BIG BROTHER TO COME HOME.
WHAT?
IS ONIITAN HOME YET?
IS...
...ONIITAN HOME YET?
OHHH!
THAT MIGHT BE HIM! ♡
BLUSH
Uh...
TH-THAT MIGHT BE HIM...
WELCOME HOME...
...ONIITAN! ♡

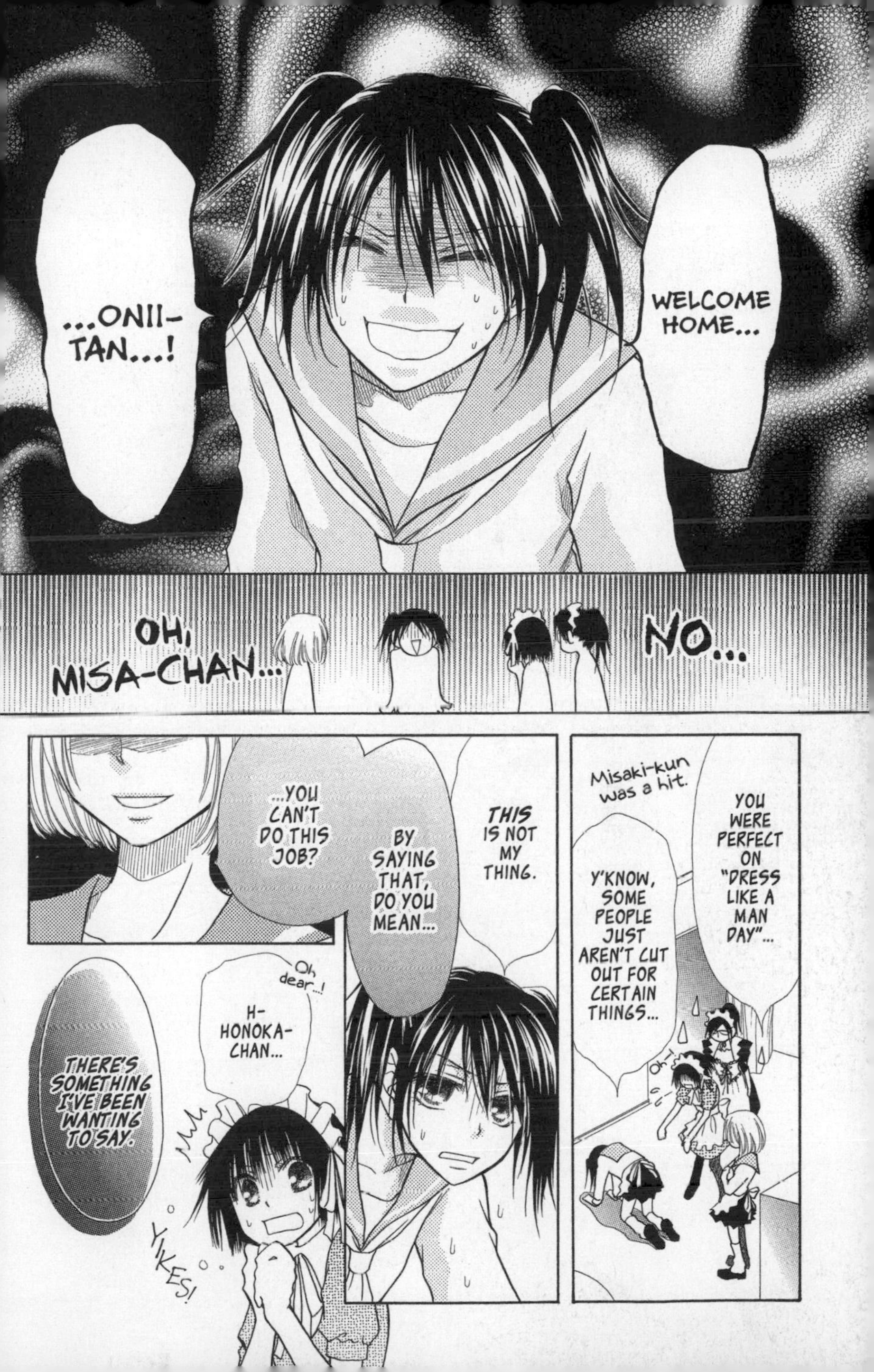
WELCOME HOME...
...ONII-TAN...!
OH, MISA-CHAN...
NO...
Misaki-kun was a hit.
YOU WERE PERFECT ON "DRESS LIKE A MAN DAY"...
Y'KNOW, SOME PEOPLE JUST AREN'T CUT OUT FOR CERTAIN THINGS...
Oh-!
THIS IS NOT MY THING.
BY SAYING THAT, DO YOU MEAN...
...YOU CAN'T DO THIS JOB?
Oh dear...!
H-HONOKA-CHAN...
YIKES!
THERE'S SOMETHING I'VE BEEN WANTING TO SAY.

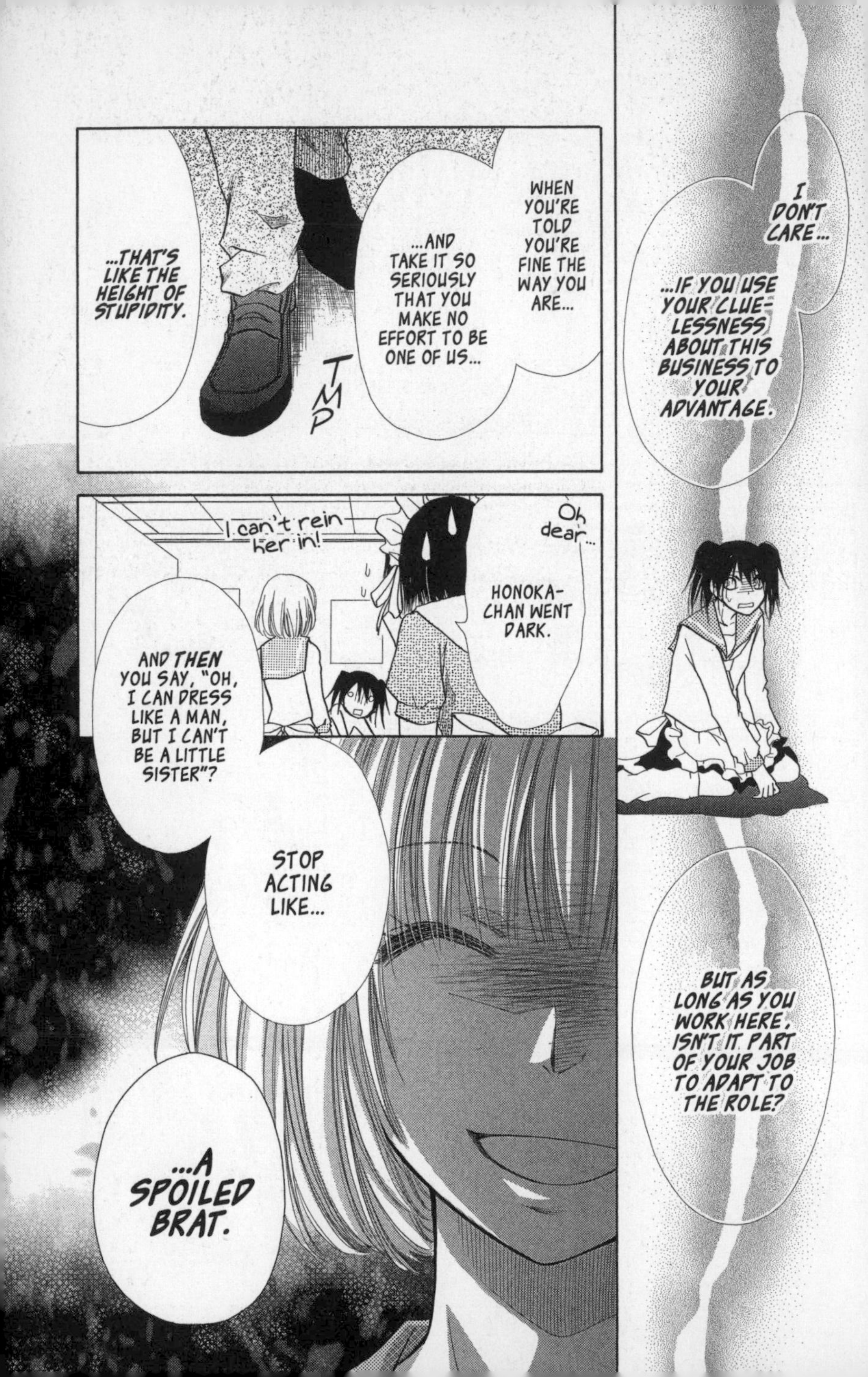
I DON'T CARE...
...IF YOU USE YOUR CLUE-LESSNESS ABOUT THIS BUSINESS TO YOUR ADVANTAGE.
BUT AS LONG AS YOU WORK HERE, ISN'T IT PART OF YOUR JOB TO ADAPT TO THE ROLE?
WHEN YOU'RE TOLD YOU'RE FINE THE WAY YOU ARE...
...AND TAKE IT SO SERIOUSLY THAT YOU MAKE NO EFFORT TO BE ONE OF US...
TMP
...THAT'S LIKE THE HEIGHT OF STUPIDITY.
Oh dear...
HONOKA-CHAN WENT DARK.
I can't rein her in!
AND THEN YOU SAY, "OH, I CAN DRESS LIKE A MAN, BUT I CAN'T BE A LITTLE SISTER"?
STOP ACTING LIKE...
...A SPOILED BRAT.

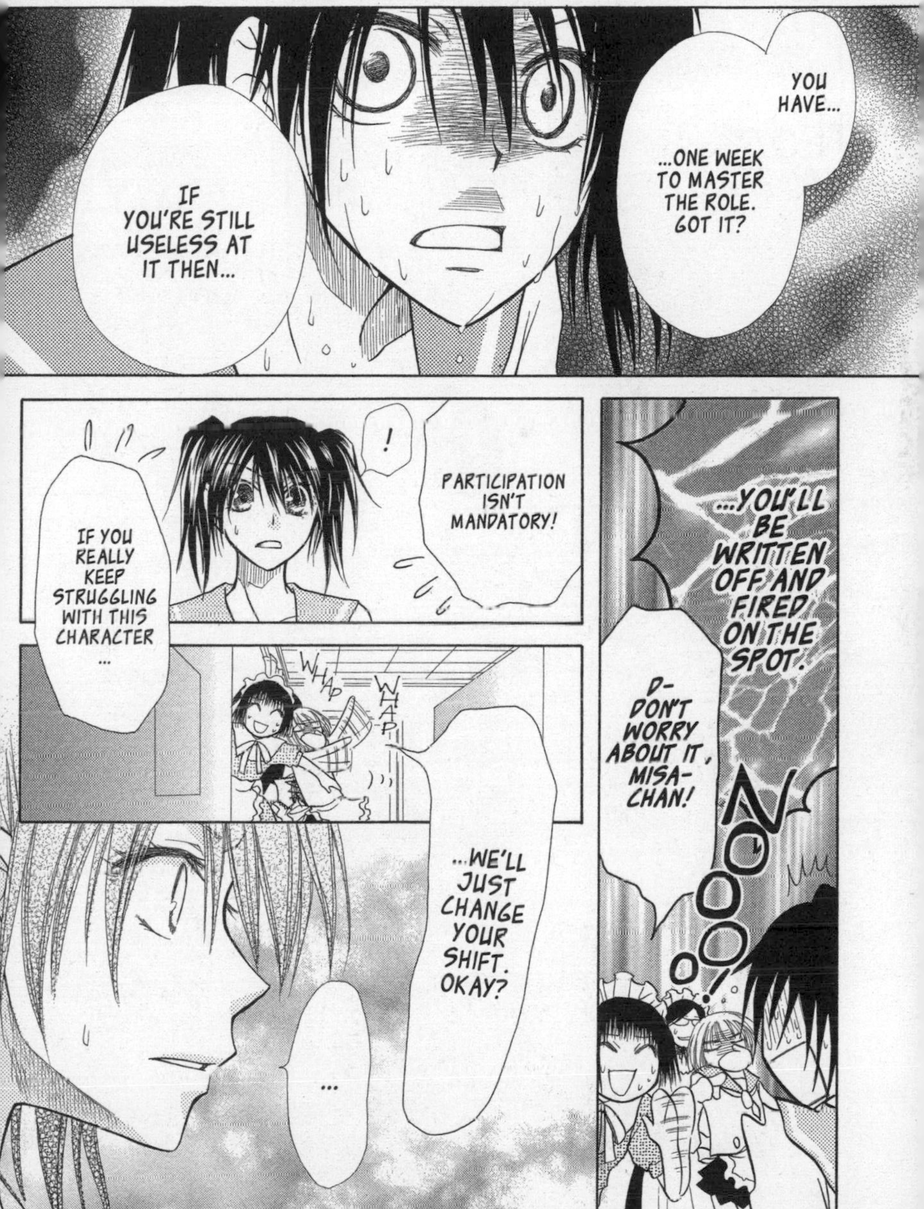
YOU HAVE...
...ONE WEEK TO MASTER THE ROLE. GOT IT?
IF YOU'RE STILL USELESS AT IT THEN...
...YOU'LL BE WRITTEN OFF AND FIRED ON THE SPOT.
NOOOOO!
D-DON'T WORRY ABOUT IT, MISA-CHAN!
!
PARTICIPATION ISN'T MANDATORY!
IF YOU REALLY KEEP STRUGGLING WITH THIS CHARACTER...
WHAP
WHAP
...WE'LL JUST CHANGE YOUR SHIFT. OKAY?
...

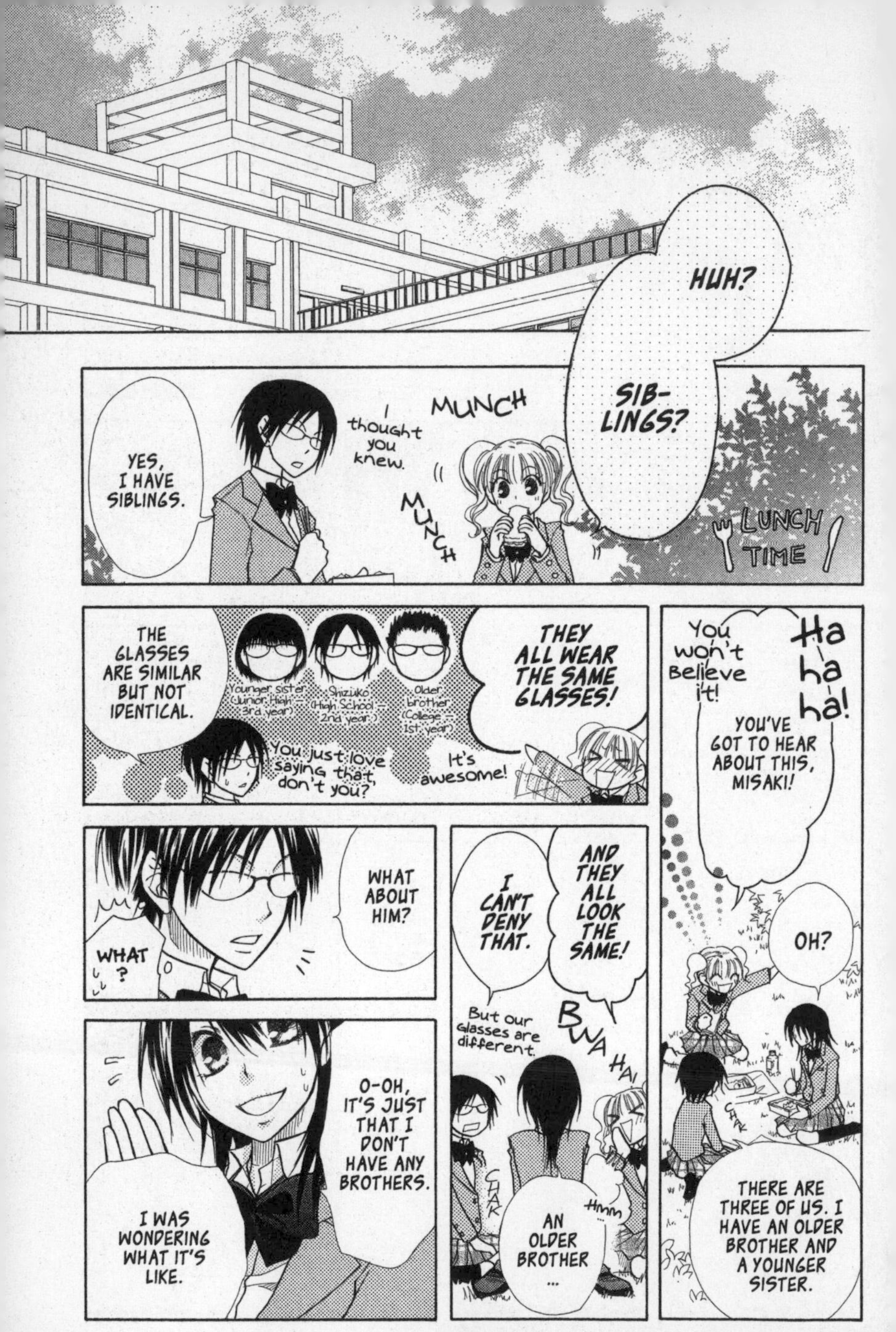
HUH?
SIB-LINGS?
LUNCH TIME
MUNCH
MUNCH
I thought you knew.
YES, I HAVE SIBLINGS.
Ha ha ha!
You won't believe it!
YOU'VE GOT TO HEAR ABOUT THIS, MISAKI!
OH?
CHAK
THERE ARE THREE OF US. I HAVE AN OLDER BROTHER AND A YOUNGER SISTER.
THEY ALL WEAR THE SAME GLASSES!
It's awesome!
Older brother (College - 1st year)
Shizuko (High School - 2nd year)
Younger sister (Junior High - 3rd year)
You just love saying that, don't you?
THE GLASSES ARE SIMILAR BUT NOT IDENTICAL.
AND THEY ALL LOOK THE SAME!
BWA HA HA
I CAN'T DENY THAT.
But our glasses are different.
Hmm...
CHAK
AN OLDER BROTHER...
WHAT ABOUT HIM?
WHAT?
O-OH, IT'S JUST THAT I DON'T HAVE ANY BROTHERS.
I WAS WONDERING WHAT IT'S LIKE.

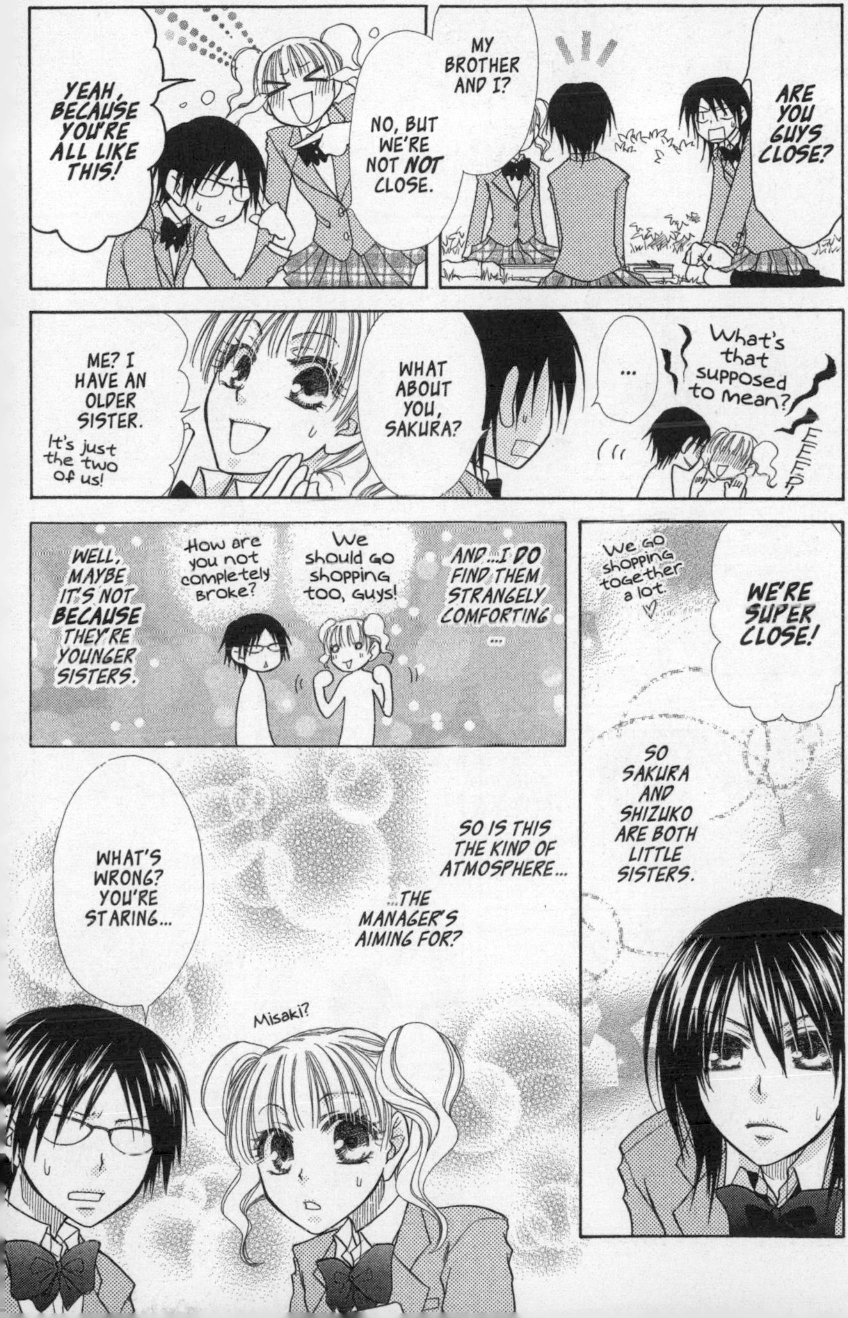
ARE YOU GUYS CLOSE?
MY BROTHER AND I?
NO, BUT WE'RE NOT NOT CLOSE.
YEAH, BECAUSE YOU'RE ALL LIKE THIS!
What's that supposed to mean?
...
EEEP!
WHAT ABOUT YOU, SAKURA?
ME? I HAVE AN OLDER SISTER.
It's just the two of us!
WE'RE SUPER CLOSE!
We go shopping together a lot ♡
SO SAKURA AND SHIZUKO ARE BOTH LITTLE SISTERS.
AND...I DO FIND THEM STRANGELY COMFORTING...
We should go shopping too, guys!
How are you not completely broke?
WELL, MAYBE IT'S NOT BECAUSE THEY'RE YOUNGER SISTERS.
SO IS THIS THE KIND OF ATMOSPHERE...
...THE MANAGER'S AIMING FOR?
Misaki?
WHAT'S WRONG? YOU'RE STARING...

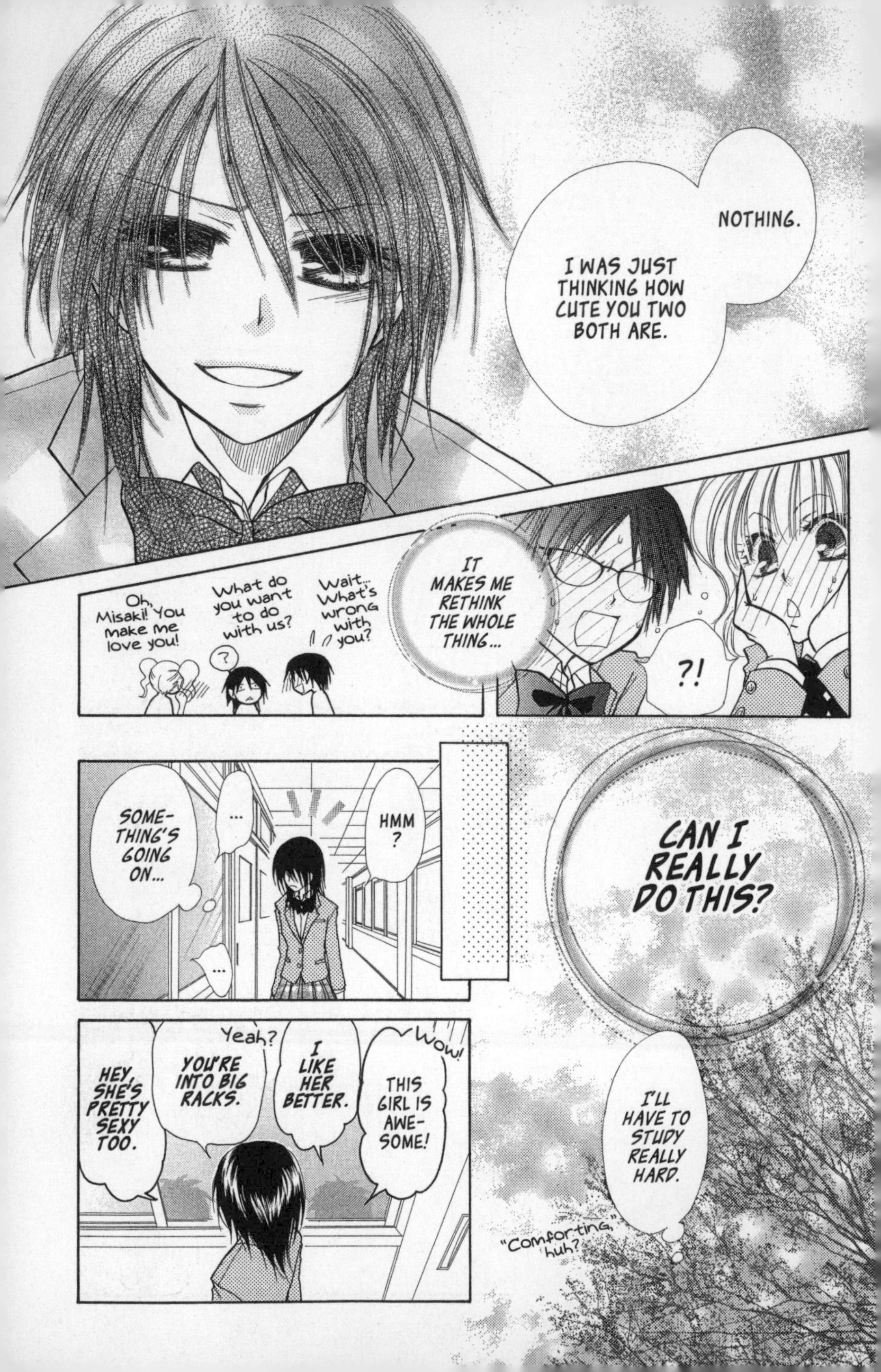
NOTHING.
I WAS JUST THINKING HOW CUTE YOU TWO BOTH ARE.
IT MAKES ME RETHINK THE WHOLE THING...
?!
Wait... What's wrong with you?
What do you want to do with us?
?
Oh, Misaki! You make me love you!
CAN I REALLY DO THIS?
I'LL HAVE TO STUDY REALLY HARD.
"Comforting," huh?
HMM?
...
SOME-THING'S GOING ON...
...
Wow!
THIS GIRL IS AWE-SOME!
I LIKE HER BETTER.
Yeah?
YOU'RE INTO BIG RACKS.
HEY, SHE'S PRETTY SEXY TOO.

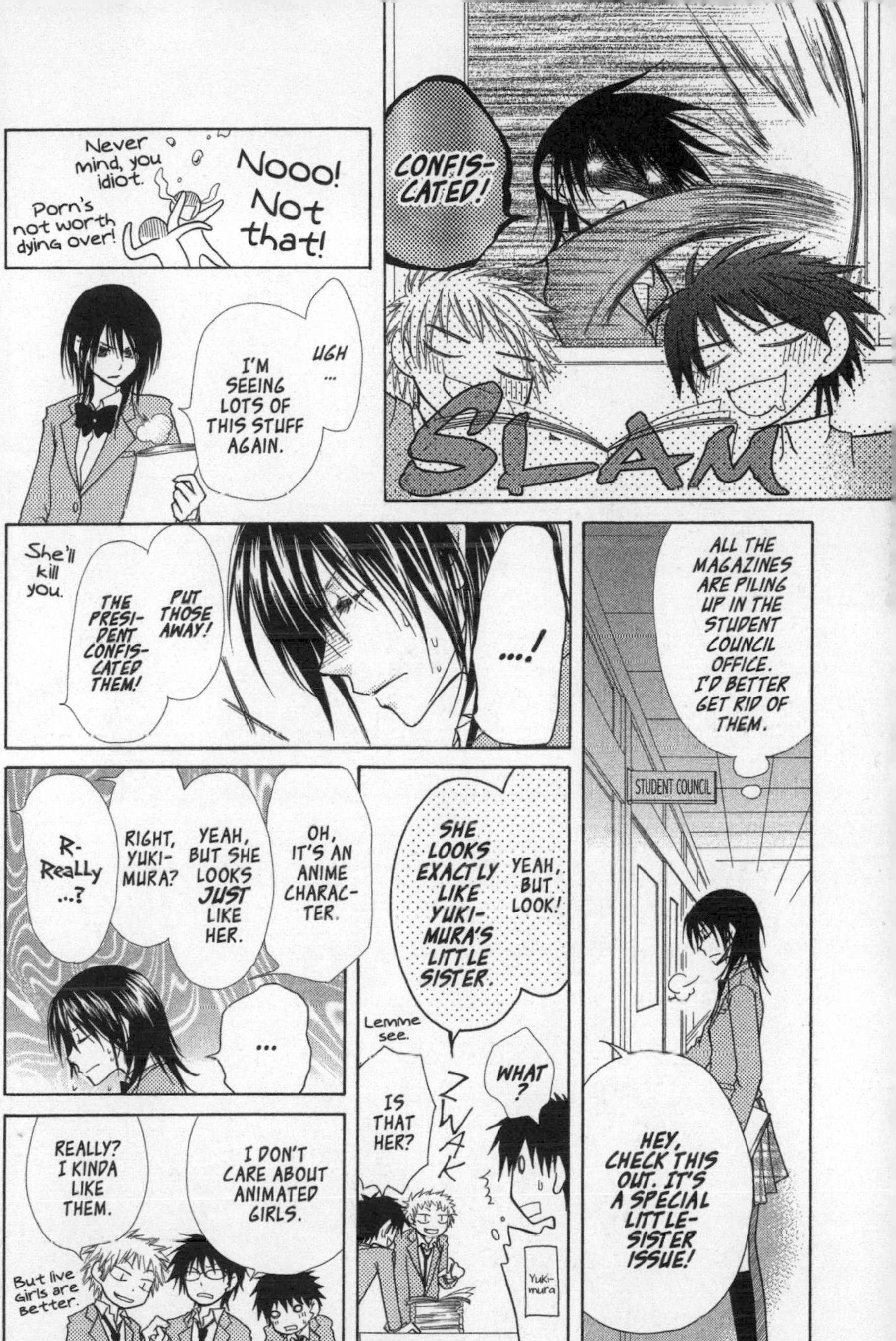
CONFISCATED!
SLAM
Never mind, you idiot.
Porn's not worth dying over!
Nooo! Not that!
UGH...
I'M SEEING LOTS OF THIS STUFF AGAIN.
ALL THE MAGAZINES ARE PILING UP IN THE STUDENT COUNCIL OFFICE. I'D BETTER GET RID OF THEM.
STUDENT COUNCIL
HEY, CHECK THIS OUT. IT'S A SPECIAL LITTLE-SISTER ISSUE!
...!
PUT THOSE AWAY!
THE PRESIDENT CONFISCATED THEM!
She'll kill you.
YEAH, BUT LOOK!
SHE LOOKS EXACTLY LIKE YUKIMURA'S LITTLE SISTER.
Lemme see.
WHAT?
ZWAK
IS THAT HER?
Yukimura
OH, IT'S AN ANIME CHARACTER.
YEAH, BUT SHE LOOKS JUST LIKE HER.
RIGHT, YUKIMURA?
R-Really ...?
...
I DON'T CARE ABOUT ANIMATED GIRLS.
REALLY? I KINDA LIKE THEM.
But live girls are better.

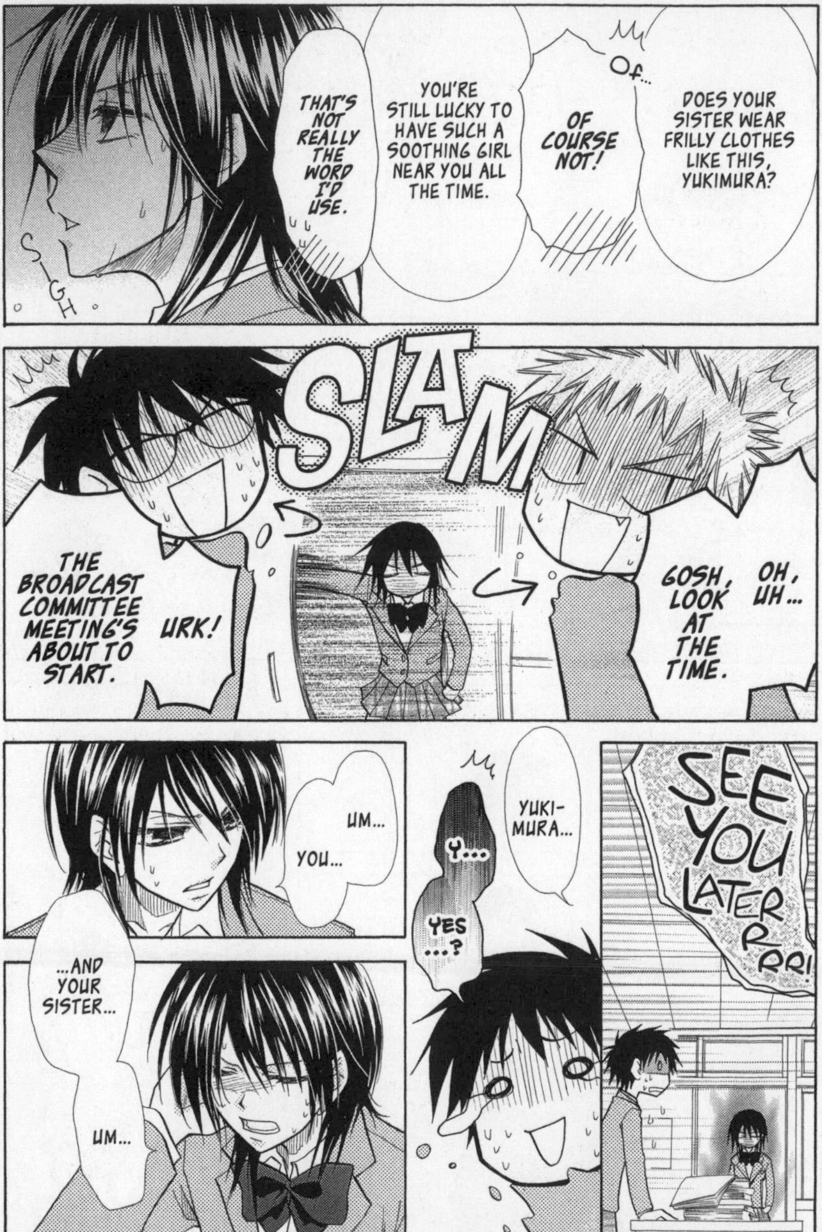
DOES YOUR SISTER WEAR FRILLY CLOTHES LIKE THIS, YUKIMURA?
Of...
OF COURSE NOT!
YOU'RE STILL LUCKY TO HAVE SUCH A SOOTHING GIRL NEAR YOU ALL THE TIME.
THAT'S NOT REALLY THE WORD I'D USE.
SIGH
SLAM
OH, UH...
GOSH, LOOK AT THE TIME.
URK!
THE BROADCAST COMMITTEE MEETING'S ABOUT TO START.
SEE YOU LATERRRR!
YUKI-MURA...
Y...
YES...?
UM...
YOU...
...AND YOUR SISTER...
UM...

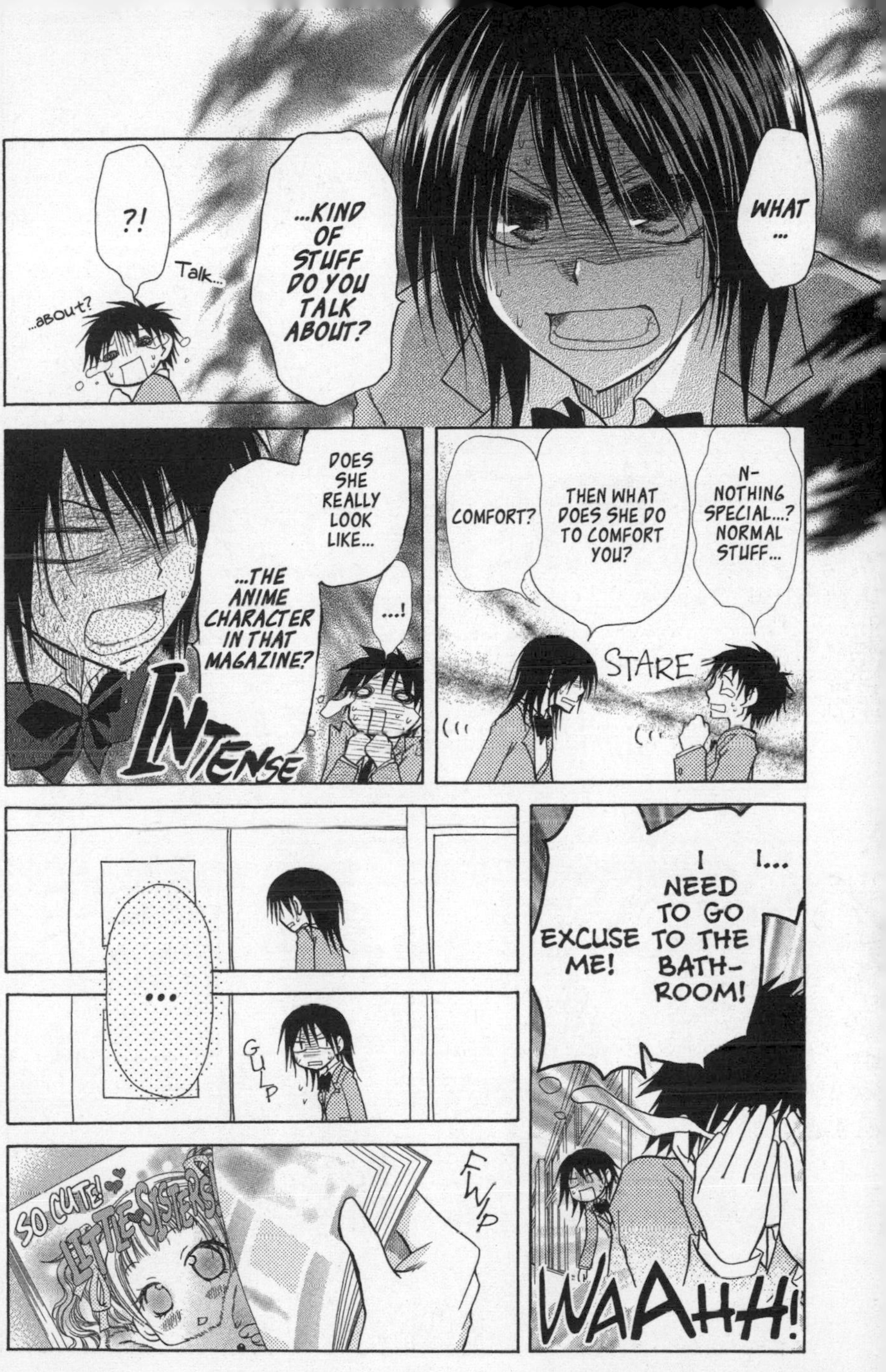
WHAT ...
...KIND OF STUFF DO YOU TALK ABOUT?
?!
Talk...
...about?
N- NOTHING SPECIAL...? NORMAL STUFF...
THEN WHAT DOES SHE DO TO COMFORT YOU?
COMFORT?
STARE
DOES SHE REALLY LOOK LIKE...
...THE ANIME CHARACTER IN THAT MAGAZINE?
...!
INTENSE
I... I NEED TO GO TO THE BATHROOM!
EXCUSE ME!
WAAHH!
...
GULP
FWIP
SO CUTE!
LITTLE SISTERS!

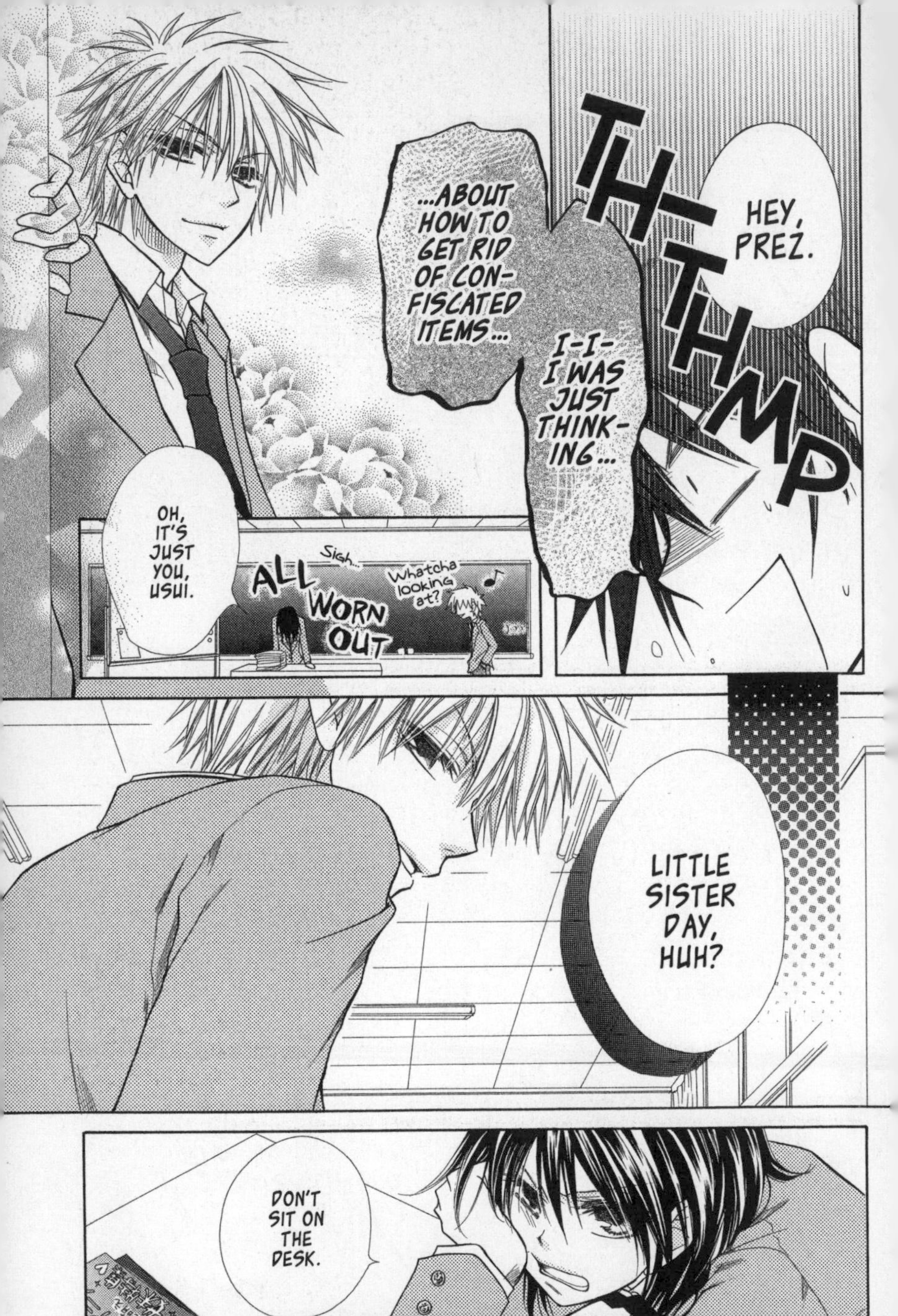

HEY, PREZ.
THTHMP
I-I-I WAS JUST THINKING...
...ABOUT HOW TO GET RID OF CON-FISCATED ITEMS...
Whatcha looking at?
Sigh...
ALL WORN OUT
OH, IT'S JUST YOU, USUI.
LITTLE SISTER DAY, HUH?
DON'T SIT ON THE DESK.

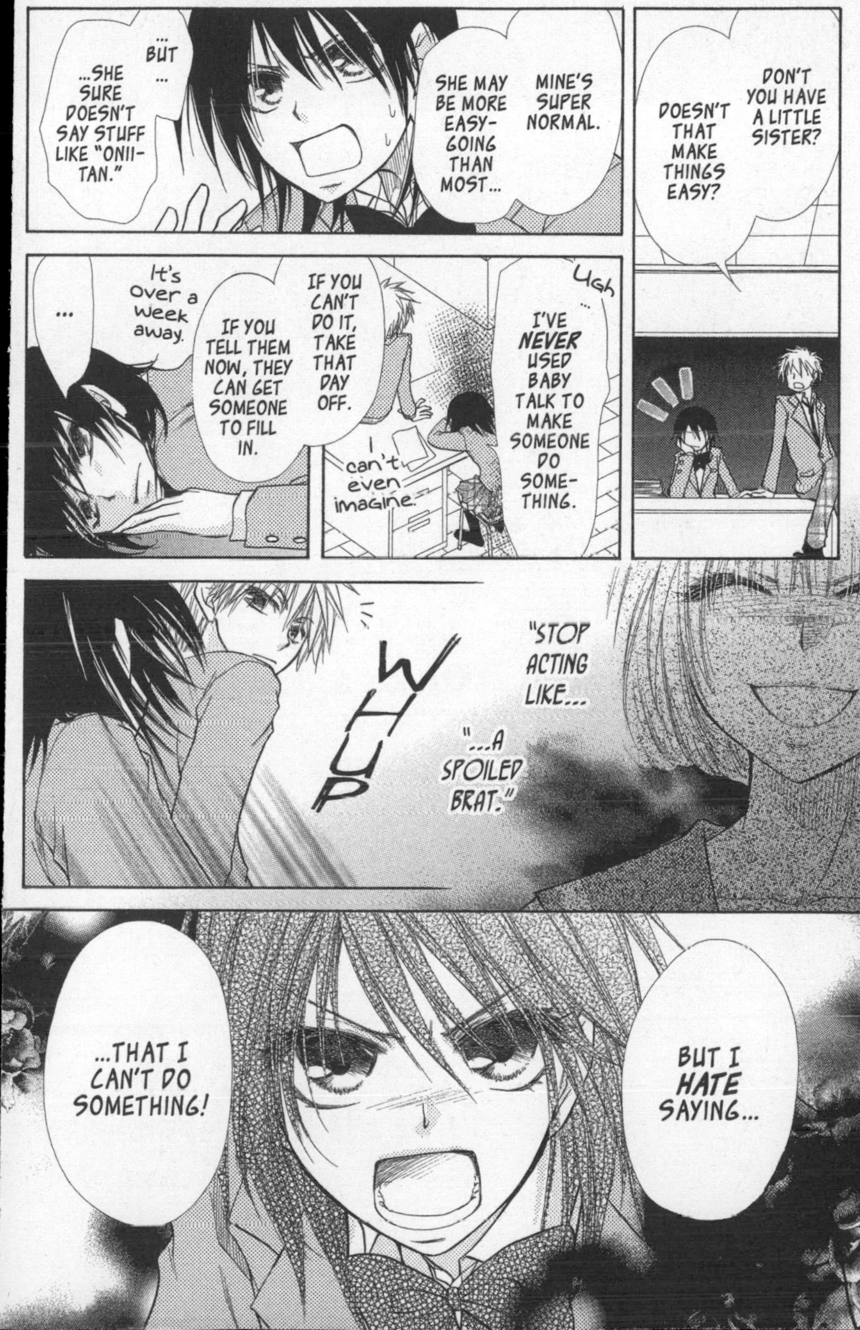
DON'T YOU HAVE A LITTLE SISTER?
DOESN'T THAT MAKE THINGS EASY?
MINE'S SUPER NORMAL.
SHE MAY BE MORE EASY-GOING THAN MOST...
...BUT...
...SHE SURE DOESN'T SAY STUFF LIKE "ONII-TAN."
Ugh...
I'VE ***NEVER*** USED BABY TALK TO MAKE SOMEONE DO SOMETHING.
I can't even imagine.
IF YOU CAN'T DO IT, TAKE THAT DAY OFF.
IF YOU TELL THEM NOW, THEY CAN GET SOMEONE TO FILL IN.
It's over a week away.
...
"STOP ACTING LIKE...
"...A SPOILED BRAT."
WHUP
BUT I ***HATE*** SAYING...
...THAT I CAN'T DO SOMETHING!

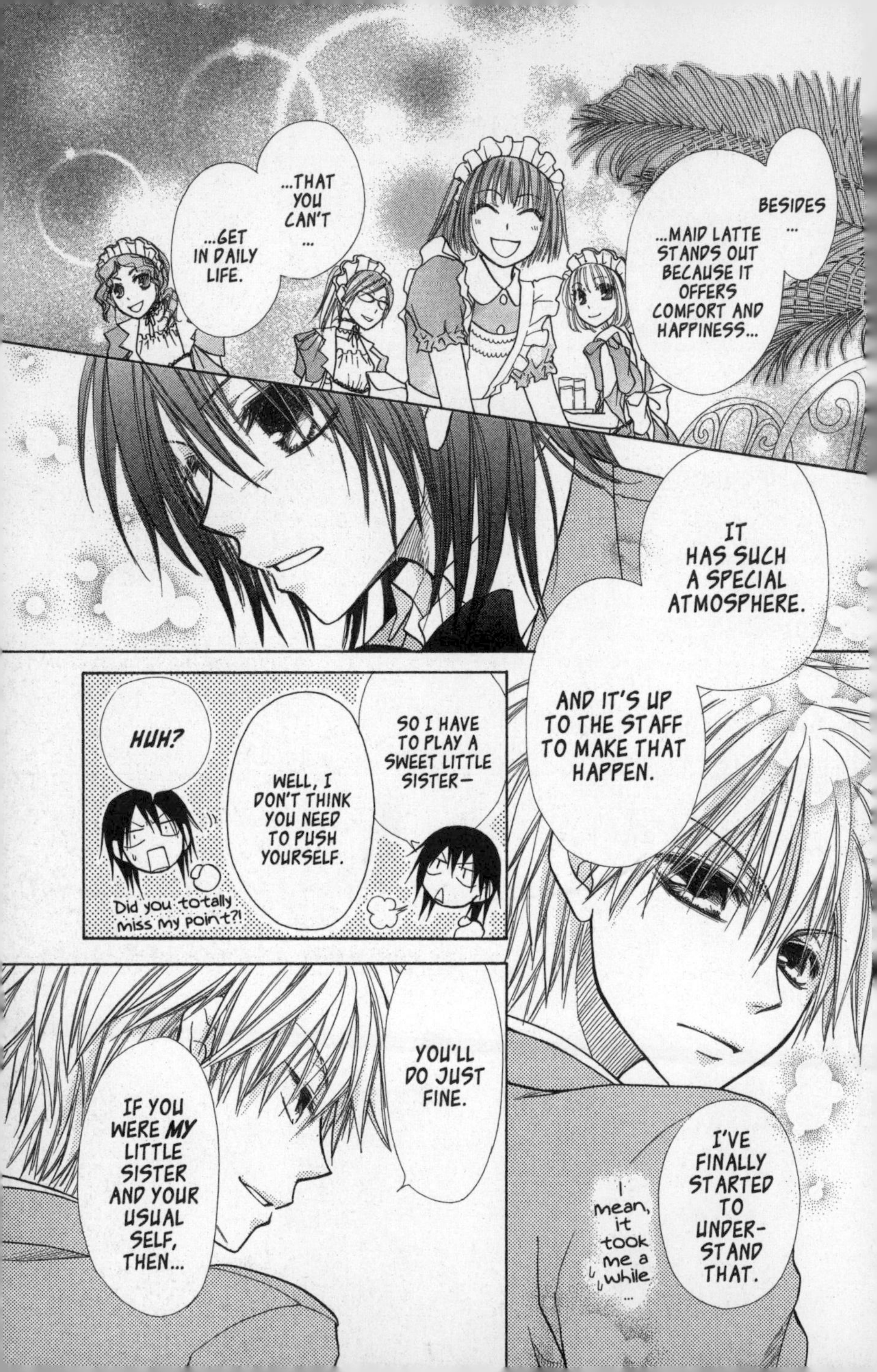
BESIDES ...
...MAID LATTE STANDS OUT BECAUSE IT OFFERS COMFORT AND HAPPINESS...
...THAT YOU CAN'T ...
...GET IN DAILY LIFE.
IT HAS SUCH A SPECIAL ATMOSPHERE.
AND IT'S UP TO THE STAFF TO MAKE THAT HAPPEN.
I'VE FINALLY STARTED TO UNDER-STAND THAT.
I mean, it took me a while ...
SO I HAVE TO PLAY A SWEET LITTLE SISTER—
WELL, I DON'T THINK YOU NEED TO PUSH YOURSELF.
HUH?
Did you totally miss my point?!
YOU'LL DO JUST FINE.
IF YOU WERE *MY* LITTLE SISTER AND YOUR USUAL SELF, THEN...

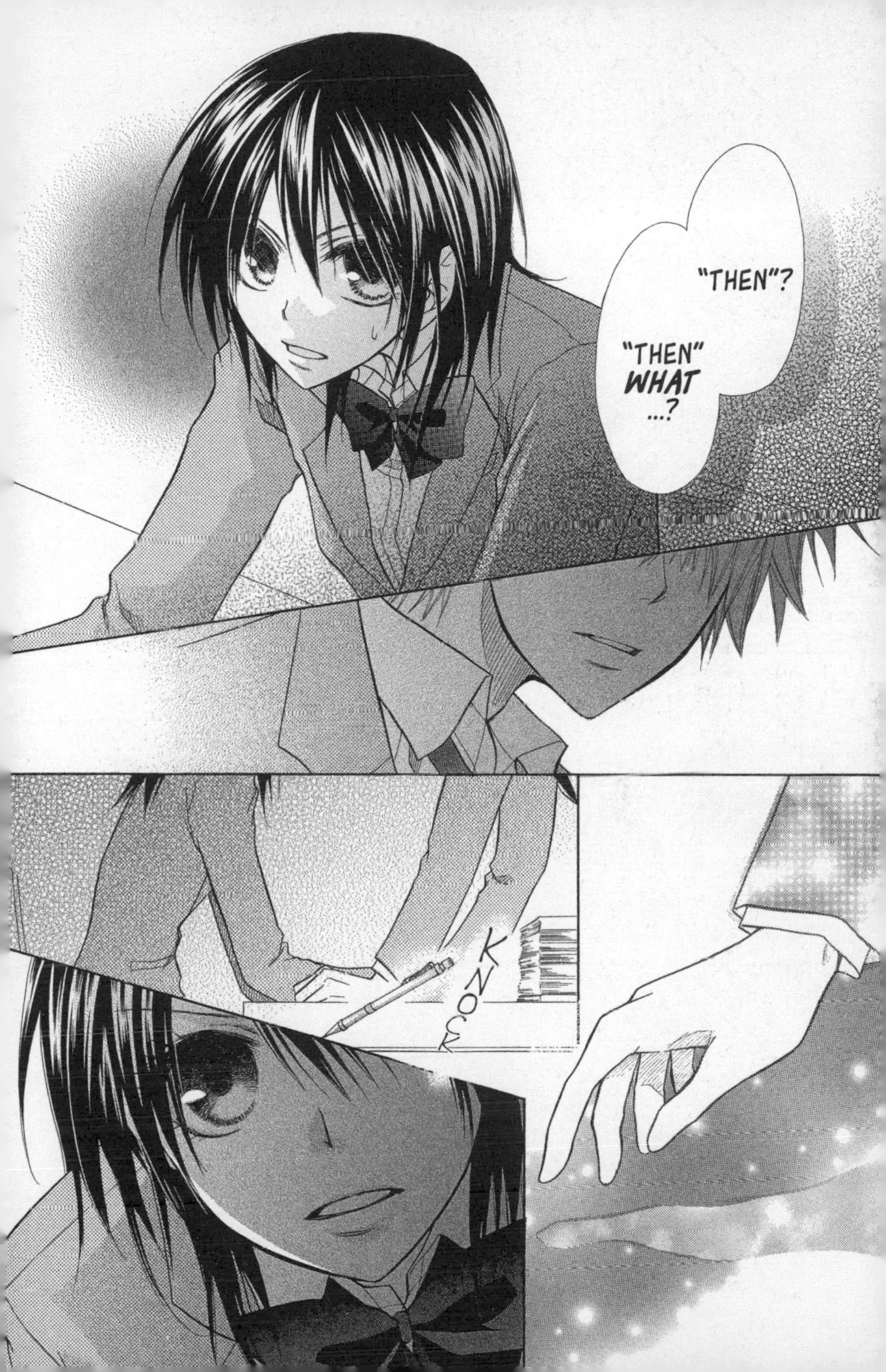
"THEN"?
"THEN" WHAT ...?
KNOCK

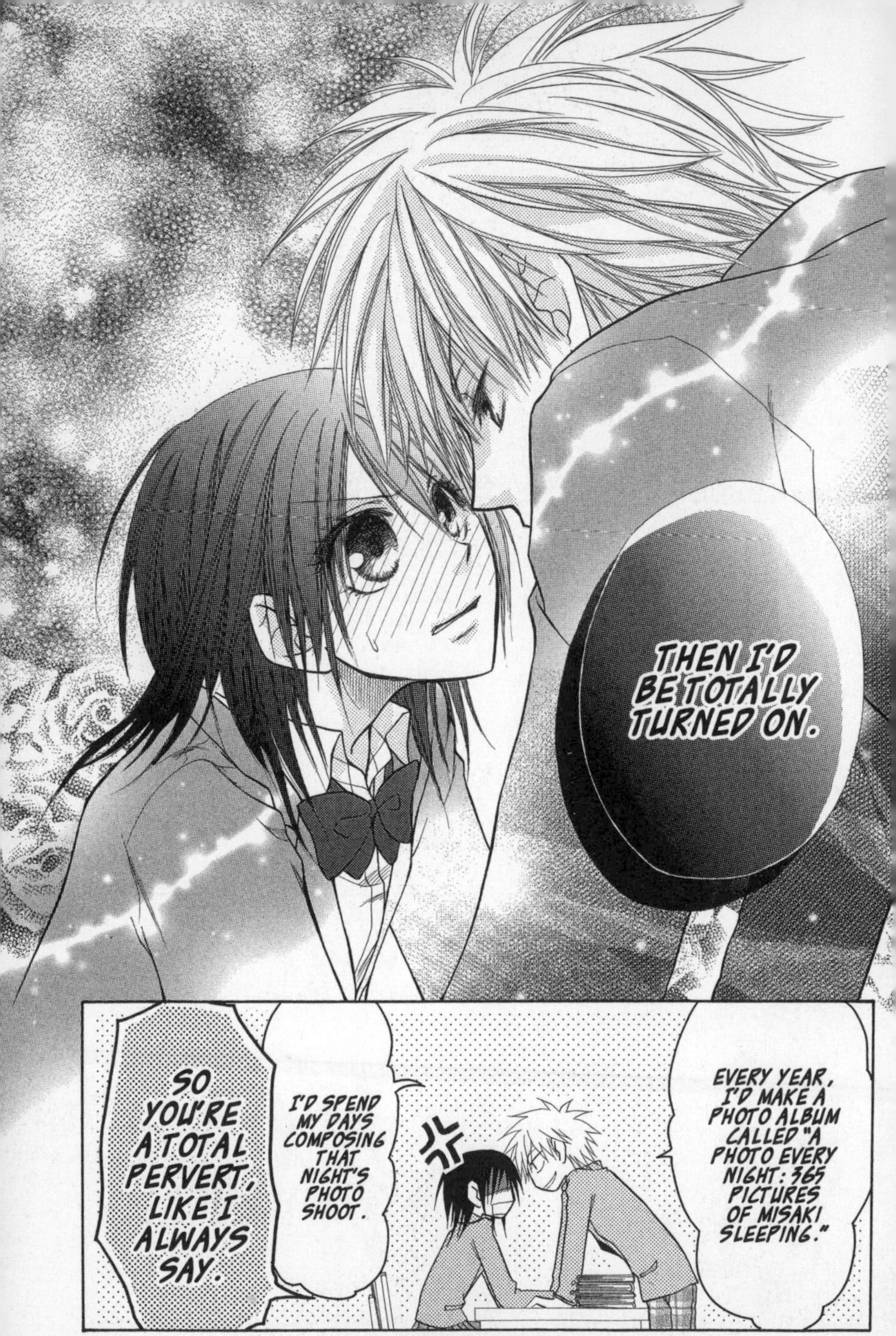
THEN I'D BE TOTALLY TURNED ON.
EVERY YEAR, I'D MAKE A PHOTO ALBUM CALLED "A PHOTO EVERY NIGHT: 365 PICTURES OF MISAKI SLEEPING."
I'D SPEND MY DAYS COMPOSING THAT NIGHT'S PHOTO SHOOT.
SO YOU'RE A TOTAL PERVERT, LIKE I ALWAYS SAY.

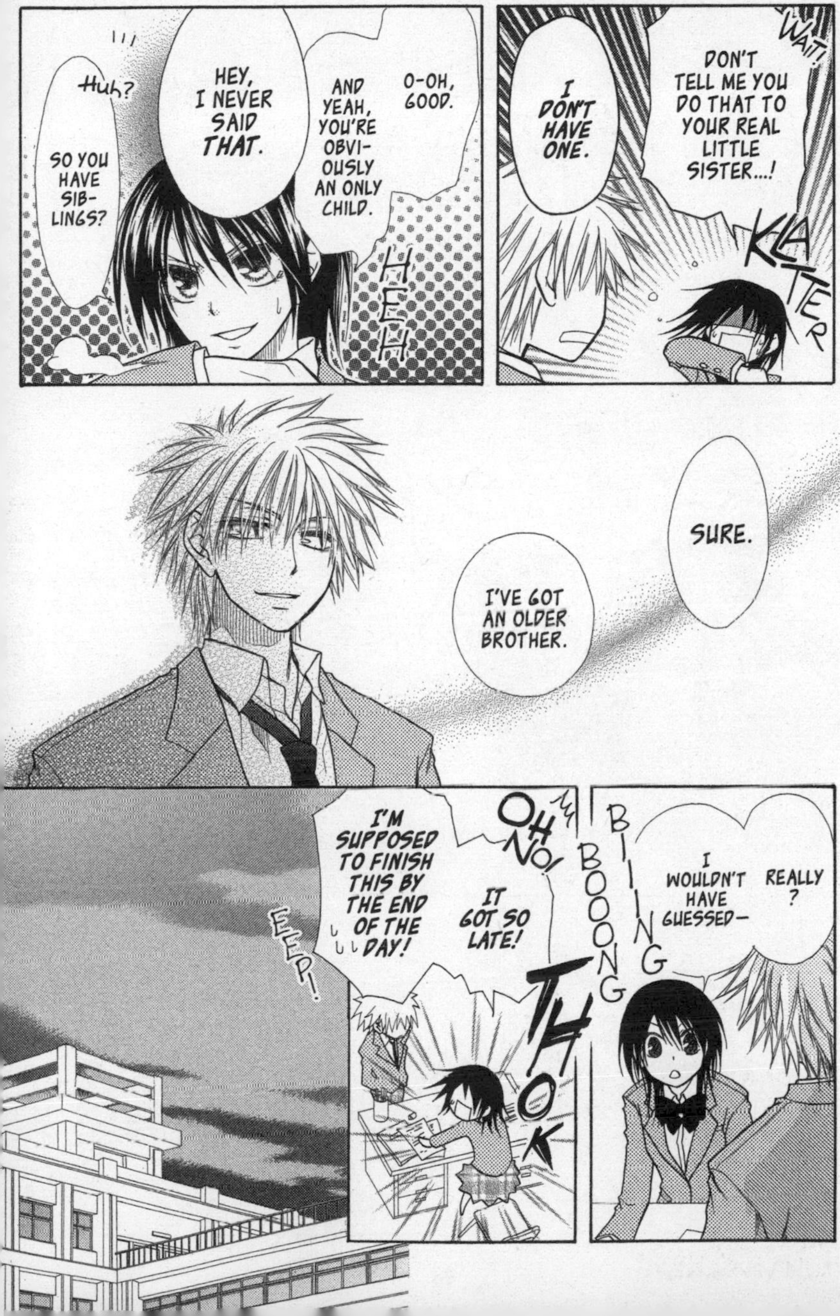
WAIT!
DON'T TELL ME YOU DO THAT TO YOUR REAL LITTLE SISTER...!
I DON'T HAVE ONE.
KLATTER
O-OH, GOOD.
AND YEAH, YOU'RE OBVI-OUSLY AN ONLY CHILD.
HEH
HEY, I NEVER SAID THAT.
Huh?
SO YOU HAVE SIB-LINGS?
SURE.
I'VE GOT AN OLDER BROTHER.
REALLY?
I WOULDN'T HAVE GUESSED—
BIIING
BOOONG
OH NO!
IT GOT SO LATE!
I'M SUPPOSED TO FINISH THIS BY THE END OF THE DAY!
THOK
EEP!

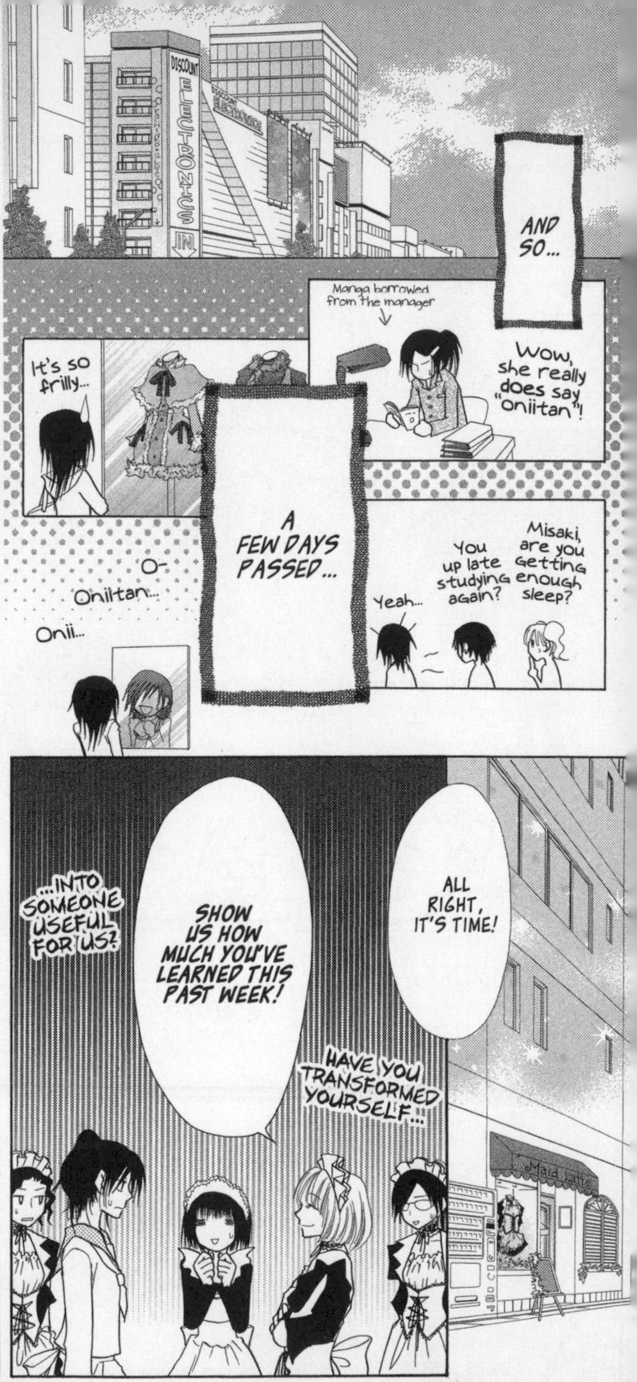
DISCOUNT
ELECTRONICS
IN
AND SO...
Manga borrowed from the manager
Wow, she really does say "oniitan"!
A FEW DAYS PASSED...
It's so frilly...
Misaki, are you getting enough sleep?
You up late studying again?
Yeah...
O- Oniitan...
Onii...
ALL RIGHT, IT'S TIME!
SHOW US HOW MUCH YOU'VE LEARNED THIS PAST WEEK!
HAVE YOU TRANSFORMED YOURSELF...
...INTO SOMEONE USEFUL FOR US?
Maid Latte

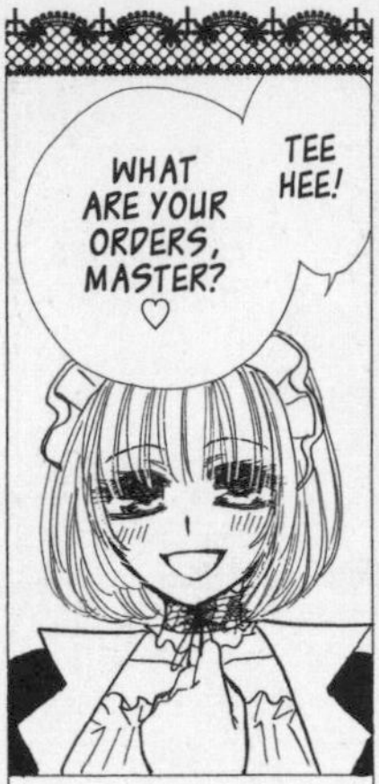
TEE HEE!
WHAT ARE YOUR ORDERS, MASTER? ♡

NAME

Honoka ♡

AGE (CLASS)

20 years old

BLOOD TYPE

B

HEIGHT

157 cm

WEIGHT

46 kg

SPECIAL SKILL

Role-playing

FAVORITE THING

MAKE-BELIEVE WORLDS

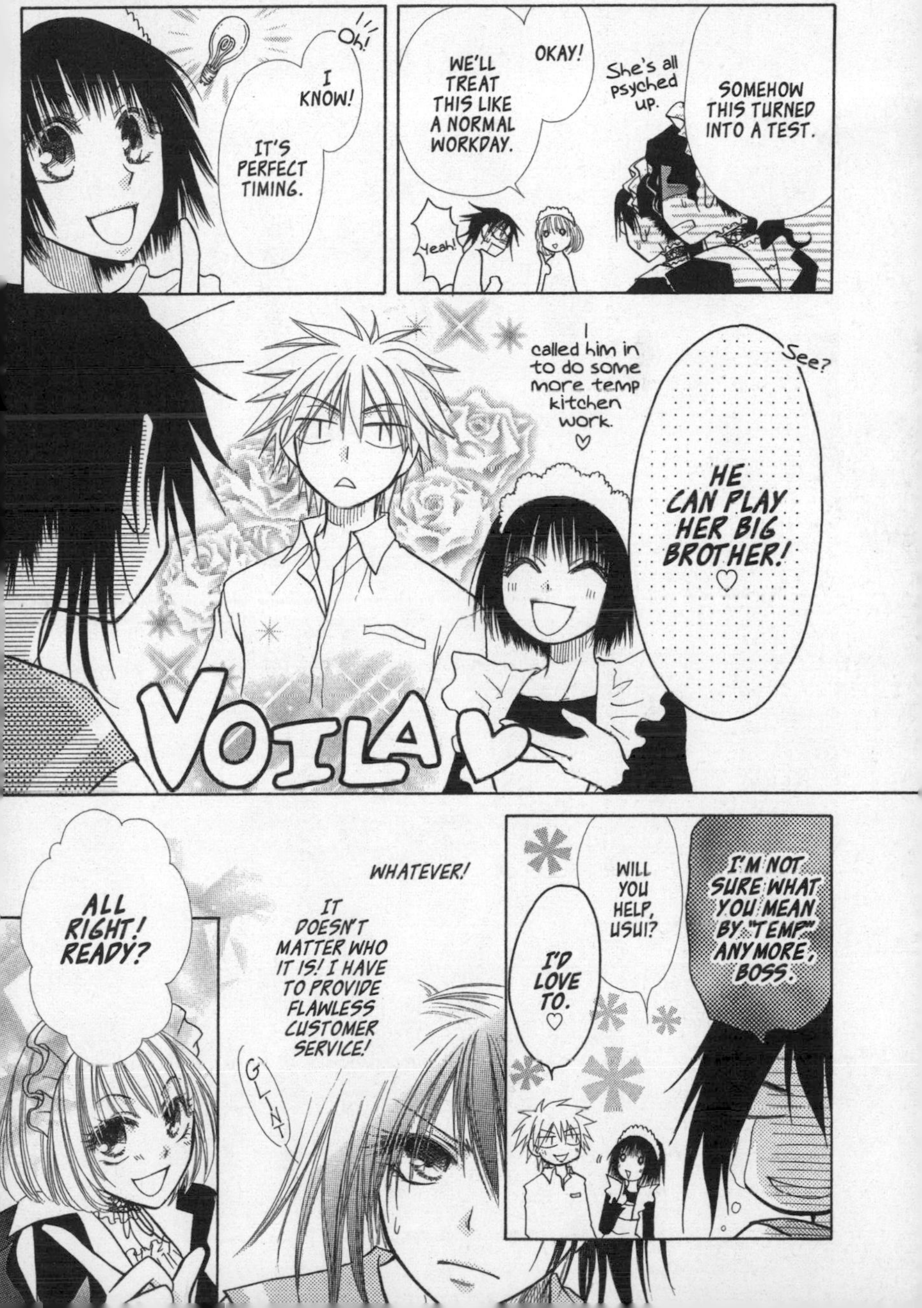
SOMEHOW THIS TURNED INTO A TEST.
She's all psyched up.
OKAY!
WE'LL TREAT THIS LIKE A NORMAL WORKDAY.
Yeah!
Oh!
I KNOW!
IT'S PERFECT TIMING.
See?
HE CAN PLAY HER BIG BROTHER! ♡
I called him in to do some more temp kitchen work. ♡
VOILA ♡
I'M NOT SURE WHAT YOU MEAN BY "TEMP" ANYMORE, BOSS.
WILL YOU HELP, USUI?
I'D LOVE TO. ♡
WHATEVER!
IT DOESN'T MATTER WHO IT IS! I HAVE TO PROVIDE FLAWLESS CUSTOMER SERVICE!
GLINT
ALL RIGHT! READY?

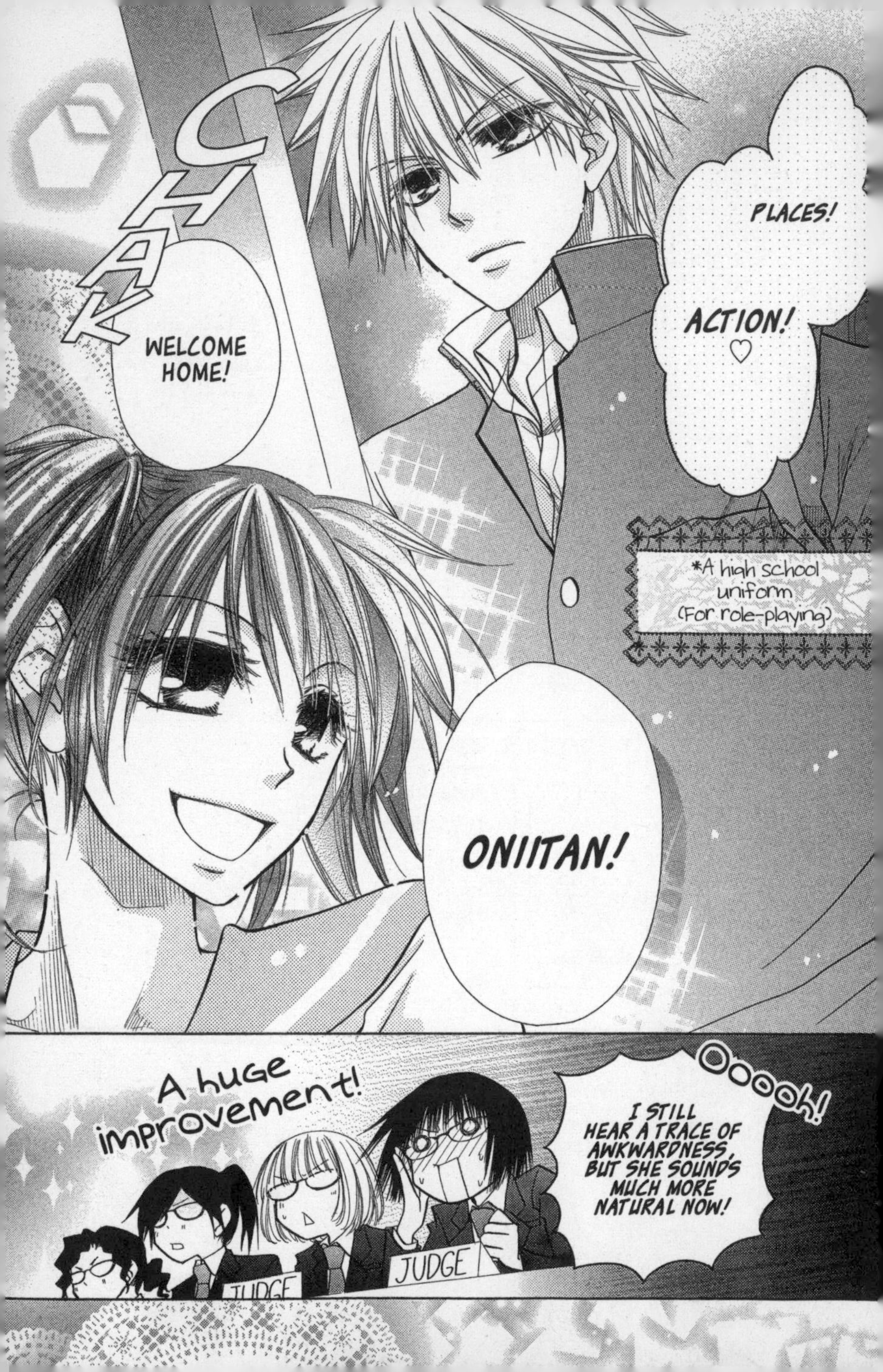
PLACES!
ACTION! ♡
CHAK
WELCOME HOME!
*A high school uniform (For role-playing)
ONIITAN!
Ooooh!
I STILL HEAR A TRACE OF AWKWARDNESS, BUT SHE SOUNDS MUCH MORE NATURAL NOW!
A huge improvement!
JUDGE
JUDGE

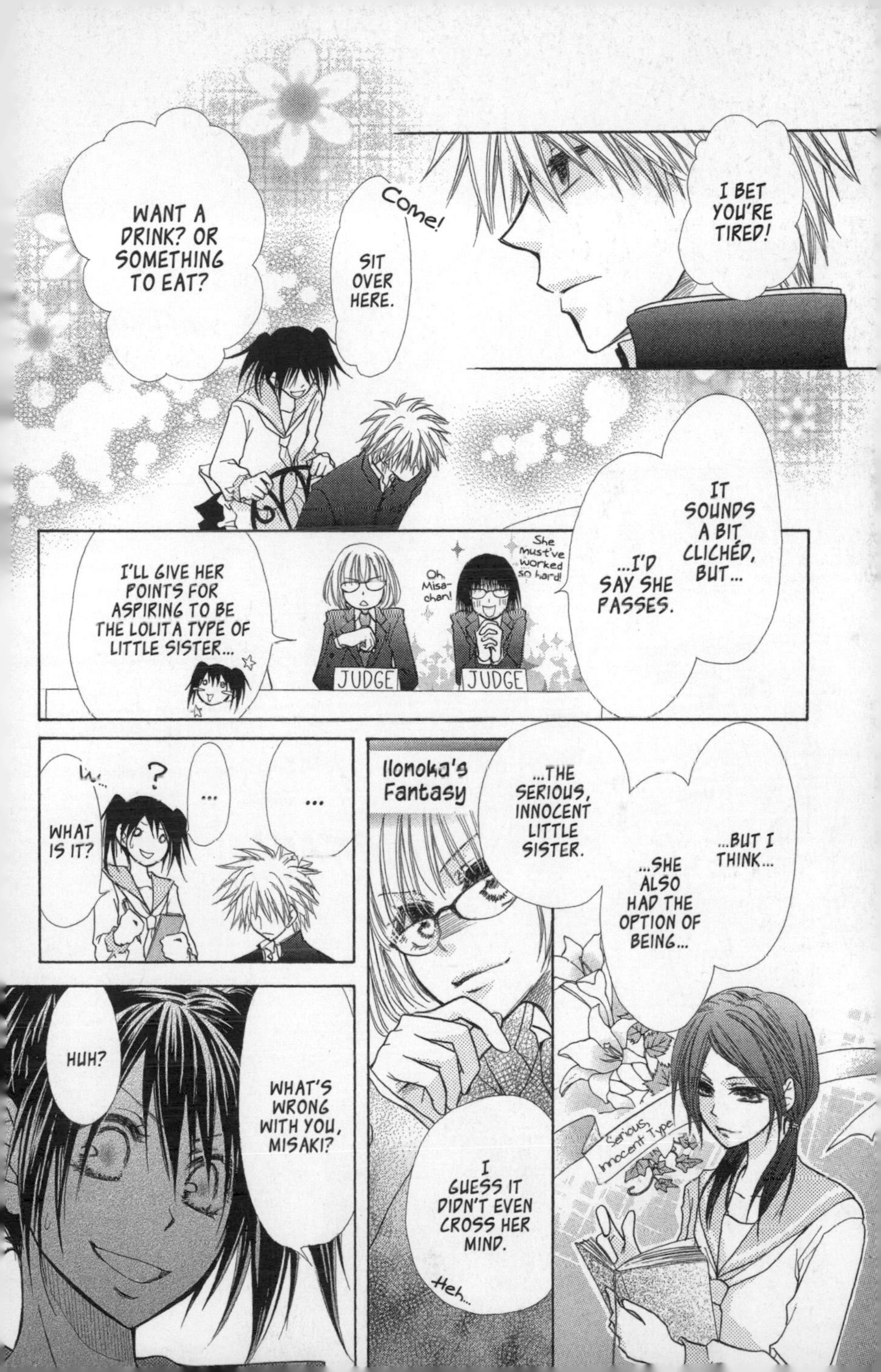
I BET YOU'RE TIRED!
Come!
SIT OVER HERE.
WANT A DRINK? OR SOMETHING TO EAT?
IT SOUNDS A BIT CLICHÉD, BUT...
...I'D SAY SHE PASSES.
She must've worked so hard!
Oh, Misa-chan!
JUDGE
JUDGE
I'LL GIVE HER POINTS FOR ASPIRING TO BE THE LOLITA TYPE OF LITTLE SISTER...
...BUT I THINK...
...SHE ALSO HAD THE OPTION OF BEING...
...THE SERIOUS, INNOCENT LITTLE SISTER.
Honoka's Fantasy
Serious, Innocent Type
I GUESS IT DIDN'T EVEN CROSS HER MIND.
Heh...
...
...
?
WHAT IS IT?
WHAT'S WRONG WITH YOU, MISAKI?
HUH?

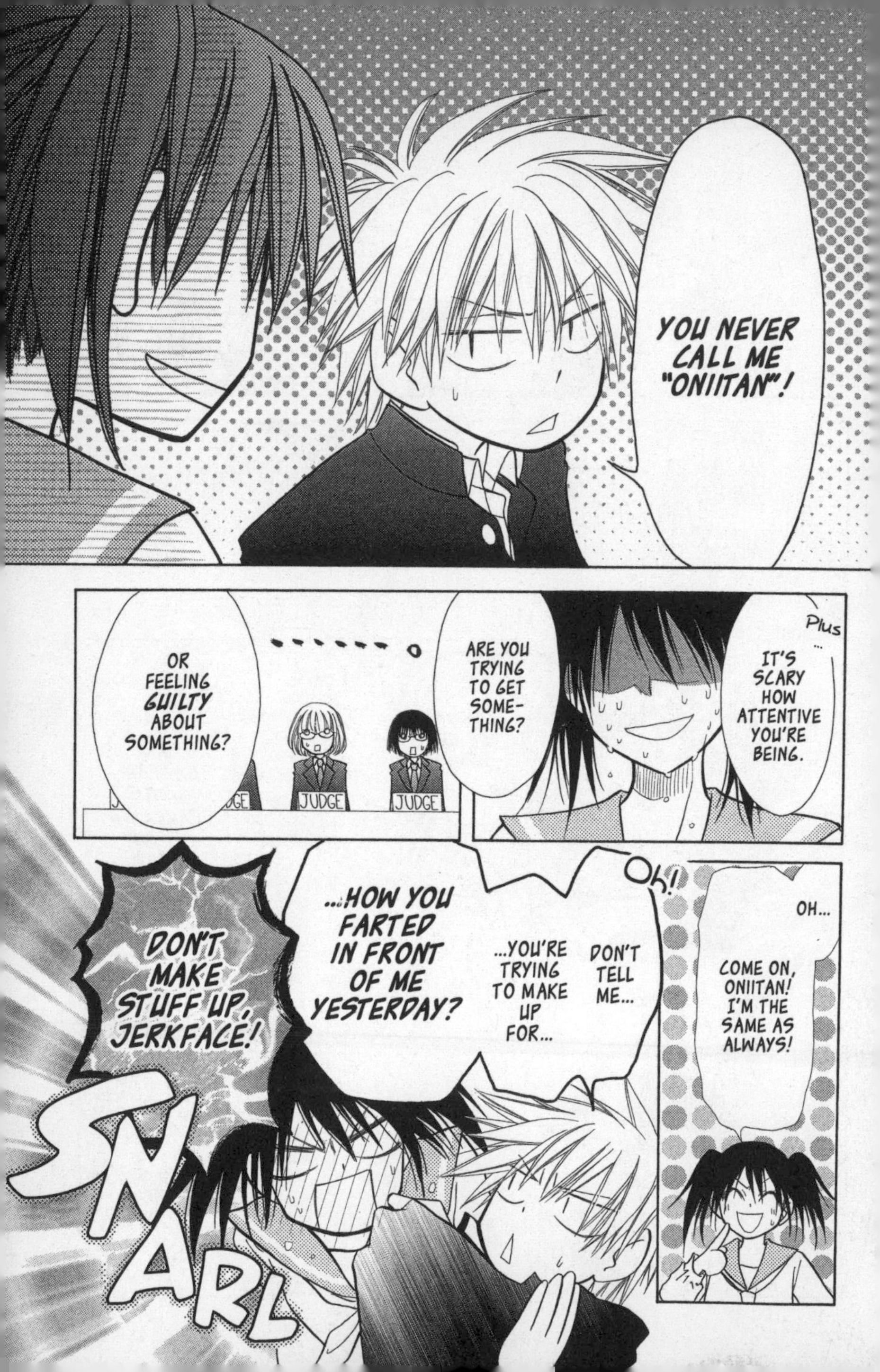
YOU NEVER CALL ME "ONIITAN"!
Plus...
IT'S SCARY HOW ATTENTIVE YOU'RE BEING.
ARE YOU TRYING TO GET SOMETHING?
......
OR FEELING GUILTY ABOUT SOMETHING?
JUDGE
JUDGE
OH...
COME ON, ONIITAN! I'M THE SAME AS ALWAYS!
Oh!
DON'T TELL ME...
...YOU'RE TRYING TO MAKE UP FOR...
...HOW YOU FARTED IN FRONT OF ME YESTERDAY?
DON'T MAKE STUFF UP, JERKFACE!
SNARL

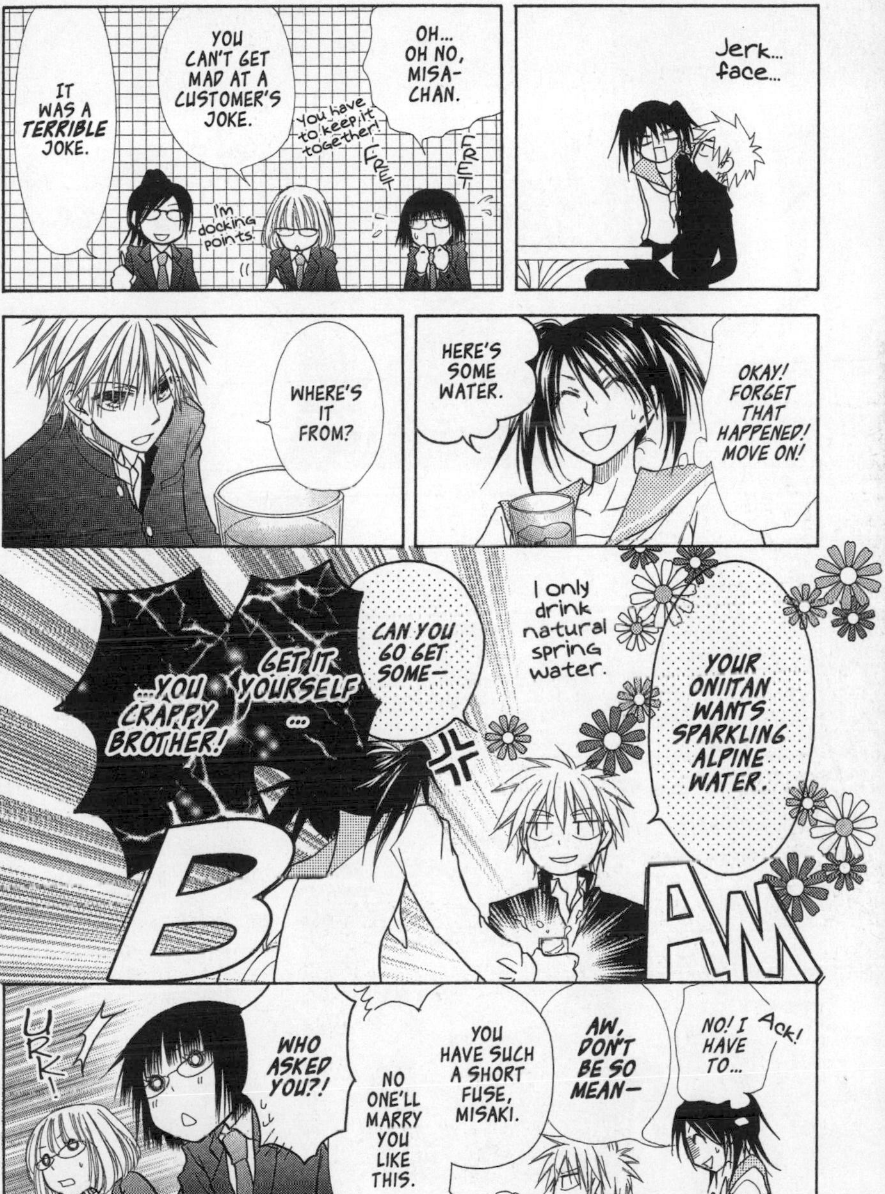
Jerk... face...
OH... OH NO, MISA-CHAN.
FRET
FRET
You have to keep it together!
YOU CAN'T GET MAD AT A CUSTOMER'S JOKE.
I'm docking points!
IT WAS A TERRIBLE JOKE.
OKAY! FORGET THAT HAPPENED! MOVE ON!
HERE'S SOME WATER.
WHERE'S IT FROM?
YOUR ONIITAN WANTS SPARKLING ALPINE WATER.
I only drink natural spring water.
CAN YOU GO GET SOME—
GET IT YOURSELF...
...YOU CRAPPY BROTHER!
BAM
Ack!
NO! I HAVE TO...
AW, DON'T BE SO MEAN—
YOU HAVE SUCH A SHORT FUSE, MISAKI.
NO ONE'LL MARRY YOU LIKE THIS.
WHO ASKED YOU?!
URK!

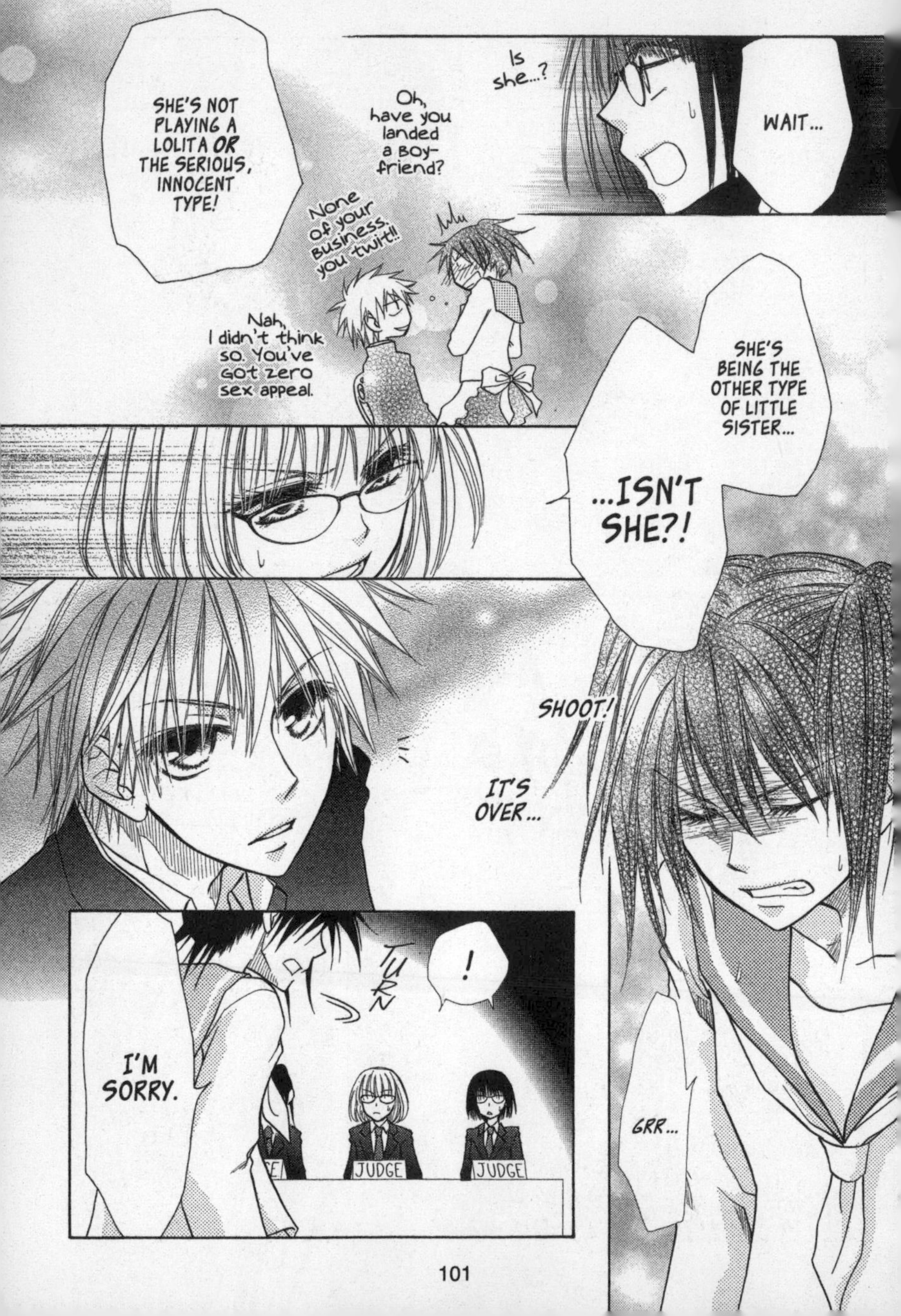
WAIT...
Is she...?
SHE'S NOT PLAYING A LOLITA OR THE SERIOUS, INNOCENT TYPE!
Oh, have you landed a boy-friend?
None of your business, you twit!!
Nah, I didn't think so. You've got zero sex appeal.
SHE'S BEING THE OTHER TYPE OF LITTLE SISTER...
...ISN'T SHE?!
SHOOT!
IT'S OVER...
GRR...
!
TURN
I'M SORRY.
JUDGE
JUDGE

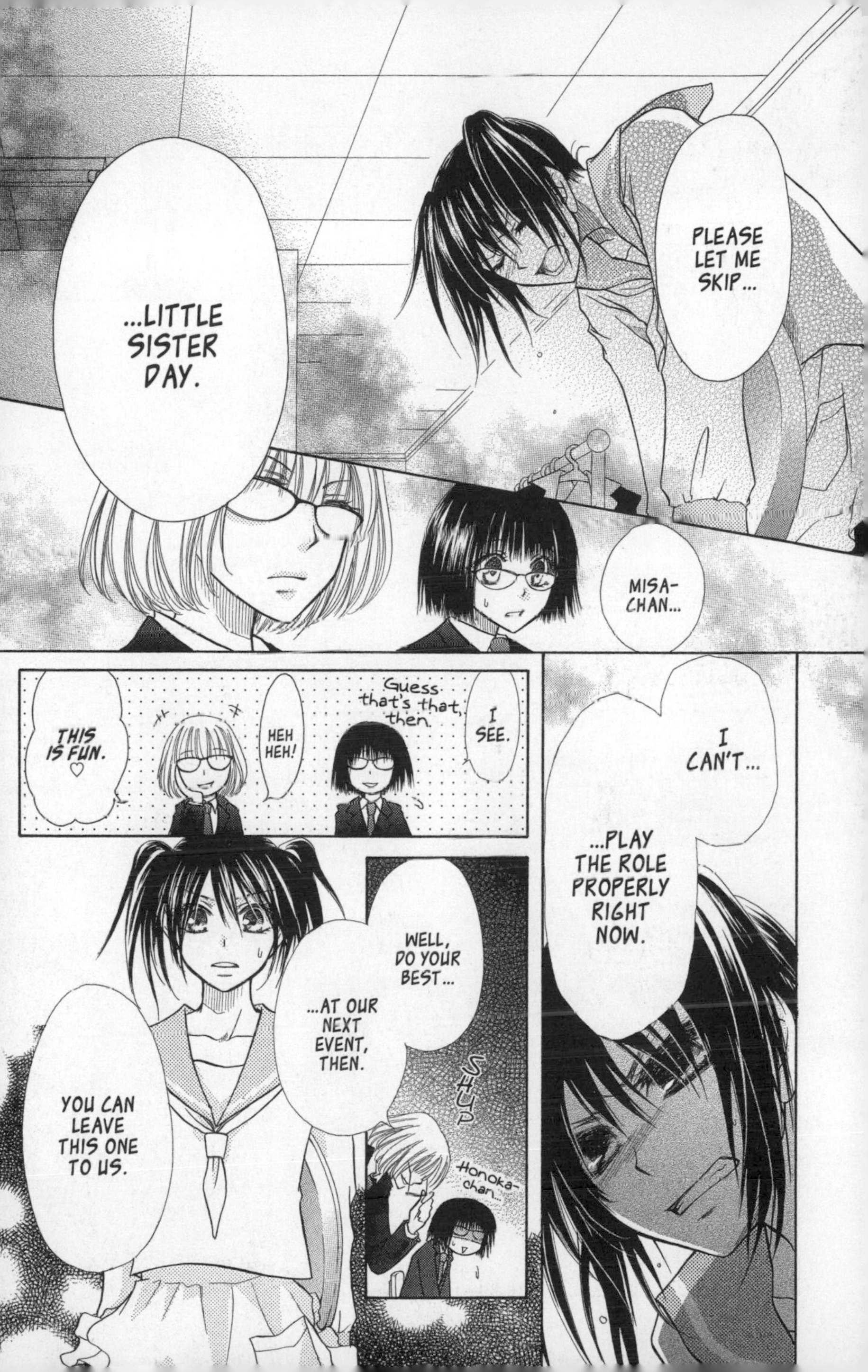
PLEASE LET ME SKIP...
...LITTLE SISTER DAY.
MISA-CHAN...
I CAN'T...
...PLAY THE ROLE PROPERLY RIGHT NOW.
I SEE.
Guess that's that, then.
HEH HEH!
THIS IS FUN. ♡
WELL, DO YOUR BEST...
...AT OUR NEXT EVENT, THEN.
SHUP
Honoka-chan...
YOU CAN LEAVE THIS ONE TO US.

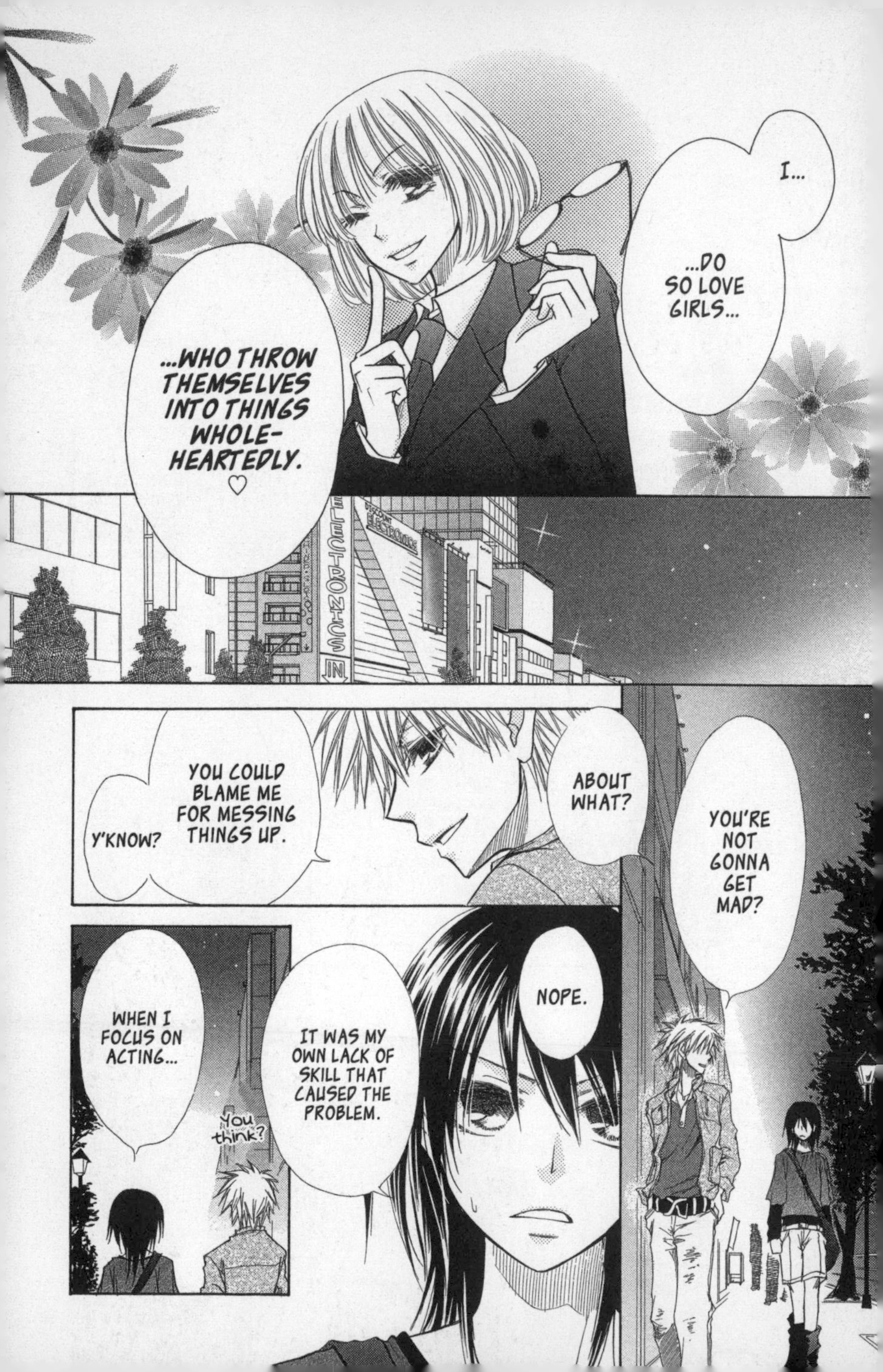
I...
...DO SO LOVE GIRLS...
...WHO THROW THEMSELVES INTO THINGS WHOLE-HEARTEDLY. ♡
ELECTRONICS
IN
YOU'RE NOT GONNA GET MAD?
ABOUT WHAT?
YOU COULD BLAME ME FOR MESSING THINGS UP.
Y'KNOW?
NOPE.
IT WAS MY OWN LACK OF SKILL THAT CAUSED THE PROBLEM.
You think?
WHEN I FOCUS ON ACTING...

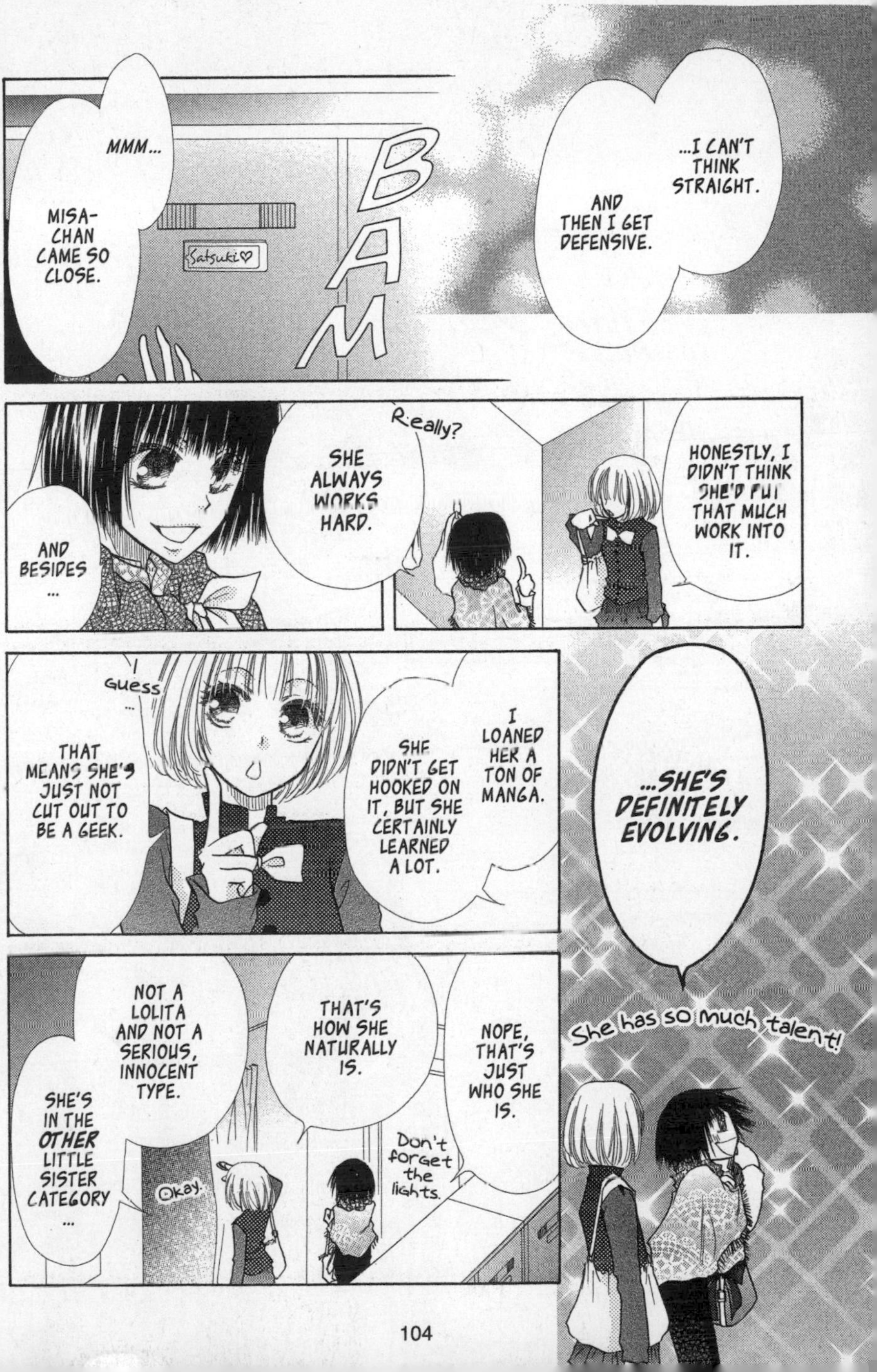
...I CAN'T THINK STRAIGHT.
AND THEN I GET DEFENSIVE.
MMM...
MISA-CHAN CAME SO CLOSE.
Satsuki♡
BAM
HONESTLY, I DIDN'T THINK SHE'D PUT THAT MUCH WORK INTO IT.
Really?
SHE ALWAYS WORKS HARD.
AND BESIDES ...
...SHE'S DEFINITELY EVOLVING.
She has so much talent!
I LOANED HER A TON OF MANGA.
SHE DIDN'T GET HOOKED ON IT, BUT SHE CERTAINLY LEARNED A LOT.
I Guess ...
THAT MEANS SHE'S JUST NOT CUT OUT TO BE A GEEK.
NOPE, THAT'S JUST WHO SHE IS.
THAT'S HOW SHE NATURALLY IS.
NOT A LOLITA AND NOT A SERIOUS, INNOCENT TYPE.
SHE'S IN THE OTHER LITTLE SISTER CATEGORY ...
Don't forget the lights.
Okay.

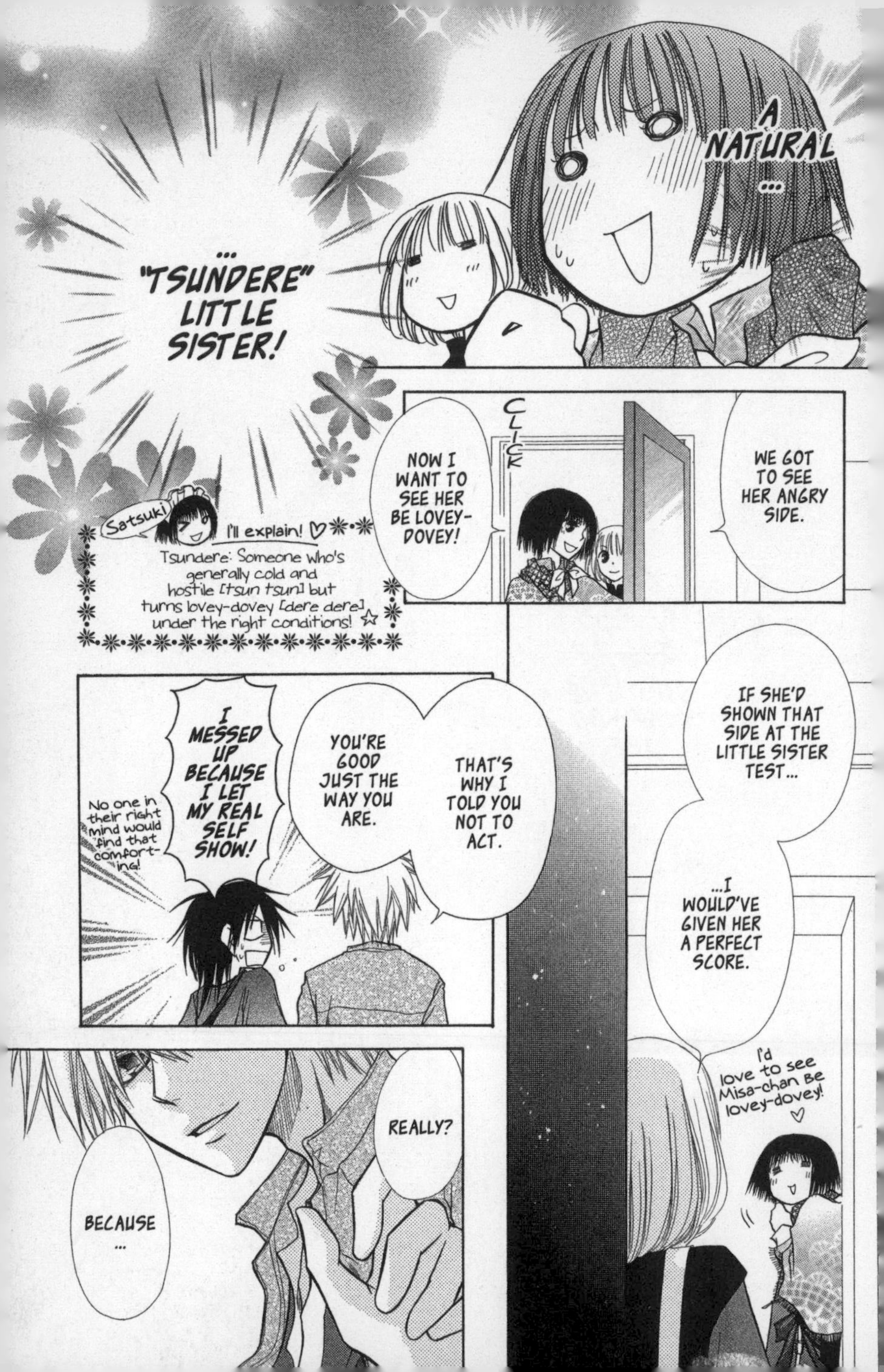
A NATURAL ...
... "TSUNDERE" LITTLE SISTER!
WE GOT TO SEE HER ANGRY SIDE.
CLICK
NOW I WANT TO SEE HER BE LOVEY-DOVEY!
Satsuki
I'll explain! ♡
Tsundere: Someone who's generally cold and hostile [tsun tsun] but turns lovey-dovey [dere dere] under the right conditions! ☆
IF SHE'D SHOWN THAT SIDE AT THE LITTLE SISTER TEST...
...I WOULD'VE GIVEN HER A PERFECT SCORE.
I'd love to see Misa-chan be lovey-dovey! ♡
THAT'S WHY I TOLD YOU NOT TO ACT.
YOU'RE GOOD JUST THE WAY YOU ARE.
I MESSED UP BECAUSE I LET MY REAL SELF SHOW!
No one in their right mind would find that comforting!
REALLY?
BECAUSE ...

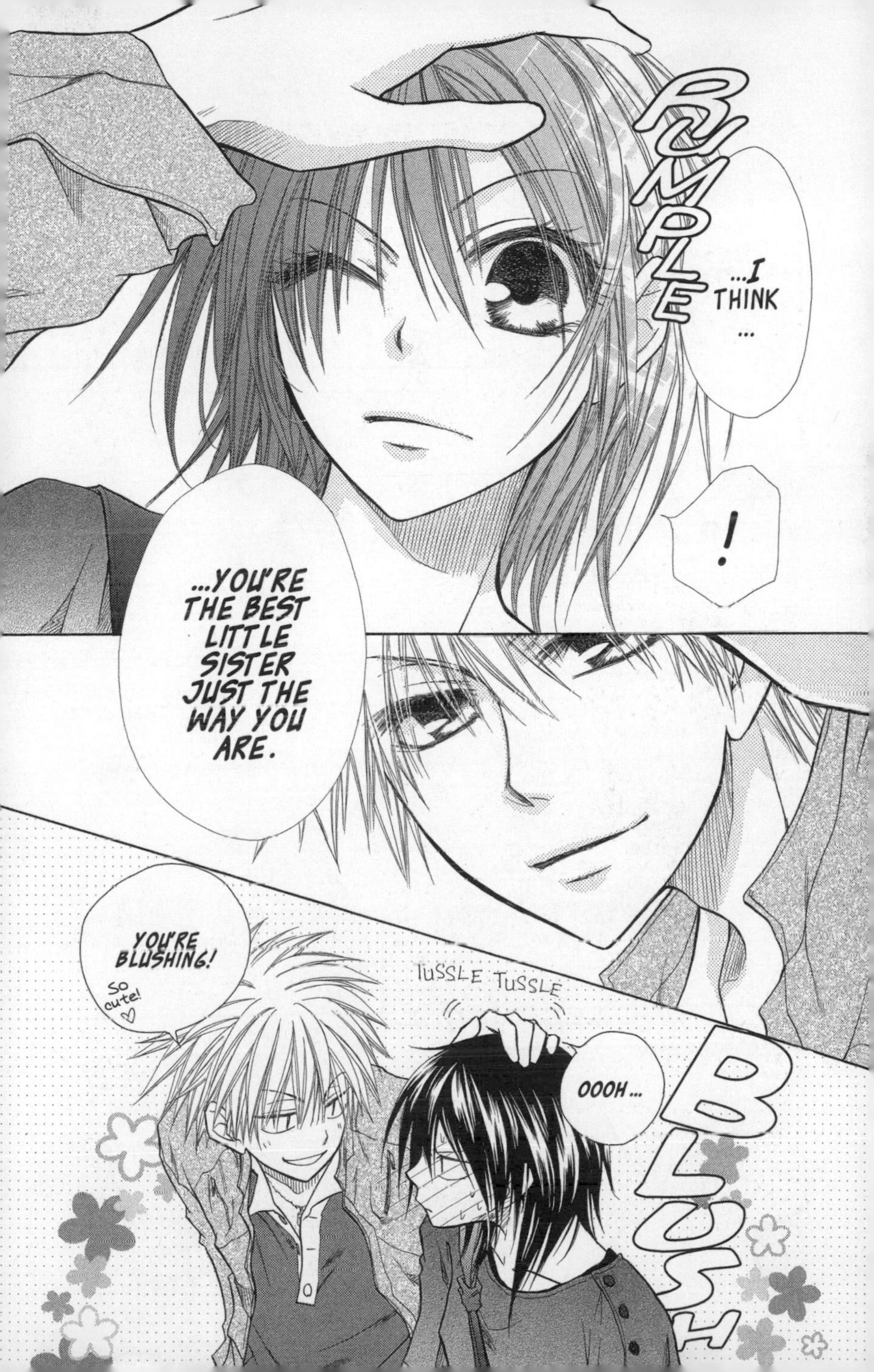
RUMPLE
...I THINK ...
!
...YOU'RE THE BEST LITTLE SISTER JUST THE WAY YOU ARE.
BLUSH
OOOH...
TUSSLE TUSSLE
YOU'RE BLUSHING!
So cute! ♥

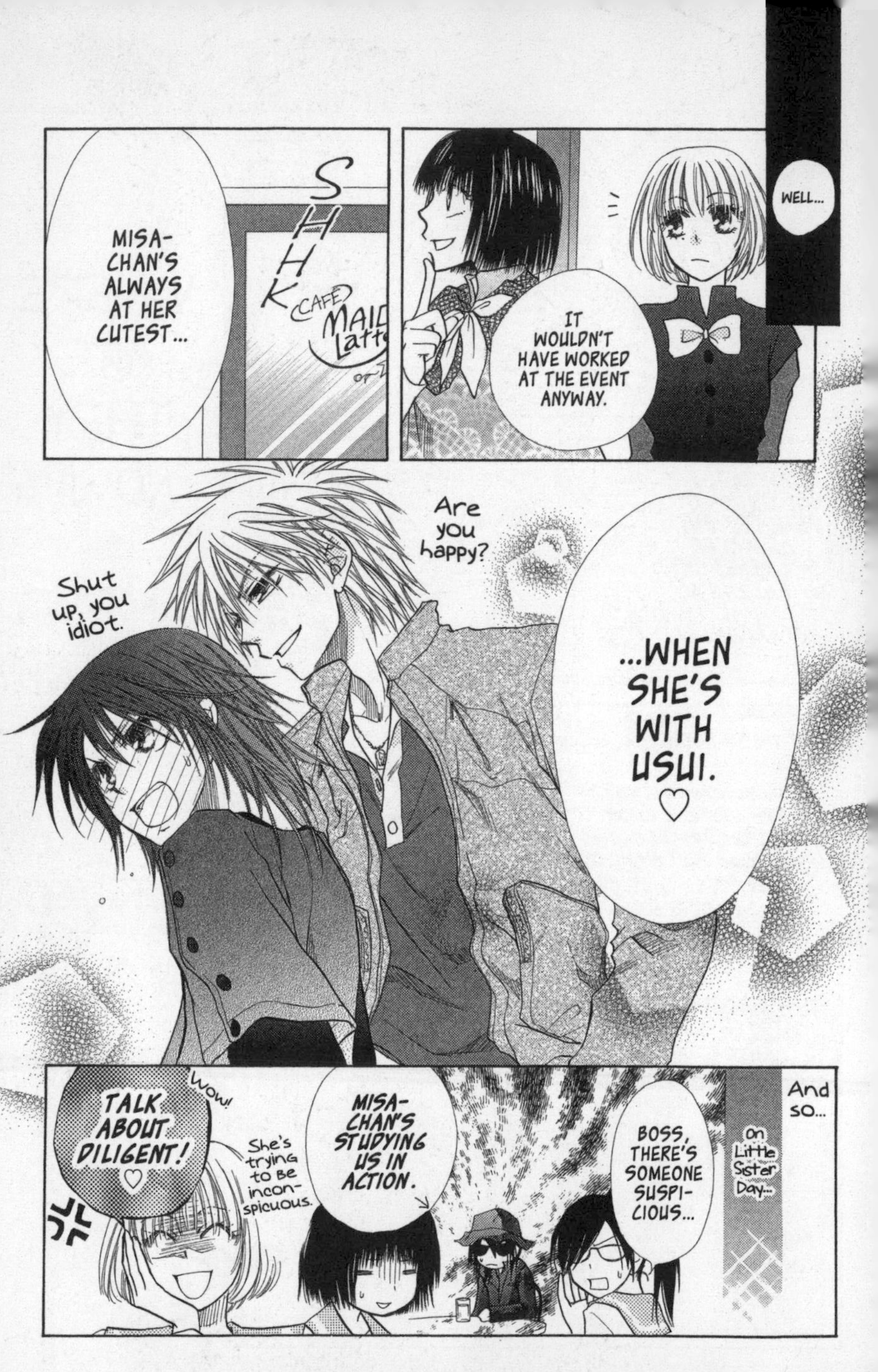
WELL...
IT WOULDN'T HAVE WORKED AT THE EVENT ANYWAY.
MISA-CHAN'S ALWAYS AT HER CUTEST...
SHHK
CAFE MAID Latte
...WHEN SHE'S WITH USUI. ♡
Are you happy?
Shut up, you idiot.
And so...
On Little Sister Day...
BOSS, THERE'S SOMEONE SUSPICIOUS...
MISA-CHAN'S STUDYING US IN ACTION.
She's trying to be inconspicuous.
WOW!
TALK ABOUT DILIGENT! ♡

WHERE ARE THEY NOW?

~ KOGANEI, THE FOUR-EYED SCOUNDREL OF MIYABI-GAOKA ~

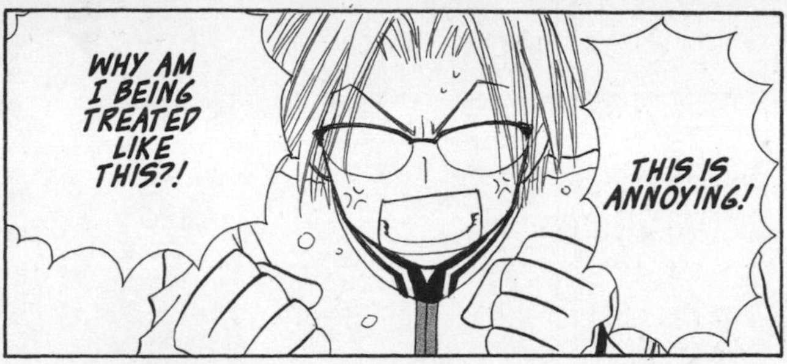
THIS IS ANNOYING!
WHY AM I BEING TREATED LIKE THIS?!

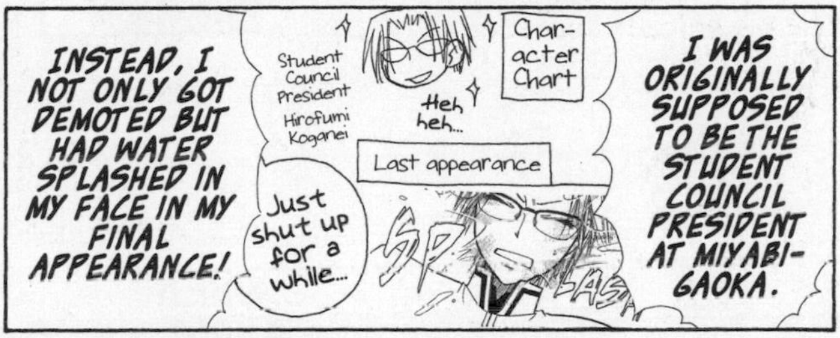
I WAS ORIGINALLY SUPPOSED TO BE THE STUDENT COUNCIL PRESIDENT AT MIYABI-GAOKA.
Character Chart
Student Council President
Hirofumi Koganei
Heh heh...
Last appearance
SPLASH
Just shut up for a while...
INSTEAD, I NOT ONLY GOT DEMOTED BUT HAD WATER SPLASHED IN MY FACE IN MY FINAL APPEARANCE!

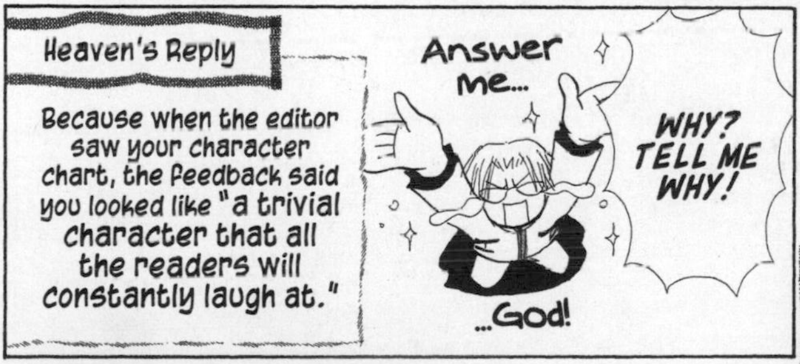
WHY? TELL ME WHY!
Answer me...
...God!
Heaven's Reply
Because when the editor saw your character chart, the feedback said you looked like "a trivial character that all the readers will constantly laugh at."

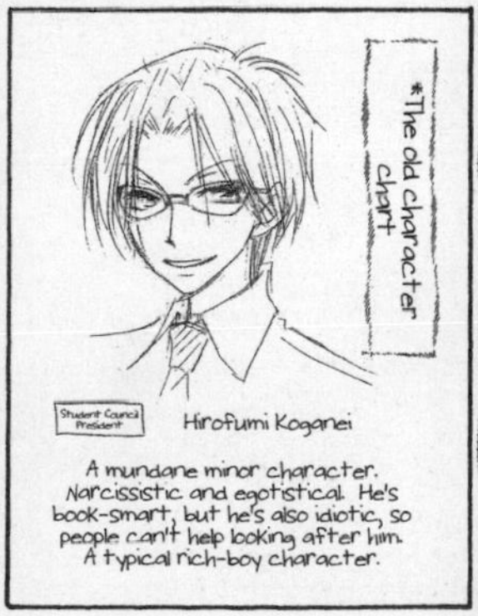
*The old character chart
Student Council President
Hirofumi Koganei
A mundane minor character. Narcissistic and egotistical. He's book-smart, but he's also idiotic, so people can't help looking after him. A typical rich-boy character.

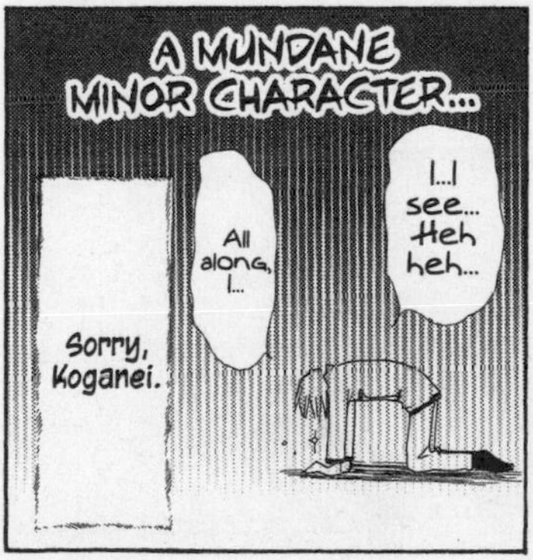
A MUNDANE MINOR CHARACTER...
I...I see... Heh heh...
All along, I...
Sorry, Koganei.

The Four-Eyes of Miyabigaoka

Appeared in volume 2, chapter 5. A student at Miyabigaoka, the prestigious private school. He had a conflict with students from Seika and demanded an apology from Misaki, but after Usui beat him in chess, he offered a snarky comment and left.

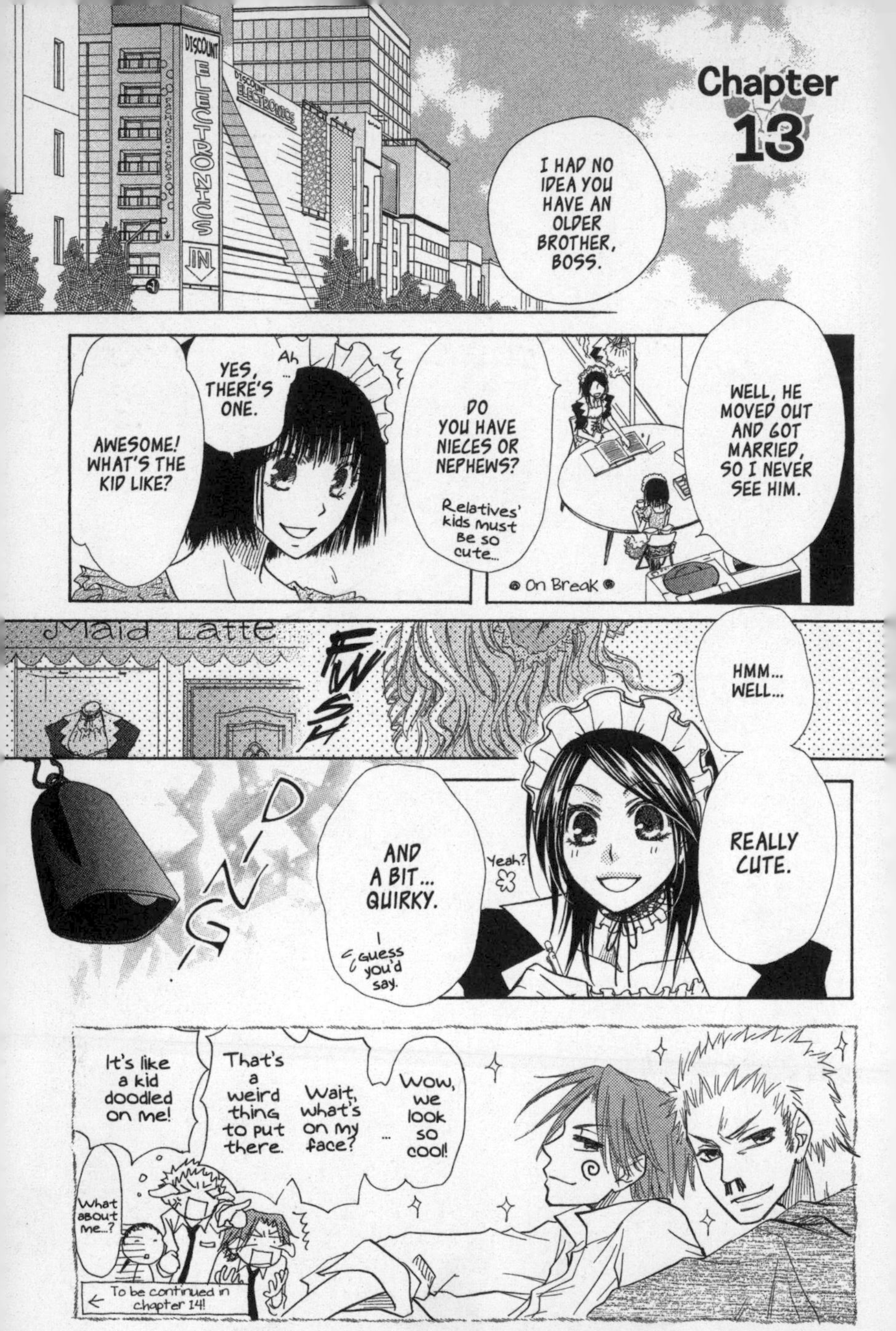
Chapter 13
I HAD NO IDEA YOU HAVE AN OLDER BROTHER, BOSS.
DISCOUNT ELECTRONICS
DISCOUNT ELECTRONICS
IN
WELL, HE MOVED OUT AND GOT MARRIED, SO I NEVER SEE HIM.
On Break
DO YOU HAVE NIECES OR NEPHEWS?
Relatives' kids must be so cute...
Ah...
YES, THERE'S ONE.
AWESOME! WHAT'S THE KID LIKE?
HMM... WELL...
Maid Latte
FWSH
REALLY CUTE.
Yeah?
AND A BIT... QUIRKY.
I guess you'd say.
DING
Wow, we look so cool!
...
Wait, what's on my face?
That's a weird thing to put there.
It's like a kid doodled on me!
What about me...?
To be continued in chapter 14!

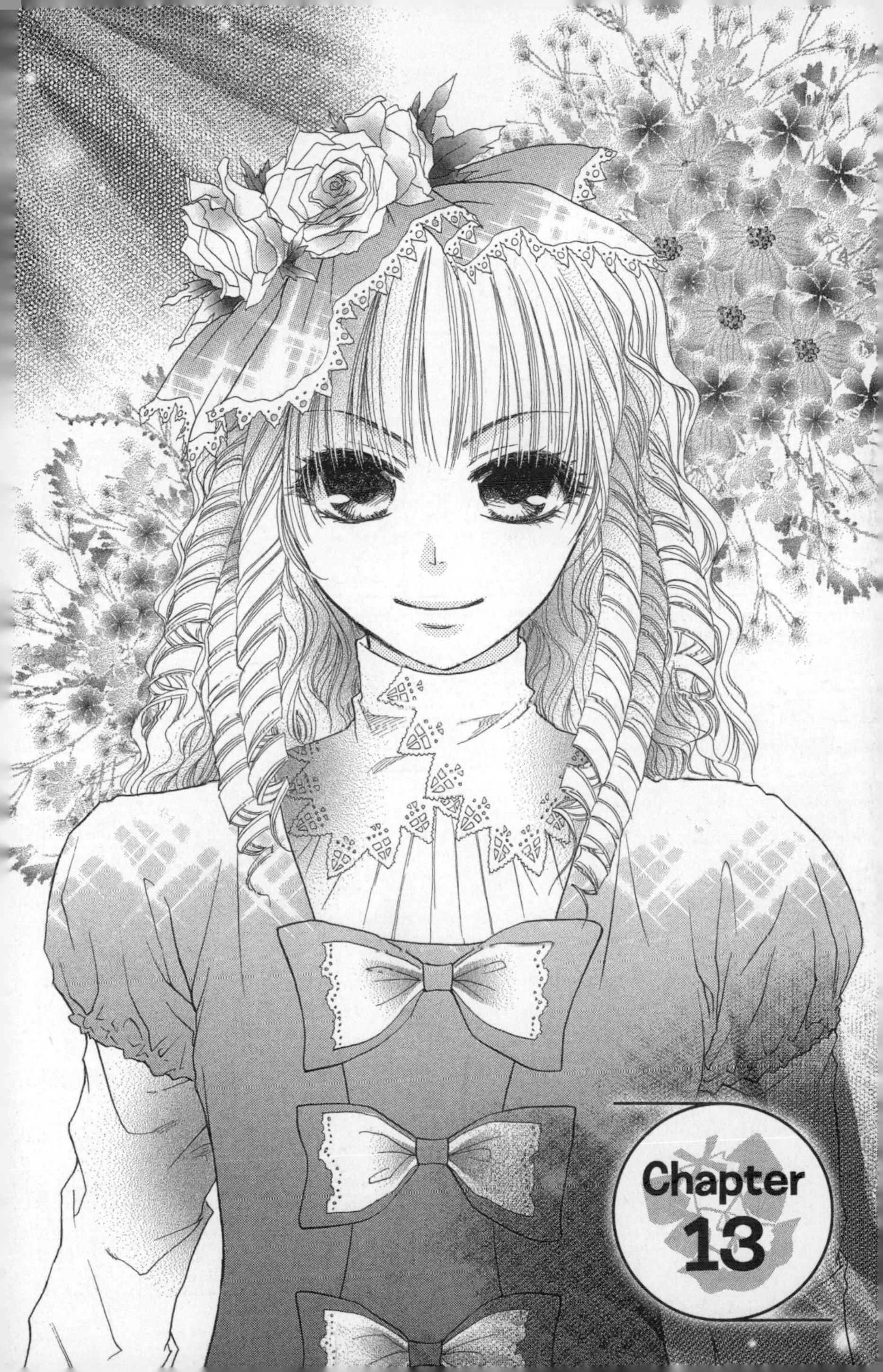
Chapter
13

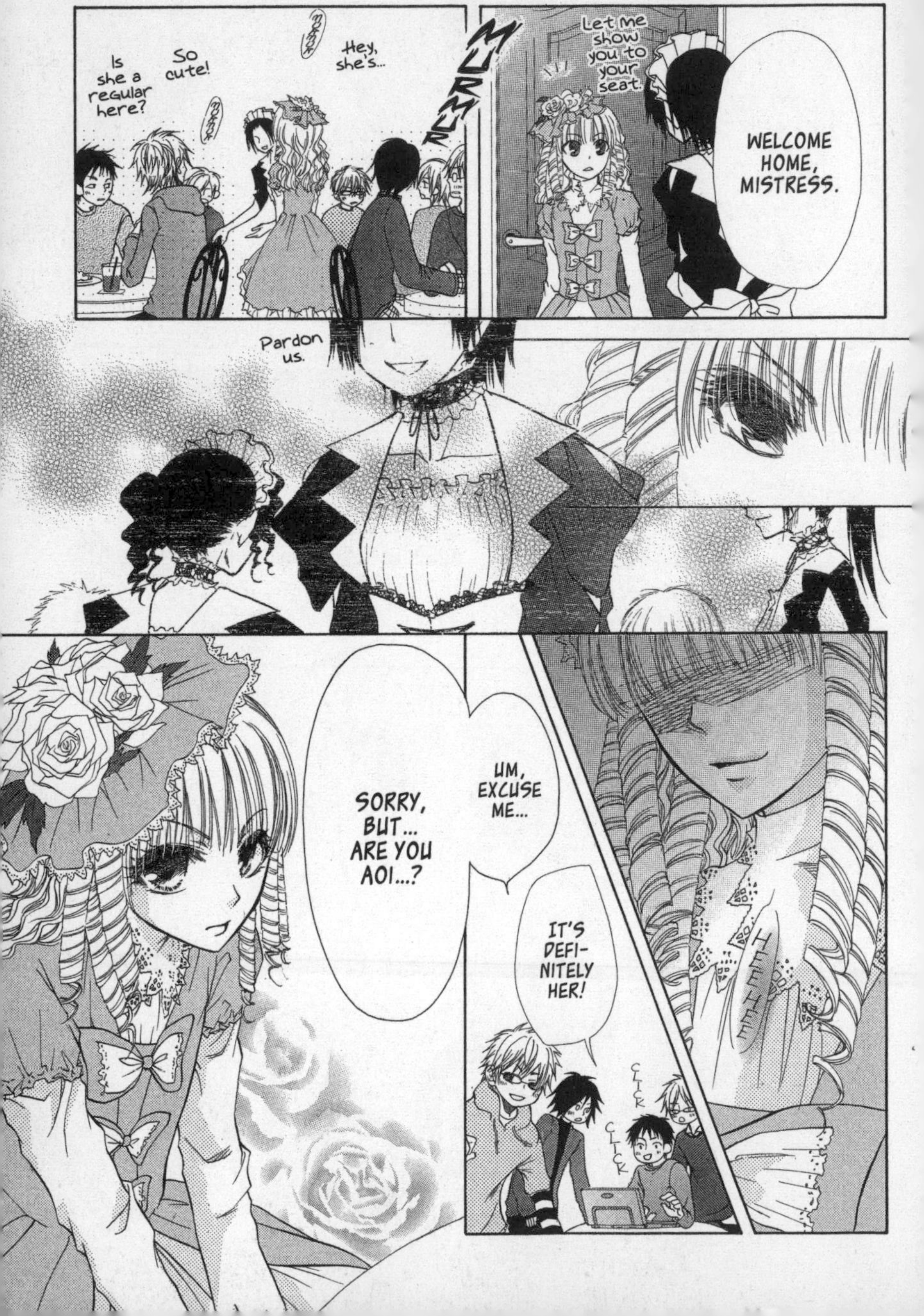
WELCOME HOME, MISTRESS.
Let me show you to your seat.
MURMUR
Hey, she's...
So cute!
Is she a regular here?
Pardon us.
HEEHEE
IT'S DEFINITELY HER!
CLICK
CLICK
UM, EXCUSE ME...
SORRY, BUT... ARE YOU AOI...?

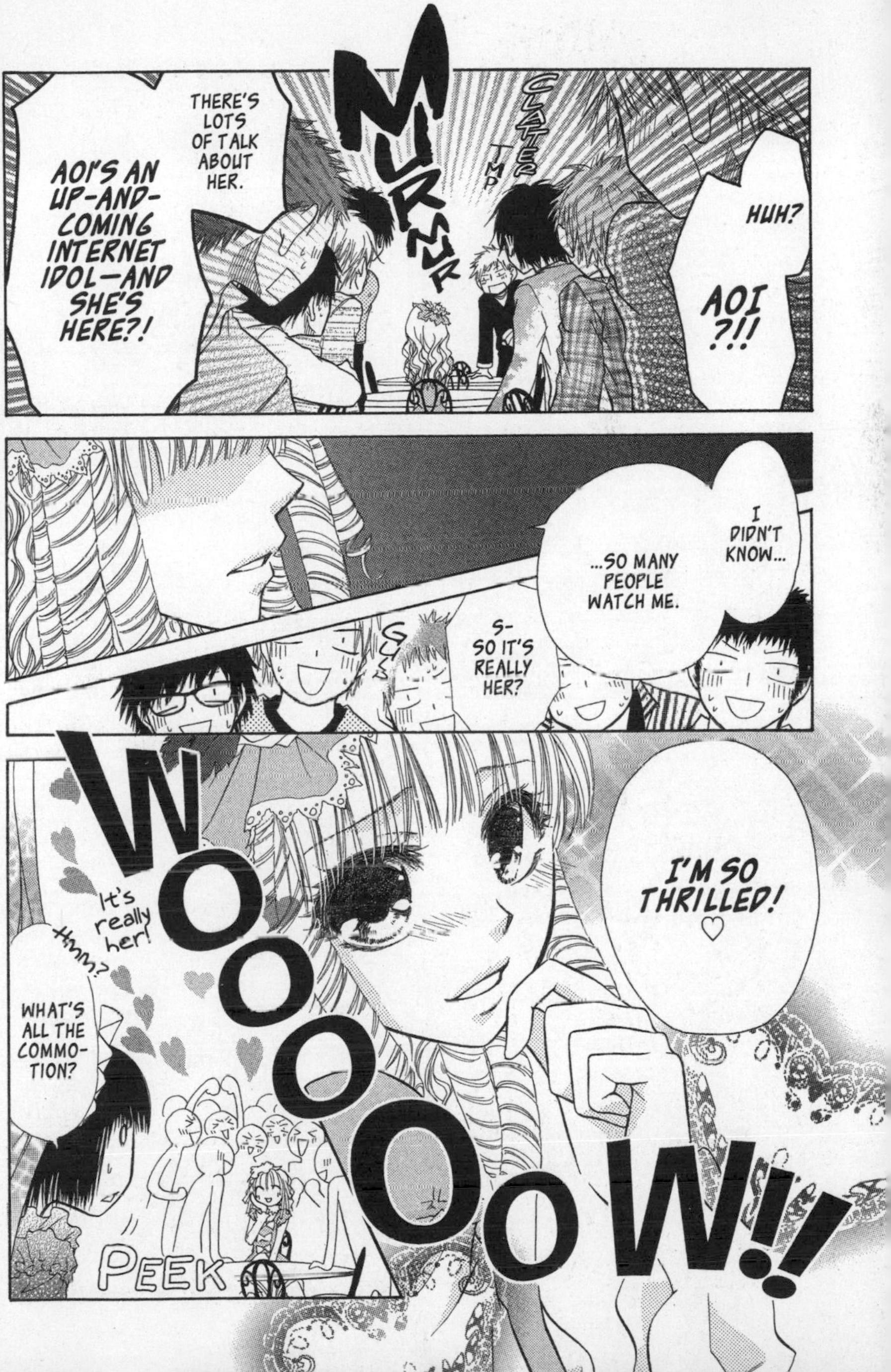
MURMUR
CLATTER
TMP
HUH?
AOI ?!!
THERE'S LOTS OF TALK ABOUT HER.
AOI'S AN UP-AND-COMING INTERNET IDOL—AND SHE'S HERE?!
I DIDN'T KNOW...
...SO MANY PEOPLE WATCH ME.
S-SO IT'S REALLY HER?
I'M SO THRILLED! ♡
WOOOOOOW!!
It's really her!
Hmm?
WHAT'S ALL THE COMMOTION?
PEEK

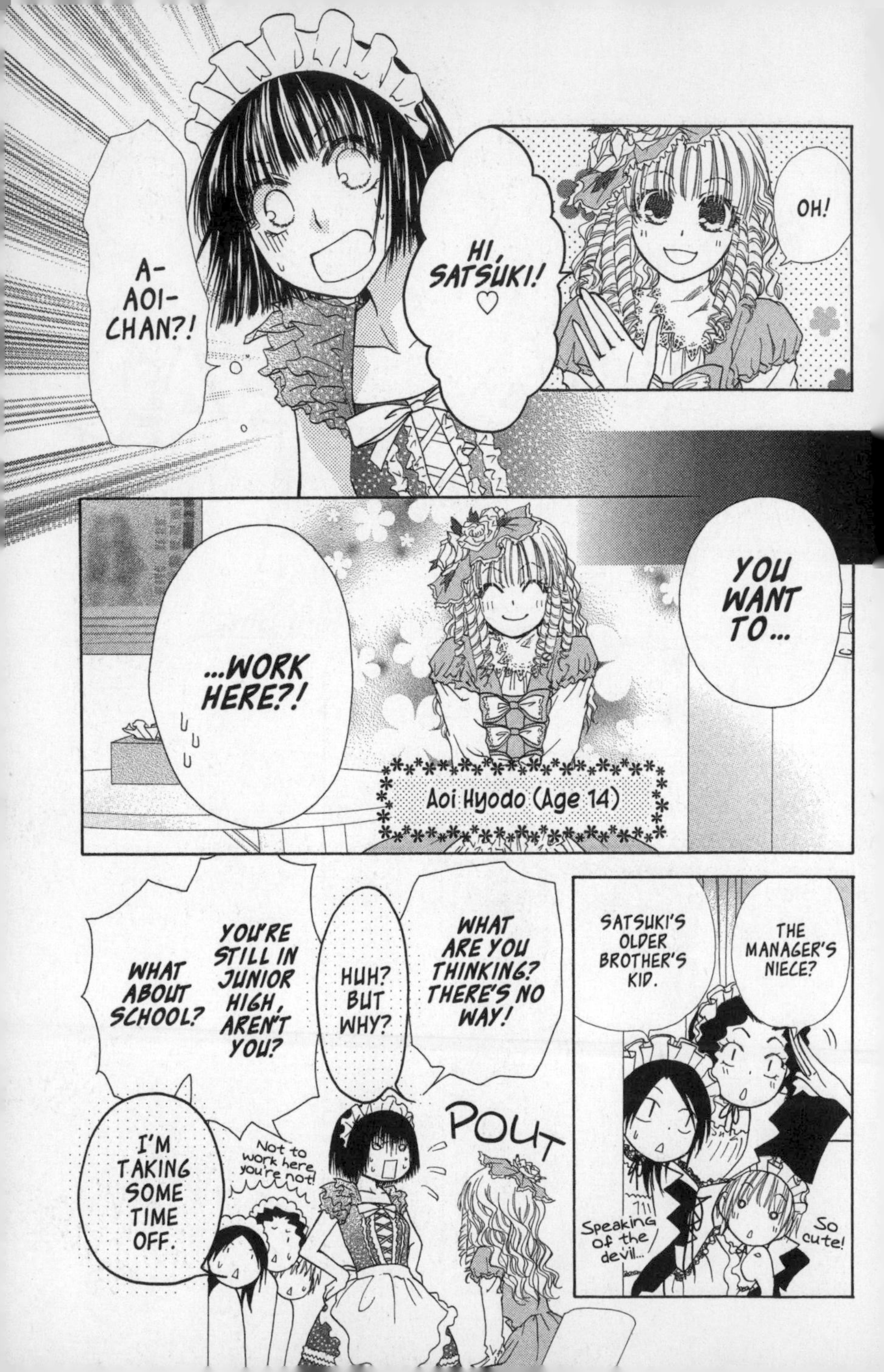

OH!
HI, SATSUKI! ♡
A-AOI-CHAN?!
YOU WANT TO...
...WORK HERE?!
Aoi Hyodo (Age 14)
THE MANAGER'S NIECE?
SATSUKI'S OLDER BROTHER'S KID.
So cute!
Speaking of the devil...
WHAT ARE YOU THINKING? THERE'S NO WAY!
HUH? BUT WHY?
YOU'RE STILL IN JUNIOR HIGH, AREN'T YOU?
WHAT ABOUT SCHOOL?
POUT
I'M TAKING SOME TIME OFF.
Not to work here you're not!

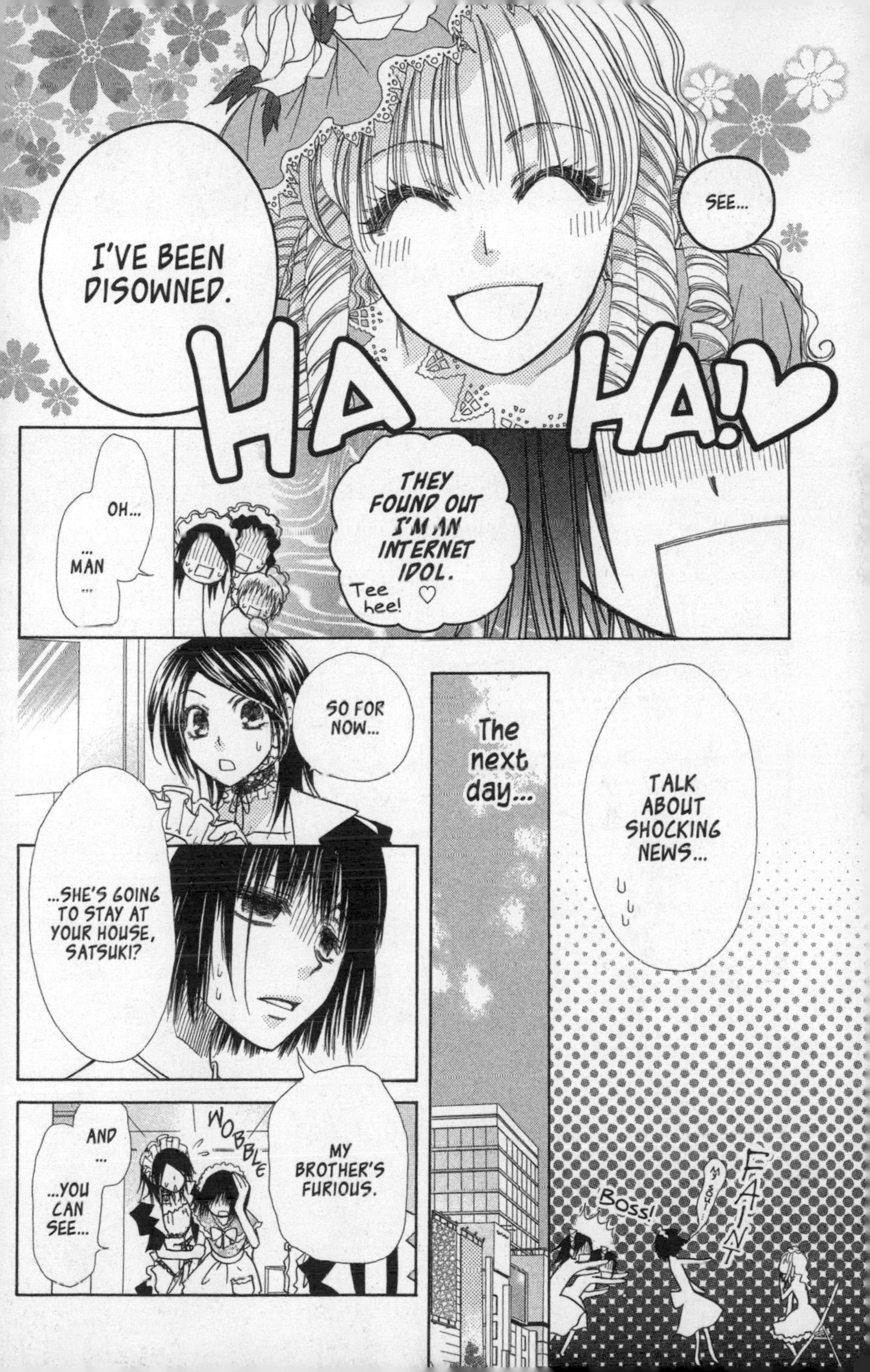
SEE...
I'VE BEEN DISOWNED.
HA HA!♥
THEY FOUND OUT I'M AN INTERNET IDOL.
Tee hee! ♡
OH... ... MAN ...
The next day...
TALK ABOUT SHOCKING NEWS...
FAINT
MY SON!...
BOSS!
SO FOR NOW...
...SHE'S GOING TO STAY AT YOUR HOUSE, SATSUKI?
MY BROTHER'S FURIOUS.
WOBBLE
AND ... ...YOU CAN SEE...

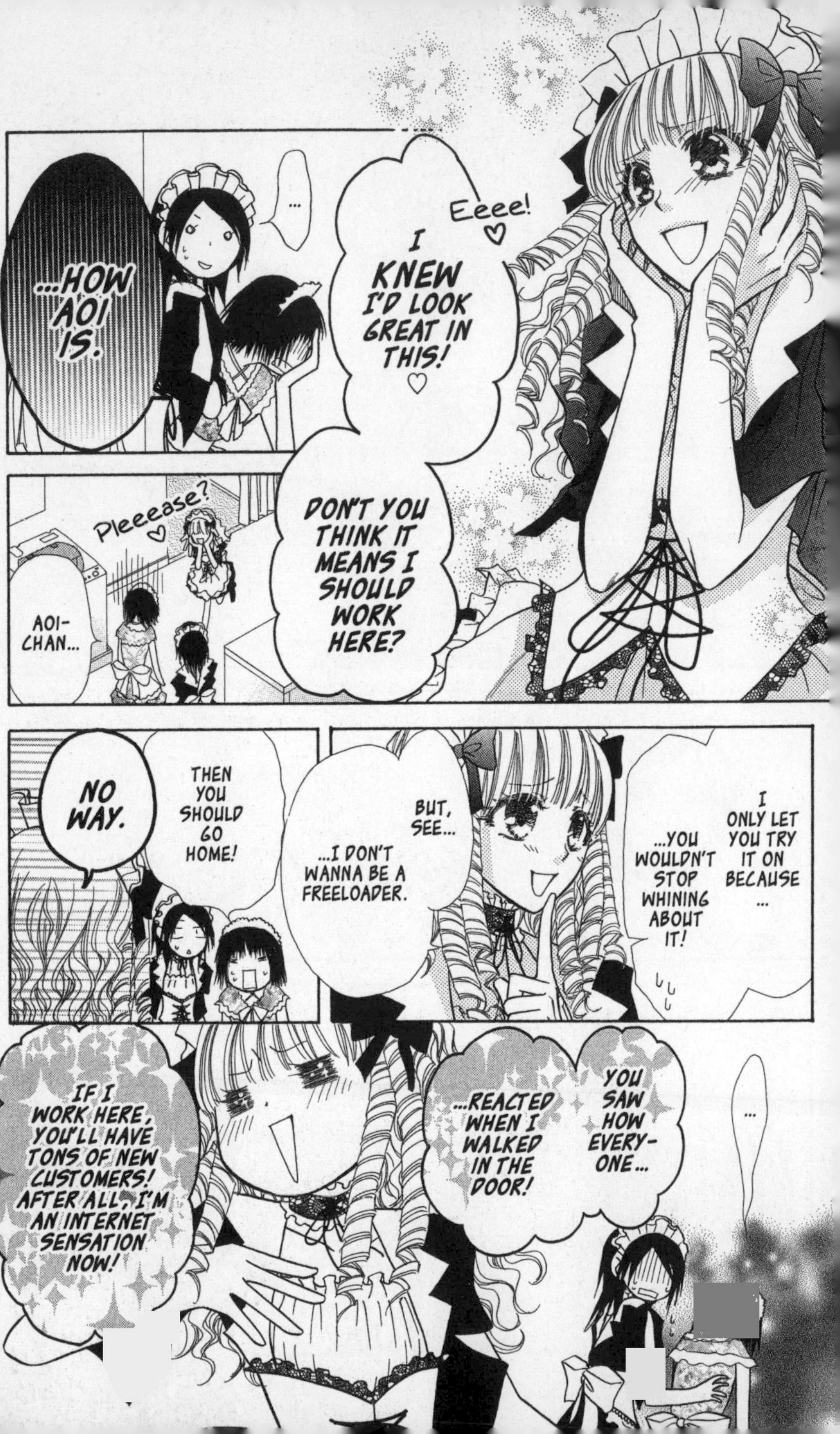
Eeee! ♡
I KNEW I'D LOOK GREAT IN THIS! ♡
DON'T YOU THINK IT MEANS I SHOULD WORK HERE?
...
...HOW AOI IS.
Pleeease? ♡
AOI-CHAN...
I ONLY LET YOU TRY IT ON BECAUSE...
...YOU WOULDN'T STOP WHINING ABOUT IT!
BUT, SEE...
...I DON'T WANNA BE A FREELOADER.
THEN YOU SHOULD GO HOME!
NO WAY.
...
YOU SAW HOW EVERY-ONE...
...REACTED WHEN I WALKED IN THE DOOR!
IF I WORK HERE, YOU'LL HAVE TONS OF NEW CUSTOMERS! AFTER ALL, I'M AN INTERNET SENSATION NOW!

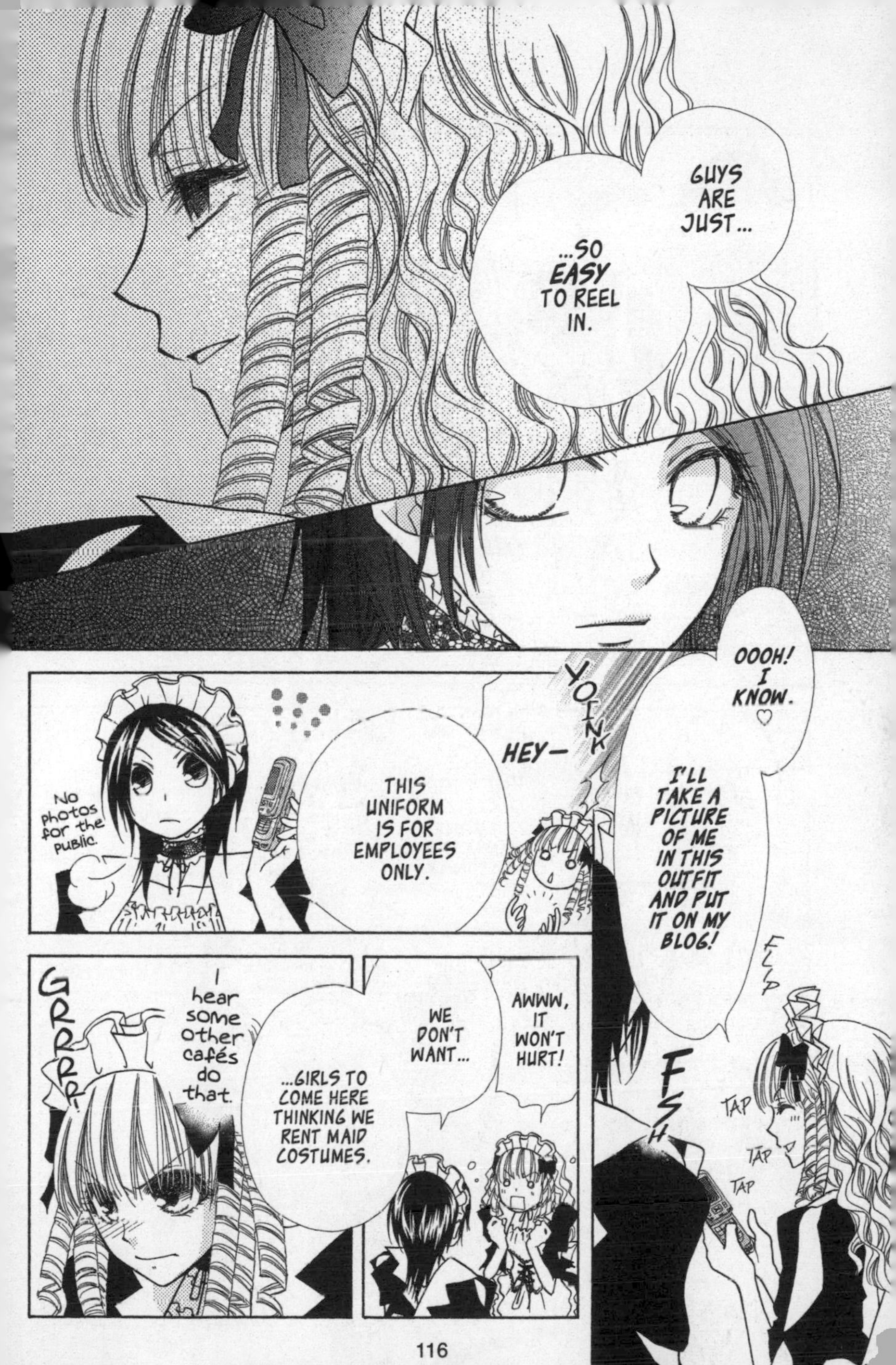
GUYS ARE JUST...
...SO EASY TO REEL IN.
OOOH! I KNOW. ♡
I'LL TAKE A PICTURE OF ME IN THIS OUTFIT AND PUT IT ON MY BLOG!
FLIP
FSH
TAP
TAP
TAP
YOINK
HEY—
THIS UNIFORM IS FOR EMPLOYEES ONLY.
No photos for the public.
AWWW, IT WON'T HURT!
WE DON'T WANT...
...GIRLS TO COME HERE THINKING WE RENT MAID COSTUMES.
I hear some other cafés do that.
GRRRR!

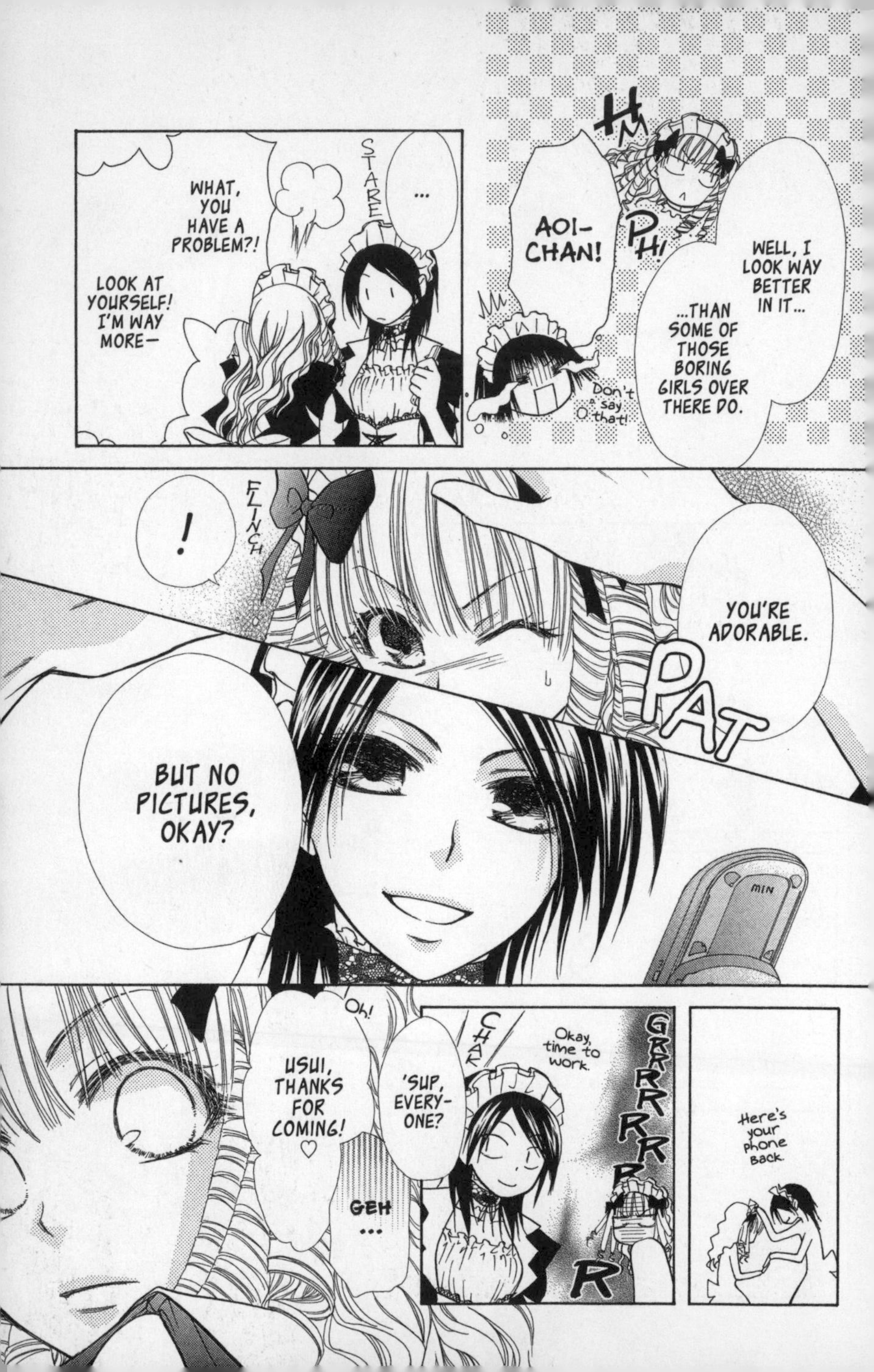
HMPH!
WELL, I LOOK WAY BETTER IN IT...
...THAN SOME OF THOSE BORING GIRLS OVER THERE DO.
AOI-CHAN!
Don't say that!
...
STARE
WHAT, YOU HAVE A PROBLEM?!
LOOK AT YOURSELF! I'M WAY MORE—
YOU'RE ADORABLE.
PAT
!
FLINCH
BUT NO PICTURES, OKAY?
MIN
Here's your phone back.
Okay, time to work.
GRRRRRRR
CHAR
'SUP, EVERYONE?
Oh!
USUI, THANKS FOR COMING! ♡
GEH ...

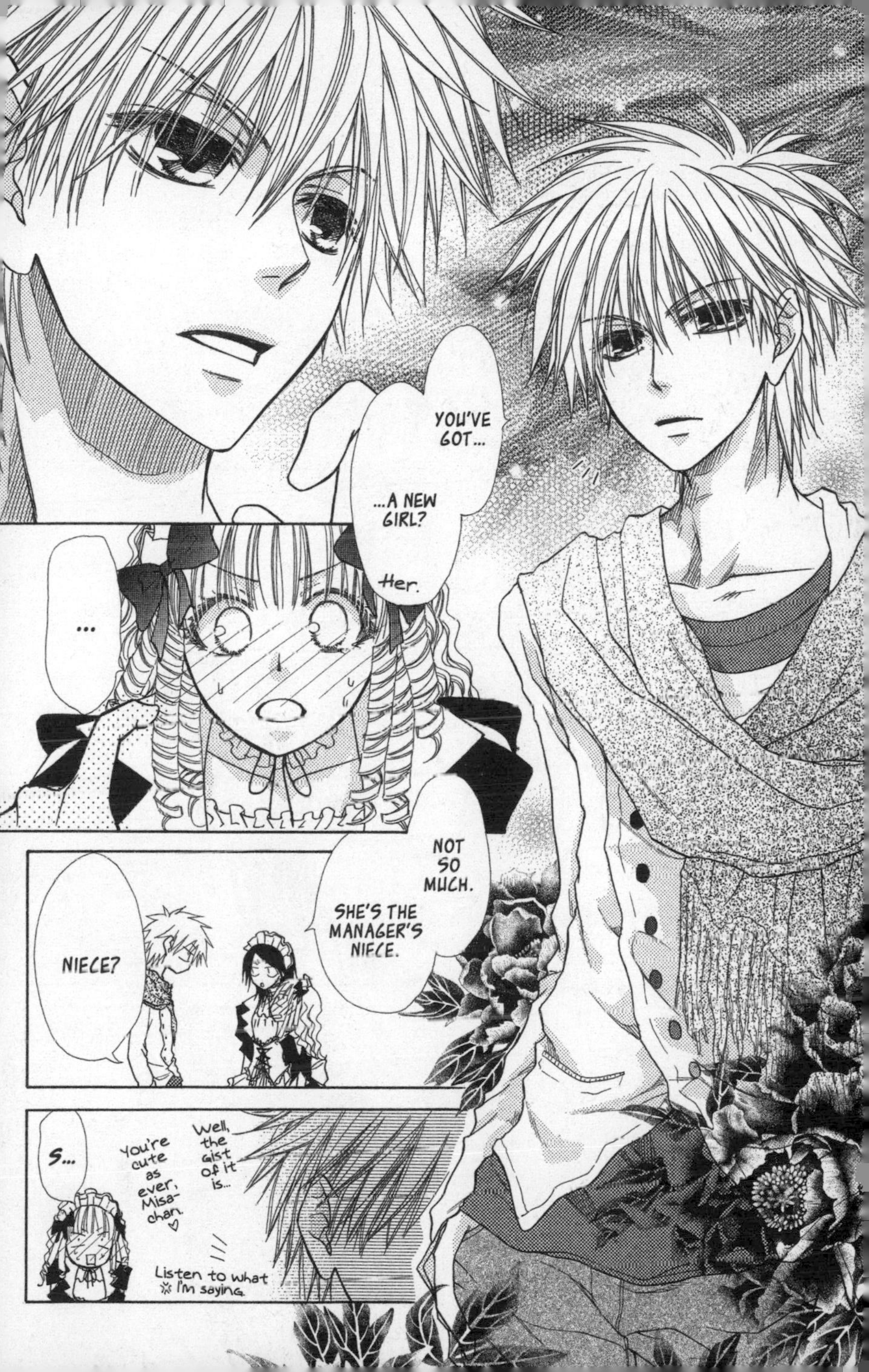
YOU'VE GOT...
...A NEW GIRL?
Her.
...
NOT SO MUCH.
SHE'S THE MANAGER'S NIECE.
NIECE?
Well, the gist of it is...
You're cute as ever, Misa-chan. ♥
S...
Listen to what I'm saying.

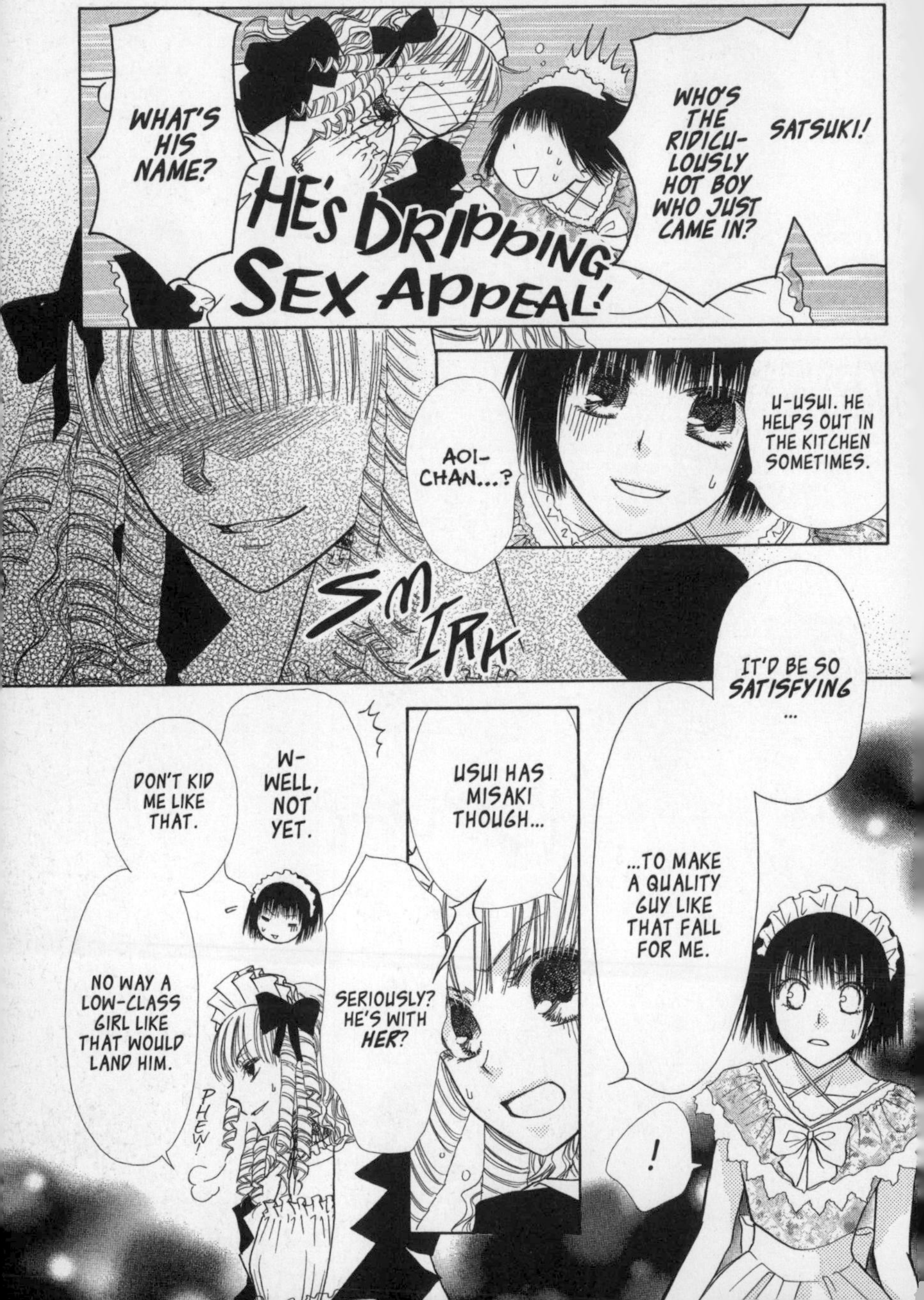
SATSUKI!
WHO'S THE RIDICU-LOUSLY HOT BOY WHO JUST CAME IN?
WHAT'S HIS NAME?
HE'S DRIPPING SEX APPEAL!
U-USUI. HE HELPS OUT IN THE KITCHEN SOMETIMES.
AOI-CHAN...?
SMIRK
IT'D BE SO SATISFYING...
...TO MAKE A QUALITY GUY LIKE THAT FALL FOR ME.
!
USUI HAS MISAKI THOUGH...
SERIOUSLY? HE'S WITH HER?
W-WELL, NOT YET.
DON'T KID ME LIKE THAT.
NO WAY A LOW-CLASS GIRL LIKE THAT WOULD LAND HIM.
PHEW!

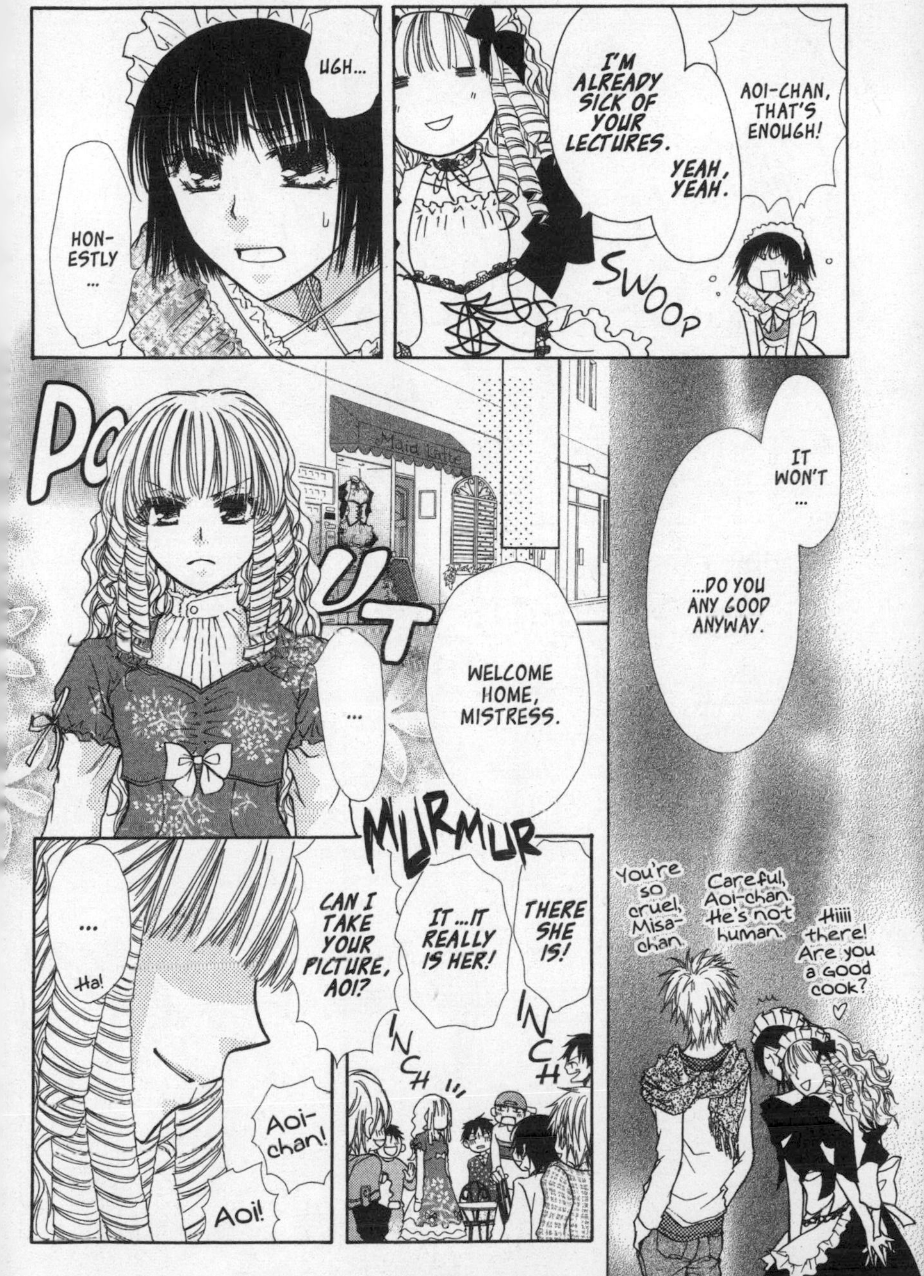
AOI-CHAN, THAT'S ENOUGH!
I'M ALREADY SICK OF YOUR LECTURES.
YEAH, YEAH.
SWOOP
UGH...
HON-ESTLY ...
IT WON'T ...
...DO YOU ANY GOOD ANYWAY.
Hiiii there! Are you a good cook?
Careful, Aoi-chan. He's not human.
You're so cruel, Misa-chan.
POUT
WELCOME HOME, MISTRESS.
...
MURMUR
THERE SHE IS!
IT ...IT REALLY IS HER!
CAN I TAKE YOUR PICTURE, AOI?
INCH
INCH
Aoi-chan!
Aoi!
...
Ha!

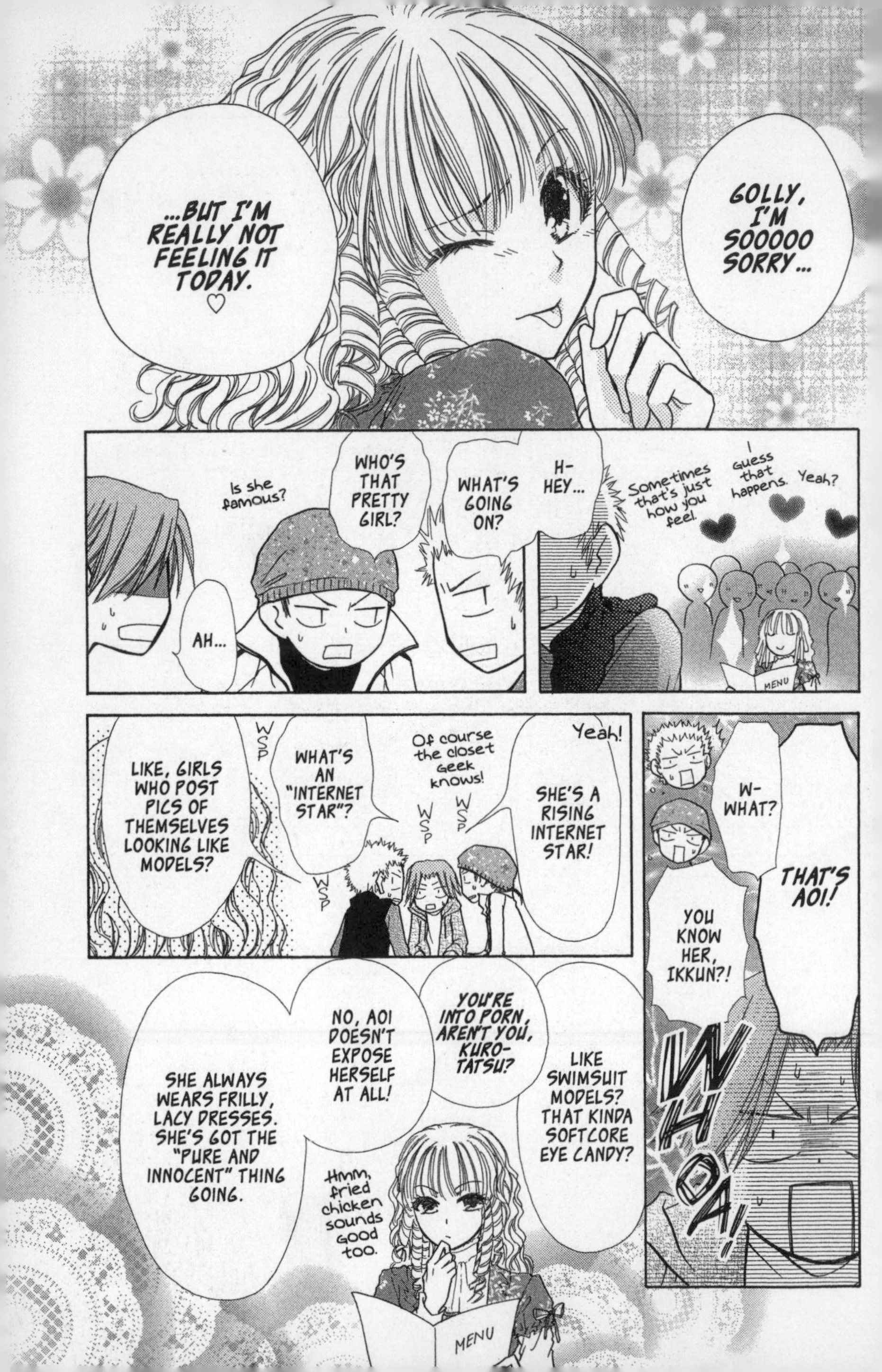
GOLLY, I'M SOOOOO SORRY...
...BUT I'M REALLY NOT FEELING IT TODAY. ♡
Yeah?
I guess that happens.
Sometimes that's just how you feel.
MENU
H-HEY...
WHAT'S GOING ON?
WHO'S THAT PRETTY GIRL?
Is she famous?
AH...
W-WHAT?
THAT'S AOI!
YOU KNOW HER, IKKUN?!
WHOA!
Yeah!
SHE'S A RISING INTERNET STAR!
Of course the closet geek knows!
WSP
WSP
WSP
WHAT'S AN "INTERNET STAR"?
WSP
WSP
LIKE, GIRLS WHO POST PICS OF THEMSELVES LOOKING LIKE MODELS?
LIKE SWIMSUIT MODELS? THAT KINDA SOFTCORE EYE CANDY?
YOU'RE INTO PORN, AREN'T YOU, KURO-TATSU?
NO, AOI DOESN'T EXPOSE HERSELF AT ALL!
SHE ALWAYS WEARS FRILLY, LACY DRESSES. SHE'S GOT THE "PURE AND INNOCENT" THING GOING.
Hmm, fried chicken sounds good too.
MENU

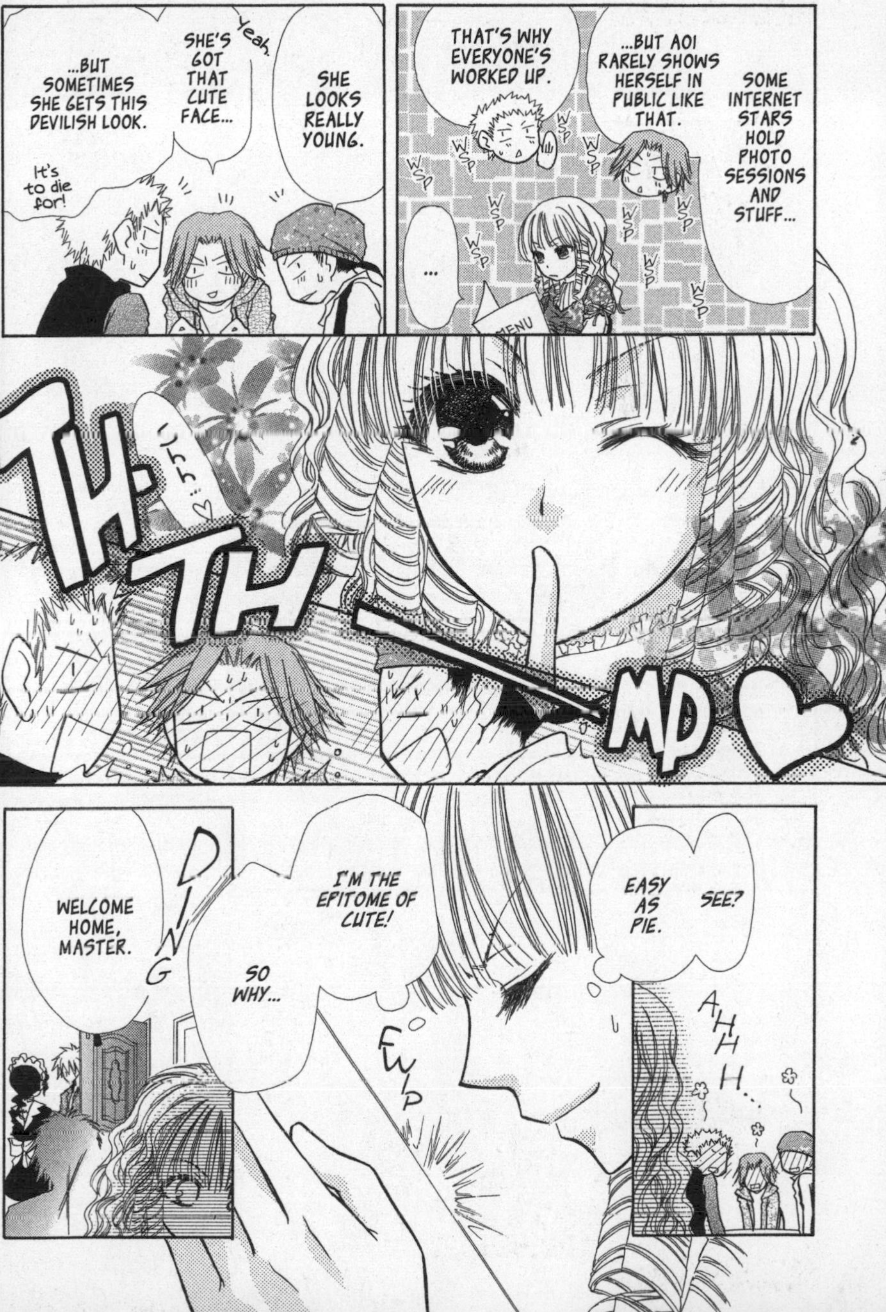
SOME INTERNET STARS HOLD PHOTO SESSIONS AND STUFF...
...BUT AOI RARELY SHOWS HERSELF IN PUBLIC LIKE THAT.
THAT'S WHY EVERYONE'S WORKED UP.
WSP WSP WSP WSP WSP WSP WSP WSP WSP
...
MENU
SHE LOOKS REALLY YOUNG.
Yeah.
SHE'S GOT THAT CUTE FACE...
...BUT SOMETIMES SHE GETS THIS DEVILISH LOOK.
It's to die for!
TH-
TH
MP ♥
SEE?
EASY AS PIE.
AHHH...
I'M THE EPITOME OF CUTE!
SO WHY...
FWIP
DING
WELCOME HOME, MASTER.

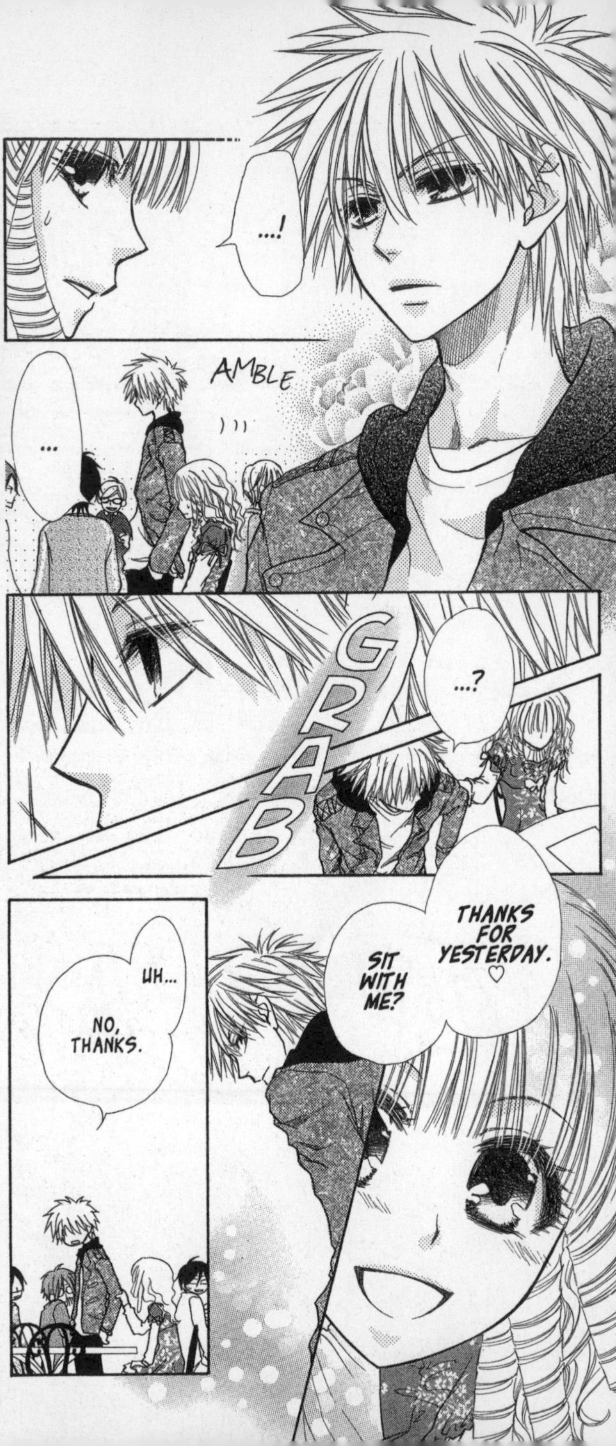
...!
AMBLE
...
GRAB
...?
THANKS FOR YESTERDAY. ♡
SIT WITH ME?
UH...
NO, THANKS.

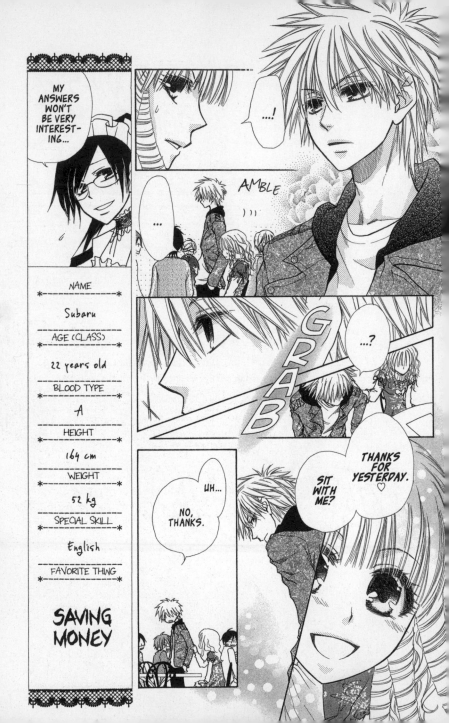

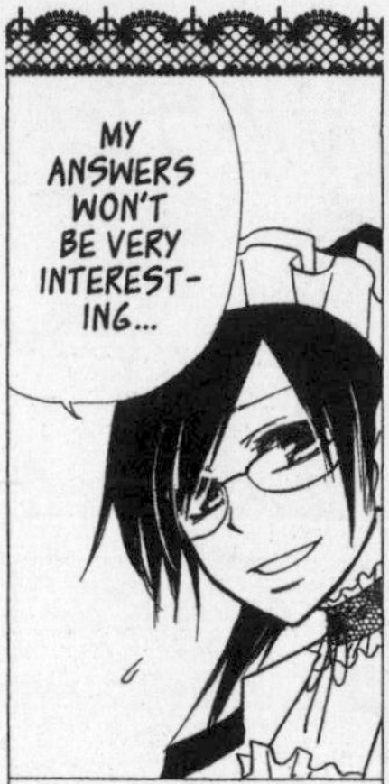
MY ANSWERS WON'T BE VERY INTEREST-ING...

NAME

Subaru

AGE (CLASS)

22 years old

BLOOD TYPE

A

HEIGHT

164 cm

WEIGHT

52 kg

SPECIAL SKILL

English

FAVORITE THING

SAVING MONEY

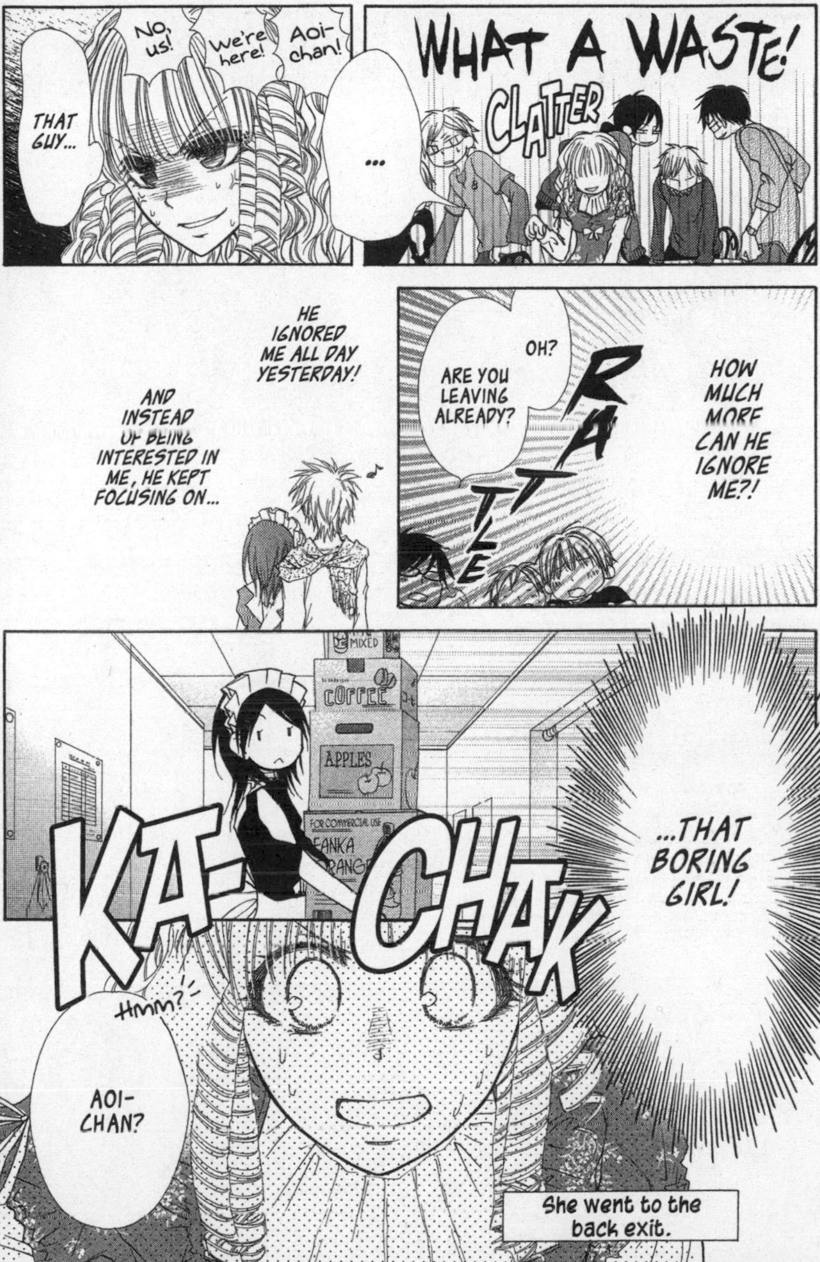
WHAT A WASTE!
CLATTER
Aoi-chan!
We're here!
No, us!
...
THAT GUY...
HOW MUCH MORE CAN HE IGNORE ME?!
OH?
ARE YOU LEAVING ALREADY?
RATTLE
HE IGNORED ME ALL DAY YESTERDAY!
AND INSTEAD OF BEING INTERESTED IN ME, HE KEPT FOCUSING ON...
...THAT BORING GIRL!
MIXED
COFFEE
APPLES
FOR COMMERCIAL USE
KA-CHAK
Hmm?
AOI-CHAN?
She went to the back exit.

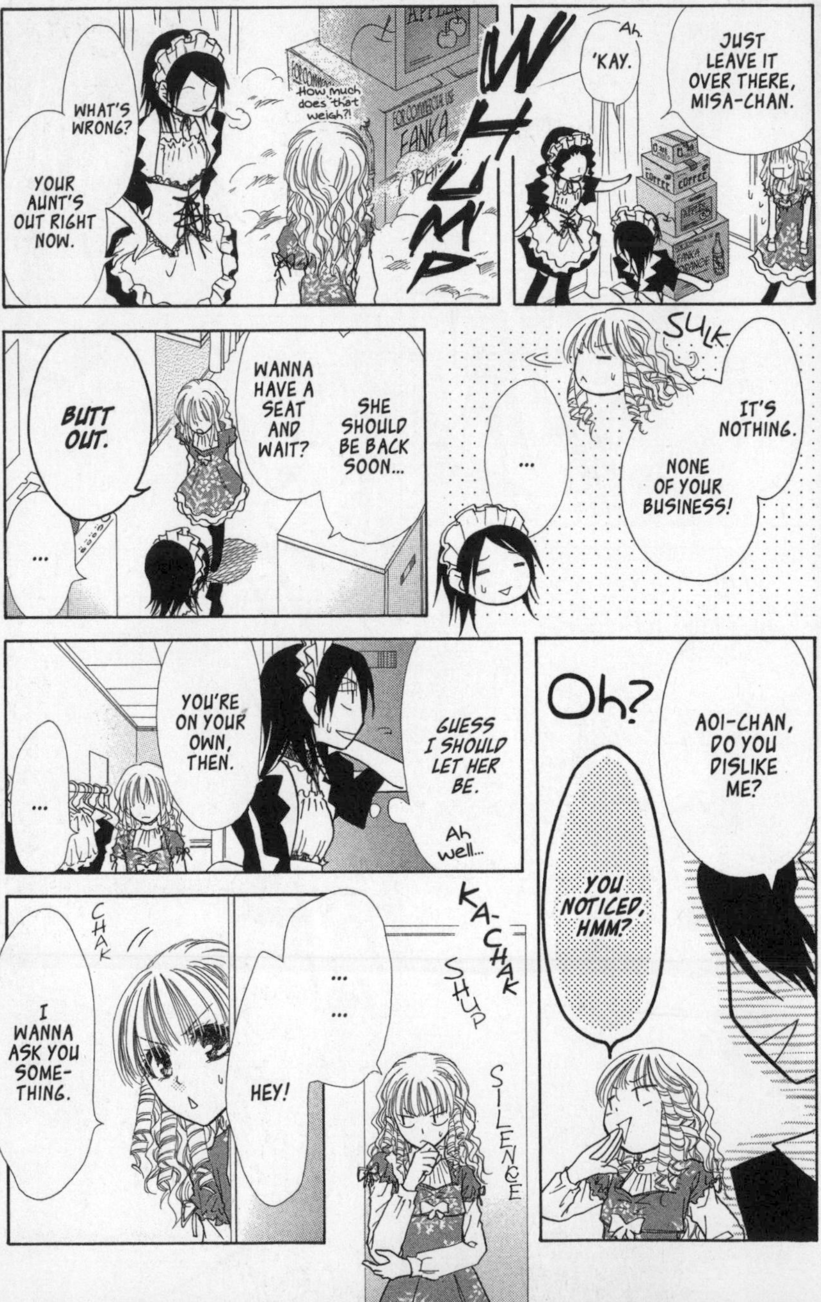
JUST LEAVE IT OVER THERE, MISA-CHAN.
Ah.
'KAY.
WHUMP
How much does that weigh?!
WHAT'S WRONG?
YOUR AUNT'S OUT RIGHT NOW.
SULK.
IT'S NOTHING.
NONE OF YOUR BUSINESS!
...
SHE SHOULD BE BACK SOON...
WANNA HAVE A SEAT AND WAIT?
BUTT OUT.
...
Oh?
AOI-CHAN, DO YOU DISLIKE ME?
YOU NOTICED, HMM?
GUESS I SHOULD LET HER BE.
Ah well...
YOU'RE ON YOUR OWN, THEN.
...
KA-CHAK
SHUP
...
...
SILENCE
HEY!
CHAK
I WANNA ASK YOU SOMETHING.

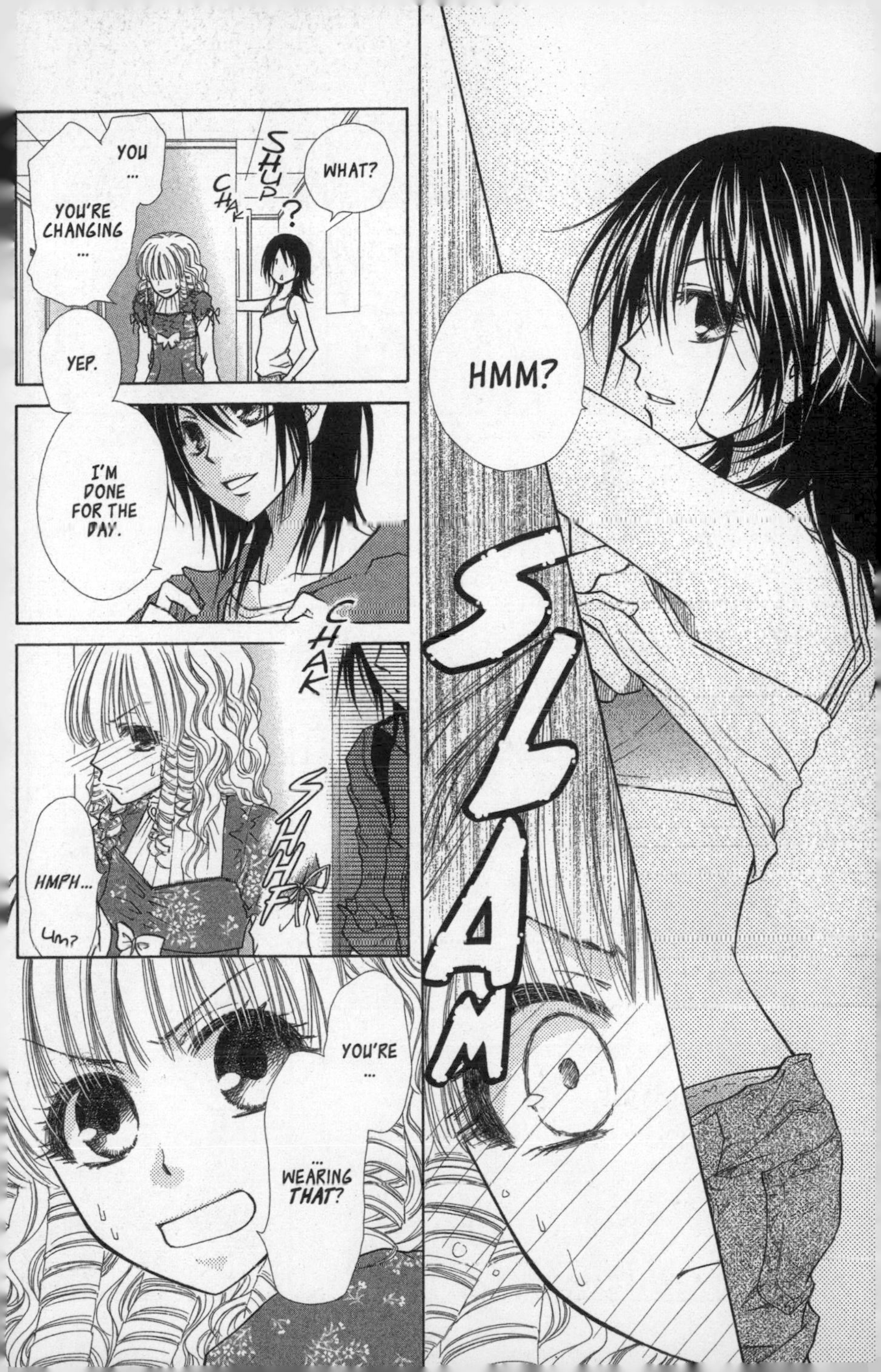
HMM?
SLAM
WHAT?
SHUP
CHAK
?
YOU ... YOU'RE CHANGING ...
YEP.
I'M DONE FOR THE DAY.
CHAK
SHHF
HMPH...
Um?
YOU'RE ... ... WEARING THAT?

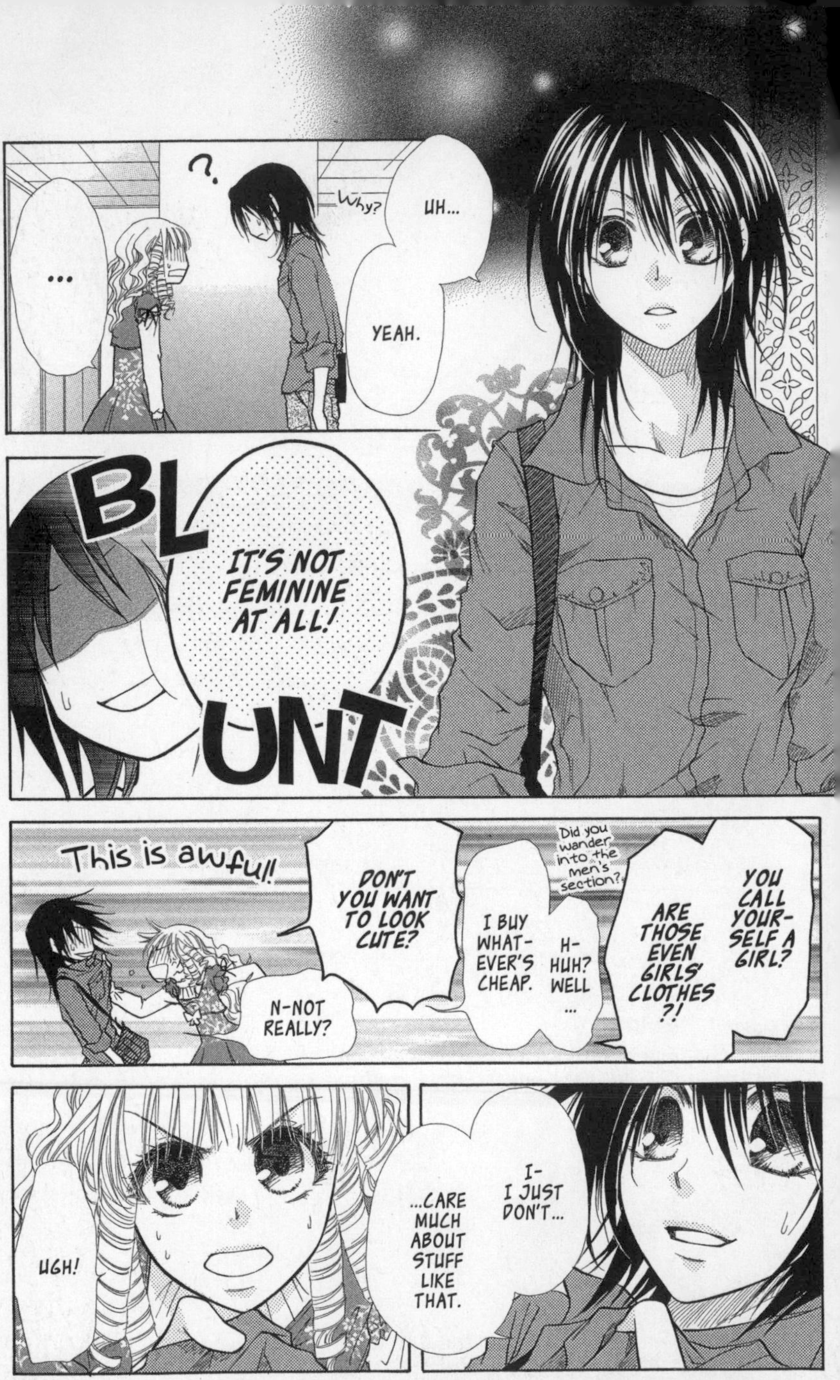
UH...
YEAH.
Why?
?
...
BLUNT
IT'S NOT FEMININE AT ALL!
YOU CALL YOURSELF A GIRL?
ARE THOSE EVEN GIRLS' CLOTHES?!
Did you wander into the men's section?
H-HUH? WELL...
I BUY WHATEVER'S CHEAP.
DON'T YOU WANT TO LOOK CUTE?
N-NOT REALLY?
This is awful!
I-I JUST DON'T...
...CARE MUCH ABOUT STUFF LIKE THAT.
UGH!

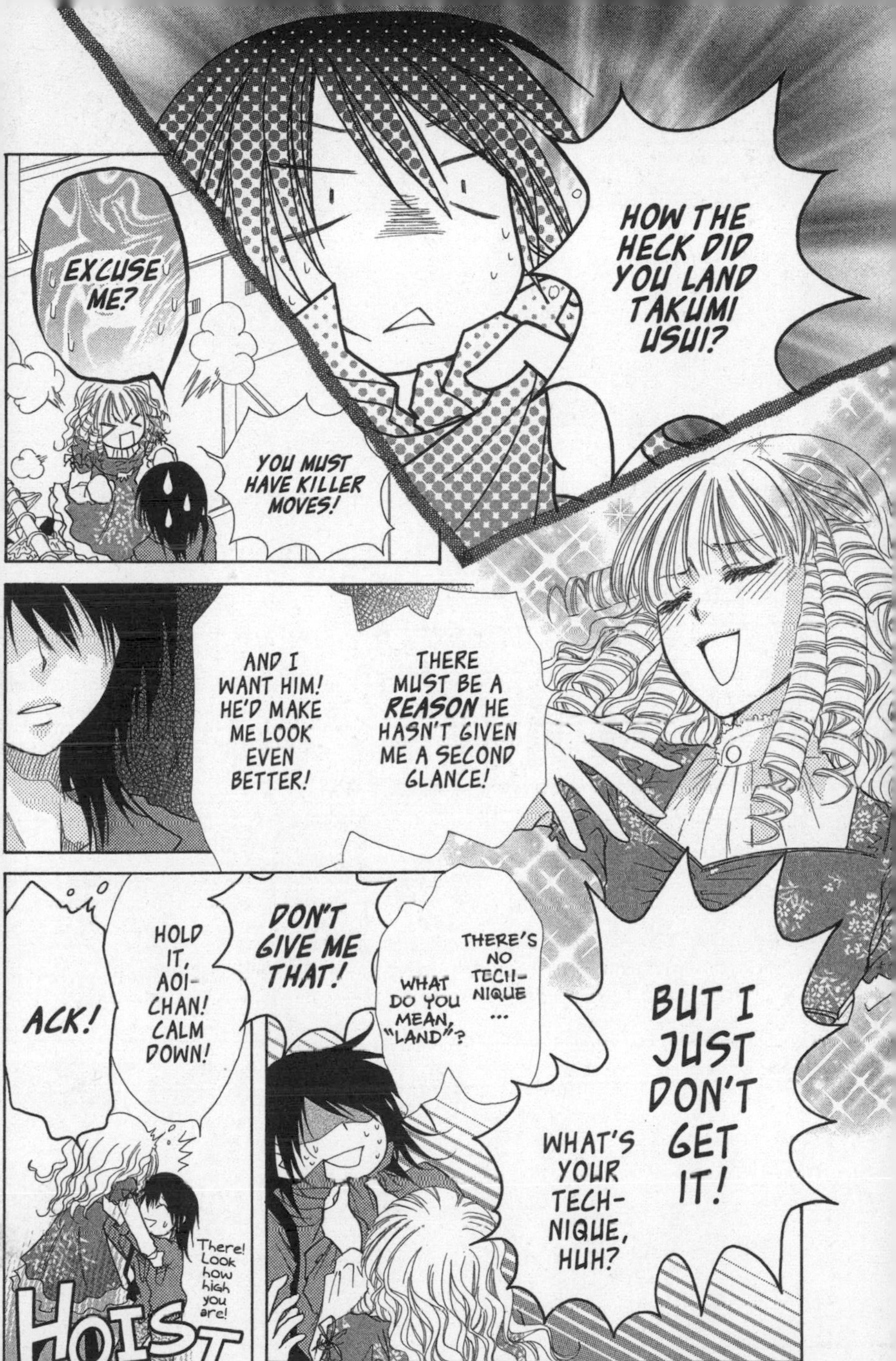
HOW THE HECK DID YOU LAND TAKUMI USUI?
EXCUSE ME?
YOU MUST HAVE KILLER MOVES!
THERE MUST BE A REASON HE HASN'T GIVEN ME A SECOND GLANCE!
AND I WANT HIM! HE'D MAKE ME LOOK EVEN BETTER!
BUT I JUST DON'T GET IT!
WHAT'S YOUR TECH-NIQUE, HUH?
THERE'S NO TECH-NIQUE...
WHAT DO YOU MEAN, "LAND"?
DON'T GIVE ME THAT!
HOLD IT, AOI-CHAN! CALM DOWN!
ACK!
There! Look how high you are!
HOIST

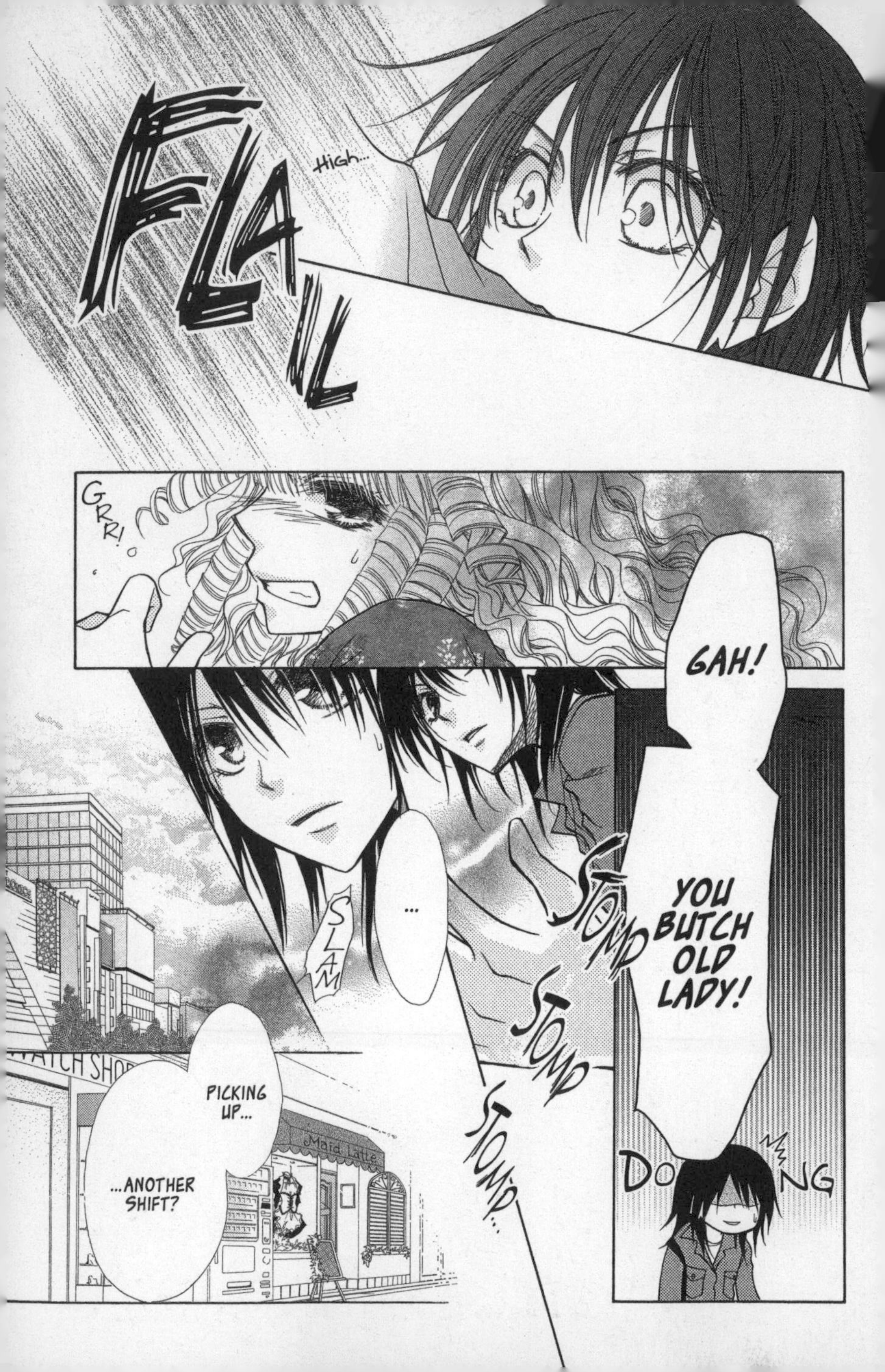
High...
FLAIL
GRR!
GAH!
YOU BUTCH OLD LADY!
DO
NG
STOMP
STOMP
STOMP...
SLAM
...
PICKING UP...
...ANOTHER SHIFT?
WATCH SHO
Maid Latte

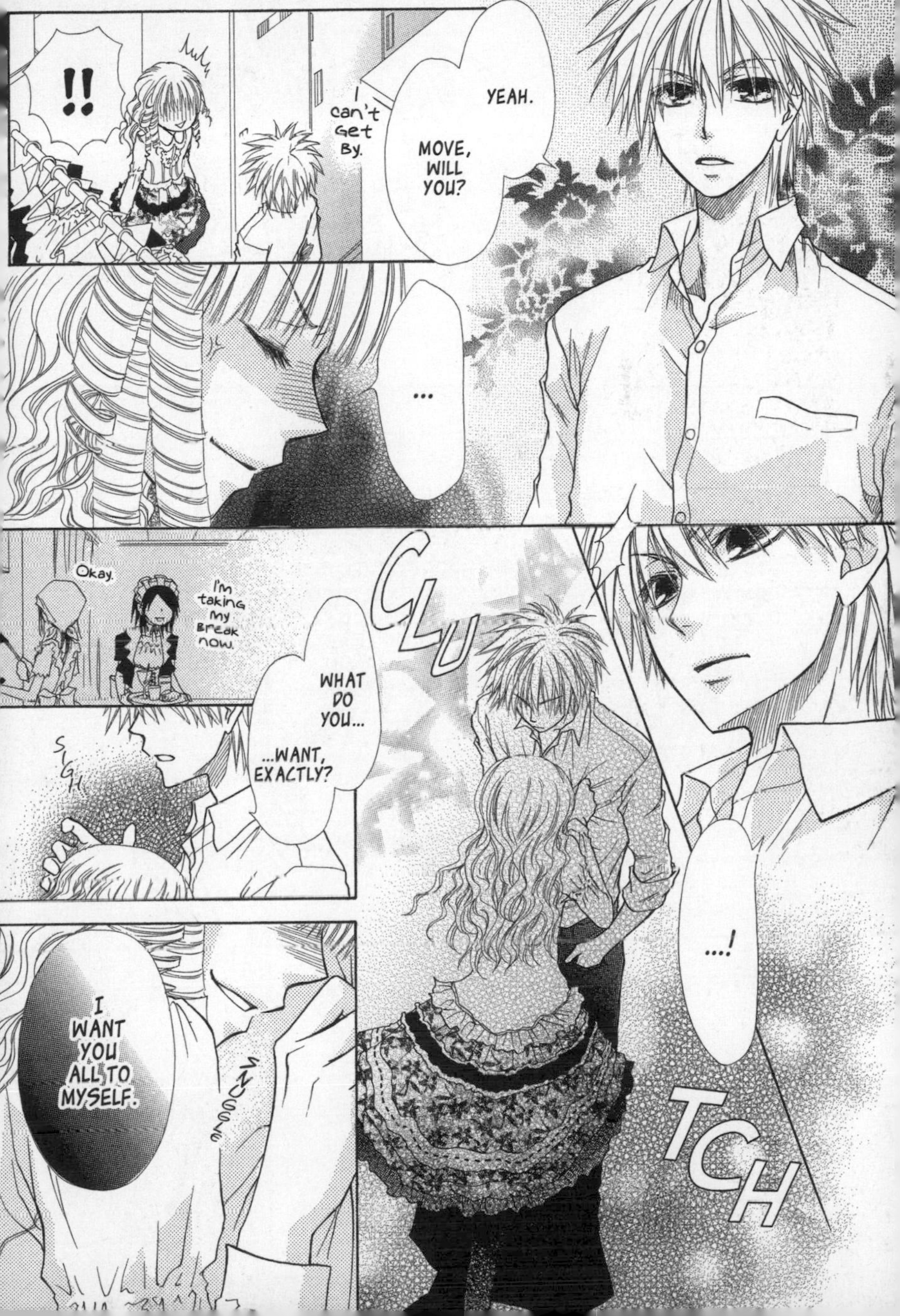
YEAH.
MOVE, WILL YOU?
I can't get by.
!!
...
CLU
TCH
...!
I'm taking my break now.
Okay.
WHAT DO YOU...
...WANT, EXACTLY?
SIGH
I WANT YOU ALL TO MYSELF.
SNUGGLE

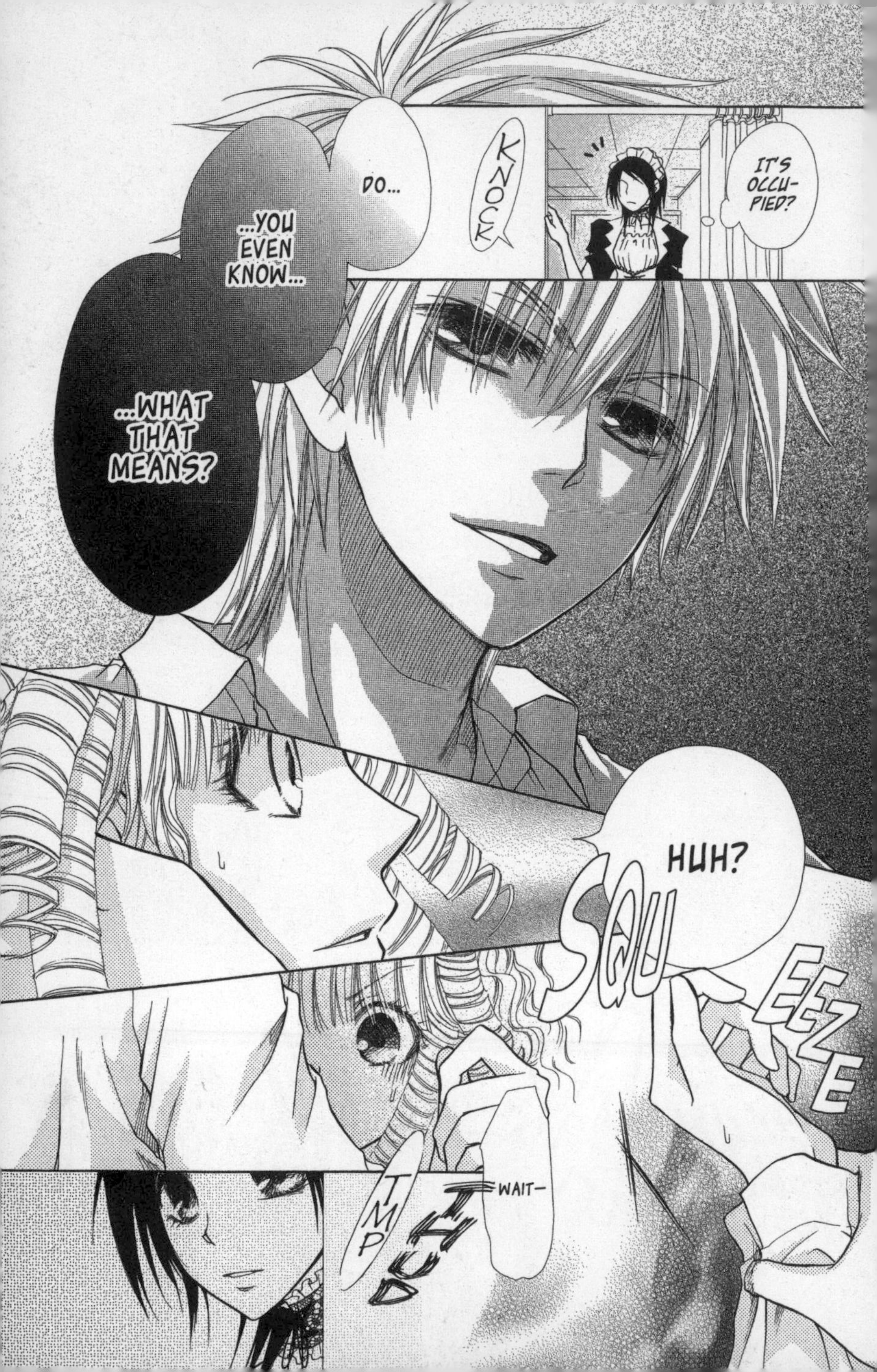
IT'S OCCUPIED?
KNOCK
DO...
...YOU EVEN KNOW...
...WHAT THAT MEANS?
HUH?
SQUEEZE
WAIT-
THUD
TMP

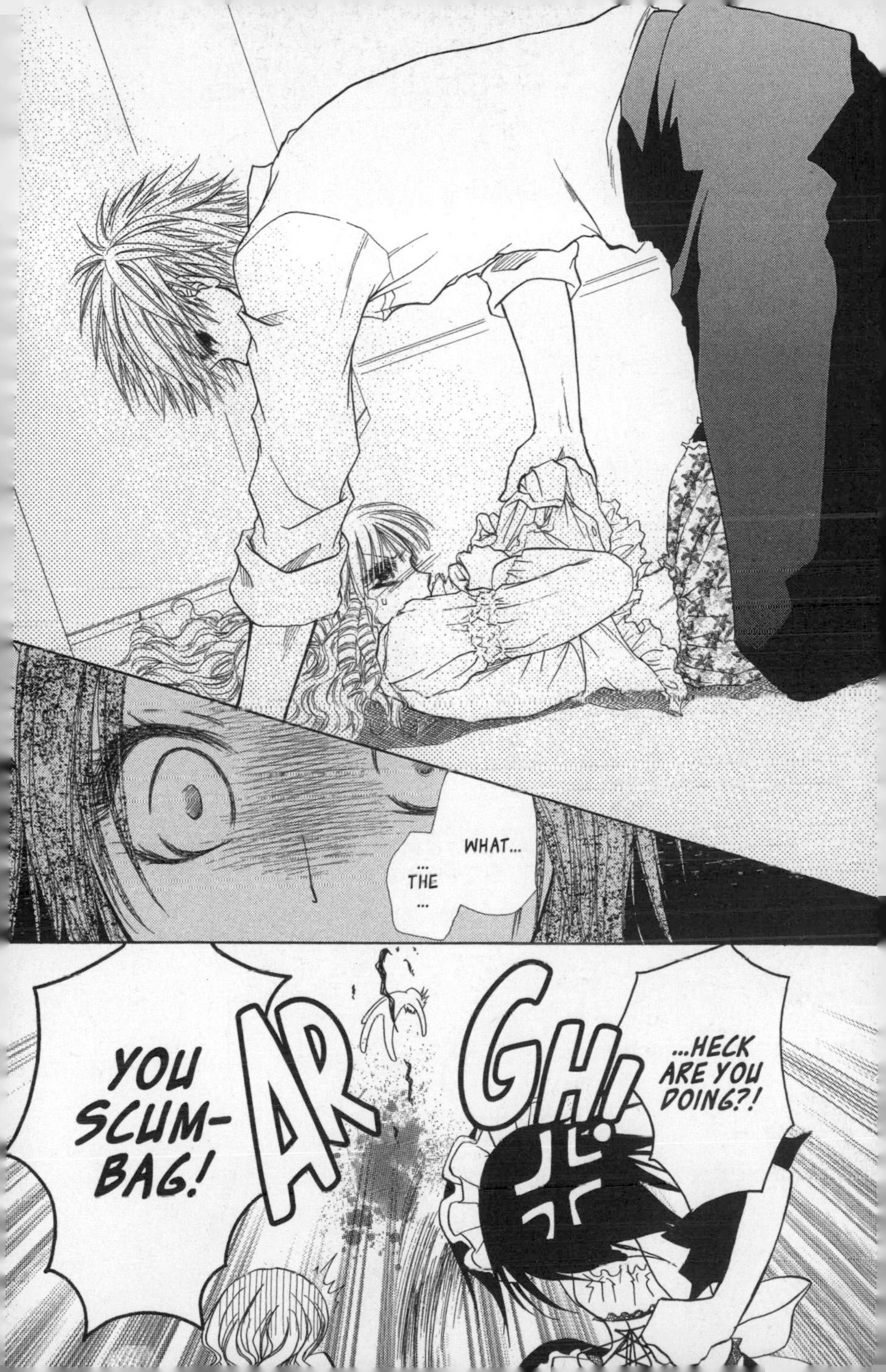
WHAT... ... THE ...
...HECK ARE YOU DOING?!
ARGH!
YOU SCUM-BAG!

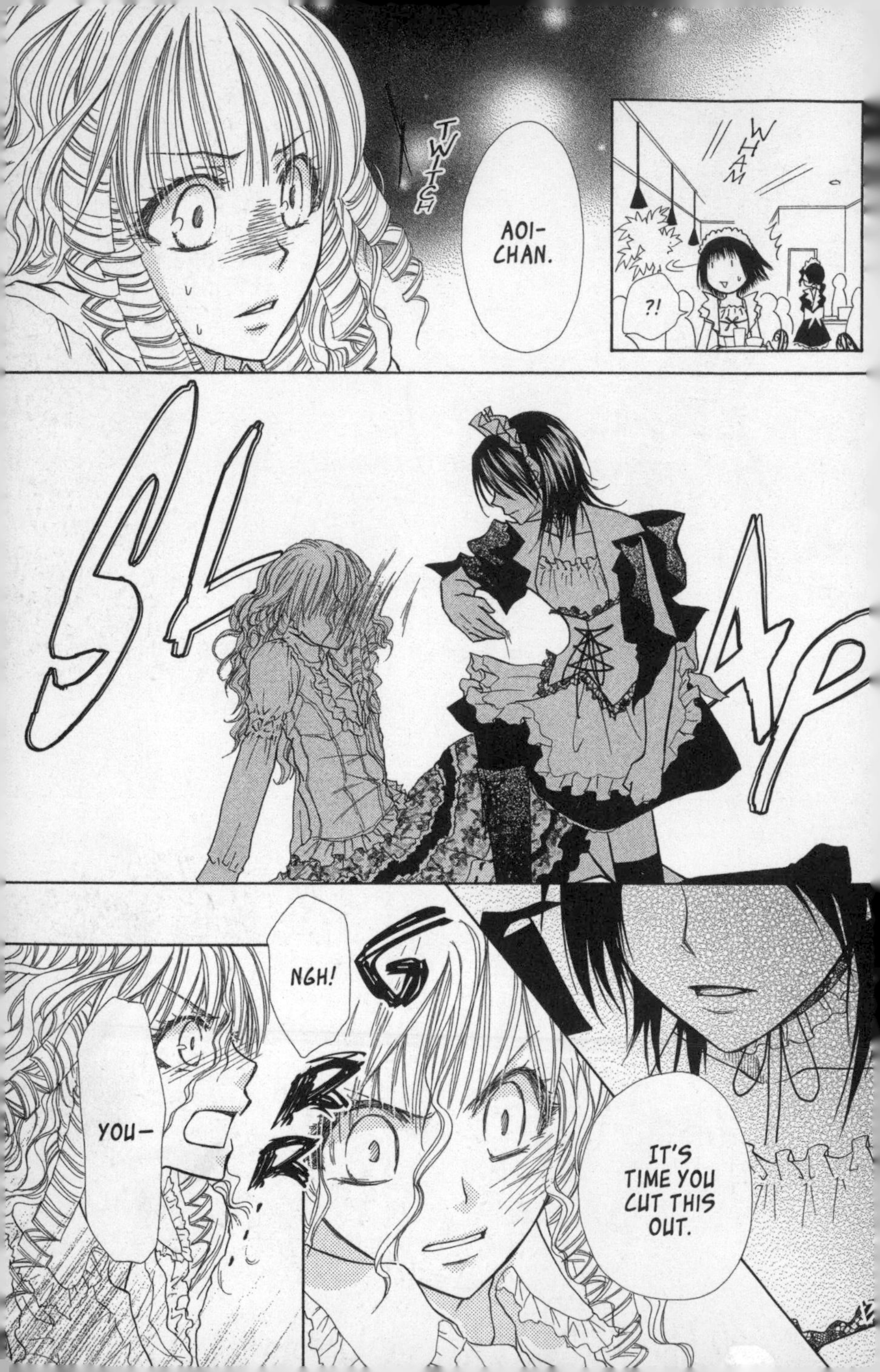
WHAM
?!
TWITCH
AOI-CHAN.
SLAP
IT'S TIME YOU CUT THIS OUT.
NGH!
YOU—

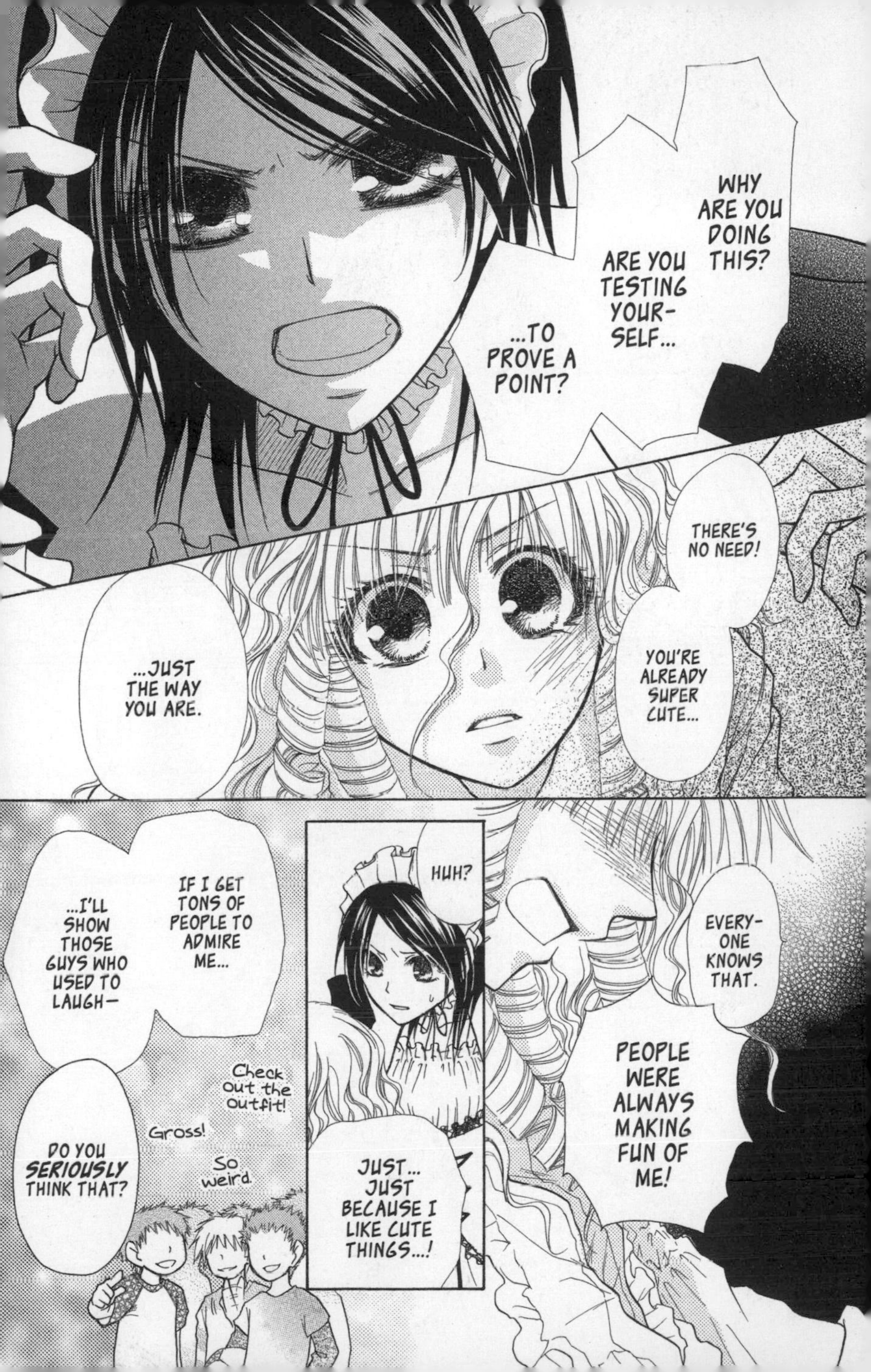
WHY ARE YOU DOING THIS?
ARE YOU TESTING YOUR-SELF...
...TO PROVE A POINT?
THERE'S NO NEED!
YOU'RE ALREADY SUPER CUTE...
...JUST THE WAY YOU ARE.
EVERY-ONE KNOWS THAT.
HUH?
PEOPLE WERE ALWAYS MAKING FUN OF ME!
JUST... JUST BECAUSE I LIKE CUTE THINGS...!
IF I GET TONS OF PEOPLE TO ADMIRE ME...
...I'LL SHOW THOSE GUYS WHO USED TO LAUGH—
Check out the outfit!
Gross!
So weird
DO YOU *SERIOUSLY* THINK THAT?

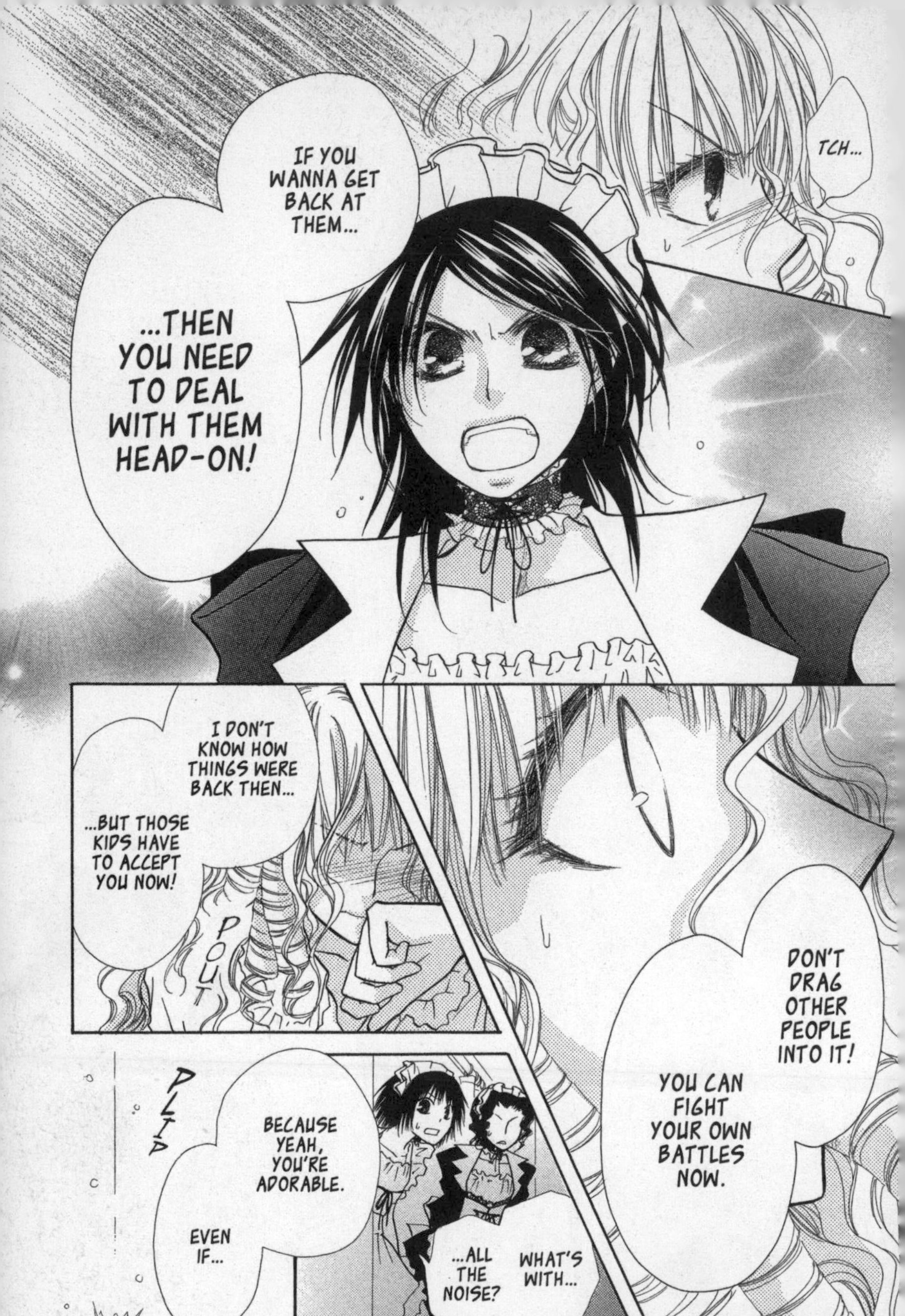
TCH...
IF YOU WANNA GET BACK AT THEM...
...THEN YOU NEED TO DEAL WITH THEM HEAD-ON!
DON'T DRAG OTHER PEOPLE INTO IT!
YOU CAN FIGHT YOUR OWN BATTLES NOW.
I DON'T KNOW HOW THINGS WERE BACK THEN...
...BUT THOSE KIDS HAVE TO ACCEPT YOU NOW!
POUT
WHAT'S WITH...
...ALL THE NOISE?
BECAUSE YEAH, YOU'RE ADORABLE.
EVEN IF...
PLIP

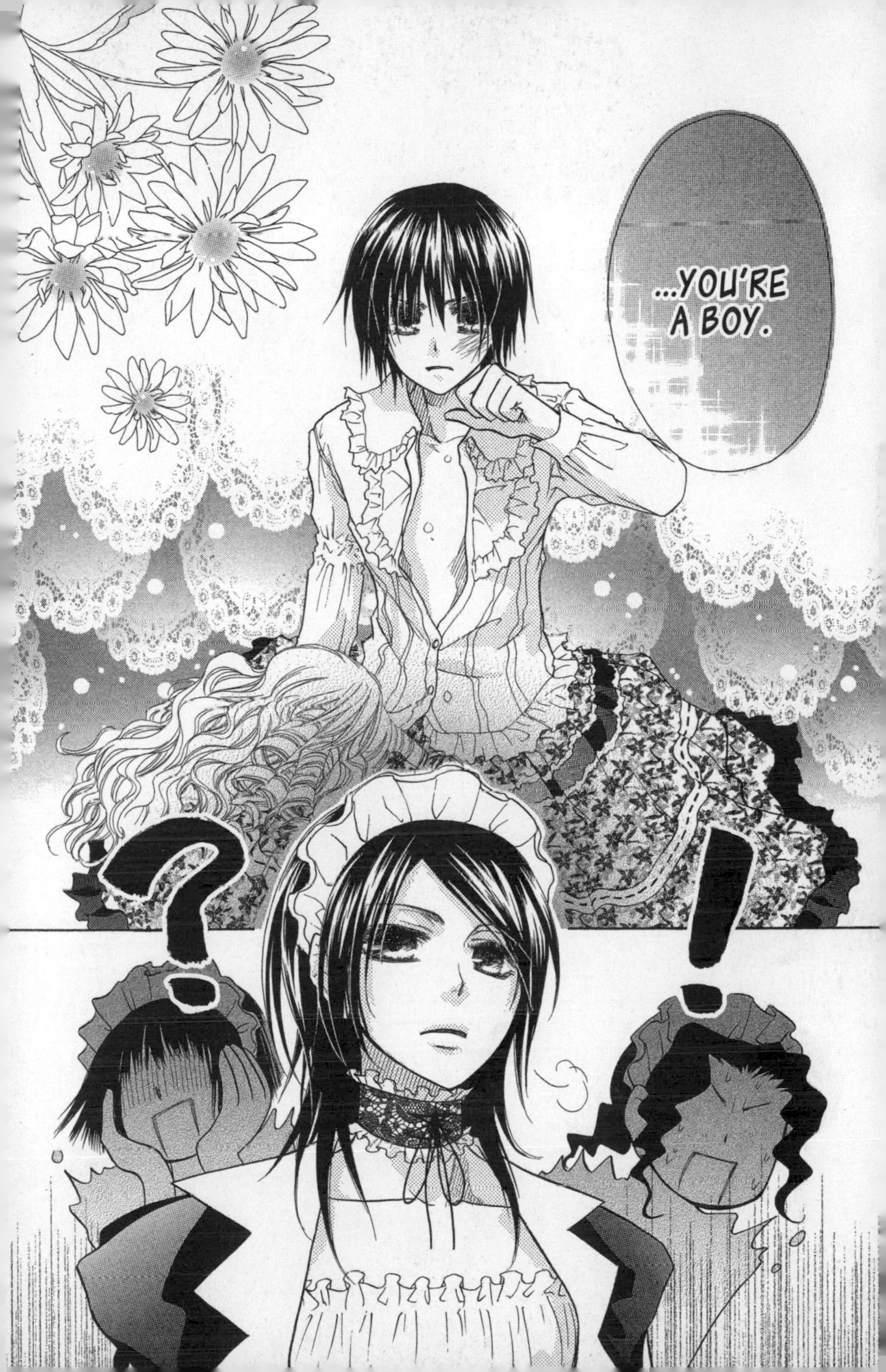
...YOU'RE A BOY.

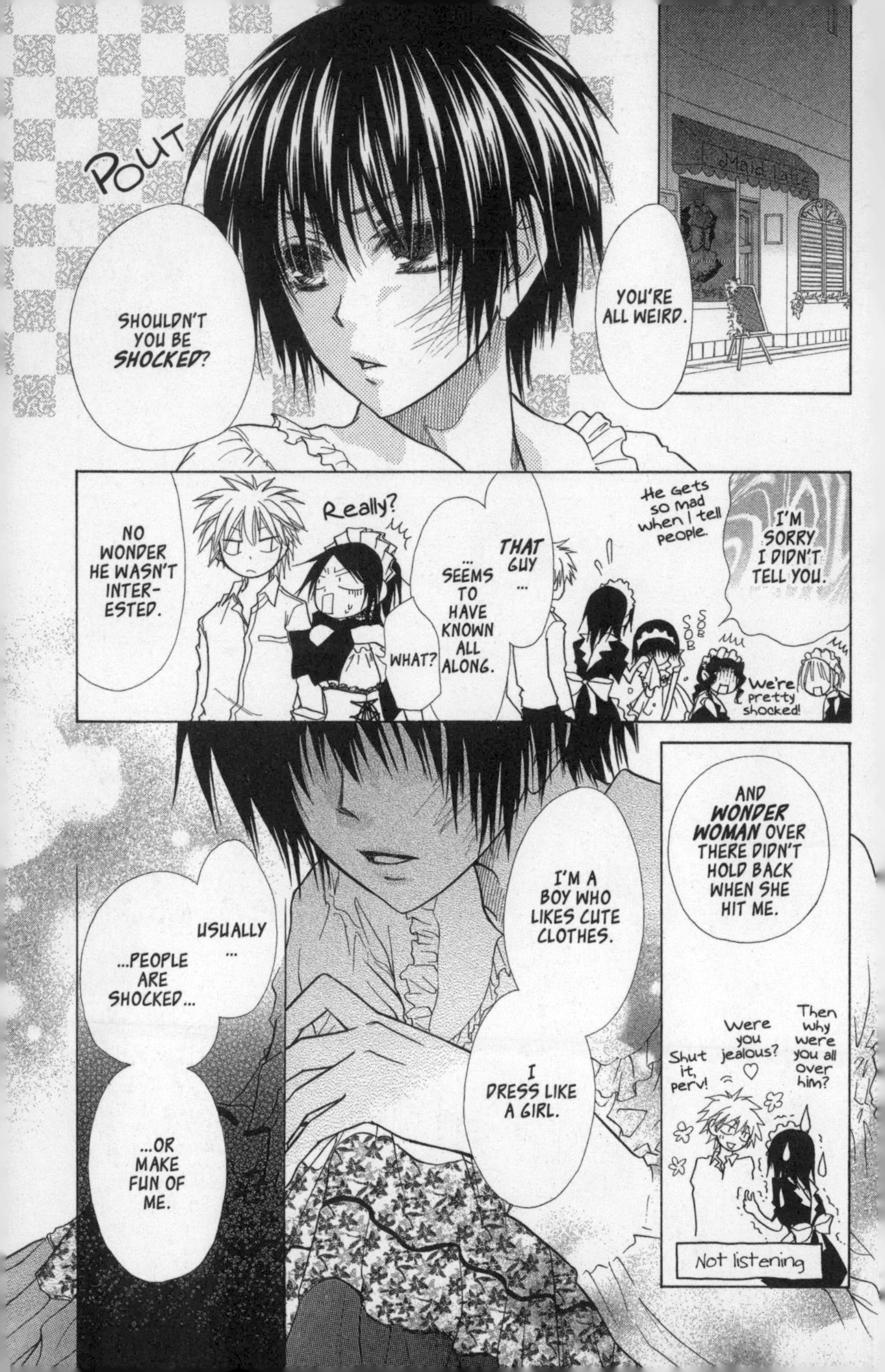
Maid latte
YOU'RE ALL WEIRD.
POUT
SHOULDN'T YOU BE **SHOCKED**?
I'M SORRY I DIDN'T TELL YOU.
He Gets so mad when I tell people.
We're pretty shocked!
SOB SOB
THAT GUY ...
... SEEMS TO HAVE KNOWN ALL ALONG.
WHAT?
Really?
NO WONDER HE WASN'T INTER-ESTED.
AND **WONDER WOMAN** OVER THERE DIDN'T HOLD BACK WHEN SHE HIT ME.
Then why were you all over him?
Were you jealous? ♡
Shut it, perv!
Not listening
I'M A BOY WHO LIKES CUTE CLOTHES.
I DRESS LIKE A GIRL.
USUALLY ...
...PEOPLE ARE SHOCKED...
...OR MAKE FUN OF ME.

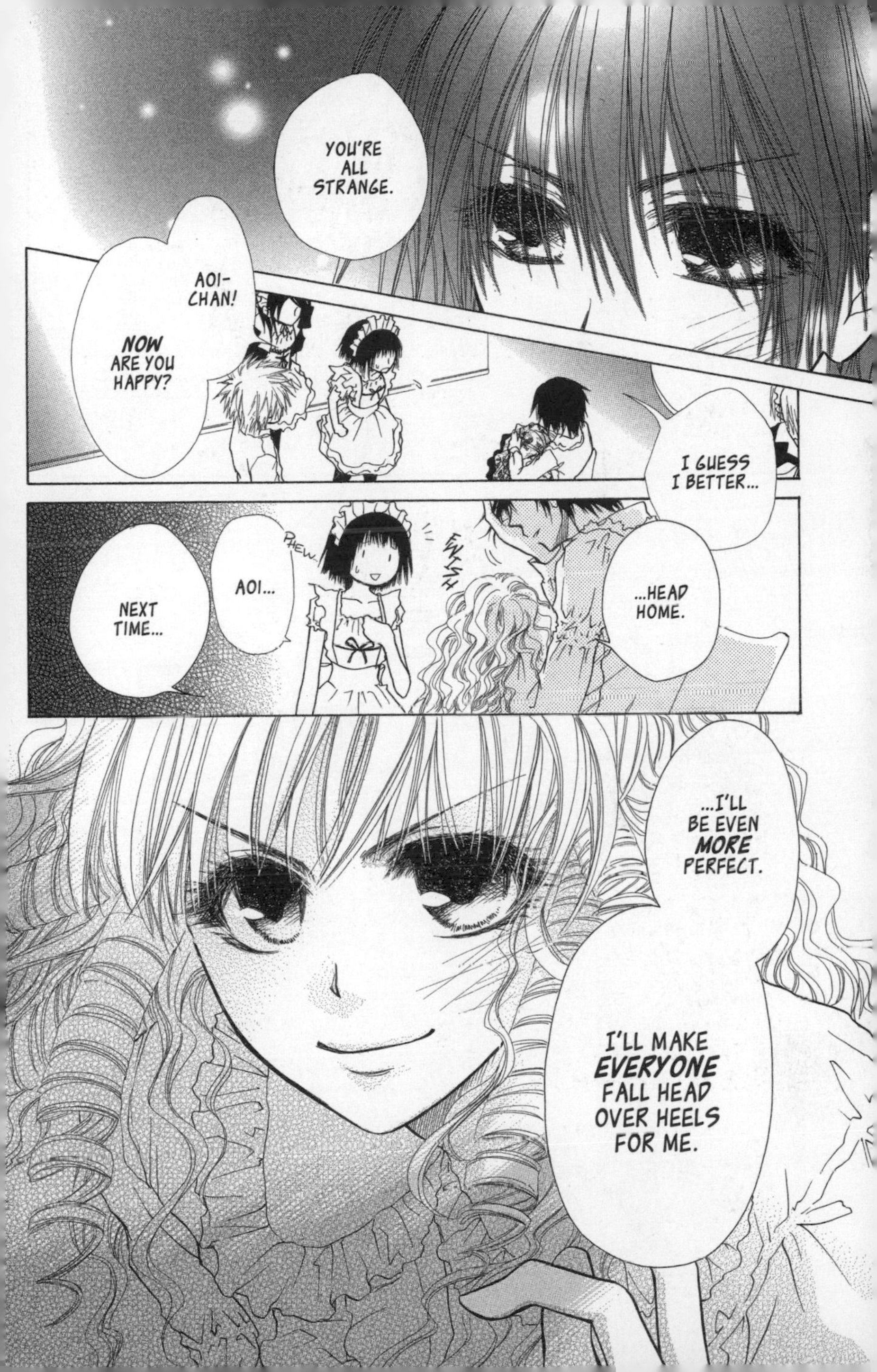
YOU'RE ALL STRANGE.
I GUESS I BETTER...
AOI-CHAN!
NOW ARE YOU HAPPY?
...HEAD HOME.
SWISH
PHEW...
AOI...
NEXT TIME...
...I'LL BE EVEN MORE PERFECT.
I'LL MAKE EVERYONE FALL HEAD OVER HEELS FOR ME.

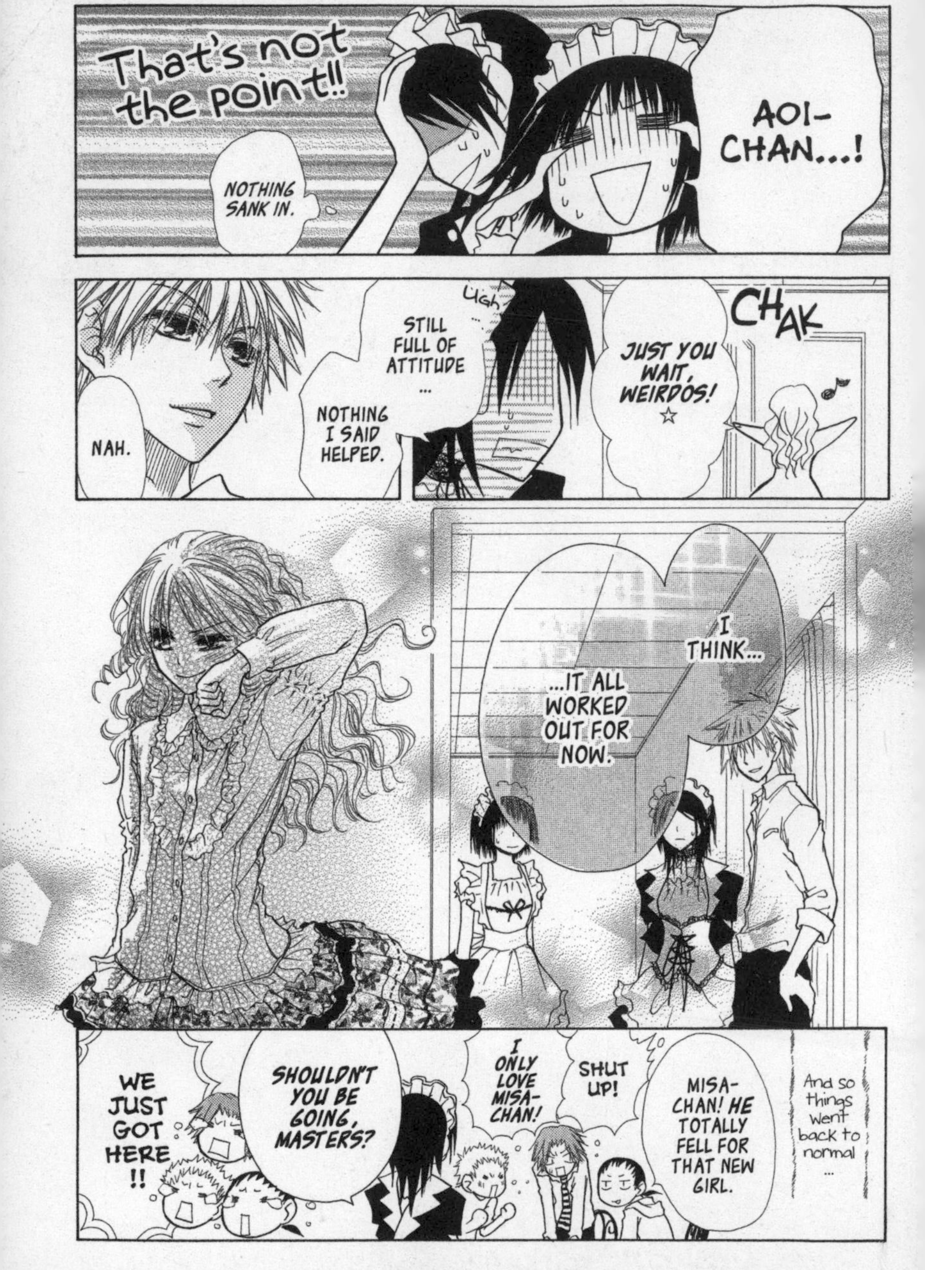
AOI-CHAN...!
That's not the point!!
NOTHING SANK IN.
CHAK
JUST YOU WAIT, WEIRDOS! ☆
Ugh...
STILL FULL OF ATTITUDE ...
NOTHING I SAID HELPED.
NAH.
I THINK...
...IT ALL WORKED OUT FOR NOW.
And so things went back to normal ...
MISA-CHAN! HE TOTALLY FELL FOR THAT NEW GIRL.
SHUT UP!
I ONLY LOVE MISA-CHAN!
SHOULDN'T YOU BE GOING, MASTERS?
WE JUST GOT HERE!!

This was published as a preview when the manga went from a one-shot to a series.

When I unearthed it, I hadn't seen it in a while. I was surprised to realize that Usui had been so thoroughly himself from the beginning.

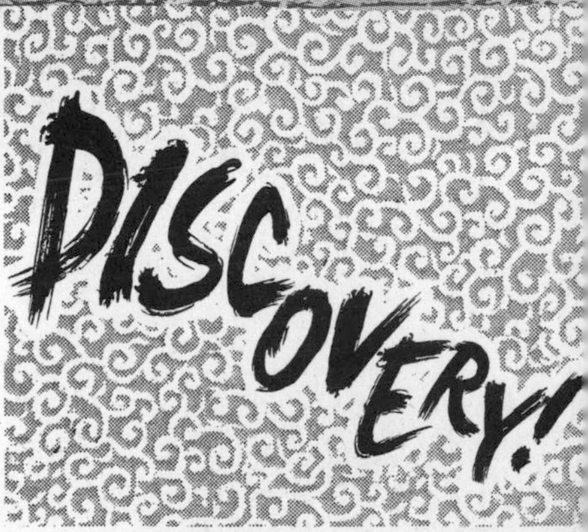
DISCOVERY!

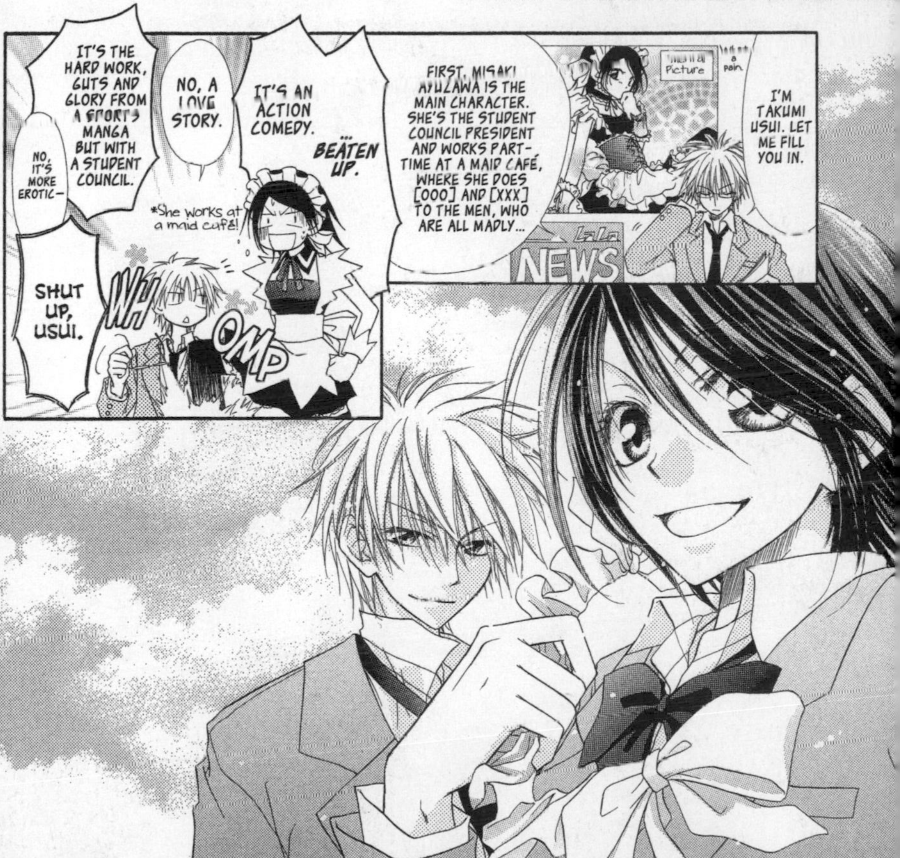
I'M TAKUMI USUI. LET ME FILL YOU IN.
a pain.
Picture
FIRST, MISAKI AYUZAWA IS THE MAIN CHARACTER. SHE'S THE STUDENT COUNCIL PRESIDENT AND WORKS PART-TIME AT A MAID CAFÉ, WHERE SHE DOES [OOO] AND [XXX] TO THE MEN, WHO ARE ALL MADLY...
NEWS
IT'S AN ACTION COMEDY.
NO, A LOVE STORY.
IT'S THE HARD WORK, GUTS AND GLORY FROM A SPORTS MANGA BUT WITH A STUDENT COUNCIL.
NO, IT'S MORE EROTIC—
... BEATEN UP.
*She works at a maid café!
SHUT UP, USUI.
WHOMP

IT'S A COMEDIC ACTION ROMANCE WITH THE GUTS AND GLORY OF SPORTS, PLUS SOME FANSERVICE!

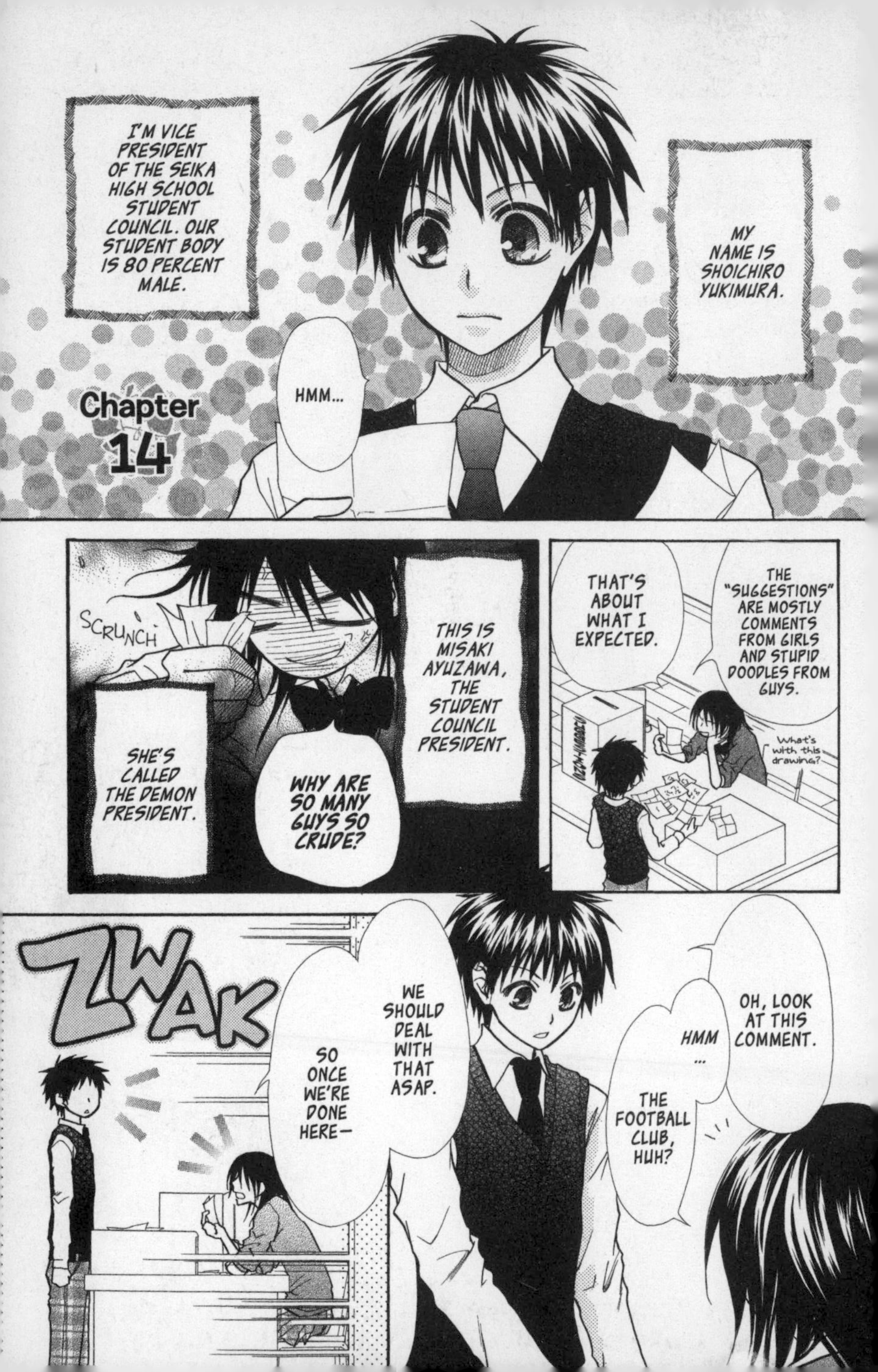
MY NAME IS SHOICHIRO YUKIMURA.
I'M VICE PRESIDENT OF THE SEIKA HIGH SCHOOL STUDENT COUNCIL. OUR STUDENT BODY IS 80 PERCENT MALE.
HMM...
Chapter 14
THE "SUGGESTIONS" ARE MOSTLY COMMENTS FROM GIRLS AND STUPID DOODLES FROM GUYS.
THAT'S ABOUT WHAT I EXPECTED.
What's with this drawing?
THIS IS MISAKI AYUZAWA, THE STUDENT COUNCIL PRESIDENT.
SCRUNCH
WHY ARE SO MANY GUYS SO CRUDE?
SHE'S CALLED THE DEMON PRESIDENT.
OH, LOOK AT THIS COMMENT.
HMM ...
THE FOOTBALL CLUB, HUH?
WE SHOULD DEAL WITH THAT ASAP.
SO ONCE WE'RE DONE HERE—
ZWAK

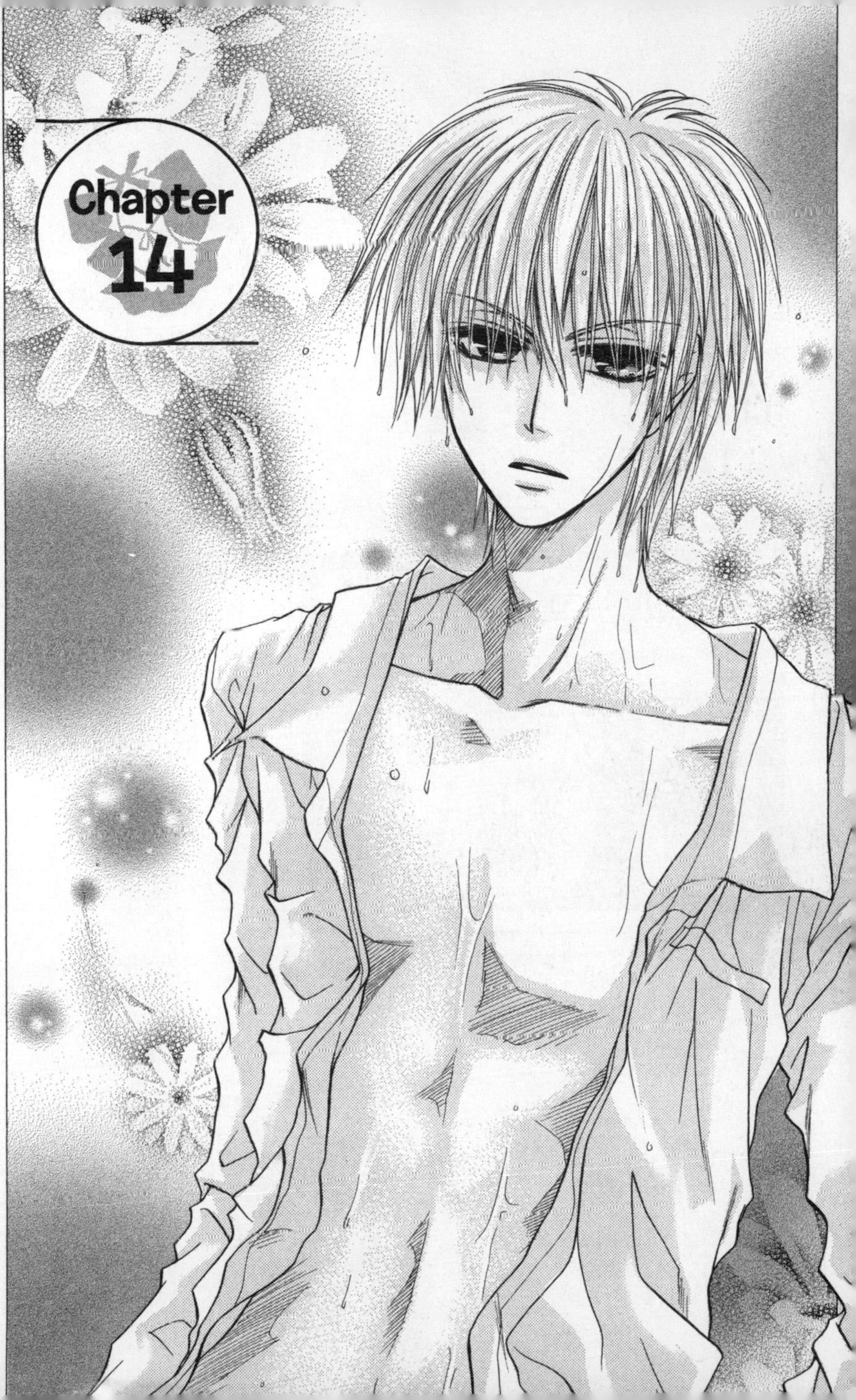
Chapter
14

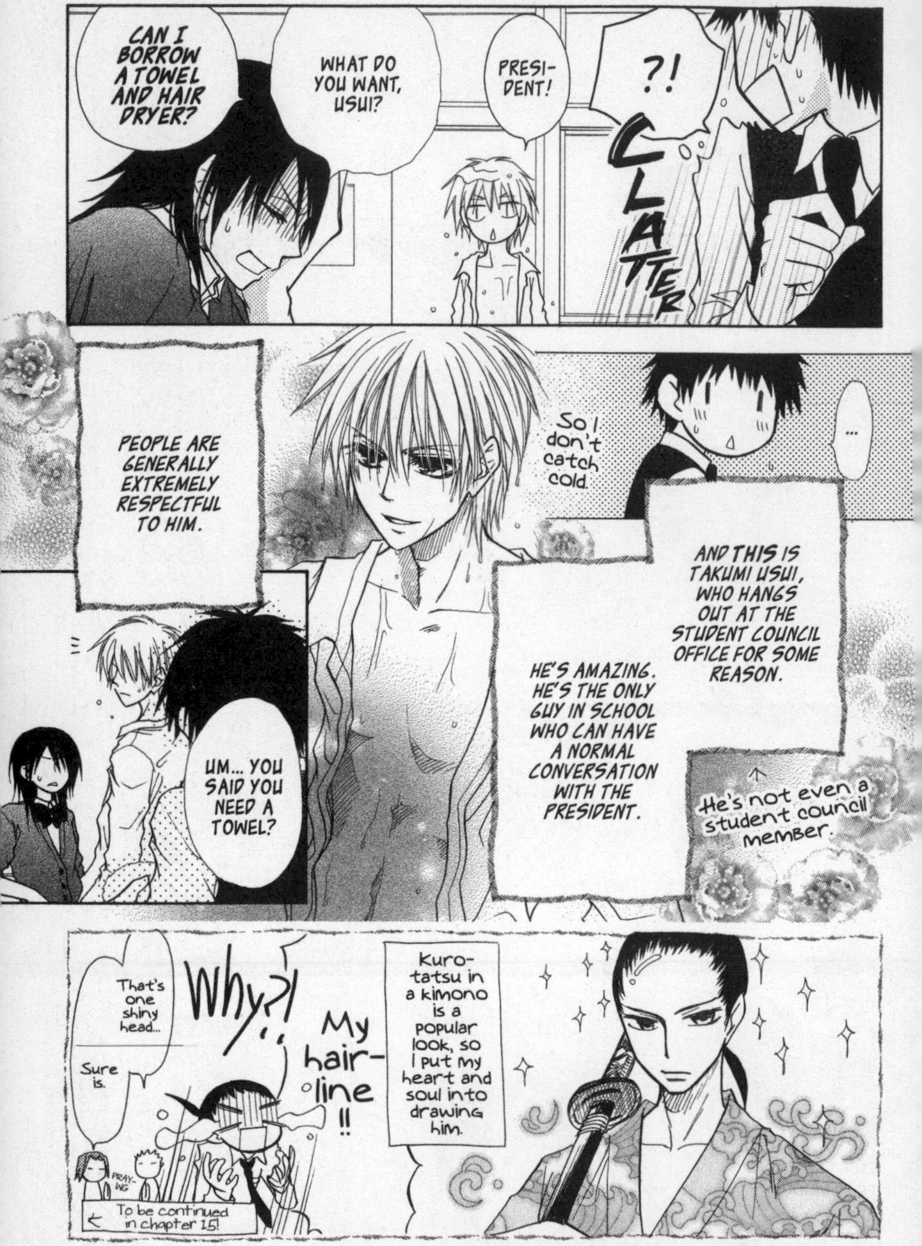
?!
CLATTER
PRESI-DENT!
WHAT DO YOU WANT, USUI?
CAN I BORROW A TOWEL AND HAIR DRYER?
...
So I don't catch cold.
AND THIS IS TAKUMI USUI, WHO HANGS OUT AT THE STUDENT COUNCIL OFFICE FOR SOME REASON.
He's not even a student council member.
PEOPLE ARE GENERALLY EXTREMELY RESPECTFUL TO HIM.
HE'S AMAZING. HE'S THE ONLY GUY IN SCHOOL WHO CAN HAVE A NORMAL CONVERSATION WITH THE PRESIDENT.
UM... YOU SAID YOU NEED A TOWEL?
Kuro-tatsu in a kimono is a popular look, so I put my heart and soul into drawing him.
My hair-line!!
Why?!
That's one shiny head...
Sure is.
PRAY-ING
To be continued in chapter 15!

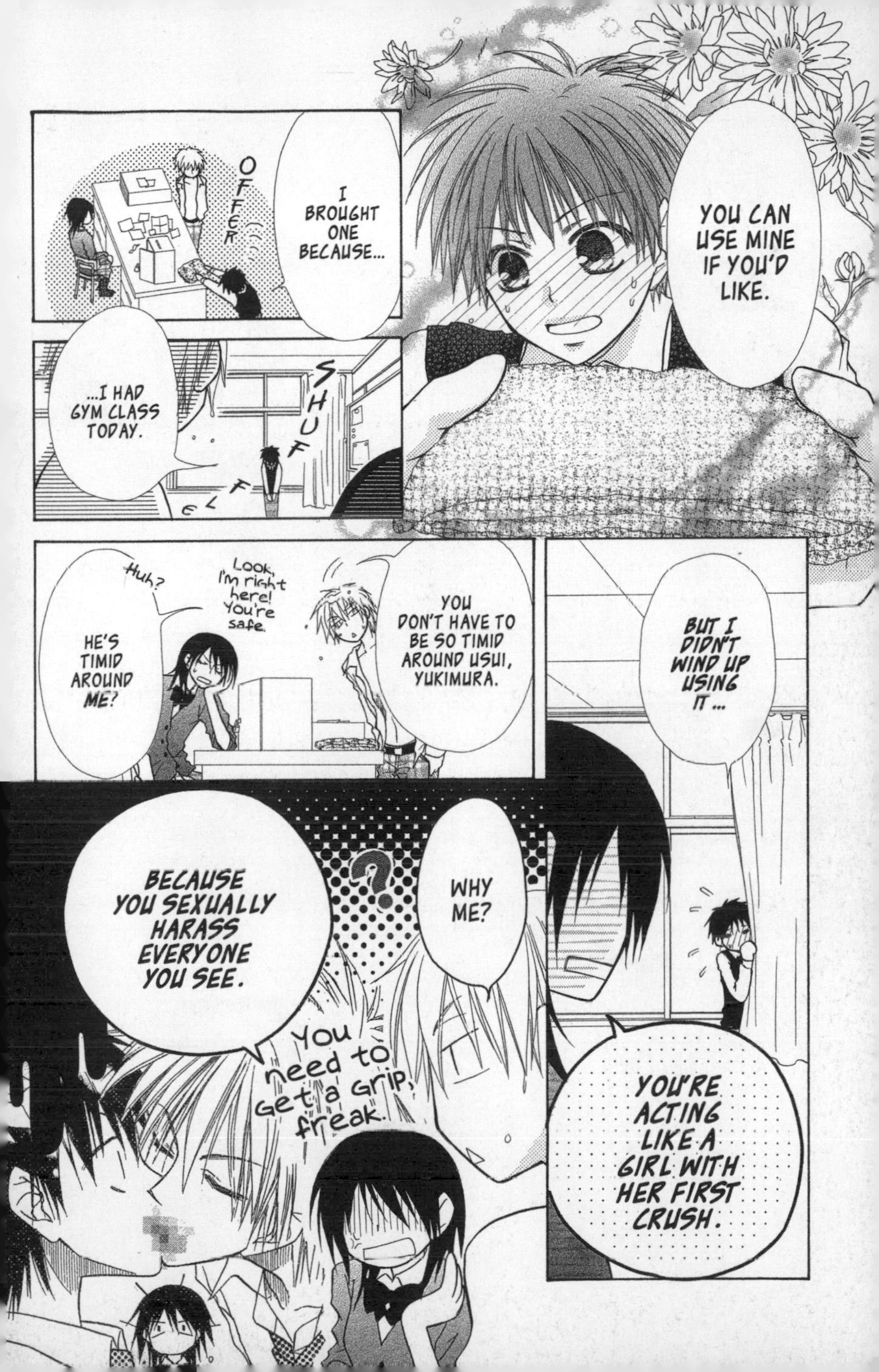
YOU CAN USE MINE IF YOU'D LIKE.
I BROUGHT ONE BECAUSE...
OFFER
...I HAD GYM CLASS TODAY.
SHUFFLE
BUT I DIDN'T WIND UP USING IT...
YOU DON'T HAVE TO BE SO TIMID AROUND USUI, YUKIMURA.
Look, I'm right here! You're safe.
Huh?
HE'S TIMID AROUND ME?
YOU'RE ACTING LIKE A GIRL WITH HER FIRST CRUSH.
WHY ME?
BECAUSE YOU SEXUALLY HARASS EVERYONE YOU SEE.
You need to get a grip, freak.

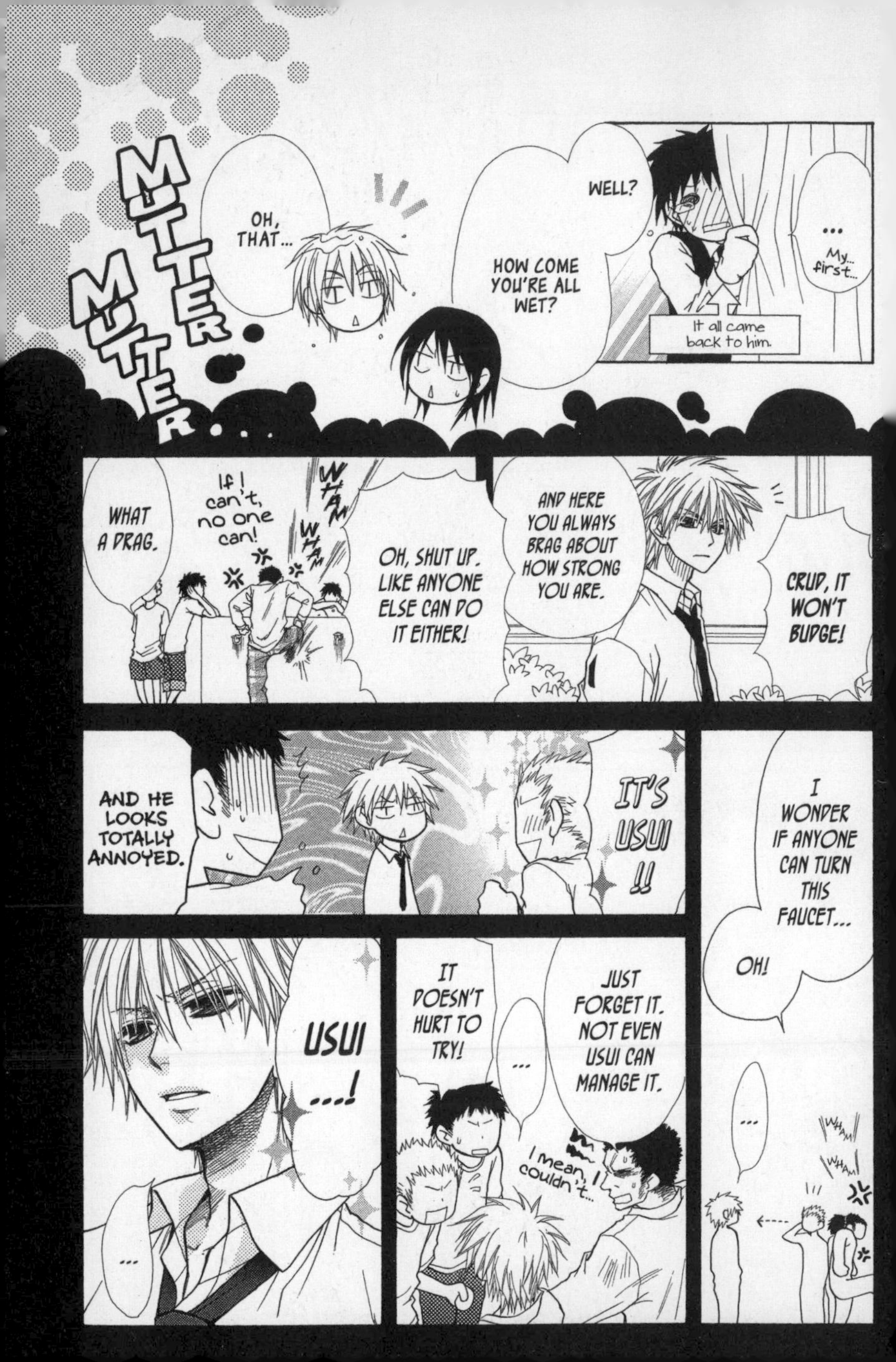
...
My... first...
It all came back to him.
WELL?
HOW COME YOU'RE ALL WET?
OH, THAT...
MUTTER MUTTER...
CRUD, IT WON'T BUDGE!
AND HERE YOU ALWAYS BRAG ABOUT HOW STRONG YOU ARE.
OH, SHUT UP. LIKE ANYONE ELSE CAN DO IT EITHER!
WHAM
WHAM
If I can't, no one can!
WHAT A DRAG.
I WONDER IF ANYONE CAN TURN THIS FAUCET...
OH!
...
WHAM
WHAM
IT'S USUI!!
AND HE LOOKS TOTALLY ANNOYED.
JUST FORGET IT. NOT EVEN USUI CAN MANAGE IT.
I mean, I couldn't...
...
IT DOESN'T HURT TO TRY!
USUI...!
...

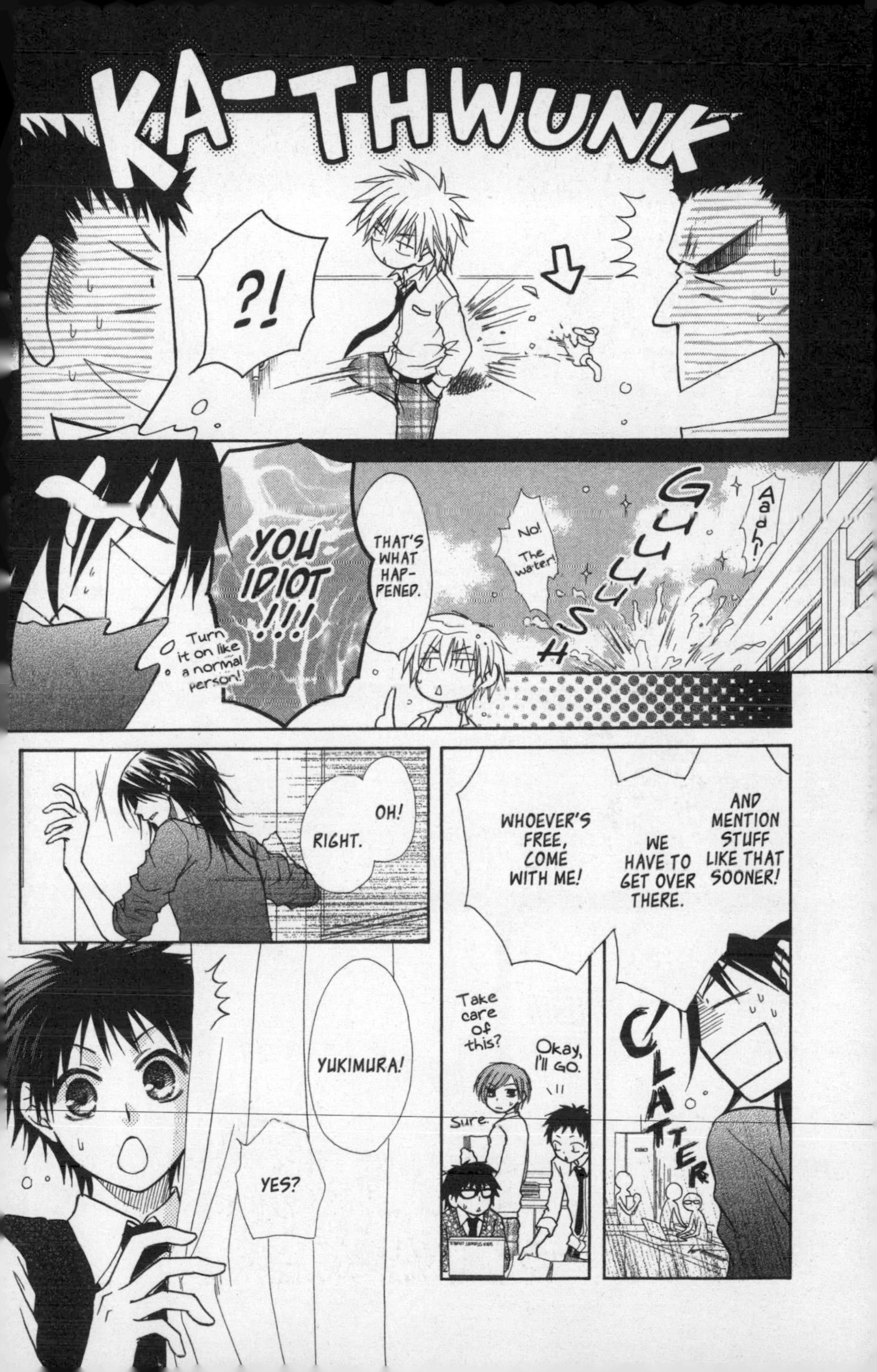
KA-THWUNK
?!
Aaah!
GUUUUSH
No! The water!
THAT'S WHAT HAP-PENED.
YOU IDIOT!!!
Turn it on like a normal person!
AND MENTION STUFF LIKE THAT SOONER!
WE HAVE TO GET OVER THERE.
WHOEVER'S FREE, COME WITH ME!
CLATTER
Take care of this?
Okay, I'll GO.
Sure.
OH!
RIGHT.
YUKIMURA!
YES?

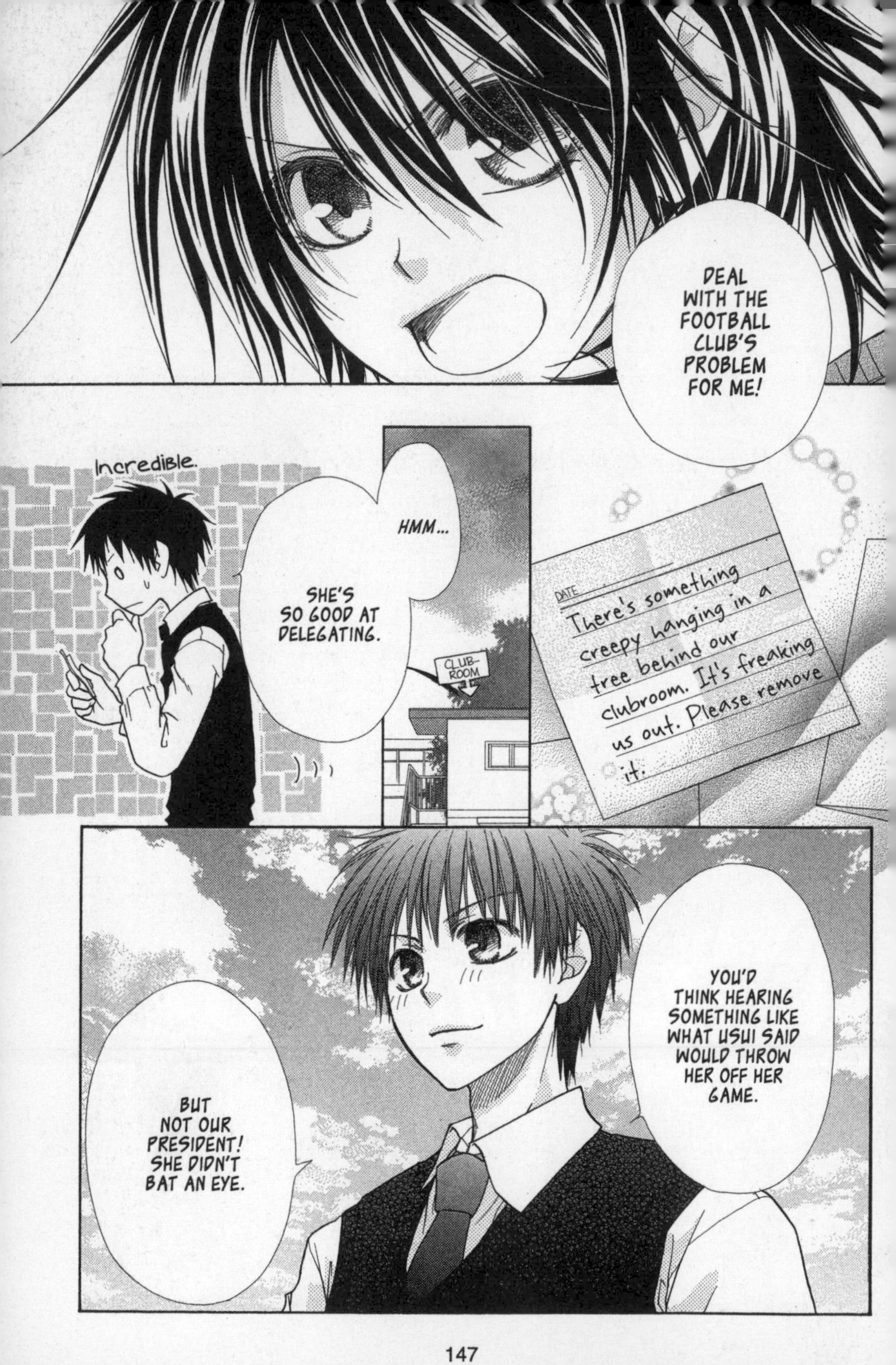
DEAL WITH THE FOOTBALL CLUB'S PROBLEM FOR ME!
DATE
There's something creepy hanging in a tree behind our clubroom. It's freaking us out. Please remove it.
CLUB-ROOM
HMM...
SHE'S SO GOOD AT DELEGATING.
Incredible.
YOU'D THINK HEARING SOMETHING LIKE WHAT USUI SAID WOULD THROW HER OFF HER GAME.
BUT NOT OUR PRESIDENT! SHE DIDN'T BAT AN EYE.

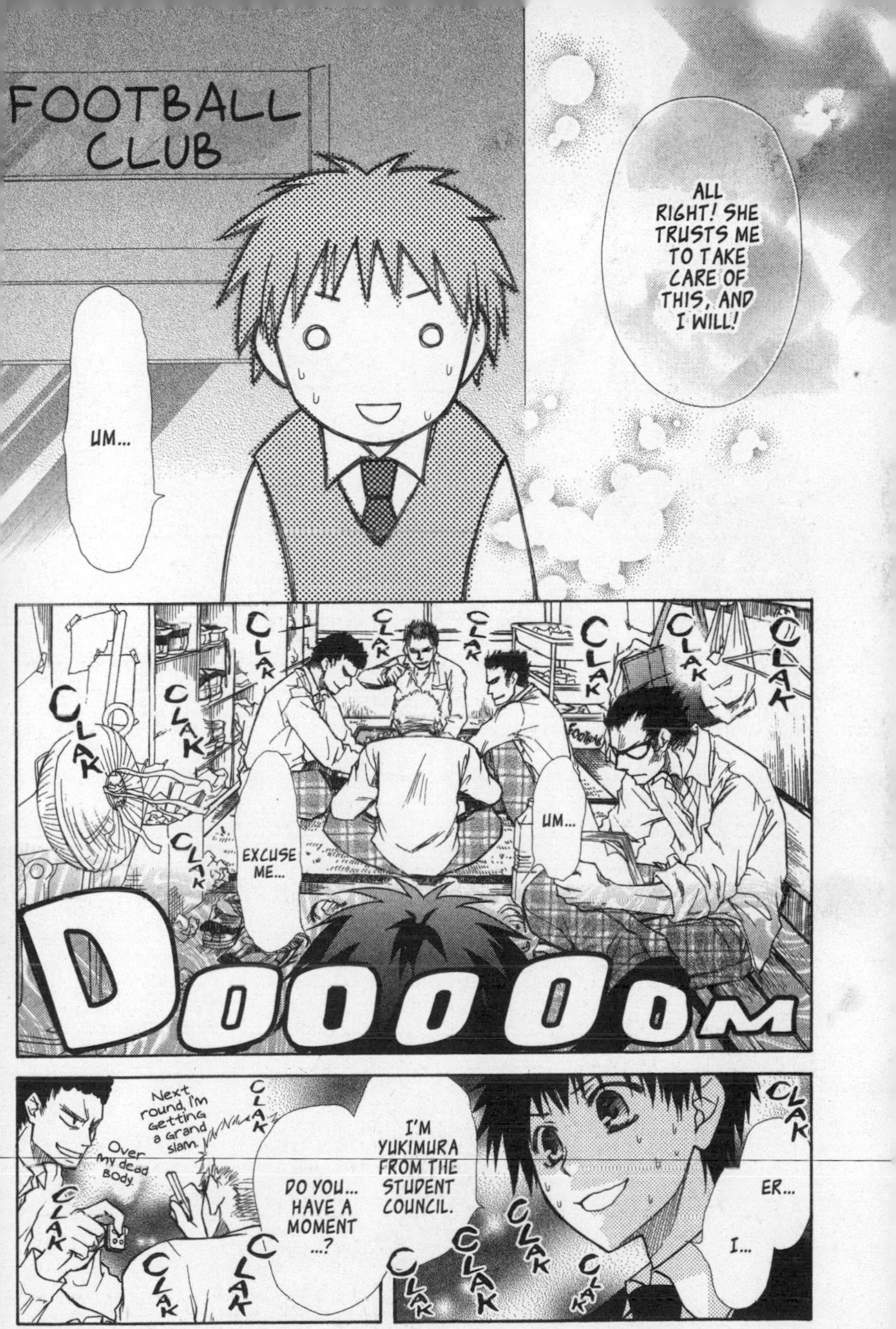
ALL RIGHT! SHE TRUSTS ME TO TAKE CARE OF THIS, AND I WILL!
FOOTBALL CLUB
UM...
CLAK
CLAK
CLAK
CLAK
CLAK
CLAK
UM...
EXCUSE ME...
CLAK
CLAK
CLAK
DOOOOOOM
CLAK
ER...
I...
CLAK
CLAK
CLAK
CLAK
I'M YUKIMURA FROM THE STUDENT COUNCIL.
DO YOU... HAVE A MOMENT ...?
CLAK
CLAK
CLAK
Next round, I'm getting a Grand slam.
Over my dead body.
CLAK

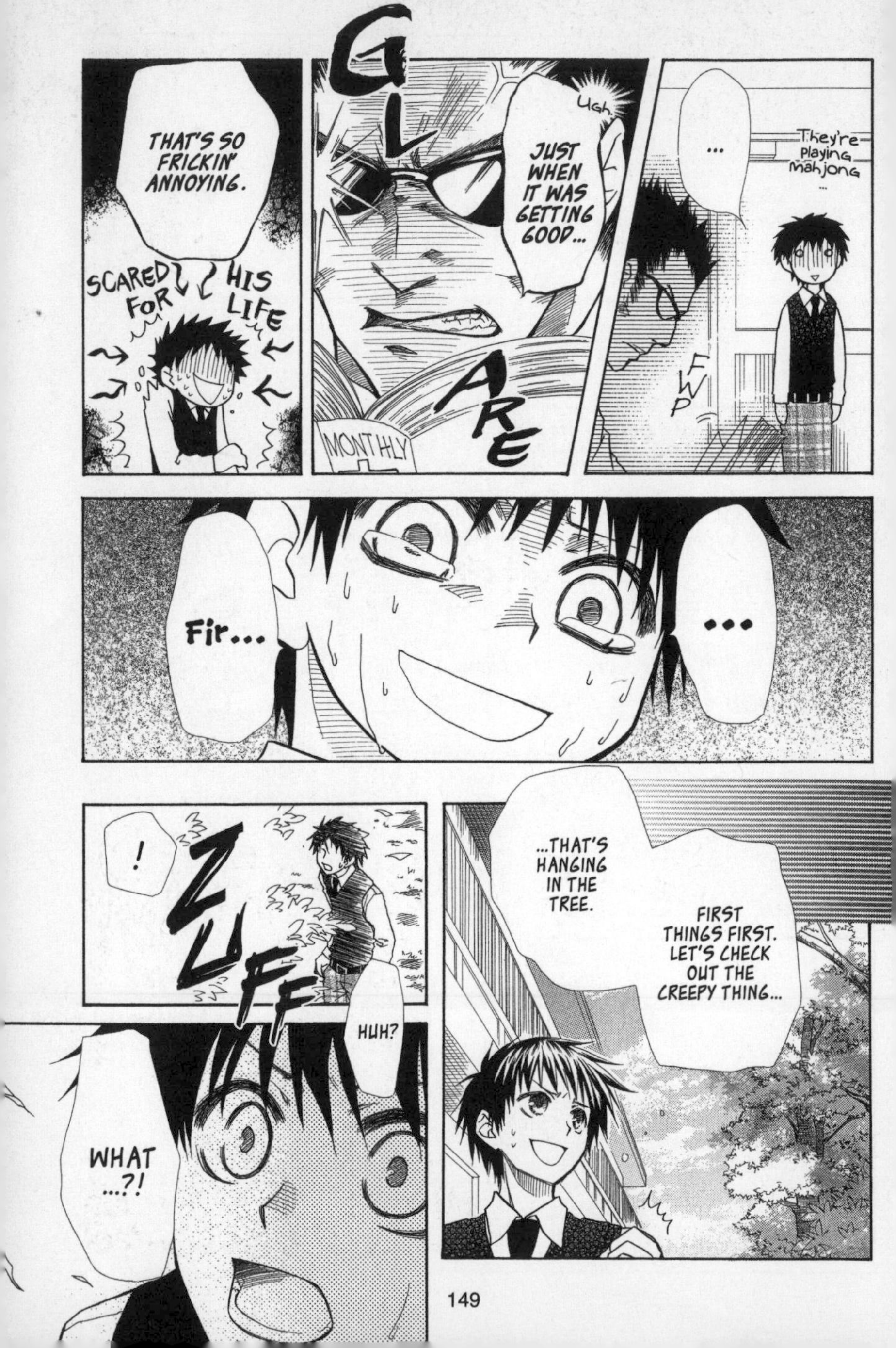
...
They're playing mahjong...
Ugh.
JUST WHEN IT WAS GETTING GOOD...
GLARE
MONTHLY
THAT'S SO FRICKIN' ANNOYING.
SCARED FOR HIS LIFE
...
Fir...
FIRST THINGS FIRST. LET'S CHECK OUT THE CREEPY THING...
...THAT'S HANGING IN THE TREE.
!
ZUFF
HUH?
WHAT ...?!

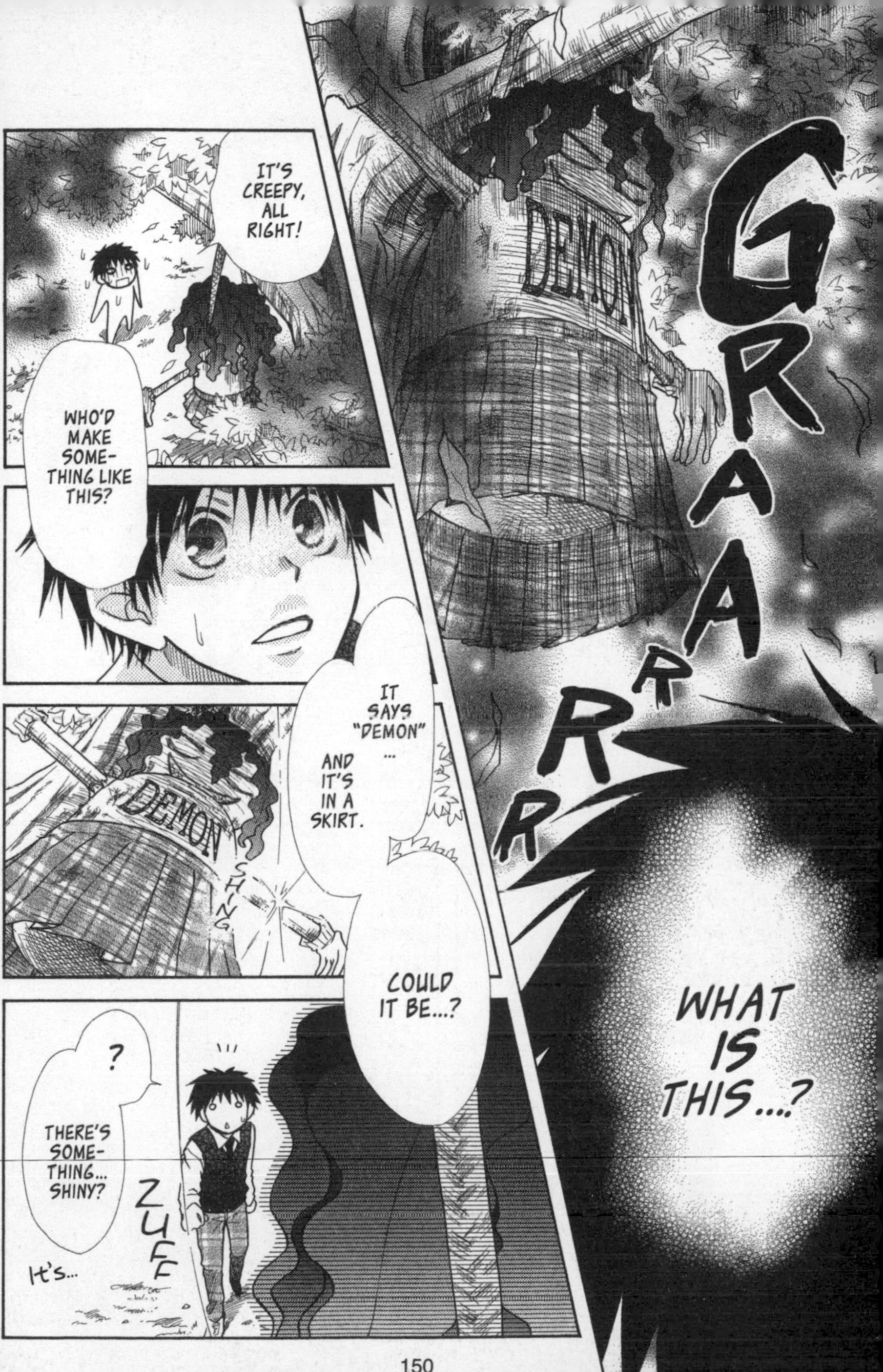
DEMON
GRAAARRRR
WHAT IS THIS...?
IT'S CREEPY, ALL RIGHT!
WHO'D MAKE SOME-THING LIKE THIS?
IT SAYS "DEMON"...
AND IT'S IN A SKIRT.
DEMON
SHING
COULD IT BE...?
?
THERE'S SOME-THING... SHINY?
ZUFF
It's...

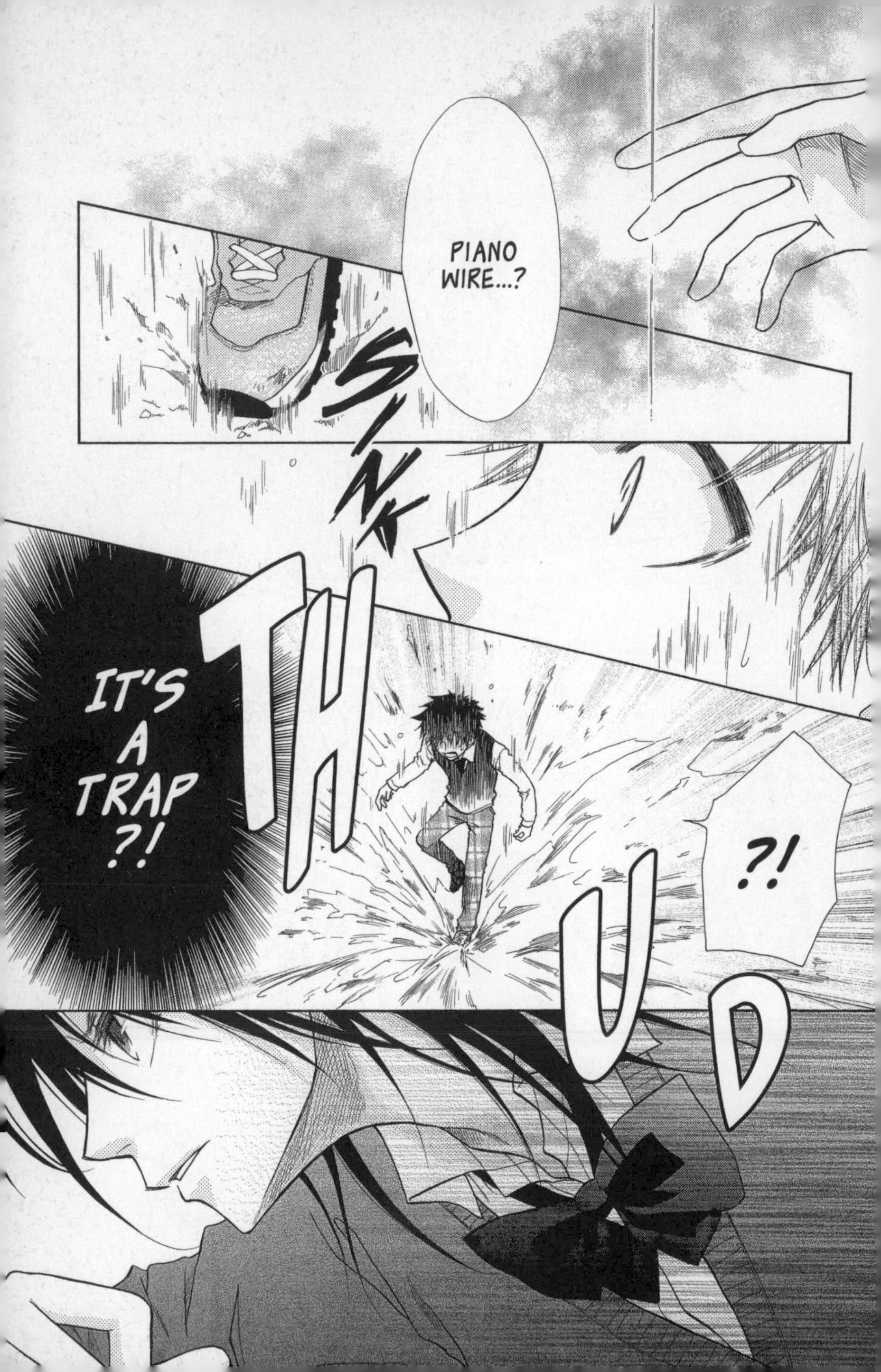
PIANO WIRE...?
SINK
THUD
?!
IT'S A TRAP ?!

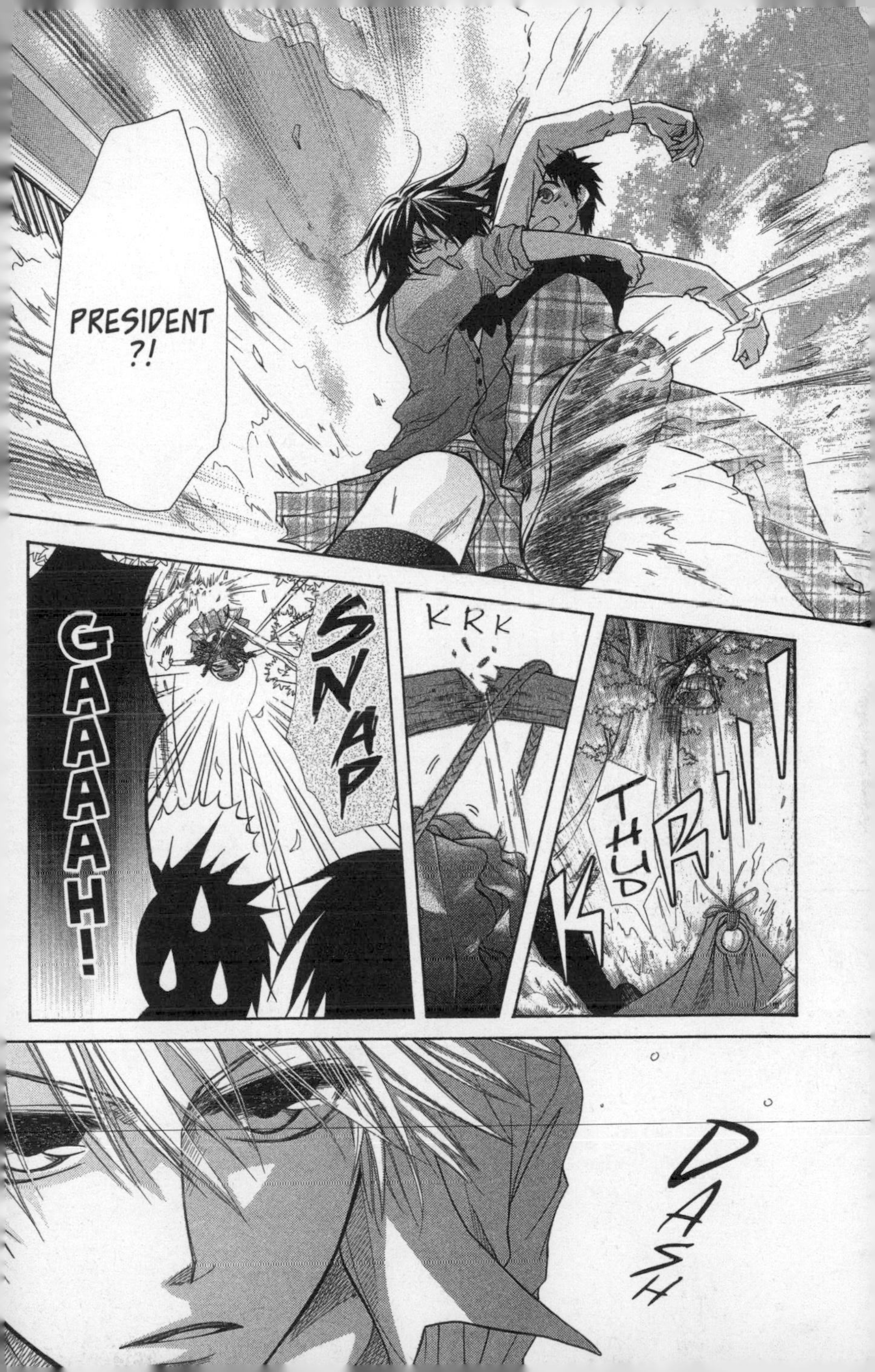
PRESIDENT ?!
THUD
TRIIK
KRK
SNAP
GAAAAAH!
DASH

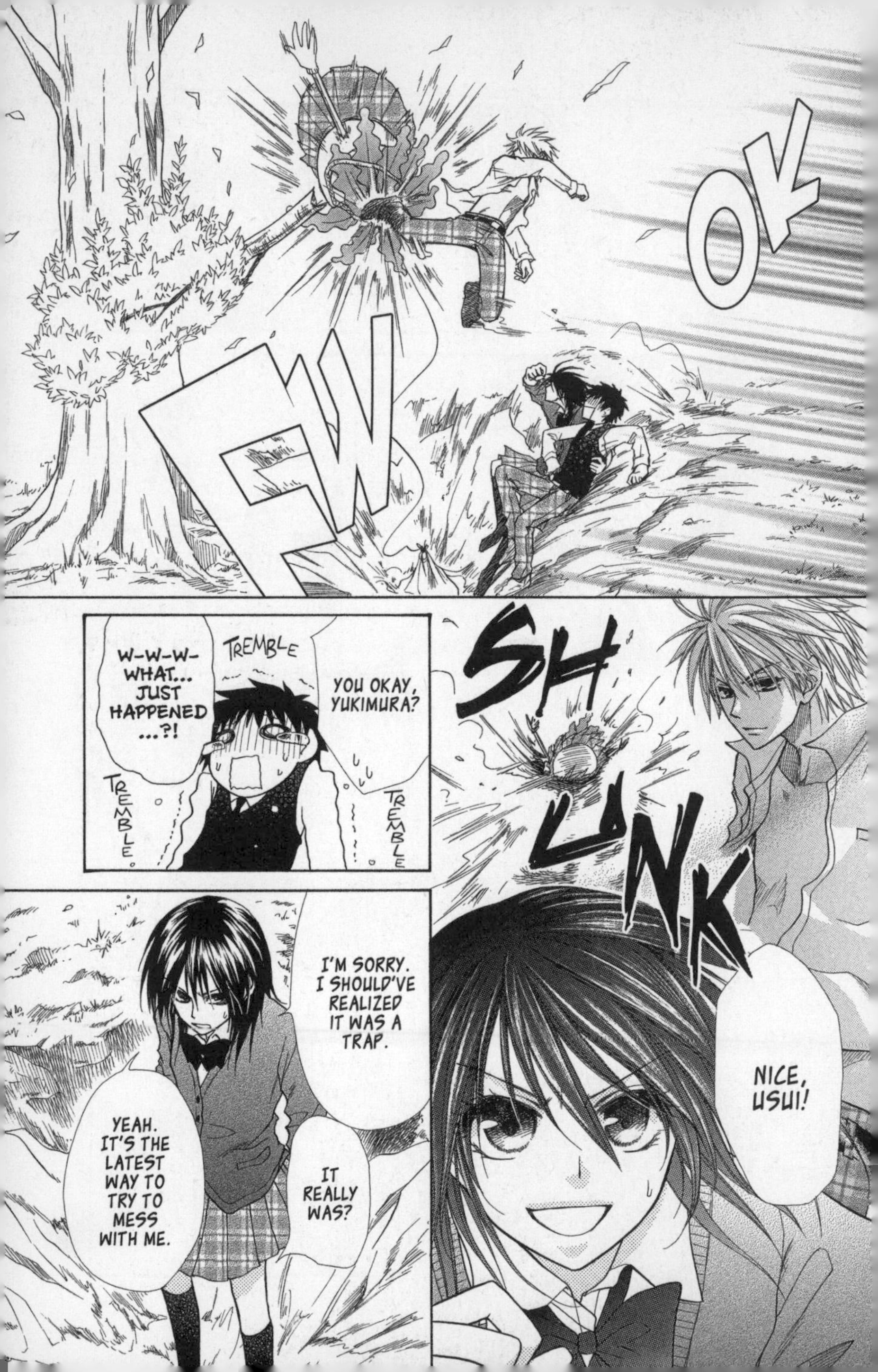
FW
OK
SHUNK
YOU OKAY, YUKIMURA?
TREMBLE
W-W-W-WHAT... JUST HAPPENED ...?!
TREMBLE
TREMBLE
NICE, USUI!
I'M SORRY. I SHOULD'VE REALIZED IT WAS A TRAP.
IT REALLY WAS?
YEAH. IT'S THE LATEST WAY TO TRY TO MESS WITH ME.

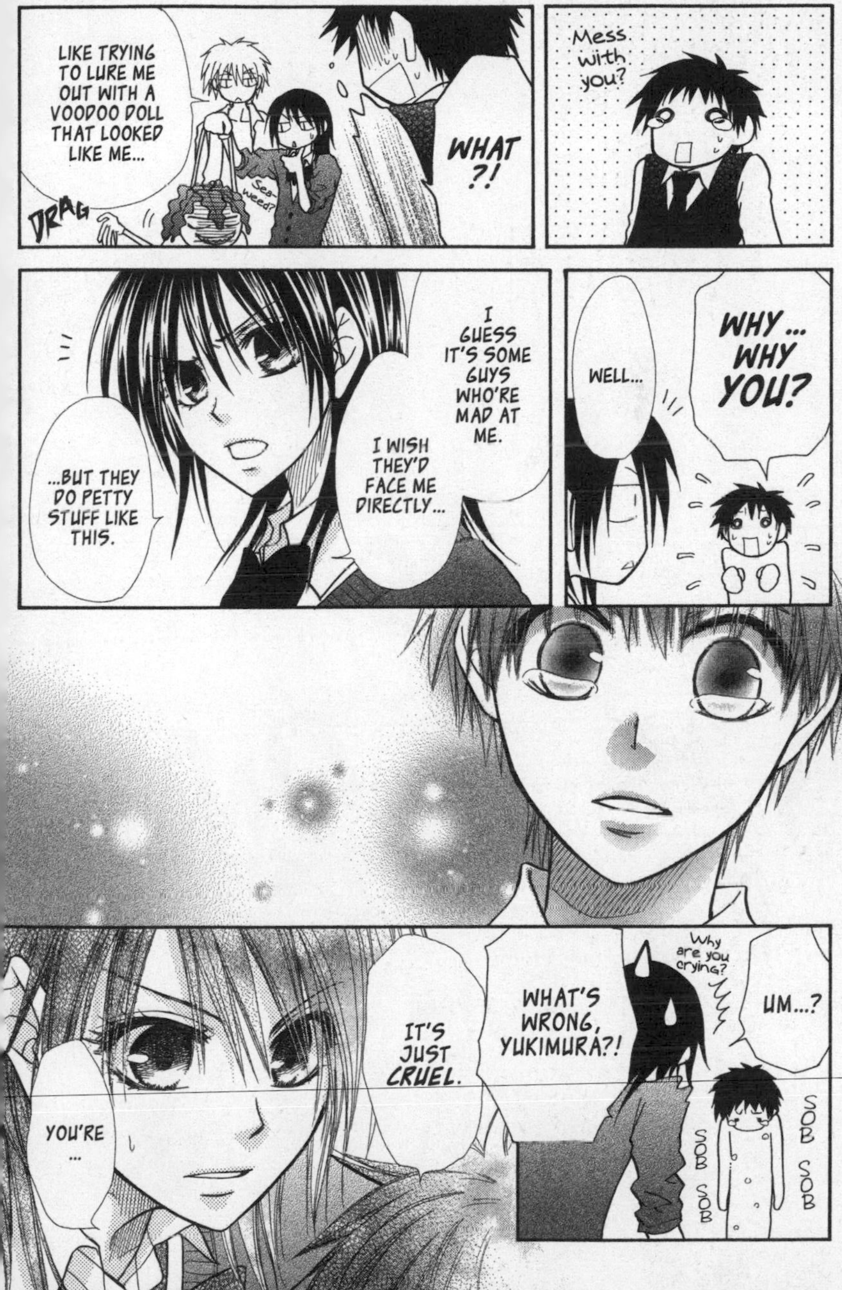
Mess with you?
WHAT ?!
LIKE TRYING TO LURE ME OUT WITH A VOODOO DOLL THAT LOOKED LIKE ME...
Sea-weed?
DRAG
WHY... WHY YOU?
WELL...
I GUESS IT'S SOME GUYS WHO'RE MAD AT ME.
I WISH THEY'D FACE ME DIRECTLY...
...BUT THEY DO PETTY STUFF LIKE THIS.
UM...?
Why are you crying?
SOB SOB
SOB SOB
WHAT'S WRONG, YUKIMURA?!
IT'S JUST CRUEL.
YOU'RE ...

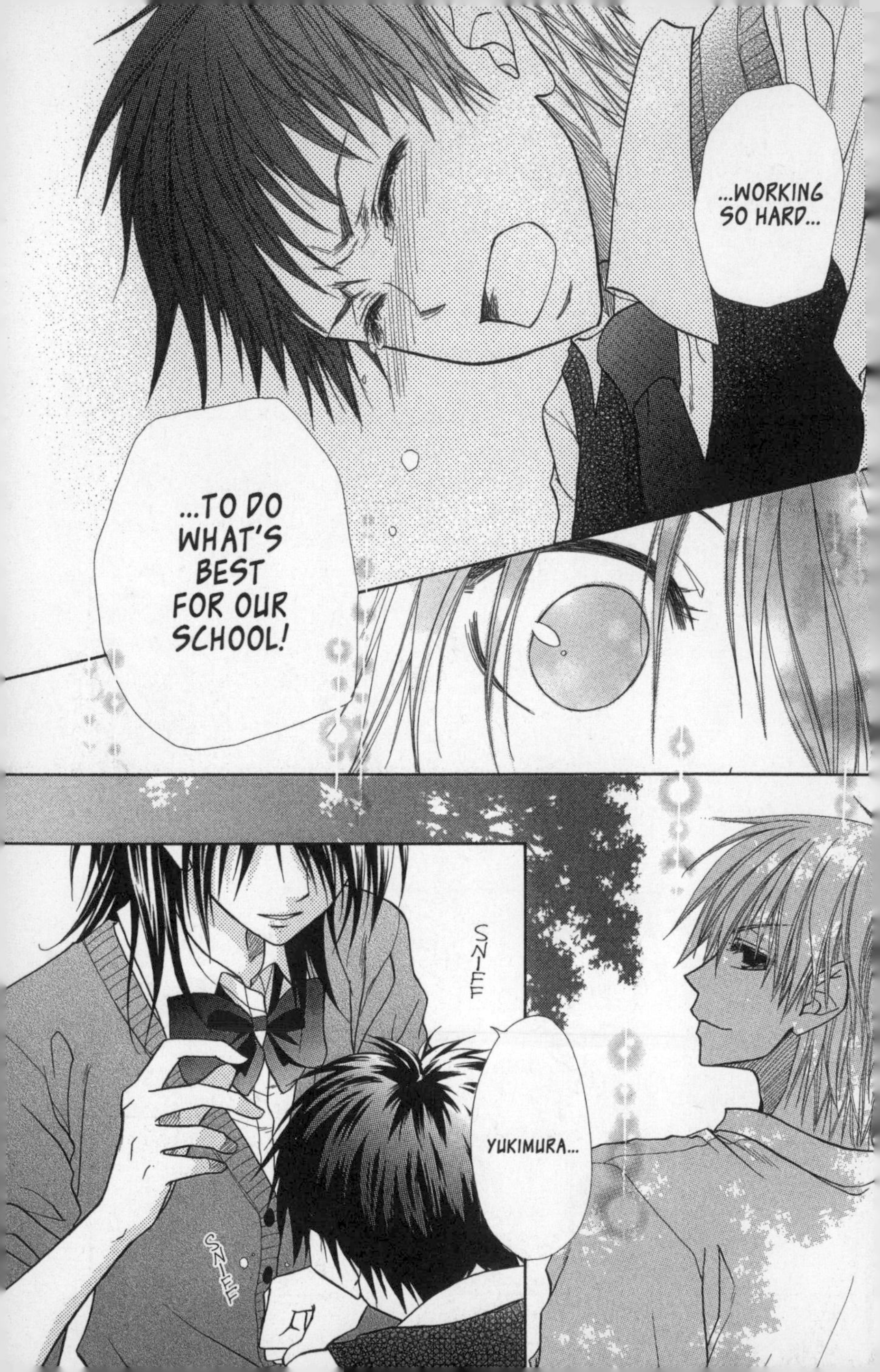
...WORKING SO HARD...
...TO DO WHAT'S BEST FOR OUR SCHOOL!
SNIFF
YUKIMURA...
SNIFF

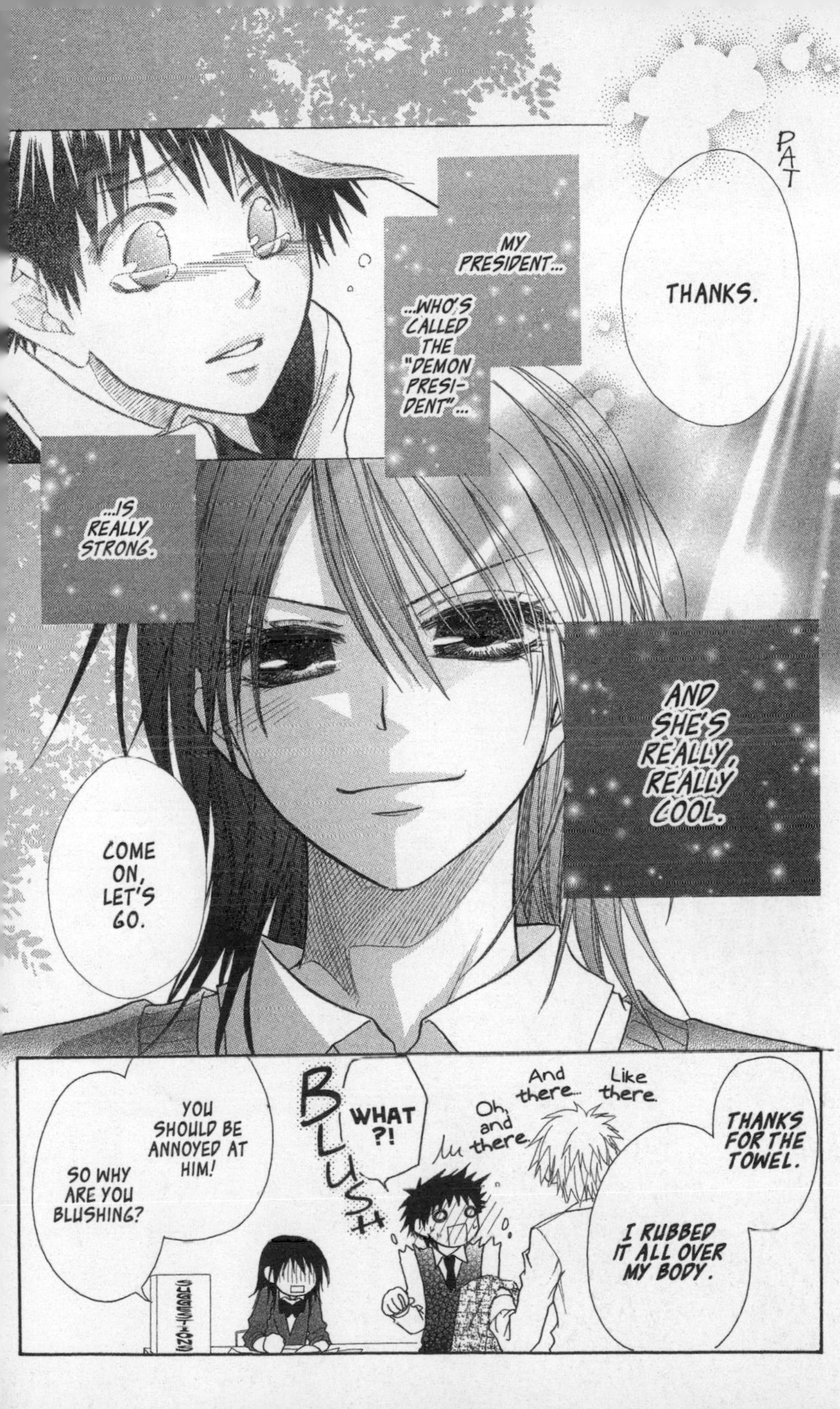
PAT
THANKS.
MY PRESIDENT...
...WHO'S CALLED THE "DEMON PRESIDENT"...
...IS REALLY STRONG.
AND SHE'S REALLY, REALLY COOL.
COME ON, LET'S GO.
THANKS FOR THE TOWEL.
I RUBBED IT ALL OVER MY BODY.
Like there.
And there...
Oh, and there.
WHAT?!
BLUSH
YOU SHOULD BE ANNOYED AT HIM!
SO WHY ARE YOU BLUSHING?

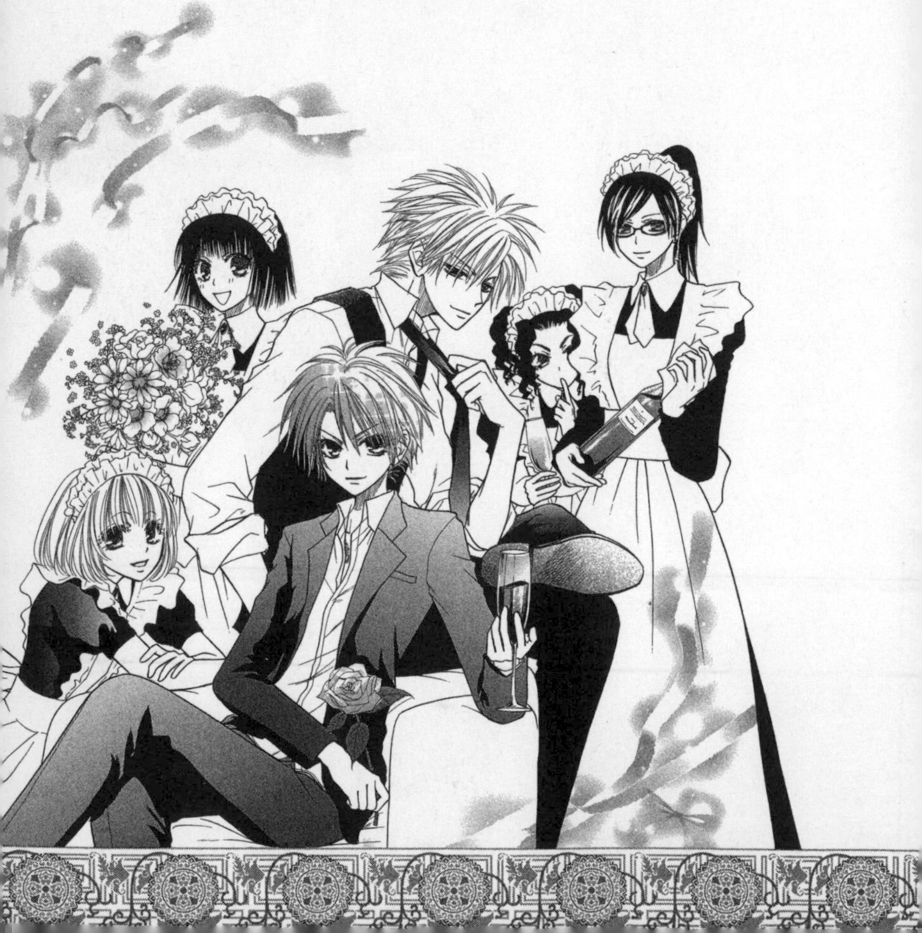

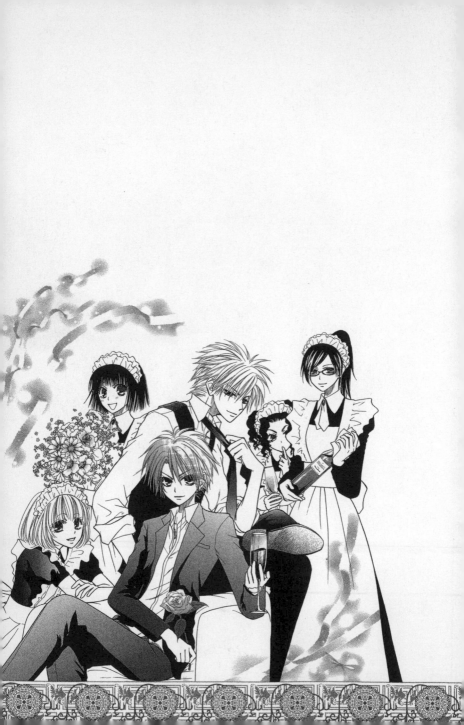

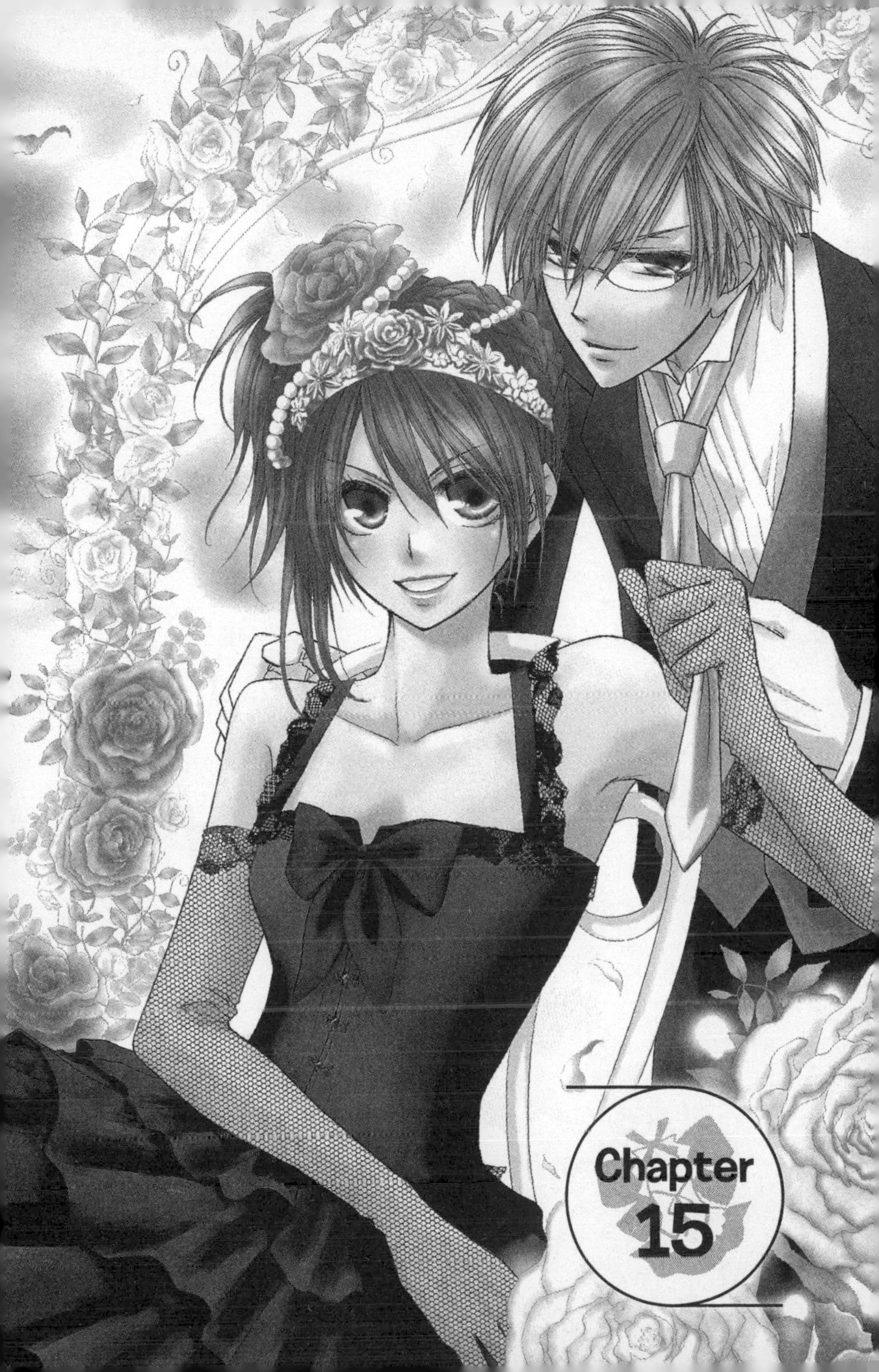
Chapter
15

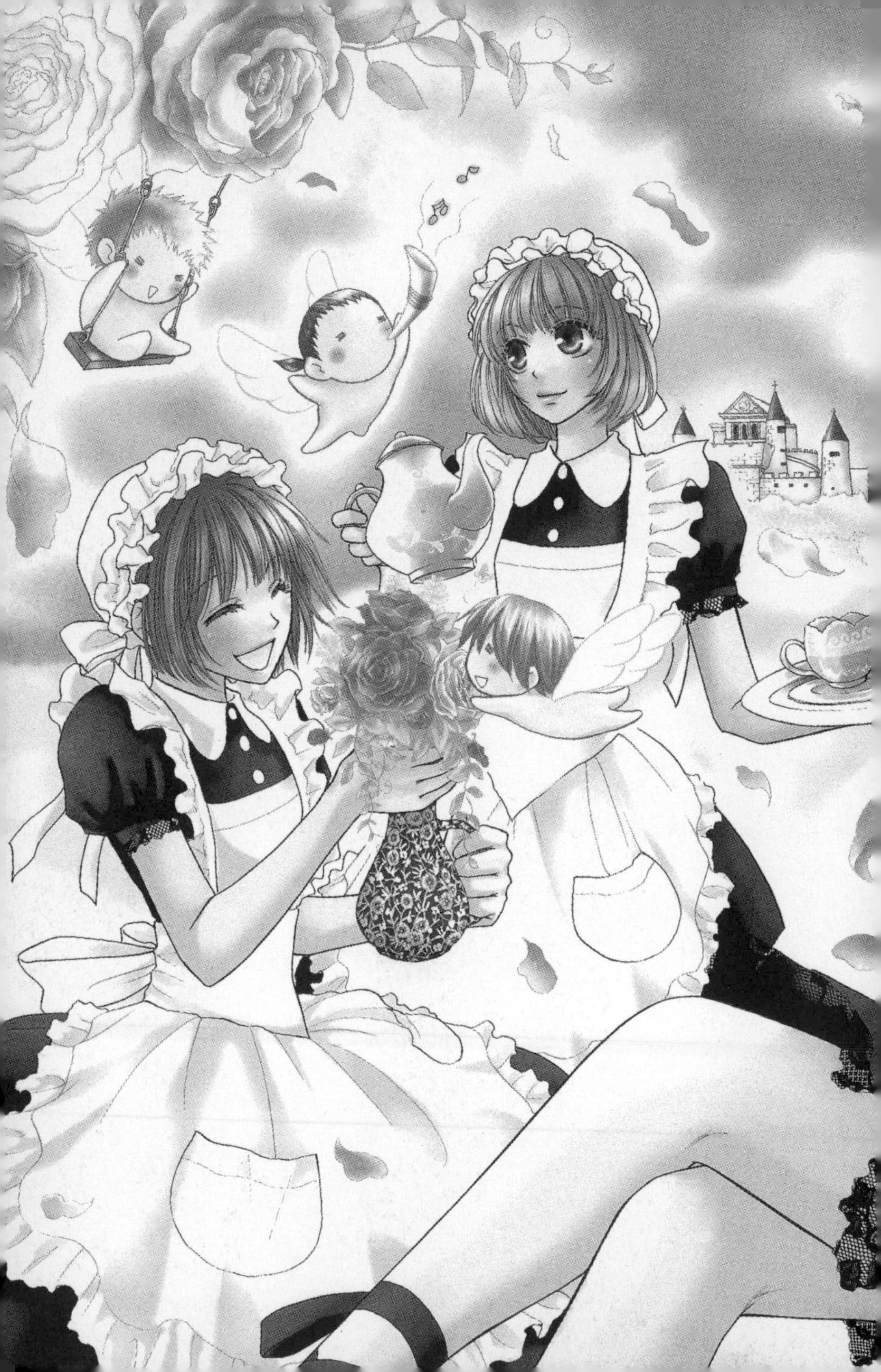

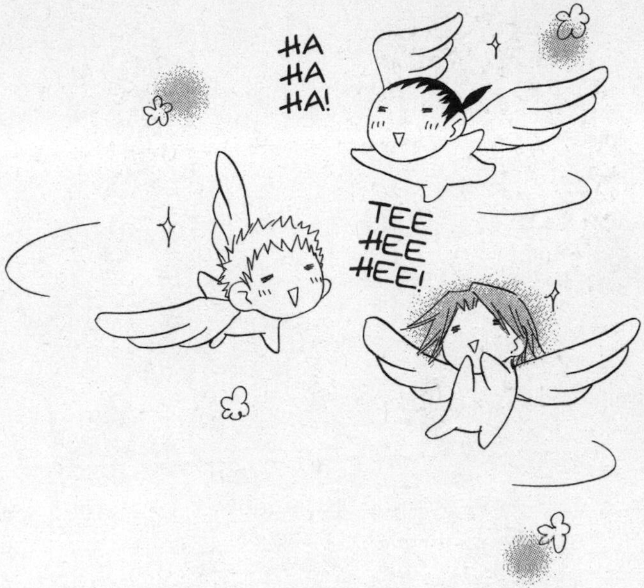
HA HA HA!
TEE HEE HEE!

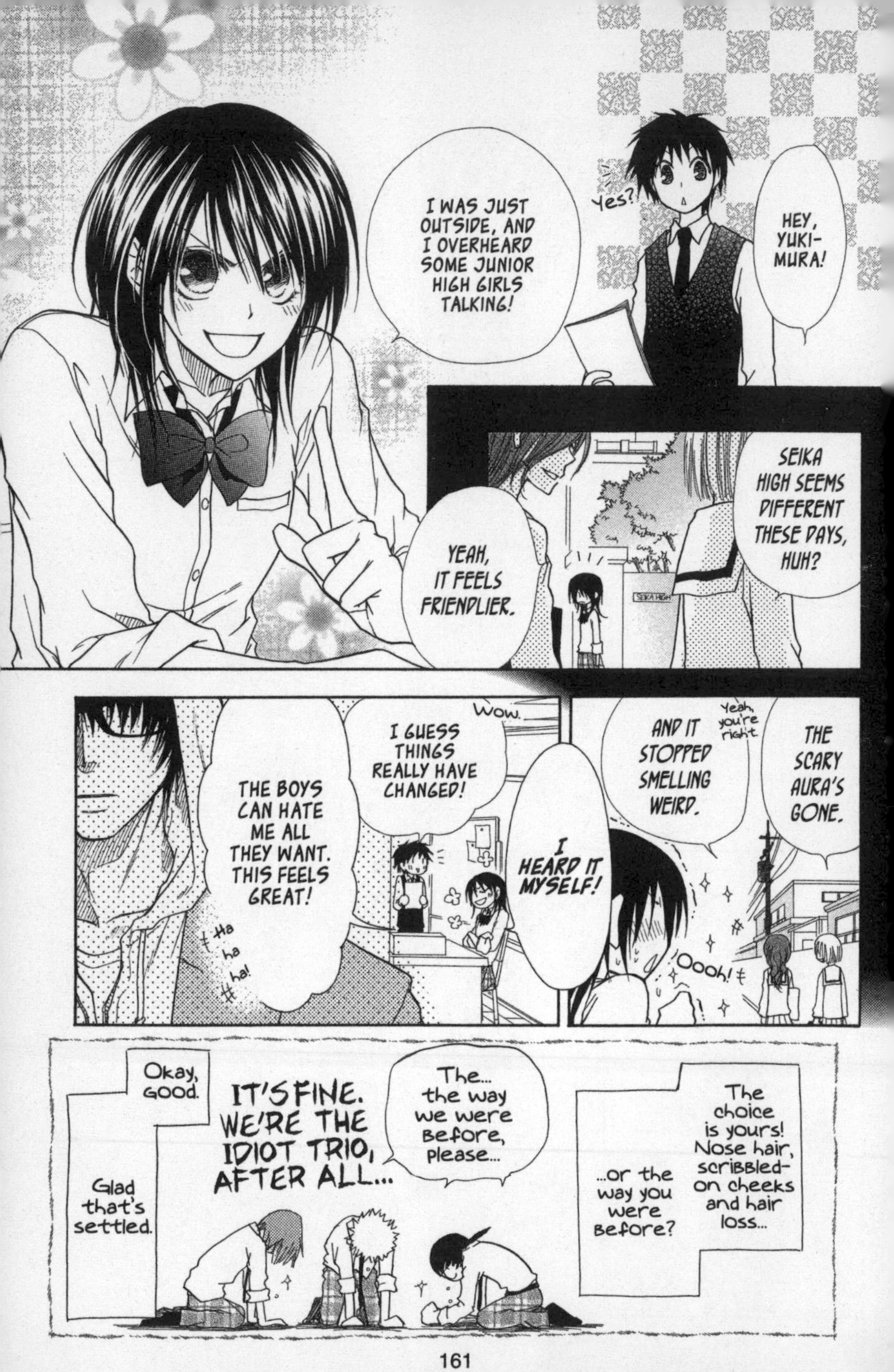
HEY, YUKI-MURA!
Yes?
SEIKA HIGH SEEMS DIFFERENT THESE DAYS, HUH?
YEAH, IT FEELS FRIENDLIER.
SEIKA HIGH
I WAS JUST OUTSIDE, AND I OVERHEARD SOME JUNIOR HIGH GIRLS TALKING!
THE SCARY AURA'S GONE.
Yeah, you're right.
AND IT STOPPED SMELLING WEIRD.
Oooh!
I HEARD IT MYSELF!
Wow.
I GUESS THINGS REALLY HAVE CHANGED!
THE BOYS CAN HATE ME ALL THEY WANT. THIS FEELS GREAT!
Ha ha ha!
The choice is yours! Nose hair, scribbled-on cheeks and hair loss...
...or the way you were before?
The... the way we were before, please...
IT'S FINE. WE'RE THE IDIOT TRIO, AFTER ALL...
Okay, good.
Glad that's settled.

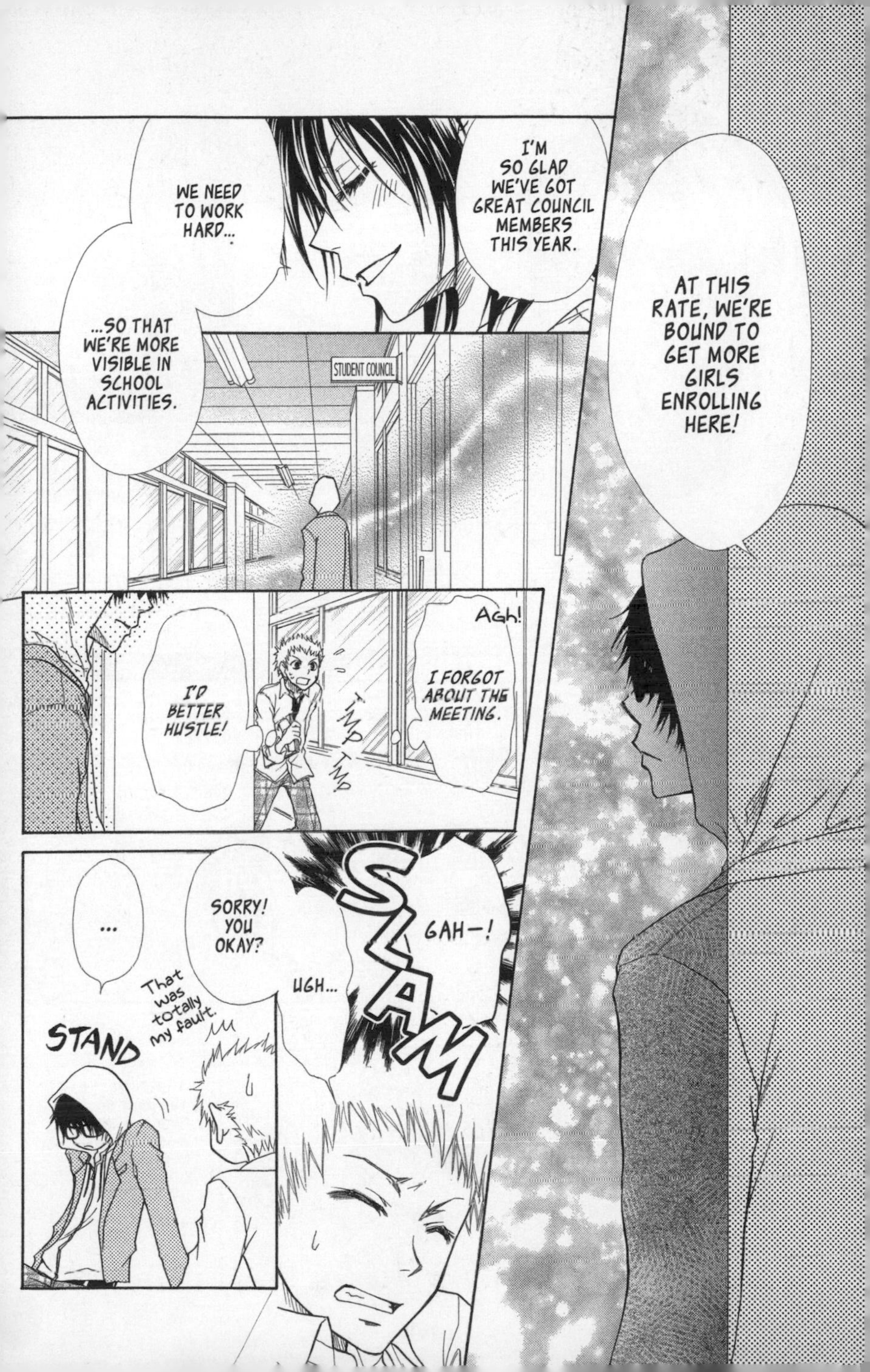
AT THIS RATE, WE'RE BOUND TO GET MORE GIRLS ENROLLING HERE!
I'M SO GLAD WE'VE GOT GREAT COUNCIL MEMBERS THIS YEAR.
WE NEED TO WORK HARD...
...SO THAT WE'RE MORE VISIBLE IN SCHOOL ACTIVITIES.
STUDENT COUNCIL
AGH!
I FORGOT ABOUT THE MEETING.
TMP TMP
I'D BETTER HUSTLE!
SLAM
GAH-!
UGH...
SORRY! YOU OKAY?
That was totally my fault.
...
STAND

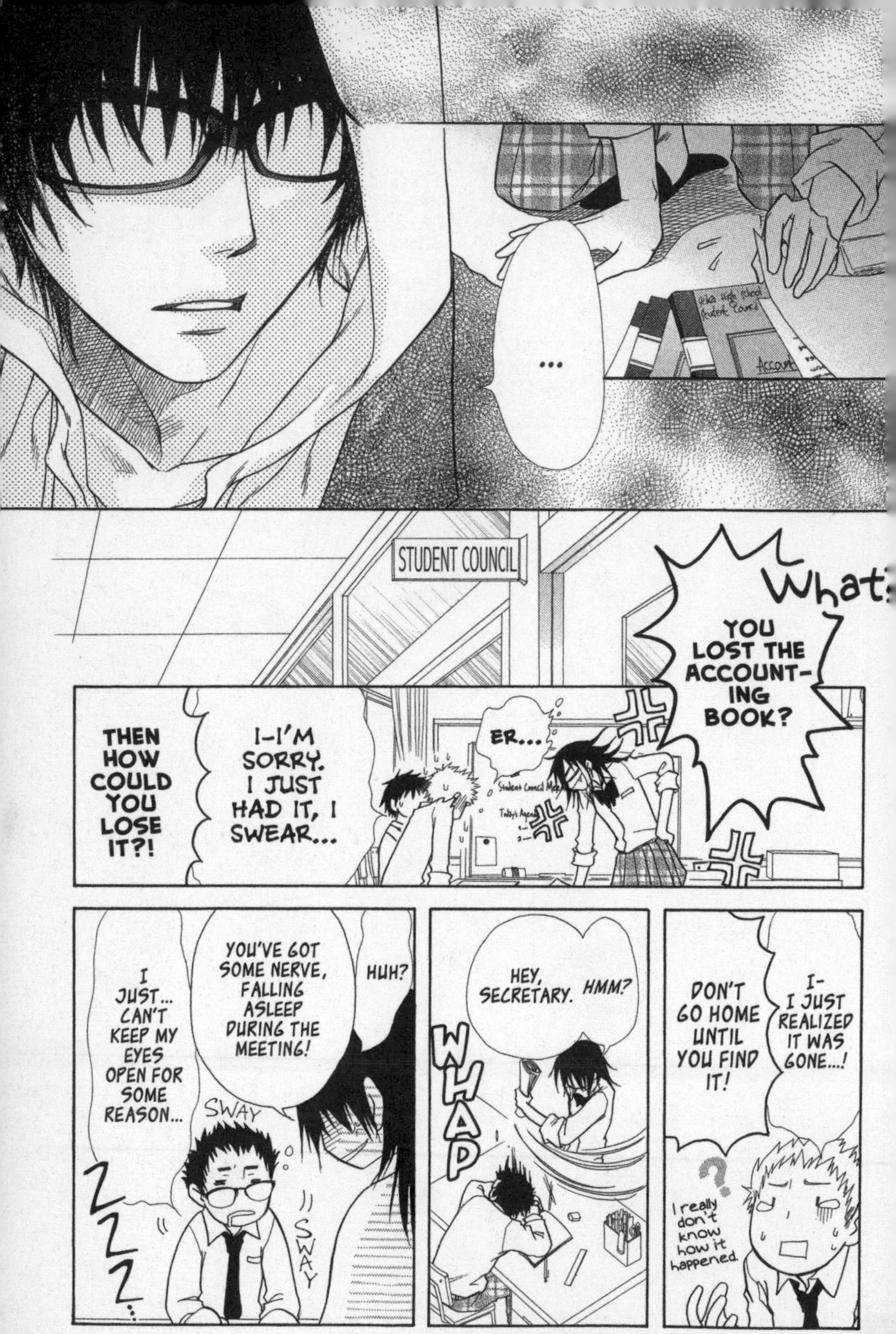
...
STUDENT COUNCIL
What
YOU LOST THE ACCOUNTING BOOK?
ER...
I-I'M SORRY. I JUST HAD IT, I SWEAR...
THEN HOW COULD YOU LOSE IT?!
I- I JUST REALIZED IT WAS GONE...!
DON'T GO HOME UNTIL YOU FIND IT!
I really don't know how it happened.
HMM?
HEY, SECRETARY.
WHAP
HUH?
YOU'VE GOT SOME NERVE, FALLING ASLEEP DURING THE MEETING!
SWAY
I JUST... CAN'T KEEP MY EYES OPEN FOR SOME REASON...
SWAY
ZZZ...

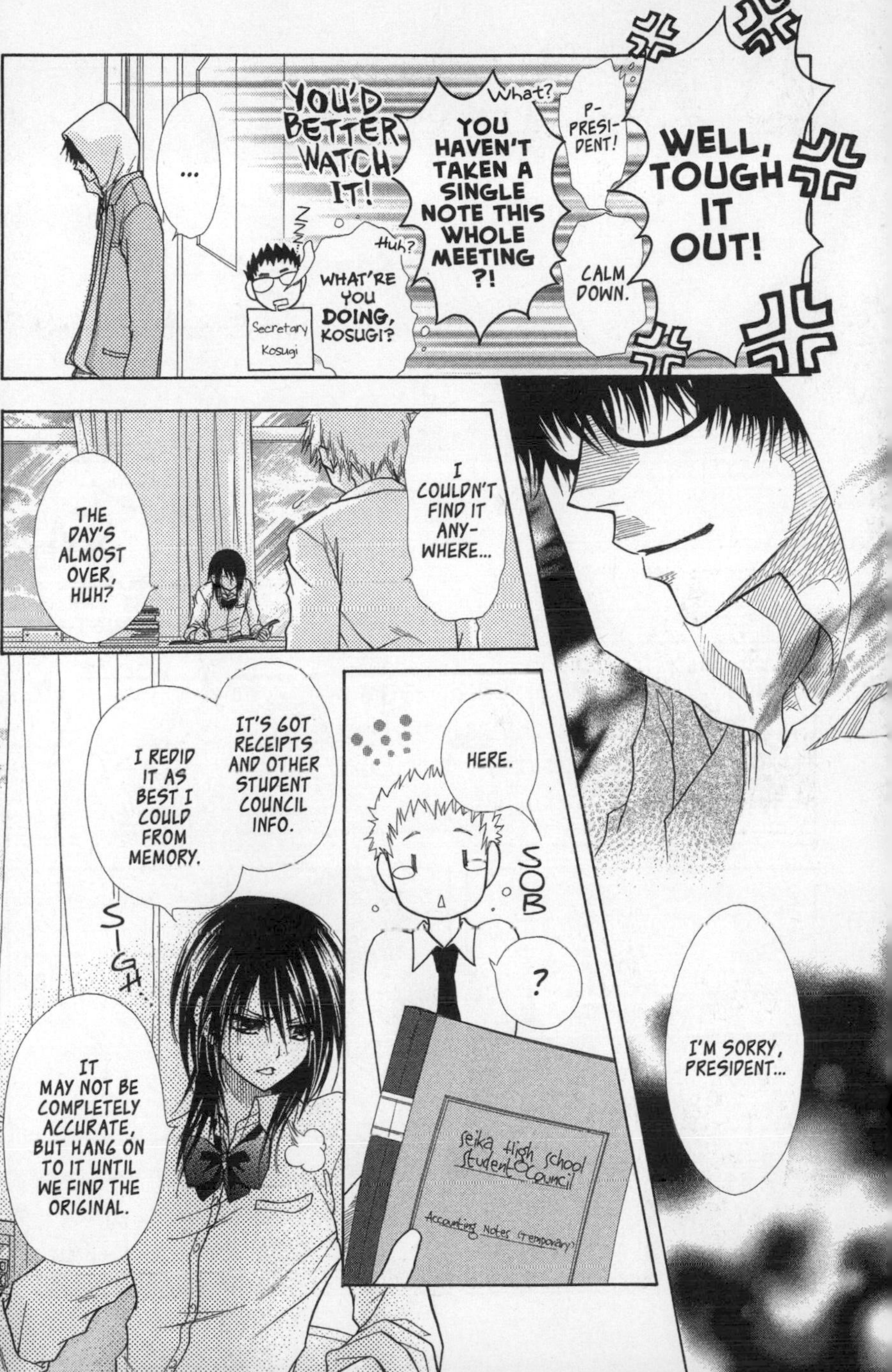
WELL, TOUGH IT OUT!
P-PRESIDENT!
CALM DOWN.
What?
YOU HAVEN'T TAKEN A SINGLE NOTE THIS WHOLE MEETING?!
YOU'D BETTER WATCH IT!
ZZZ
Huh?
WHAT'RE YOU DOING, KOSUGI?
Secretary Kosugi
...
I'M SORRY, PRESIDENT...
I COULDN'T FIND IT ANYWHERE...
THE DAY'S ALMOST OVER, HUH?
HERE.
SOB
?
Seika High School Student Council
Accounting Notes (Temporary)
IT'S GOT RECEIPTS AND OTHER STUDENT COUNCIL INFO.
I REDID IT AS BEST I COULD FROM MEMORY.
SIGH...
IT MAY NOT BE COMPLETELY ACCURATE, BUT HANG ON TO IT UNTIL WE FIND THE ORIGINAL.

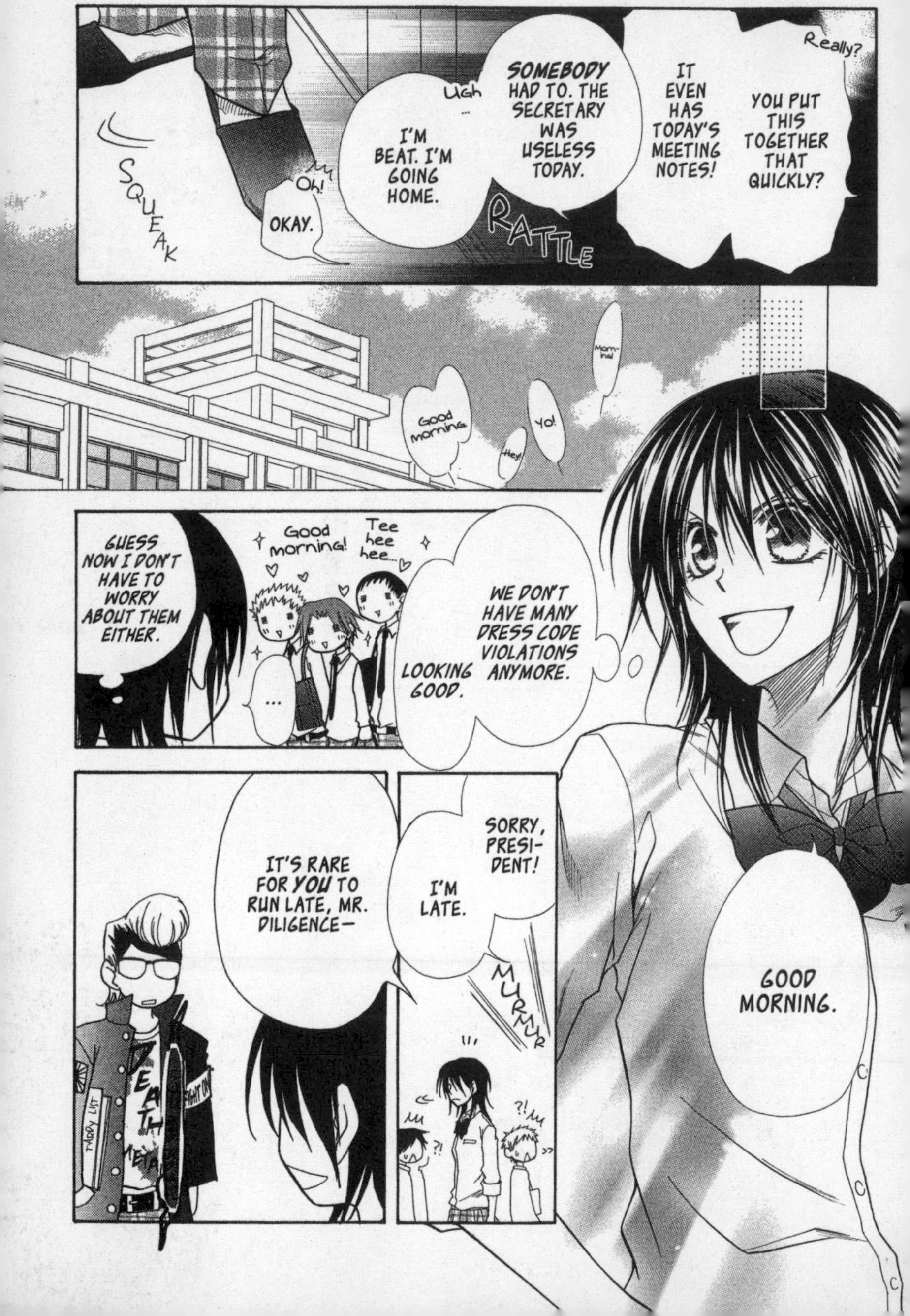
Really?
YOU PUT THIS TOGETHER THAT QUICKLY?
IT EVEN HAS TODAY'S MEETING NOTES!
RATTLE
SOMEBODY HAD TO. THE SECRETARY WAS USELESS TODAY.
Ugh...
I'M BEAT. I'M GOING HOME.
Oh!
OKAY.
SQUEAK
Morn-ing!
Yo!
Hey!
Good morning
GOOD MORNING.
WE DON'T HAVE MANY DRESS CODE VIOLATIONS ANYMORE.
LOOKING GOOD.
Tee hee hee...
Good morning!
GUESS NOW I DON'T HAVE TO WORRY ABOUT THEM EITHER.
...
SORRY, PRESIDENT!
I'M LATE.
MURMUR
IT'S RARE FOR YOU TO RUN LATE, MR. DILIGENCE—

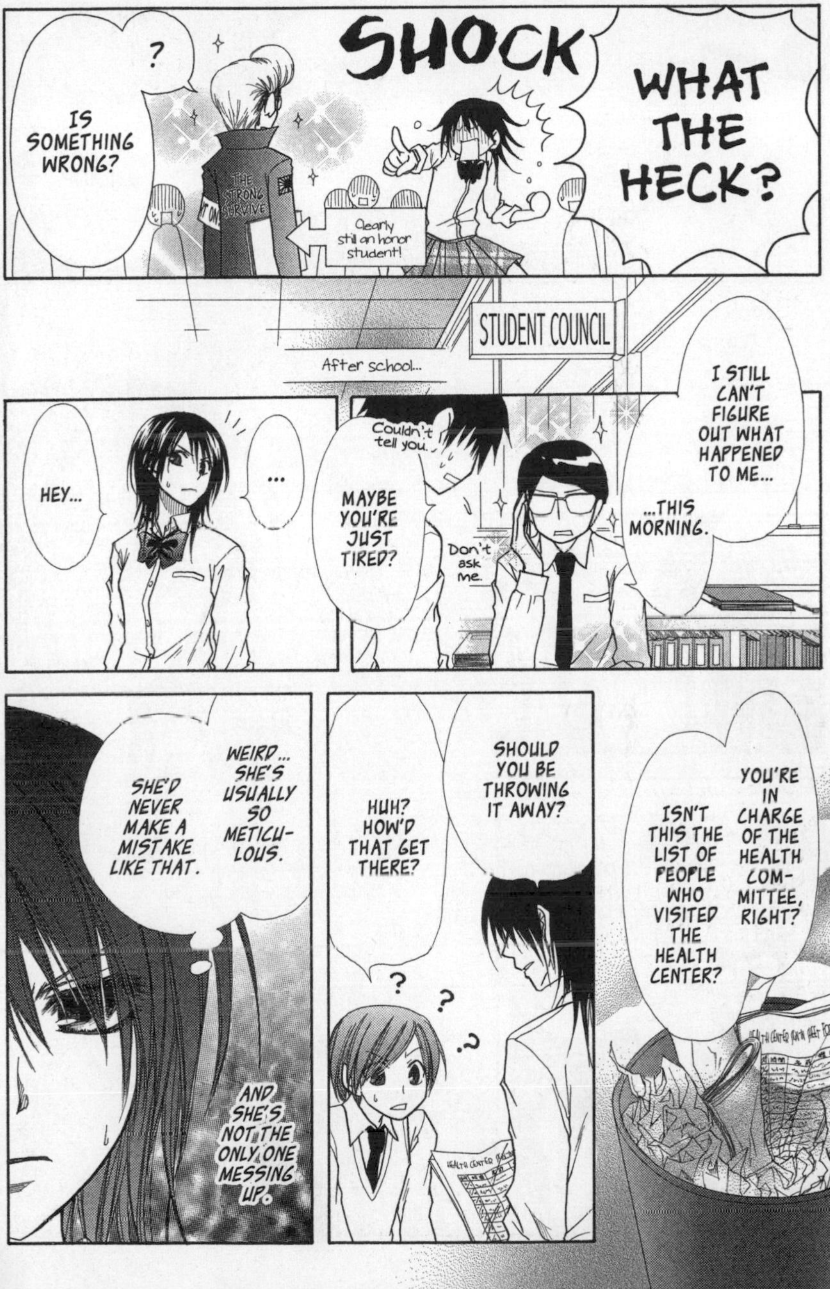
WHAT THE HECK?
SHOCK
Clearly still an honor student!
THE STRONG SURVIVE
?
IS SOMETHING WRONG?
STUDENT COUNCIL
After school...
I STILL CAN'T FIGURE OUT WHAT HAPPENED TO ME...
...THIS MORNING.
Couldn't tell you.
MAYBE YOU'RE JUST TIRED?
Don't ask me.
...
HEY...
YOU'RE IN CHARGE OF THE HEALTH COMMITTEE, RIGHT?
ISN'T THIS THE LIST OF PEOPLE WHO VISITED THE HEALTH CENTER?
SHOULD YOU BE THROWING IT AWAY?
HUH? HOW'D THAT GET THERE?
WEIRD... SHE'S USUALLY SO METICULOUS.
SHE'D NEVER MAKE A MISTAKE LIKE THAT.
AND SHE'S NOT THE ONLY ONE MESSING UP.

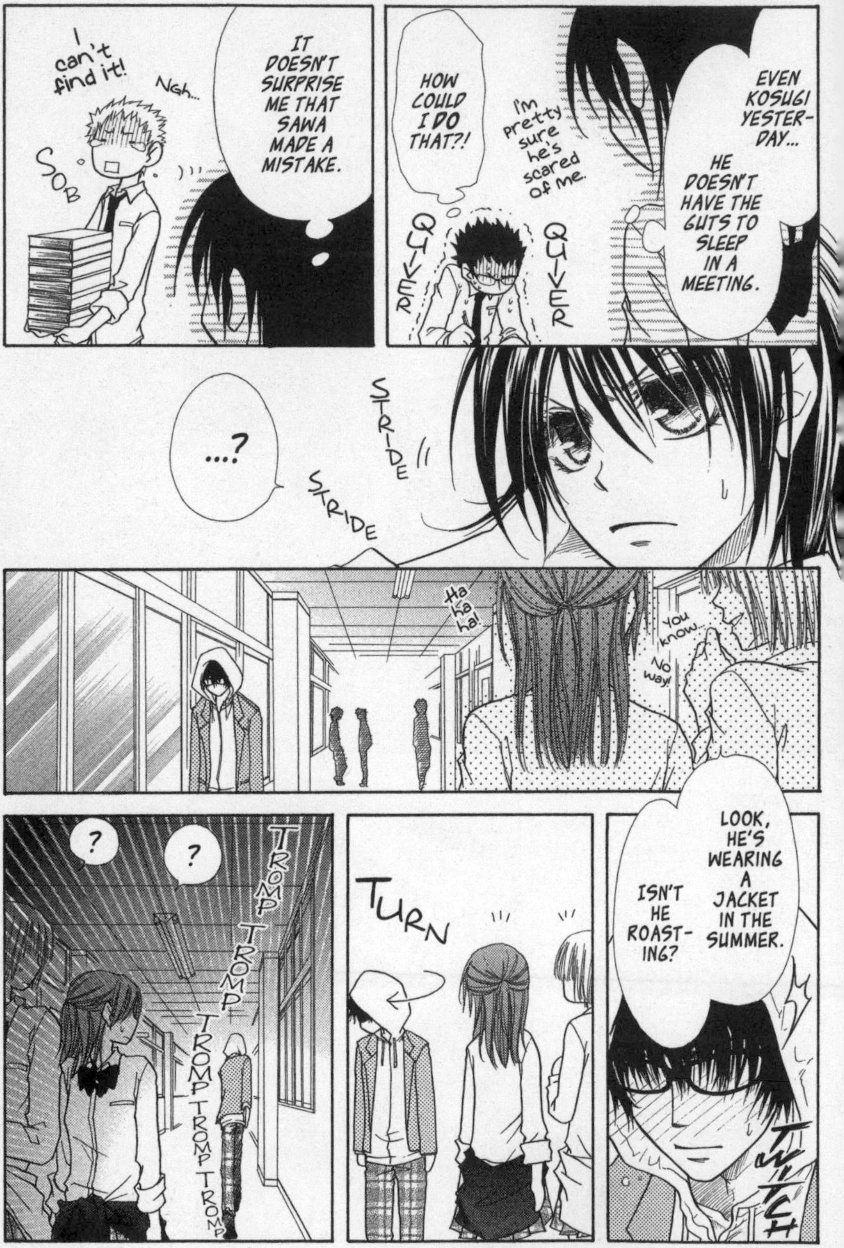
EVEN KOSUGI YESTER-DAY...
HE DOESN'T HAVE THE GUTS TO SLEEP IN A MEETING.
I'm pretty sure he's scared of me.
HOW COULD I DO THAT?!
QUIVER
QUIVER
IT DOESN'T SURPRISE ME THAT SAWA MADE A MISTAKE.
Ngh...
I can't find it!
SOB
STRIDE
STRIDE
...?
You know...
No way!
Ha ha ha!
LOOK, HE'S WEARING A JACKET IN THE SUMMER.
ISN'T HE ROASTING?
TWITCH
TURN
?
?
TROMP TROMP TROMP TROMP TROMP

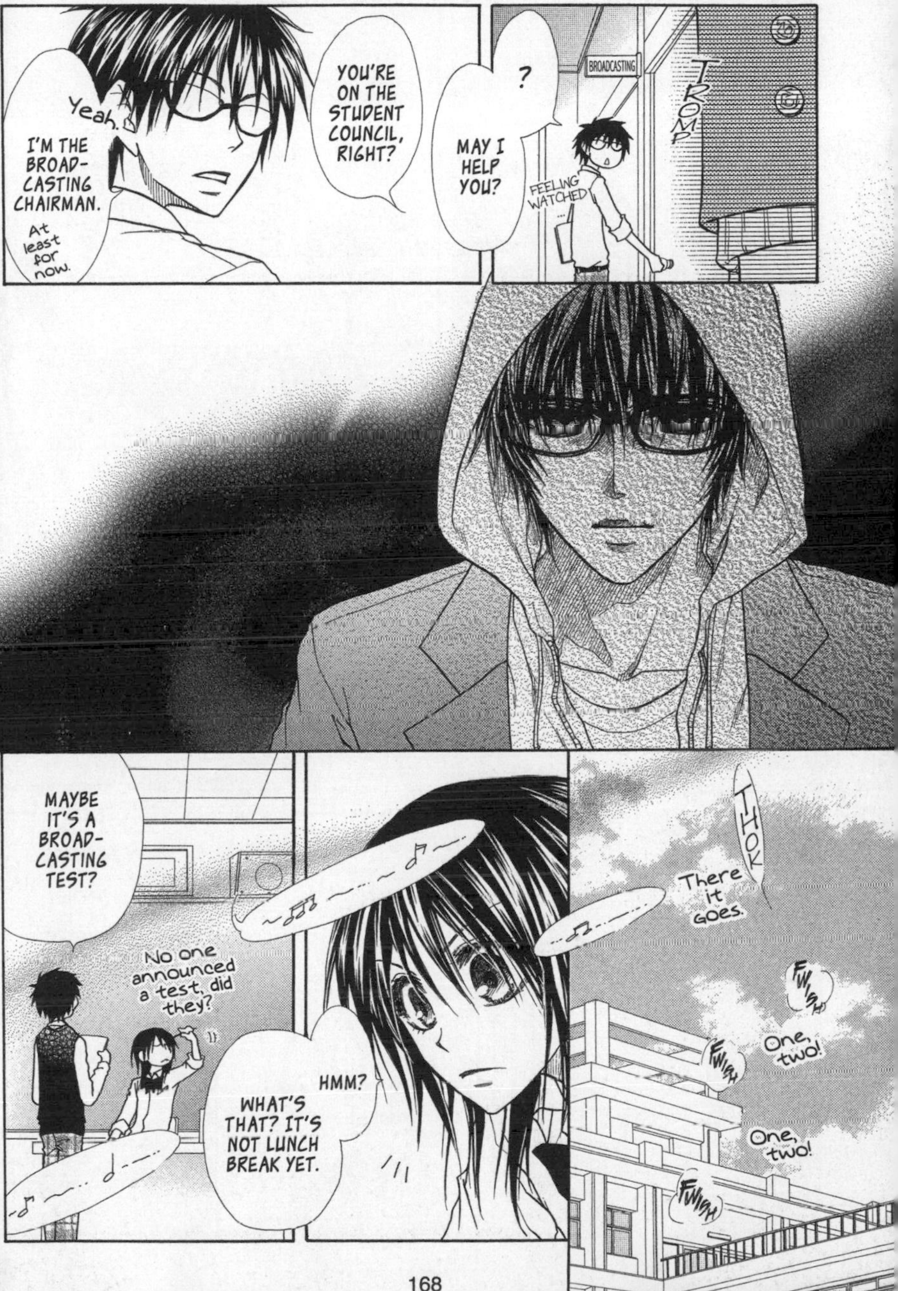
?
MAY I HELP YOU?
BROADCASTING
TROMP
FEELING WATCHED...
YOU'RE ON THE STUDENT COUNCIL, RIGHT?
Yeah.
I'M THE BROAD-CASTING CHAIRMAN.
At least for now.
THOK
There it goes.
FWISH
One, two!
FWISH
One, two!
FWISH
HMM?
WHAT'S THAT? IT'S NOT LUNCH BREAK YET.
MAYBE IT'S A BROAD-CASTING TEST?
No one announced a test, did they?

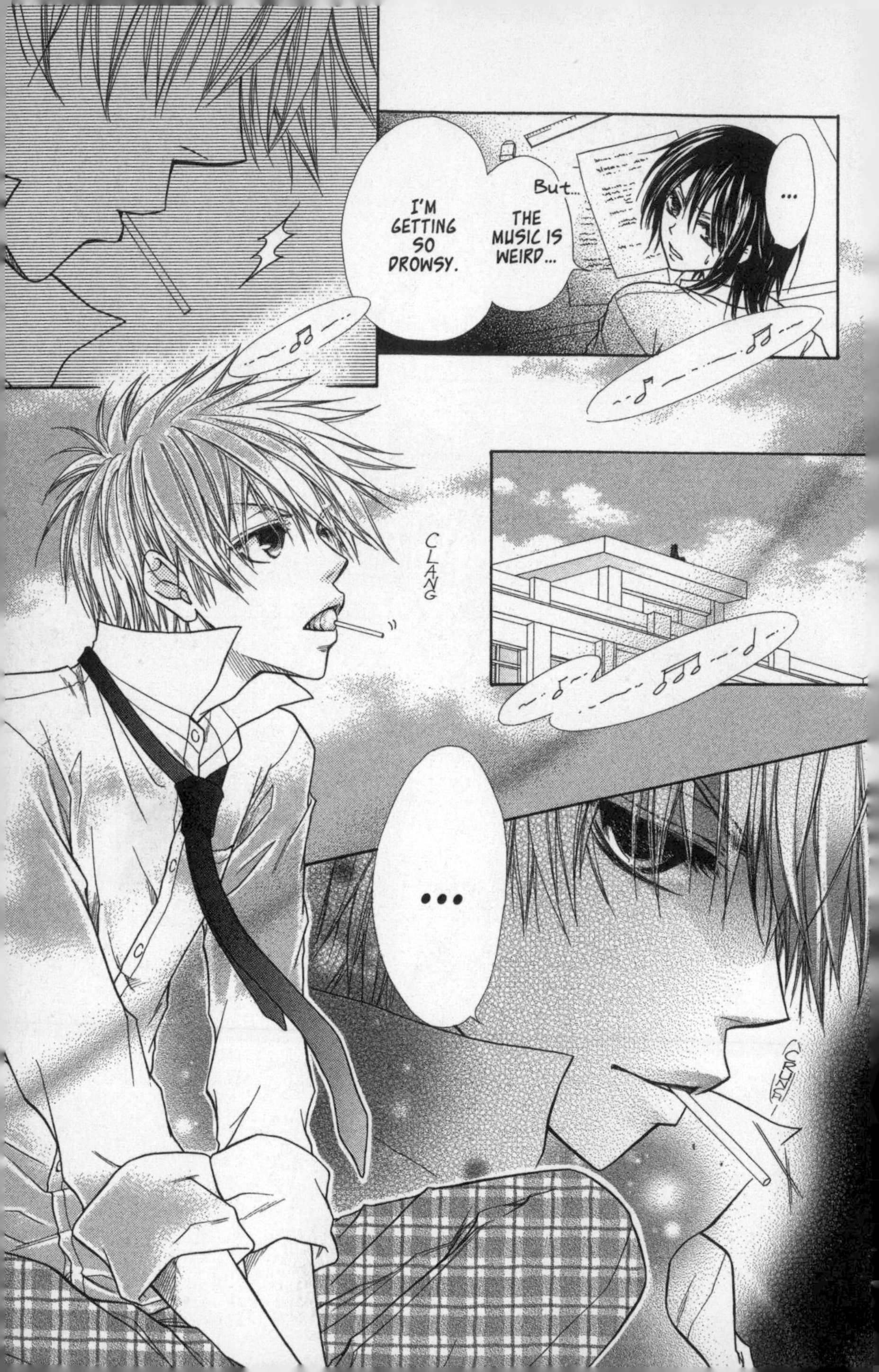
...
But...
THE MUSIC IS WEIRD...
I'M GETTING SO DROWSY.
CLANG
...
CRUNCH

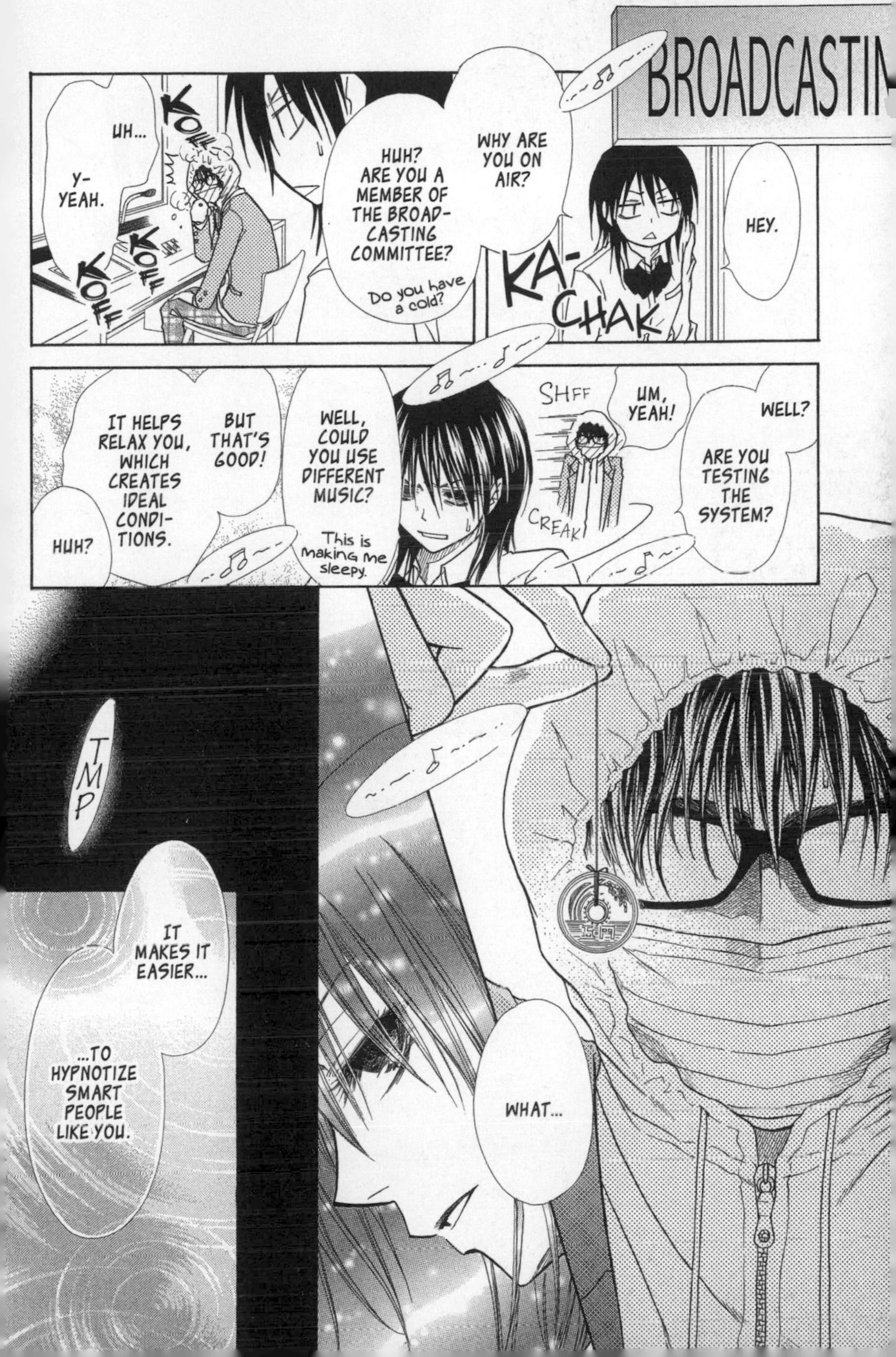
BROADCASTIN
HEY.
KA-CHAK
WHY ARE YOU ON AIR?
HUH? ARE YOU A MEMBER OF THE BROAD-CASTING COMMITTEE?
Do you have a cold?
KOFF
KOFF KOFF KOFF
UH...
Y-YEAH.
WELL?
ARE YOU TESTING THE SYSTEM?
UM, YEAH!
SHFF
CREAK
WELL, COULD YOU USE DIFFERENT MUSIC?
This is making me sleepy.
BUT THAT'S GOOD!
IT HELPS RELAX YOU, WHICH CREATES IDEAL CONDI-TIONS.
HUH?
WHAT...
TMP
IT MAKES IT EASIER...
...TO HYPNOTIZE SMART PEOPLE LIKE YOU.

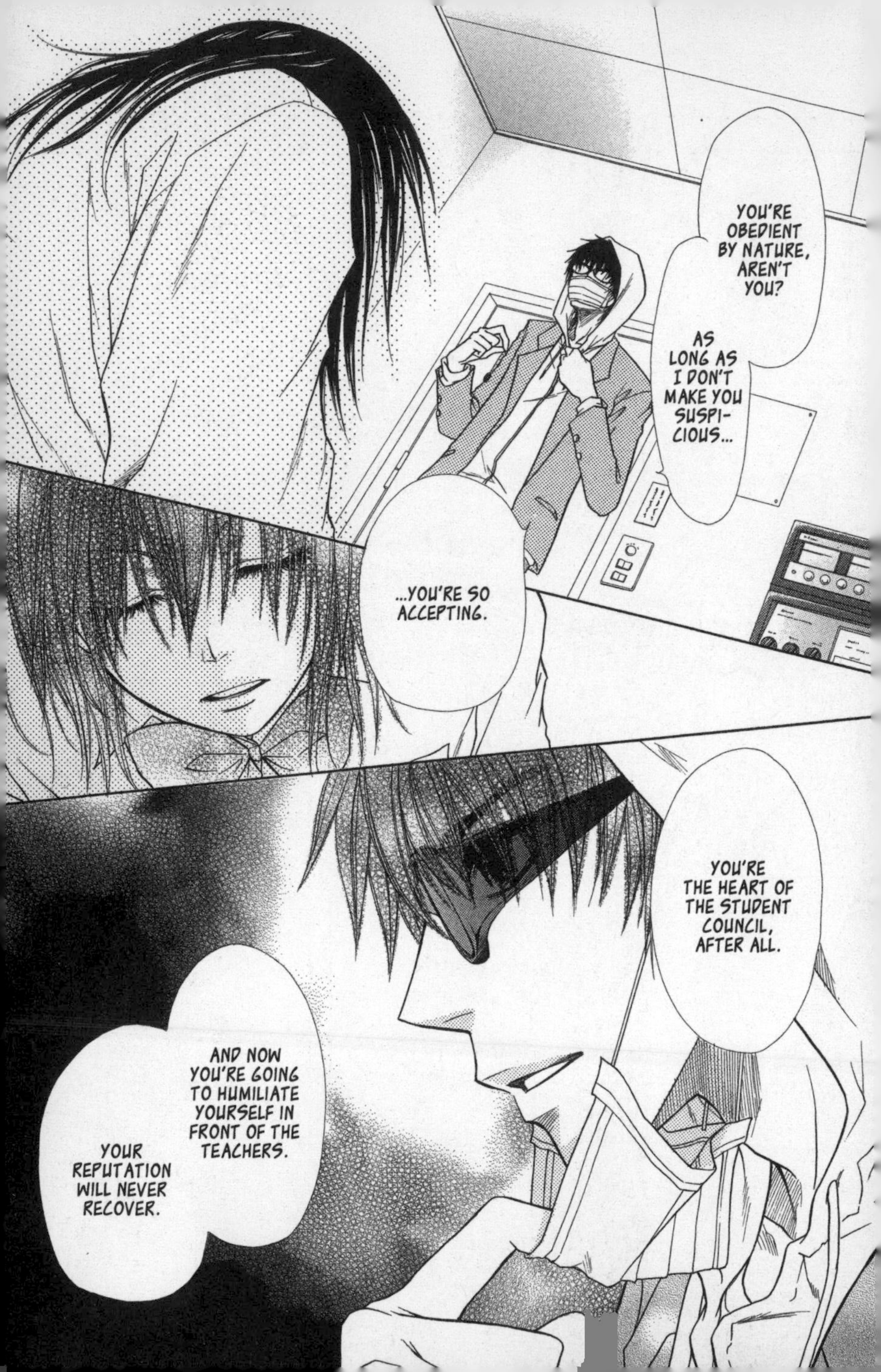
YOU'RE OBEDIENT BY NATURE, AREN'T YOU?
AS LONG AS I DON'T MAKE YOU SUSPI-CIOUS...
...YOU'RE SO ACCEPTING.
YOU'RE THE HEART OF THE STUDENT COUNCIL, AFTER ALL.
AND NOW YOU'RE GOING TO HUMILIATE YOURSELF IN FRONT OF THE TEACHERS.
YOUR REPUTATION WILL NEVER RECOVER.

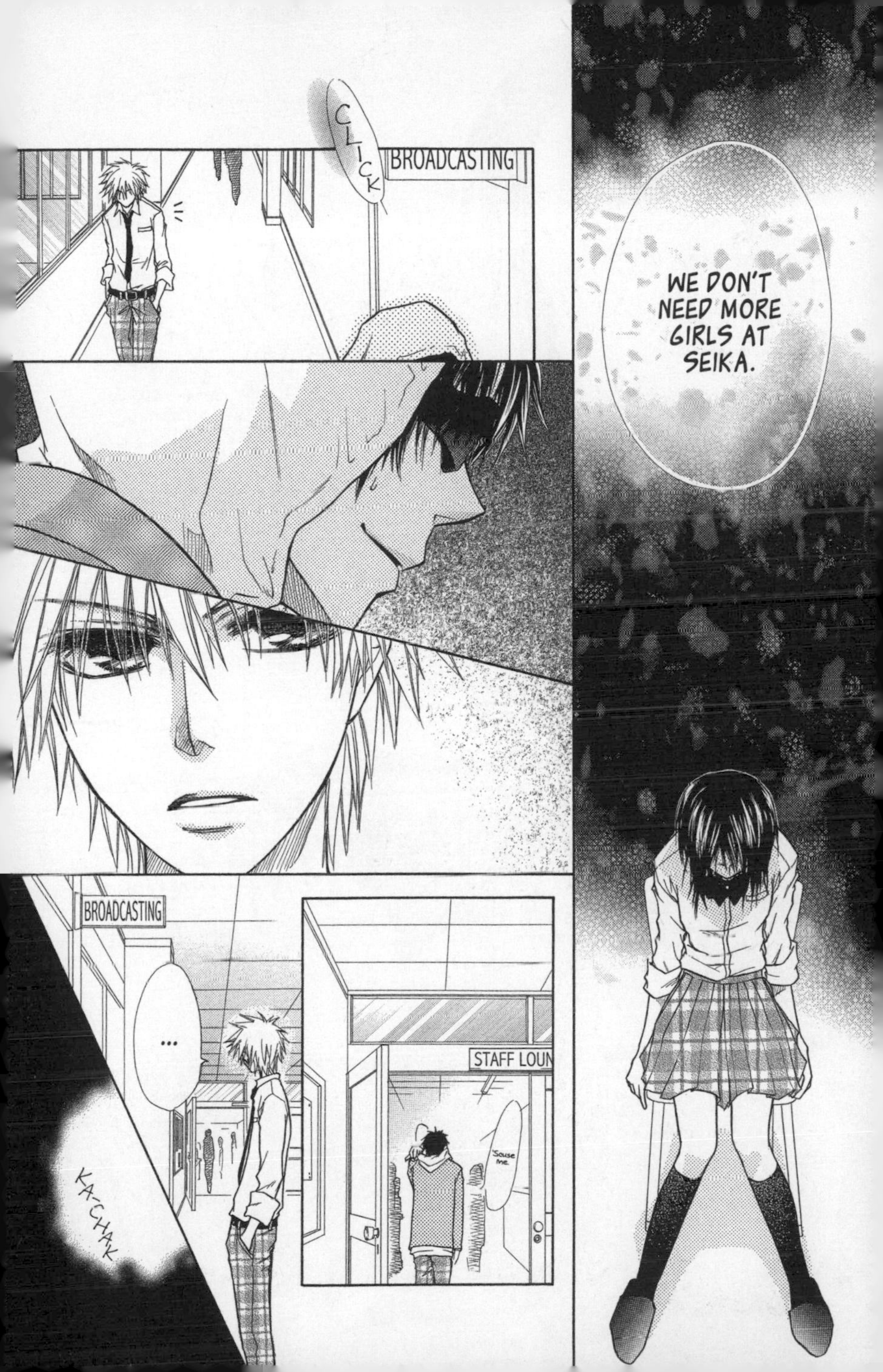
WE DON'T NEED MORE GIRLS AT SEIKA.
CLICK
BROADCASTING
STAFF LOUN
'Scouse me.
BROADCASTING
...
KA-CHAK

WORDS OF APPRECIATION!

Hi, it's Fujiwara!

Thanks again for continuing to read my weirdly-named manga. It's been over a year since it became a series, and I've started receiving more fan mail. Every single letter thrills me, but I get especially excited when I see such amazing *Maid-Sama!* fan art.

It's interesting that most drawings of Usui show him smiling, while Misaki usually looks mad. Looks like you all understand them pretty well!

Whether you send artwork or not, I'm thrilled by all the mail, so please keep it coming!

I'll see you again at the end of this volume...

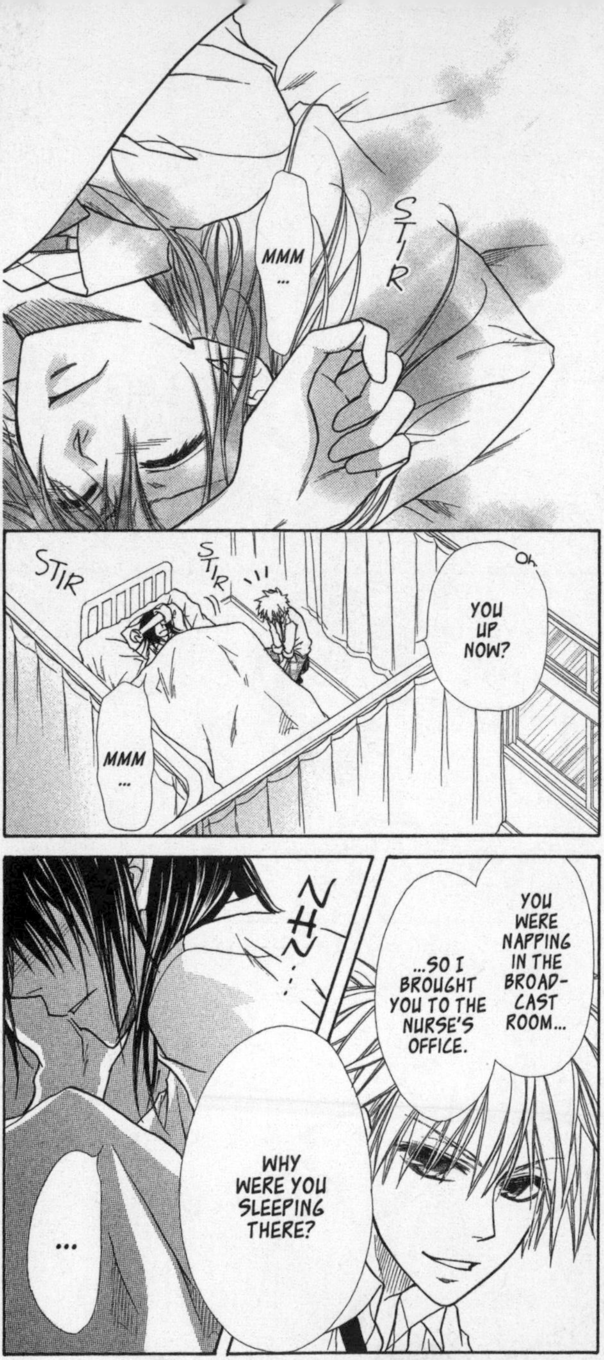
STIR
MMM...
Oh
YOU UP NOW?
STIR
STIR
MMM...
YOU WERE NAPPING IN THE BROADCAST ROOM...
...SO I BROUGHT YOU TO THE NURSE'S OFFICE.
WHY WERE YOU SLEEPING THERE?
NHN..
...

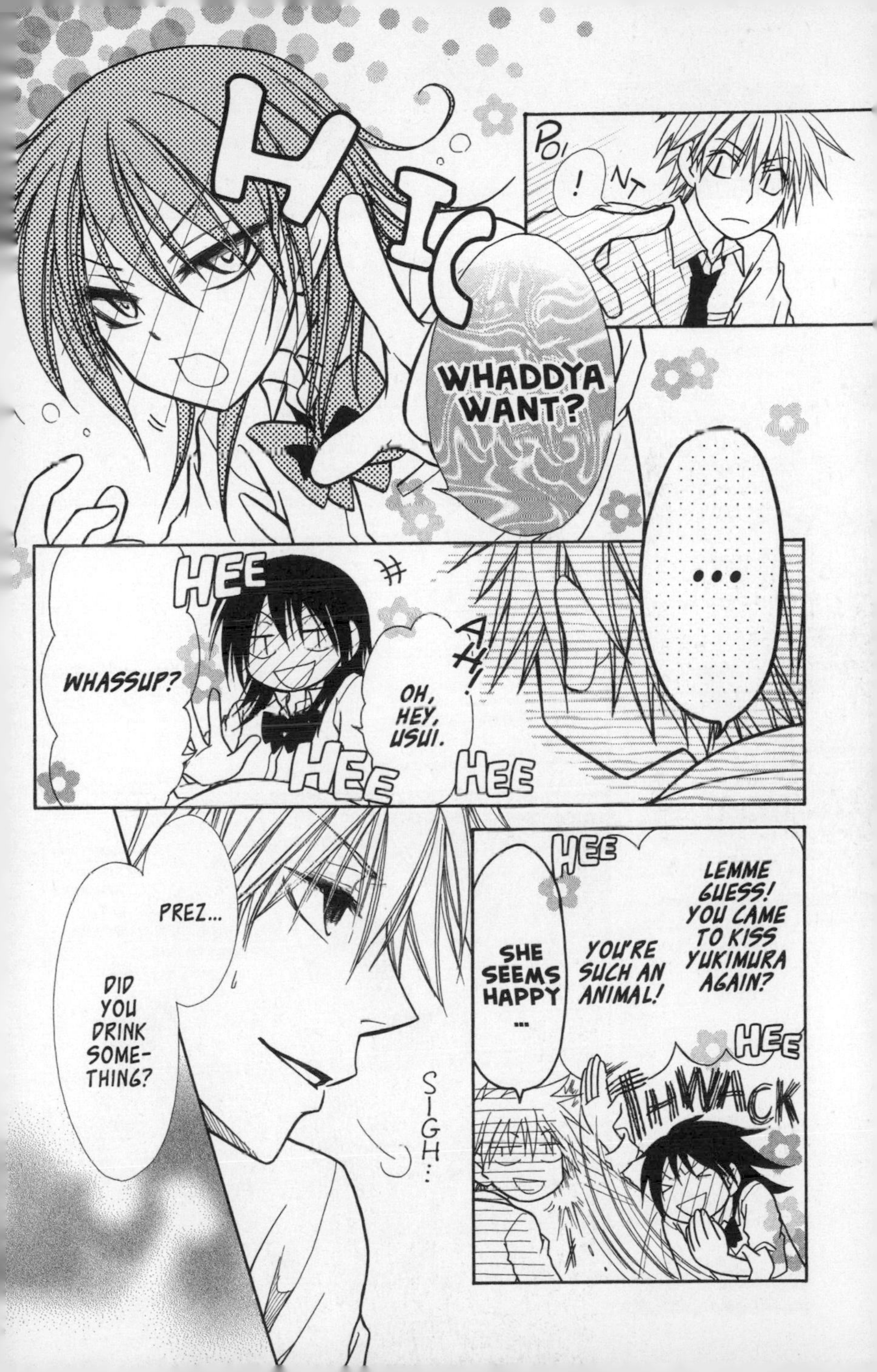
POINT
!
HIC
WHADDYA WANT?
...
AH!
OH, HEY, USUI.
HEE
WHASSUP?
HEE
HEE
HEE
LEMME GUESS! YOU CAME TO KISS YUKIMURA AGAIN?
YOU'RE SUCH AN ANIMAL!
SHE SEEMS HAPPY ...
HEE
THWACK
PREZ...
DID YOU DRINK SOME-THING?
SIGH...

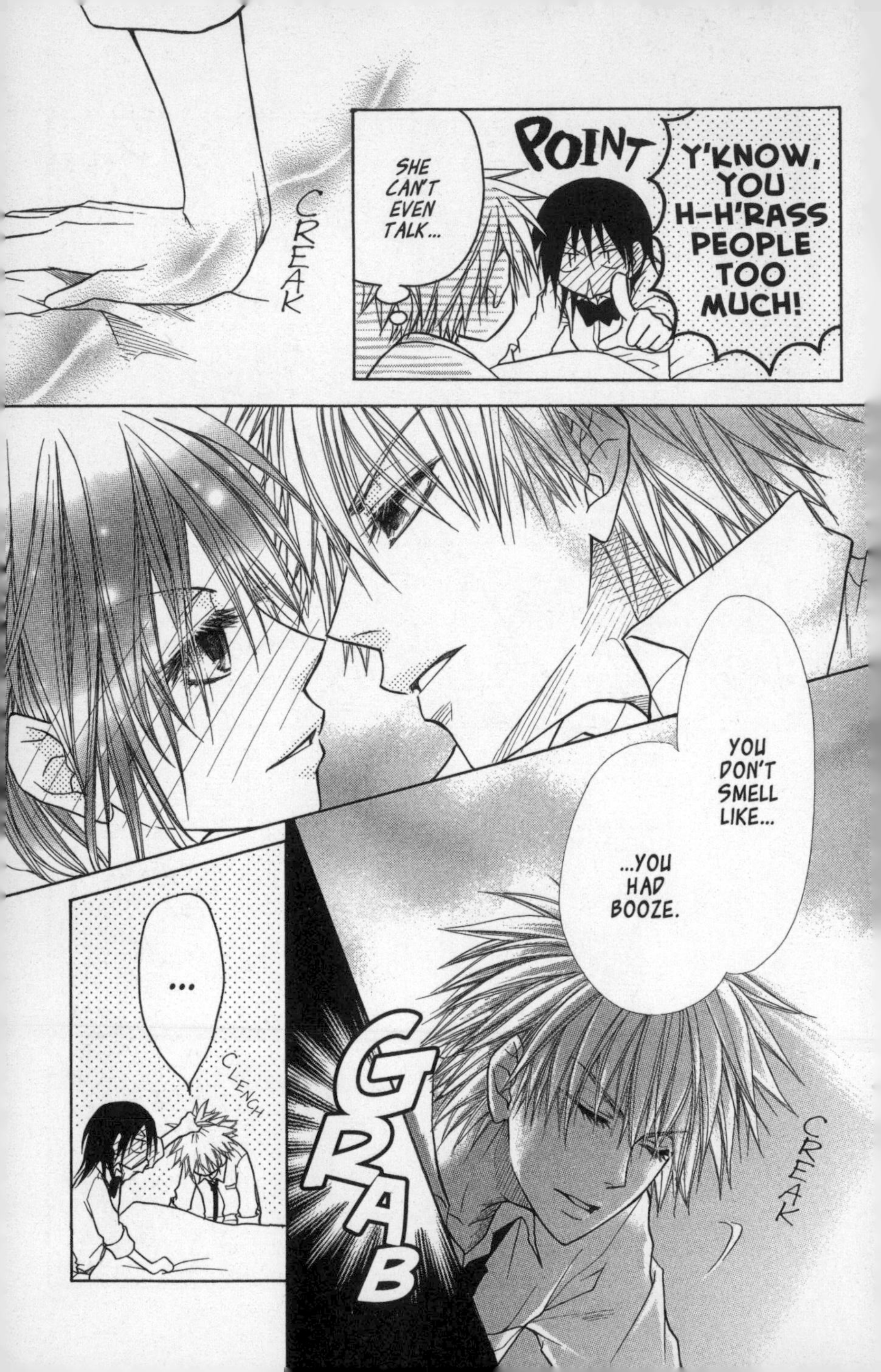
Y'KNOW, YOU H-H'RASS PEOPLE TOO MUCH!
POINT
SHE CAN'T EVEN TALK...
CREAK
YOU DON'T SMELL LIKE...
...YOU HAD BOOZE.
CREAK
GRAB
...
CLENCH

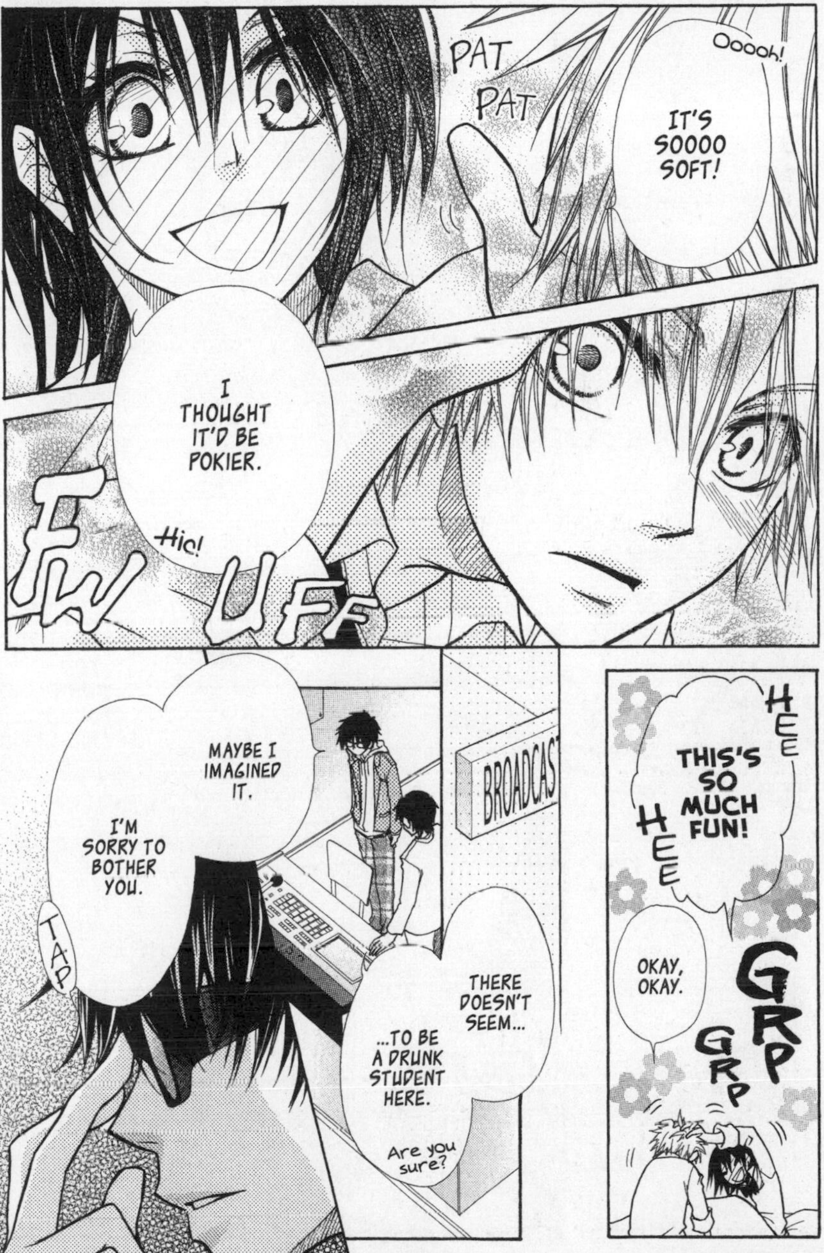
PAT PAT
Ooooh!
IT'S SOOOO SOFT!
I THOUGHT IT'D BE POKIER.
Hic!
FWUFF
HEE HEE
THIS'S SO MUCH FUN!
OKAY, OKAY.
GRP GRP
BROADCAST
THERE DOESN'T SEEM...
...TO BE A DRUNK STUDENT HERE.
Are you sure?
MAYBE I IMAGINED IT.
I'M SORRY TO BOTHER YOU.
TAP

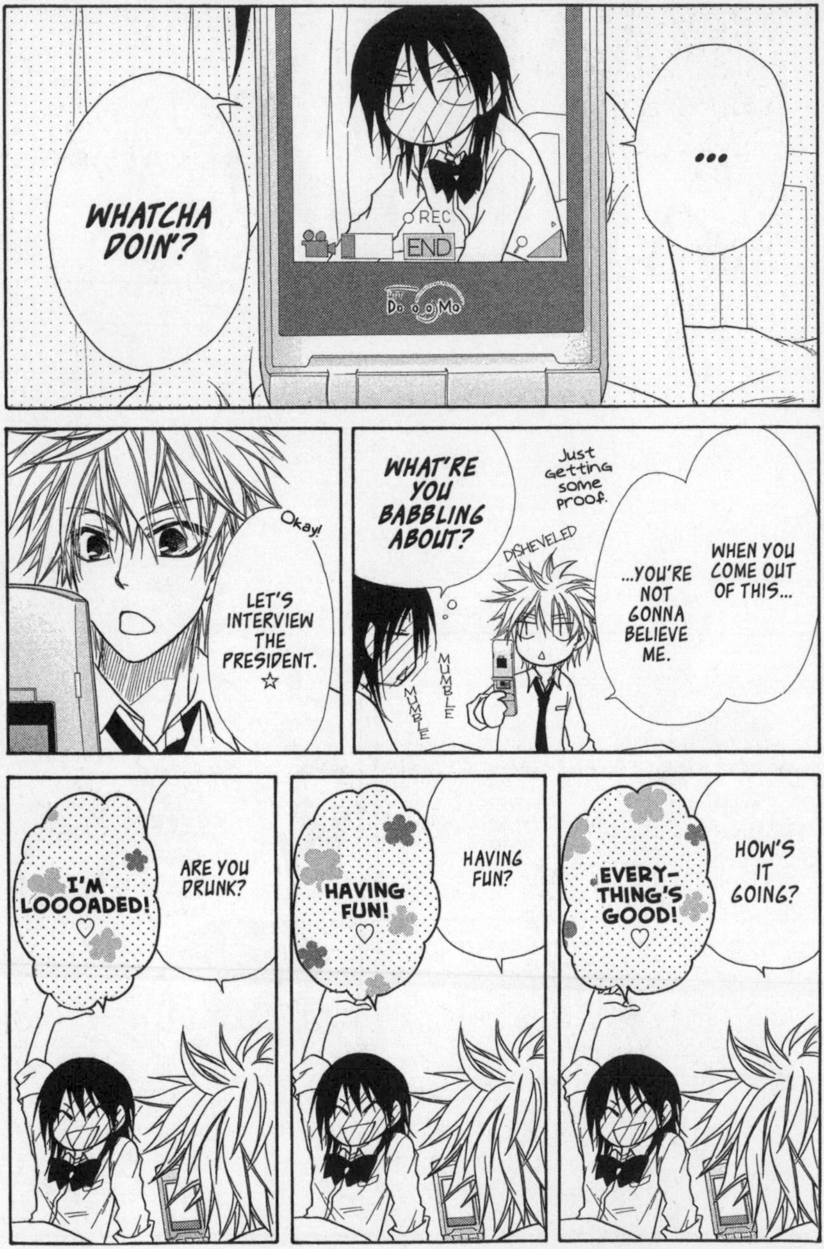
...
REC
END
WHATCHA DOIN'?
WHEN YOU COME OUT OF THIS...
...YOU'RE NOT GONNA BELIEVE ME.
Just getting some proof.
DISHEVELED
WHAT'RE YOU BABBLING ABOUT?
MUMBLE MUMBLE
Okay!
LET'S INTERVIEW THE PRESIDENT. ☆
HOW'S IT GOING?
EVERY-THING'S GOOD! ♡
HAVING FUN?
HAVING FUN! ♡
ARE YOU DRUNK?
I'M LOOOADED! ♡

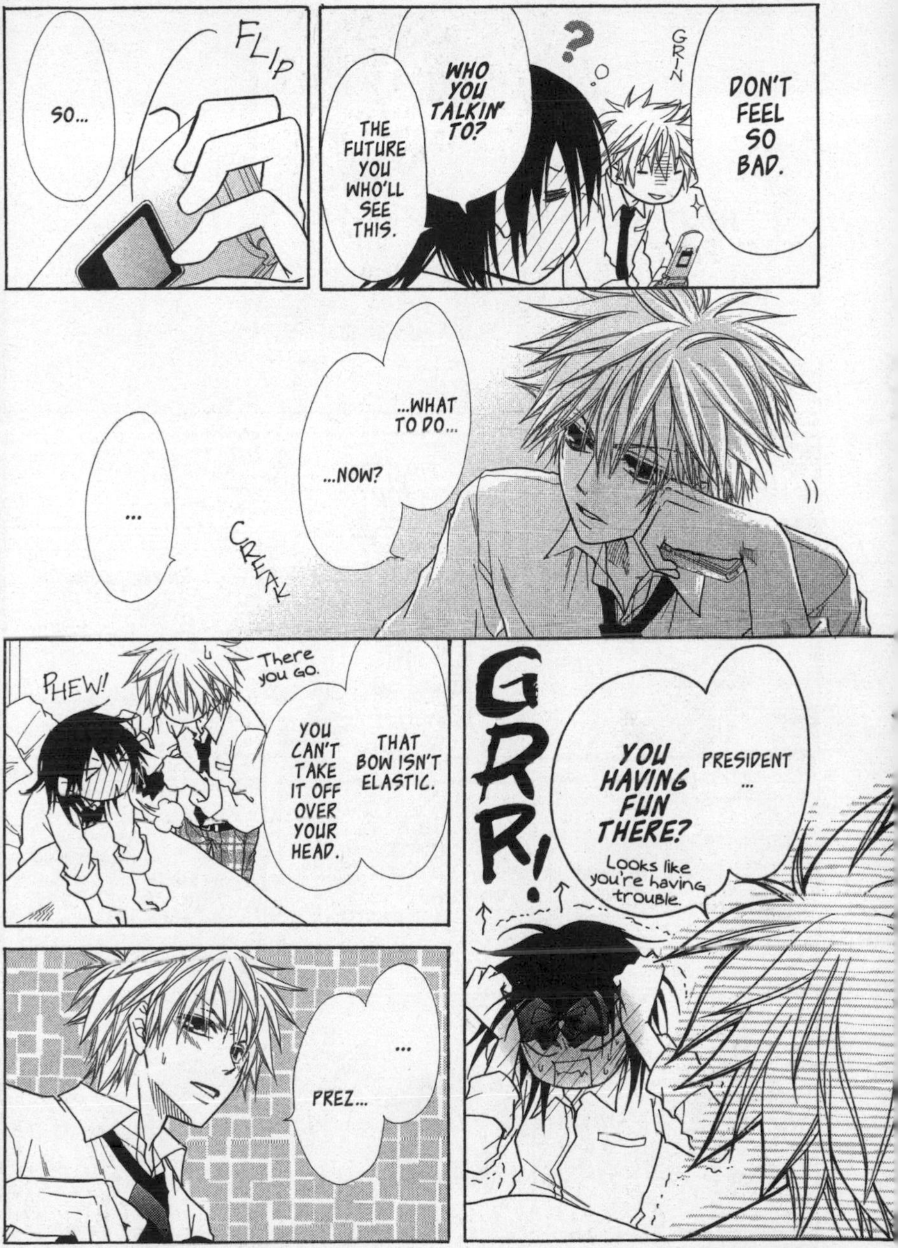
GRIN
DON'T FEEL SO BAD.
?
WHO YOU TALKIN' TO?
THE FUTURE YOU WHO'LL SEE THIS.
FLIP
SO...
...WHAT TO DO...
...NOW?
CREAK
...
GRR!
PRESIDENT...
YOU HAVING FUN THERE?
Looks like you're having trouble.
There you go.
THAT BOW ISN'T ELASTIC.
YOU CAN'T TAKE IT OFF OVER YOUR HEAD.
PHEW!
...
PREZ...

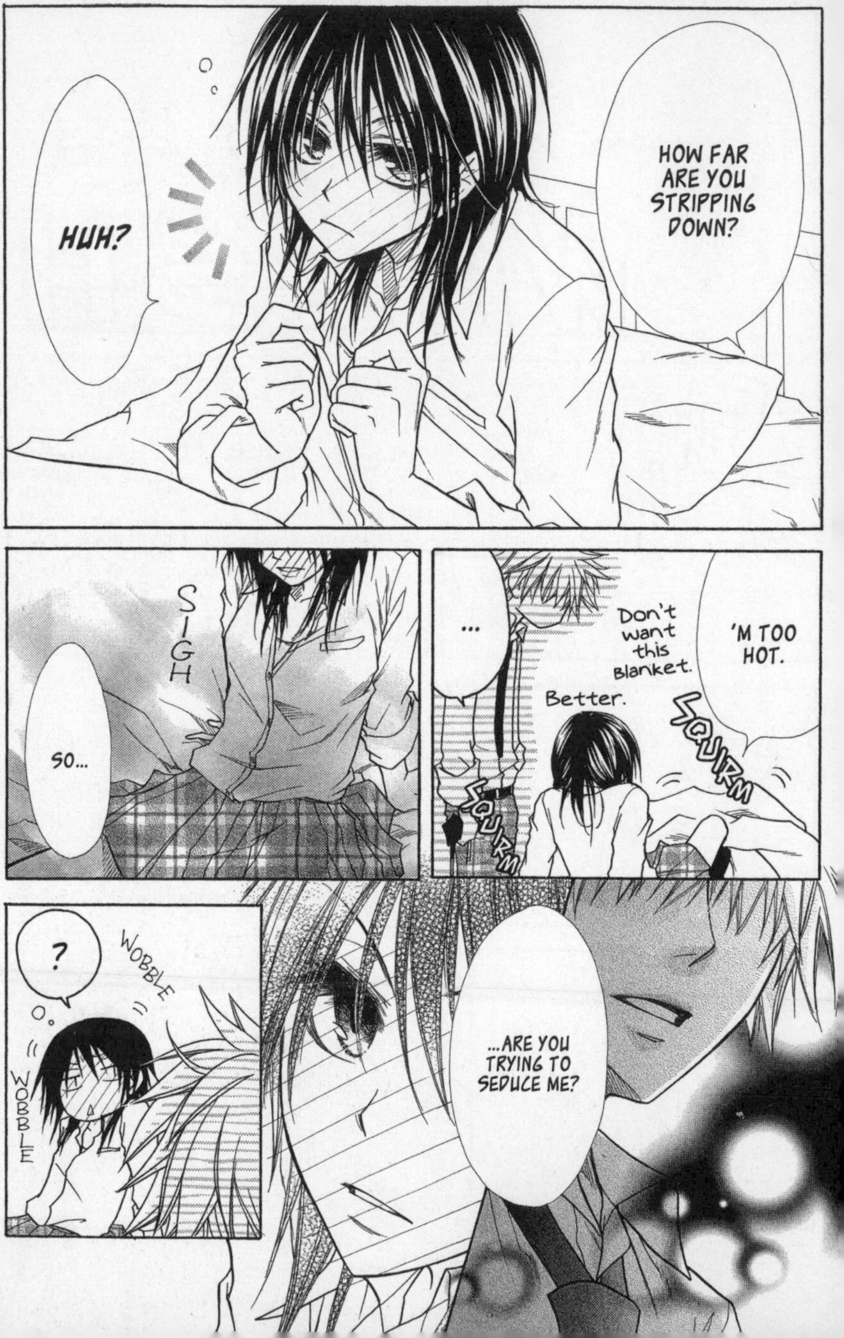
HOW FAR ARE YOU STRIPPING DOWN?
HUH?
'M TOO HOT.
SQUIRM
Don't want this Blanket.
Better.
...
SQUIRM
SIGH
SO...
...ARE YOU TRYING TO SEDUCE ME?
?
WOBBLE
WOBBLE

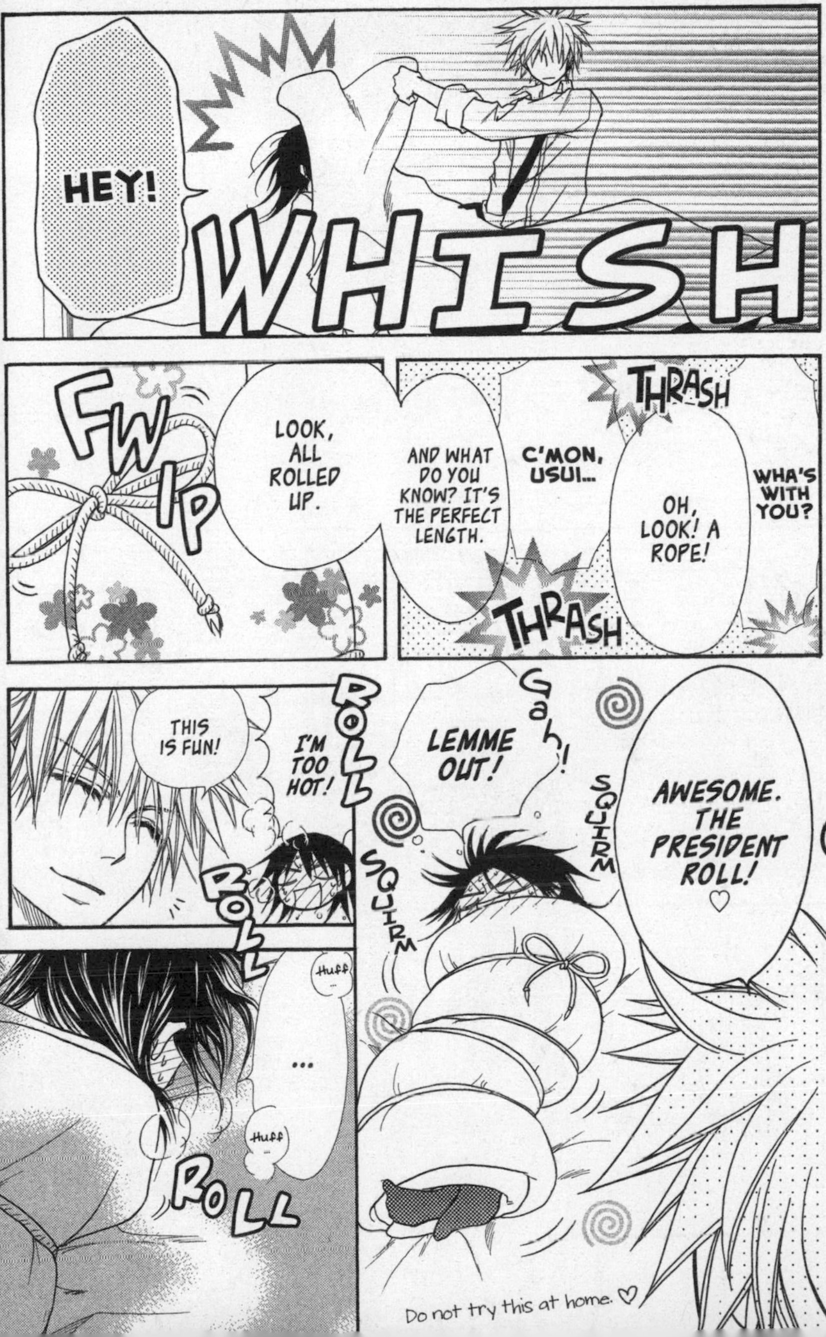
HEY!
WHISH
WHA'S WITH YOU?
THRASH
OH, LOOK! A ROPE!
C'MON, USUI...
THRASH
AND WHAT DO YOU KNOW? IT'S THE PERFECT LENGTH.
LOOK, ALL ROLLED UP.
FWIP
AWESOME. THE PRESIDENT ROLL! ♡
SQUIRM
Gah!
LEMME OUT!
SQUIRM
ROLL
I'M TOO HOT!
THIS IS FUN!
ROLL
Huff...
...
Huff...
ROLL
Do not try this at home. ♡

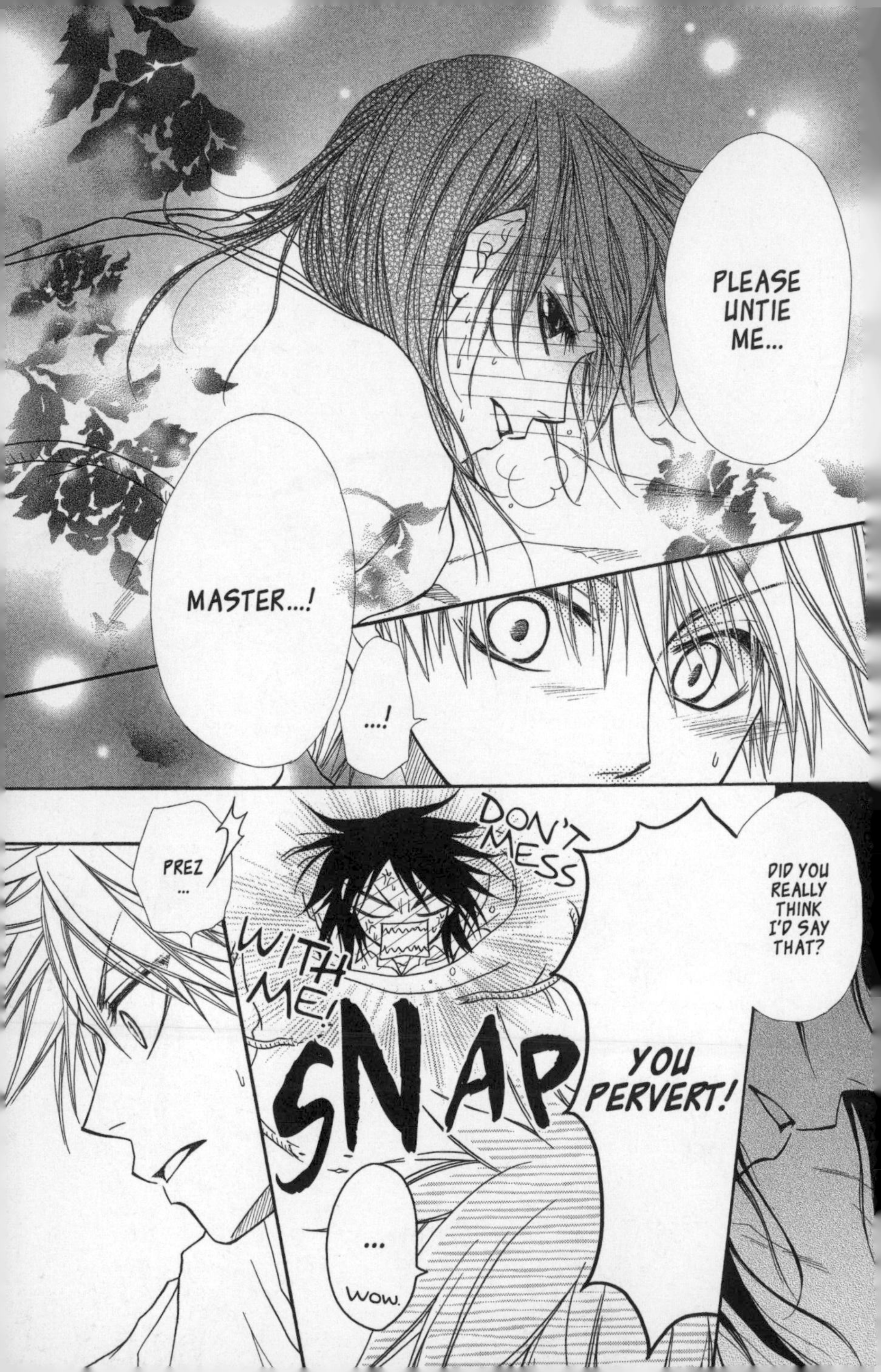
PLEASE UNTIE ME...
MASTER...!
...!
DID YOU REALLY THINK I'D SAY THAT?
DON'T MESS WITH ME!
PREZ ...
YOU PERVERT!
SNAP
...
WOW.

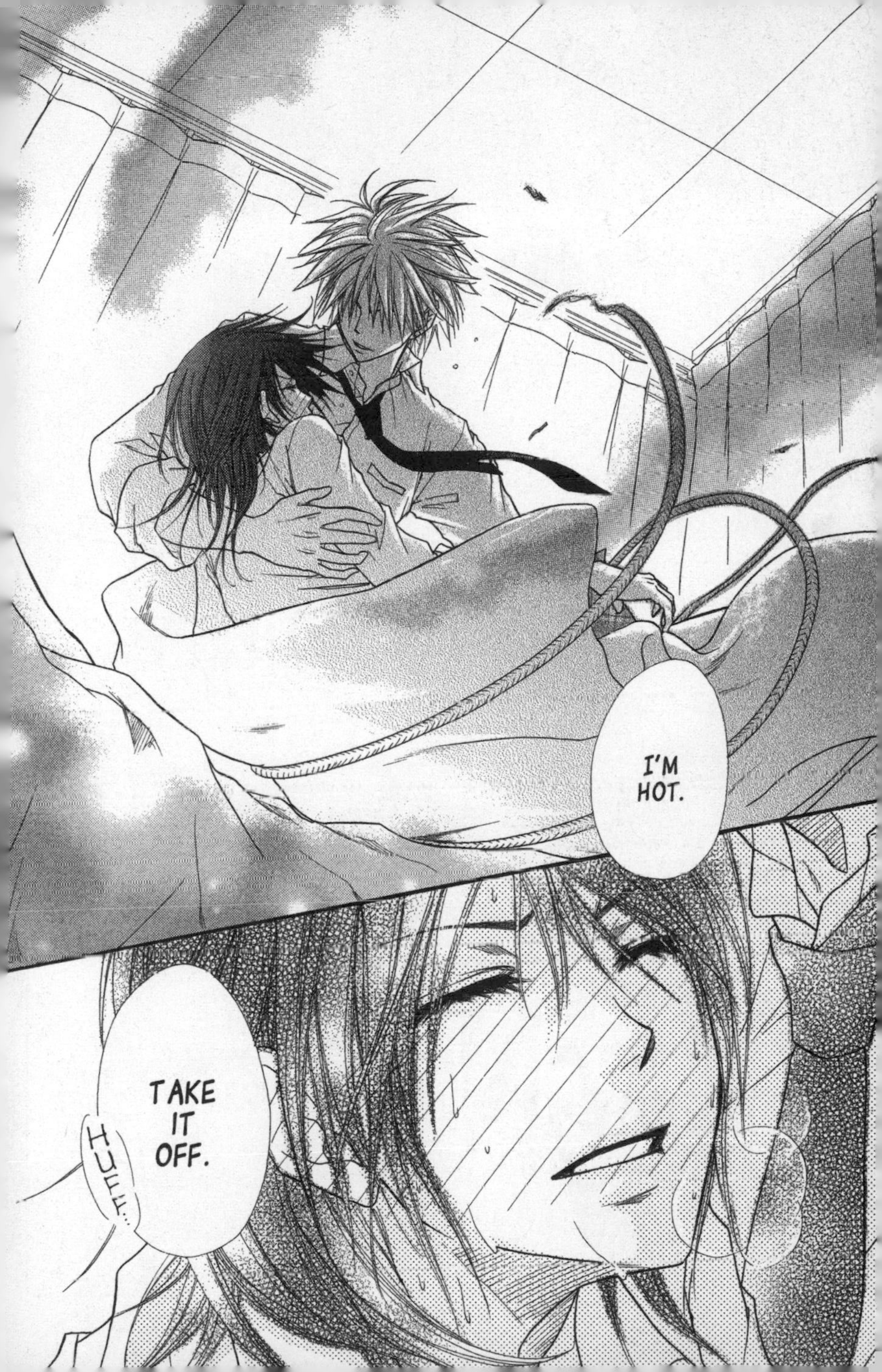
I'M HOT.
TAKE IT OFF.
HUFF...

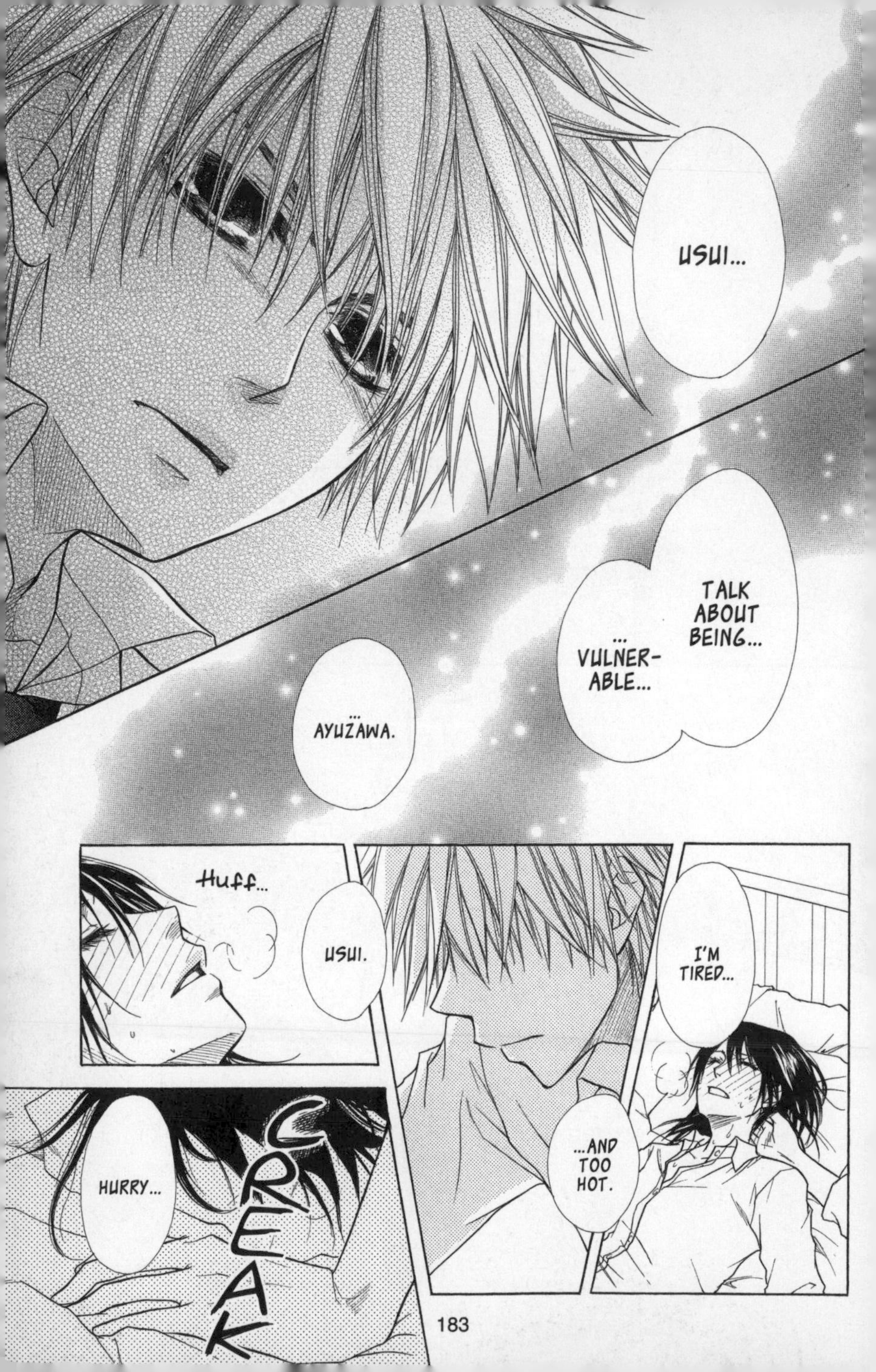
USUI...
TALK ABOUT BEING... ...VULNER-ABLE...
...AYUZAWA.
I'M TIRED...
...AND TOO HOT.
Huff...
USUI.
HURRY...
CREAK

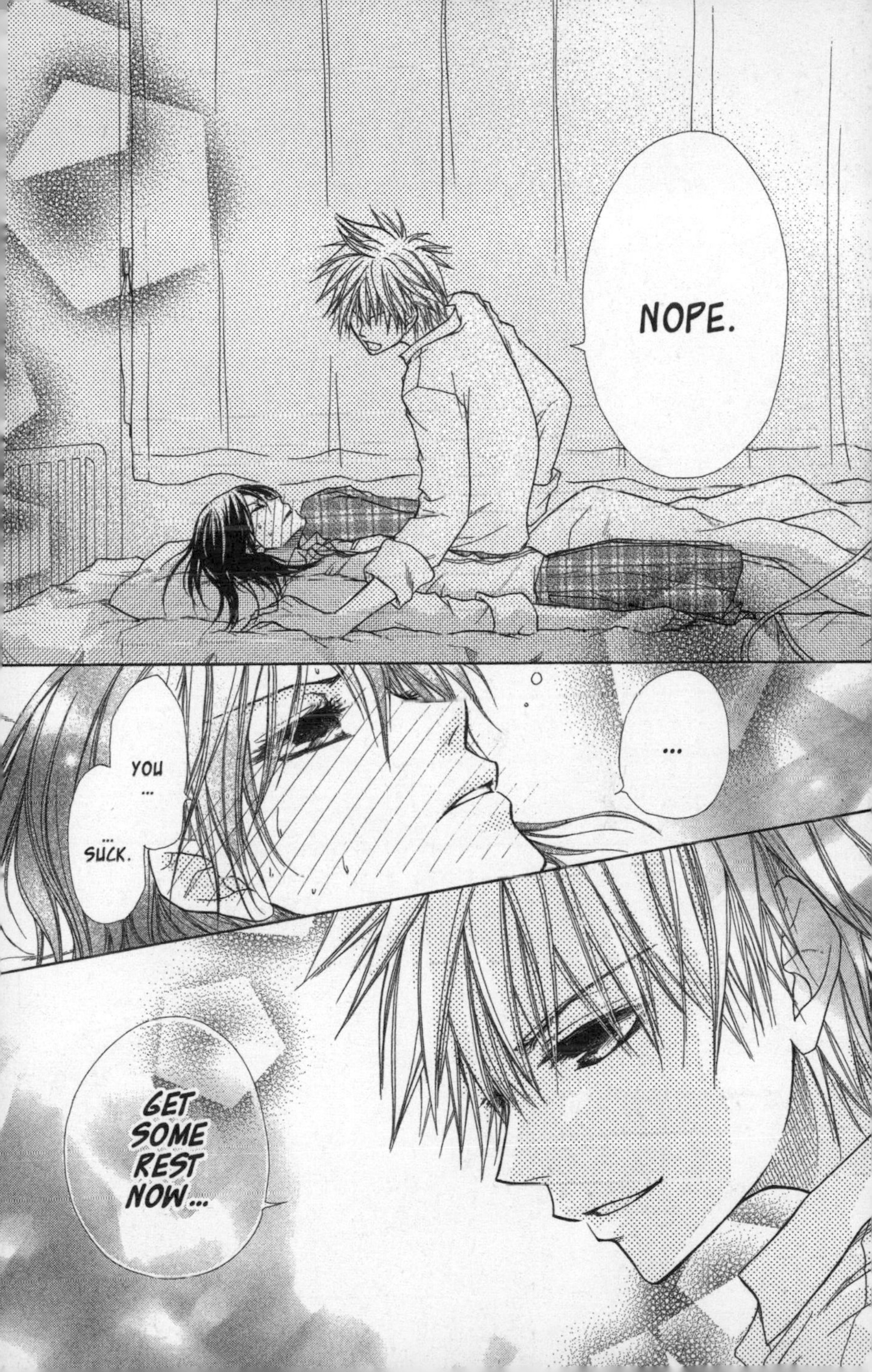
NOPE.
...
YOU ... ... SUCK.
GET SOME REST NOW...

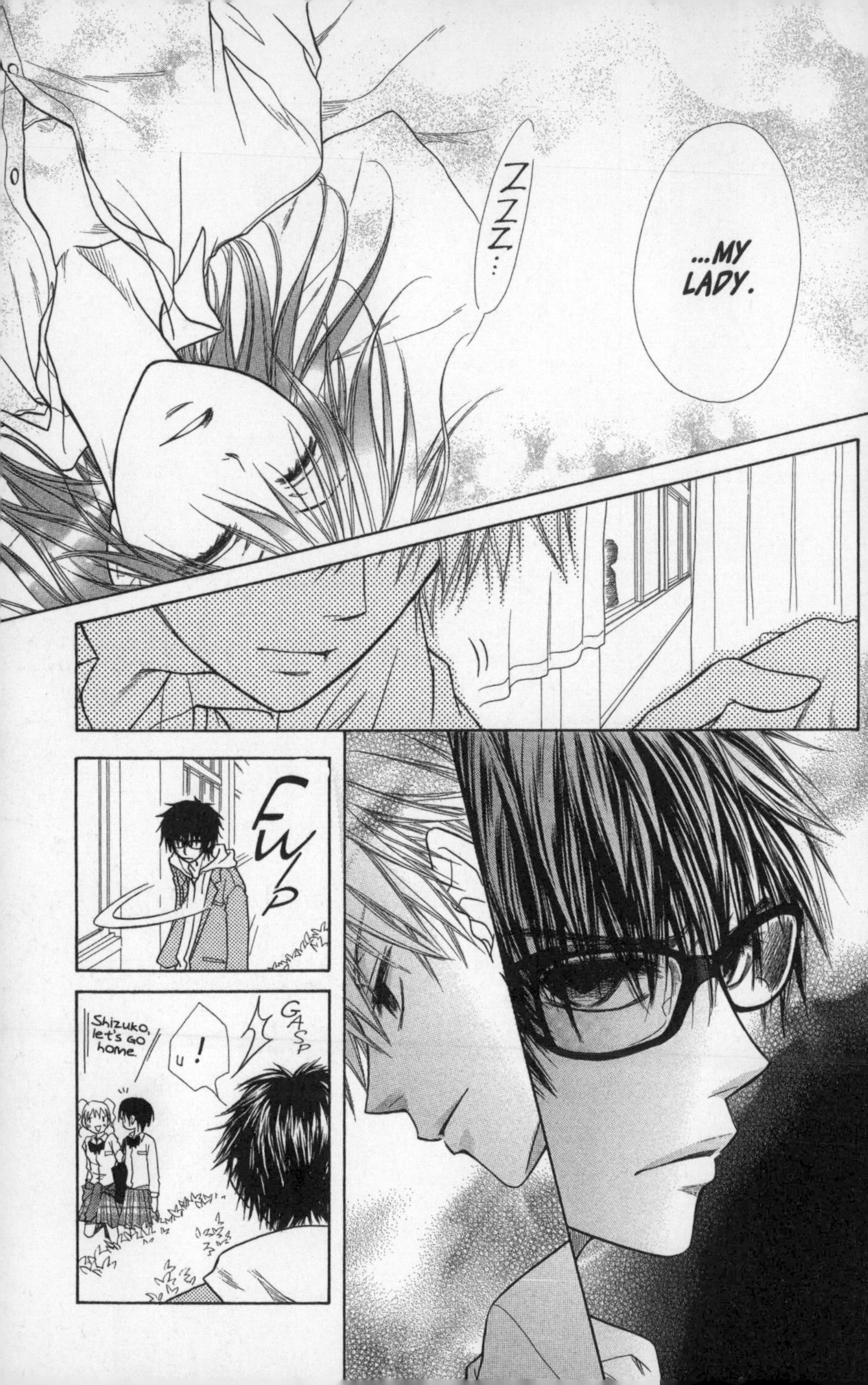
...MY LADY.
ZZZ...
FWP
GASP
!
Shizuko, let's GO home.

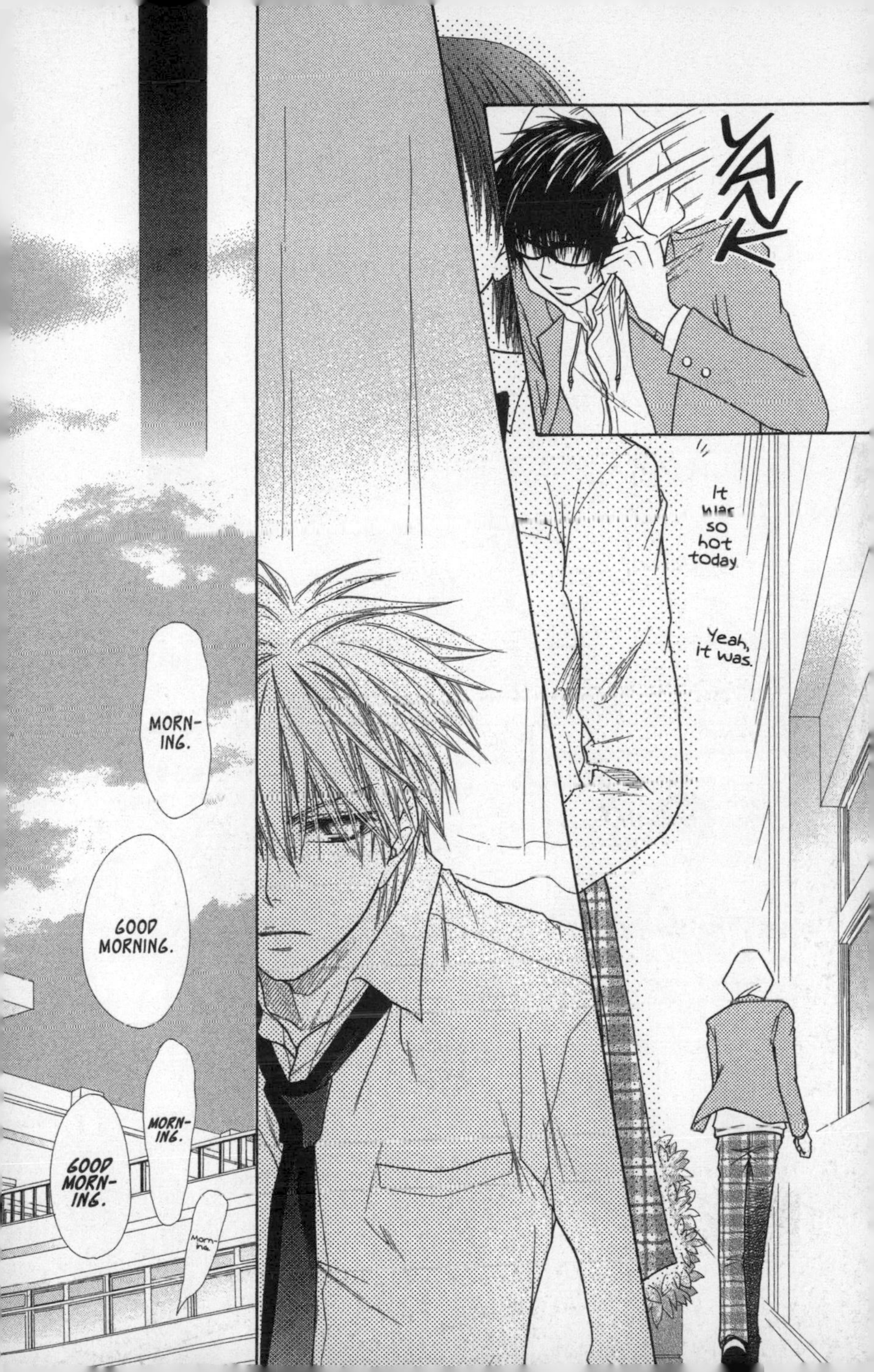
YANK
It was so hot today.
Yeah, it was.
MORN-ING.
GOOD MORNING.
MORN-ING.
GOOD MORN-ING.
Morn-ing.

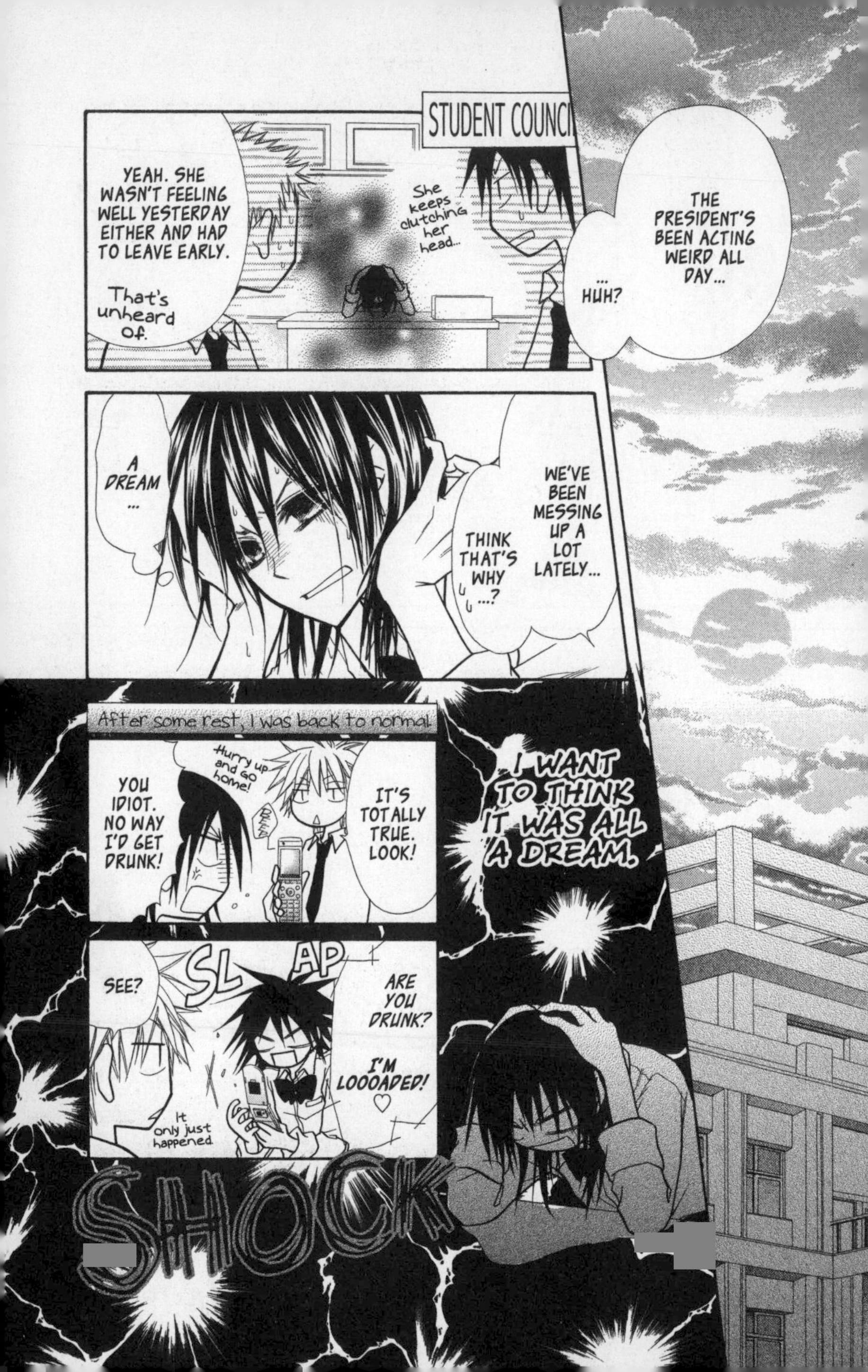
STUDENT COUNCI
THE PRESIDENT'S BEEN ACTING WEIRD ALL DAY...
... HUH?
She keeps clutching her head...
YEAH. SHE WASN'T FEELING WELL YESTERDAY EITHER AND HAD TO LEAVE EARLY.
That's unheard of.
WE'VE BEEN MESSING UP A LOT LATELY...
THINK THAT'S WHY ...?
A DREAM ...
I WANT TO THINK IT WAS ALL A DREAM.
After some rest, I was back to normal.
IT'S TOTALLY TRUE. LOOK!
Hurry up and go home!
YOU IDIOT. NO WAY I'D GET DRUNK!
ARE YOU DRUNK?
I'M LOOOADED! ♡
SLAP
SEE?
It only just happened
SHOCK

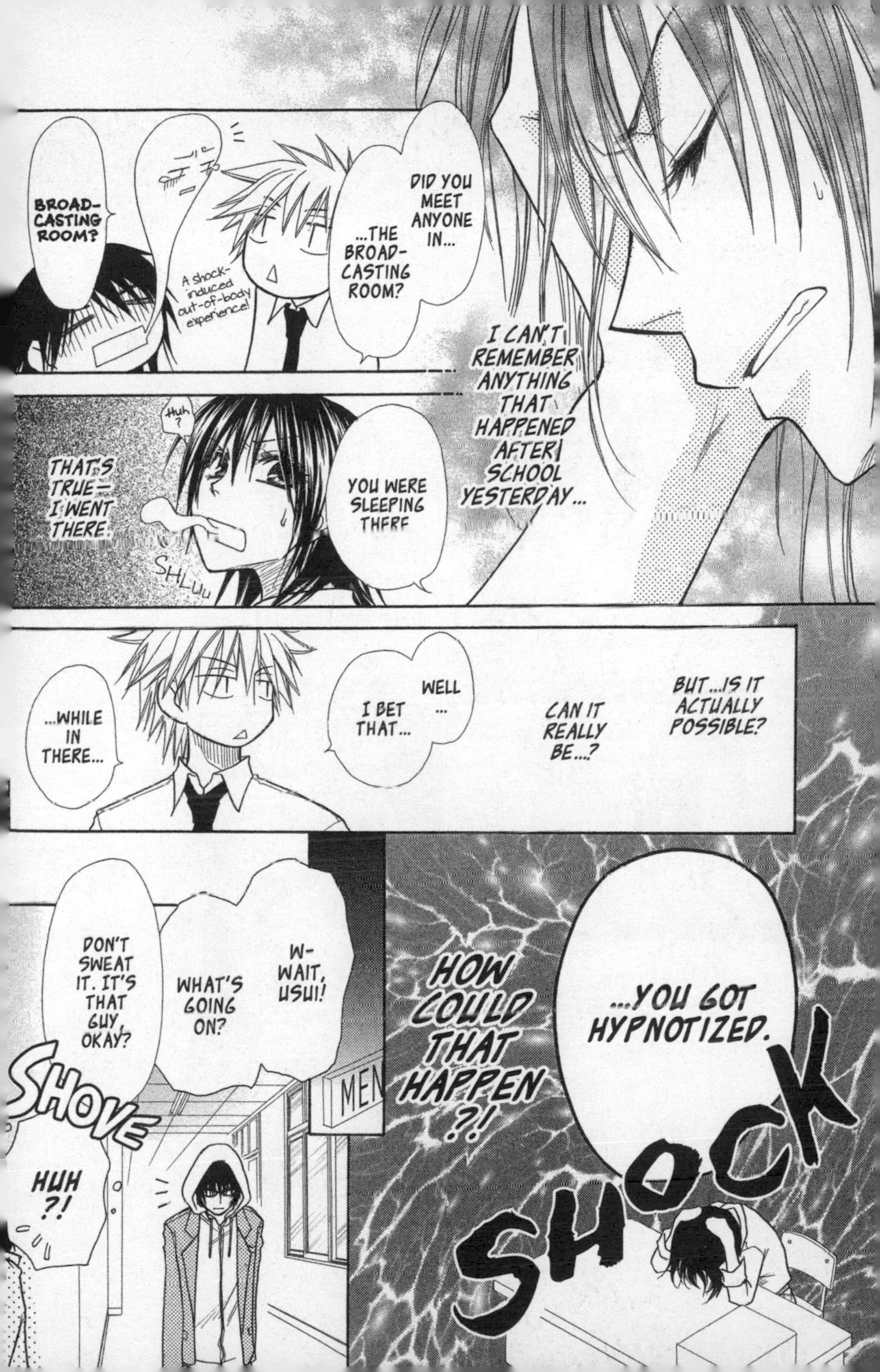
I CAN'T REMEMBER ANYTHING THAT HAPPENED AFTER SCHOOL YESTERDAY...
DID YOU MEET ANYONE IN...
...THE BROAD-CASTING ROOM?
A shock-induced out-of-body experience!
BROAD-CASTING ROOM?
YOU WERE SLEEPING THERE
Huh?
THAT'S TRUE— I WENT THERE.
SHLUU
BUT...IS IT ACTUALLY POSSIBLE?
CAN IT REALLY BE...?
WELL...
I BET THAT...
...WHILE IN THERE...
...YOU GOT HYPNOTIZED.
HOW COULD THAT HAPPEN?!
SHOCK
W-WAIT, USUI!
WHAT'S GOING ON?
DON'T SWEAT IT. IT'S THAT GUY, OKAY?
SHOVE
HUH?!
MEN

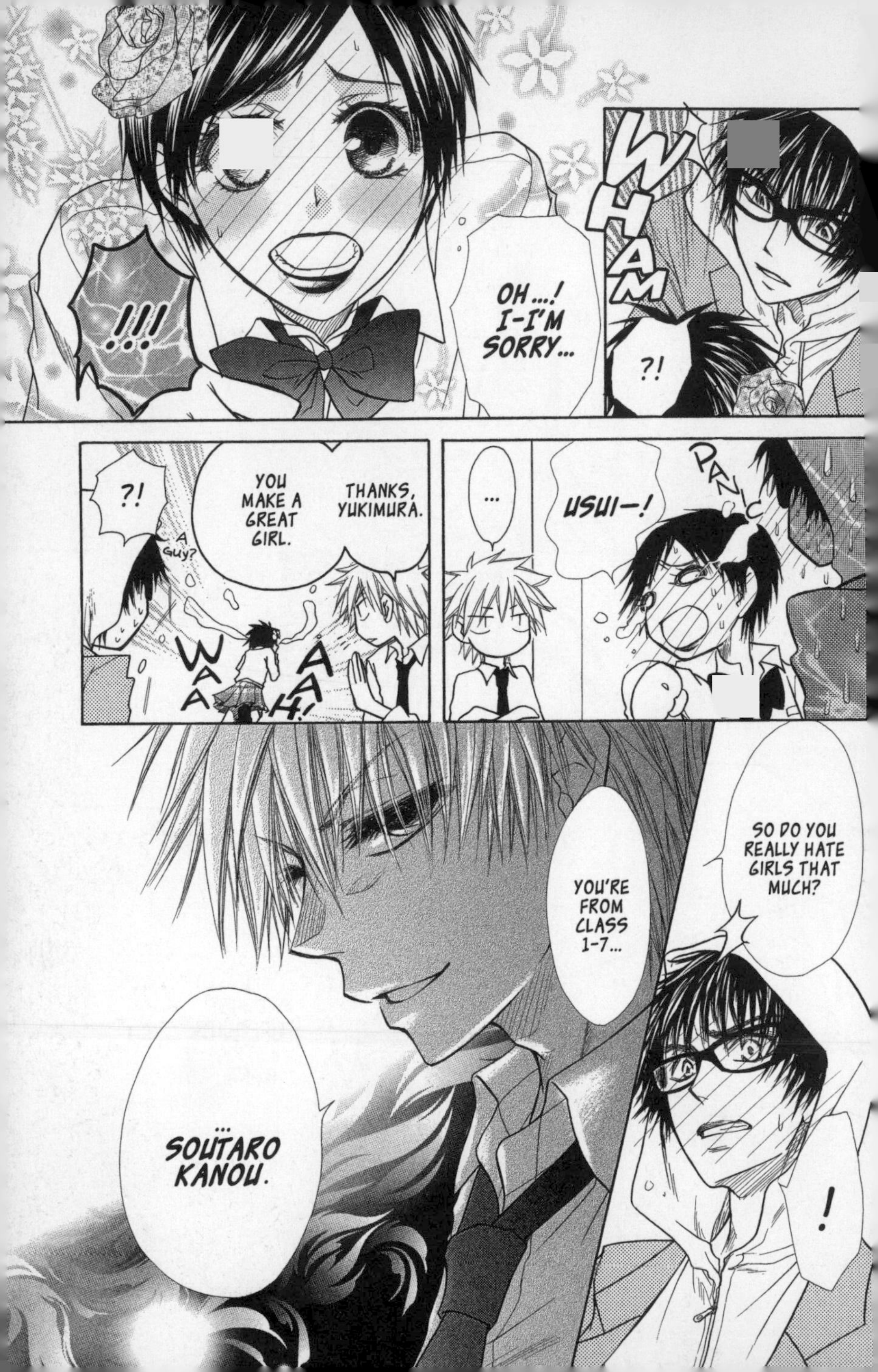
WHAM
?!
OH...! I-I'M SORRY...
!!!
PANIC
USUI—!
...
THANKS, YUKIMURA.
YOU MAKE A GREAT GIRL.
?!
A Guy?
WAAAAH!
SO DO YOU REALLY HATE GIRLS THAT MUCH?
YOU'RE FROM CLASS 1-7...
!
... SOUTARO KANOU.

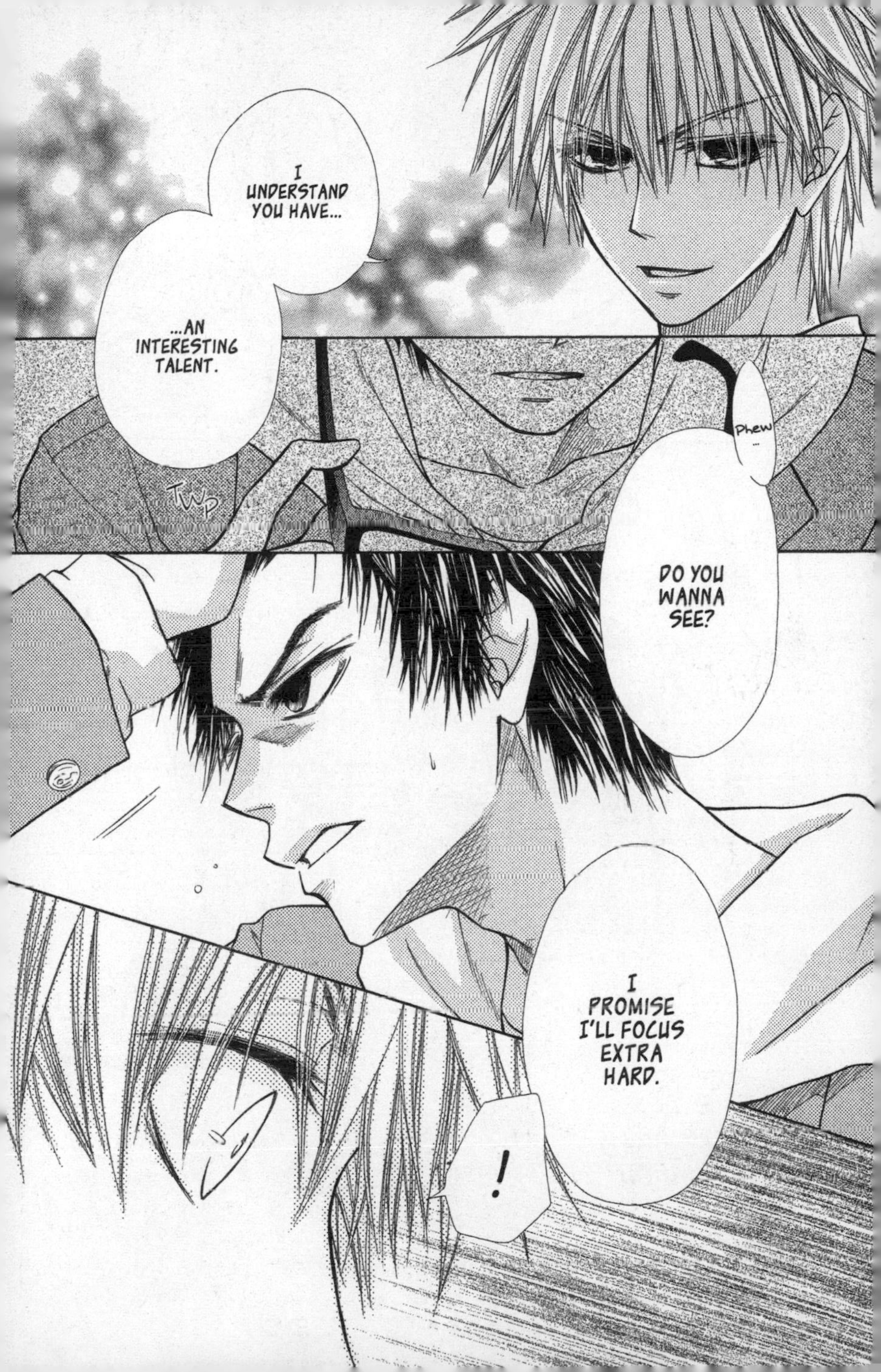
I UNDERSTAND YOU HAVE...
...AN INTERESTING TALENT.
Phew...
TWP
DO YOU WANNA SEE?
I PROMISE I'LL FOCUS EXTRA HARD.
!

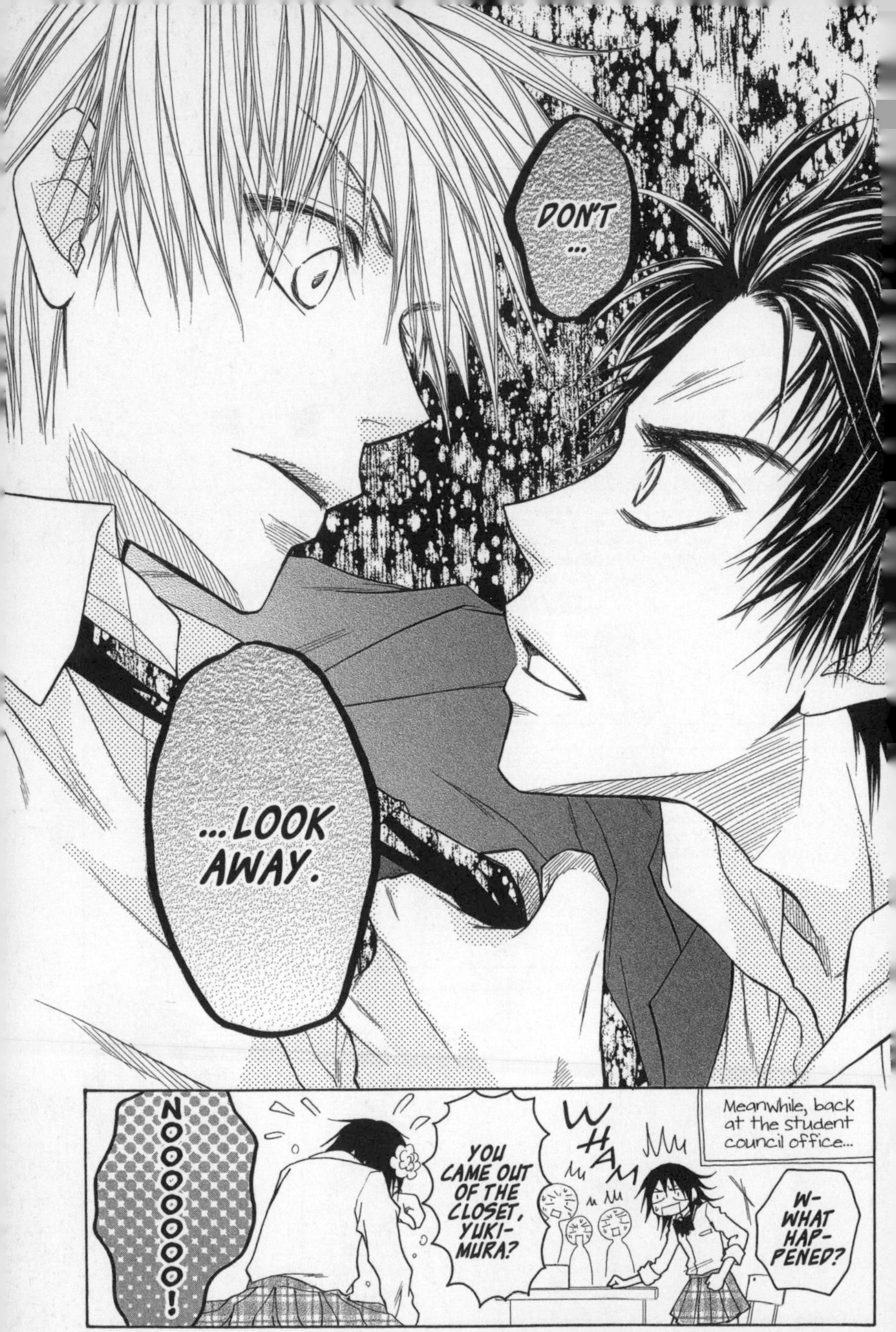
DON'T ...
...LOOK AWAY.
Meanwhile, back at the student council office...
W-WHAT HAPPENED?
WHAM
YOU CAME OUT OF THE CLOSET, YUKIMURA?
NOOOOOOO!

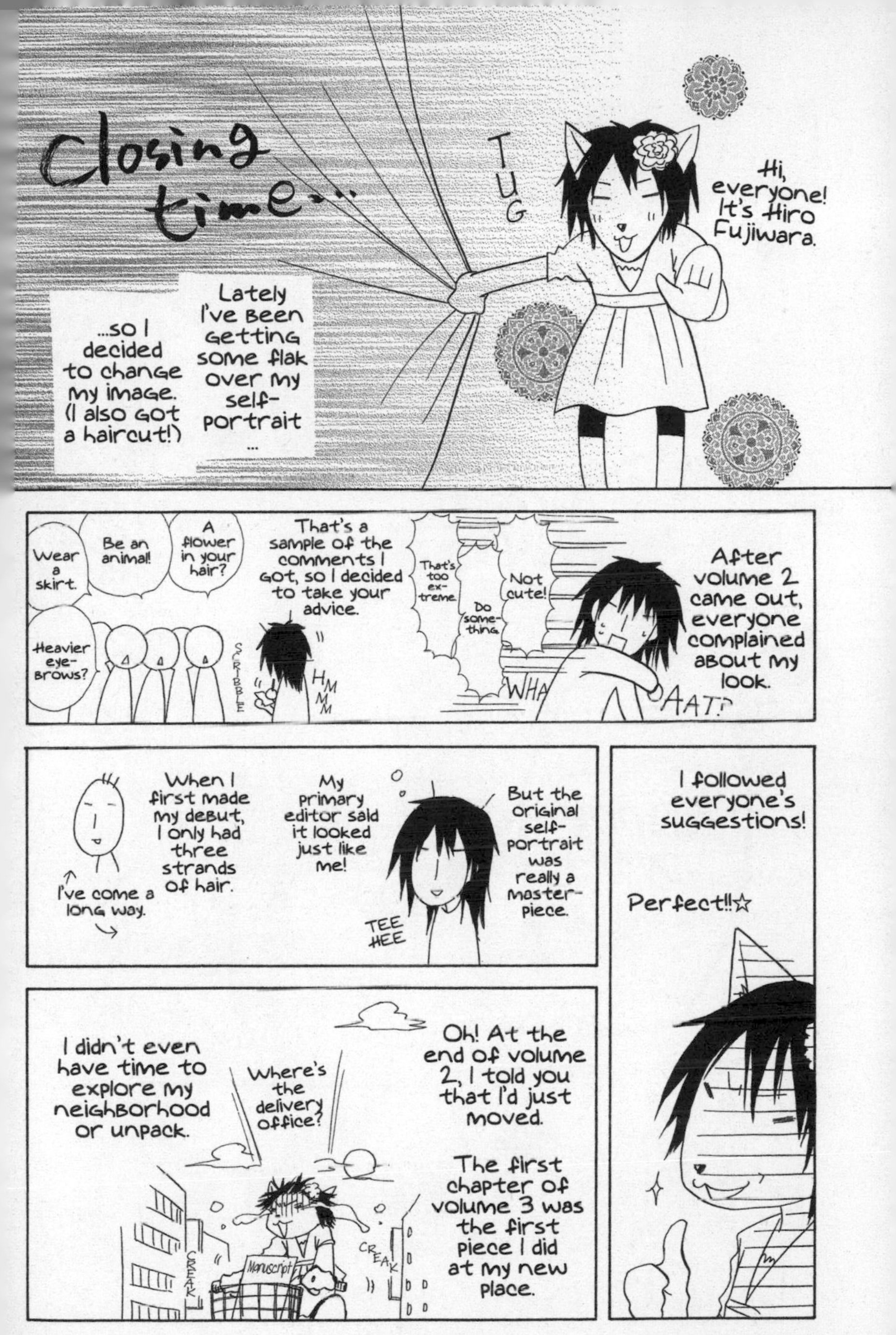
Hi, everyone! It's Hiro Fujiwara.
TUG
Closing time...
Lately I've been getting some flak over my self-portrait...
...so I decided to change my image. (I also got a haircut!)
After volume 2 came out, everyone complained about my look.
Not cute!
That's too extreme.
Do something.
WHAAAT!?
That's a sample of the comments I got, so I decided to take your advice.
HMMM
SCRIBBLE
A flower in your hair?
Be an animal!
Wear a skirt.
Heavier eyebrows?
I followed everyone's suggestions!
Perfect!!☆
But the original self-portrait was really a masterpiece.
TEE HEE
My primary editor said it looked just like me!
When I first made my debut, I only had three strands of hair.
I've come a long way.
Oh! At the end of volume 2, I told you that I'd just moved.
The first chapter of volume 3 was the first piece I did at my new place.
Where's the delivery office?
CREAK
Manuscript
CREAK
I didn't even have time to explore my neighborhood or unpack.

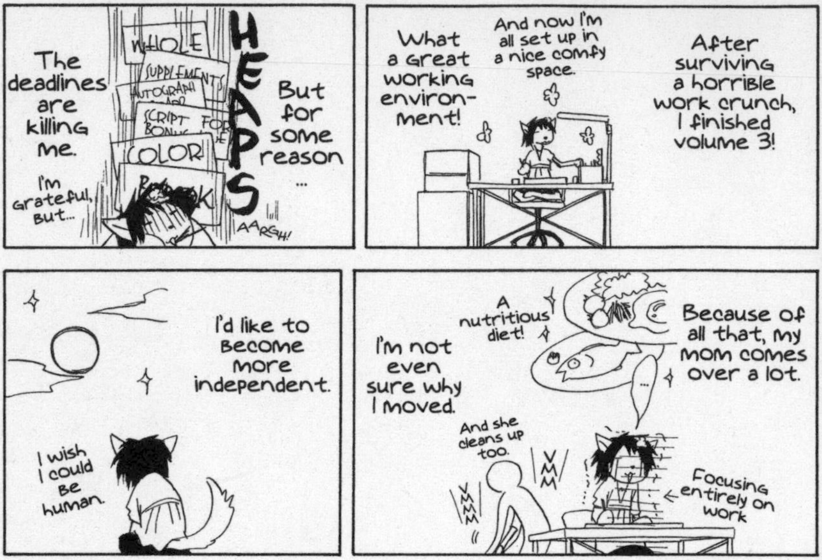
After surviving a horrible work crunch, I finished volume 3!
And now I'm all set up in a nice comfy space.
What a great working environment!
But for some reason...
HEAPS
WHOLE
SUPPLEMENTS
COLOR
The deadlines are killing me.
I'm grateful, but...
AARGH!
Because of all that, my mom comes over a lot.
A nutritious diet!
...
I'm not even sure why I moved.
Focusing entirely on work
VMM
And she cleans up too.
VMM
I'd like to become more independent.
I wish I could be human.

Well, I came to you today as a fox, but since it's kinda creepy, I won't do that again.

Thank you for reading this far!

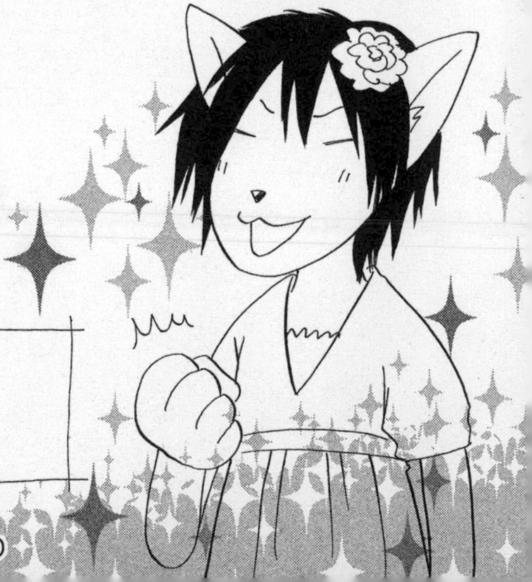

Special Thanks!

- NAMINO
- ERI MINAKAMI
- RIKORO TSUJITA
- YUKI FUJITSUKA
- SUDDOCHI
- MU-KYO
- EDITOR IN CHARGE
- MOTHER

PLEASE SEND YOUR LETTERS HERE ↓

HIRO FUJIWARA
C/O MAID-SAMA! EDITOR
VIZ MEDIA
P.O. BOX 77010
SAN FRANCISCO, CA
94107

CLOSING TIME... / THE END

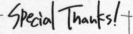

Shojo Beat

Maid-sama!

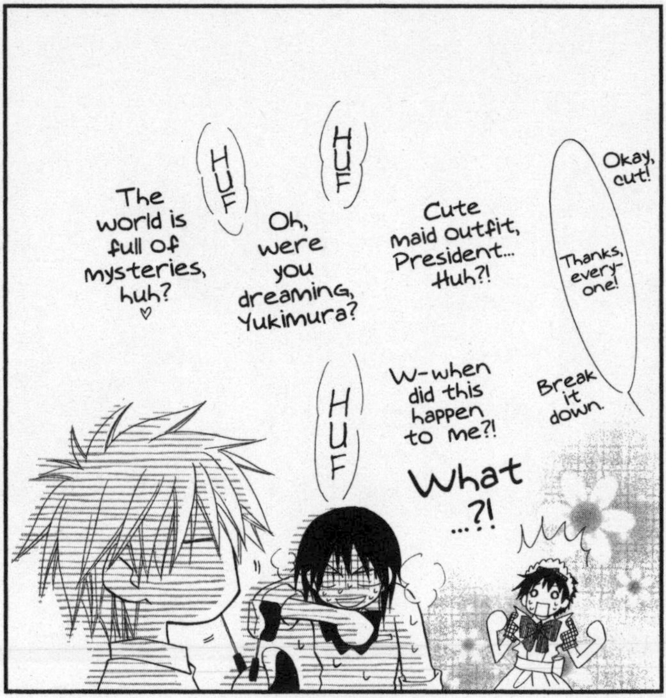
Okay, cut! Thanks, every-one!
HUF
Cute maid outfit, President... Huh?!
Oh, were you dreaming, Yukimura?
HUF
The world is full of mysteries, huh? ♡
Break it down.
W-when did this happen to me?!
What ...?!
HUF

Vol.4

Story & Art by

Hiro Fujiwara

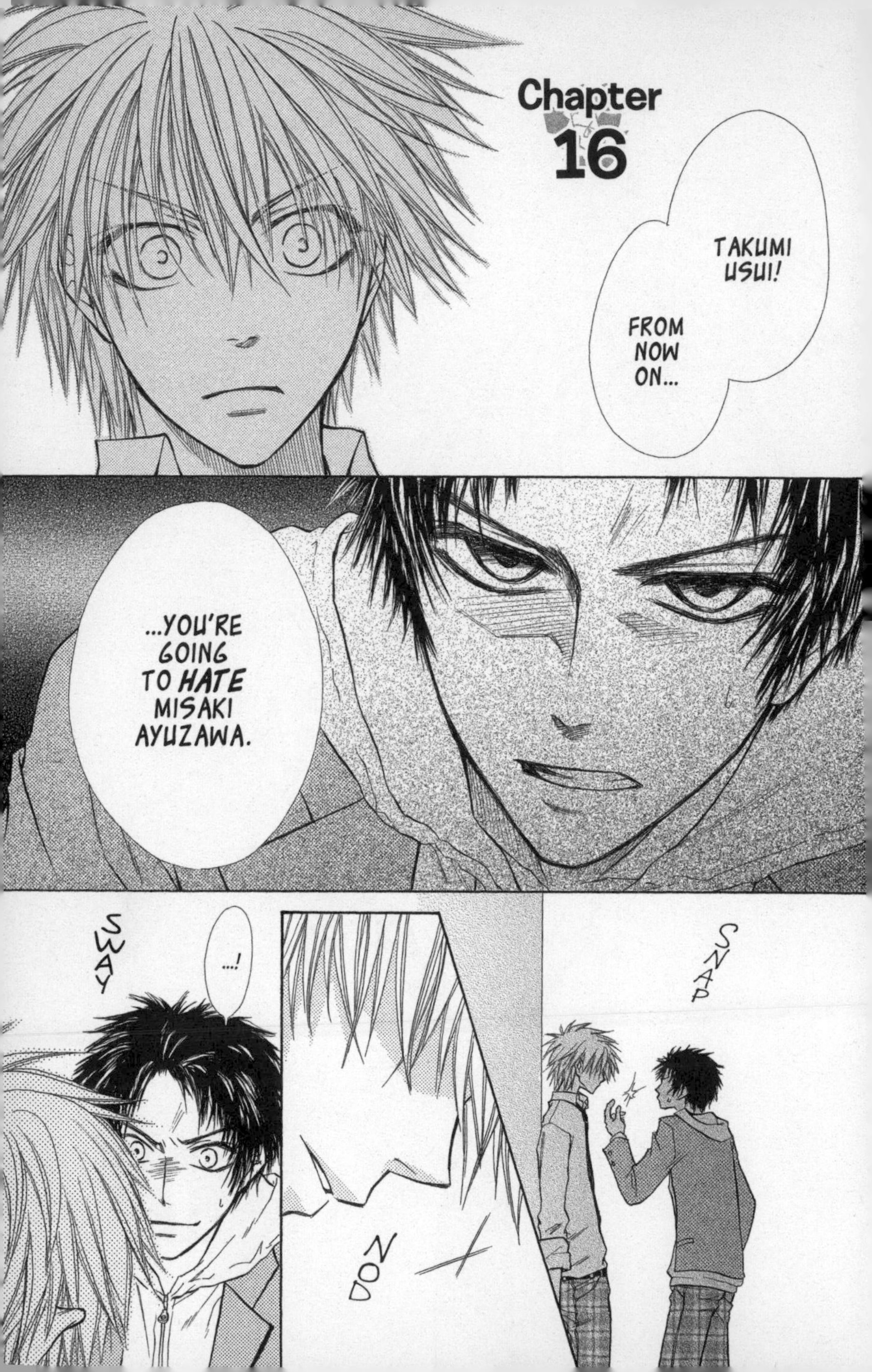
Chapter 16
TAKUMI USUI!
FROM NOW ON...
...YOU'RE GOING TO HATE MISAKI AYUZAWA.
SNAP
NOD
SWAY
...!

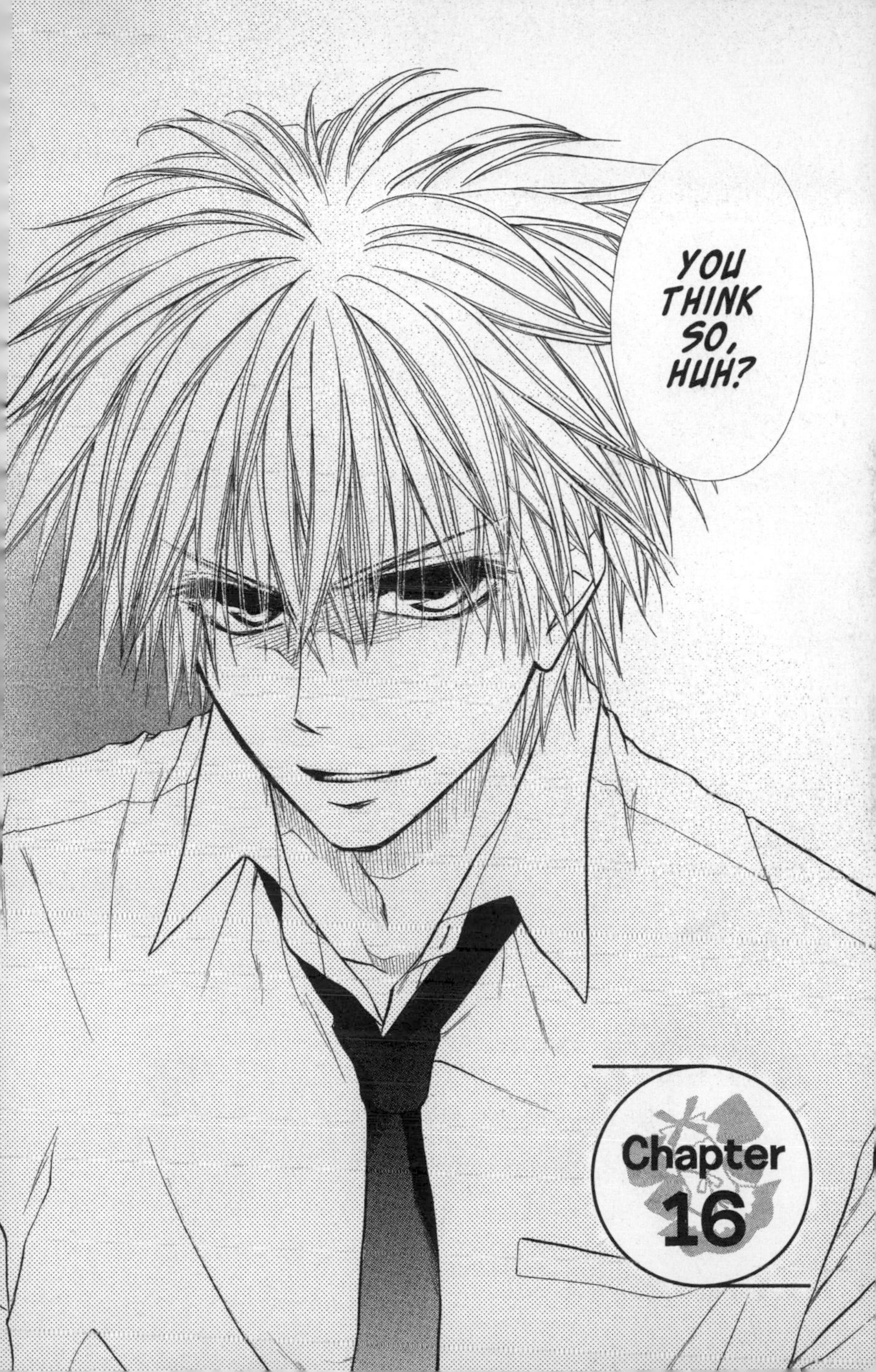
YOU THINK SO, HUH?
Chapter 16

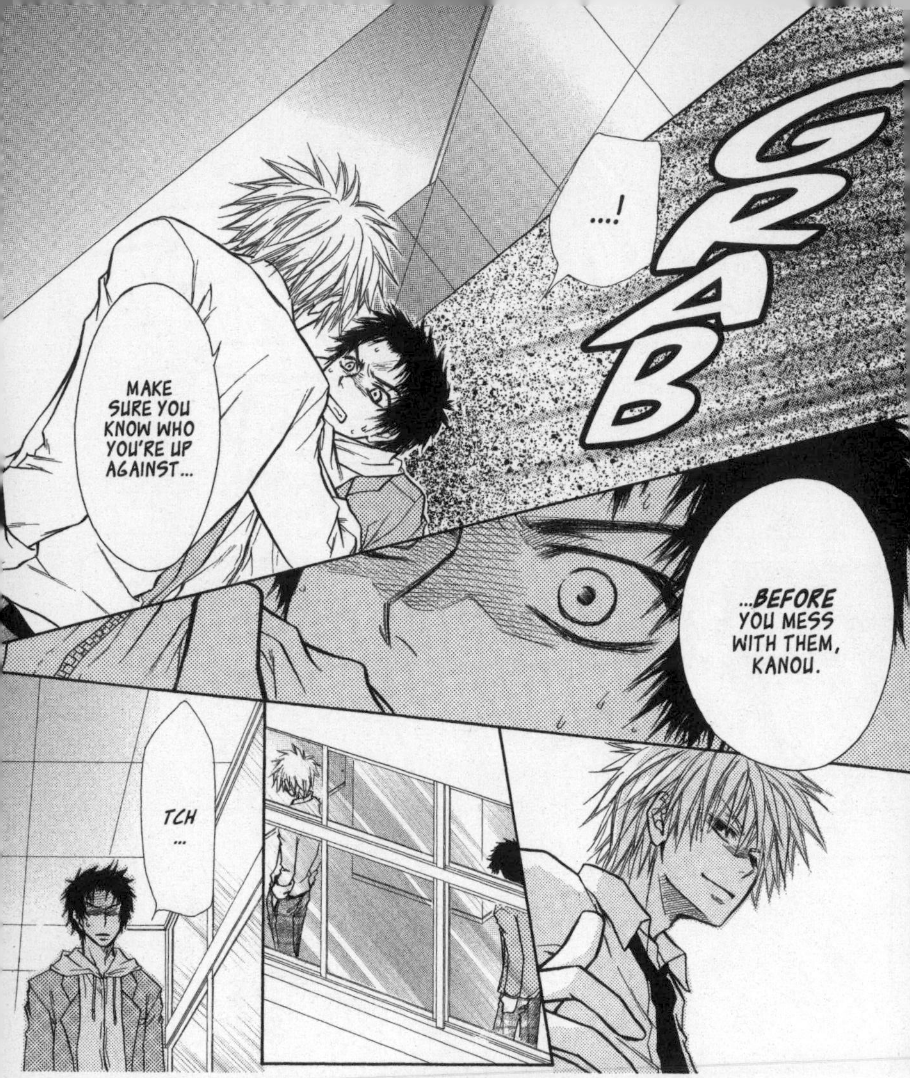
GRAB
...!
MAKE SURE YOU KNOW WHO YOU'RE UP AGAINST...
...BEFORE YOU MESS WITH THEM, KANOU.
TCH ...

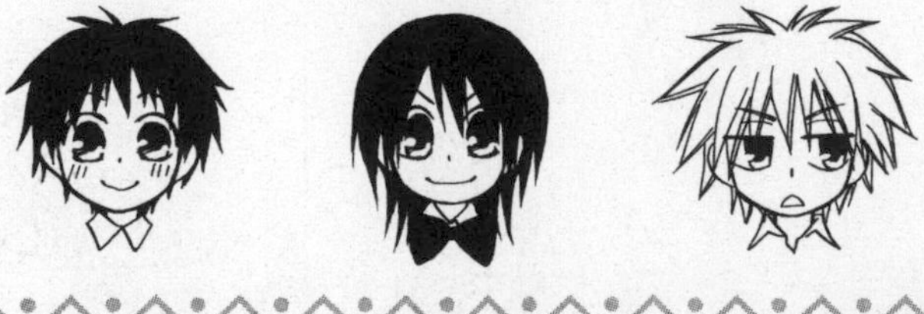

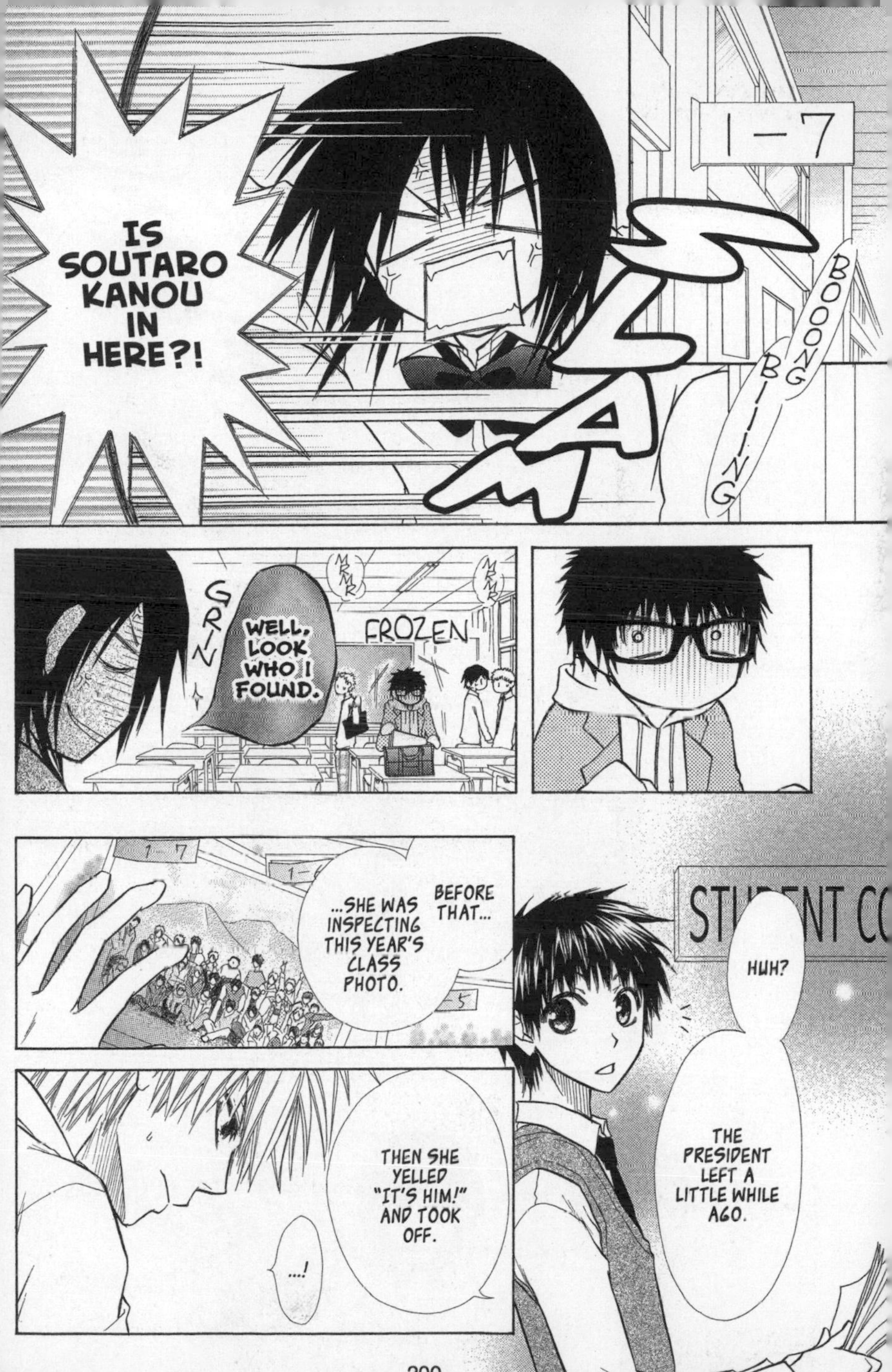
1-7
BOOOONG
BIIIING
SLAM
IS SOUTARO KANOU IN HERE?!
MRMR
MRMR
FROZEN
WELL, LOOK WHO I FOUND.
GRIN
HUH?
THE PRESIDENT LEFT A LITTLE WHILE AGO.
BEFORE THAT...
...SHE WAS INSPECTING THIS YEAR'S CLASS PHOTO.
THEN SHE YELLED "IT'S HIM!" AND TOOK OFF.
...!

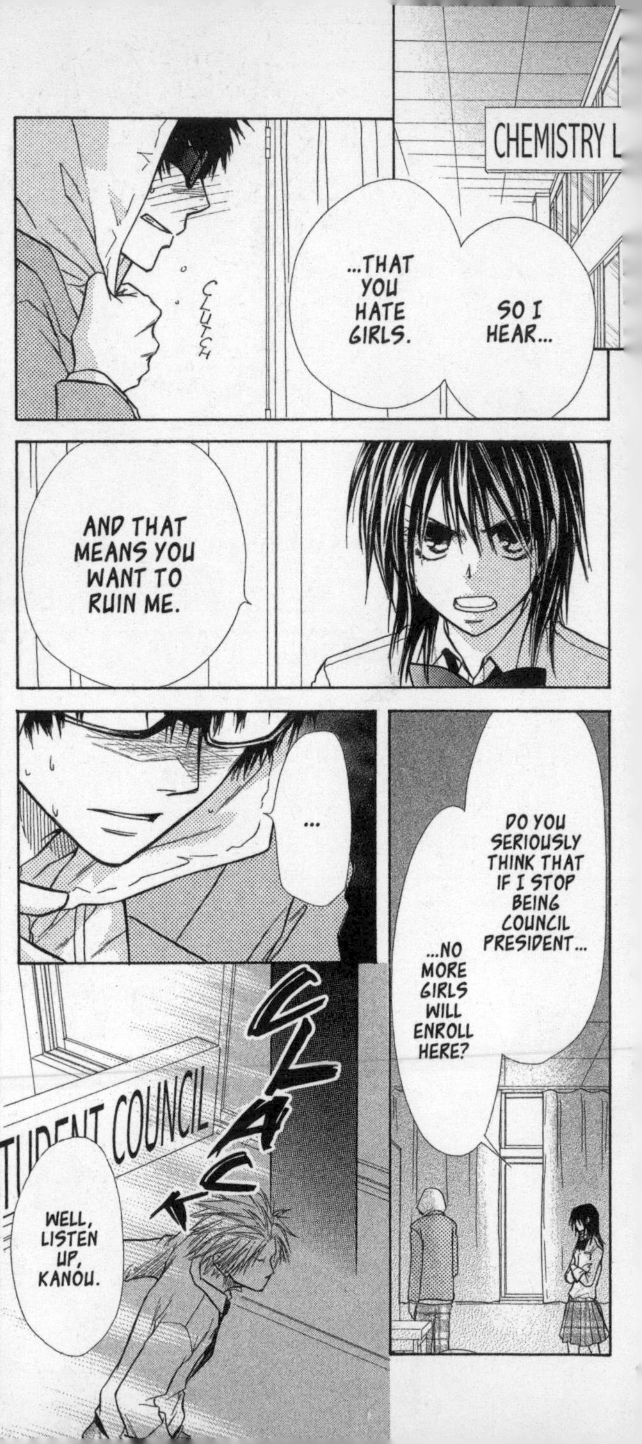
CHEMISTRY L
SO I HEAR...
...THAT YOU HATE GIRLS.
CLUTCH
AND THAT MEANS YOU WANT TO RUIN ME.
DO YOU SERIOUSLY THINK THAT IF I STOP BEING COUNCIL PRESIDENT...
...NO MORE GIRLS WILL ENROLL HERE?
...
CLACK
TUDENT COUNCIL
WELL, LISTEN UP, KANOU.

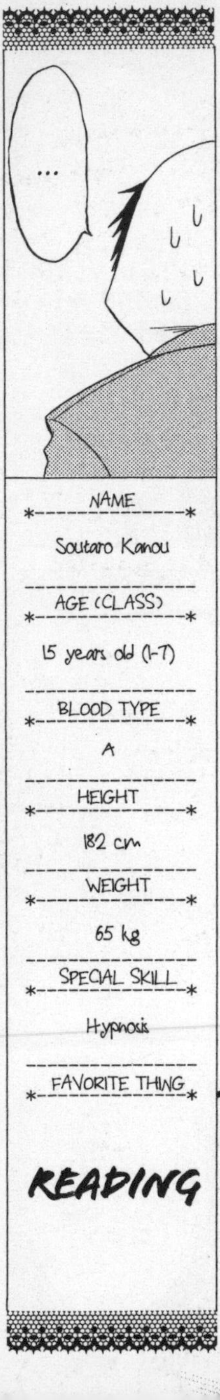
...

NAME

Soutaro Kanou

AGE (CLASS)

15 years old (1-7)

BLOOD TYPE

A

HEIGHT

182 cm

WEIGHT

65 kg

SPECIAL SKILL

Hypnosis

FAVORITE THING

READING

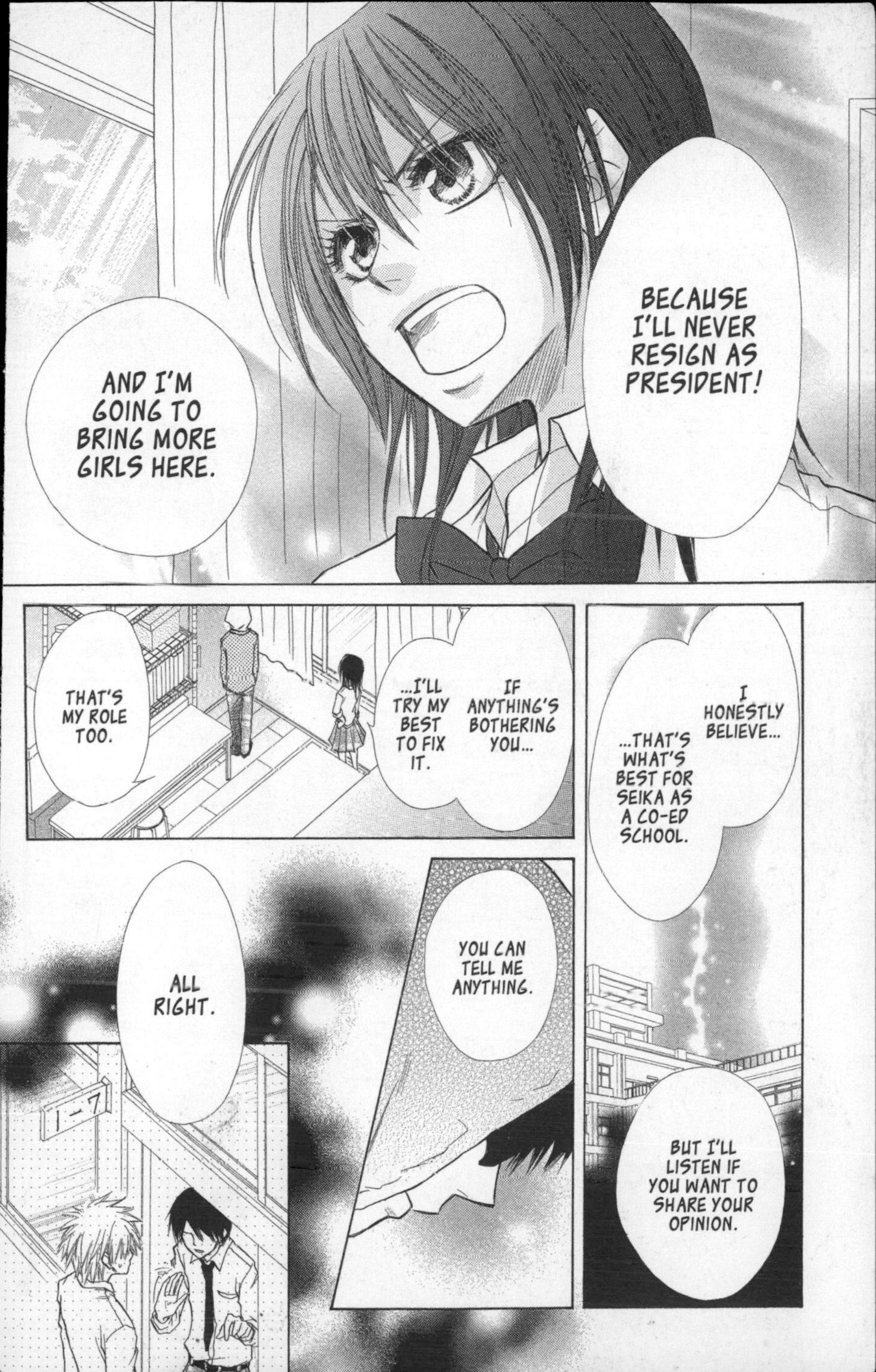
BECAUSE I'LL NEVER RESIGN AS PRESIDENT!
AND I'M GOING TO BRING MORE GIRLS HERE.
I HONESTLY BELIEVE...
...THAT'S WHAT'S BEST FOR SEIKA AS A CO-ED SCHOOL.
BUT I'LL LISTEN IF YOU WANT TO SHARE YOUR OPINION.
IF ANYTHING'S BOTHERING YOU...
...I'LL TRY MY BEST TO FIX IT.
THAT'S MY ROLE TOO.
YOU CAN TELL ME ANYTHING.
ALL RIGHT.
1-7

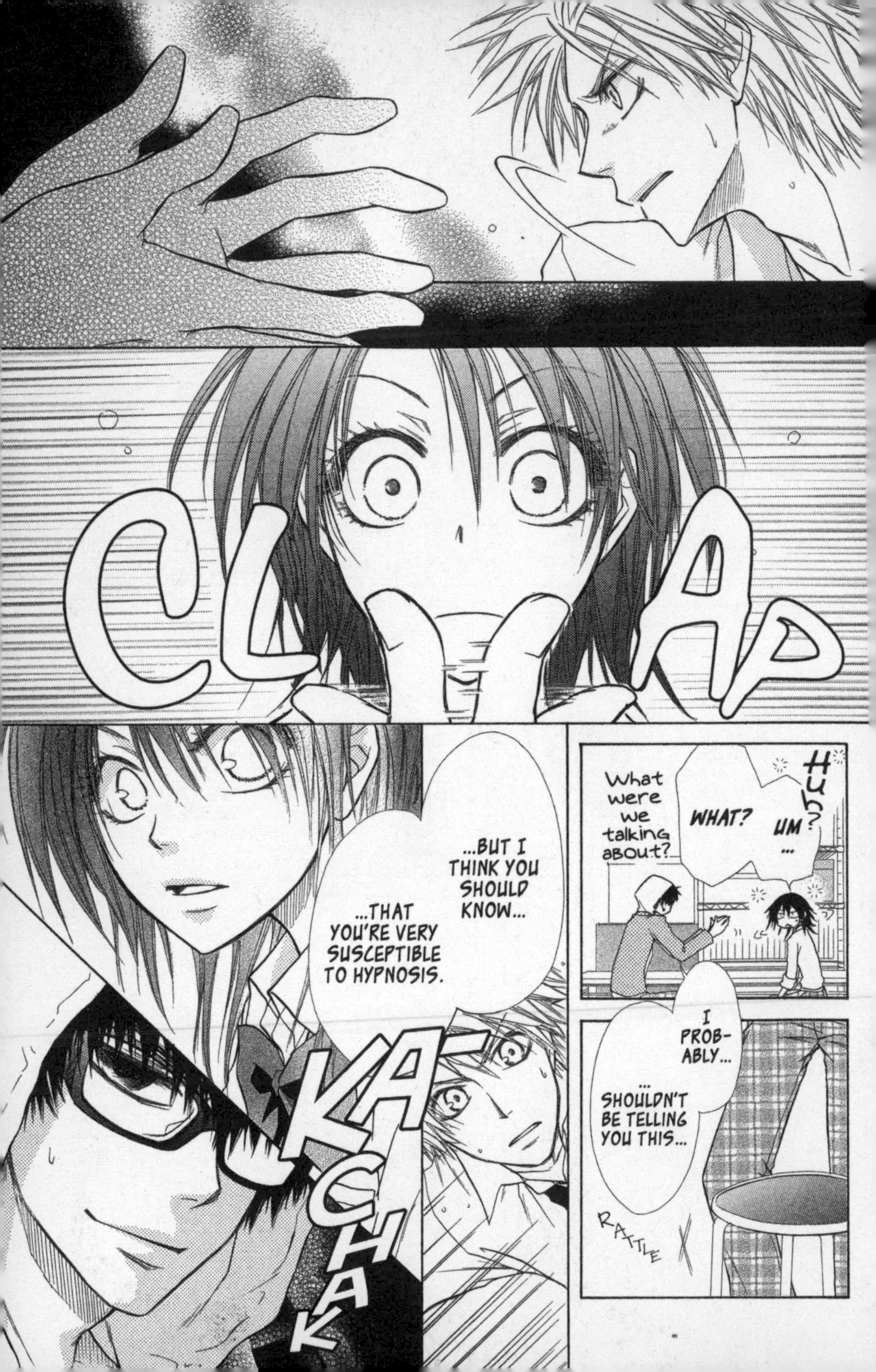
CLAP
Huh?
UM...
WHAT?
What were we talking about?
I PROBABLY...
...SHOULDN'T BE TELLING YOU THIS...
RATTLE
...BUT I THINK YOU SHOULD KNOW...
...THAT YOU'RE VERY SUSCEPTIBLE TO HYPNOSIS.
KA-CHAK

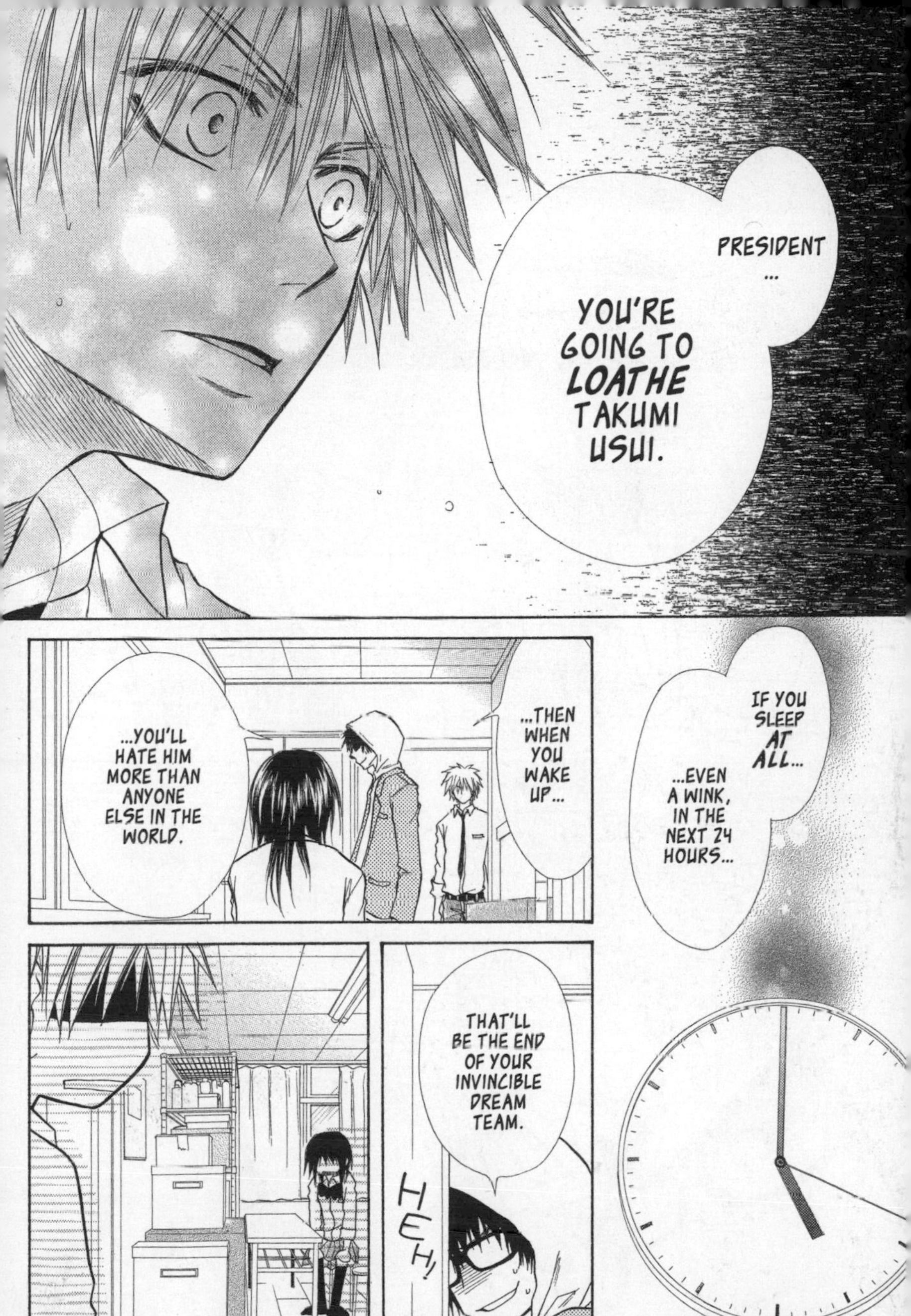
PRESIDENT ...
YOU'RE GOING TO LOATHE TAKUMI USUI.
IF YOU SLEEP AT ALL...
...EVEN A WINK, IN THE NEXT 24 HOURS...
...THEN WHEN YOU WAKE UP...
...YOU'LL HATE HIM MORE THAN ANYONE ELSE IN THE WORLD.
THAT'LL BE THE END OF YOUR INVINCIBLE DREAM TEAM.
HEH!

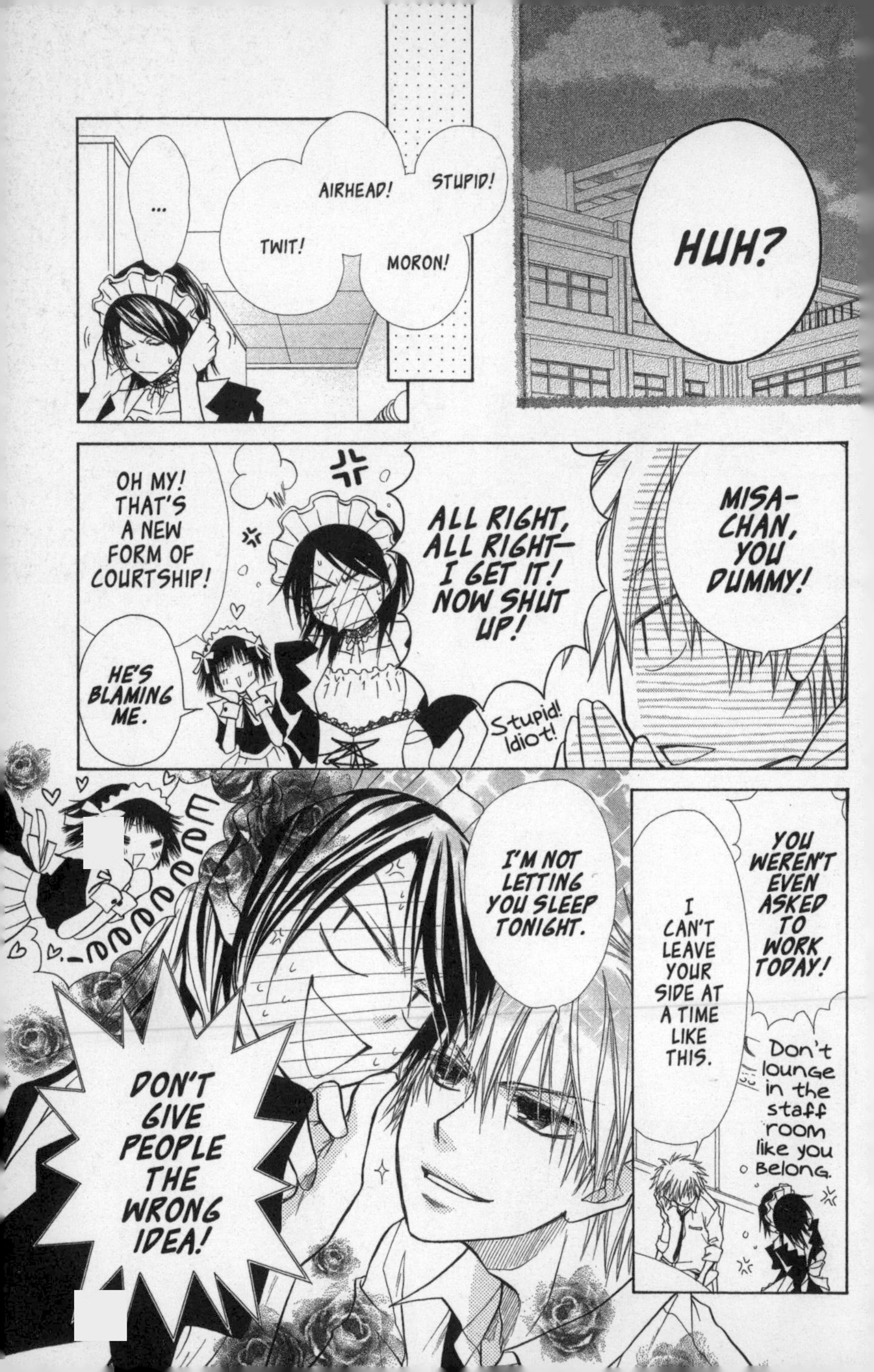
HUH?
STUPID!
AIRHEAD!
MORON!
TWIT!
...
MISA-CHAN, YOU DUMMY!
Stupid! Idiot!
ALL RIGHT, ALL RIGHT— I GET IT! NOW SHUT UP!
OH MY! THAT'S A NEW FORM OF COURTSHIP!
HE'S BLAMING ME.
YOU WEREN'T EVEN ASKED TO WORK TODAY!
I CAN'T LEAVE YOUR SIDE AT A TIME LIKE THIS.
Don't lounge in the staff room like you belong.
I'M NOT LETTING YOU SLEEP TONIGHT.
Eeeeeeee-eeeee
DON'T GIVE PEOPLE THE WRONG IDEA!

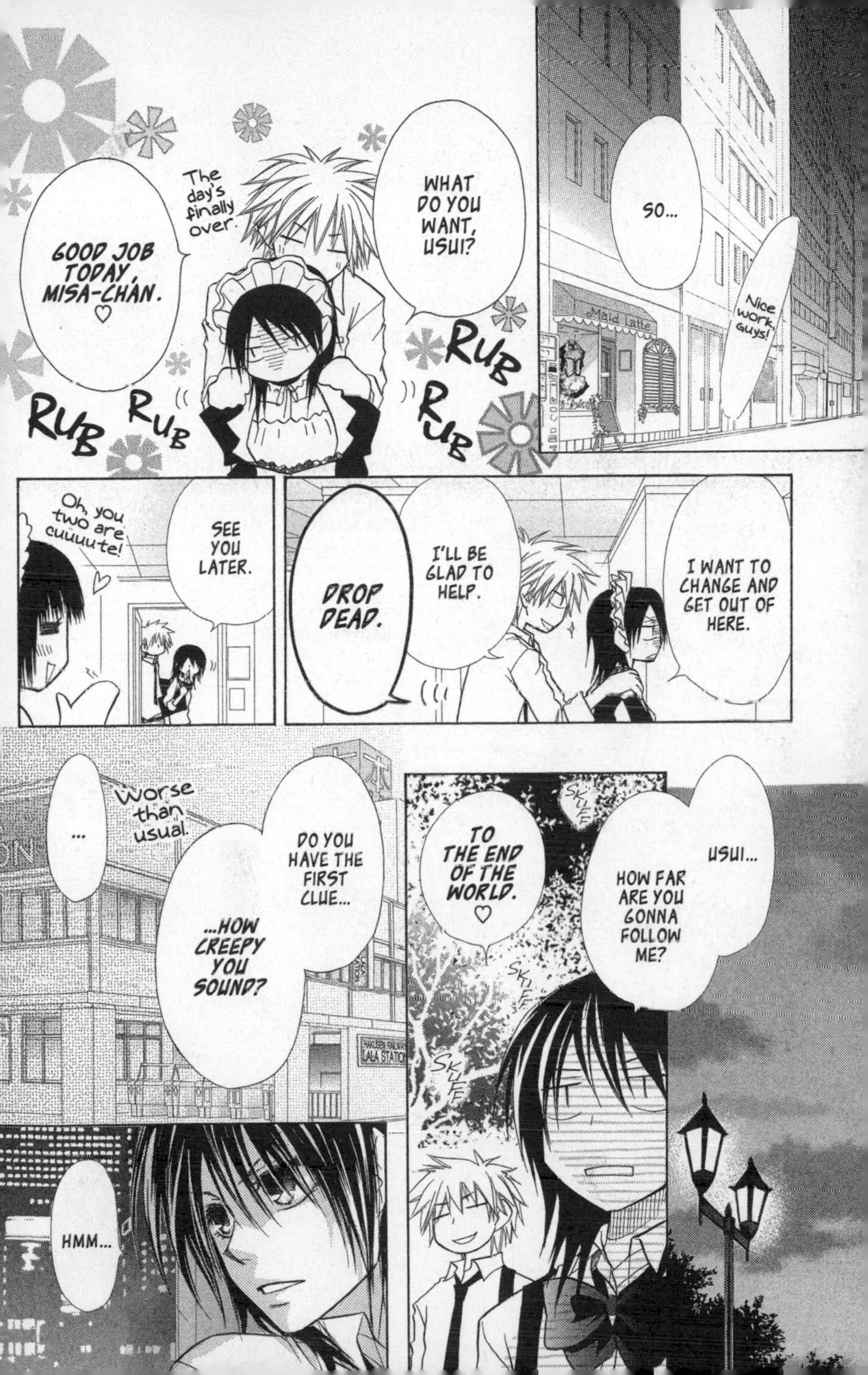
SO...
Nice work, guys!
Maid Latte
WHAT DO YOU WANT, USUI?
The day's finally over.
GOOD JOB TODAY, MISA-CHAN. ♡
RUB
RUB
RUB
RUB
I WANT TO CHANGE AND GET OUT OF HERE.
I'LL BE GLAD TO HELP.
DROP DEAD.
SEE YOU LATER.
Oh, you two are cuuuute! ♡
USUI...
HOW FAR ARE YOU GONNA FOLLOW ME?
TO THE END OF THE WORLD. ♡
SKUFF
SKUFF
SKUFF
DO YOU HAVE THE FIRST CLUE...
...HOW CREEPY YOU SOUND?
Worse than usual.
...
LALA STATION
HMM...

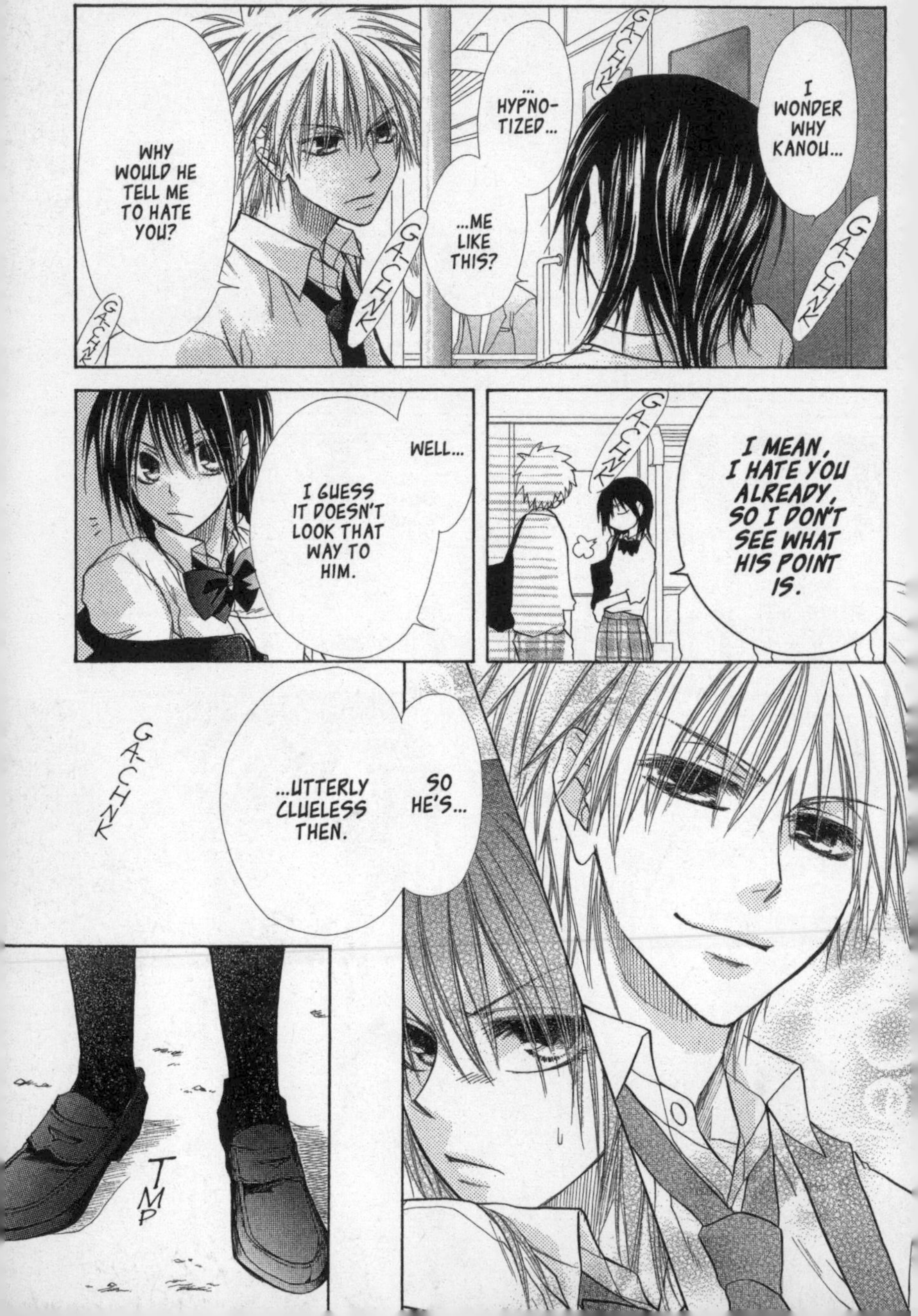
I WONDER WHY KANOU...
GACHNK
... HYPNO-TIZED...
GACHNK
...ME LIKE THIS?
GACHNK
WHY WOULD HE TELL ME TO HATE YOU?
GACHNK
GACHNK
I MEAN, I HATE YOU ALREADY, SO I DON'T SEE WHAT HIS POINT IS.
WELL...
I GUESS IT DOESN'T LOOK THAT WAY TO HIM.
SO HE'S...
...UTTERLY CLUELESS THEN.
GACHNK
TMP

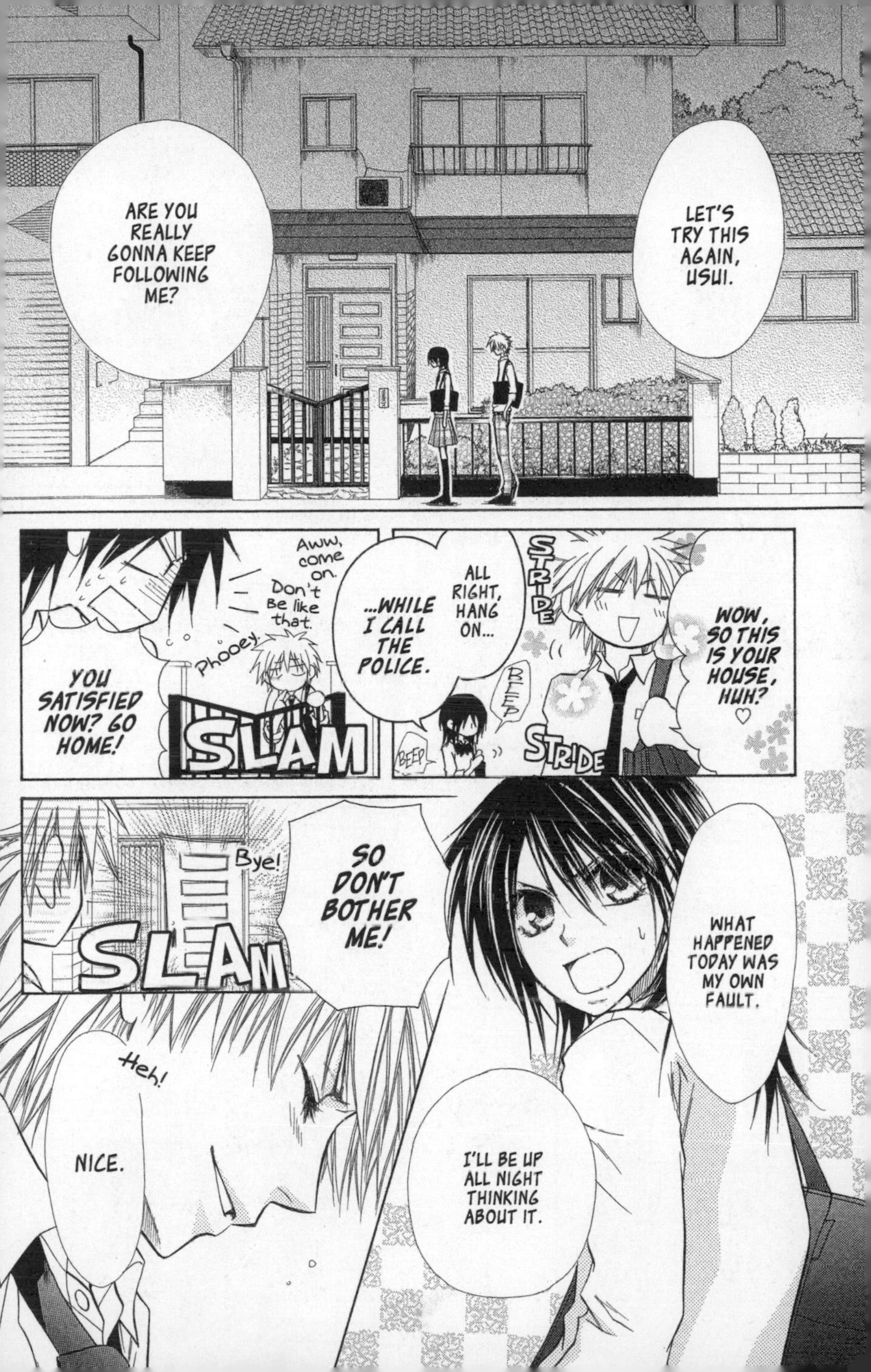
LET'S TRY THIS AGAIN, USUI.
ARE YOU REALLY GONNA KEEP FOLLOWING ME?
STRIDE
WOW, SO THIS IS YOUR HOUSE, HUH? ♡
STRIDE
BLEEP
BEEP
ALL RIGHT, HANG ON...
...WHILE I CALL THE POLICE.
Aww, come on. Don't be like that.
Phooey.
YOU SATISFIED NOW? GO HOME!
SLAM
WHAT HAPPENED TODAY WAS MY OWN FAULT.
SO DON'T BOTHER ME!
Bye!
SLAM
I'LL BE UP ALL NIGHT THINKING ABOUT IT.
Heh!
NICE.

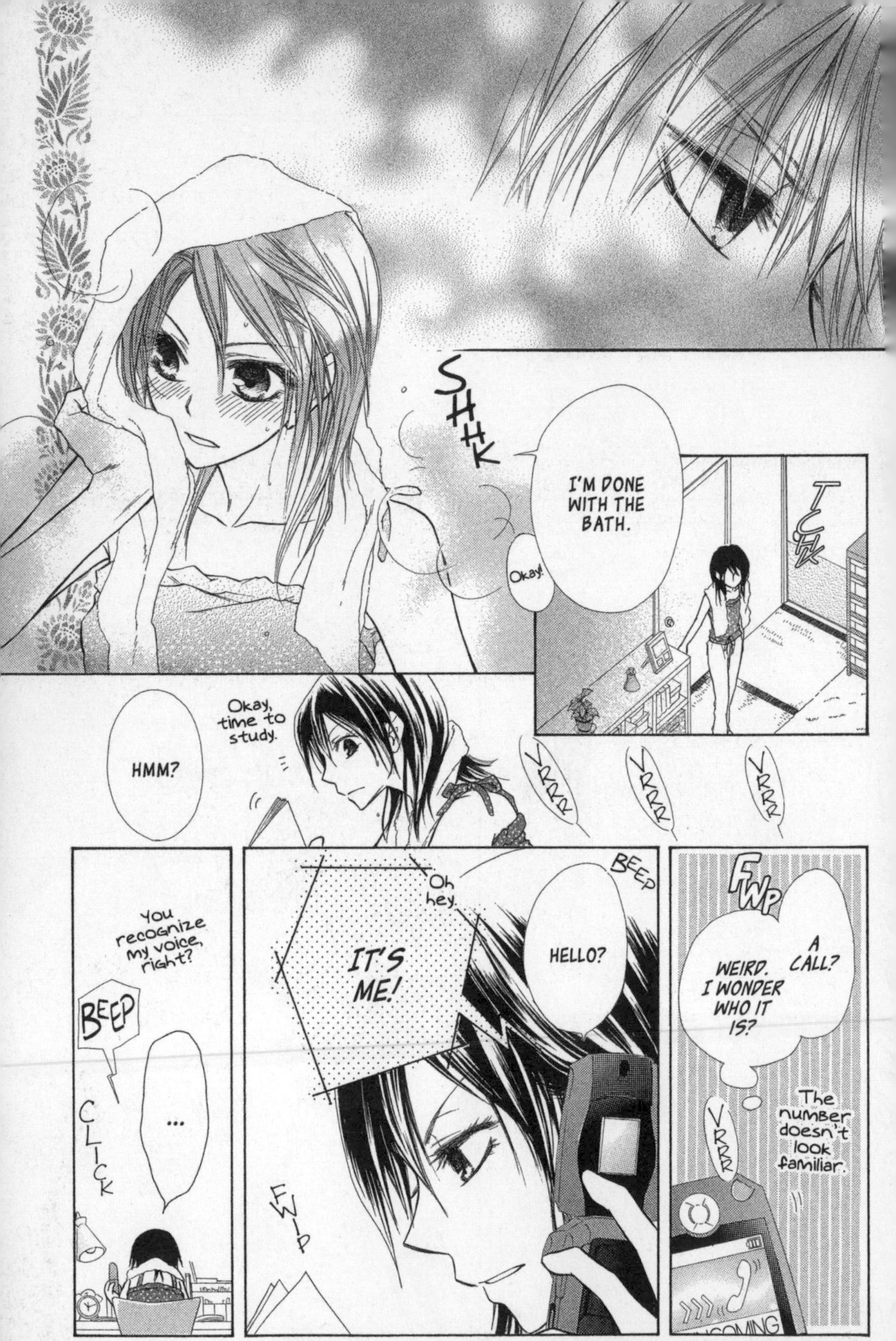
TCHK
I'M DONE WITH THE BATH.
SHHK
Okay!
VRRR
VRRR
VRRR
Okay, time to study.
HMM?
FWP
A CALL?
WEIRD. I WONDER WHO IT IS?
VRRR
The number doesn't look familiar.
BEEP
HELLO?
Oh hey.
IT'S ME!
FWIP
You recognize my voice, right?
BEEP
CLICK
...

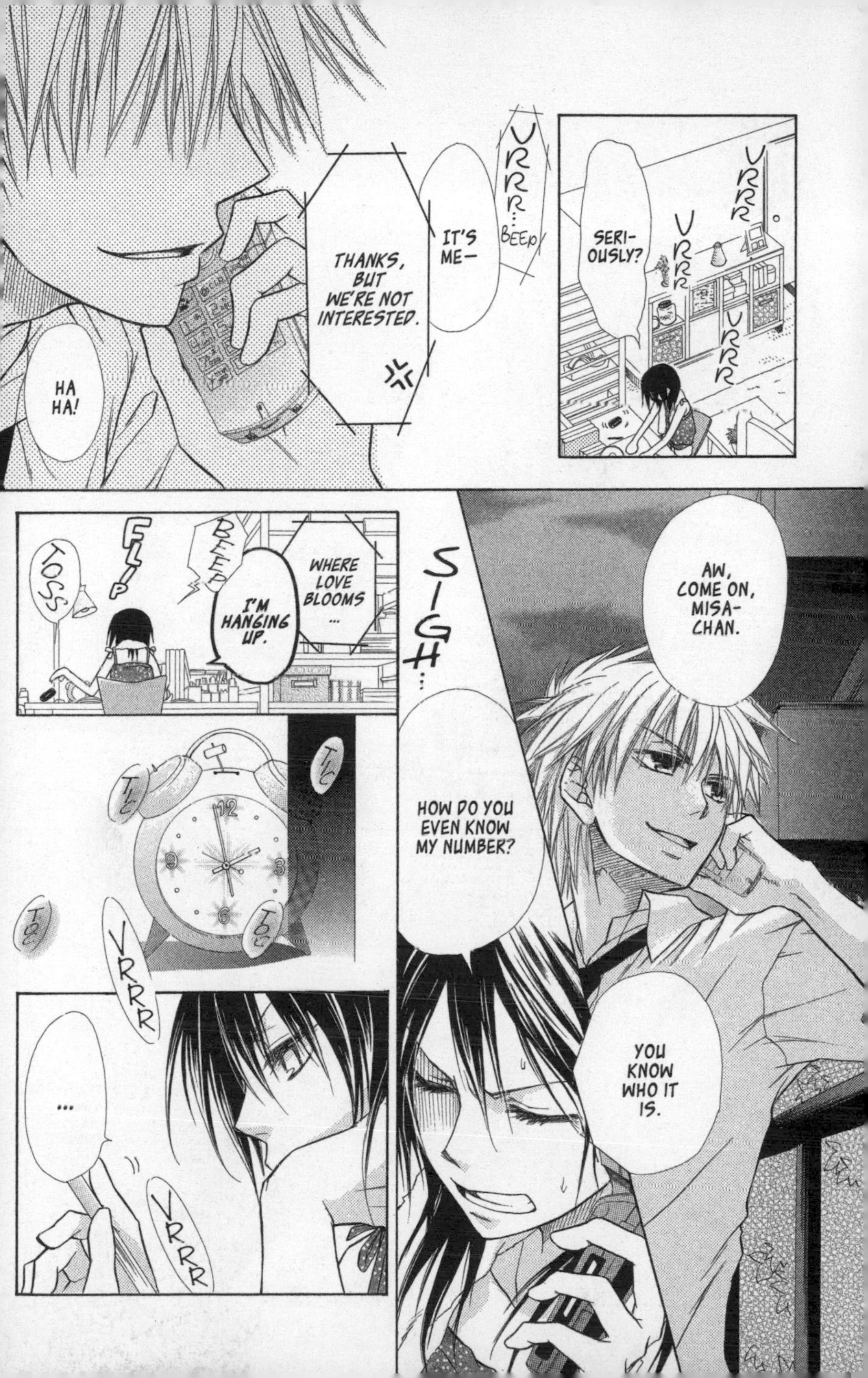
VRRR
VRRR
VRRR
SERI-OUSLY?
VRRR... BEEP
IT'S ME—
THANKS, BUT WE'RE NOT INTERESTED.
HA HA!
AW, COME ON, MISA-CHAN.
HOW DO YOU EVEN KNOW MY NUMBER?
YOU KNOW WHO IT IS.
WHERE LOVE BLOOMS ...
I'M HANGING UP.
BEEP
FLIP
TOSS
SIGH...
TIC
TIC
TOC
TOC
VRRR
...
VRRR

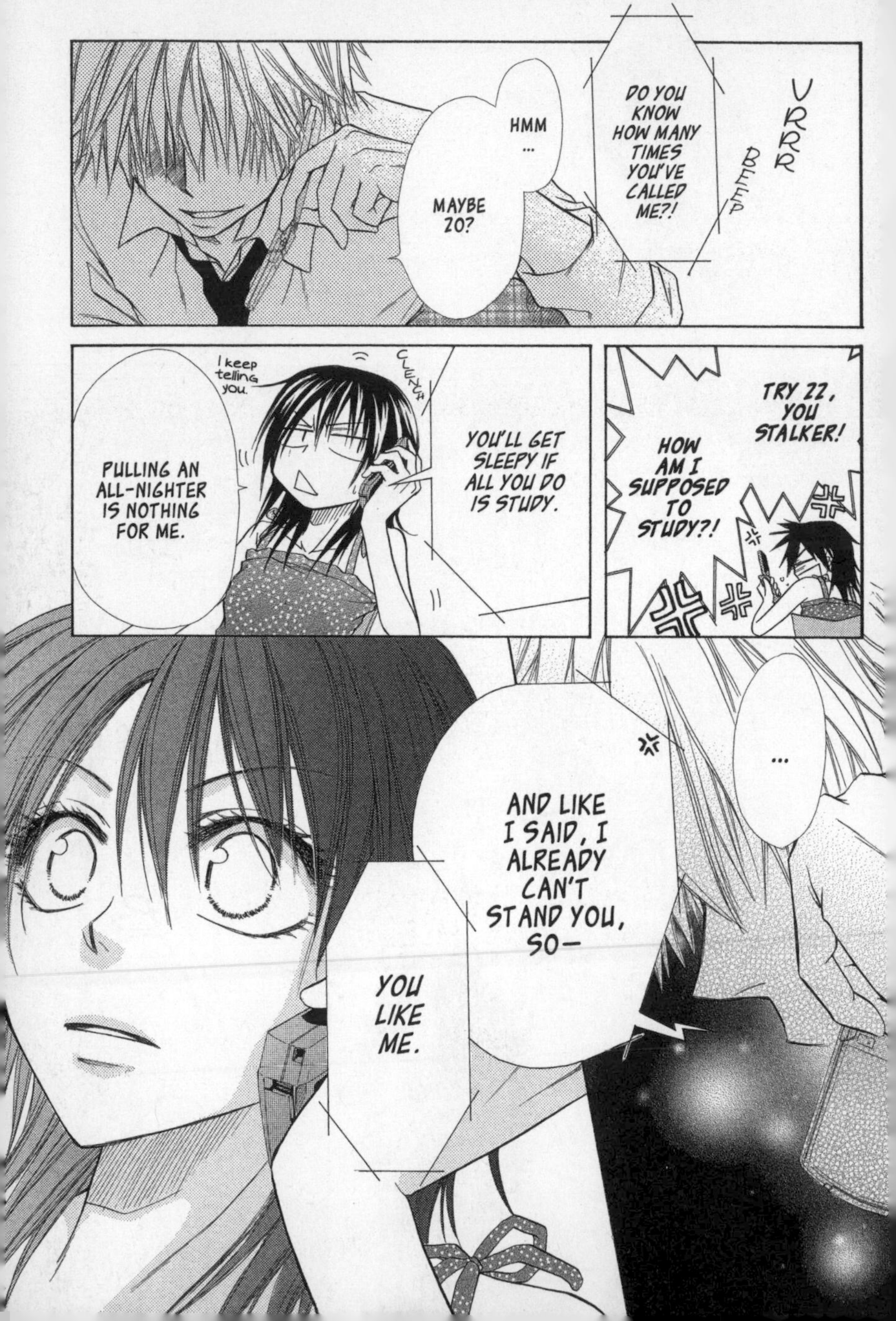
VRRR
BEEP
DO YOU KNOW HOW MANY TIMES YOU'VE CALLED ME?!
HMM...
MAYBE 20?
TRY 22, YOU STALKER!
HOW AM I SUPPOSED TO STUDY?!
CLENCH
YOU'LL GET SLEEPY IF ALL YOU DO IS STUDY.
I keep telling you.
PULLING AN ALL-NIGHTER IS NOTHING FOR ME.
...
AND LIKE I SAID, I ALREADY CAN'T STAND YOU, SO—
YOU LIKE ME.

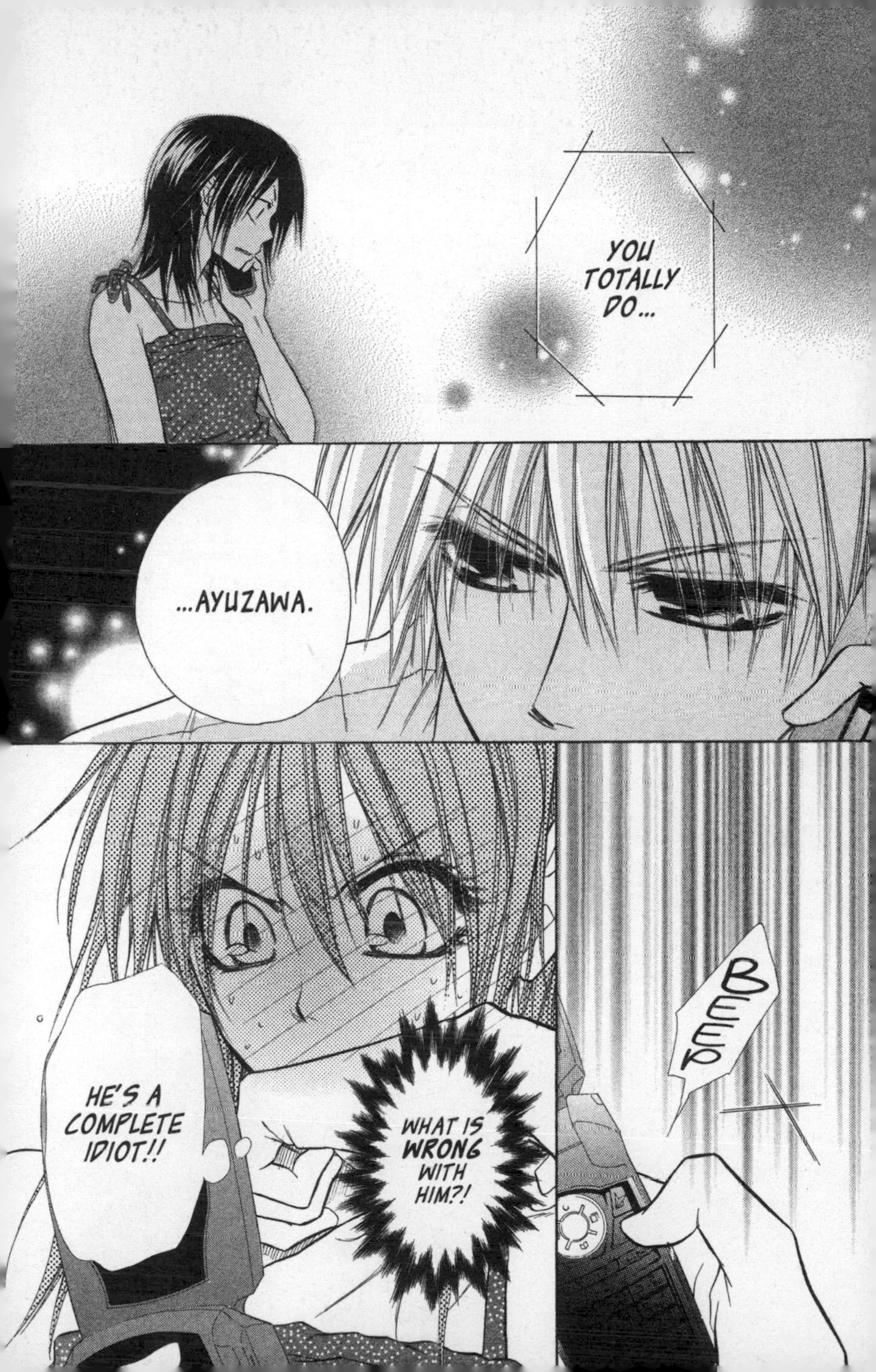
YOU TOTALLY DO...
...AYUZAWA.
BEEP
WHAT IS WRONG WITH HIM?!
HE'S A COMPLETE IDIOT!!

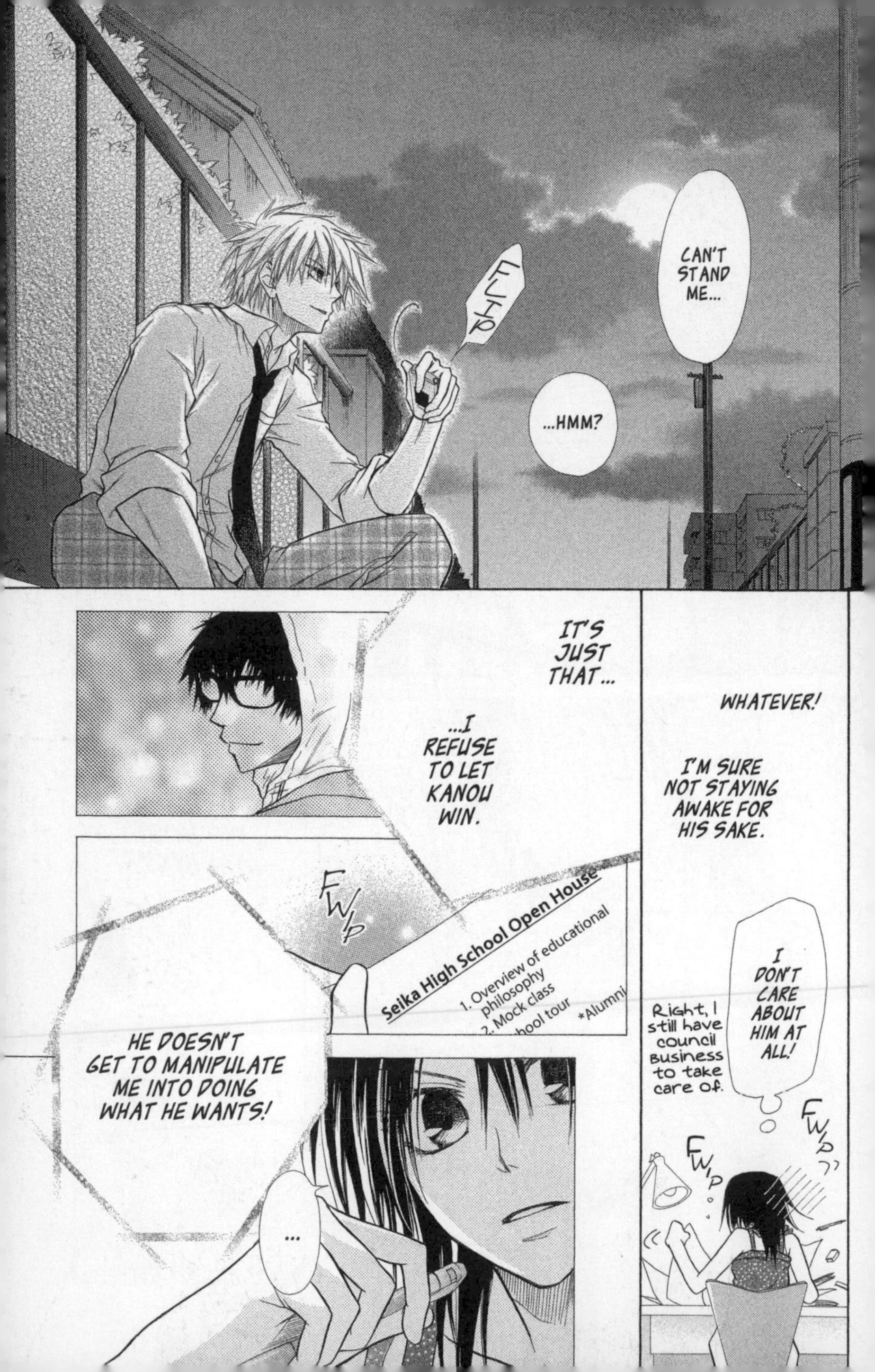
CAN'T STAND ME...
...HMM?
FLIP
WHATEVER!
I'M SURE NOT STAYING AWAKE FOR HIS SAKE.
I DON'T CARE ABOUT HIM AT ALL!
Right, I still have council business to take care of.
FWIP
FWIP
IT'S JUST THAT...
...I REFUSE TO LET KANOU WIN.
FWIP
Seika High School Open House
1. Overview of educational philosophy
2. Mock class
*Alumni
HE DOESN'T GET TO MANIPULATE ME INTO DOING WHAT HE WANTS!
...

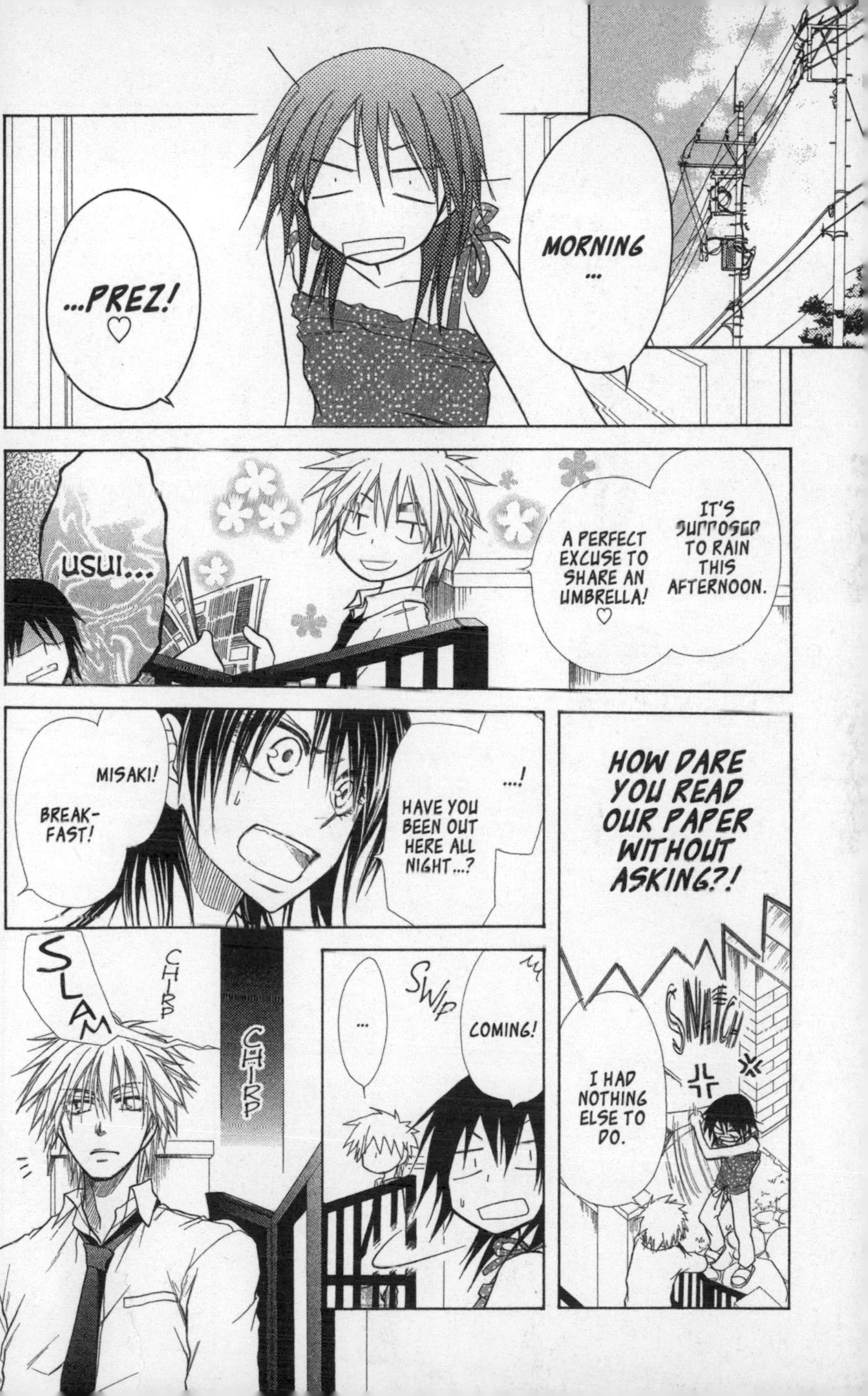
MORNING ...
...PREZ! ♡
IT'S SUPPOSED TO RAIN THIS AFTERNOON.
A PERFECT EXCUSE TO SHARE AN UMBRELLA! ♡
USUI...
HOW DARE YOU READ OUR PAPER WITHOUT ASKING?!
...!
HAVE YOU BEEN OUT HERE ALL NIGHT...?
MISAKI!
BREAK-FAST!
SNATCH
I HAD NOTHING ELSE TO DO.
COMING!
SWIP
...
CHIRP
CHIRP
SLAM

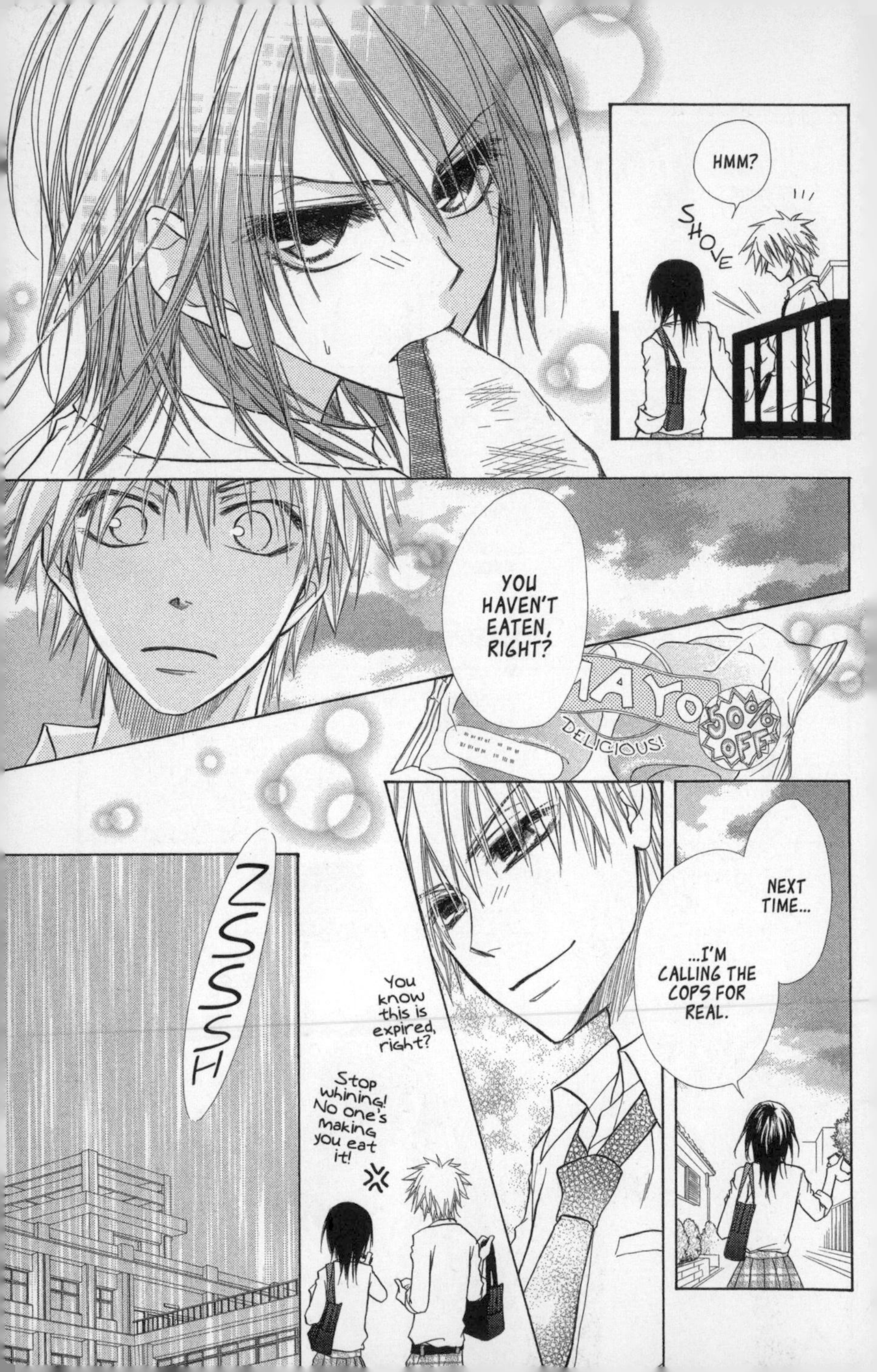
HMM?
SHOVE
YOU HAVEN'T EATEN, RIGHT?
MAYO
DELICIOUS!
50% OFF
NEXT TIME...
...I'M CALLING THE COPS FOR REAL.
ZSSSH
You know this is expired, right?
Stop whining! No one's making you eat it!

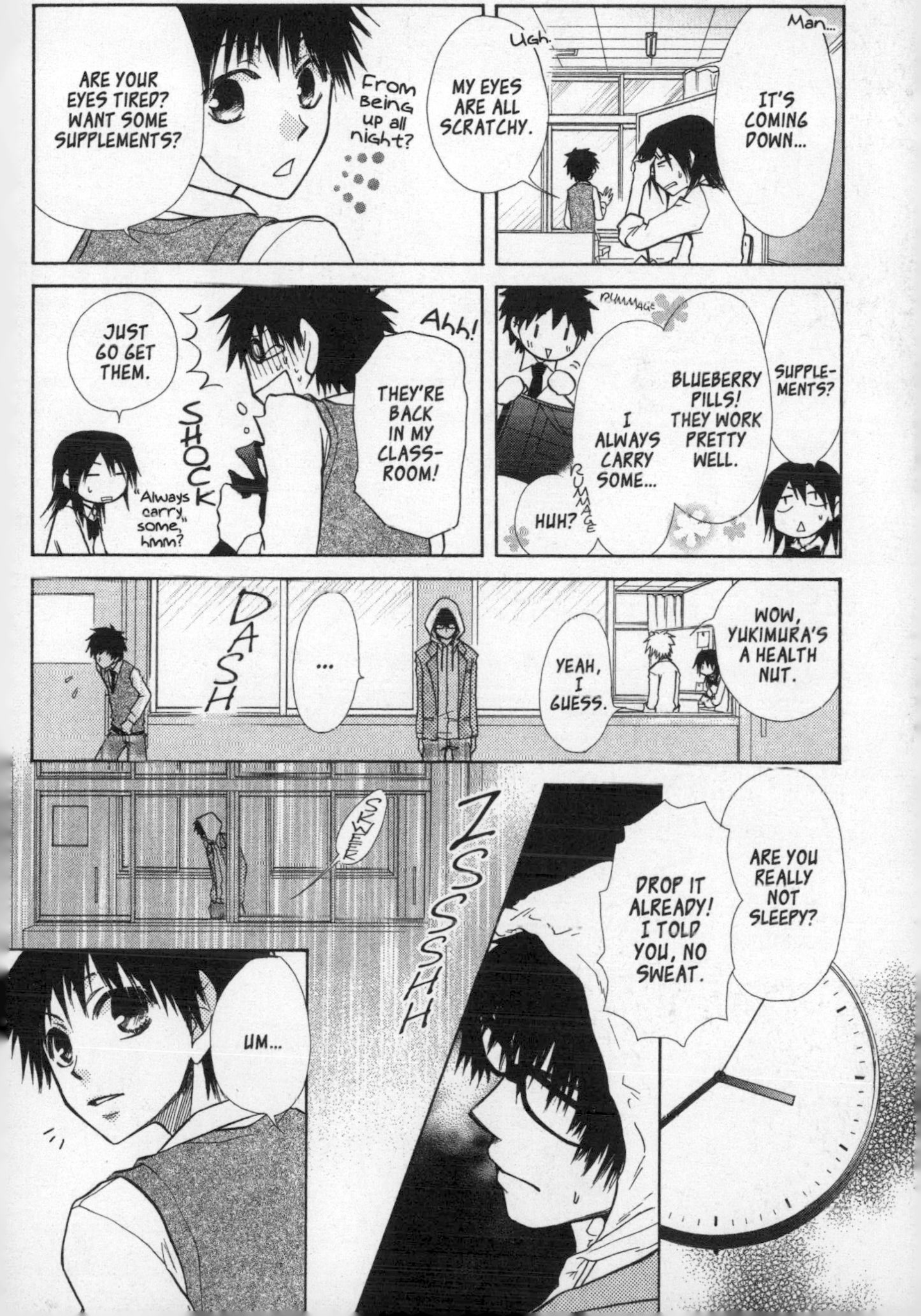
Man...
IT'S COMING DOWN...
Ugh.
MY EYES ARE ALL SCRATCHY.
From being up all night?
ARE YOUR EYES TIRED? WANT SOME SUPPLEMENTS?
SUPPLEMENTS?
BLUEBERRY PILLS! THEY WORK PRETTY WELL.
RUMMAGE
I ALWAYS CARRY SOME...
RUMMAGE
HUH?
Ahh!
THEY'RE BACK IN MY CLASSROOM!
SHOCK
JUST GO GET THEM.
"Always carry some," hmm?
WOW, YUKIMURA'S A HEALTH NUT.
YEAH, I GUESS.
...
DASH
ARE YOU REALLY NOT SLEEPY?
DROP IT ALREADY! I TOLD YOU, NO SWEAT.
ZSSSSHH
SKWEEK
UM...

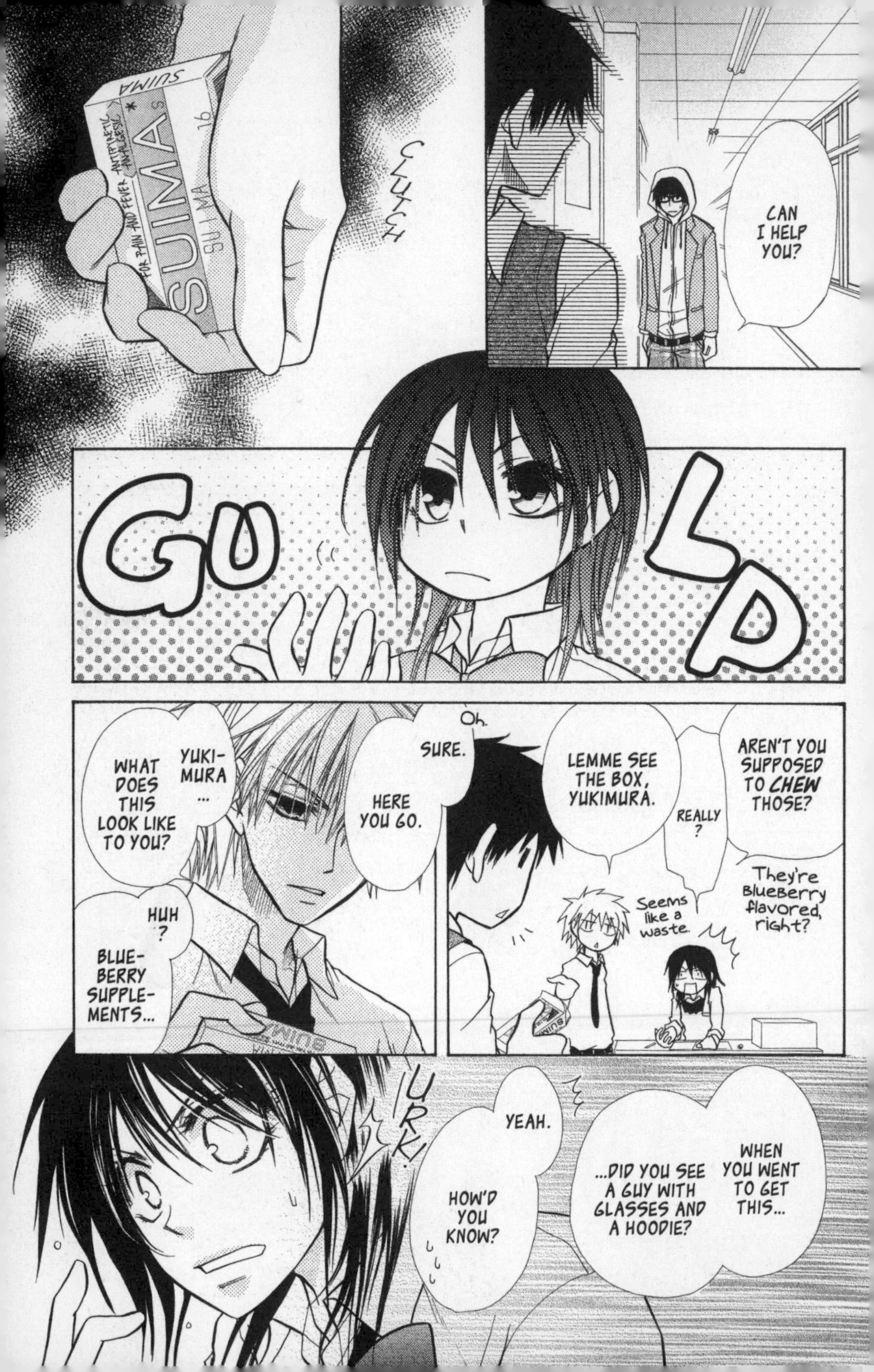
CAN I HELP YOU?
SUIMA
FOR PAIN AND FEVER
ANTIPYRETIC ANALGESIC
CLUTCH
GULP
AREN'T YOU SUPPOSED TO *CHEW* THOSE?
LEMME SEE THE BOX, YUKIMURA.
REALLY?
They're Blueberry flavored, right?
Seems like a waste.
Oh.
SURE.
HERE YOU GO.
YUKIMURA...
WHAT DOES THIS LOOK LIKE TO YOU?
HUH?
BLUEBERRY SUPPLEMENTS...
WHEN YOU WENT TO GET THIS...
...DID YOU SEE A GUY WITH GLASSES AND A HOODIE?
YEAH.
URK!
HOW'D YOU KNOW?

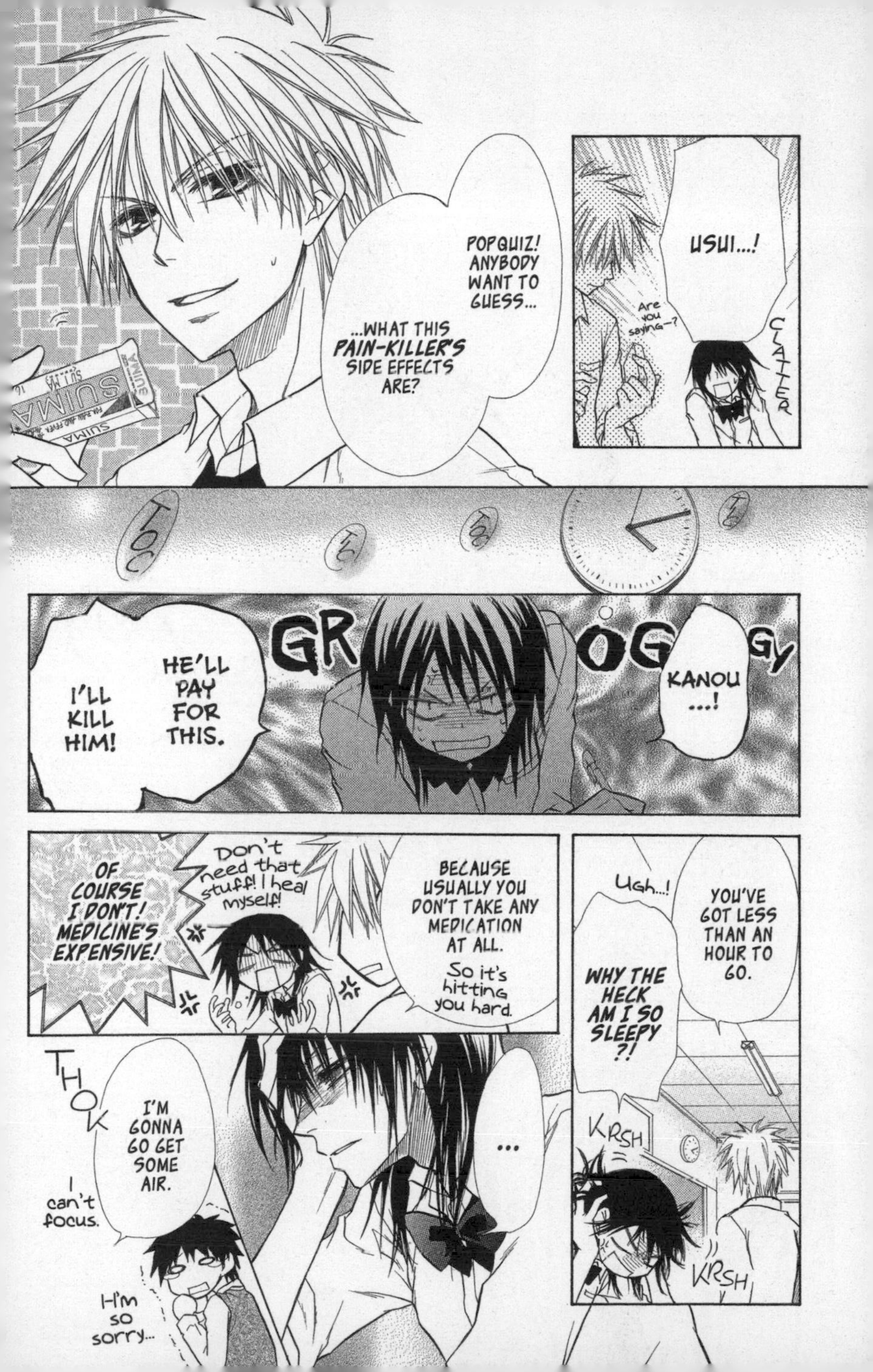
USUI...!
Are you saying--?
CLATTER
POPQUIZ! ANYBODY WANT TO GUESS...
...WHAT THIS PAIN-KILLER'S SIDE EFFECTS ARE?
SUIMA
TIC
TOC
TIC
TOC
KANOU ...!
GROGGY
HE'LL PAY FOR THIS.
I'LL KILL HIM!
YOU'VE GOT LESS THAN AN HOUR TO GO.
Ugh...!
WHY THE HECK AM I SO SLEEPY?!
KRSH
KRSH
BECAUSE USUALLY YOU DON'T TAKE ANY MEDICATION AT ALL.
So it's hitting you hard.
Don't need that stuff! I heal myself!
OF COURSE I DON'T! MEDICINE'S EXPENSIVE!
...
I'M GONNA GO GET SOME AIR.
I can't focus.
THOK
I'm so sorry...

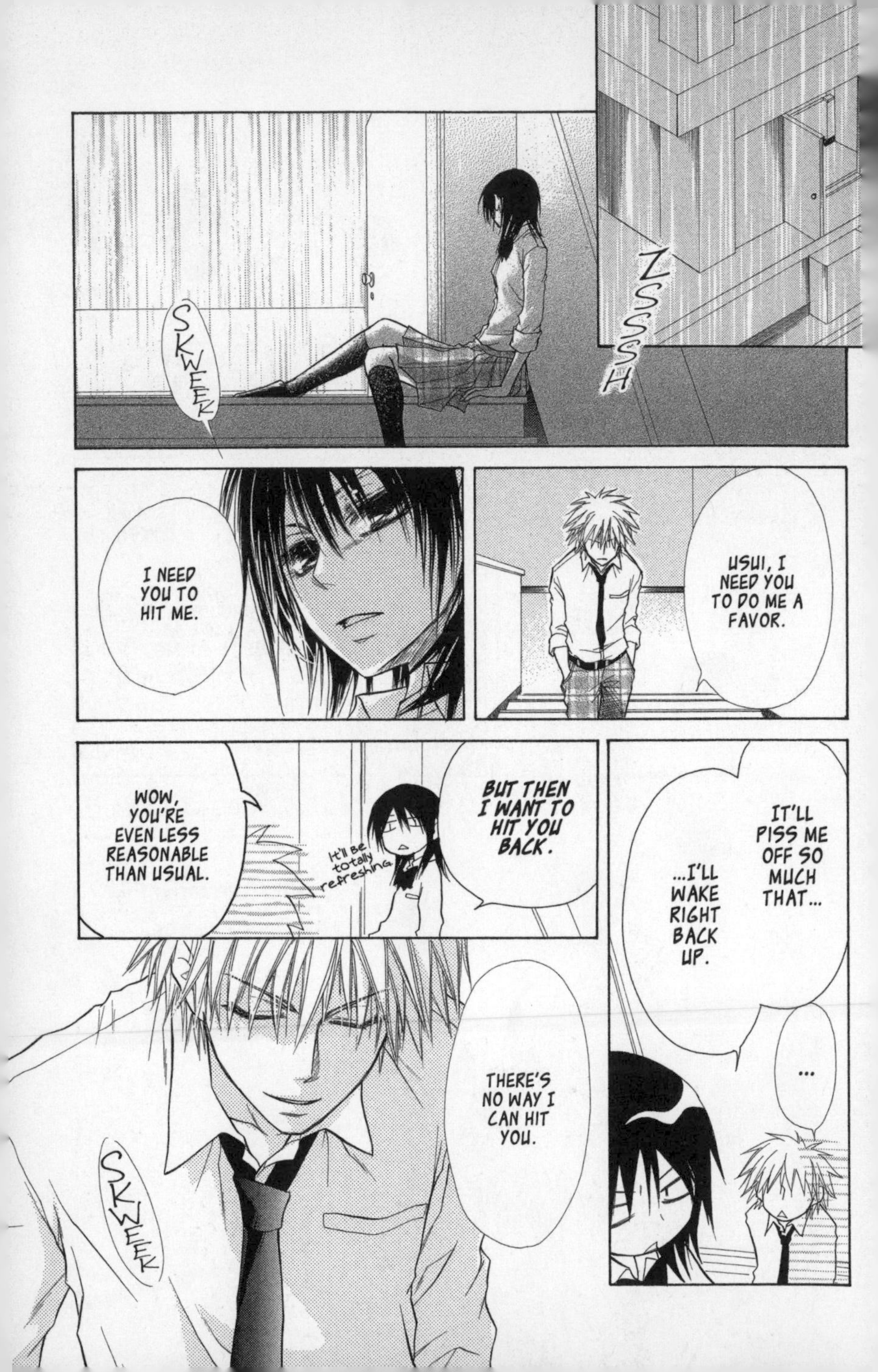
ZSSSH
SKWEEK
USUI, I NEED YOU TO DO ME A FAVOR.
I NEED YOU TO HIT ME.
IT'LL PISS ME OFF SO MUCH THAT...
...I'LL WAKE RIGHT BACK UP.
...
BUT THEN I WANT TO HIT YOU BACK.
It'll be totally refreshing.
WOW, YOU'RE EVEN LESS REASONABLE THAN USUAL.
THERE'S NO WAY I CAN HIT YOU.
SKWEEK

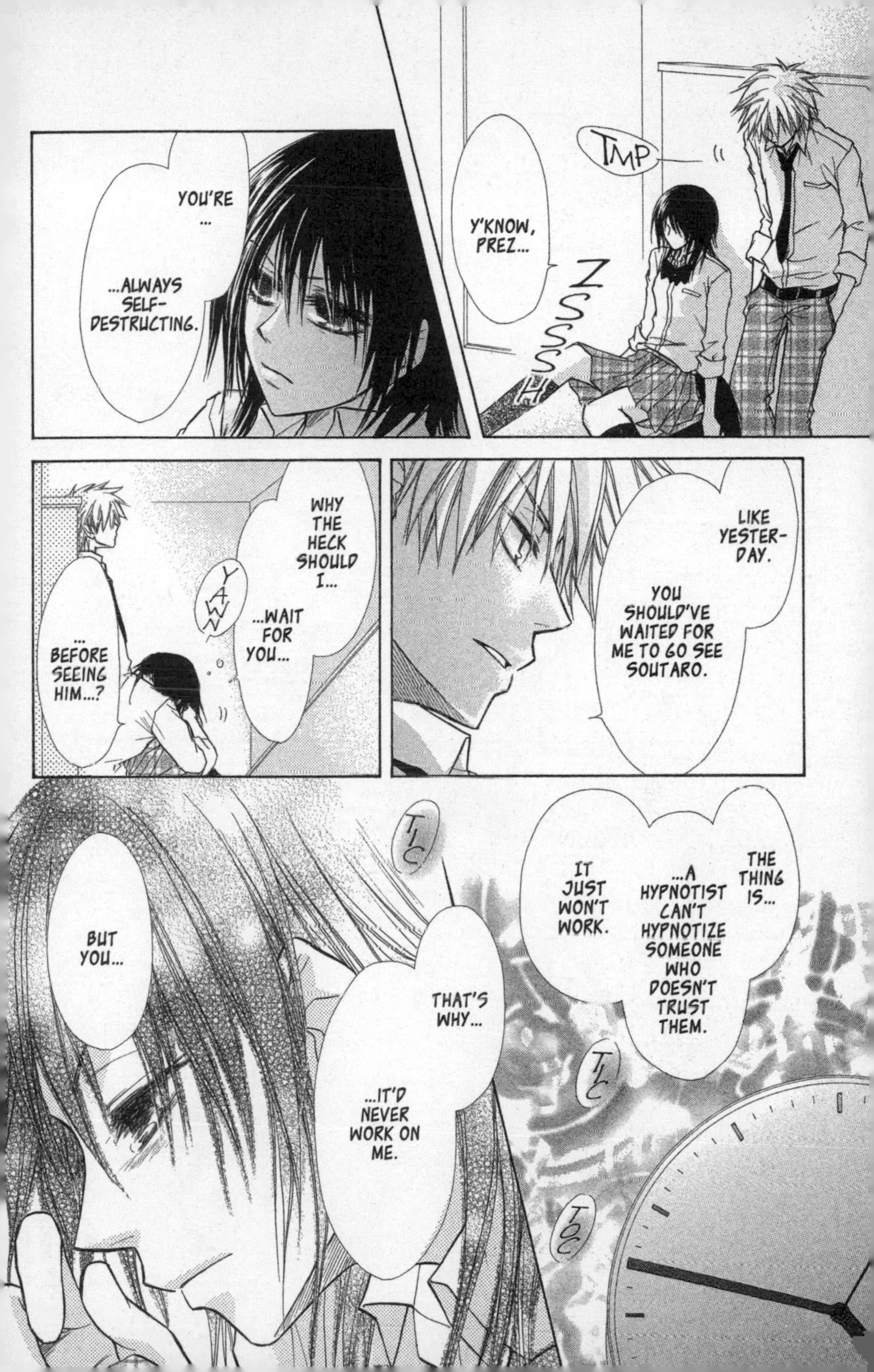
TMP
Y'KNOW, PREZ...
ZSSSH
YOU'RE ...
...ALWAYS SELF-DESTRUCTING.
LIKE YESTER-DAY.
YOU SHOULD'VE WAITED FOR ME TO GO SEE SOUTARO.
WHY THE HECK SHOULD I...
...WAIT FOR YOU...
YAWN
... BEFORE SEEING HIM...?
THE THING IS...
...A HYPNOTIST CAN'T HYPNOTIZE SOMEONE WHO DOESN'T TRUST THEM.
IT JUST WON'T WORK.
TIC
TIC
TOC
THAT'S WHY...
...IT'D NEVER WORK ON ME.
BUT YOU...

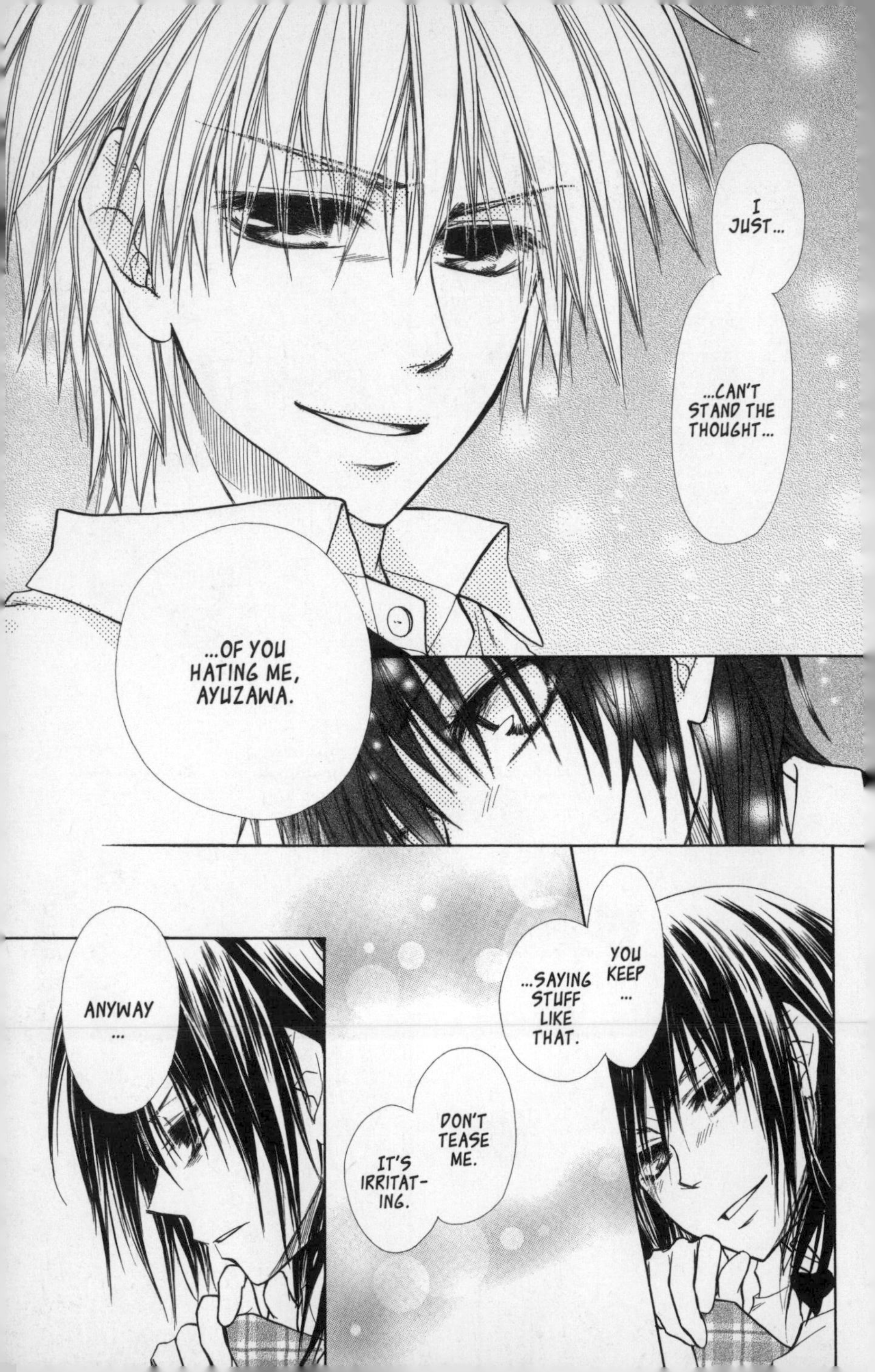
I JUST...
...CAN'T STAND THE THOUGHT...
...OF YOU HATING ME, AYUZAWA.
YOU KEEP ...
...SAYING STUFF LIKE THAT.
DON'T TEASE ME.
IT'S IRRITAT-ING.
ANYWAY ...

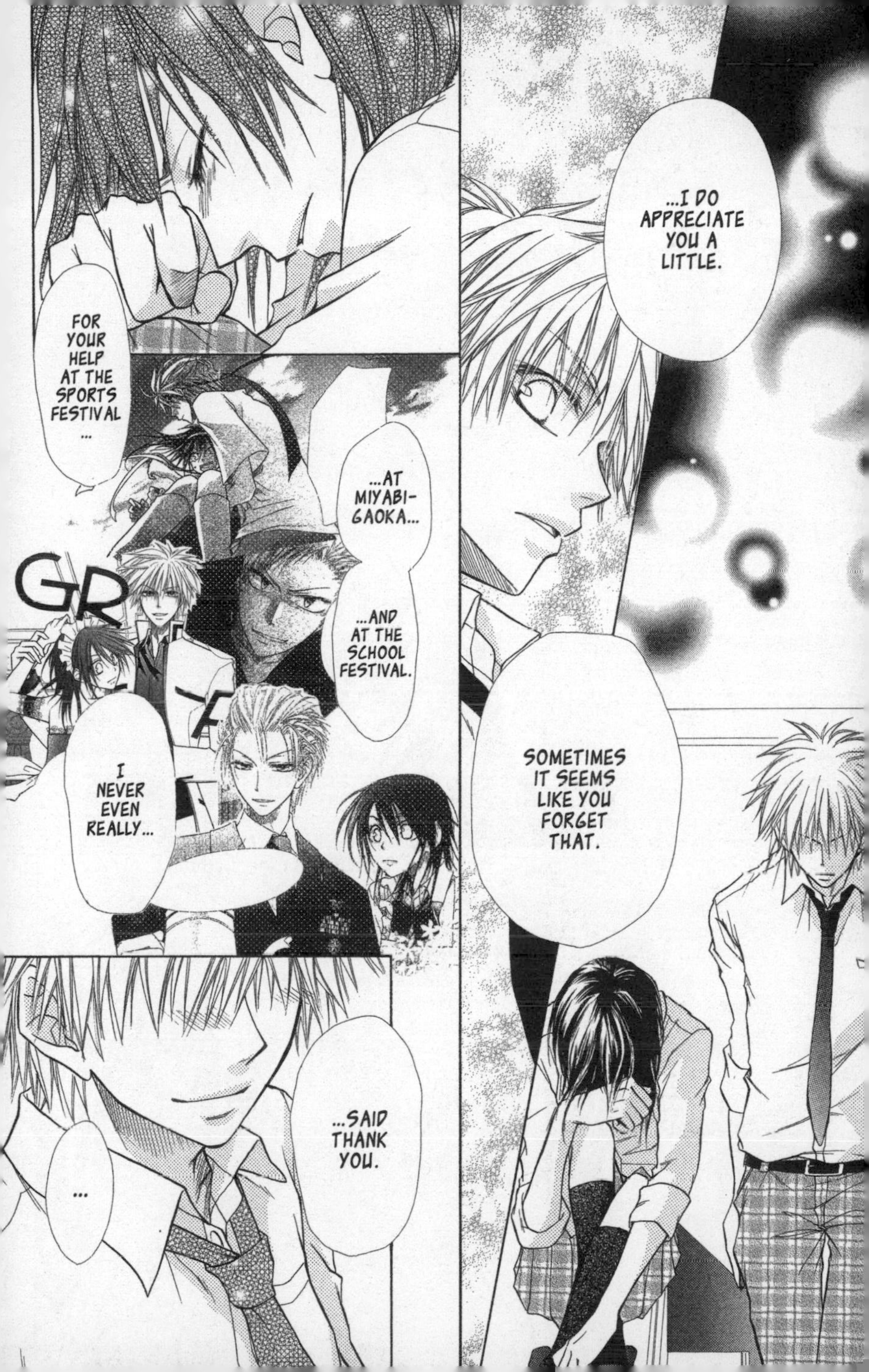
...I DO APPRECIATE YOU A LITTLE.
SOMETIMES IT SEEMS LIKE YOU FORGET THAT.
FOR YOUR HELP AT THE SPORTS FESTIVAL...
...AT MIYABI-GAOKA...
GR
...AND AT THE SCHOOL FESTIVAL.
I NEVER EVEN REALLY...
...SAID THANK YOU.
...

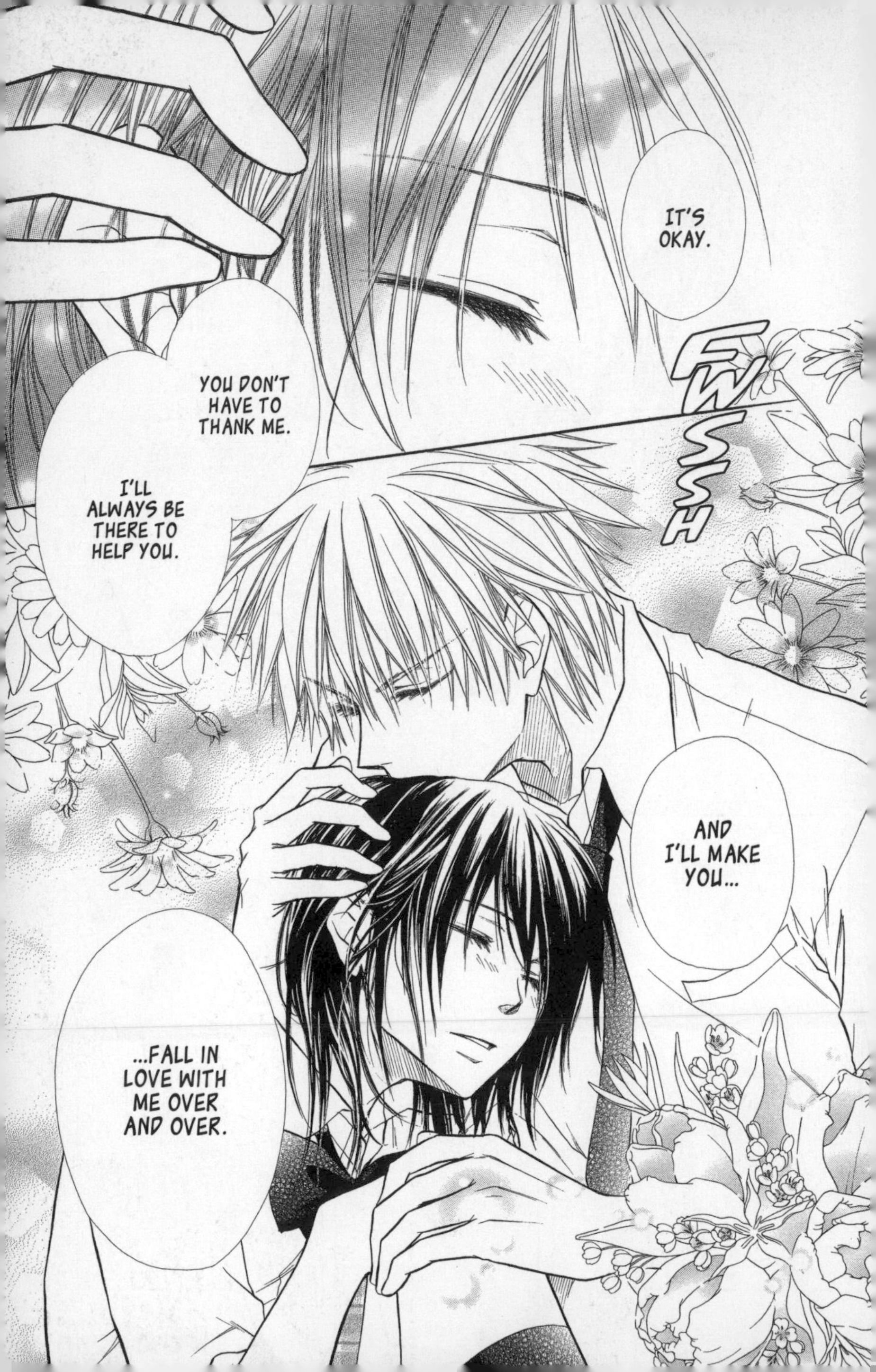
IT'S OKAY.
FWSSH
YOU DON'T HAVE TO THANK ME.
I'LL ALWAYS BE THERE TO HELP YOU.
AND I'LL MAKE YOU...
...FALL IN LOVE WITH ME OVER AND OVER.

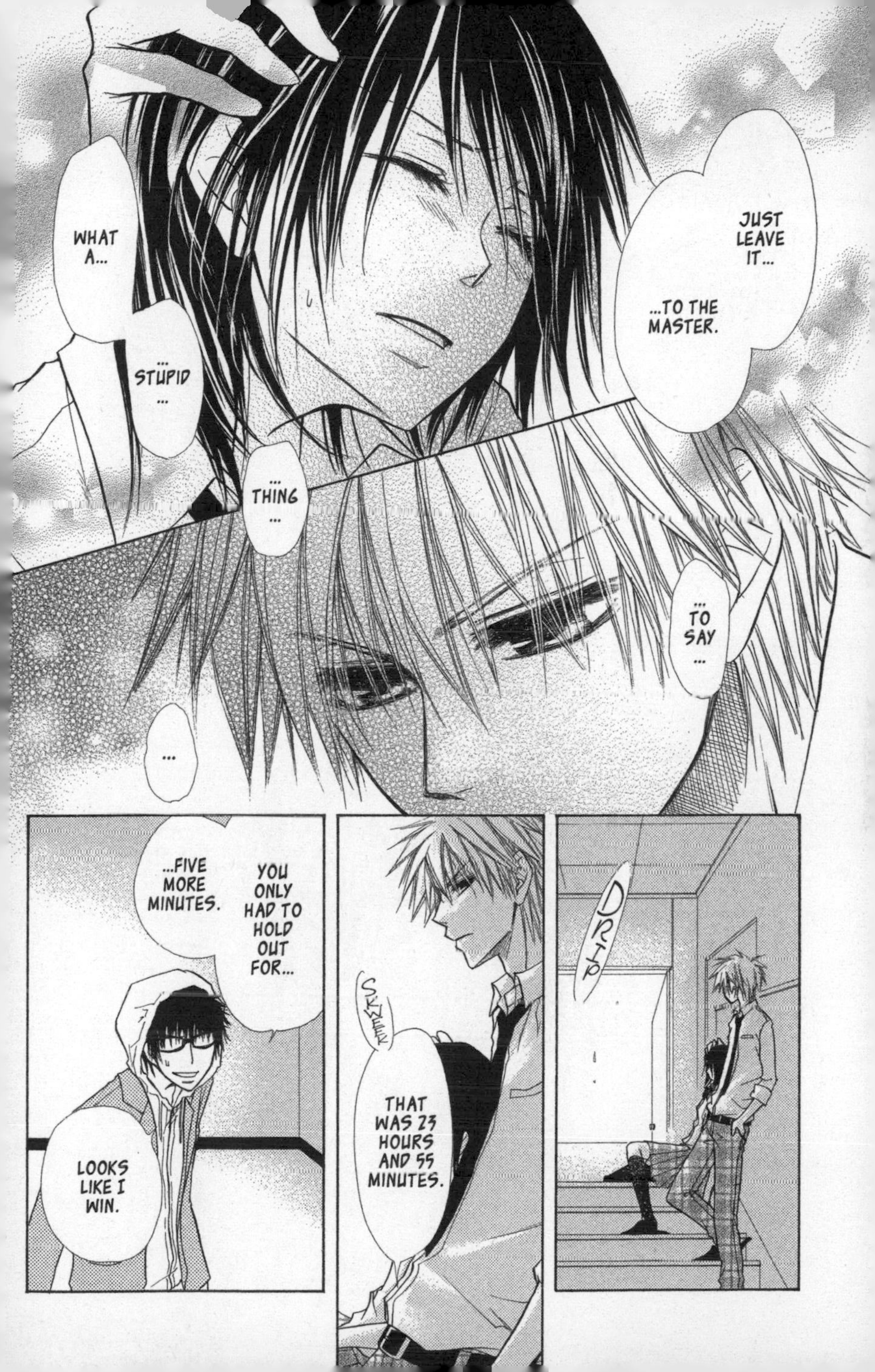
JUST LEAVE IT...
...TO THE MASTER.
WHAT A...
...STUPID...
...THING...
...TO SAY...
...
DRIP
SKWEEK
THAT WAS 23 HOURS AND 55 MINUTES.
YOU ONLY HAD TO HOLD OUT FOR...
...FIVE MORE MINUTES.
LOOKS LIKE I WIN.

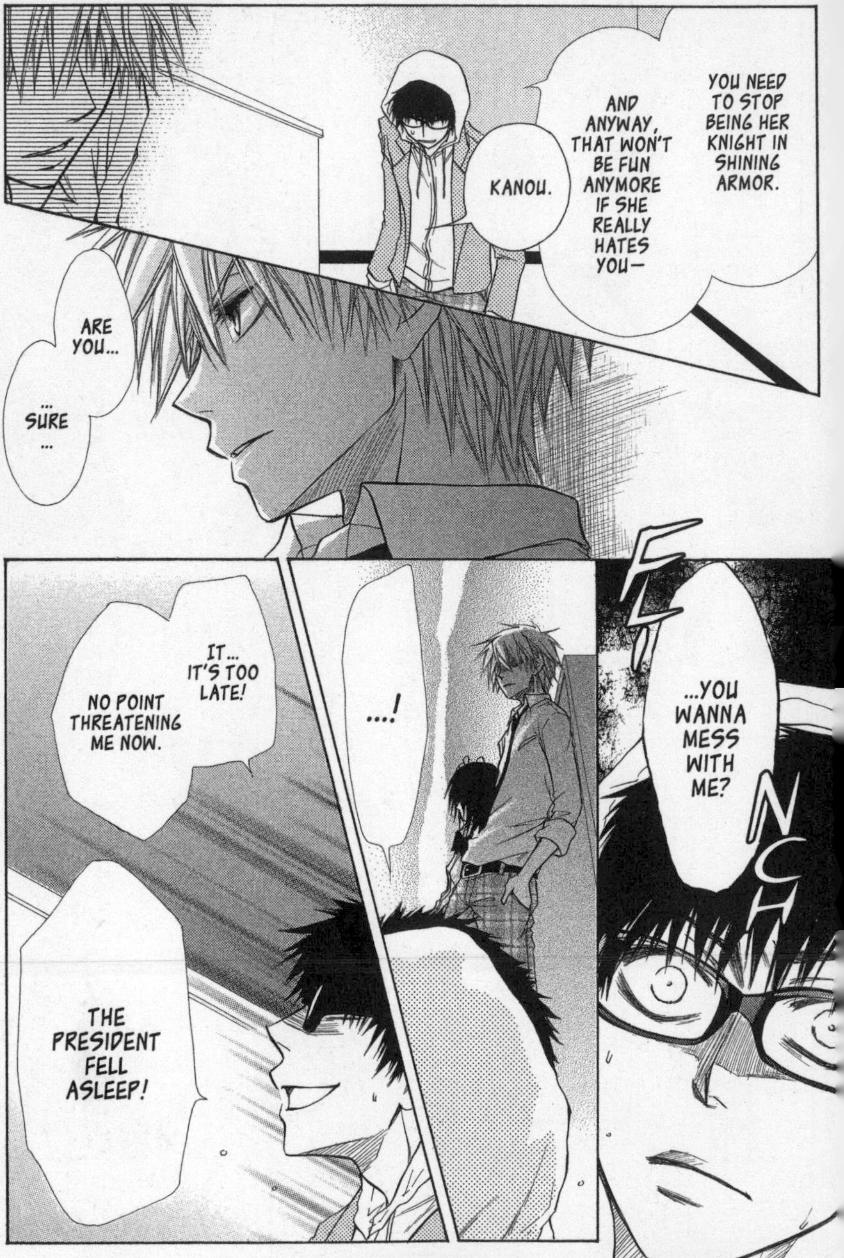
YOU NEED TO STOP BEING HER KNIGHT IN SHINING ARMOR.
AND ANYWAY, THAT WON'T BE FUN ANYMORE IF SHE REALLY HATES YOU—
KANOU.
ARE YOU...
...SURE...
FLINCH
...YOU WANNA MESS WITH ME?
...!
IT... IT'S TOO LATE!
NO POINT THREATENING ME NOW.
THE PRESIDENT FELL ASLEEP!

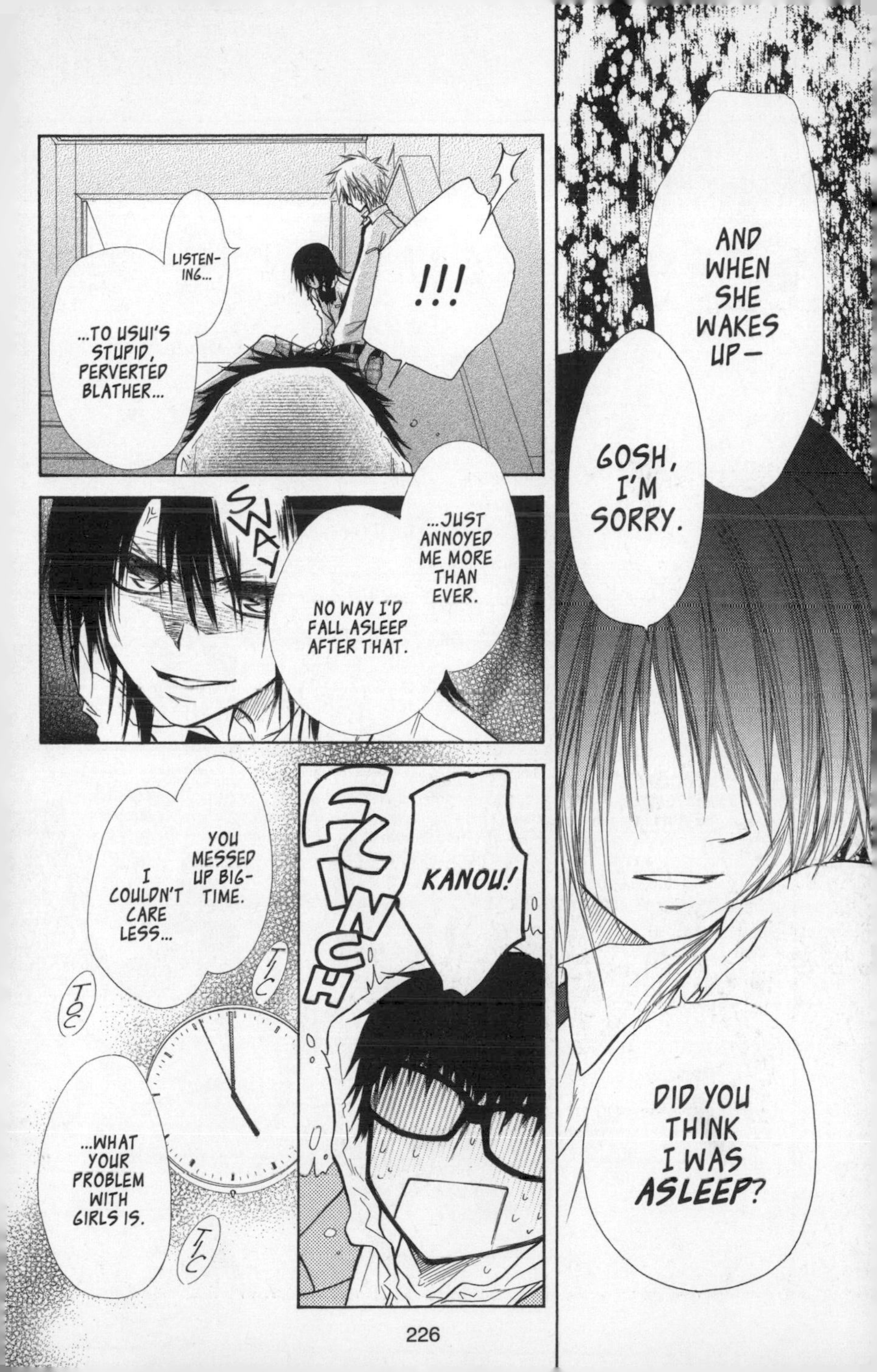
AND WHEN SHE WAKES UP—
GOSH, I'M SORRY.
DID YOU THINK I WAS ASLEEP?
!!!
LISTEN-ING...
...TO USUI'S STUPID, PERVERTED BLATHER...
SWAT
...JUST ANNOYED ME MORE THAN EVER.
NO WAY I'D FALL ASLEEP AFTER THAT.
FLINCH
KANOU!
YOU MESSED UP BIG-TIME.
I COULDN'T CARE LESS...
TIC
TOC
...WHAT YOUR PROBLEM WITH GIRLS IS.
TIC

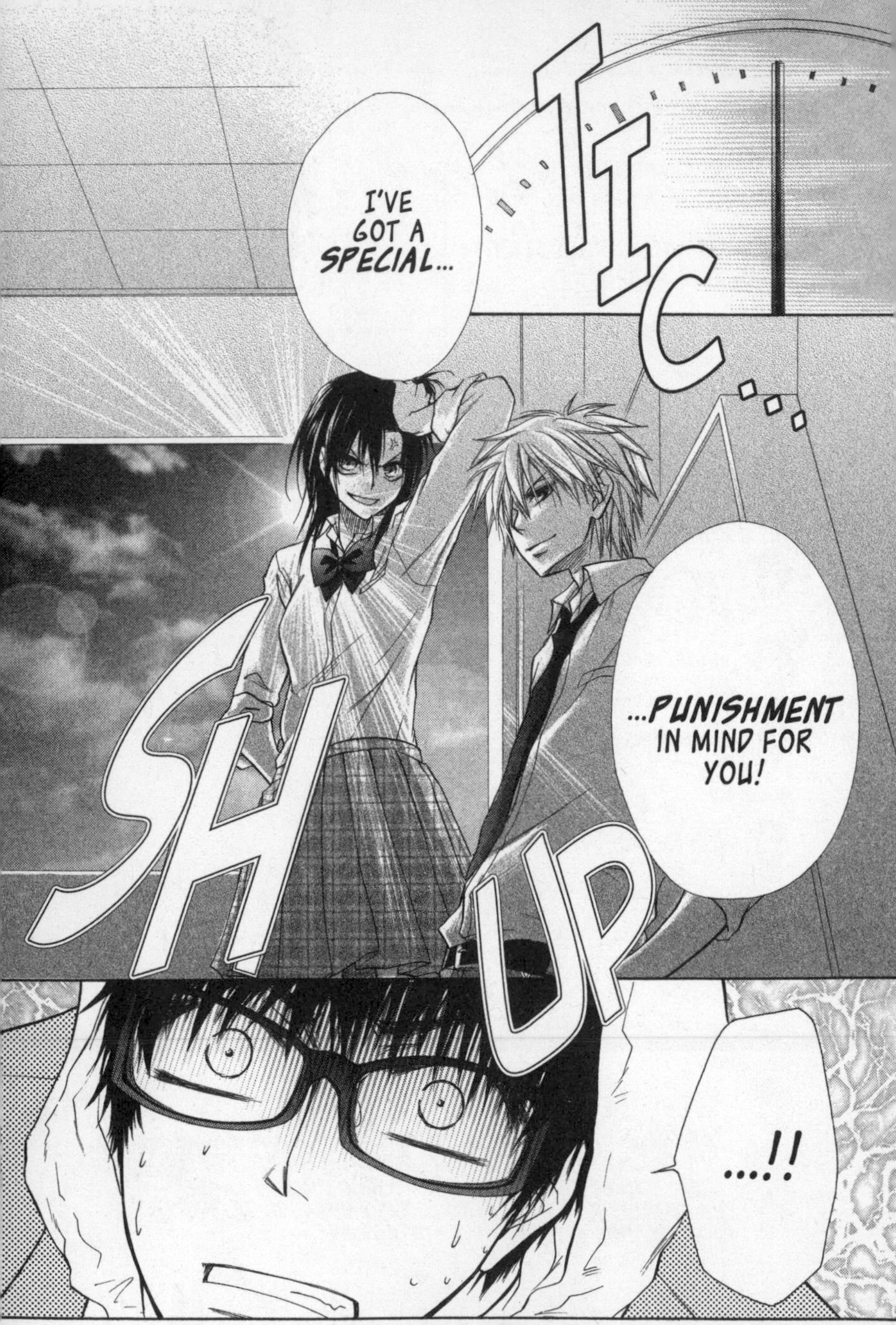
TIC...
I'VE GOT A SPECIAL...
...PUNISHMENT IN MIND FOR YOU!
SHUP
...!!

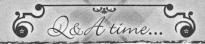

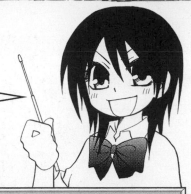

OKAY, LET'S JUMP RIGHT IN! WE'RE STARTING A NEW SEGMENT!

I'M GOING TO ANSWER QUESTIONS SENT IN BY OUR READERS.

LET'S START THINGS OFF.

 OUR FIRST QUESTION IS...

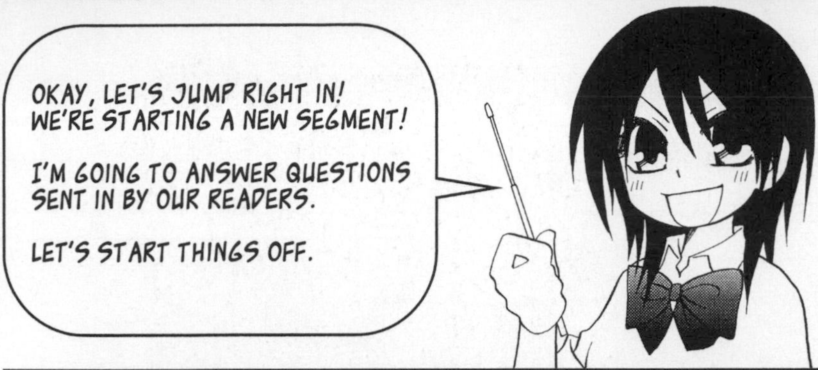

QUESTION 1: "WHAT THE HELL IS USUI?"

 ERR... WE'RE STARTING BY TALKING ABOUT *HIM*?

QUESTION 2: "IS HE AN ALIEN?"

 WHAT? HANG ON A SEC...

QUESTION 3: "IS THERE ANYTHING USUI CAN'T DO?"

 NO, SERIOUSLY, WAIT—

QUESTION 4: "IS USUI RICH? HOW MUCH DOES HE SPEND AT THE MAID CAFÉ?"

 WHO KNOWS?

QUESTION 5: "DOES USUI HAVE A FAN CLUB?"

 WHAT WOULD YOU DO IF I SAID YES?

QUESTION 6: "WHAT'S USUI'S FAMILY LIKE?"

 WHY ARE ALL THE QUESTIONS ABOUT USUI?

QUESTION 7: "WHY IS USUI A PERFECT HUMAN BEING WHO CAN DO ANYTHING?"

ALL RIGHT, ALL RIGHT—I'LL ANSWER YOU! LISTEN UP.

TAKUMI USUI IS A PERVERTED ALIEN WHO CAME FROM THE PLANET PHEROMONE AND SEXUALLY HARASSES EVERYONE HE MEETS. HE CAN DO ANYTHING BECAUSE HE COMES FROM PHEROMONE. REMEMBER, EVERYBODY: DON'T TRUST ALIENS! HE'S NOT HUMAN!

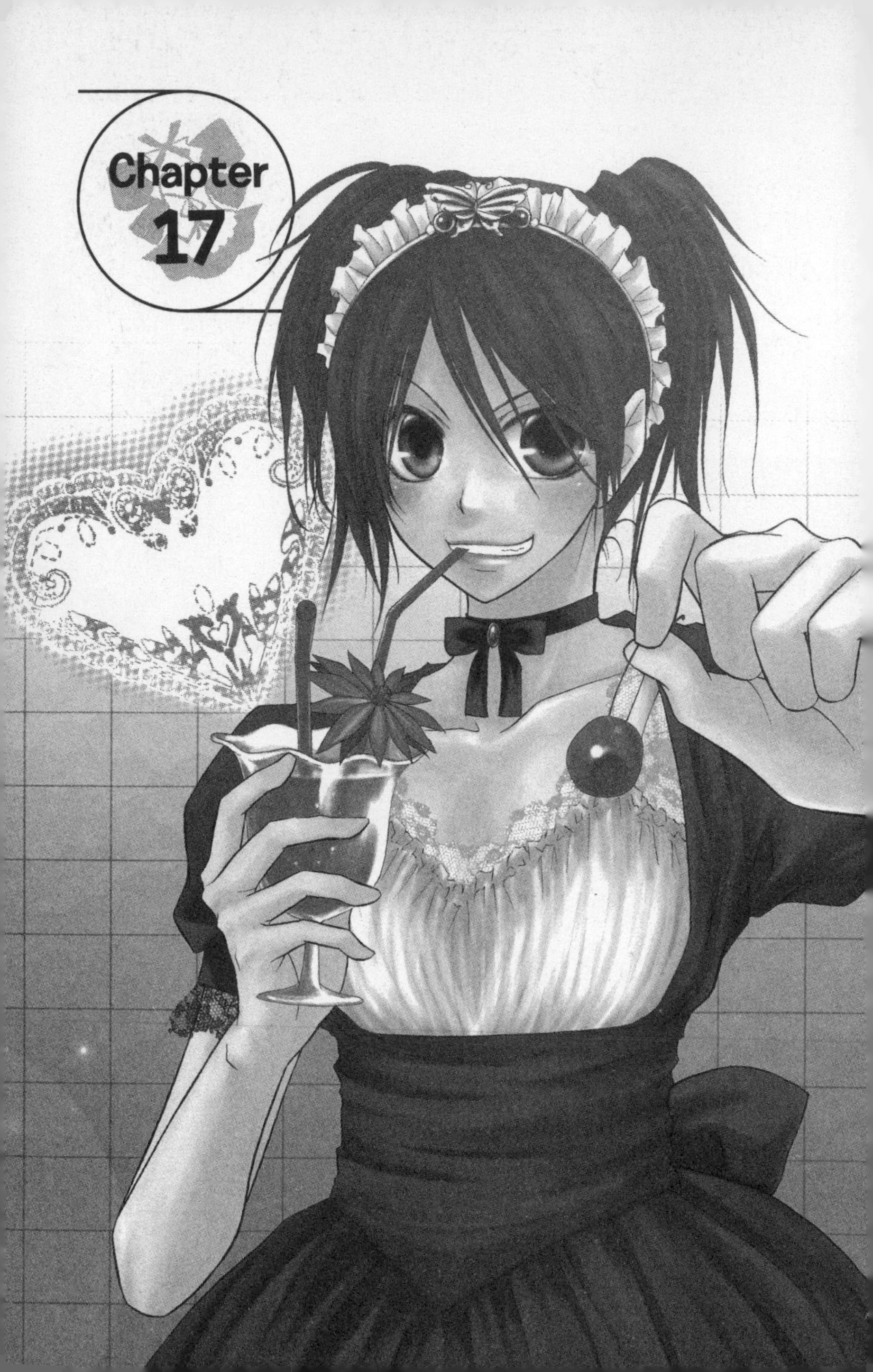
Chapter
17

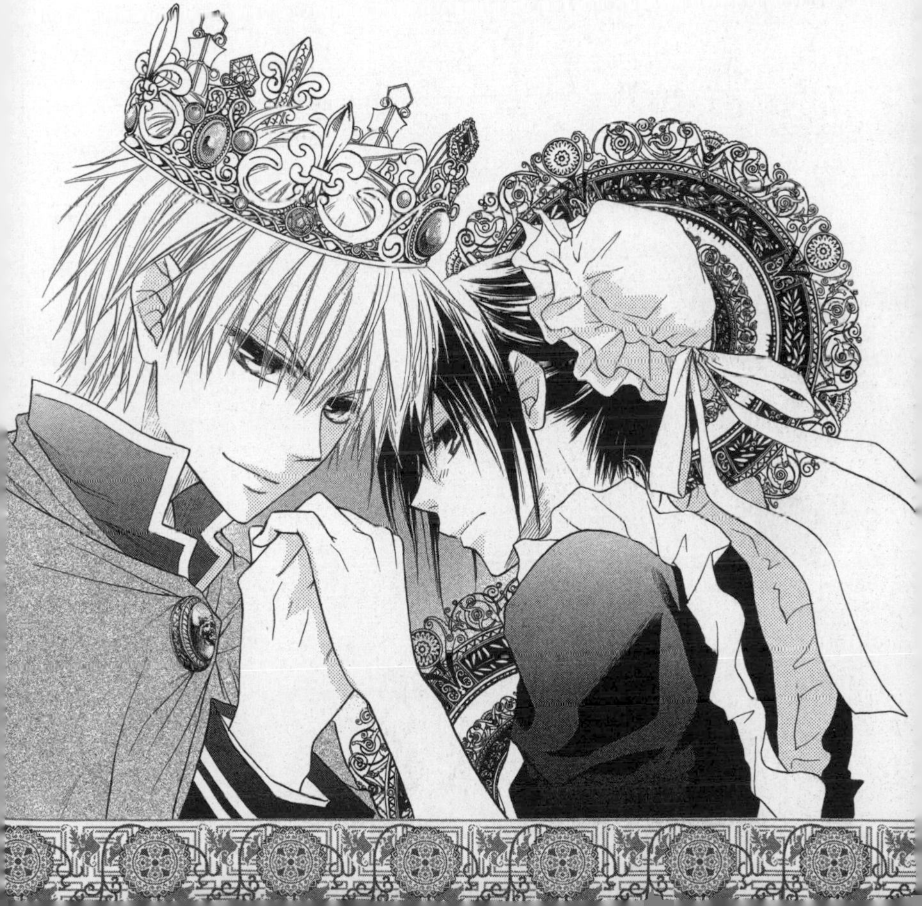

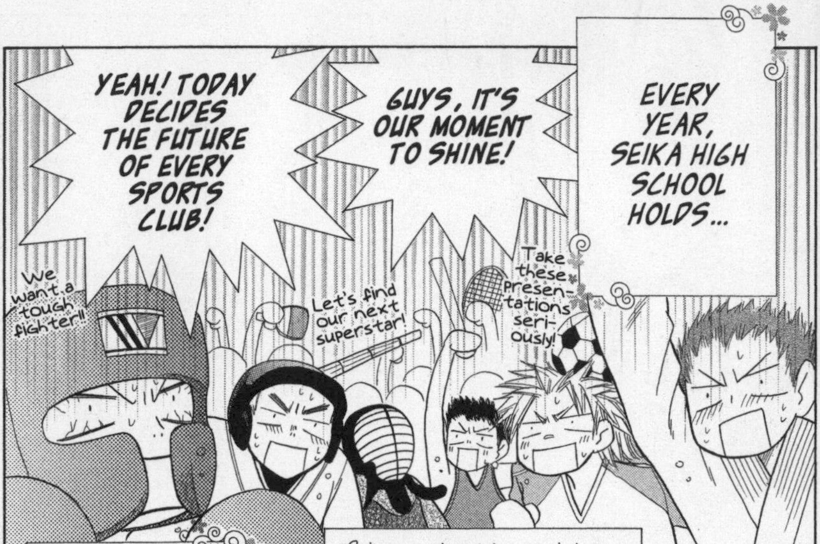
EVERY YEAR, SEIKA HIGH SCHOOL HOLDS...
GUYS, IT'S OUR MOMENT TO SHINE!
YEAH! TODAY DECIDES THE FUTURE OF EVERY SPORTS CLUB!
Take these presentations seriously!
Let's find our next superstar!
We want a tough fighter!!
*Seika sports clubs are intense.
(Even between various clubs, it's a dog-eat-dog world!)
...AN OPEN HOUSE FOR THIRD-YEAR JUNIOR HIGH STUDENTS.
WOW, THIS LOOKS LIKE FUN!
WE HAVE CAFETERIA DUTY!

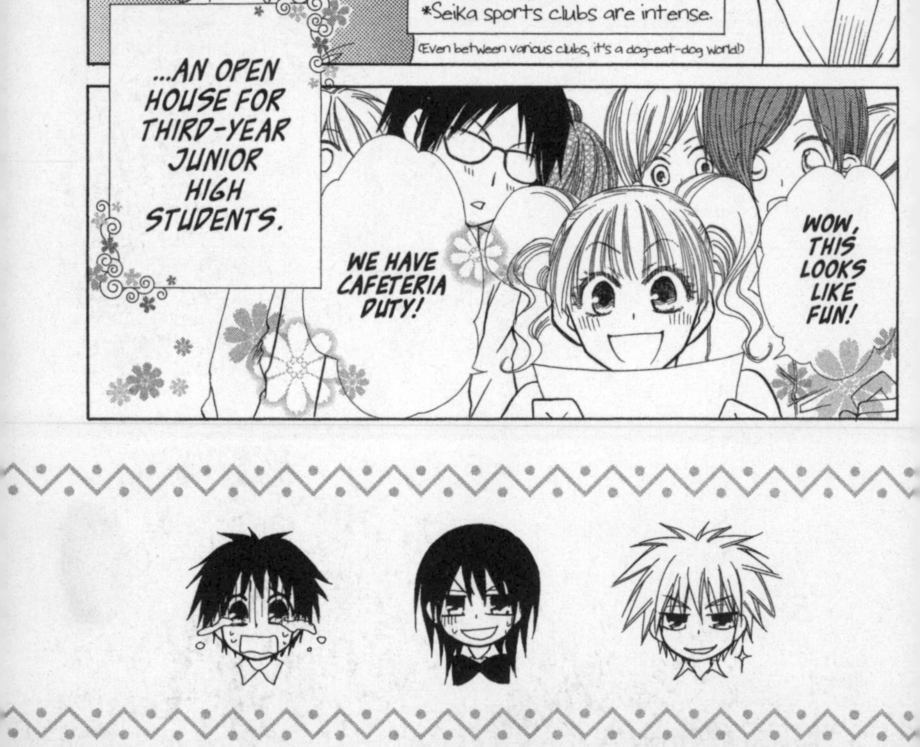

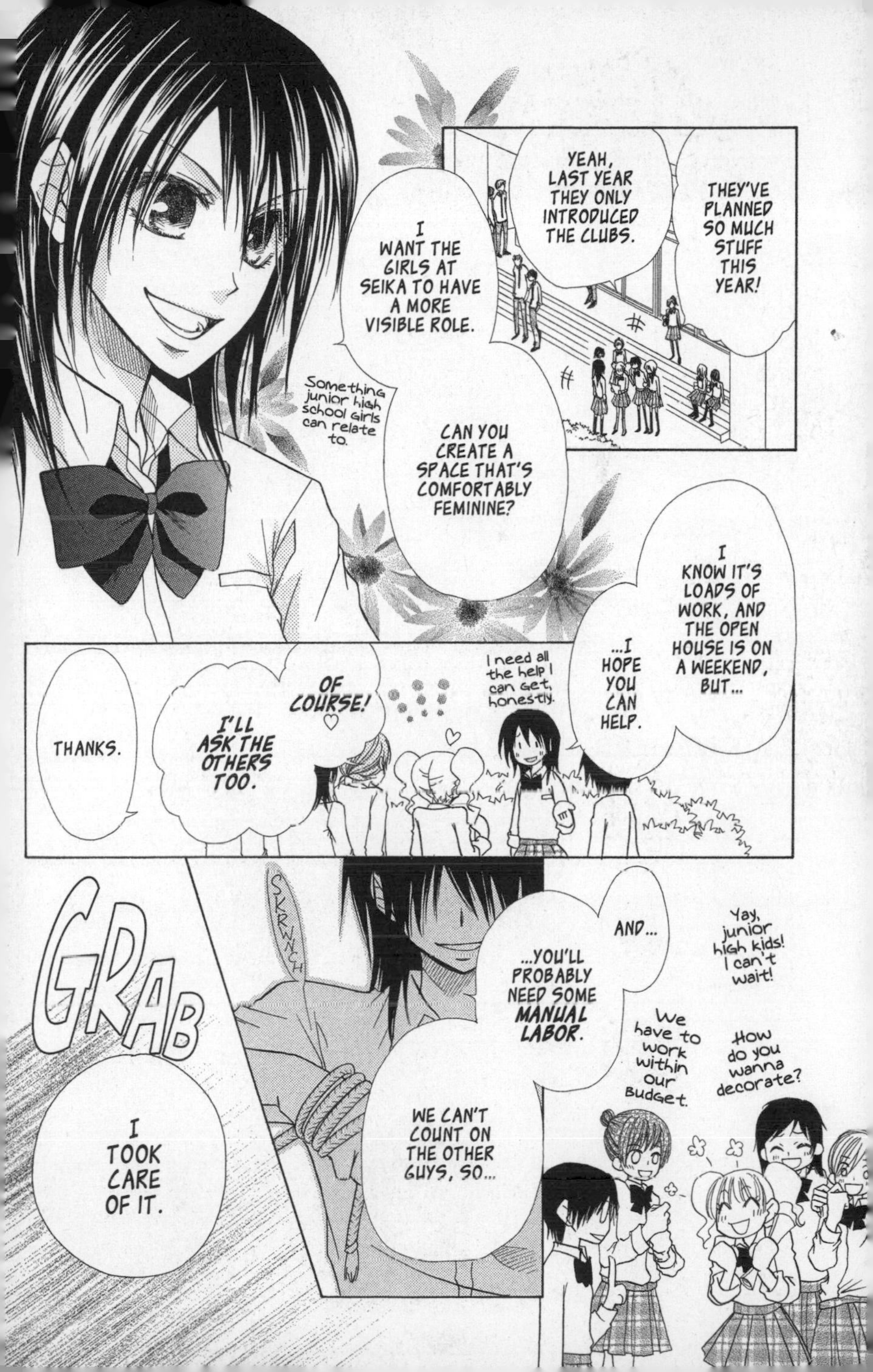

THEY'VE PLANNED SO MUCH STUFF THIS YEAR!
YEAH, LAST YEAR THEY ONLY INTRODUCED THE CLUBS.
I WANT THE GIRLS AT SEIKA TO HAVE A MORE VISIBLE ROLE.
Something junior high school girls can relate to.
CAN YOU CREATE A SPACE THAT'S COMFORTABLY FEMININE?
I KNOW IT'S LOADS OF WORK, AND THE OPEN HOUSE IS ON A WEEKEND, BUT...
...I HOPE YOU CAN HELP.
I need all the help I can get, honestly.
OF COURSE! ♡
I'LL ASK THE OTHERS TOO.
THANKS.
Yay, junior high kids! I can't wait!
How do you wanna decorate?
We have to work within our budget.
AND...
...YOU'LL PROBABLY NEED SOME **MANUAL LABOR**.
WE CAN'T COUNT ON THE OTHER GUYS, SO...
SKRWNCH
GRAB
I TOOK CARE OF IT.

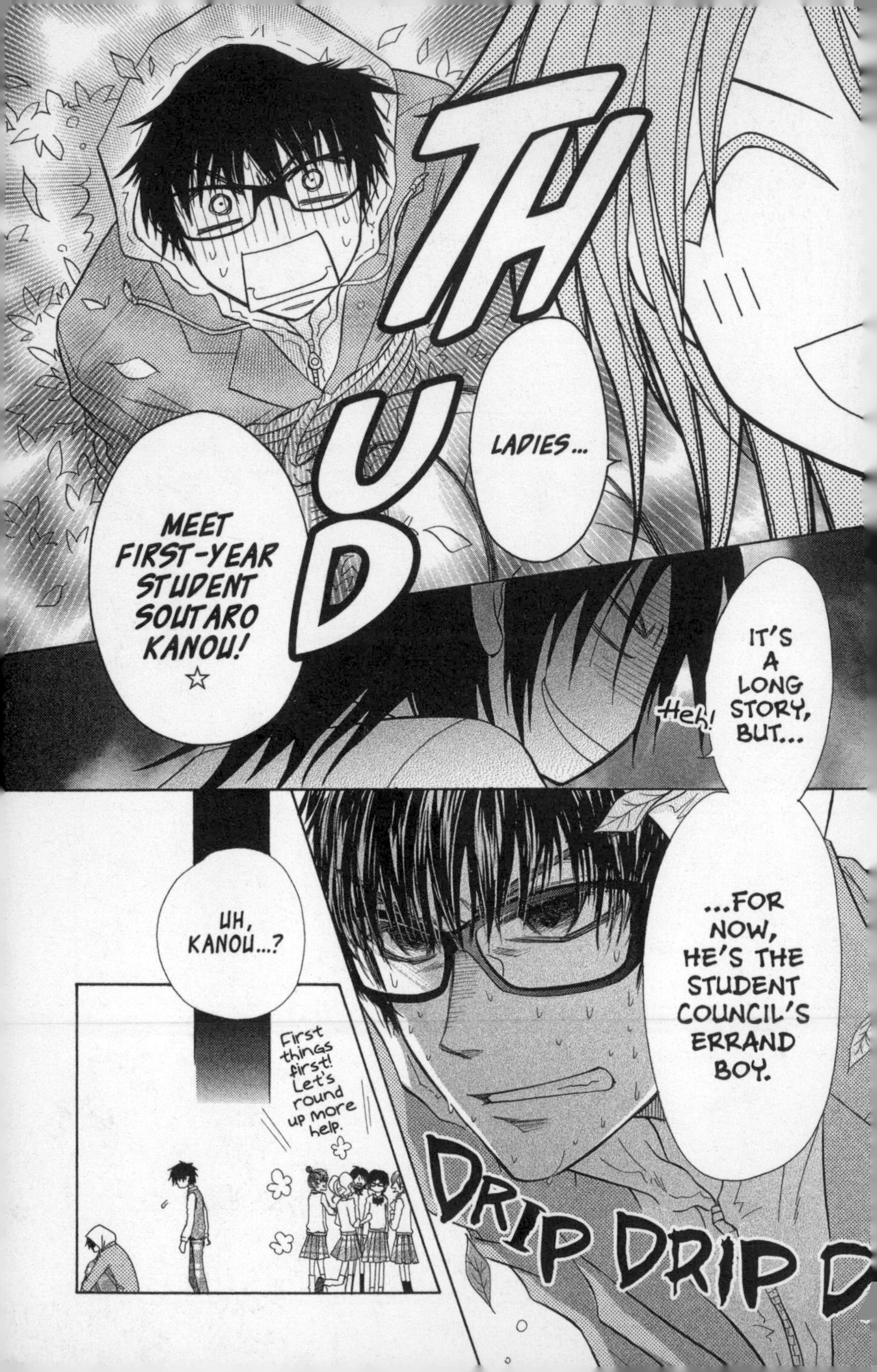
THUD
LADIES...
MEET FIRST-YEAR STUDENT SOUTARO KANOU! ☆
IT'S A LONG STORY, BUT...
Heh!
...FOR NOW, HE'S THE STUDENT COUNCIL'S ERRAND BOY.
DRIP DRIP D
UH, KANOU...?
First things first! Let's round up more help.

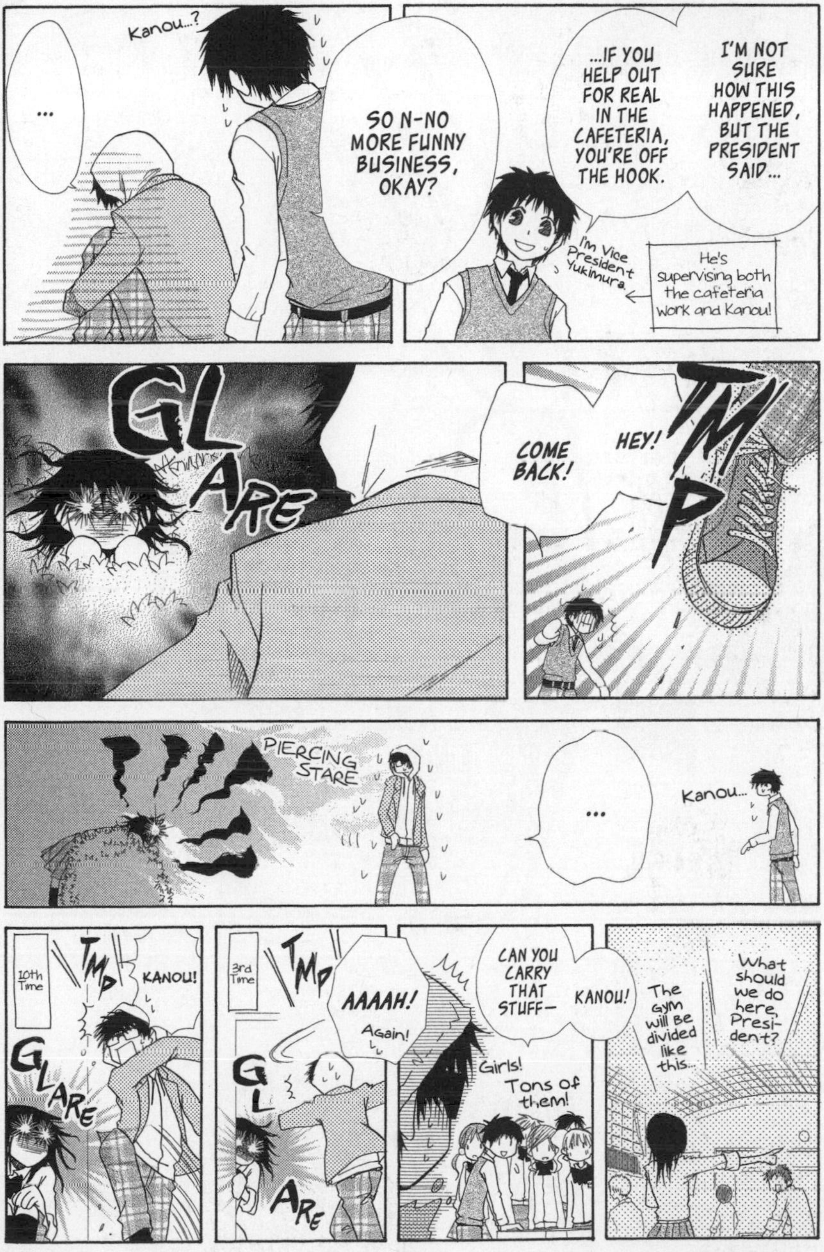
I'M NOT SURE HOW THIS HAPPENED, BUT THE PRESIDENT SAID...
...IF YOU HELP OUT FOR REAL IN THE CAFETERIA, YOU'RE OFF THE HOOK.
I'm Vice President Yukimura.
He's supervising both the cafeteria work and Kanou!
SO N-NO MORE FUNNY BUSINESS, OKAY?
Kanou...?
...
TMP
HEY!
COME BACK!
GLARE
Kanou...
...
PIERCING STARE
What should we do here, President?
The gym will be divided like this...
CAN YOU CARRY THAT STUFF—
KANOU!
Girls! Tons of them!
3rd Time
TMP
AAAAH!
Again!
GLARE
10th Time
TMP
KANOU!
GLARE

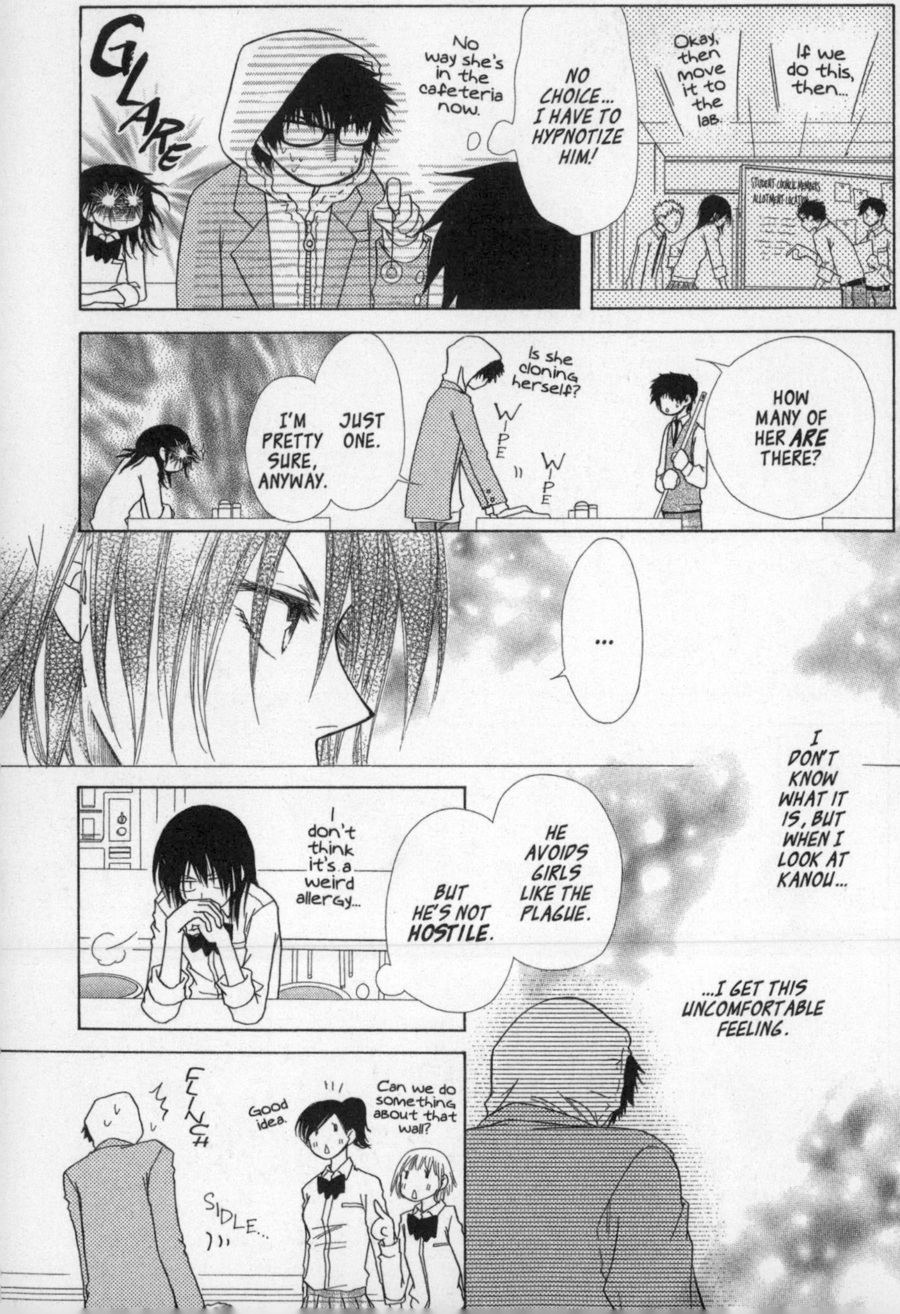
If we do this, then...
Okay, then move it to the lab.
NO CHOICE... I HAVE TO HYPNOTIZE HIM!
No way she's in the cafeteria now.
GLARE
HOW MANY OF HER ARE THERE?
Is she cloning herself?
WIPE WIPE
JUST ONE.
I'M PRETTY SURE, ANYWAY.
...
I DON'T KNOW WHAT IT IS, BUT WHEN I LOOK AT KANOU...
HE AVOIDS GIRLS LIKE THE PLAGUE.
BUT HE'S NOT HOSTILE.
I don't think it's a weird allergy...
...I GET THIS UNCOMFORTABLE FEELING.
Can we do something about that wall?
Good idea.
FLINCH
SIDLE...

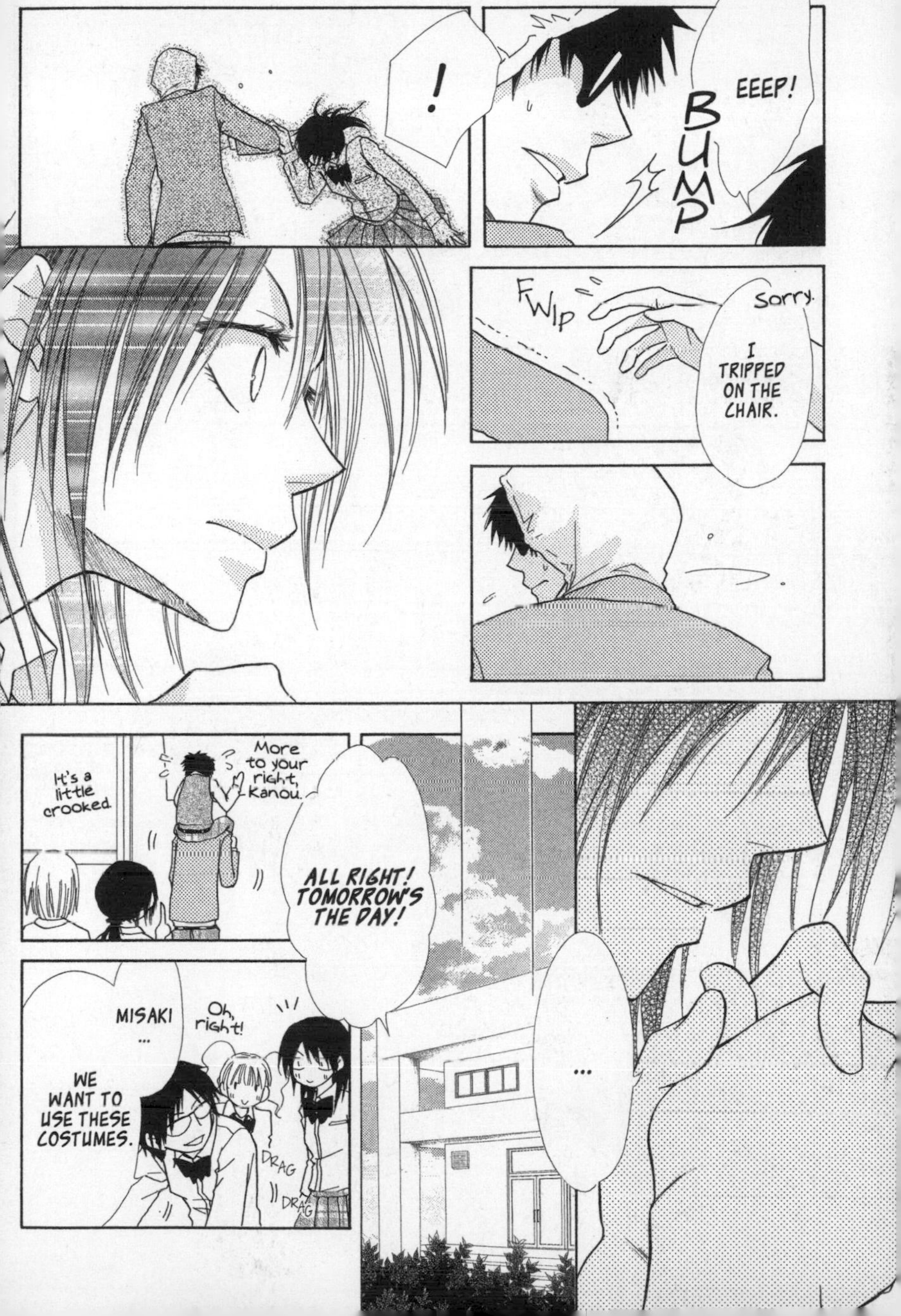
EEEP!
BUMP
!
FWIP
Sorry.
I TRIPPED ON THE CHAIR.
...
ALL RIGHT! TOMORROW'S THE DAY!
More to your right, Kanou.
It's a little crooked.
Oh, right!
MISAKI ...
WE WANT TO USE THESE COSTUMES.
DRAG
DRAG

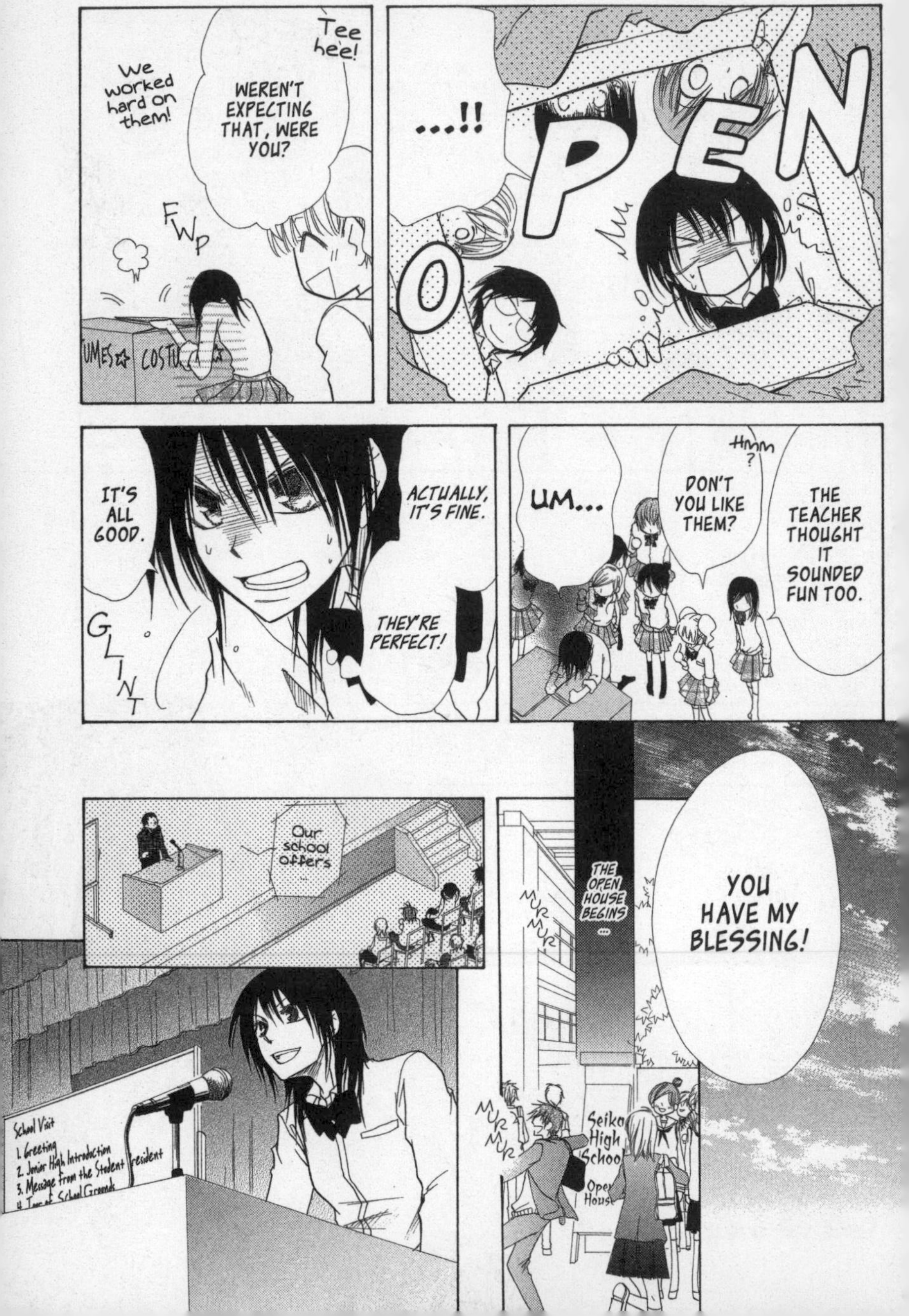
...!!
OPEN
Tee hee!
WEREN'T EXPECTING THAT, WERE YOU?
We worked hard on them!
FWP
THE TEACHER THOUGHT IT SOUNDED FUN TOO.
Hmm?
DON'T YOU LIKE THEM?
UM...
ACTUALLY, IT'S FINE.
THEY'RE PERFECT!
IT'S ALL GOOD.
GLINT
YOU HAVE MY BLESSING!
THE OPEN HOUSE BEGINS...
MUR MUR
Seika High School
MUR MUR
Our school offers...
School Visit
1. Greeting
2. Junior High Introduction
3. Message from the Student President
4. Tour of School Grounds

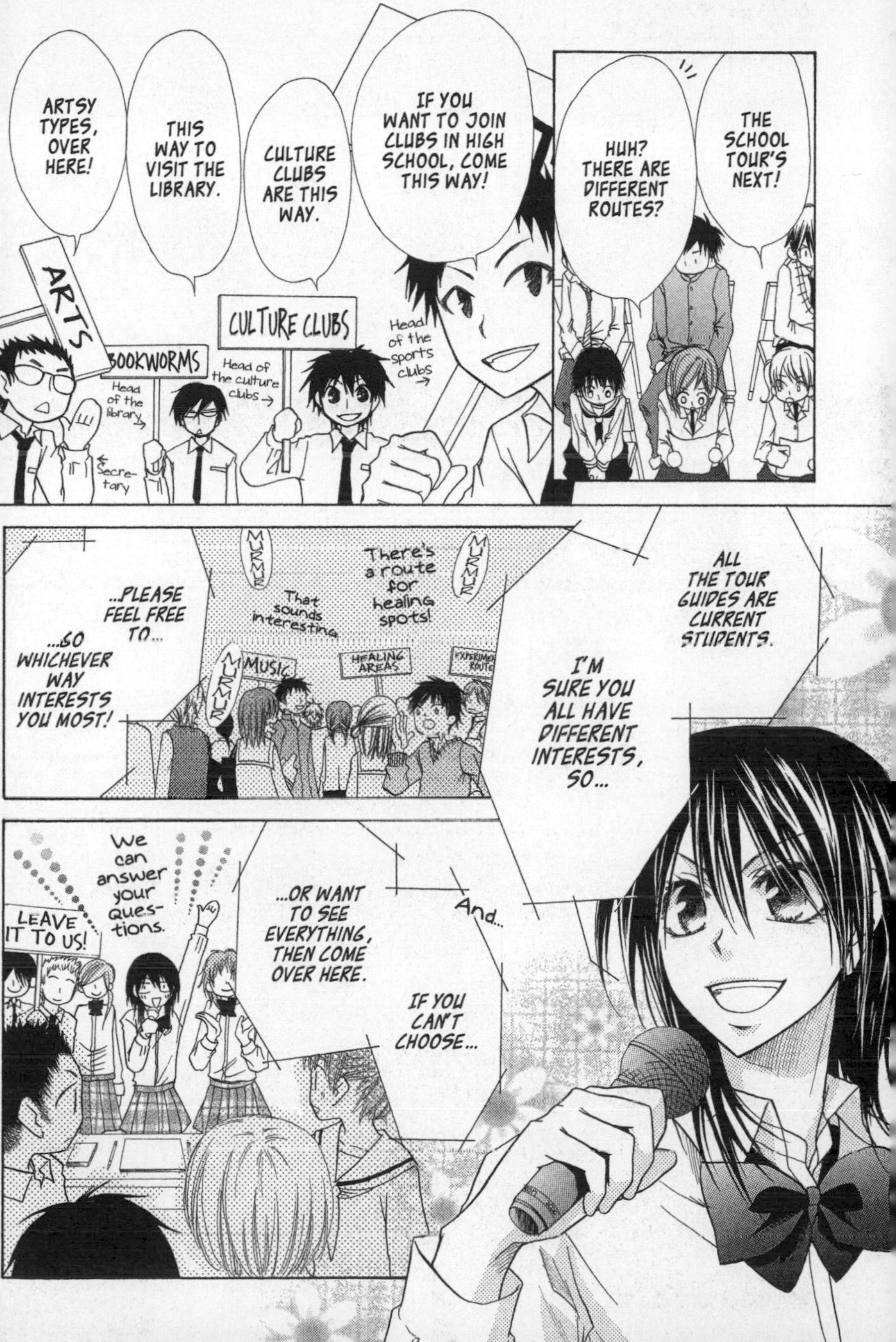
THE SCHOOL TOUR'S NEXT!
HUH? THERE ARE DIFFERENT ROUTES?
IF YOU WANT TO JOIN CLUBS IN HIGH SCHOOL, COME THIS WAY!
Head of the sports clubs
CULTURE CLUBS ARE THIS WAY.
CULTURE CLUBS
Head of the culture clubs
THIS WAY TO VISIT THE LIBRARY.
BOOKWORMS
Head of the library
ARTSY TYPES, OVER HERE!
ARTS
Secretary
ALL THE TOUR GUIDES ARE CURRENT STUDENTS.
I'M SURE YOU ALL HAVE DIFFERENT INTERESTS, SO...
MURMUR
There's a route for healing spots!
MURMUR
That sounds interesting.
EXPERIMENT ROUTE
HEALING AREAS
MUSIC
MURMUR
...PLEASE FEEL FREE TO...
...SO WHICHEVER WAY INTERESTS YOU MOST!
And...
IF YOU CAN'T CHOOSE...
...OR WANT TO SEE EVERYTHING, THEN COME OVER HERE.
We can answer your questions.
LEAVE IT TO US!

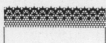

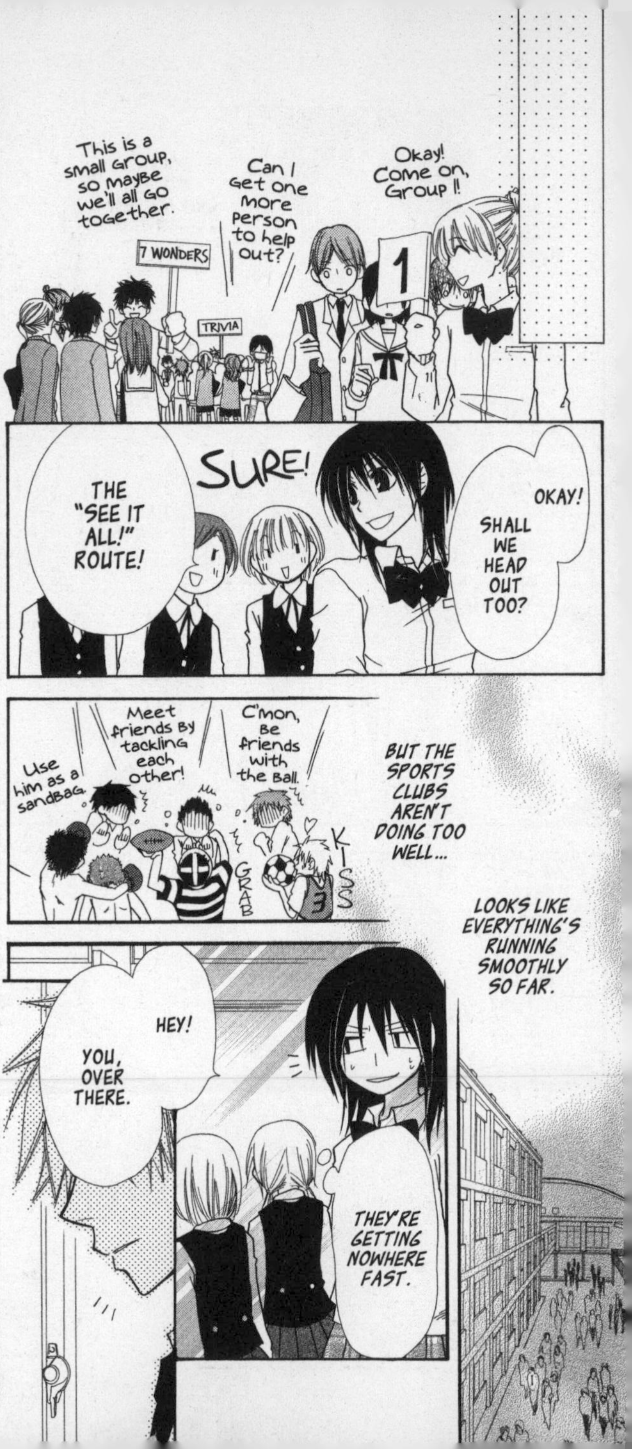
Okay! Come on, Group 1!
Can I get one more person to help out?
This is a small group, so maybe we'll all go together.
7 WONDERS
TRIVIA
1
OKAY! SHALL WE HEAD OUT TOO?
SURE!
THE "SEE IT ALL!" ROUTE!
BUT THE SPORTS CLUBS AREN'T DOING TOO WELL...
C'mon, be friends with the ball.
Meet friends by tackling each other!
Use him as a sandbag.
KISS
GRAB
LOOKS LIKE EVERYTHING'S RUNNING SMOOTHLY SO FAR.
HEY!
YOU, OVER THERE.
THEY'RE GETTING NOWHERE FAST.

Memories from junior high...

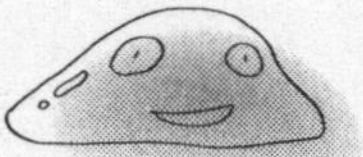

I made slime at the high school open house!

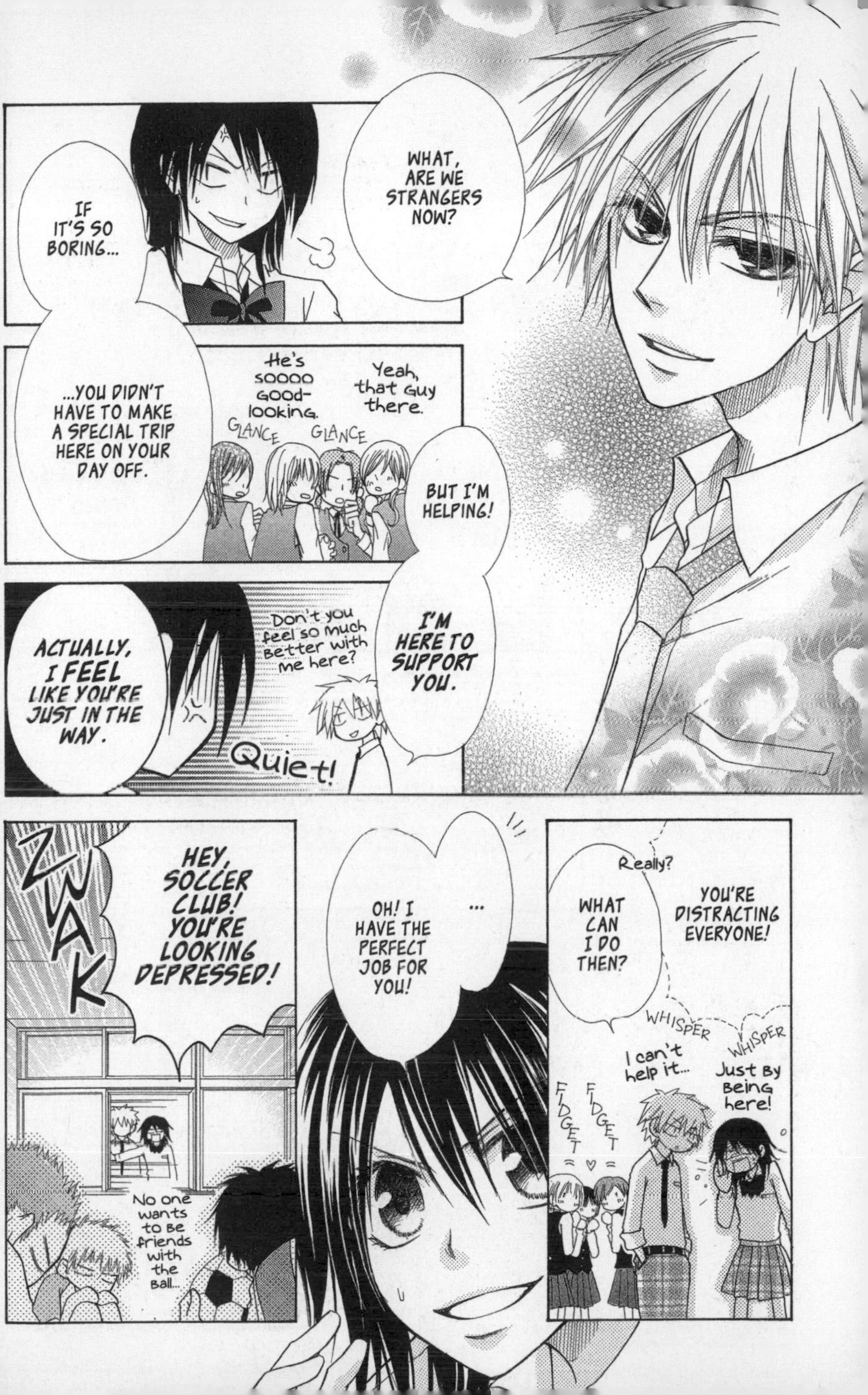
WHAT, ARE WE STRANGERS NOW?
IF IT'S SO BORING...
...YOU DIDN'T HAVE TO MAKE A SPECIAL TRIP HERE ON YOUR DAY OFF.
Yeah, that guy there.
He's soooo good-looking.
GLANCE
GLANCE
BUT I'M HELPING!
I'M HERE TO SUPPORT YOU.
Don't you feel so much better with me here?
ACTUALLY, I FEEL LIKE YOU'RE JUST IN THE WAY.
Quiet!
YOU'RE DISTRACTING EVERYONE!
Really?
WHAT CAN I DO THEN?
WHISPER
WHISPER
Just by being here!
I can't help it...
FIDGET
FIDGET
...
OH! I HAVE THE PERFECT JOB FOR YOU!
ZWAK
HEY, SOCCER CLUB! YOU'RE LOOKING DEPRESSED!
No one wants to be friends with the ball...

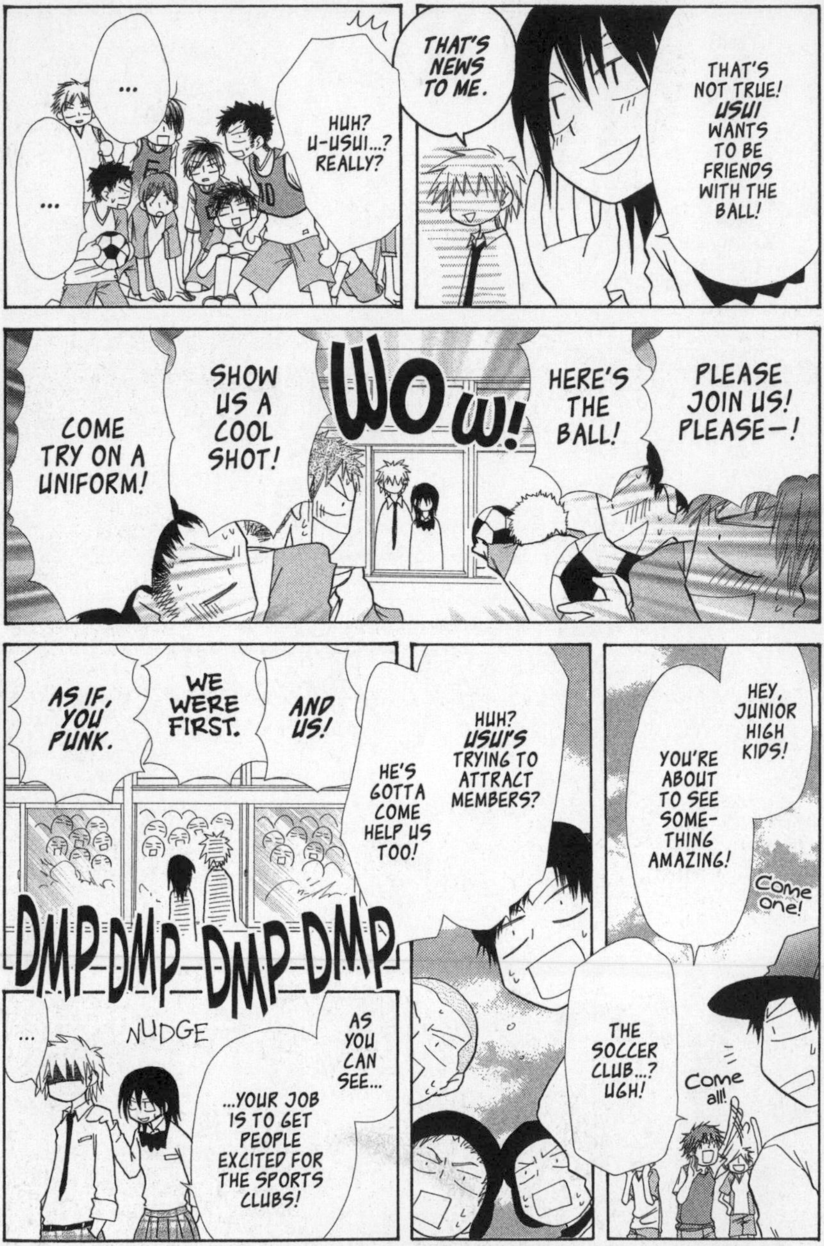
THAT'S NOT TRUE! USUI WANTS TO BE FRIENDS WITH THE BALL!
THAT'S NEWS TO ME.
HUH? U-USUI...? REALLY?
...
...
PLEASE JOIN US! PLEASE—!
HERE'S THE BALL!
WOW!
SHOW US A COOL SHOT!
COME TRY ON A UNIFORM!
HEY, JUNIOR HIGH KIDS!
YOU'RE ABOUT TO SEE SOME-THING AMAZING!
Come one!
Come all!
THE SOCCER CLUB...? UGH!
HUH? USUI'S TRYING TO ATTRACT MEMBERS?
HE'S GOTTA COME HELP US TOO!
AND US!
WE WERE FIRST.
AS IF, YOU PUNK.
DMP DMP DMP DMP
AS YOU CAN SEE...
...YOUR JOB IS TO GET PEOPLE EXCITED FOR THE SPORTS CLUBS!
NUDGE
...

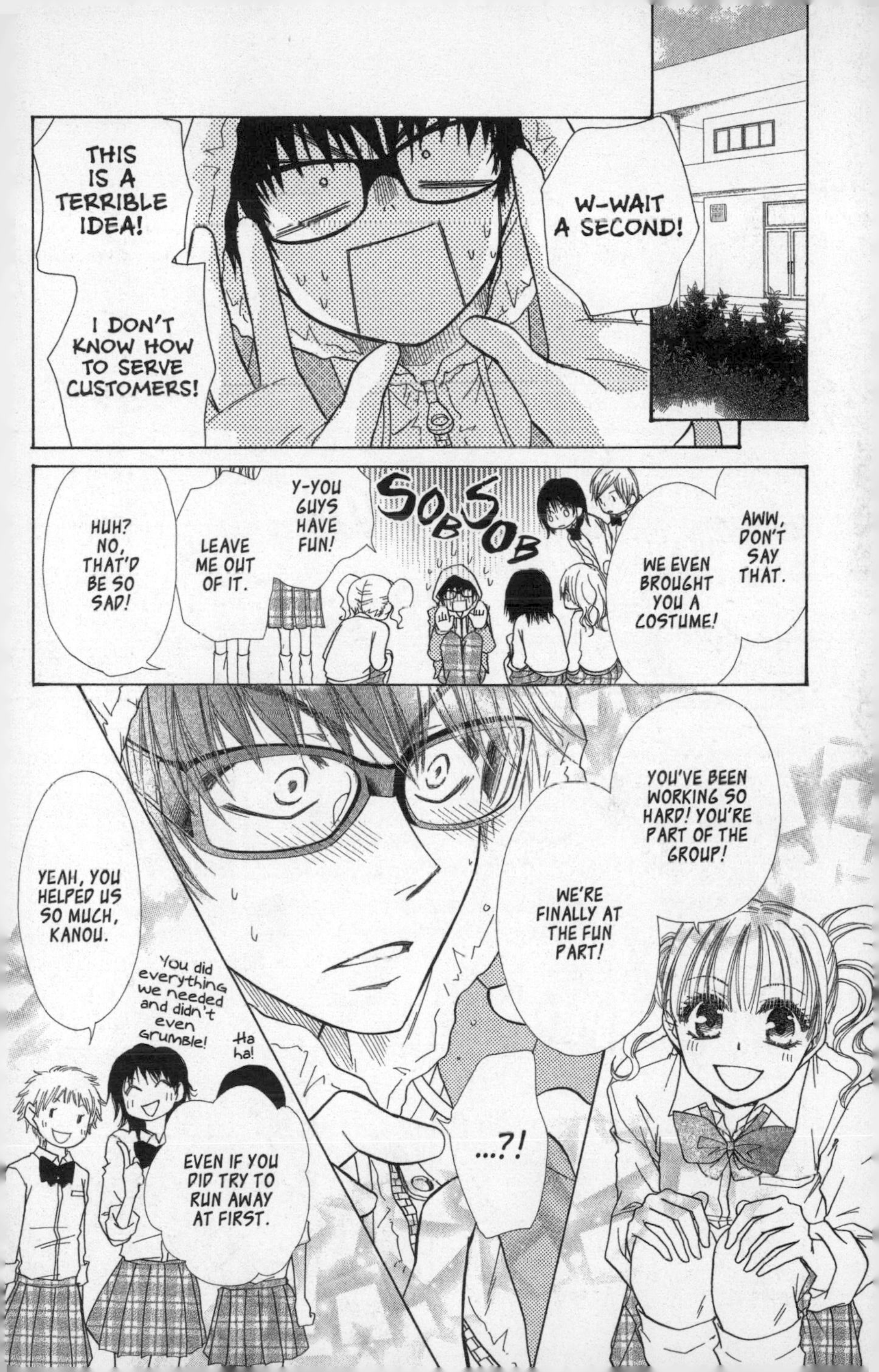
W-WAIT A SECOND!
THIS IS A TERRIBLE IDEA!
I DON'T KNOW HOW TO SERVE CUSTOMERS!
AWW, DON'T SAY THAT.
WE EVEN BROUGHT YOU A COSTUME!
SOB SOB
Y-YOU GUYS HAVE FUN!
LEAVE ME OUT OF IT.
HUH? NO, THAT'D BE SO SAD!
YOU'VE BEEN WORKING SO HARD! YOU'RE PART OF THE GROUP!
WE'RE FINALLY AT THE FUN PART!
...?!
YEAH, YOU HELPED US SO MUCH, KANOU.
You did everything we needed and didn't even grumble!
Ha ha!
EVEN IF YOU DID TRY TO RUN AWAY AT FIRST.

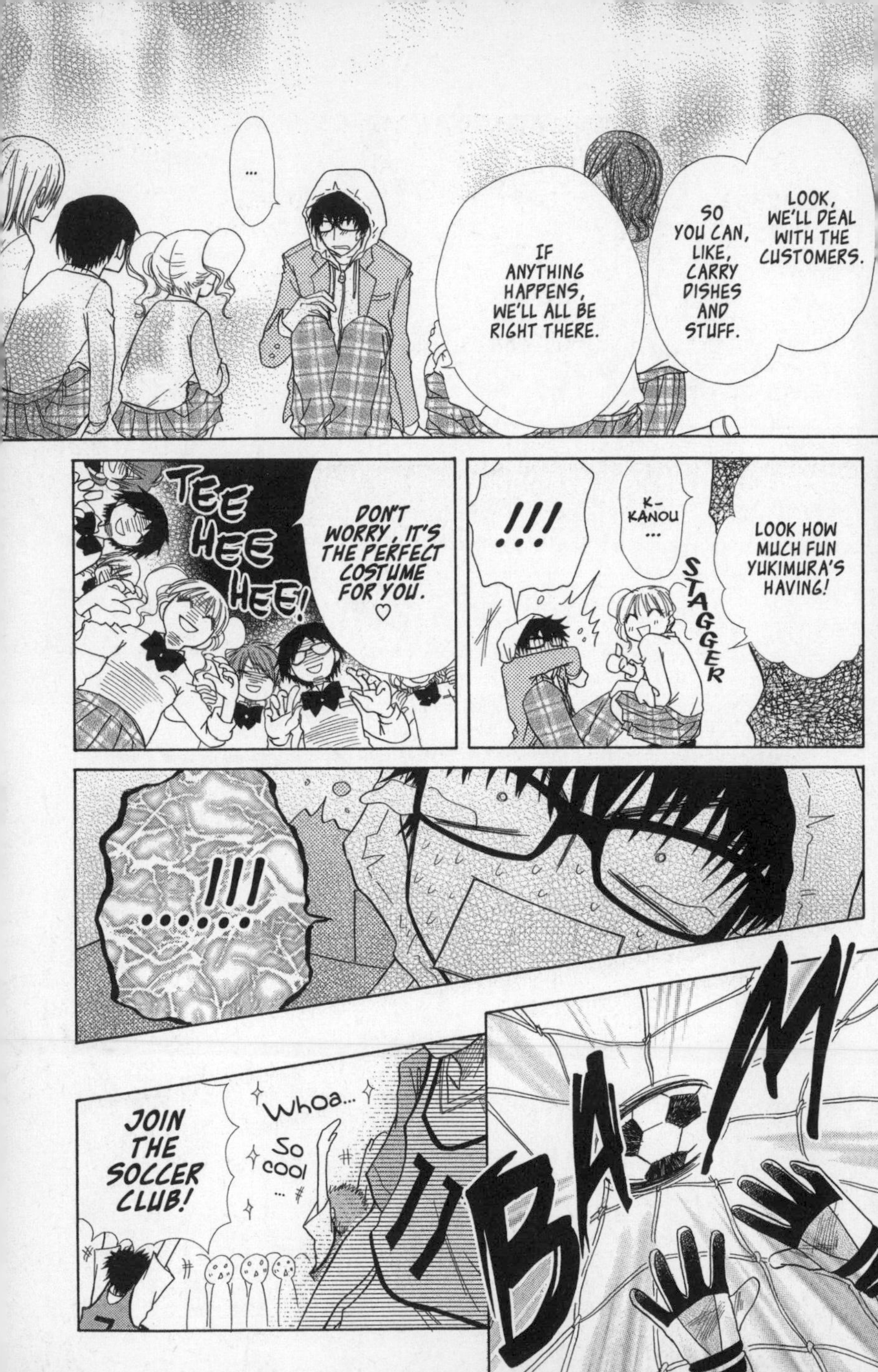
LOOK, WE'LL DEAL WITH THE CUSTOMERS.
SO YOU CAN, LIKE, CARRY DISHES AND STUFF.
IF ANYTHING HAPPENS, WE'LL ALL BE RIGHT THERE.
...
LOOK HOW MUCH FUN YUKIMURA'S HAVING!
STAGGER
K-KANOU ...
!!!
DON'T WORRY, IT'S THE PERFECT COSTUME FOR YOU. ♡
TEE HEE HEE!
!!!
......
BAM
Whoa...
So cool ...
JOIN THE SOCCER CLUB!

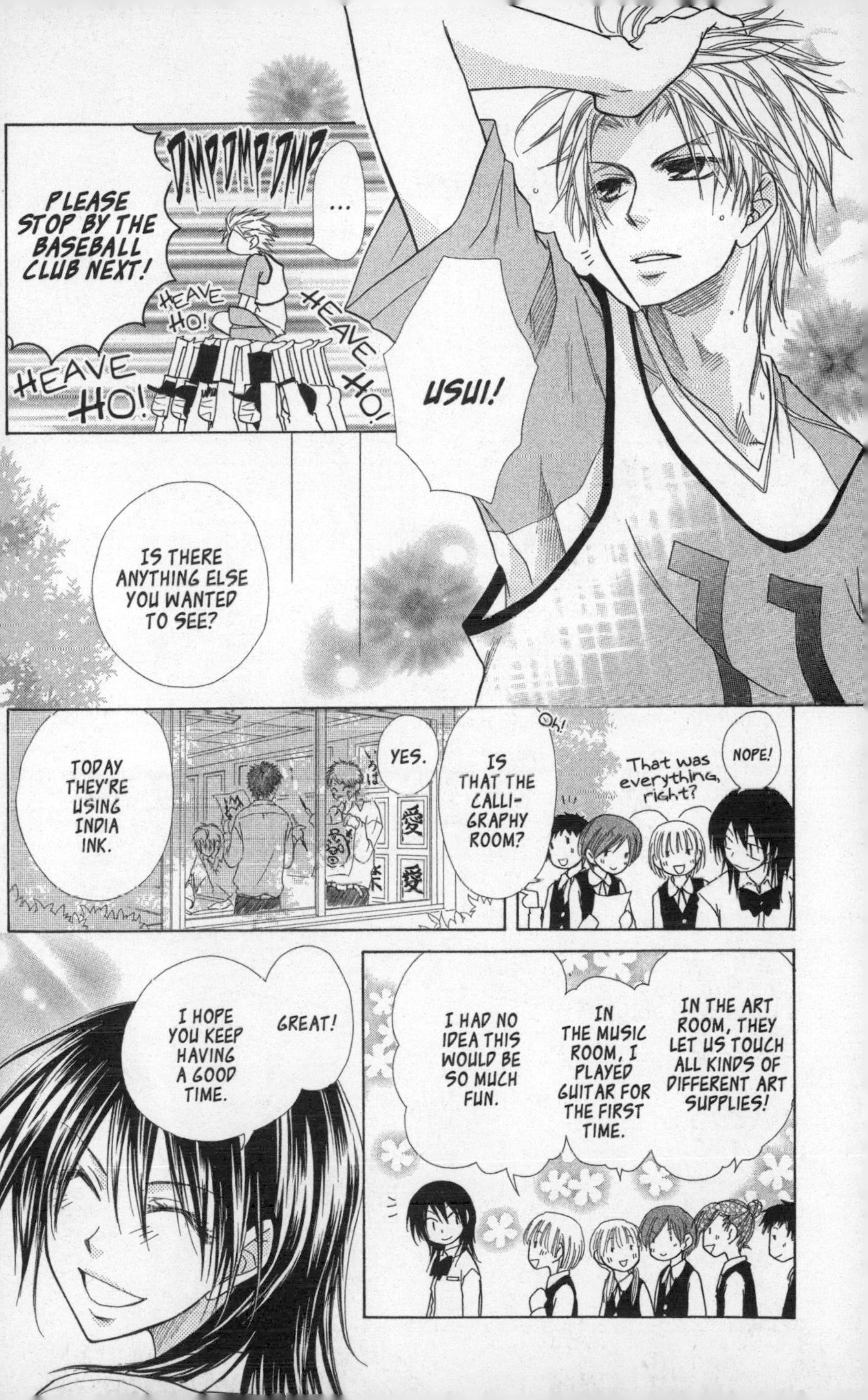
USUI!
PLEASE STOP BY THE BASEBALL CLUB NEXT!
DMP DMP DMP
...
HEAVE HO!
HEAVE HO!
HEAVE HO!
HEAVE HO!
IS THERE ANYTHING ELSE YOU WANTED TO SEE?
That was everything, right?
NOPE!
Oh!
IS THAT THE CALLI-GRAPHY ROOM?
YES.
TODAY THEY'RE USING INDIA INK.
IN THE ART ROOM, THEY LET US TOUCH ALL KINDS OF DIFFERENT ART SUPPLIES!
IN THE MUSIC ROOM, I PLAYED GUITAR FOR THE FIRST TIME.
I HAD NO IDEA THIS WOULD BE SO MUCH FUN.
GREAT!
I HOPE YOU KEEP HAVING A GOOD TIME.

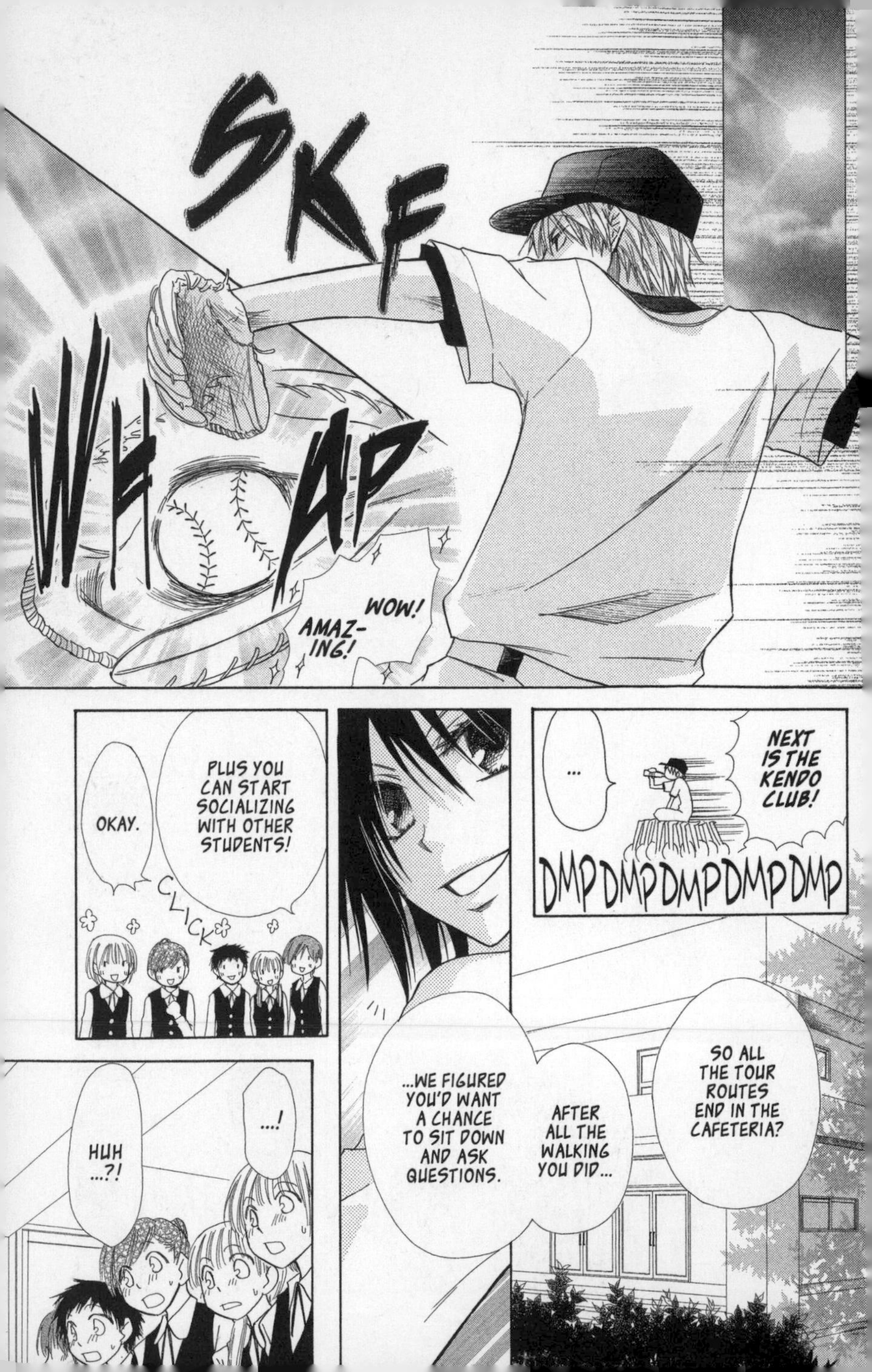
SKF
WHAP
WOW!
AMAZ-
ING!
...
NEXT IS THE KENDO CLUB!
DMP DMP DMP DMP DMP
SO ALL THE TOUR ROUTES END IN THE CAFETERIA?
AFTER ALL THE WALKING YOU DID...
...WE FIGURED YOU'D WANT A CHANCE TO SIT DOWN AND ASK QUESTIONS.
PLUS YOU CAN START SOCIALIZING WITH OTHER STUDENTS!
OKAY.
CLICK
...!
HUH ...?!

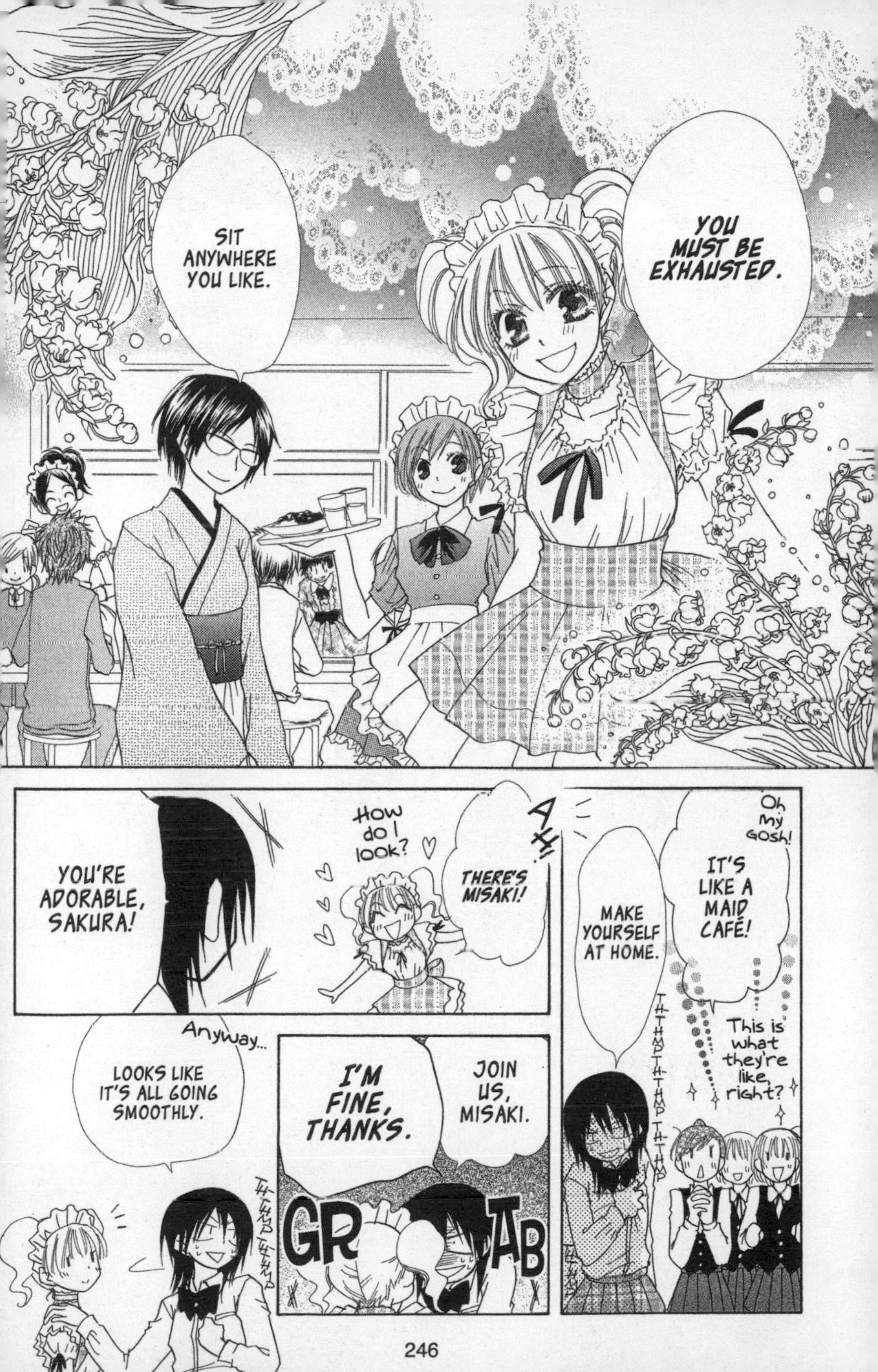
YOU MUST BE EXHAUSTED.
SIT ANYWHERE YOU LIKE.
Oh my gosh!
IT'S LIKE A MAID CAFÉ!
MAKE YOURSELF AT HOME.
This is what they're like, right?
THTHMP THTHMP THTHMP
AH!
THERE'S MISAKI!
How do I look?
YOU'RE ADORABLE, SAKURA!
JOIN US, MISAKI.
I'M FINE, THANKS.
GRAB
Anyway...
LOOKS LIKE IT'S ALL GOING SMOOTHLY.
THTHMP THTHMP

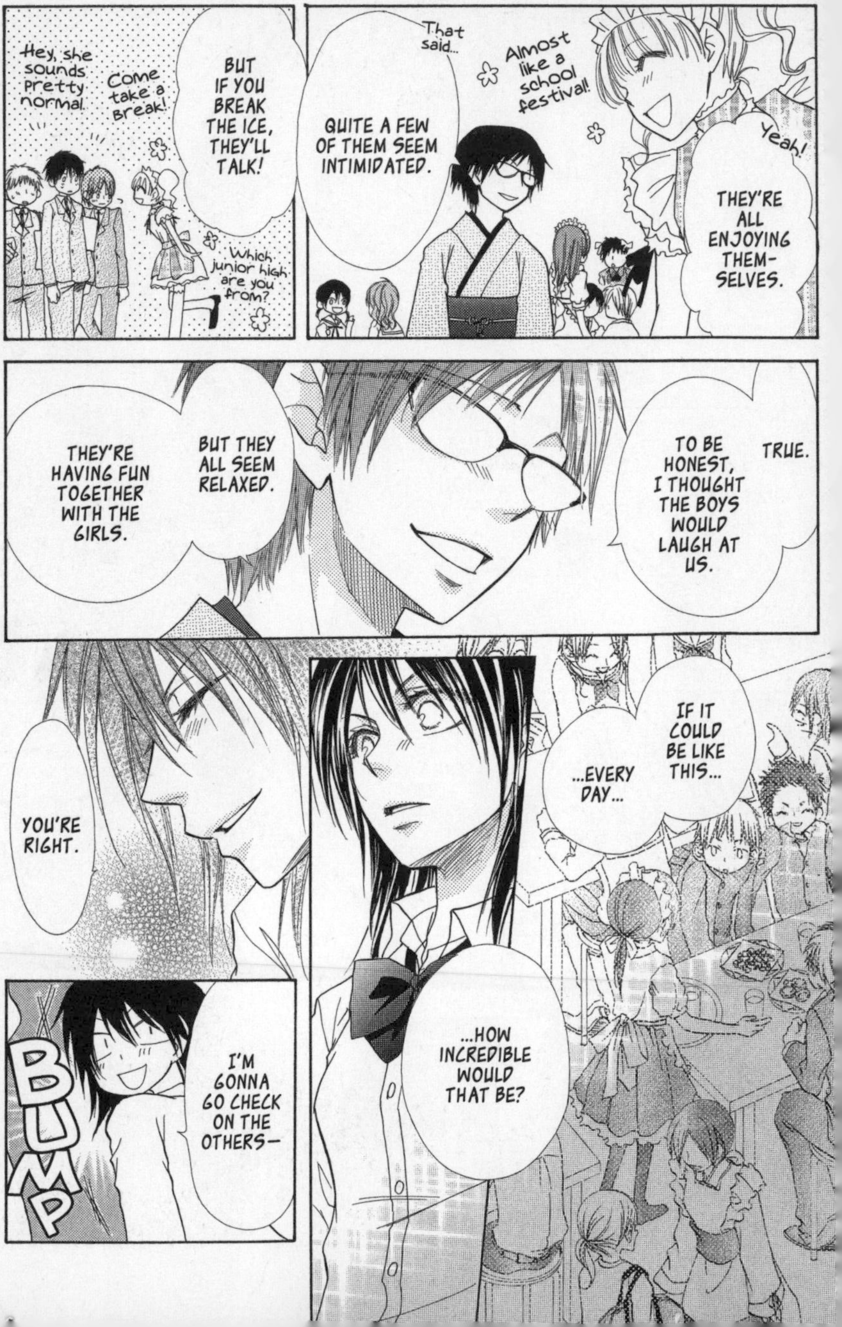
Yeah!
THEY'RE ALL ENJOYING THEMSELVES.
Almost like a school festival!
That said...
QUITE A FEW OF THEM SEEM INTIMIDATED.
BUT IF YOU BREAK THE ICE, THEY'LL TALK!
Come take a break!
Hey, she sounds pretty normal.
Which junior high are you from?
TRUE.
TO BE HONEST, I THOUGHT THE BOYS WOULD LAUGH AT US.
BUT THEY ALL SEEM RELAXED.
THEY'RE HAVING FUN TOGETHER WITH THE GIRLS.
IF IT COULD BE LIKE THIS...
...EVERY DAY...
...HOW INCREDIBLE WOULD THAT BE?
YOU'RE RIGHT.
I'M GONNA GO CHECK ON THE OTHERS—
BUMP

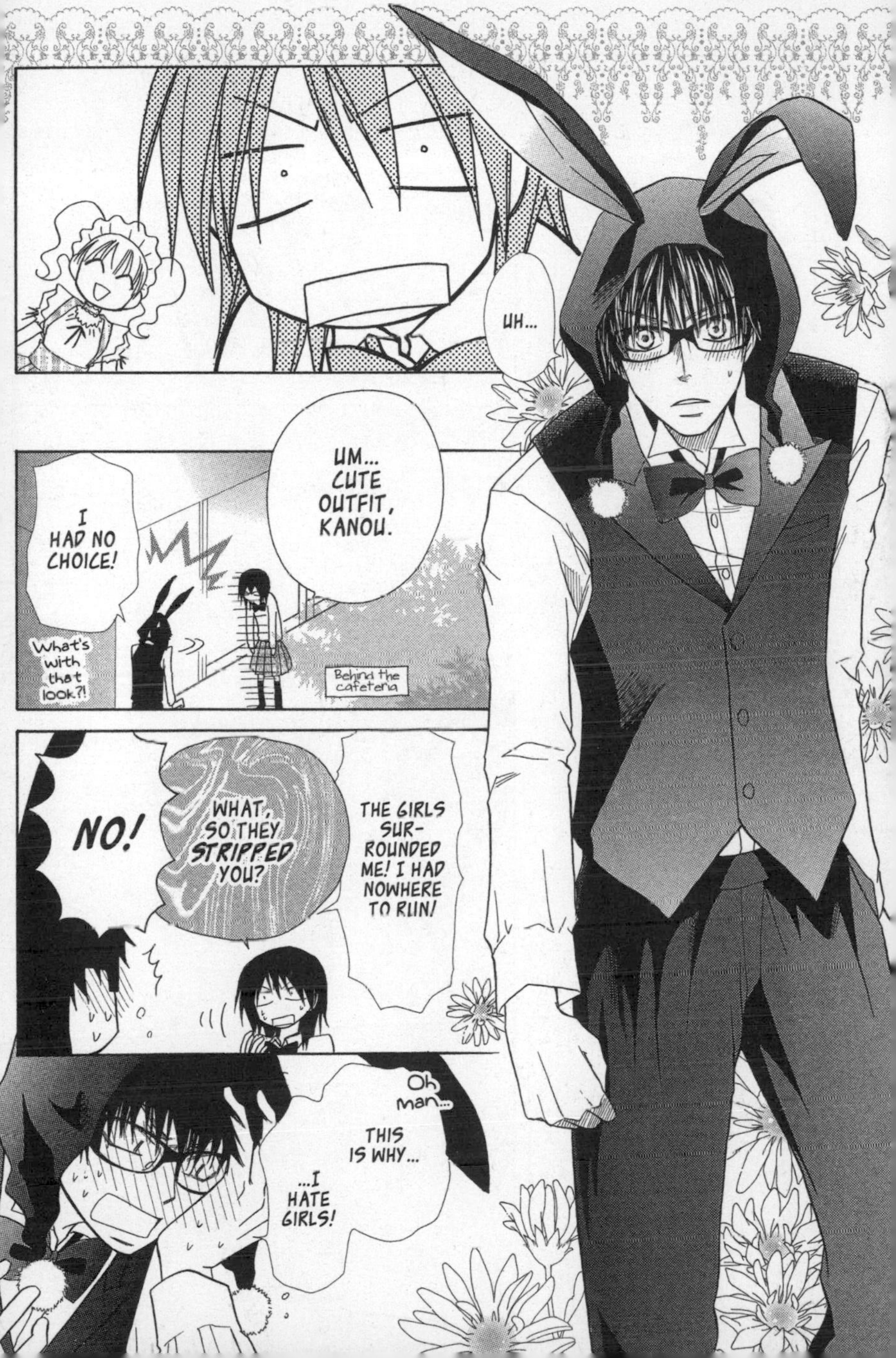
UH...
UM... CUTE OUTFIT, KANOU.
I HAD NO CHOICE!
What's with that look?!
Behind the cafeteria
THE GIRLS SUR-ROUNDED ME! I HAD NOWHERE TO RUN!
WHAT, SO THEY STRIPPED YOU?
NO!
Oh man...
THIS IS WHY...
...I HATE GIRLS!

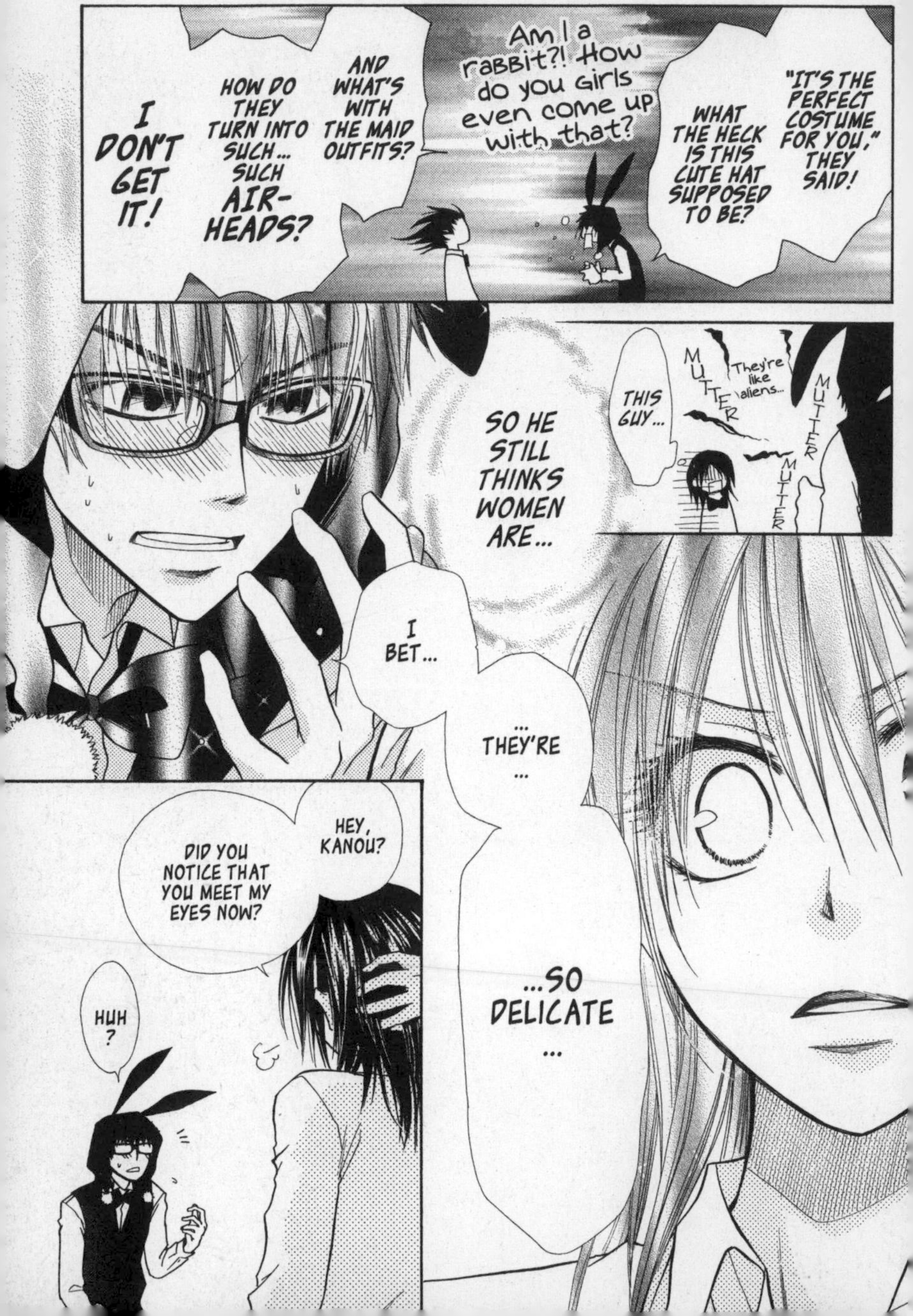
"IT'S THE PERFECT COSTUME FOR YOU," THEY SAID!
WHAT THE HECK IS THIS CUTE HAT SUPPOSED TO BE?
Am I a rabbit?! How do you girls even come up with that?
AND WHAT'S WITH THE MAID OUTFITS?
HOW DO THEY TURN INTO SUCH... SUCH AIR-HEADS?
I DON'T GET IT!
MUTTER
They're like aliens...
MUTTER
MUTTER
THIS GUY...
SO HE STILL THINKS WOMEN ARE...
I BET...
...THEY'RE...
...SO DELICATE...
HEY, KANOU?
DID YOU NOTICE THAT YOU MEET MY EYES NOW?
HUH?

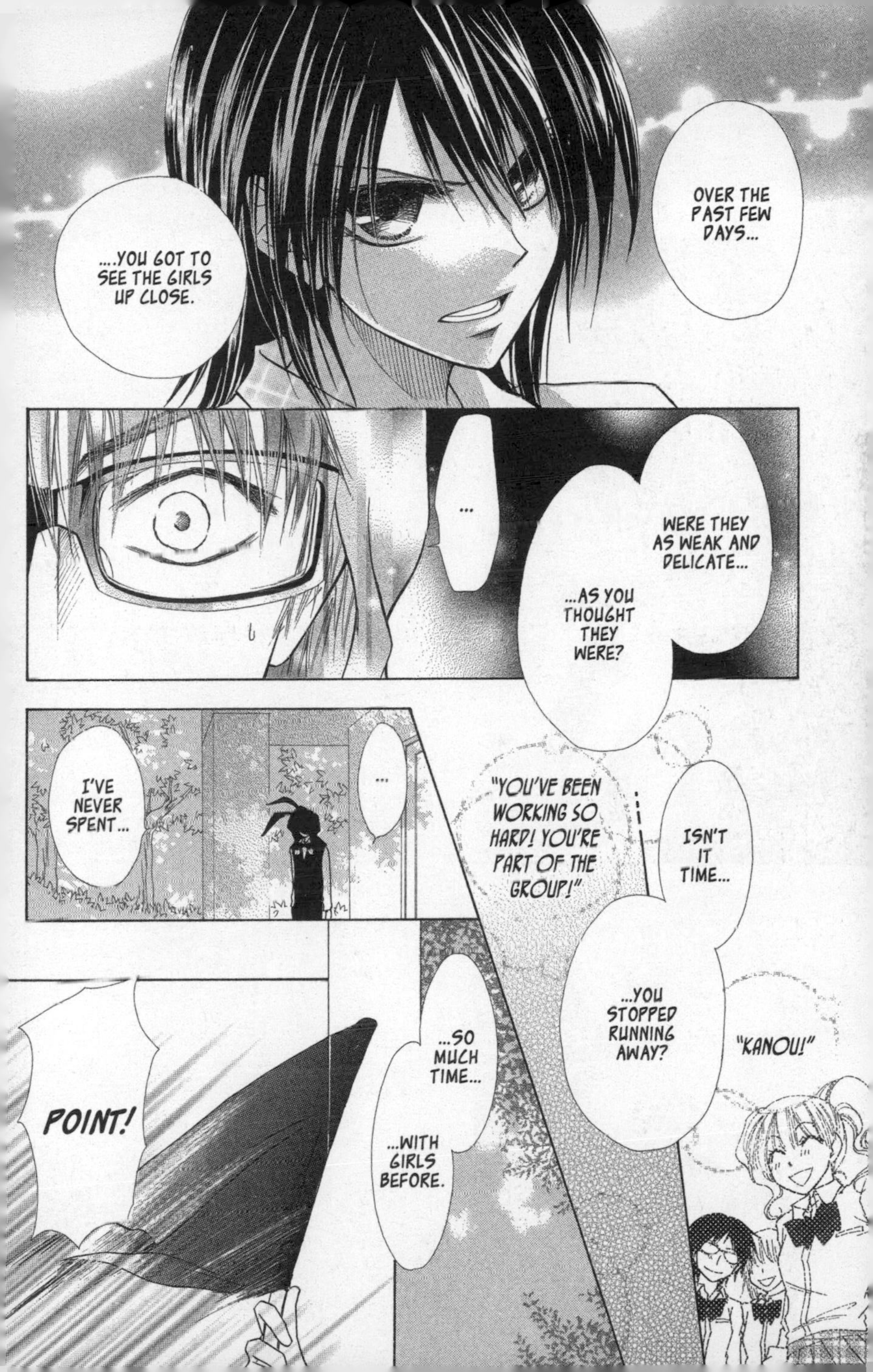
OVER THE PAST FEW DAYS...
....YOU GOT TO SEE THE GIRLS UP CLOSE.
WERE THEY AS WEAK AND DELICATE...
...AS YOU THOUGHT THEY WERE?
...
ISN'T IT TIME...
...YOU STOPPED RUNNING AWAY?
"YOU'VE BEEN WORKING SO HARD! YOU'RE PART OF THE GROUP!"
"KANOU!"
...
I'VE NEVER SPENT...
...SO MUCH TIME...
...WITH GIRLS BEFORE.
POINT!

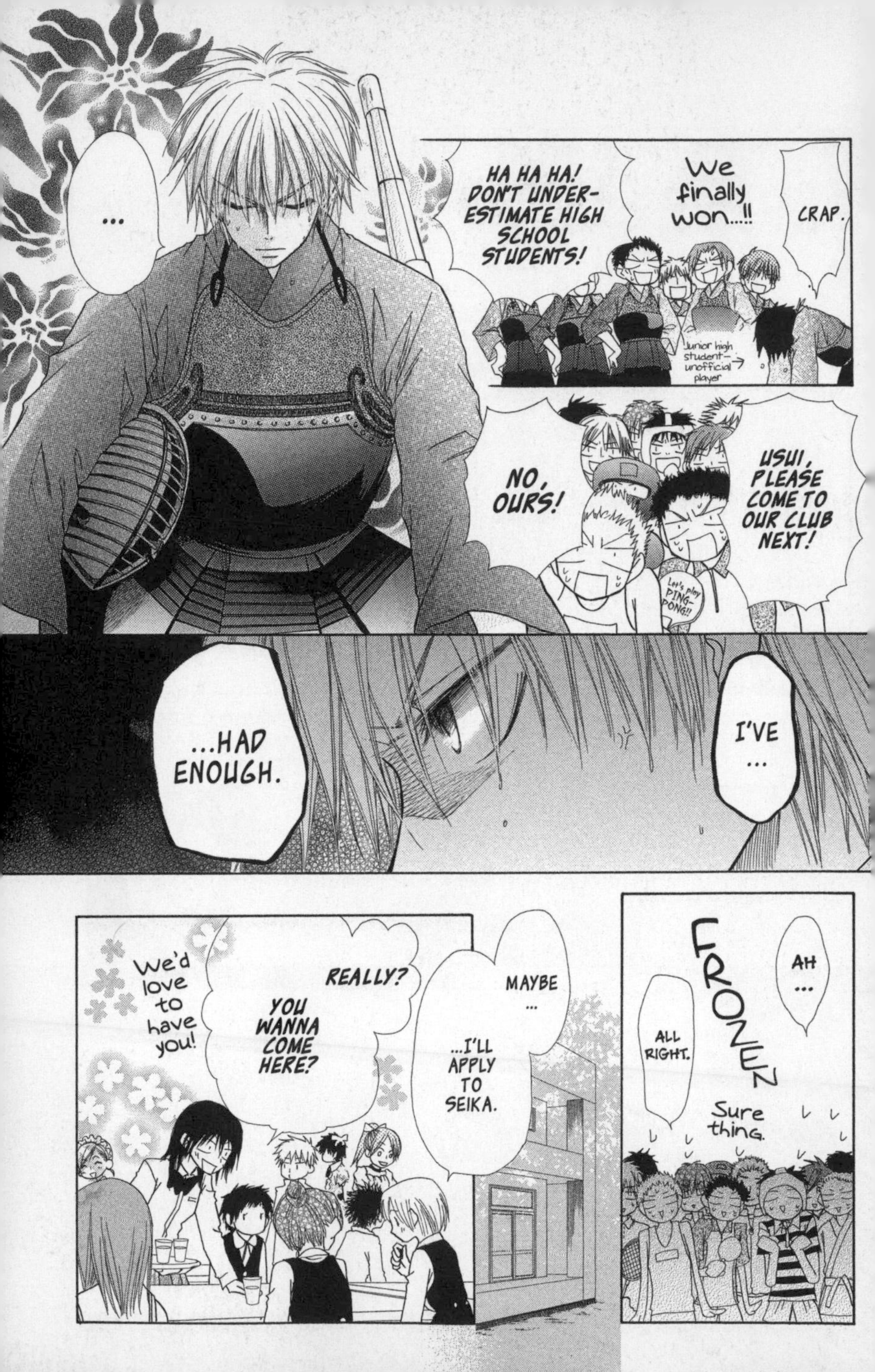
CRAP.
We finally won...!!
HA HA HA! DON'T UNDER-ESTIMATE HIGH SCHOOL STUDENTS!
Junior high student—unofficial player
USUI, PLEASE COME TO OUR CLUB NEXT!
NO, OURS!
Let's play PING-PONG!!
...
I'VE ...
...HAD ENOUGH.
AH ...
FROZEN
ALL RIGHT.
Sure thing.
MAYBE ...
...I'LL APPLY TO SEIKA.
REALLY?
YOU WANNA COME HERE?
We'd love to have you!

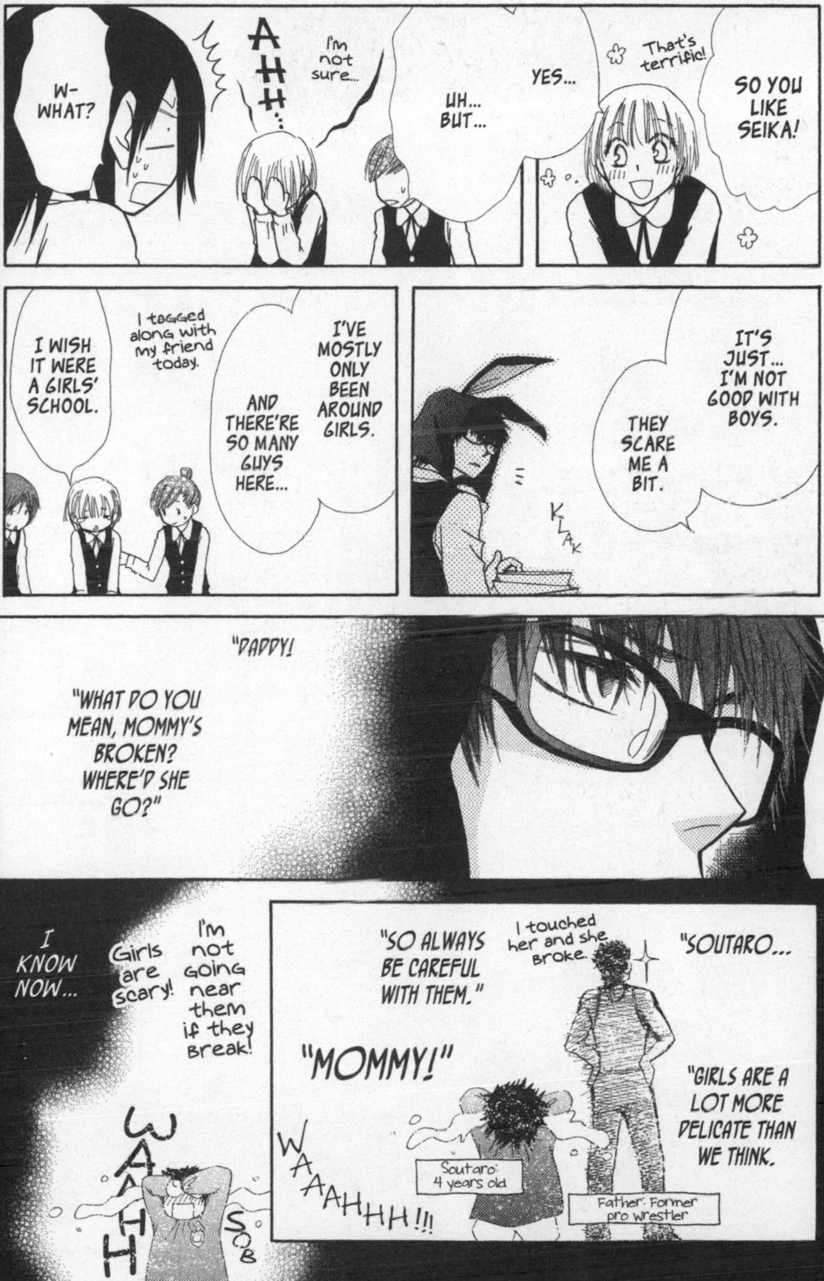
SO YOU LIKE SEIKA!
That's terrific!
YES...
UH... BUT...
I'm not sure...
AHH...
W-WHAT?
IT'S JUST... I'M NOT GOOD WITH BOYS.
THEY SCARE ME A BIT.
KLAK
I'VE MOSTLY ONLY BEEN AROUND GIRLS.
AND THERE'RE SO MANY GUYS HERE...
I tagged along with my friend today.
I WISH IT WERE A GIRLS' SCHOOL.
"DADDY!
"WHAT DO YOU MEAN, MOMMY'S BROKEN? WHERE'D SHE GO?"
"SOUTARO...
I touched her and she broke.
"SO ALWAYS BE CAREFUL WITH THEM."
"GIRLS ARE A LOT MORE DELICATE THAN WE THINK.
"MOMMY!"
WAAAHHH!!!
Soutaro: 4 years old
Father: Former pro wrestler
I'm not going near them if they break!
Girls are scary!
I KNOW NOW...
WAAAHH
SOB

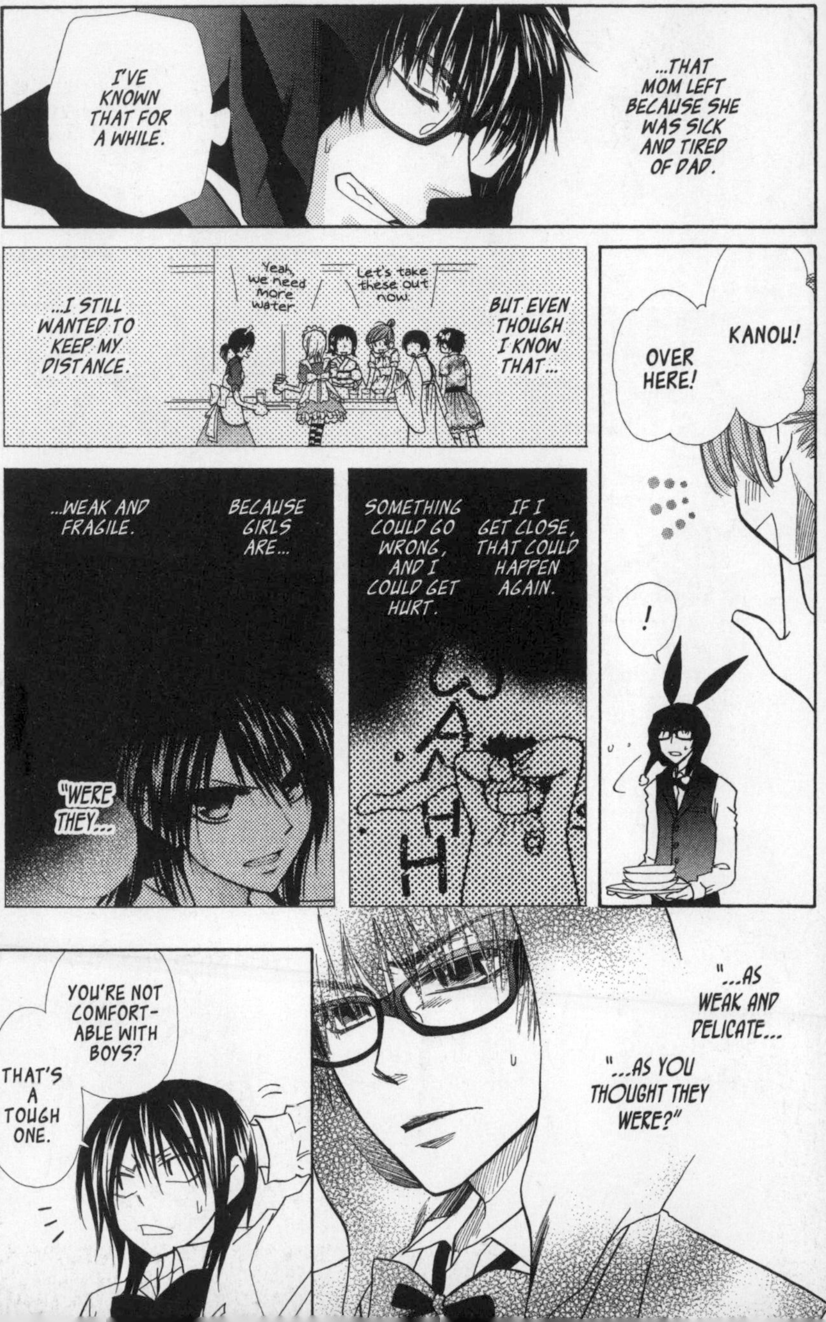
I'VE KNOWN THAT FOR A WHILE.
...THAT MOM LEFT BECAUSE SHE WAS SICK AND TIRED OF DAD.
KANOU!
OVER HERE!
!
BUT EVEN THOUGH I KNOW THAT...
Let's take these out now.
Yeah, we need more water.
...I STILL WANTED TO KEEP MY DISTANCE.
IF I GET CLOSE, THAT COULD HAPPEN AGAIN.
SOMETHING COULD GO WRONG, AND I COULD GET HURT.
BECAUSE GIRLS ARE...
...WEAK AND FRAGILE.
"WERE THEY...
"...AS WEAK AND DELICATE...
"...AS YOU THOUGHT THEY WERE?"
YOU'RE NOT COMFORTABLE WITH BOYS?
THAT'S A TOUGH ONE.

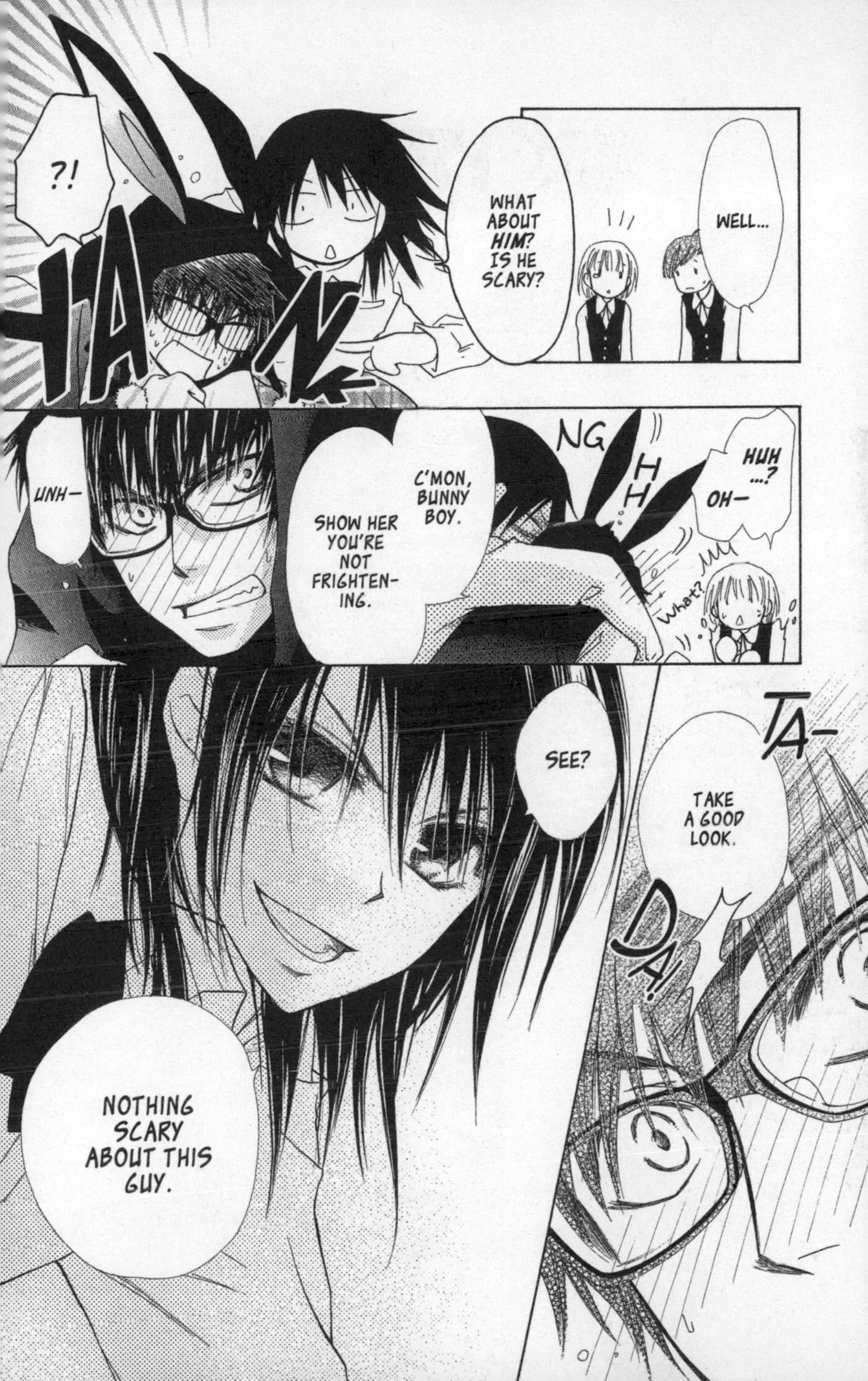
WELL...
WHAT ABOUT HIM? IS HE SCARY?
?!
HUH ...?
OH—
What?
NGHH
C'MON, BUNNY BOY.
SHOW HER YOU'RE NOT FRIGHTEN-ING.
UNH—
TA-
TAKE A GOOD LOOK.
DA!
SEE?
NOTHING SCARY ABOUT THIS GUY.

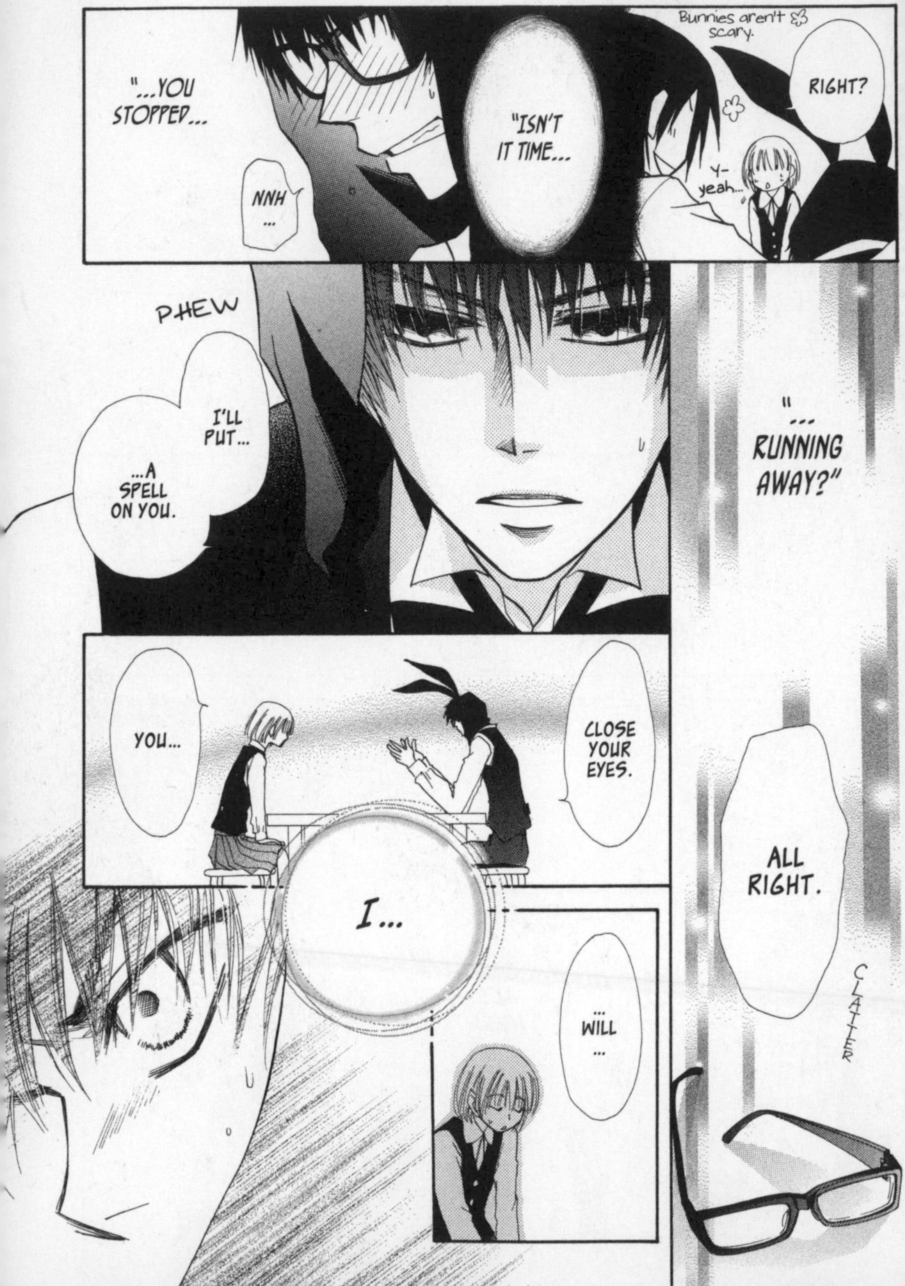
Bunnies aren't scary.
RIGHT?
Y-yeah...
"ISN'T IT TIME...
"...YOU STOPPED...
NNH ...
"... RUNNING AWAY?"
ALL RIGHT.
CLATTER
PHEW
I'LL PUT...
...A SPELL ON YOU.
CLOSE YOUR EYES.
YOU...
I...
... WILL ...

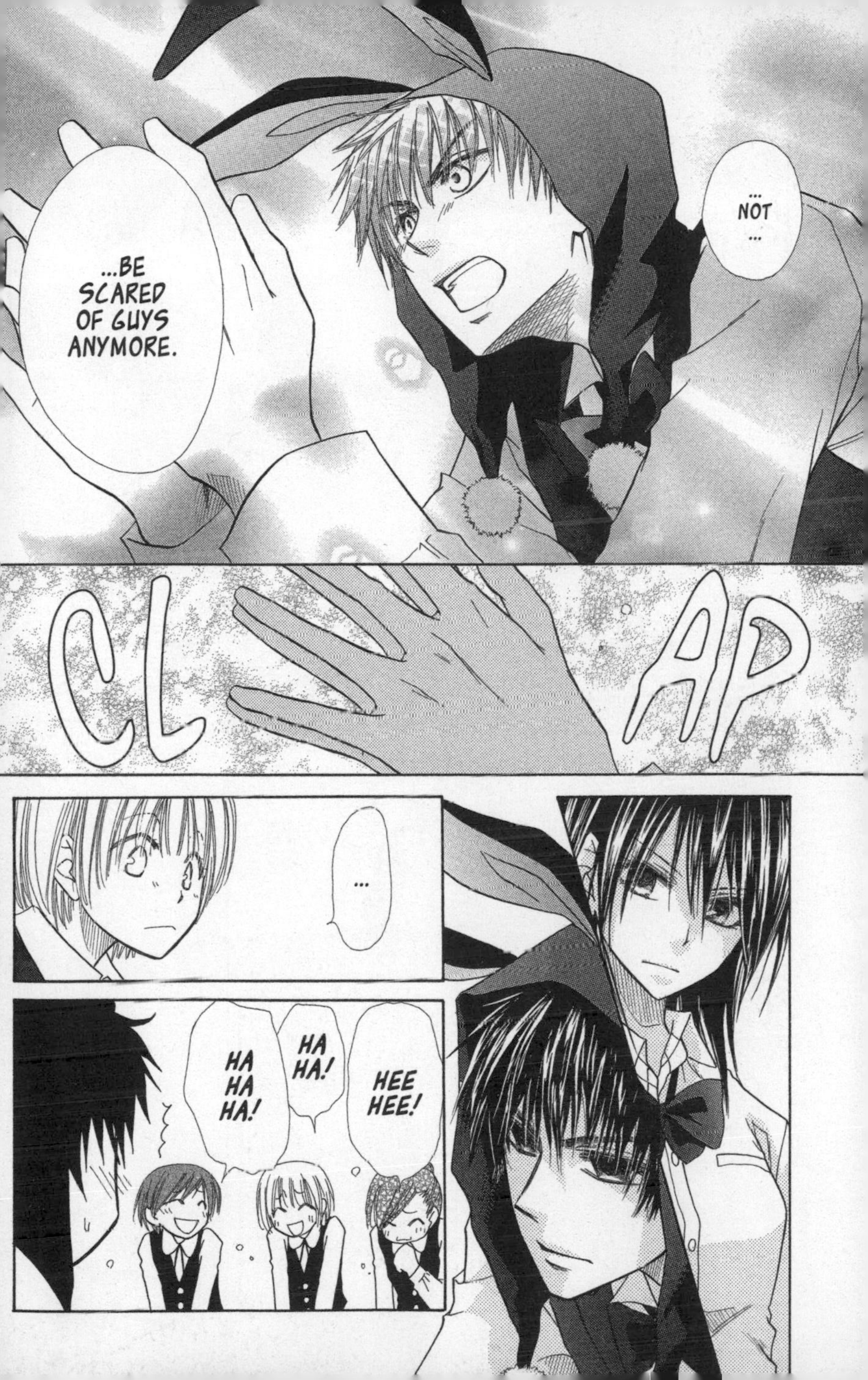
...NOT...
...BE SCARED OF GUYS ANYMORE.
CLAP
...
HEE HEE!
HA HA!
HA HA HA!

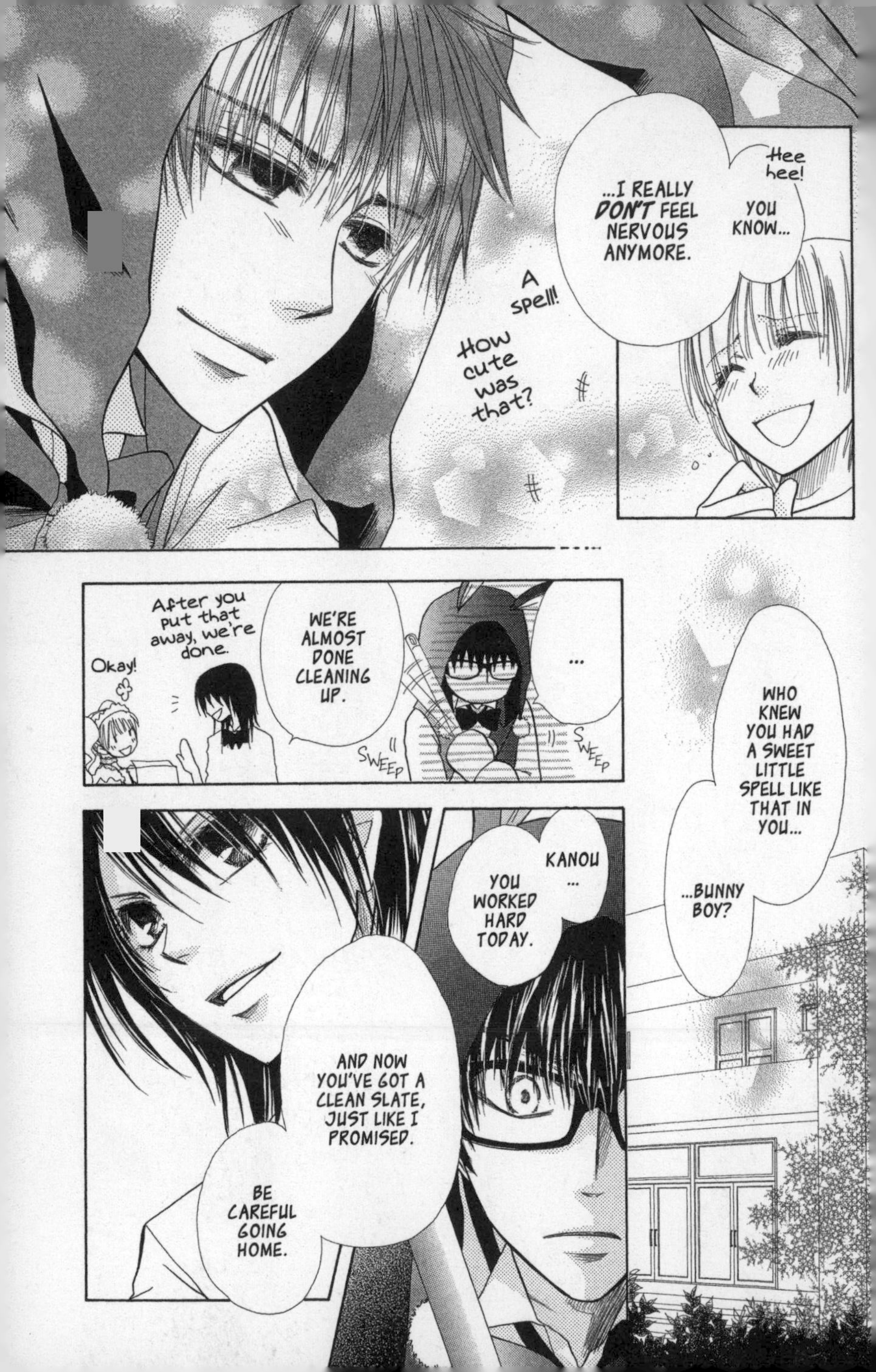
Hee hee!
You know...
...I really DON'T feel nervous anymore.
A spell!
How cute was that?
Who knew you had a sweet little spell like that in you...
...bunny boy?
...
We're almost done cleaning up.
After you put that away, we're done.
Okay!
Sweep
Sweep
Kanou...
You worked hard today.
And now you've got a clean slate, just like I promised.
Be careful going home.

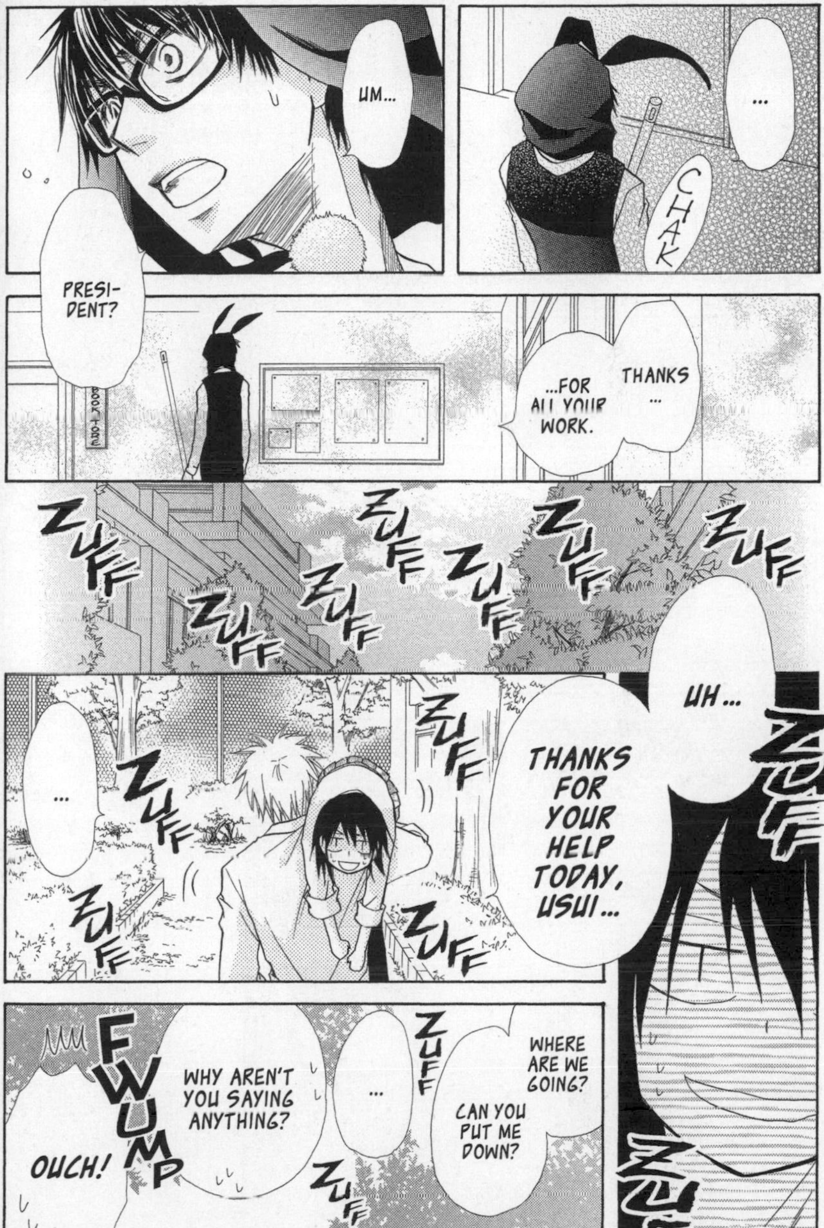
...
CHAK
UM...
PRESI-DENT?
THANKS...
...FOR ALL YOUR WORK.
ZUFF ZUFF ZUFF ZUFF ZUFF ZUFF ZUFF
UH...
THANKS FOR YOUR HELP TODAY, USUI...
ZUFF
ZUFF
ZUFF ZUFF ZUFF ZUFF
...
ZUFF
WHERE ARE WE GOING?
CAN YOU PUT ME DOWN?
ZUFF ZUFF
...
WHY AREN'T YOU SAYING ANYTHING?
FWUMP
OUCH!

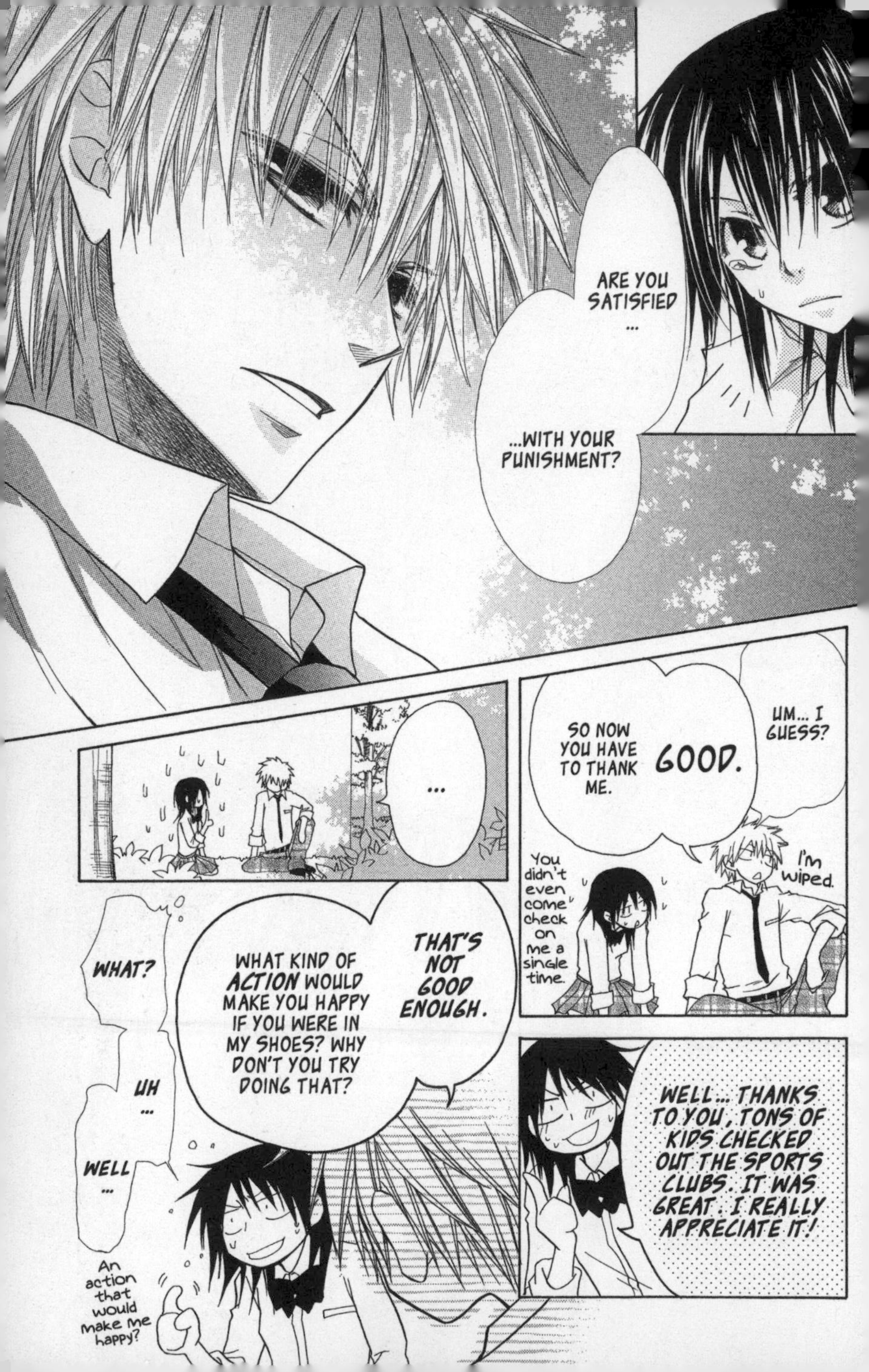
ARE YOU SATISFIED ...
...WITH YOUR PUNISHMENT?
UM... I GUESS?
GOOD.
SO NOW YOU HAVE TO THANK ME.
I'm wiped.
You didn't even come check on me a single time.
...
WELL... THANKS TO YOU, TONS OF KIDS CHECKED OUT THE SPORTS CLUBS. IT WAS GREAT. I REALLY APPRECIATE IT!
THAT'S NOT GOOD ENOUGH.
WHAT KIND OF ACTION WOULD MAKE YOU HAPPY IF YOU WERE IN MY SHOES? WHY DON'T YOU TRY DOING THAT?
WHAT?
UH ...
WELL ...
An action that would make me happy?

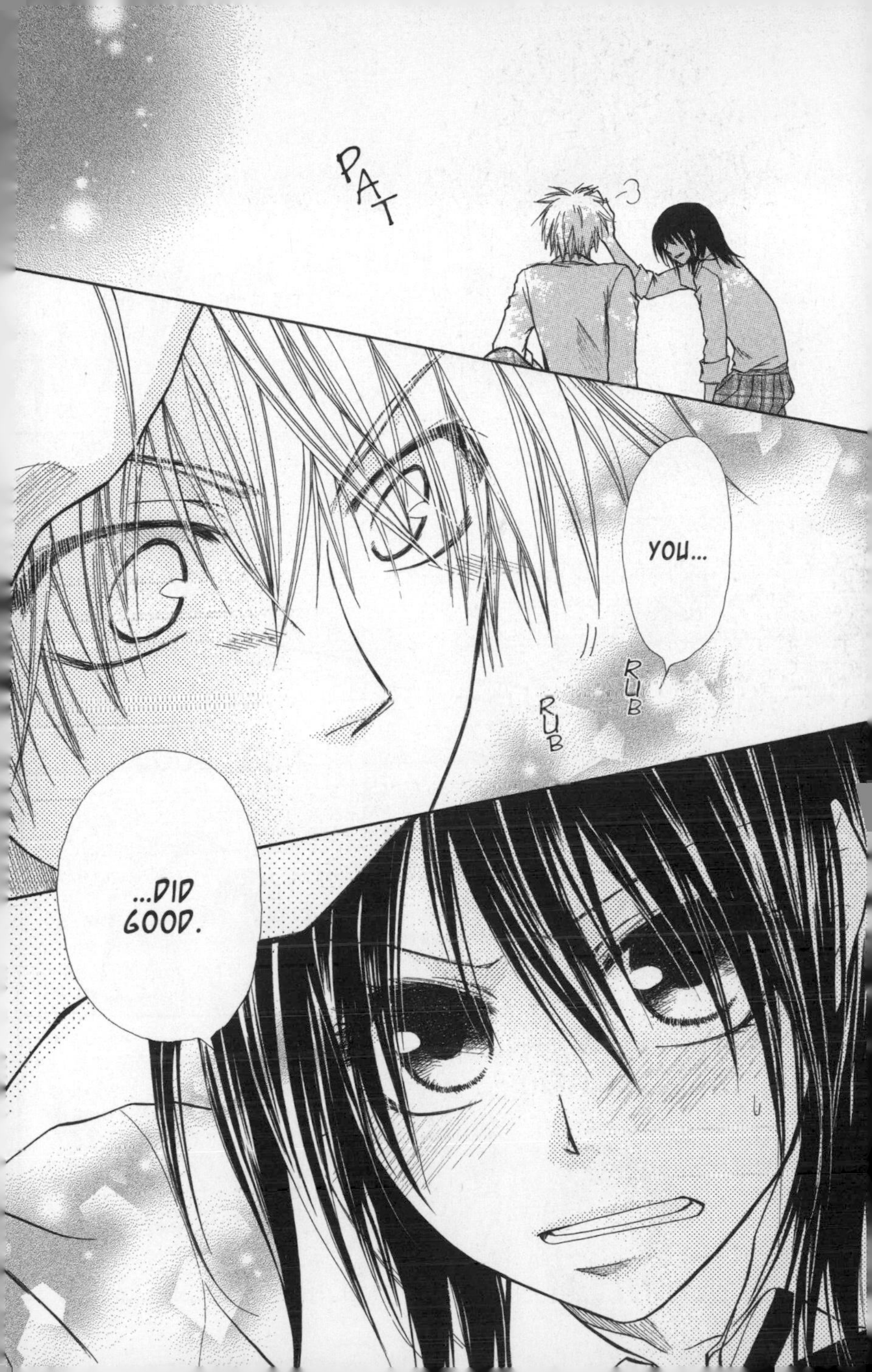
PAT
YOU...
RUB
RUB
...DID GOOD.

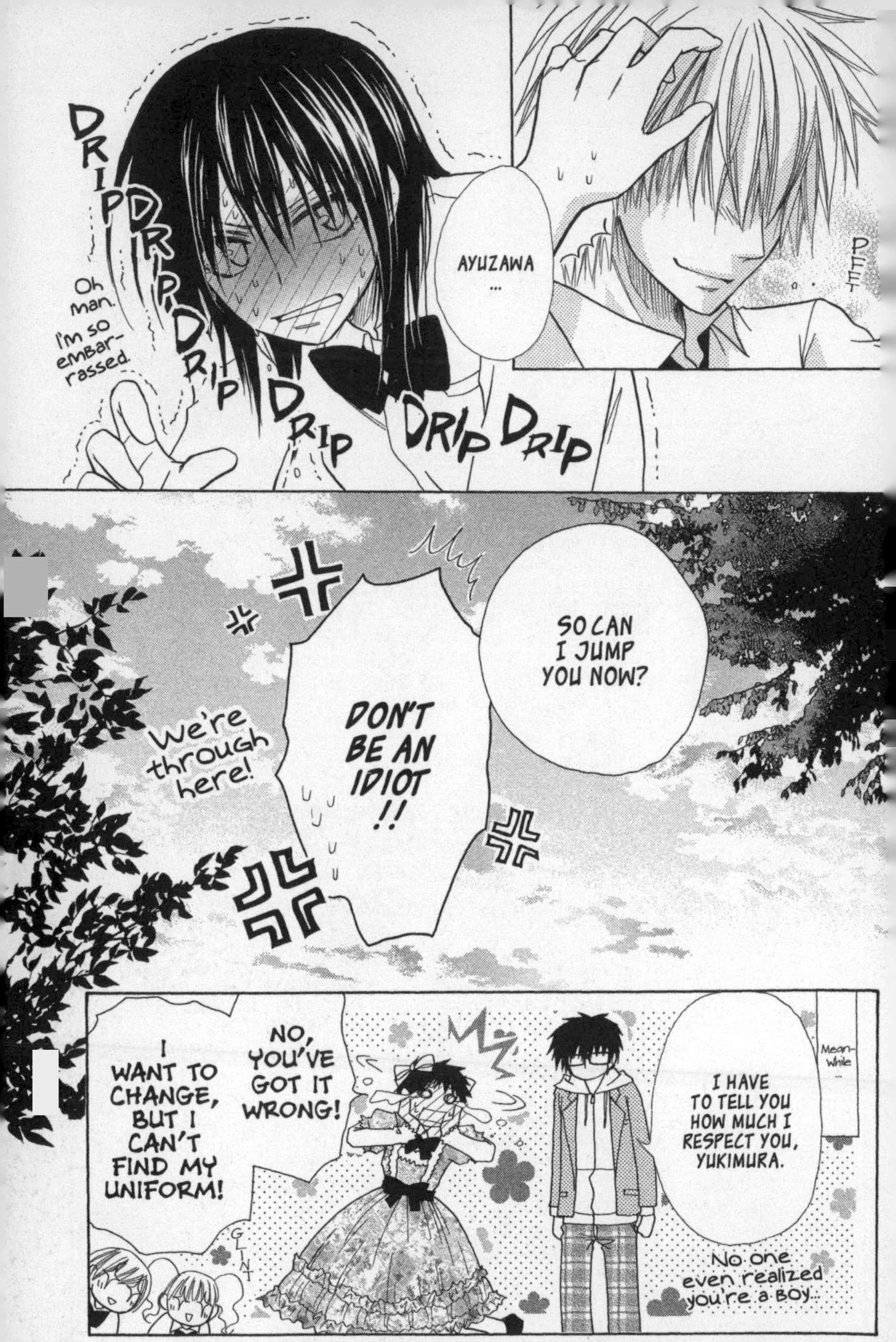
PFFT
AYUZAWA ...
DRIP DRIP DRIP DRIP DRIP DRIP DRIP DRIP
Oh man. I'm so embarrassed.
SO CAN I JUMP YOU NOW?
DON'T BE AN IDIOT !!
We're through here!
Meanwhile ...
I HAVE TO TELL YOU HOW MUCH I RESPECT YOU, YUKIMURA.
No one even realized you're a boy...
NO, YOU'VE GOT IT WRONG!
I WANT TO CHANGE, BUT I CAN'T FIND MY UNIFORM!
GLINT

Q&A time...

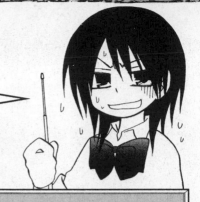

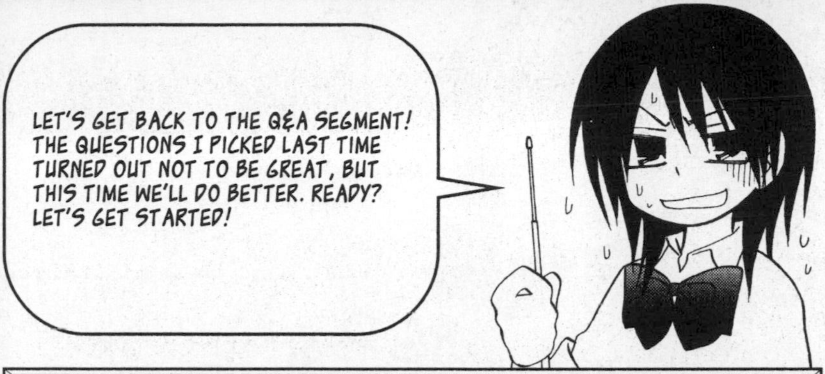

LET'S GET BACK TO THE Q&A SEGMENT! THE QUESTIONS I PICKED LAST TIME TURNED OUT NOT TO BE GREAT, BUT THIS TIME WE'LL DO BETTER. READY? LET'S GET STARTED!

 (THERE HAVE TO BE **SOME** QUESTIONS THAT AREN'T ABOUT USUI...)

QUESTION 8: "THE SIZE OF MISAKI'S CHEST SEEMS TO CHANGE DEPENDING ON WHAT SHE'S WEARING. WHAT'S HER ACTUAL BRA SIZE?"

 ...

OKAY, I'LL GRANT YOU THAT IT'S NOT A QUESTION ABOUT USUI, BUT... REALLY? YOU REALLY WANNA GO THERE?

FINE, WHATEVER. I'LL ANSWER. IN THIS VOLUME YOU'LL SEE ME IN A SWIMSUIT, SO I THINK THE ACTUAL SIZE OF MY CHEST WILL BE OBVIOUS.

AS FOR WHY IT CHANGES FROM OUTFIT TO OUTFIT, I THINK WE CAN CHALK THAT UP TO *THE AUTHOR'S DRAWING ABILITY.* EVERYONE'S A CRITIC!

QUESTION 9: "WHY DOES MISAKI HAVE SUCH A GREAT BODY?"

 WOW, THAT'S FLATTERING. BUT WHY IS EVERYONE ASKING ABOUT MY BODY?

WELL, LET'S SEE. I DON'T DO ANYTHING IN PARTICULAR, SO I GUESS IT'S BECAUSE *I WORK OUT EVERY NIGHT BEFORE BED. I'M ALSO CAREFUL TO HAVE GOOD POSTURE,* BECAUSE THAT CONTRIBUTES TO A HEALTHY MIND AND A HEALTHY BODY. *GOOD POSTURE IS SO IMPORTANT!*

 HMM? THAT'S THE END OF MY TURN?

WAIT, WHO'S UP NEXT? USUI IS?!

NUH-UH, NOT HAPPENING. THERE'S NO WAY HE'LL TAKE THIS SERIOUSLY!!

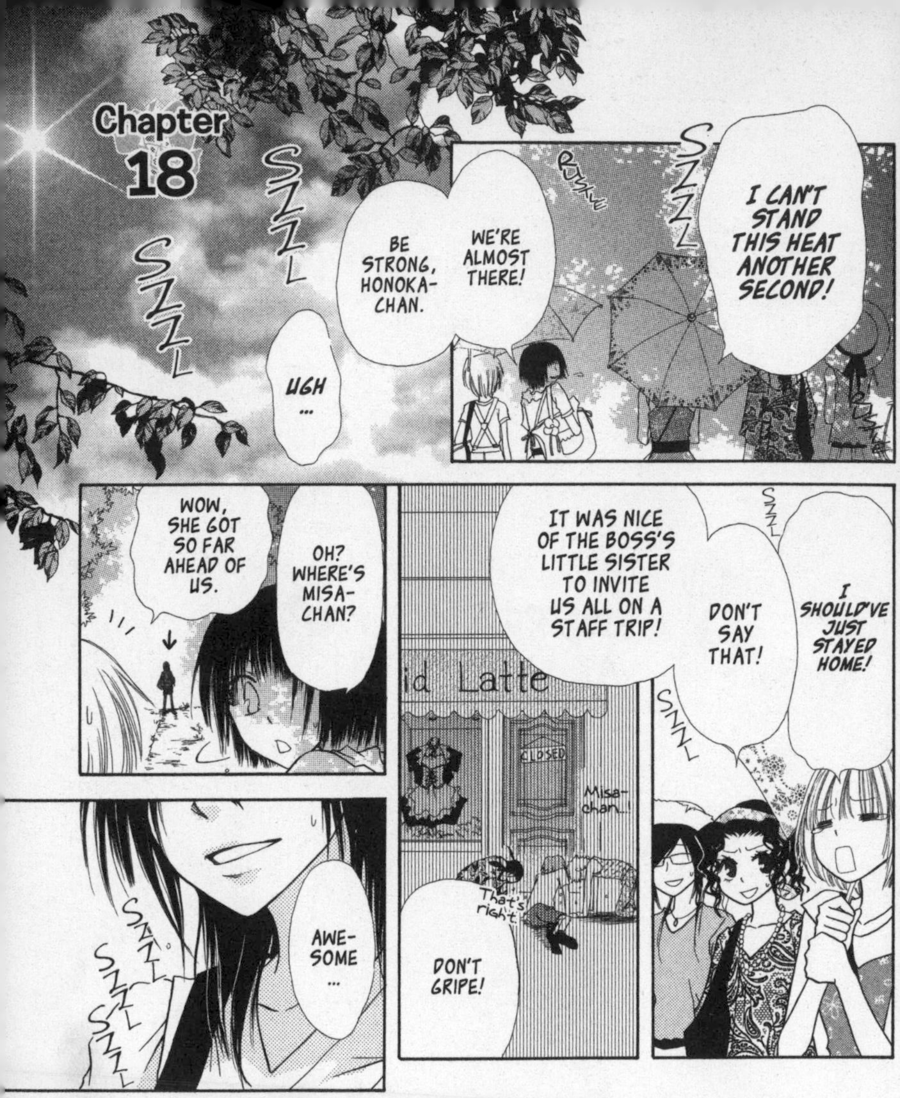
I CAN'T STAND THIS HEAT ANOTHER SECOND!
SZZZL
RUSTLE
WE'RE ALMOST THERE!
BE STRONG, HONOKA-CHAN.
UGH ...
Chapter 18
SZZZL
SZZZL
I SHOULD'VE JUST STAYED HOME!
SZZL
DON'T SAY THAT!
IT WAS NICE OF THE BOSS'S LITTLE SISTER TO INVITE US ALL ON A STAFF TRIP!
SZZL
CLOSED
Misa-chan...!
That's right.
DON'T GRIPE!
OH? WHERE'S MISA-CHAN?
WOW, SHE GOT SO FAR AHEAD OF US.
AWE-SOME ...
SZZZL
SZZZL
SZZZL

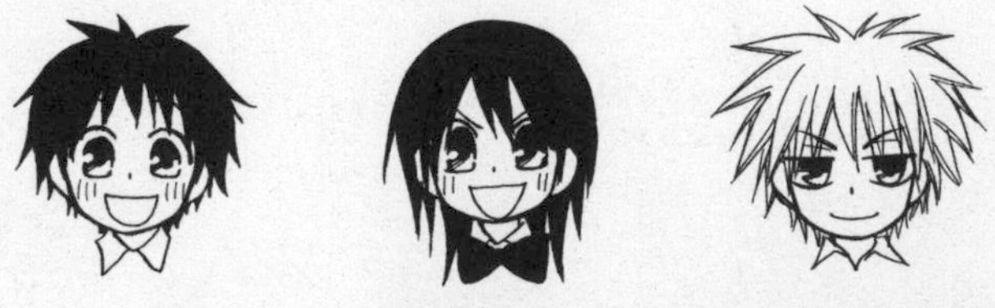

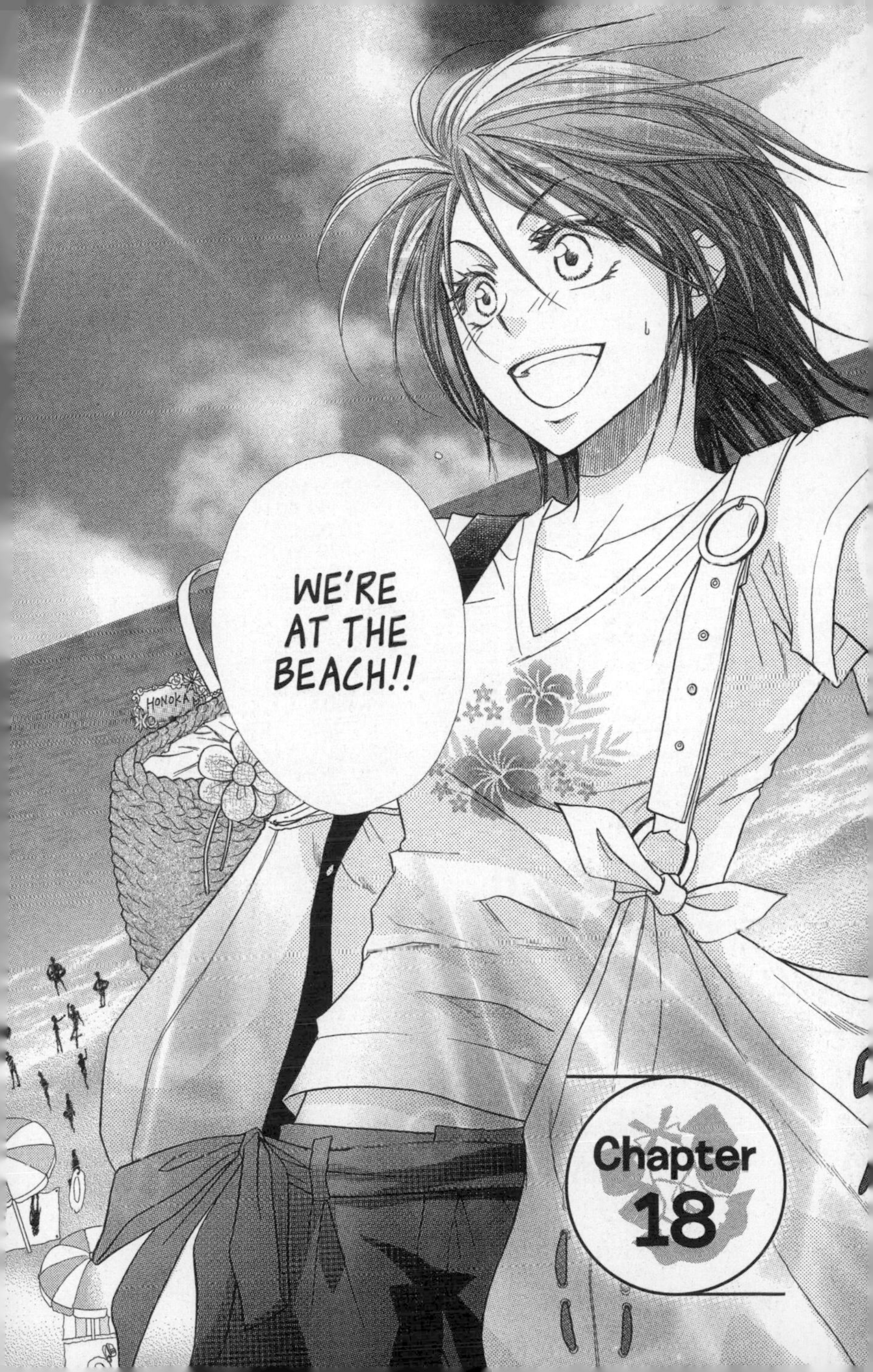
WE'RE AT THE BEACH!!
HONOKA
Chapter 18

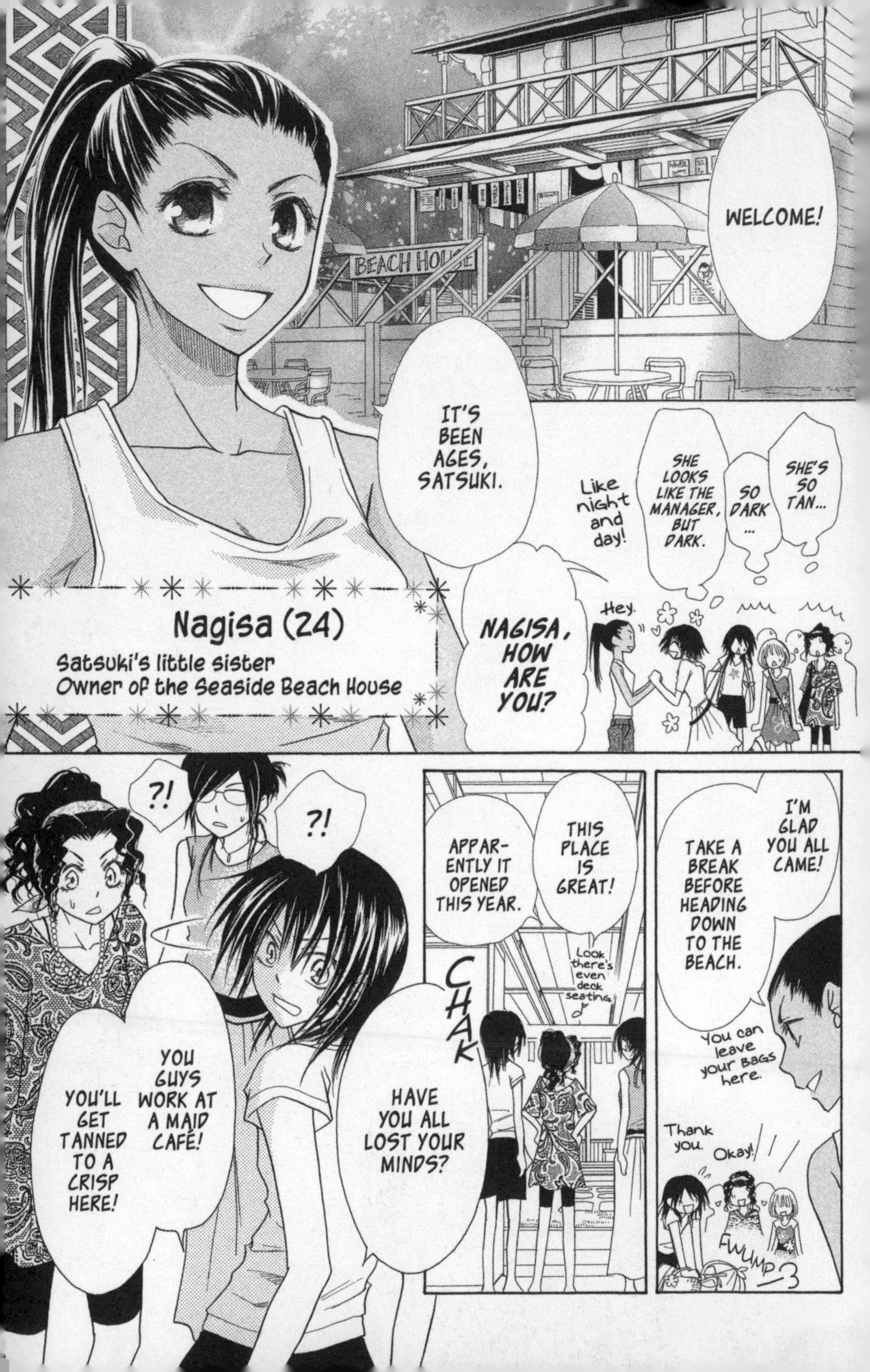
WELCOME!
IT'S BEEN AGES, SATSUKI.
SHE'S SO TAN...
SO DARK...
SHE LOOKS LIKE THE MANAGER, BUT DARK.
Like night and day!
NAGISA, HOW ARE YOU?
Hey.
Nagisa (24)
Satsuki's little sister
Owner of the Seaside Beach House
I'M GLAD YOU ALL CAME!
TAKE A BREAK BEFORE HEADING DOWN TO THE BEACH.
You can leave your bags here.
Okay!
Thank you.
FWUMP
THIS PLACE IS GREAT!
APPARENTLY IT OPENED THIS YEAR.
Look there's even deck seating.
CHAK
?!
?!
HAVE YOU ALL LOST YOUR MINDS?
YOU GUYS WORK AT A MAID CAFÉ!
YOU'LL GET TANNED TO A CRISP HERE!

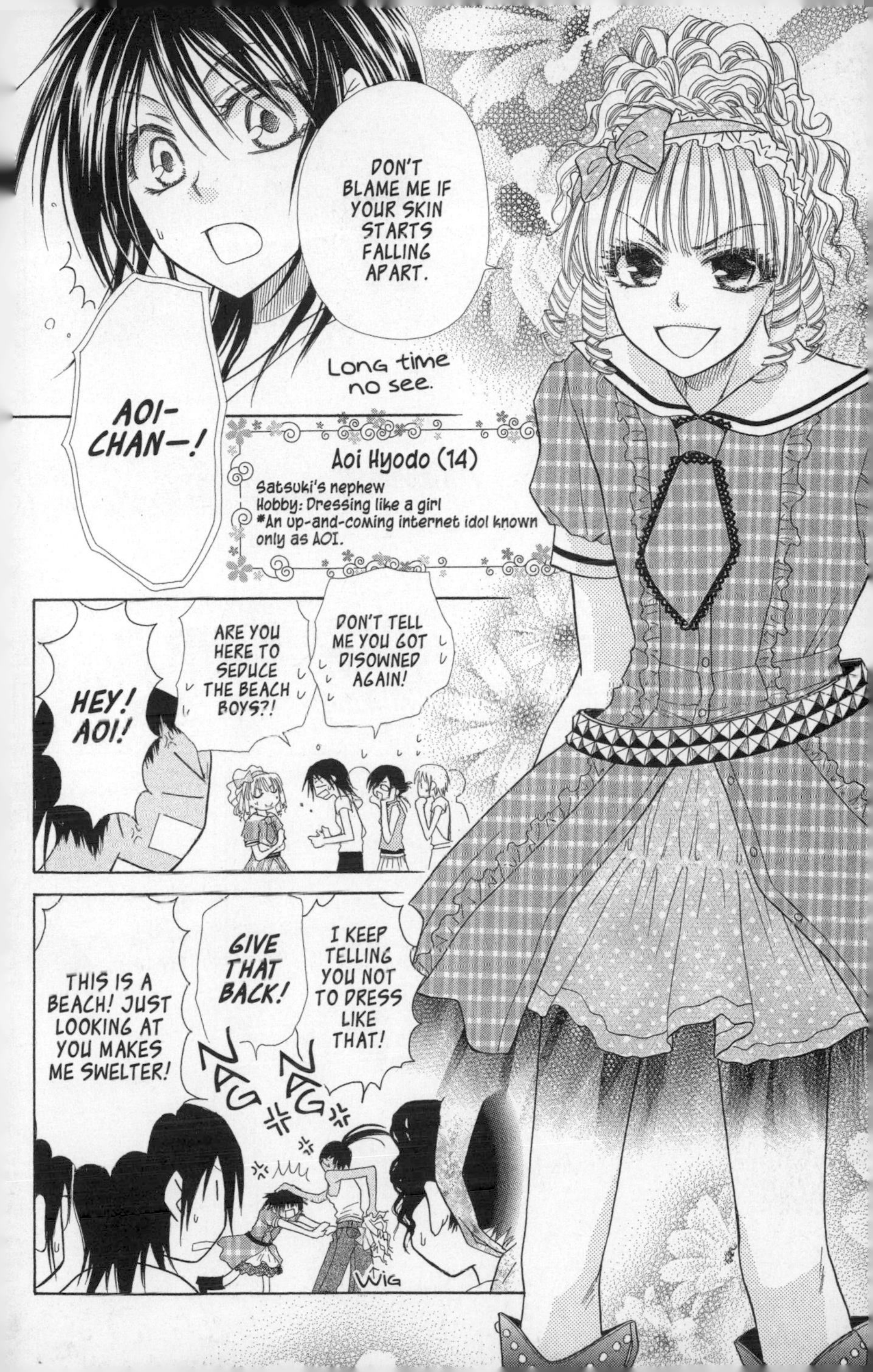
Long time no see.
Aoi Hyodo (14)
Satsuki's nephew
Hobby: Dressing like a girl
*An up-and-coming internet idol known only as AOI.
DON'T BLAME ME IF YOUR SKIN STARTS FALLING APART.
AOI-CHAN—!
DON'T TELL ME YOU GOT DISOWNED AGAIN!
ARE YOU HERE TO SEDUCE THE BEACH BOYS?!
HEY! AOI!
I KEEP TELLING YOU NOT TO DRESS LIKE THAT!
GIVE THAT BACK!
THIS IS A BEACH! JUST LOOKING AT YOU MAKES ME SWELTER!
ZAG ZAG
WIG

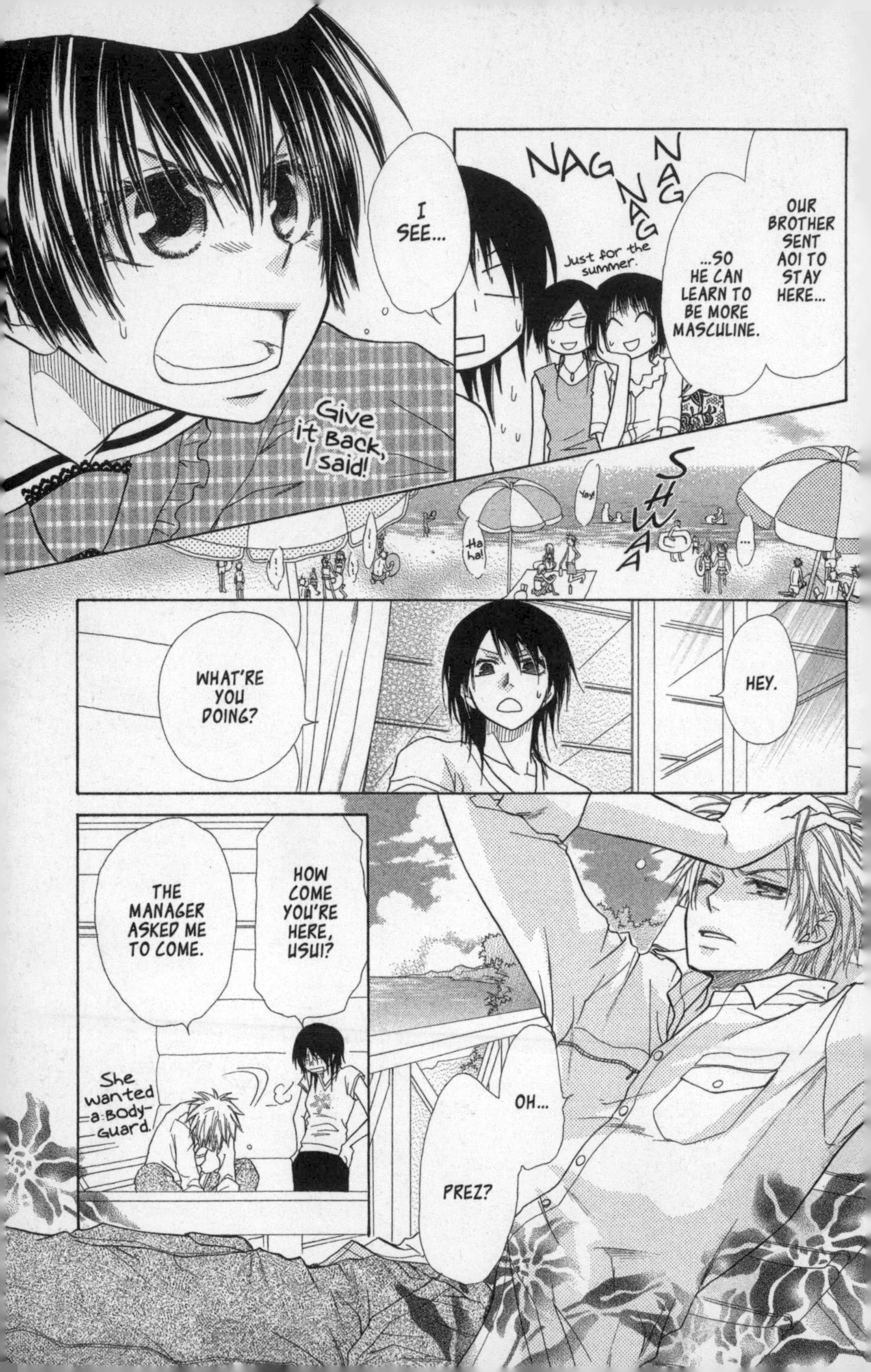
NAG NAG NAG NAG
OUR BROTHER SENT AOI TO STAY HERE...
...SO HE CAN LEARN TO BE MORE MASCULINE.
Just for the summer.
I SEE...
Give it Back, I said!
SHWAA
Yay!
Ha ha!
HEY.
WHAT'RE YOU DOING?
OH...
PREZ?
HOW COME YOU'RE HERE, USUI?
THE MANAGER ASKED ME TO COME.
She wanted a body-guard.

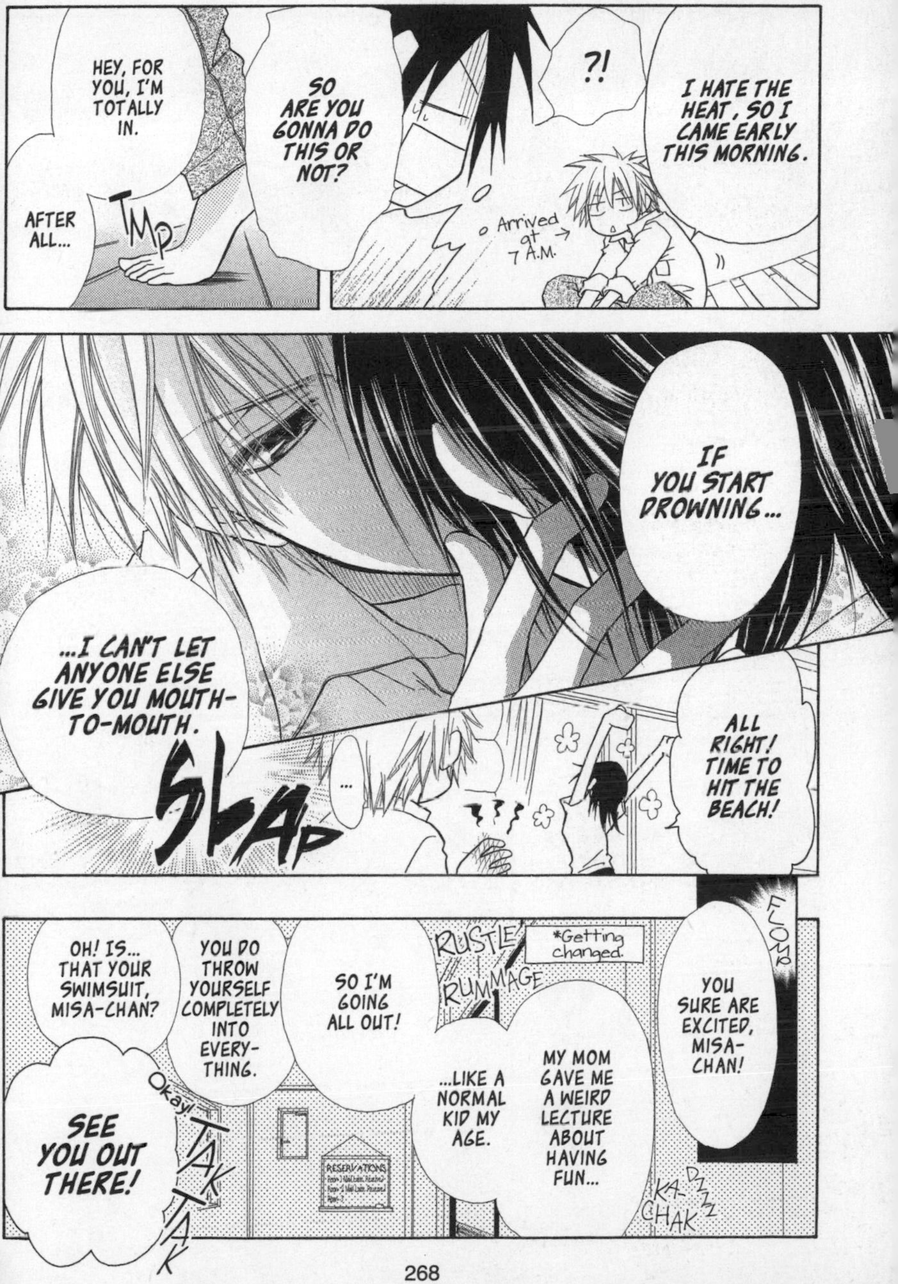
?!
I HATE THE HEAT, SO I CAME EARLY THIS MORNING.
Arrived at 7 A.M.
SO ARE YOU GONNA DO THIS OR NOT?
HEY, FOR YOU, I'M TOTALLY IN.
TMP
AFTER ALL...
IF YOU START DROWNING...
...I CAN'T LET ANYONE ELSE GIVE YOU MOUTH-TO-MOUTH.
SLAP
ALL RIGHT! TIME TO HIT THE BEACH!
...
FLOMP
YOU SURE ARE EXCITED, MISA-CHAN!
KA-CHAK
MY MOM GAVE ME A WEIRD LECTURE ABOUT HAVING FUN...
...LIKE A NORMAL KID MY AGE.
*Getting changed.
RUSTLE RUMMAGE
SO I'M GOING ALL OUT!
YOU DO THROW YOURSELF COMPLETELY INTO EVERY-THING.
OH! IS... THAT YOUR SWIMSUIT, MISA-CHAN?
SEE YOU OUT THERE!
Okay!
TAK TAK
RESERVATIONS

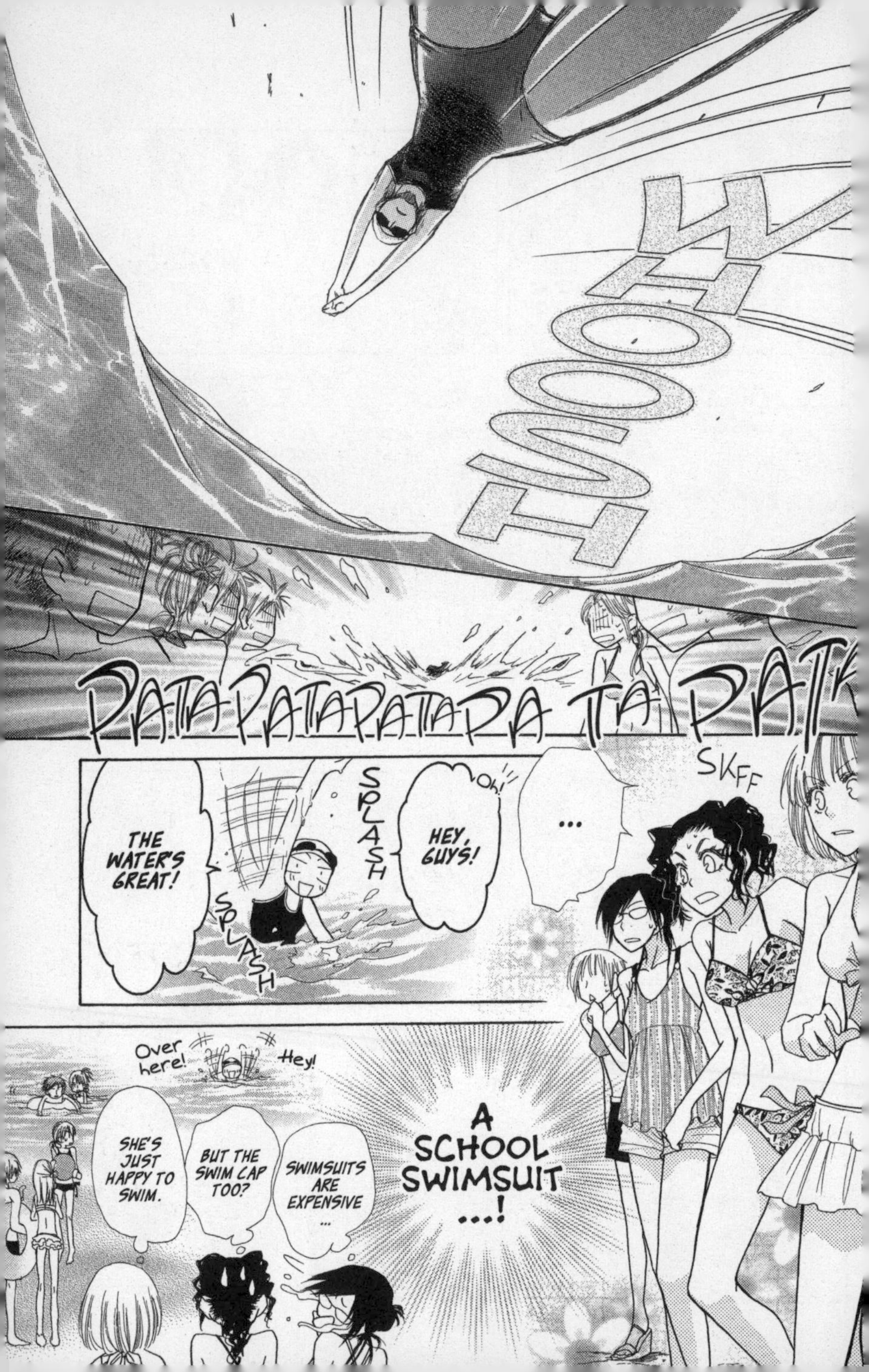
WHOOSH
PATAPATAPATAPA TA PAT
...
SKFF
Oh!
HEY, GUYS!
SPLASH
THE WATER'S GREAT!
SPLASH
A SCHOOL SWIMSUIT ...!
Over here!
Hey!
SWIMSUITS ARE EXPENSIVE ...
BUT THE SWIM CAP TOO?
SHE'S JUST HAPPY TO SWIM.

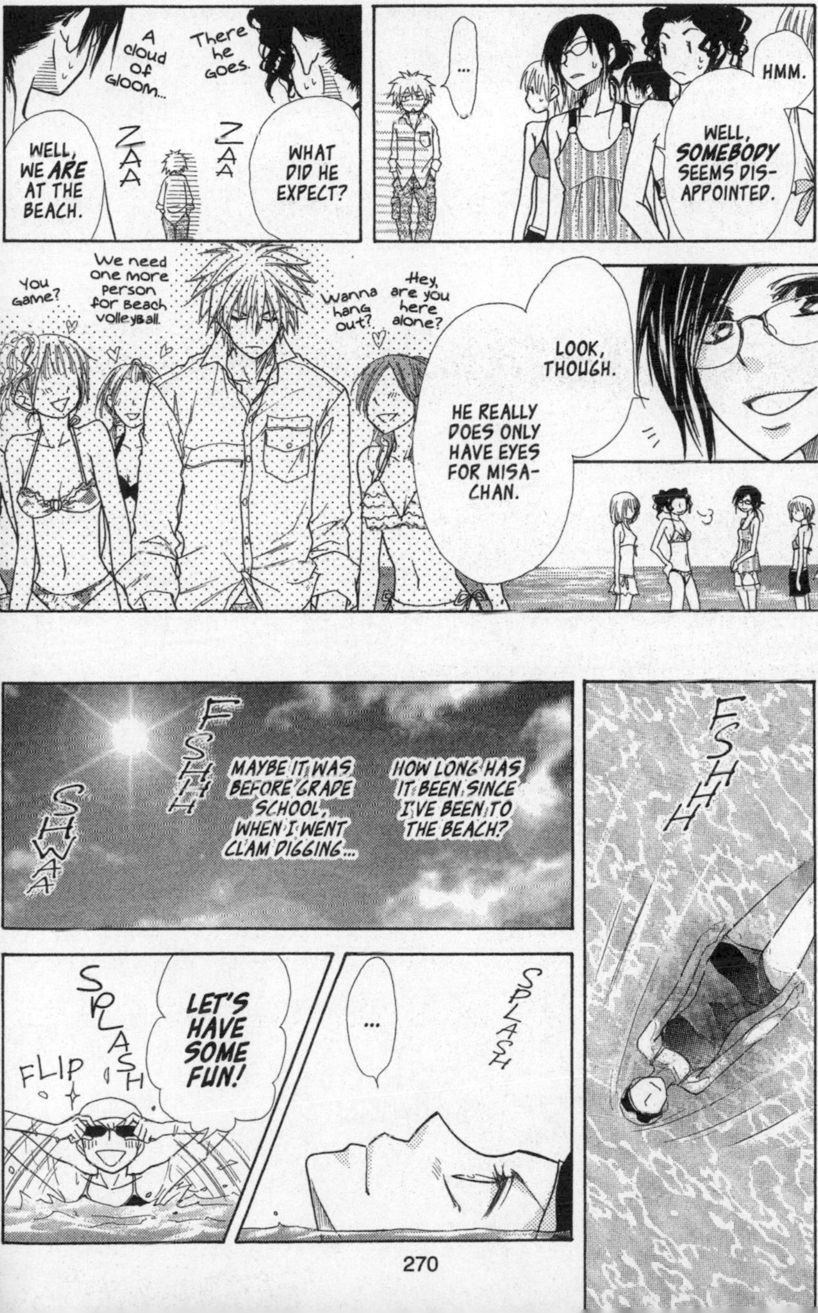
HMM.
WELL, SOMEBODY SEEMS DIS-APPOINTED.
...
WHAT DID HE EXPECT?
There he goes.
ZAA
ZAA
A cloud of gloom...
WELL, WE ARE AT THE BEACH.
LOOK, THOUGH.
HE REALLY DOES ONLY HAVE EYES FOR MISA-CHAN.
Hey, are you here alone?
Wanna hang out?
We need one more person for beach volleyball.
You game?
FSHHH
HOW LONG HAS IT BEEN SINCE I'VE BEEN TO THE BEACH?
MAYBE IT WAS BEFORE GRADE SCHOOL, WHEN I WENT CLAM DIGGING...
FSHHH
SHWAA
SPLASH
...
LET'S HAVE SOME FUN!
SPLASH
FLIP

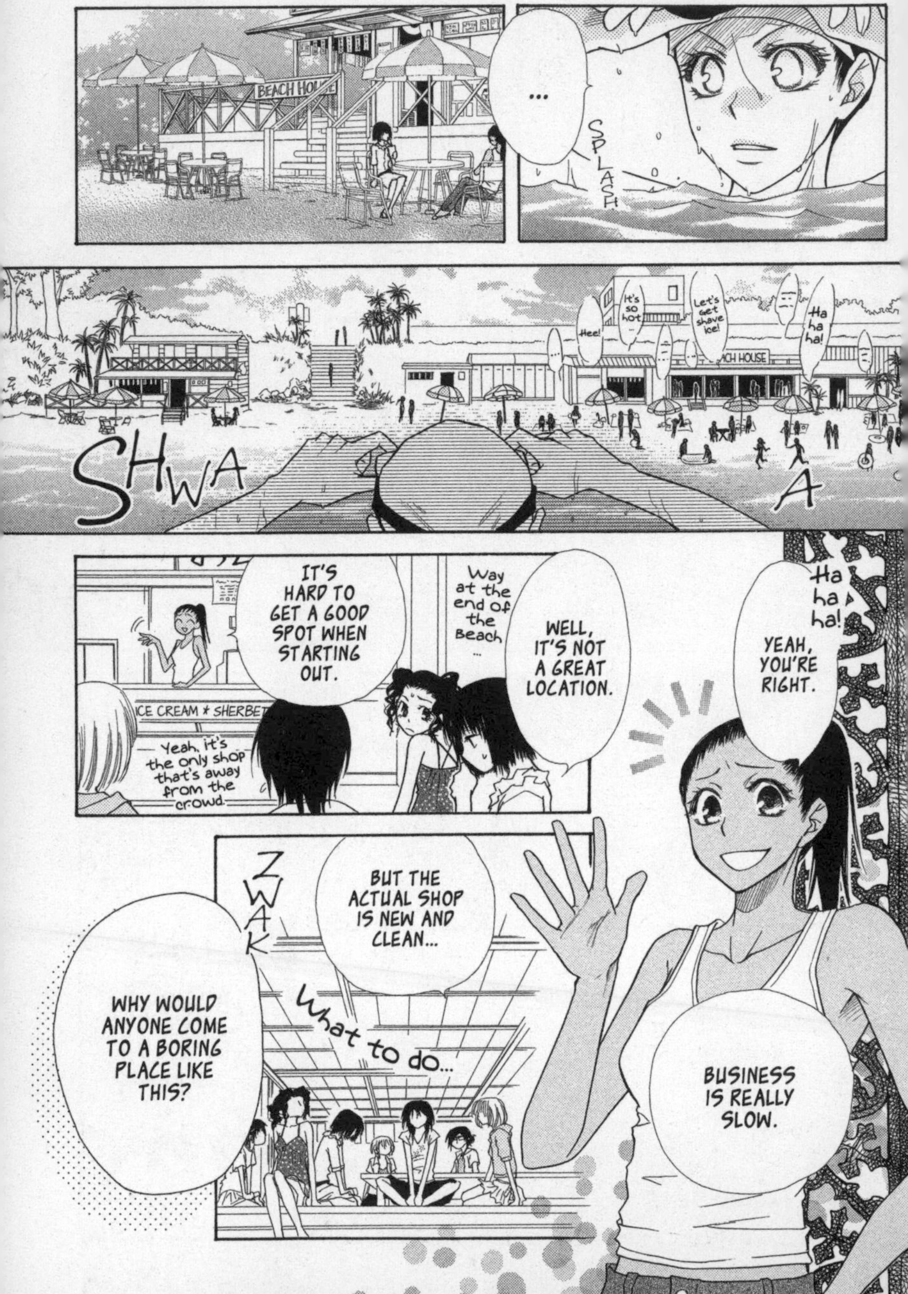
...
SPLASH
BEACH HOUSE
Ha ha ha!
Let's get shave ice!
It's so hot ...
Hee!
SHWA
A
Ha ha ha!
YEAH, YOU'RE RIGHT.
BUSINESS IS REALLY SLOW.
WELL, IT'S NOT A GREAT LOCATION.
Way at the end of the Beach ...
IT'S HARD TO GET A GOOD SPOT WHEN STARTING OUT.
ICE CREAM * SHERBET
Yeah, it's the only shop that's away from the crowd.
BUT THE ACTUAL SHOP IS NEW AND CLEAN...
ZWAK
What to do...
WHY WOULD ANYONE COME TO A BORING PLACE LIKE THIS?

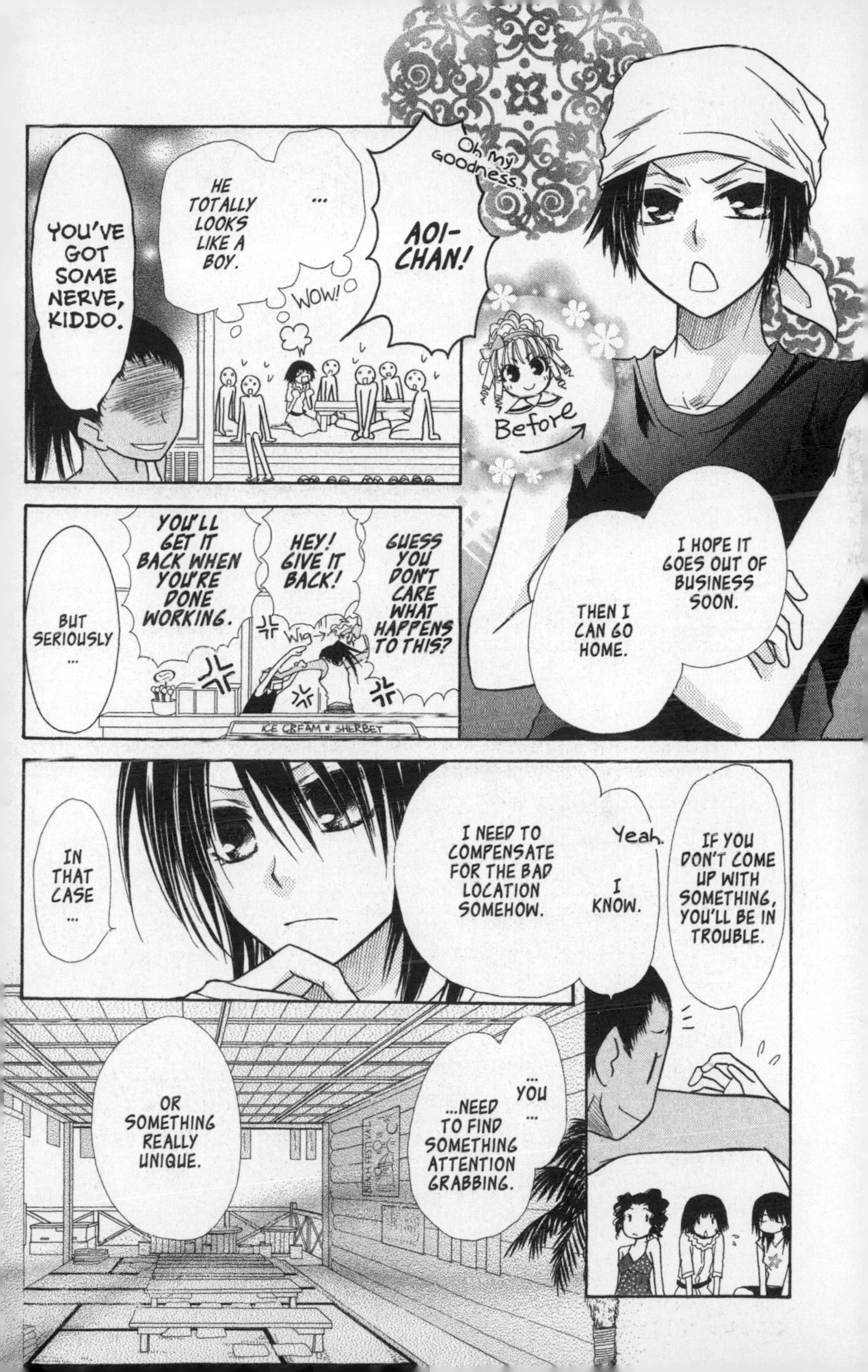
Oh my goodness...
Before
I HOPE IT GOES OUT OF BUSINESS SOON.
THEN I CAN GO HOME.
AOI-CHAN!
...
WOW!
HE TOTALLY LOOKS LIKE A BOY.
YOU'VE GOT SOME NERVE, KIDDO.
GUESS YOU DON'T CARE WHAT HAPPENS TO THIS?
HEY! GIVE IT BACK!
Wig
YOU'LL GET IT BACK WHEN YOU'RE DONE WORKING.
BUT SERIOUSLY ...
ICE CREAM & SHERBET
IF YOU DON'T COME UP WITH SOMETHING, YOU'LL BE IN TROUBLE.
Yeah.
I KNOW.
I NEED TO COMPENSATE FOR THE BAD LOCATION SOMEHOW.
IN THAT CASE ...
... YOU ...
...NEED TO FIND SOMETHING ATTENTION GRABBING.
OR SOMETHING REALLY UNIQUE.

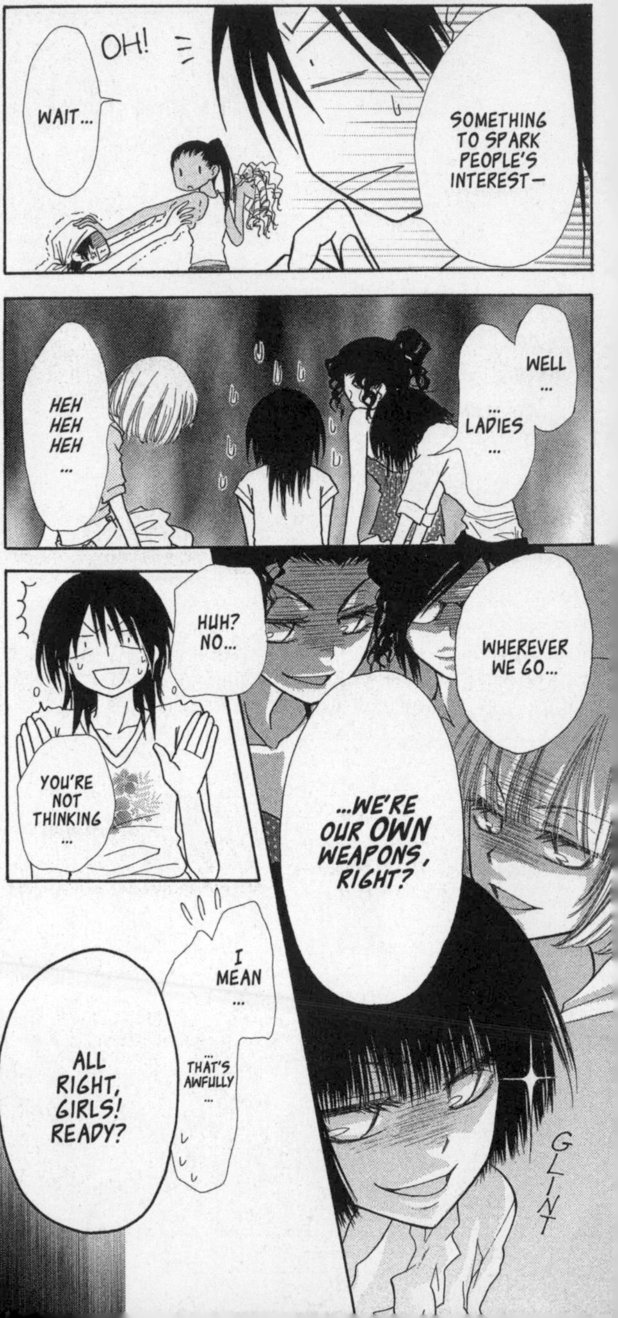
SOMETHING TO SPARK PEOPLE'S INTEREST—
OH!
WAIT...
WELL ... ... LADIES ...
HEH HEH HEH ...
WHEREVER WE GO...
...WE'RE OUR OWN WEAPONS, RIGHT?
GLINT
HUH? NO...
YOU'RE NOT THINKING ...
I MEAN ...
... THAT'S AWFULLY ...
ALL RIGHT, GIRLS! READY?

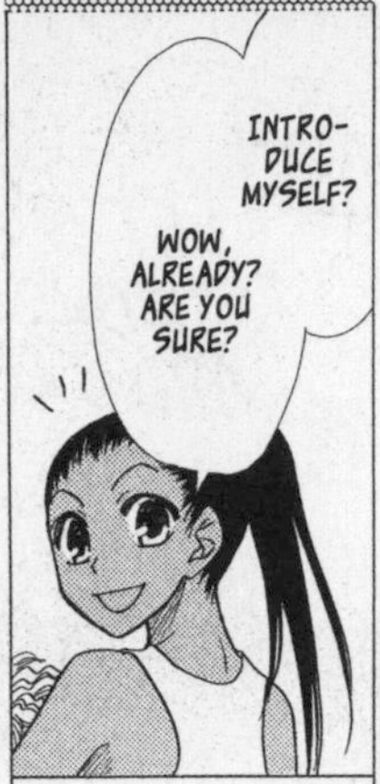
INTRODUCE MYSELF?
WOW, ALREADY? ARE YOU SURE?

NAME

Nagisa Hyodo

AGE (CLASS)

24 years old

BLOOD TYPE

B

HEIGHT

162 cm

WEIGHT

49 kg

SPECIAL SKILL

Beach volleyball

FAVORITE THING

THE OCEAN

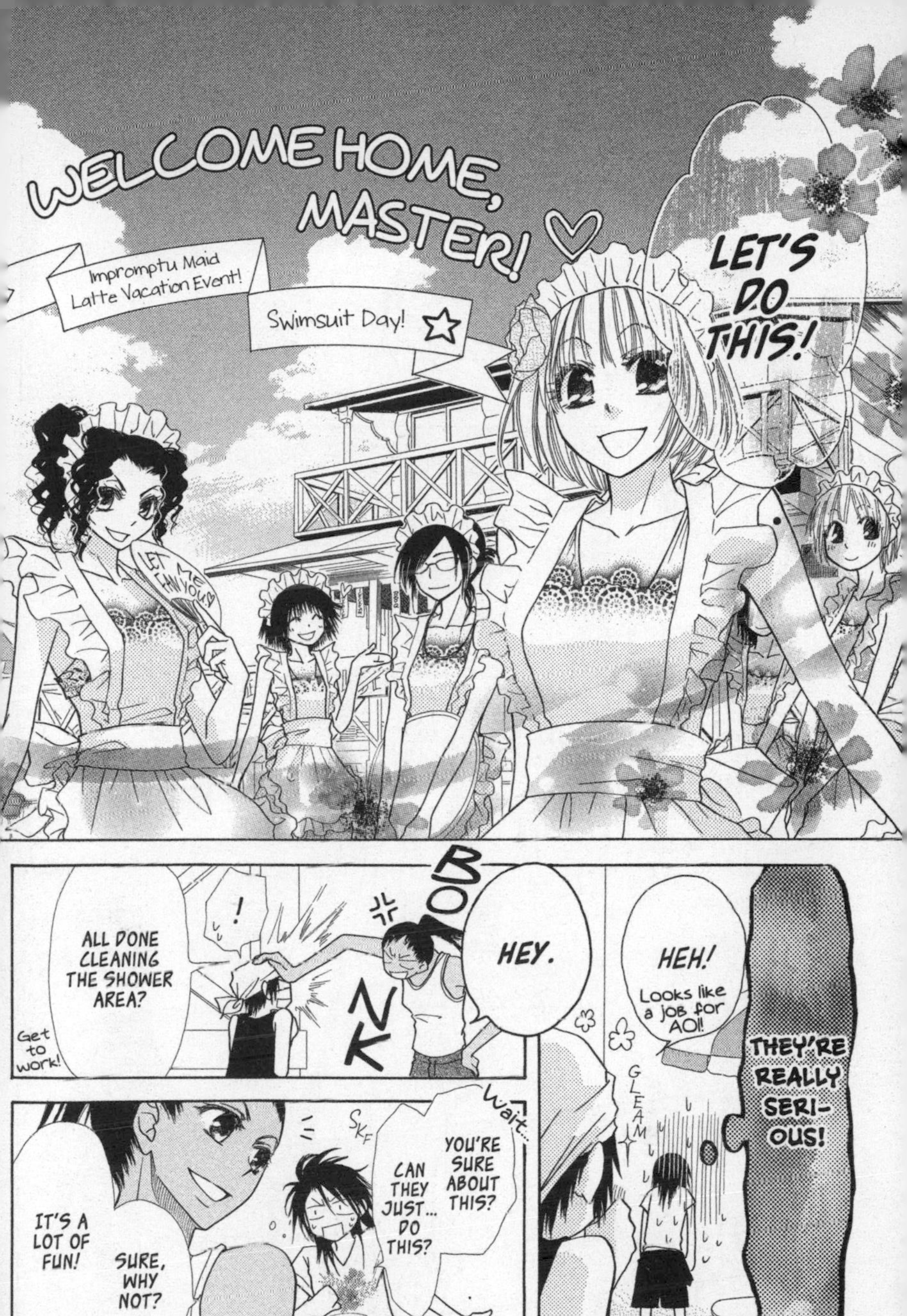
LET'S DO THIS!
WELCOME HOME, MASTER! ♡
Impromptu Maid Latte Vacation Event!
Swimsuit Day! ☆
LET ME FAN YOU
THEY'RE REALLY SERI-OUS!
HEH!
Looks like a job for AOI!
GLEAM
HEY.
BONK
!
ALL DONE CLEANING THE SHOWER AREA?
Get to work!
Wait...
YOU'RE SURE ABOUT THIS?
CAN THEY JUST... DO THIS?
SKF
SURE, WHY NOT?
IT'S A LOT OF FUN!

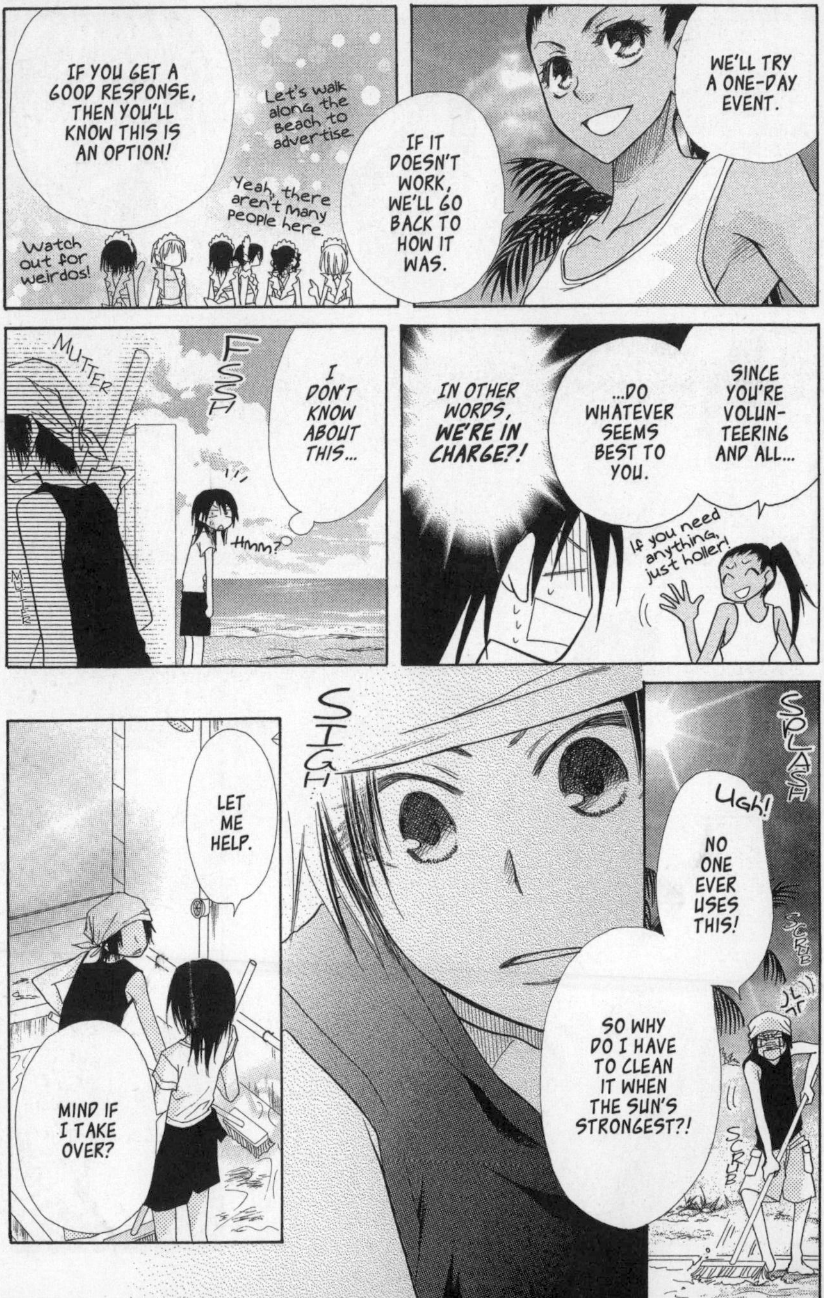
WE'LL TRY A ONE-DAY EVENT.
IF IT DOESN'T WORK, WE'LL GO BACK TO HOW IT WAS.
IF YOU GET A GOOD RESPONSE, THEN YOU'LL KNOW THIS IS AN OPTION!
Let's walk along the beach to advertise
Yeah, there aren't many people here.
Watch out for weirdos!
SINCE YOU'RE VOLUN-TEERING AND ALL...
...DO WHATEVER SEEMS BEST TO YOU.
IN OTHER WORDS, WE'RE IN CHARGE?!
If you need anything, just holler!
FSSH
MUTTER
I DON'T KNOW ABOUT THIS...
Hmm?
MUTTER
SPLASH
Ugh!
NO ONE EVER USES THIS!
SCRUB
SO WHY DO I HAVE TO CLEAN IT WHEN THE SUN'S STRONGEST?!
SCRUB
SIGH
LET ME HELP.
MIND IF I TAKE OVER?

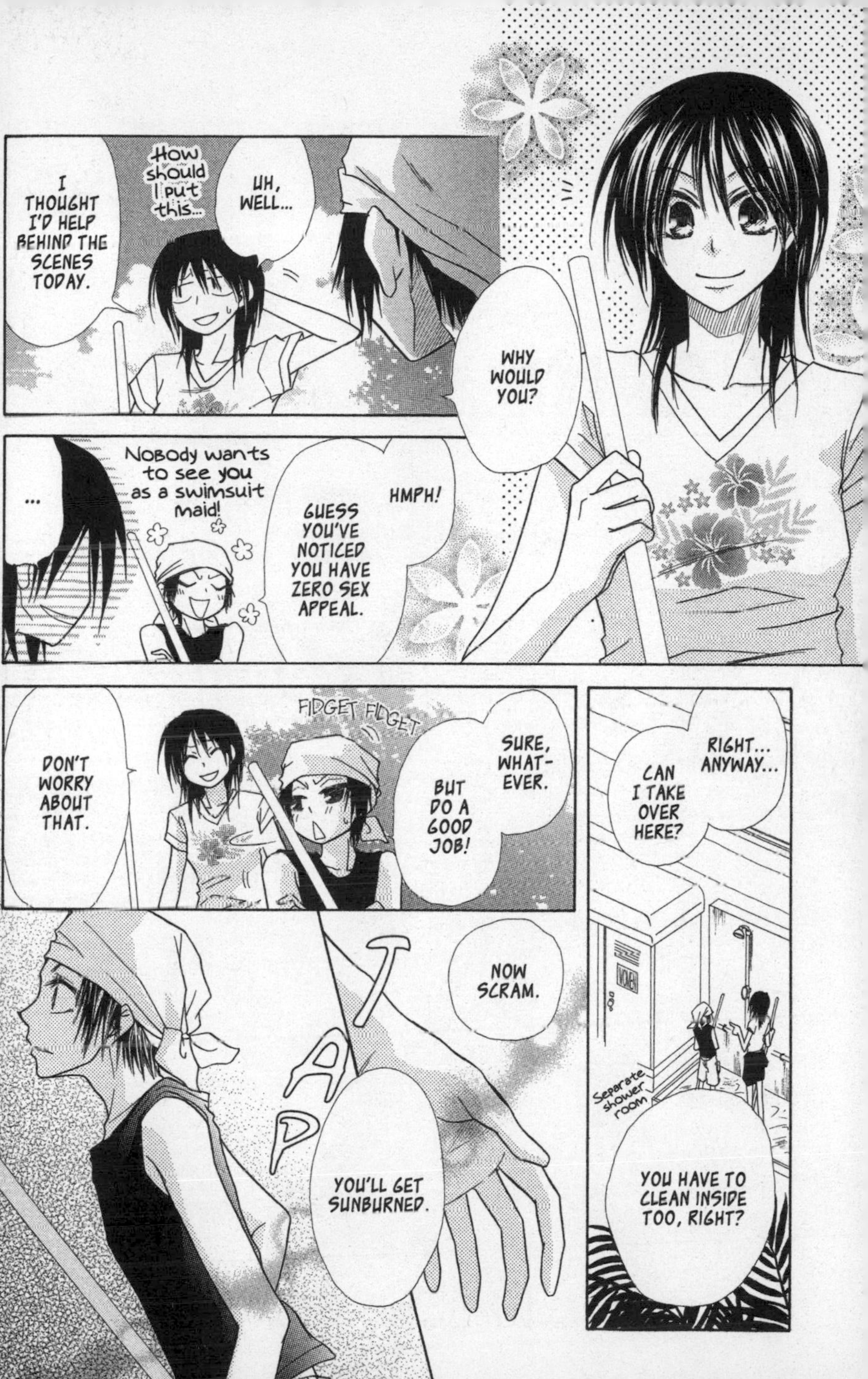
WHY WOULD YOU?
UH, WELL...
How should I put this...
I THOUGHT I'D HELP BEHIND THE SCENES TODAY.
HMPH!
GUESS YOU'VE NOTICED YOU HAVE ZERO SEX APPEAL.
Nobody wants to see you as a swimsuit maid!
...
RIGHT... ANYWAY...
CAN I TAKE OVER HERE?
WOMEN
Separate shower room
YOU HAVE TO CLEAN INSIDE TOO, RIGHT?
SURE, WHATEVER.
BUT DO A GOOD JOB!
FIDGET FIDGET
DON'T WORRY ABOUT THAT.
NOW SCRAM.
TAP
YOU'LL GET SUNBURNED.

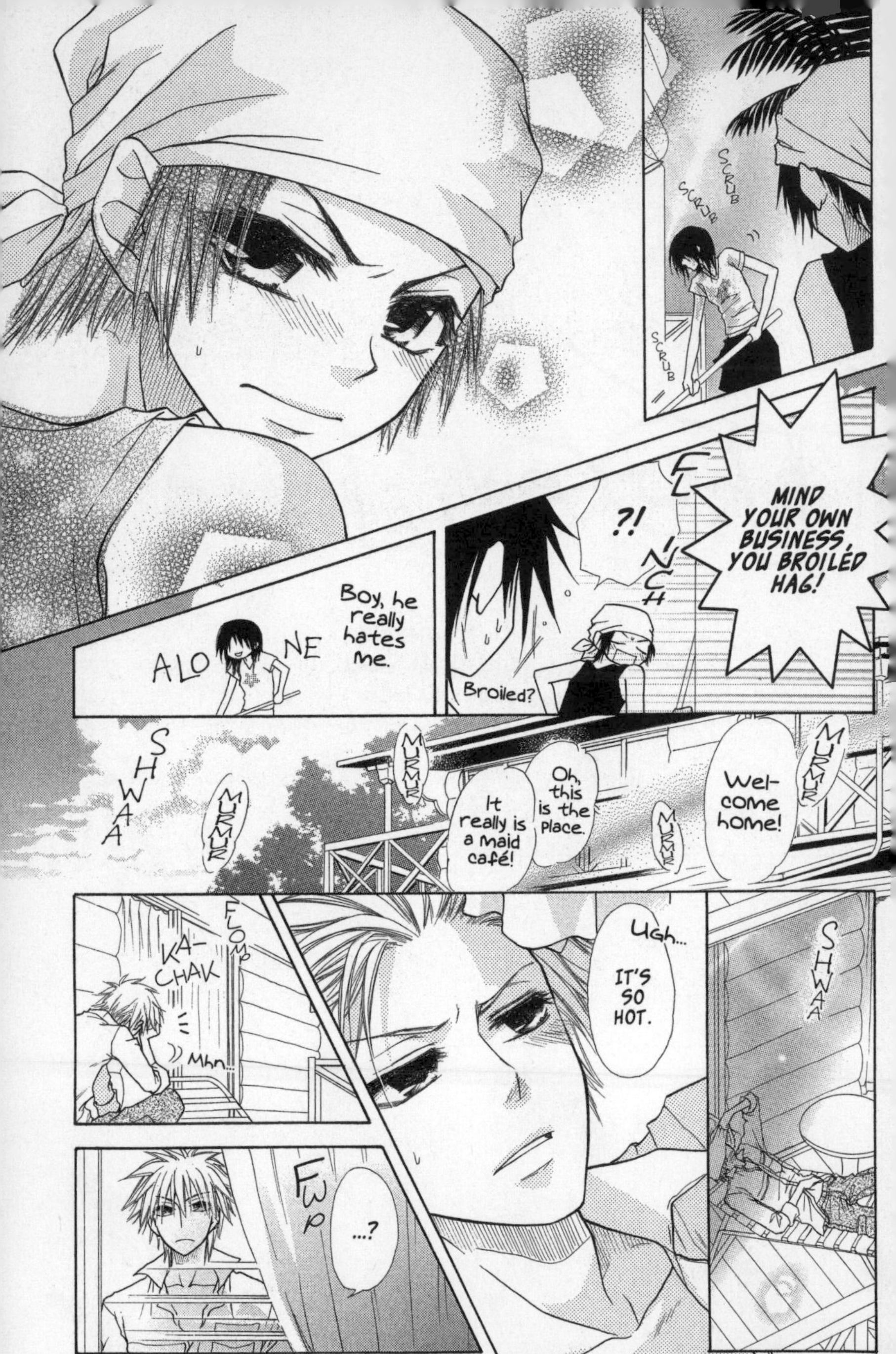
SCRUB
SCRUB
SCRUB
MIND YOUR OWN BUSINESS, YOU BROILED HAG!
FLINCH
?!
Broiled?
ALONE
Boy, he really hates me.
MURMUR
Wel-come home!
MURMUR
Oh, this is the place.
It really is a maid café!
MURMUR
SHWAA
SHWAA
Ugh...
IT'S SO HOT.
FLOMP
KA-CHAK
Mhn...
FWP
...?

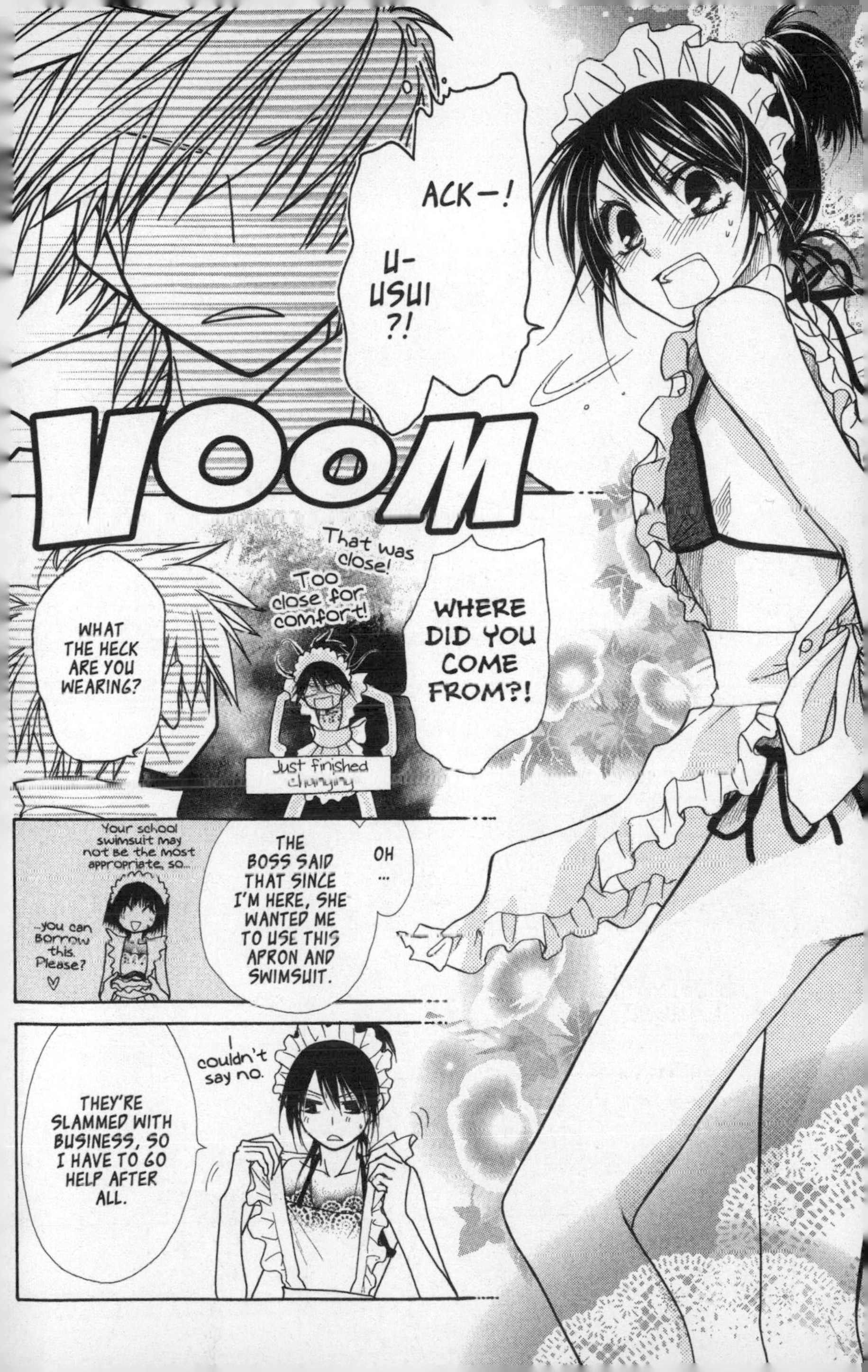
ACK—!
U-USUI ?!
VOOM
WHERE DID YOU COME FROM?!
That was close! Too close for comfort!
WHAT THE HECK ARE YOU WEARING?
Just finished changing
OH ...
THE BOSS SAID THAT SINCE I'M HERE, SHE WANTED ME TO USE THIS APRON AND SWIMSUIT.
Your school swimsuit may not be the most appropriate, so...
...you can borrow this. Please? ♥
I couldn't say no.
THEY'RE SLAMMED WITH BUSINESS, SO I HAVE TO GO HELP AFTER ALL.

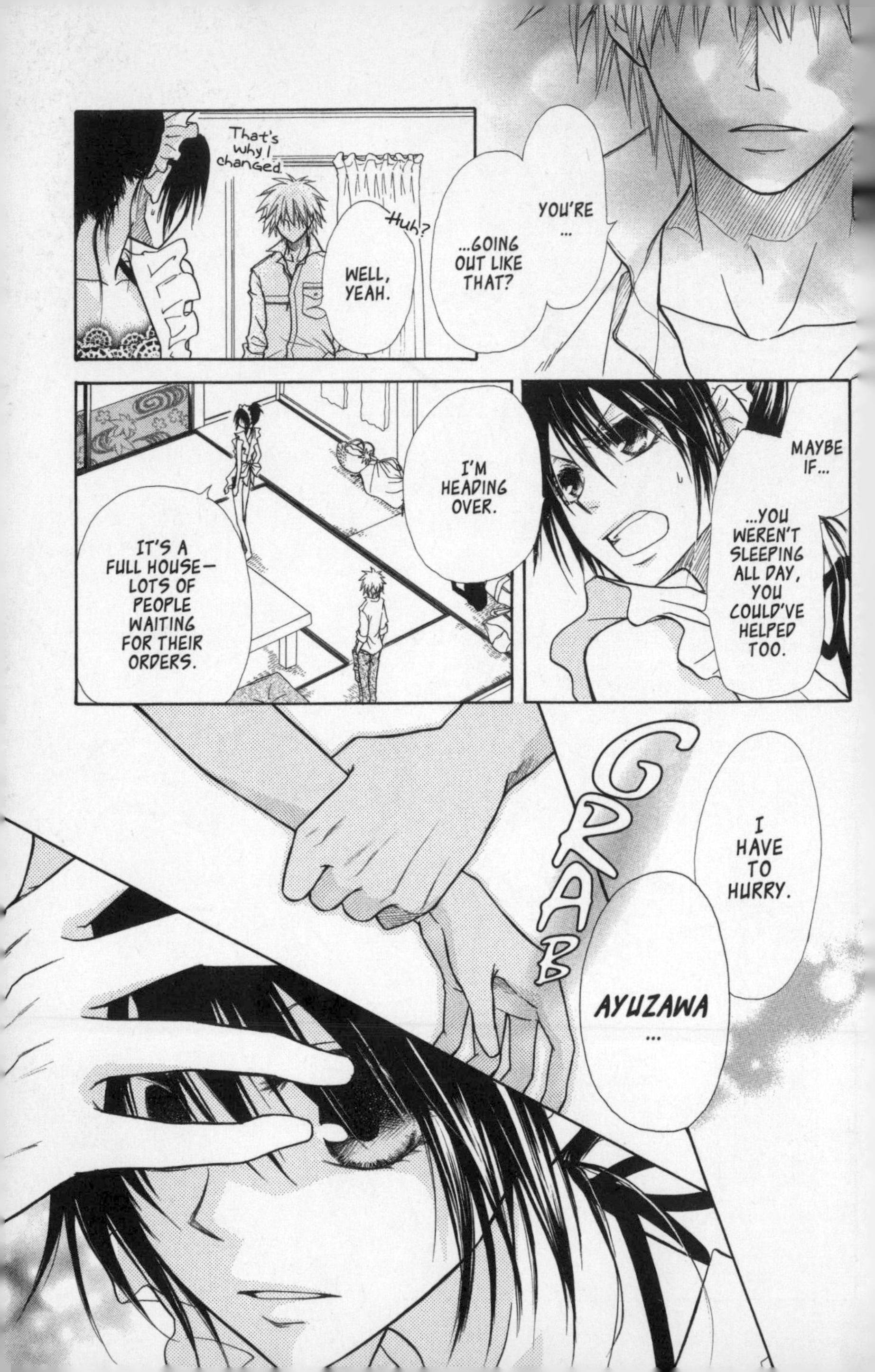
YOU'RE ...
...GOING OUT LIKE THAT?
Huh?
WELL, YEAH.
That's why I changed.
MAYBE IF...
...YOU WEREN'T SLEEPING ALL DAY, YOU COULD'VE HELPED TOO.
I'M HEADING OVER.
IT'S A FULL HOUSE—LOTS OF PEOPLE WAITING FOR THEIR ORDERS.
I HAVE TO HURRY.
GRAB
AYUZAWA ...

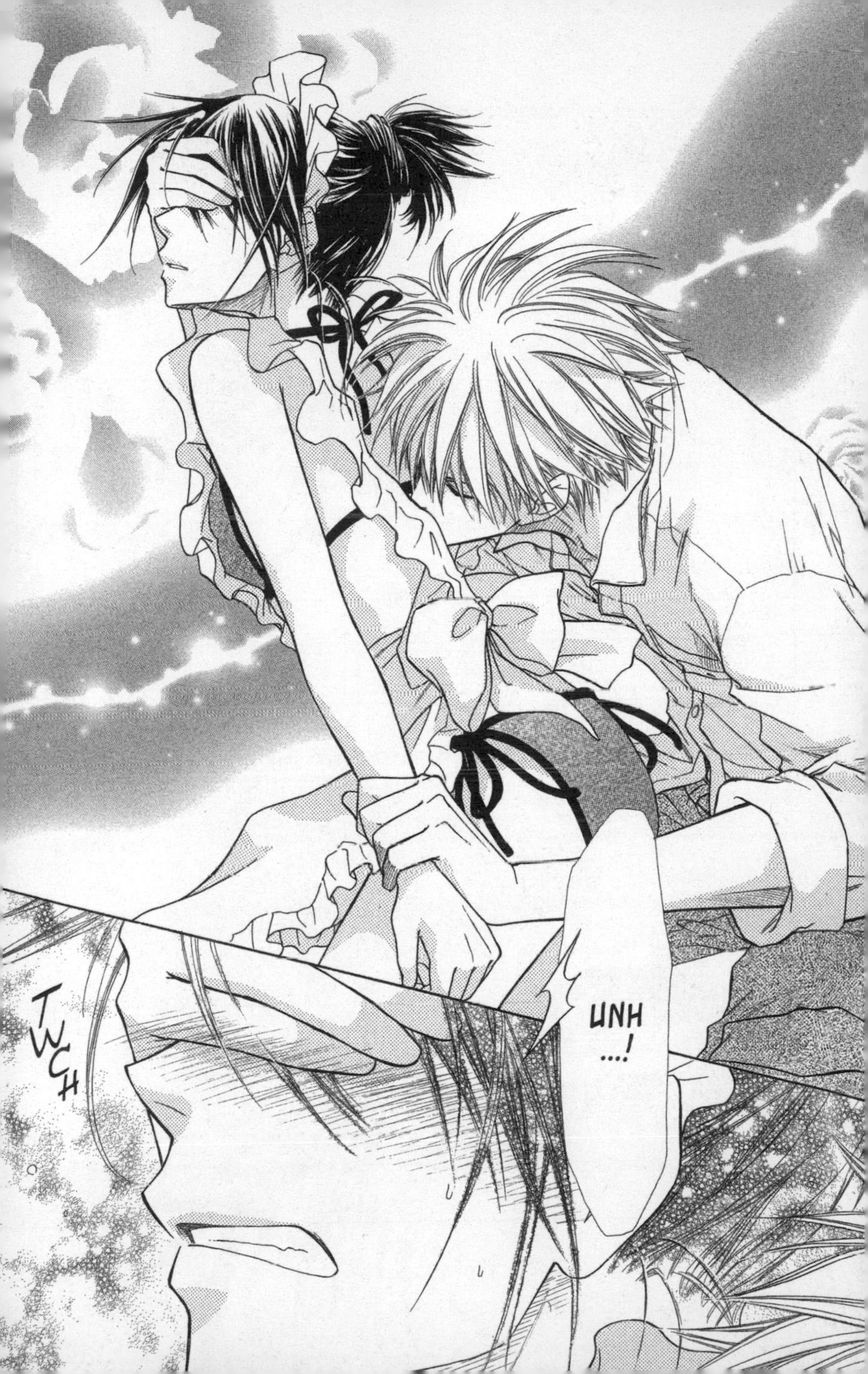
UNH ...!
TWCH

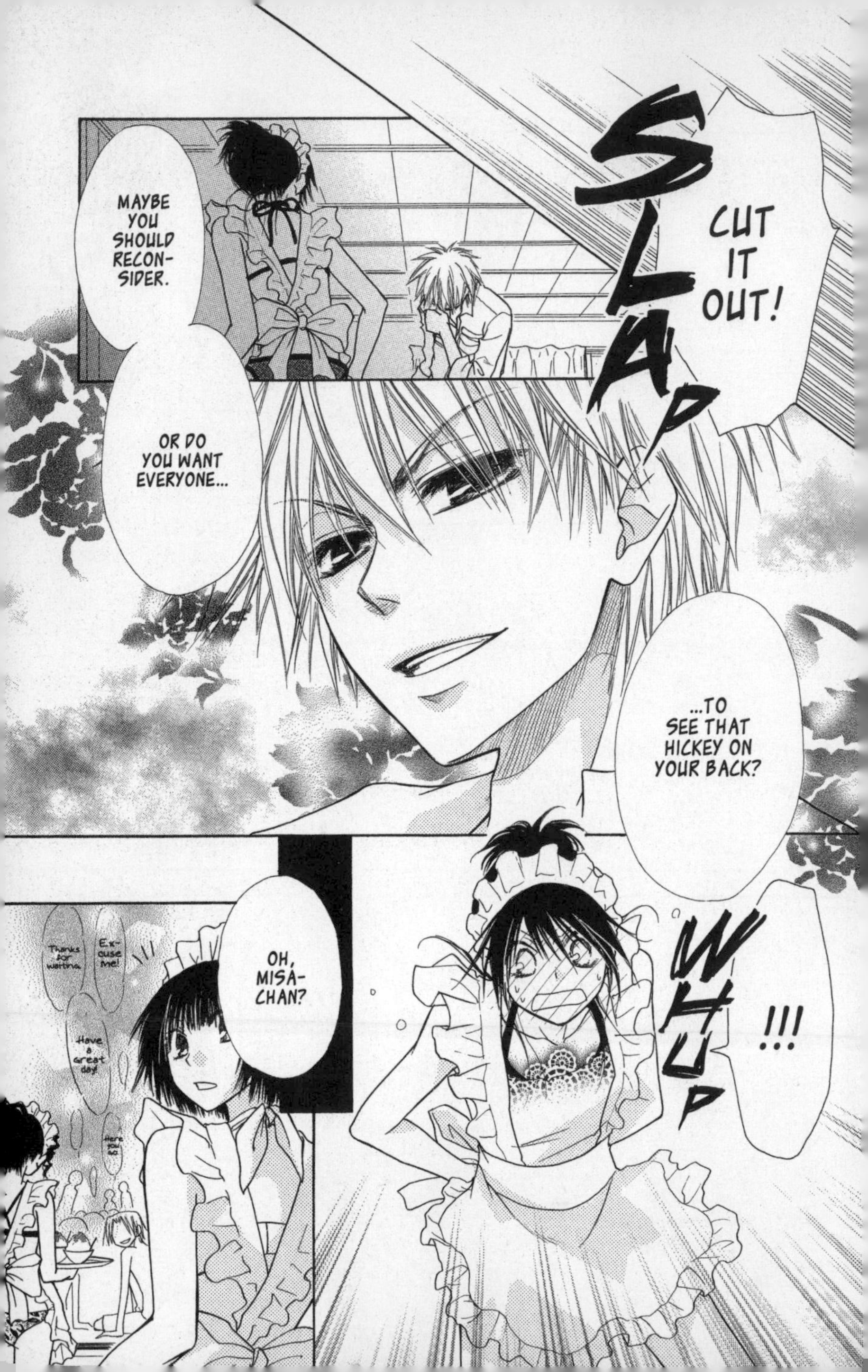
SLAP
CUT IT OUT!
MAYBE YOU SHOULD RECON-SIDER.
OR DO YOU WANT EVERYONE...
...TO SEE THAT HICKEY ON YOUR BACK?
WHUP
!!!
OH, MISA-CHAN?
Ex-cuse me!
Thanks for waiting
Have a great day!
Here you go.

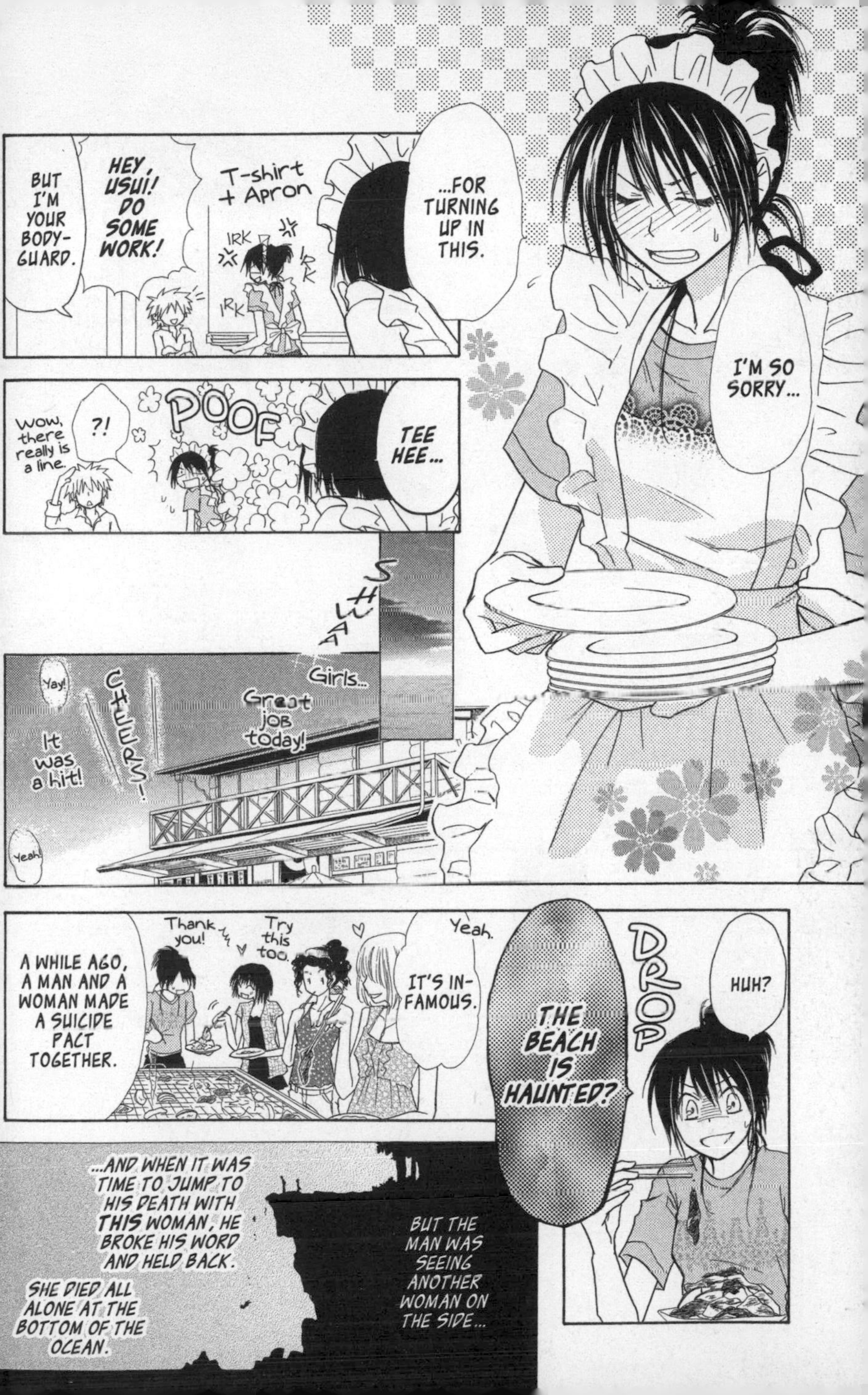
I'M SO SORRY...
...FOR TURNING UP IN THIS.
T-shirt + Apron
IRK IRK IRK
HEY, USUI! DO SOME WORK!
BUT I'M YOUR BODY-GUARD.
TEE HEE...
POOF
?!
Wow, there really is a line.
SHWAA
Girls... Great job today!
CHEERS!
Yay!
It was a hit!
Yeah!
HUH?
DROP
THE BEACH IS HAUNTED?
Yeah.
IT'S IN-FAMOUS.
Try this too.
Thank you!
A WHILE AGO, A MAN AND A WOMAN MADE A SUICIDE PACT TOGETHER.
BUT THE MAN WAS SEEING ANOTHER WOMAN ON THE SIDE...
...AND WHEN IT WAS TIME TO JUMP TO HIS DEATH WITH THIS WOMAN, HE BROKE HIS WORD AND HELD BACK.
SHE DIED ALL ALONE AT THE BOTTOM OF THE OCEAN.

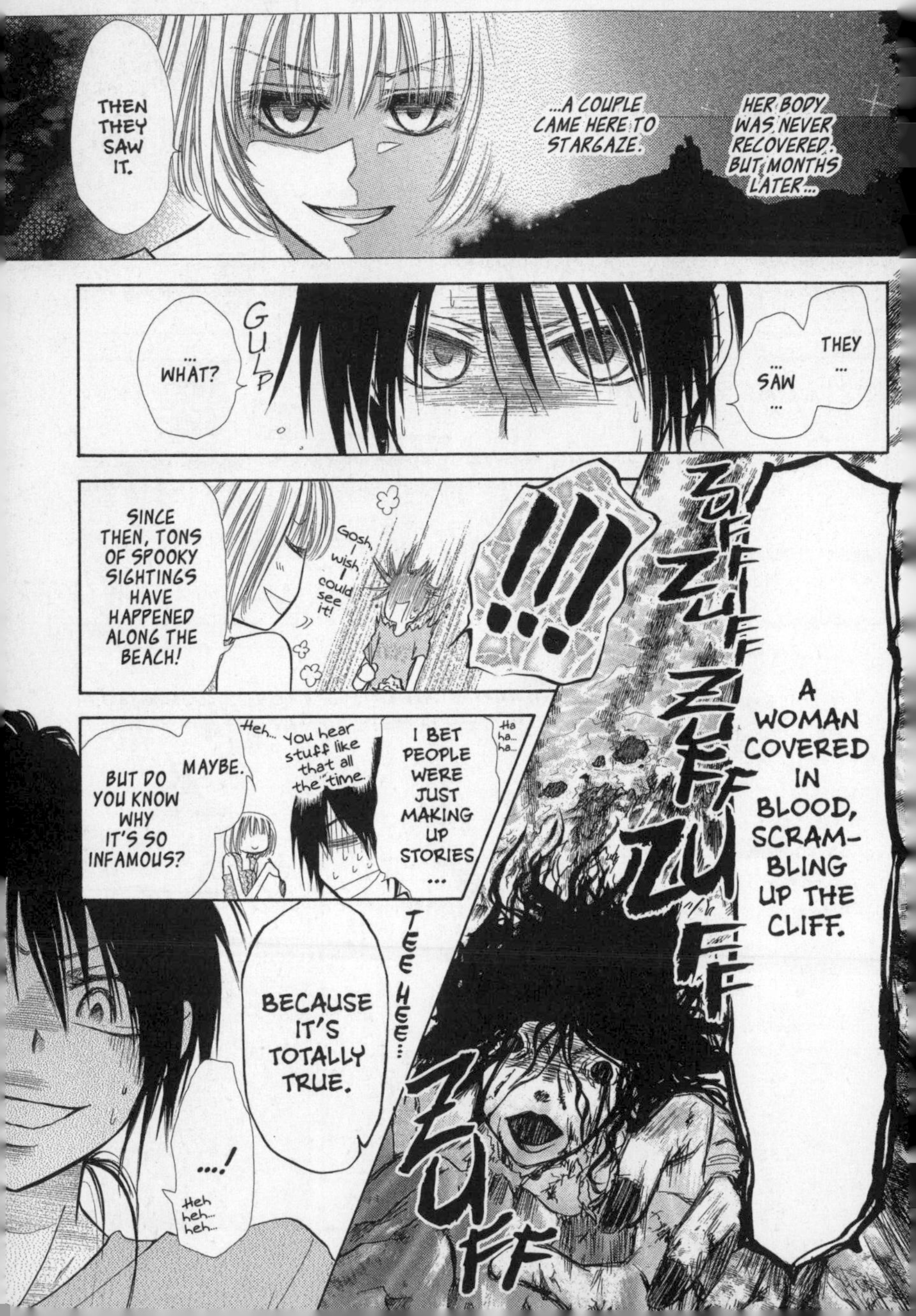
HER BODY WAS NEVER RECOVERED. BUT MONTHS LATER...
...A COUPLE CAME HERE TO STARGAZE.
THEN THEY SAW IT.
THEY ... SAW ...
GULP
... WHAT?
!!!
ZUFF ZUFF ZUFF ZUFF
A WOMAN COVERED IN BLOOD, SCRAMBLING UP THE CLIFF.
ZUFF
SINCE THEN, TONS OF SPOOKY SIGHTINGS HAVE HAPPENED ALONG THE BEACH!
Gosh, I wish I could see it!
I BET PEOPLE WERE JUST MAKING UP STORIES ...
Ha ha... ha...
You hear stuff like that all the time.
Heh...
MAYBE.
BUT DO YOU KNOW WHY IT'S SO INFAMOUS?
TEE HEE...
BECAUSE IT'S TOTALLY TRUE.
...!
Heh heh... heh...

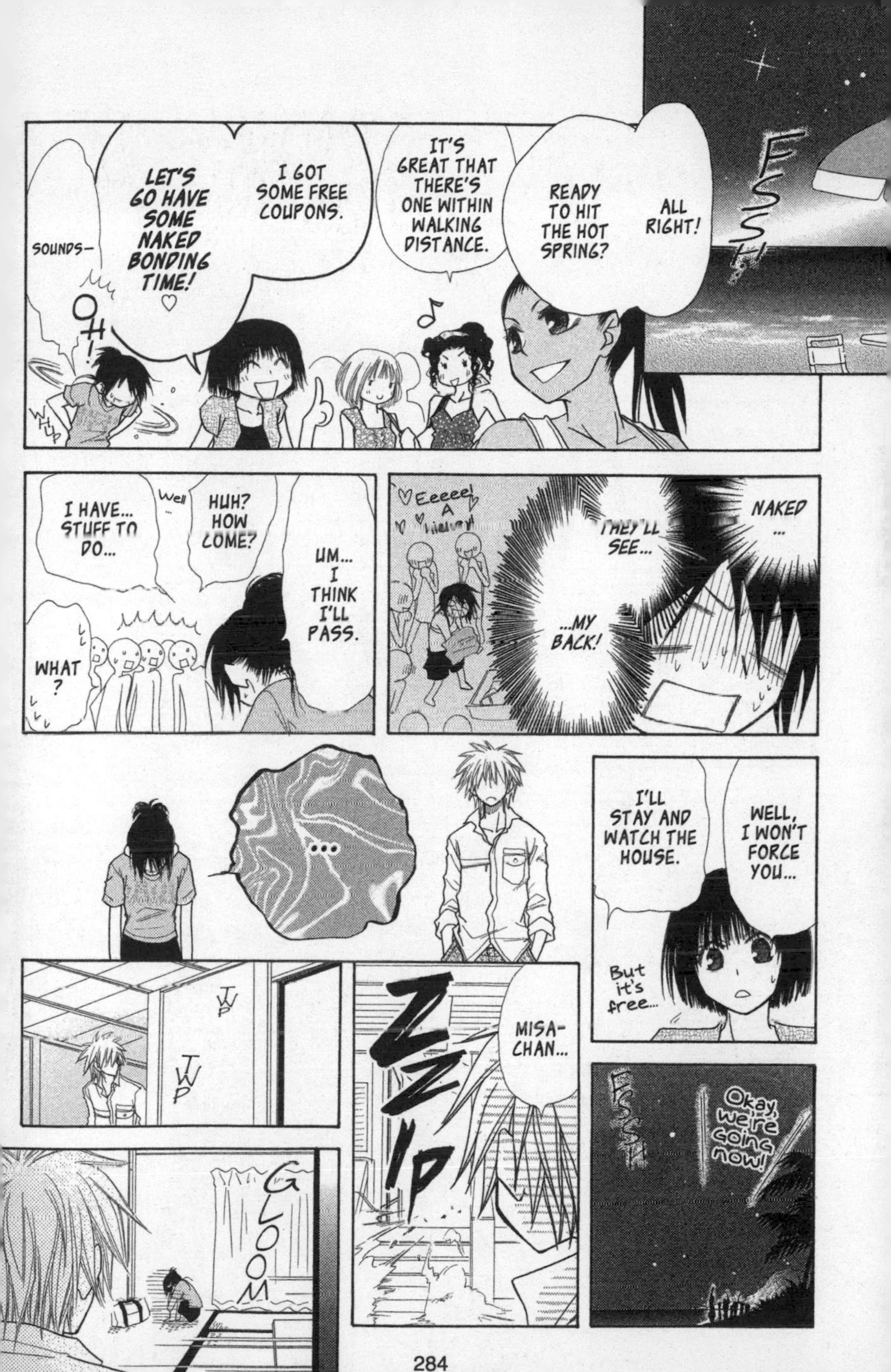

FSSH
ALL RIGHT!
READY TO HIT THE HOT SPRING?
IT'S GREAT THAT THERE'S ONE WITHIN WALKING DISTANCE.
I GOT SOME FREE COUPONS.
LET'S GO HAVE SOME NAKED BONDING TIME!
SOUNDS—
OH!
WHUP
NAKED...
THEY'LL SEE...
...MY BACK!
Eeeee! A
UM... I THINK I'LL PASS.
HUH? HOW COME?
Well...
I HAVE... STUFF TO DO...
WHAT?
WELL, I WON'T FORCE YOU...
I'LL STAY AND WATCH THE HOUSE.
But it's free...
...
FSSH
Okay, we're going now!
MISA-CHAN...
ZZIP
TWP
TWP
GLOOM

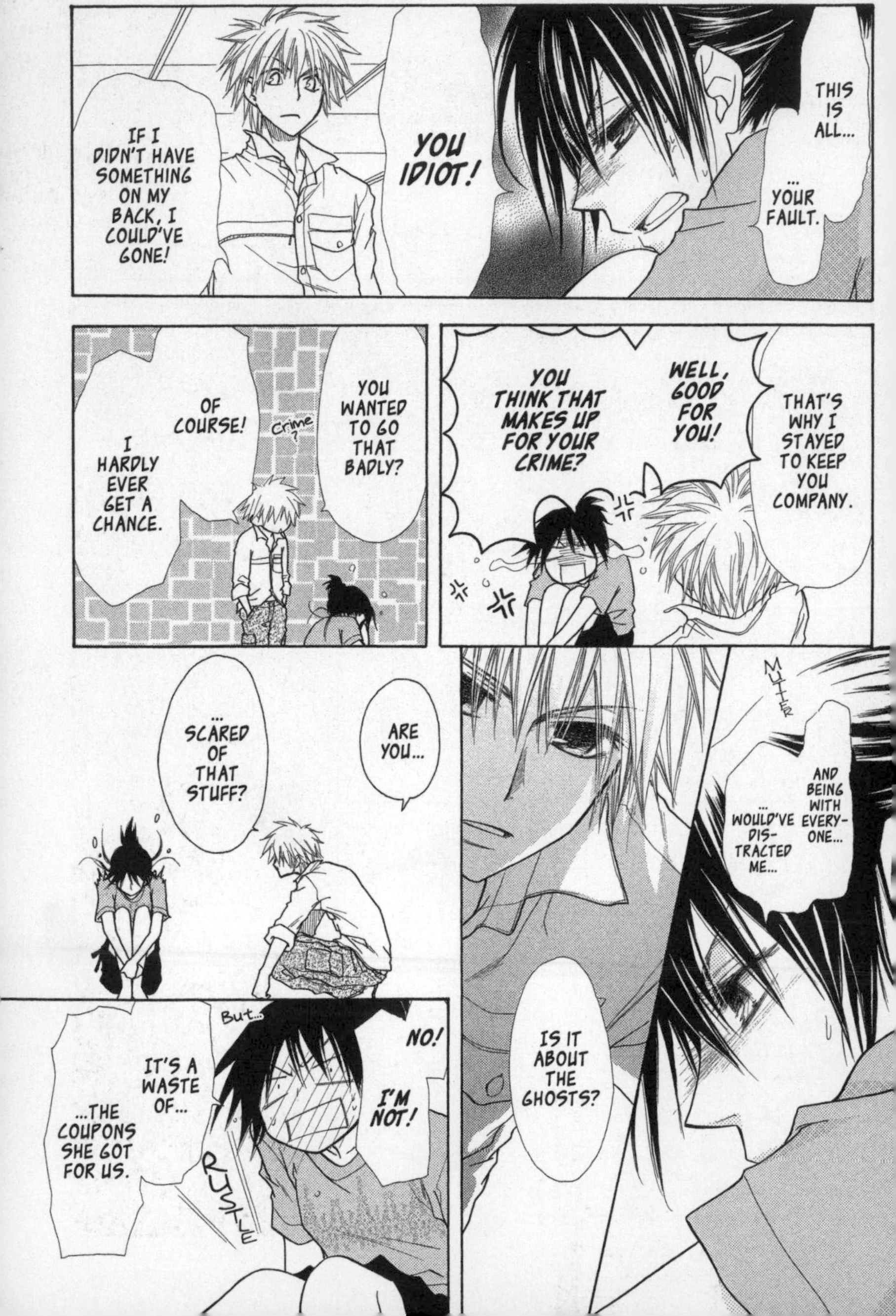

THIS IS ALL...
... YOUR FAULT.
YOU IDIOT!
IF I DIDN'T HAVE SOMETHING ON MY BACK, I COULD'VE GONE!
THAT'S WHY I STAYED TO KEEP YOU COMPANY.
WELL, GOOD FOR YOU!
YOU THINK THAT MAKES UP FOR YOUR CRIME?
YOU WANTED TO GO THAT BADLY?
Crime?
OF COURSE!
I HARDLY EVER GET A CHANCE.
MUTTER
AND BEING WITH EVERY-ONE...
... WOULD'VE DIS-TRACTED ME...
IS IT ABOUT THE GHOSTS?
ARE YOU...
... SCARED OF THAT STUFF?
NO!
I'M NOT!
But...
IT'S A WASTE OF...
...THE COUPONS SHE GOT FOR US.
RUSTLE

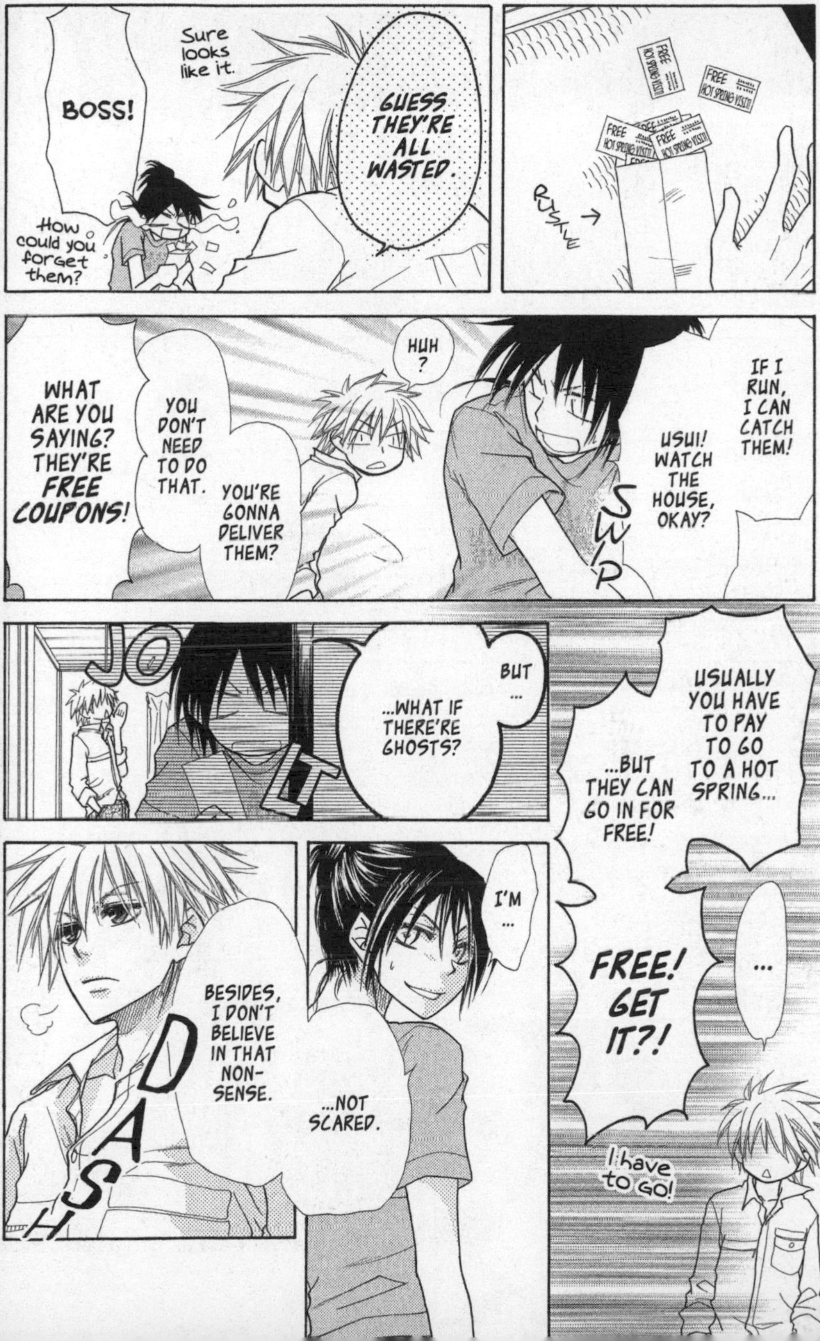
FREE HOT SPRING VISIT!!
RUSTLE
GUESS THEY'RE ALL WASTED.
Sure looks like it.
BOSS!
How could you forget them?
IF I RUN, I CAN CATCH THEM!
USUI! WATCH THE HOUSE, OKAY?
SWIP
HUH?
YOU DON'T NEED TO DO THAT.
YOU'RE GONNA DELIVER THEM?
WHAT ARE YOU SAYING? THEY'RE FREE COUPONS!
USUALLY YOU HAVE TO PAY TO GO TO A HOT SPRING...
...BUT THEY CAN GO IN FOR FREE!
FREE! GET IT?!
...
I have to go!
BUT...
...WHAT IF THERE'RE GHOSTS?
JOLT
I'M...
...NOT SCARED.
BESIDES, I DON'T BELIEVE IN THAT NON-SENSE.
DASH

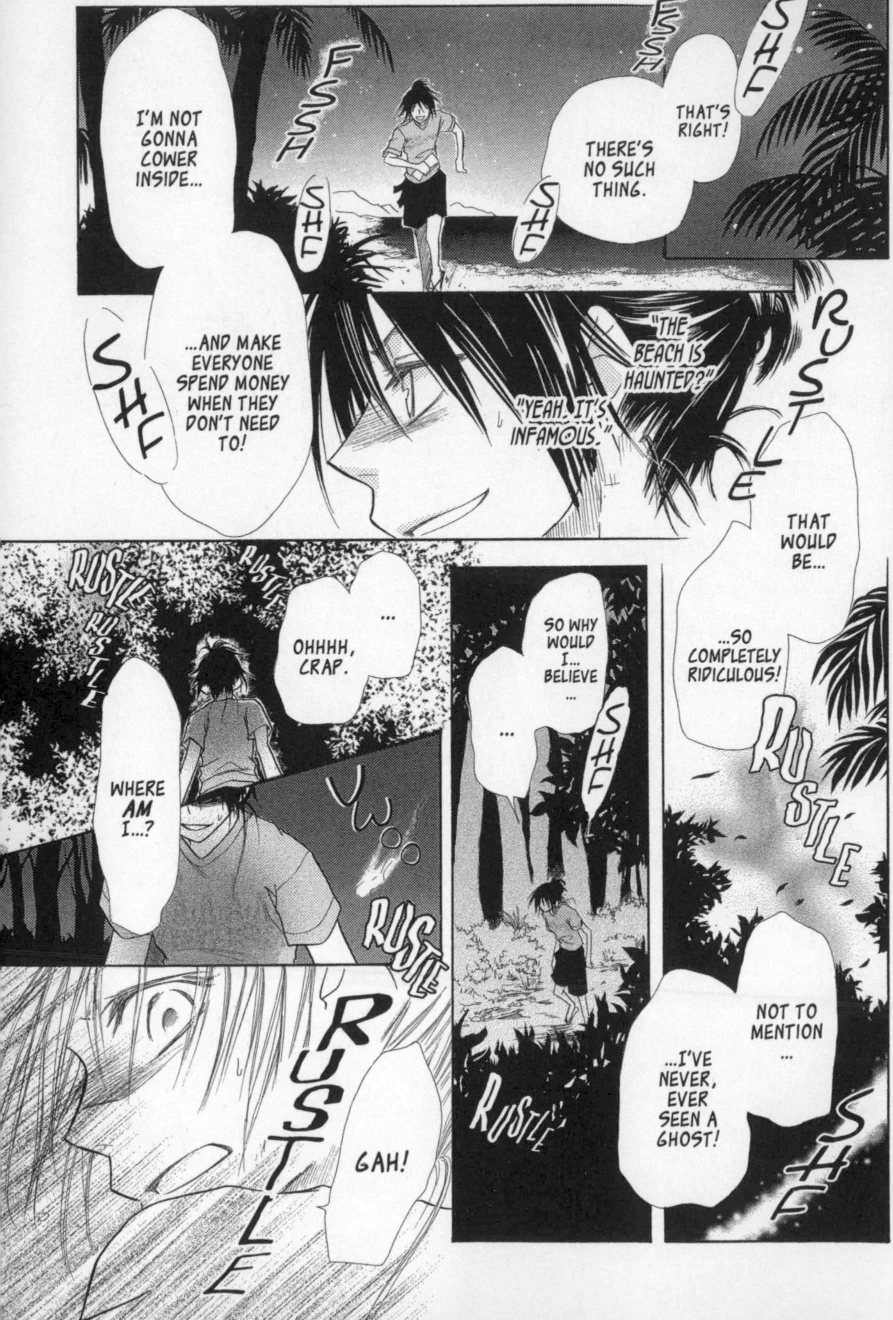
SHF
FSSH
THAT'S RIGHT!
THERE'S NO SUCH THING.
SHF
FSSH
SHF
I'M NOT GONNA COWER INSIDE...
...AND MAKE EVERYONE SPEND MONEY WHEN THEY DON'T NEED TO!
SHF
RUSTLE
"THE BEACH IS HAUNTED?"
"YEAH. IT'S INFAMOUS."
THAT WOULD BE...
...SO COMPLETELY RIDICULOUS!
RUSTLE
NOT TO MENTION...
...I'VE NEVER, EVER SEEN A GHOST!
SHF
SO WHY WOULD I... BELIEVE...
...
SHF
RUSTLE
...
OHHHH, CRAP.
RUSTLE
RUSTLE
RUSTLE
WHERE AM I...?
VWOO
RUSTLE
RUSTLE
GAH!

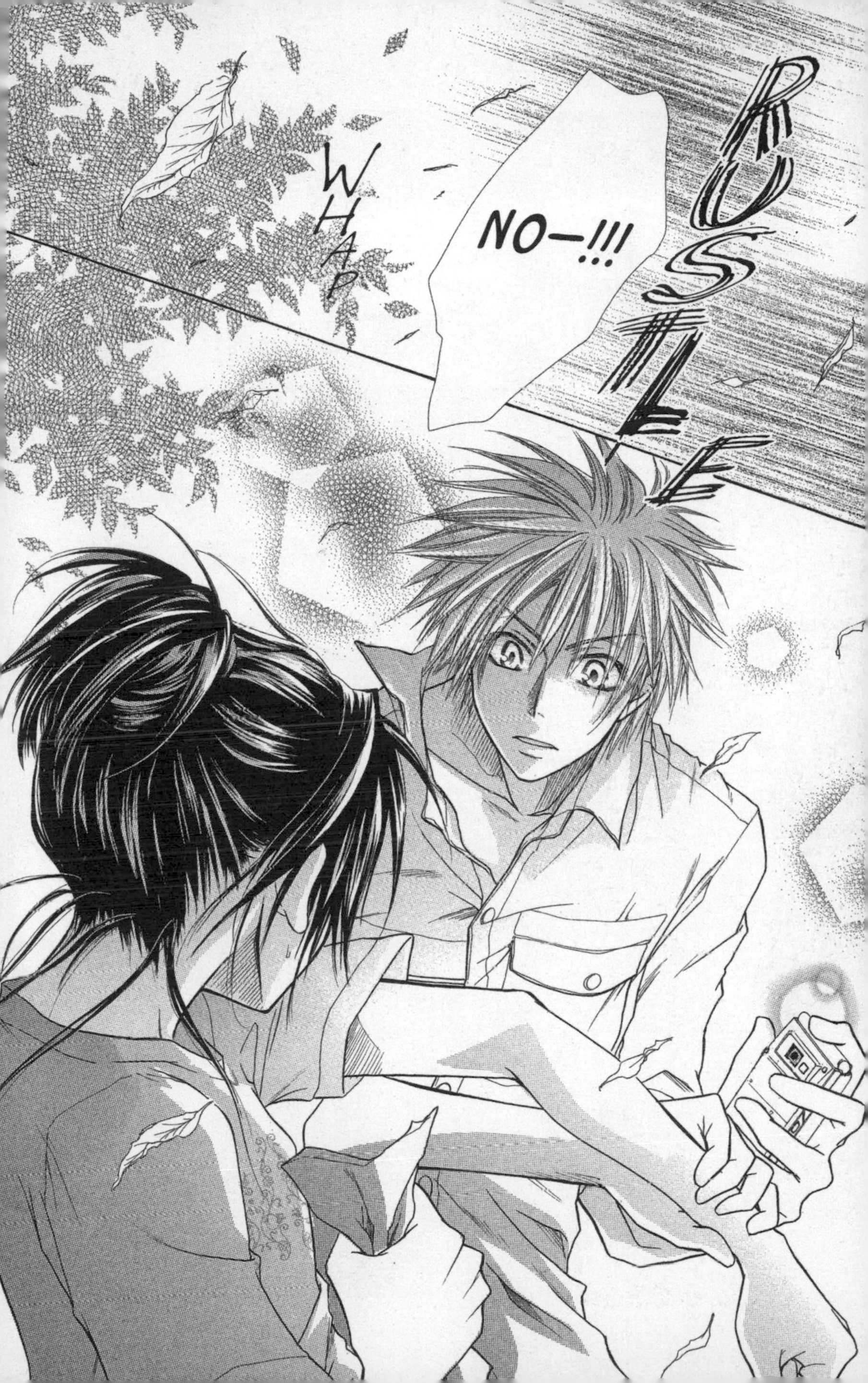
RUSTLE
NO—!!!
WHAP

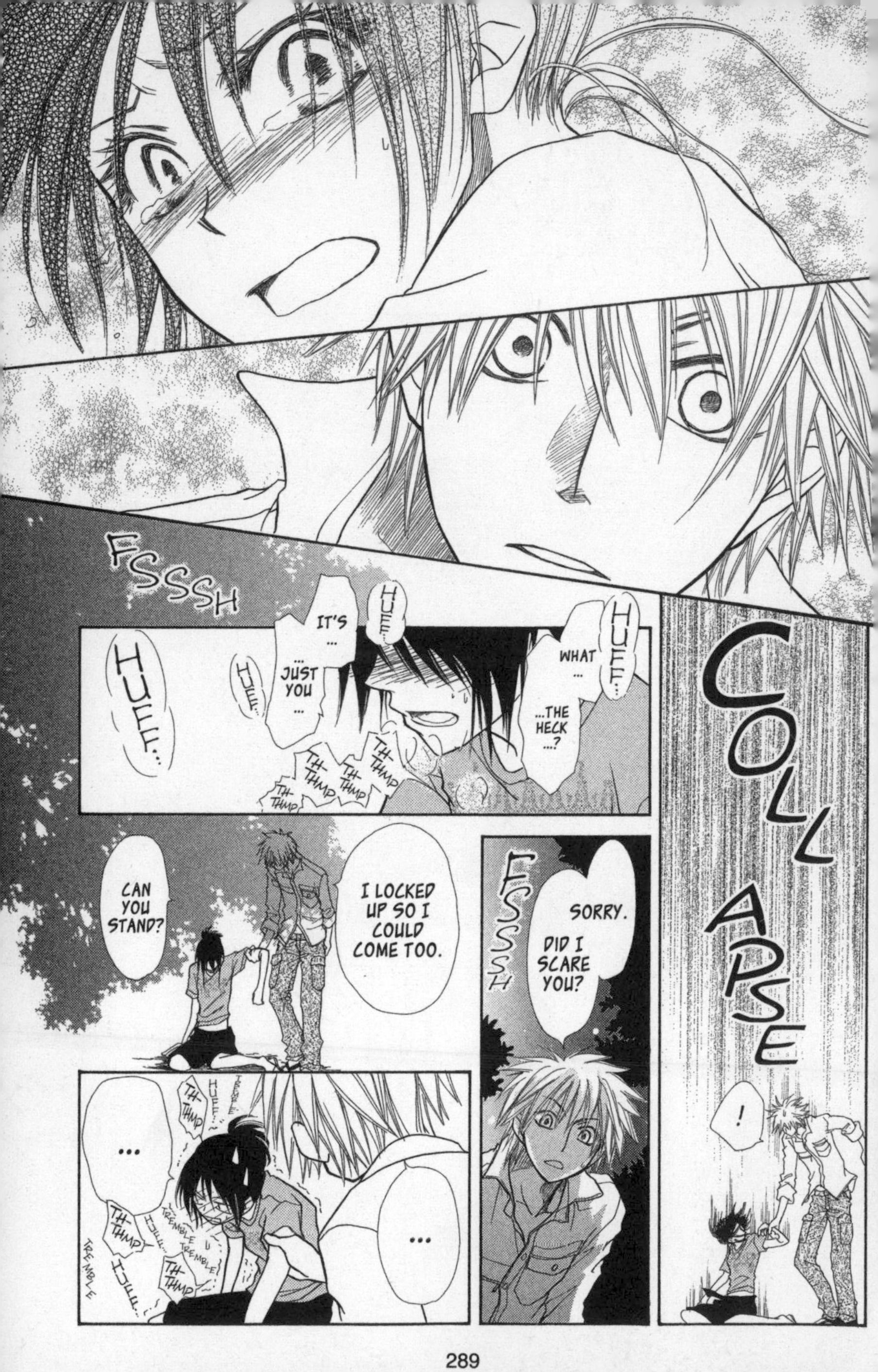
FSSSH
COLLAPSE
!
HUFF...
WHAT...
...THE HECK...?
HUFF...
IT'S...
...JUST YOU...
HUFF...
HUFF...
TH-THMP TH-THMP TH-THMP TH-THMP
FSSSH
SORRY.
DID I SCARE YOU?
I LOCKED UP SO I COULD COME TOO.
CAN YOU STAND?
...
HUFF...
TREMBLE
TH-THMP
...
TREMBLE TREMBLE TREMBLE
HUFF... HUFF...
TH-THMP TH-THMP TH-THMP

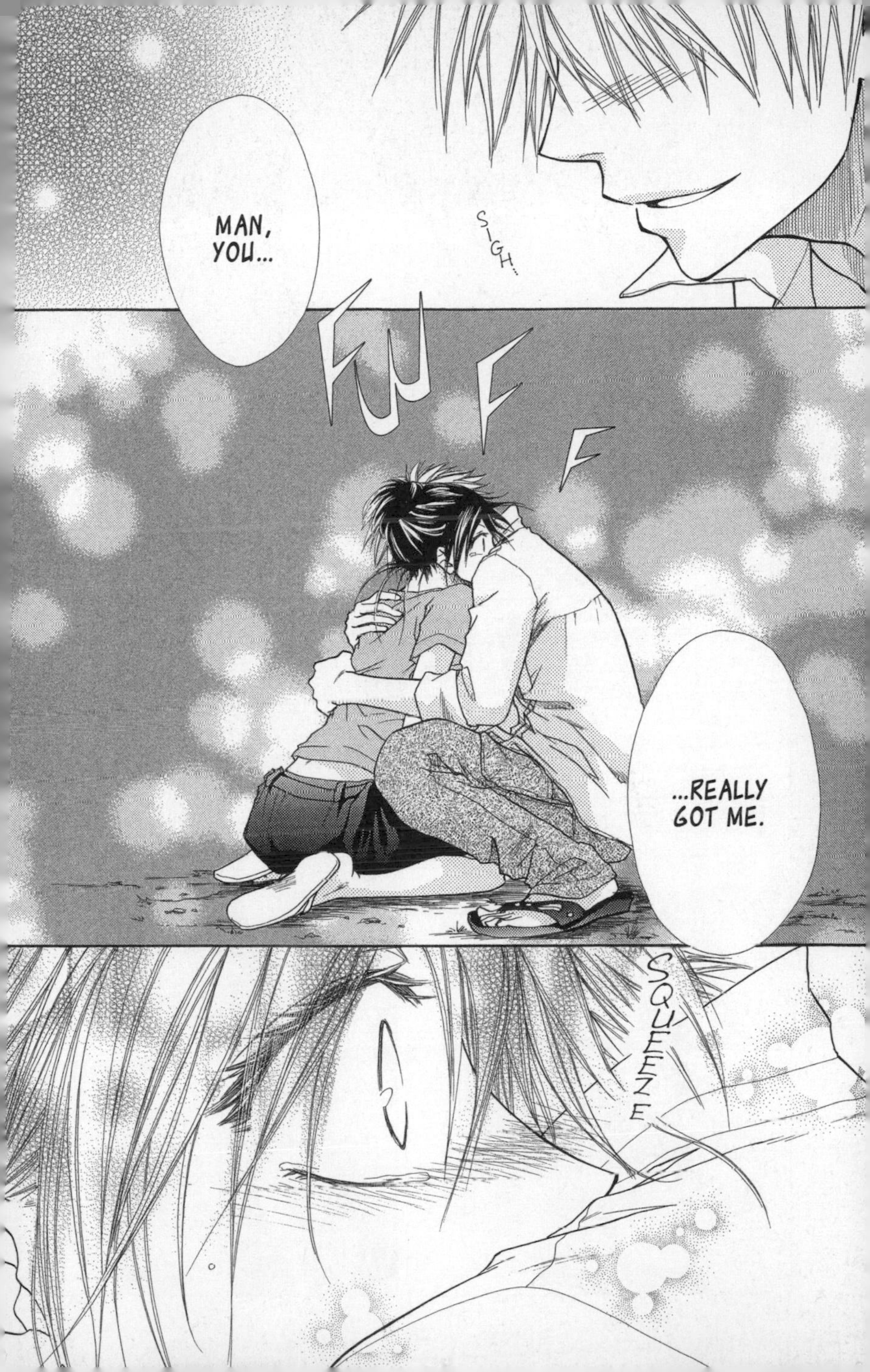
SIGH...
MAN, YOU...
FUFF
...REALLY GOT ME.
SQUEEZE

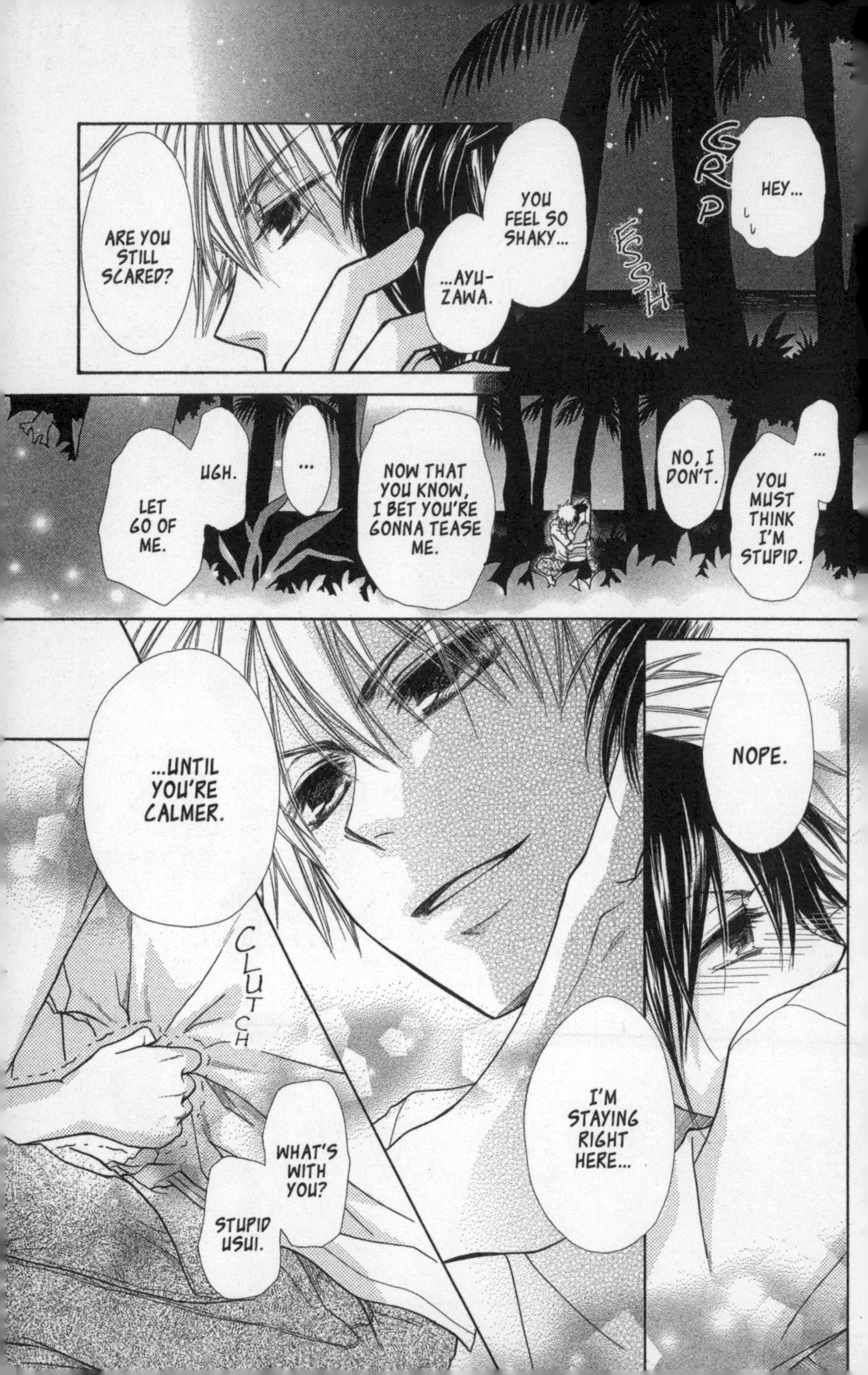
GRP
HEY...
FSSH
YOU FEEL SO SHAKY...
...AYU-ZAWA.
ARE YOU STILL SCARED?
...
YOU MUST THINK I'M STUPID.
NO, I DON'T.
NOW THAT YOU KNOW, I BET YOU'RE GONNA TEASE ME.
...
UGH.
LET GO OF ME.
NOPE.
I'M STAYING RIGHT HERE...
...UNTIL YOU'RE CALMER.
CLUTCH
WHAT'S WITH YOU?
STUPID USUI.

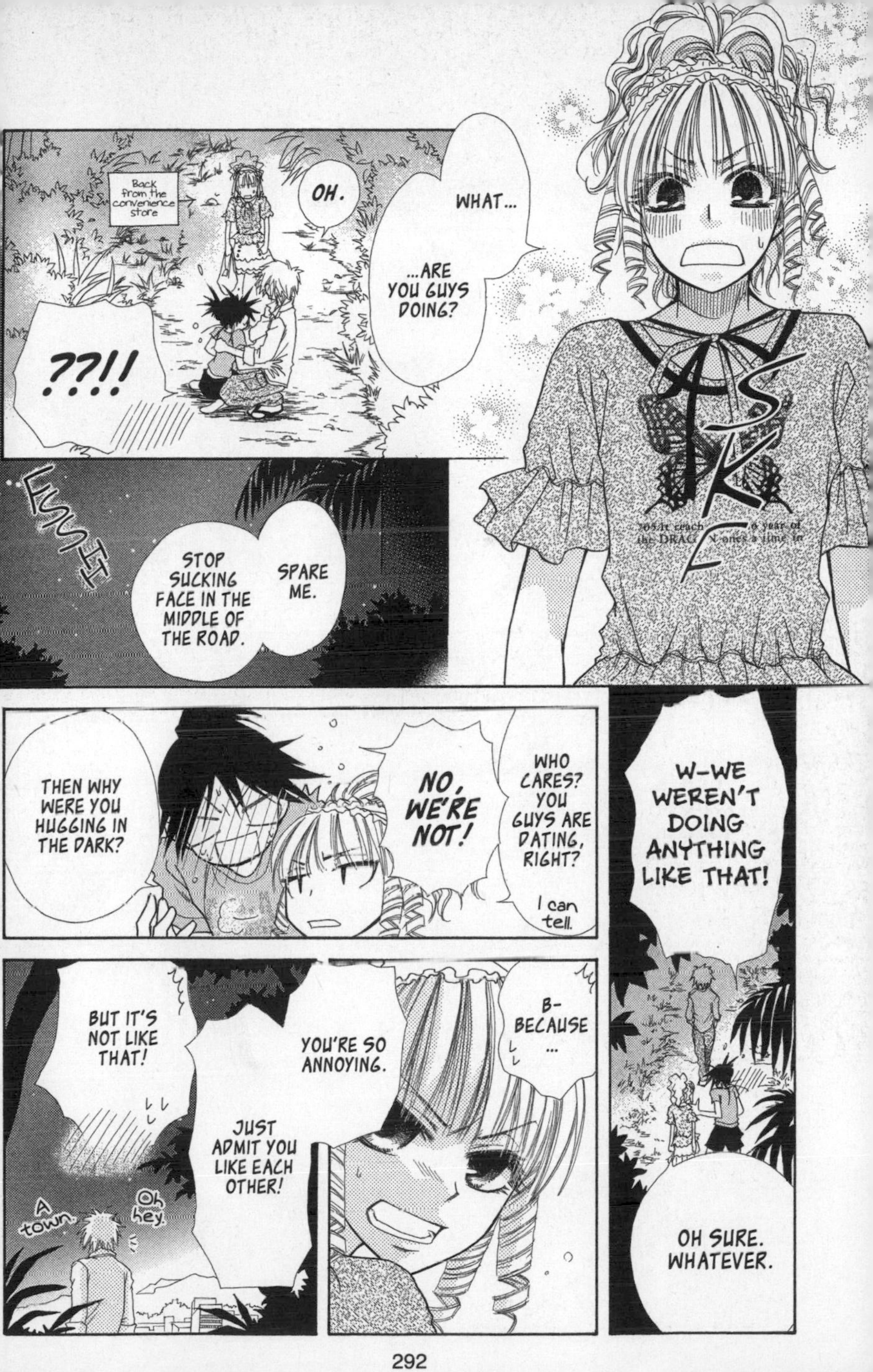
ASK
WHAT...
...ARE YOU GUYS DOING?
OH.
Back from the convenience store
??!!
SPARE ME.
STOP SUCKING FACE IN THE MIDDLE OF THE ROAD.
W-WE WEREN'T DOING ANYTHING LIKE THAT!
OH SURE. WHATEVER.
WHO CARES? YOU GUYS ARE DATING, RIGHT?
I can tell.
NO, WE'RE NOT!
THEN WHY WERE YOU HUGGING IN THE DARK?
B-BECAUSE ...
YOU'RE SO ANNOYING.
JUST ADMIT YOU LIKE EACH OTHER!
BUT IT'S NOT LIKE THAT!
Oh hey.
A town.

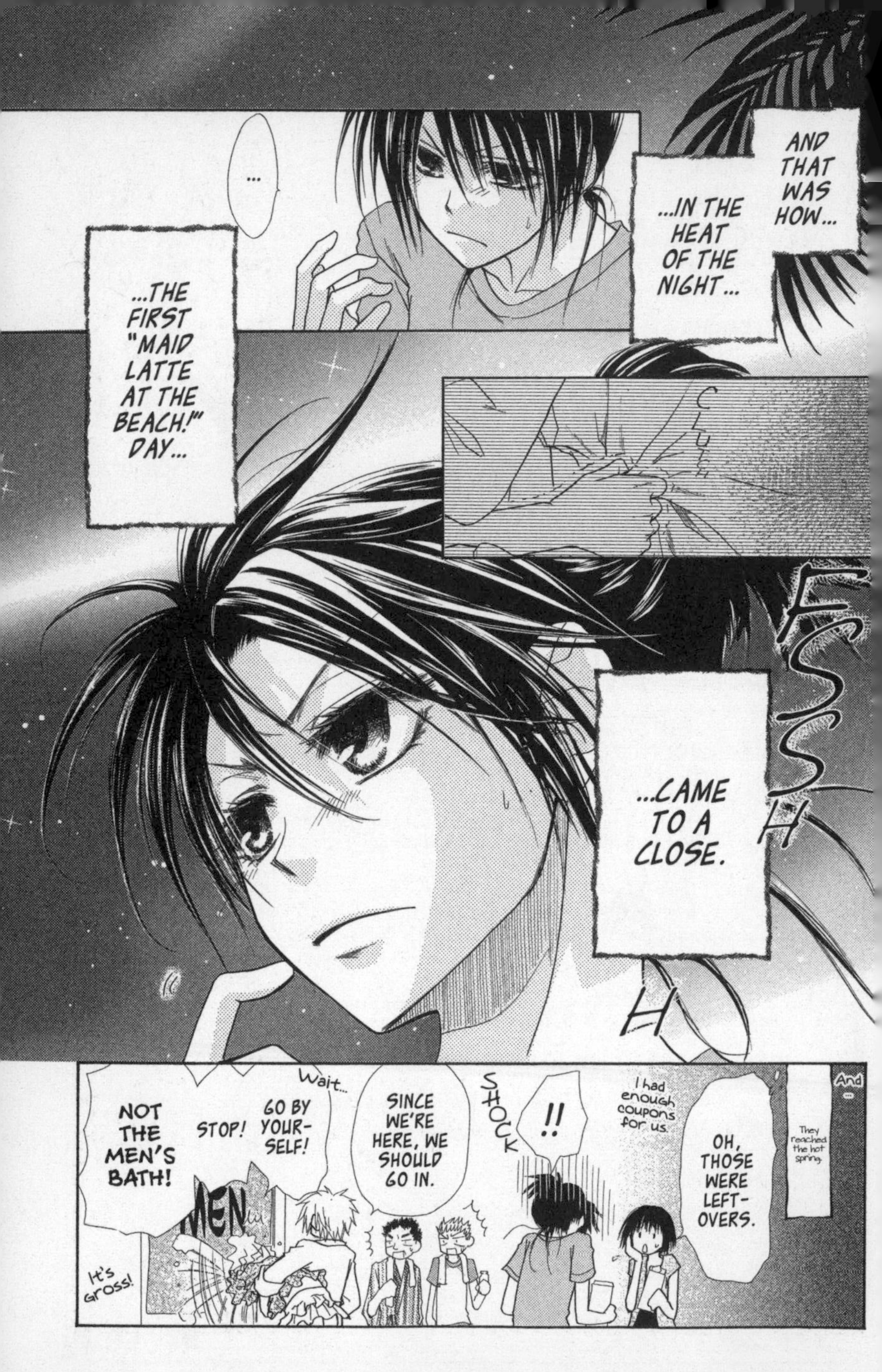
AND THAT WAS HOW...
...IN THE HEAT OF THE NIGHT...
...
...THE FIRST "MAID LATTE AT THE BEACH!" DAY...
CLUTCH
FSSSH
...CAME TO A CLOSE.
And...
They reached the hot spring.
OH, THOSE WERE LEFT-OVERS.
I had enough coupons for us.
!!
SHOCK
SINCE WE'RE HERE, WE SHOULD GO IN.
Wait...
GO BY YOUR-SELF!
STOP!
NOT THE MEN'S BATH!
MEN
It's gross!

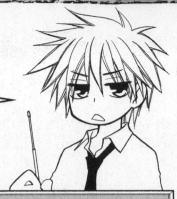

I'M TAKUMI USUI. A LOT OF PEOPLE THINK THE "I" IN MY FAMILY NAME USES THE CHARACTER FOR "WATER WELL," BUT MY NAME IS WRITTEN WITH THE CHARACTER FOR "ICE."

UMM... (DRAWING A BLANK.)

LET'S GO TO THE QUESTIONS.

QUESTION 10: "WHEN ARE MISAKI AND USUI'S BIRTHDAYS?"

 THAT'S A SECRET.

QUESTION 11: "DOES SAKURA EVER TALK ABOUT LOVE OR BOYS SHE LIKES?"

 HOW WOULD I KNOW?

QUESTION 12: "DOES IT TAKE COURAGE TO WALK INTO A MAID CAFÉ?"

 WHY WOULD IT?

QUESTION 13: "HAS MISAKI EVER FALLEN IN LOVE?"

 I HAVE NO IDEA.

QUESTION 14: "I WANT TO SEE YOUR BROTHER!"

 HMM...

QUESTION 15: "WHAT IS MISAKI'S WEAKNESS?"

 THAT'S FOR ME TO KNOW AND NO ONE ELSE TO FIND OUT.

I'M GETTING BORED. LET YUKIMURA TAKE OVER.

 W-WHAT? WAIT, USUI! IT'S TOO SOON!

UM... OKAY...

KEEP THE QUESTIONS COMING, I GUESS!

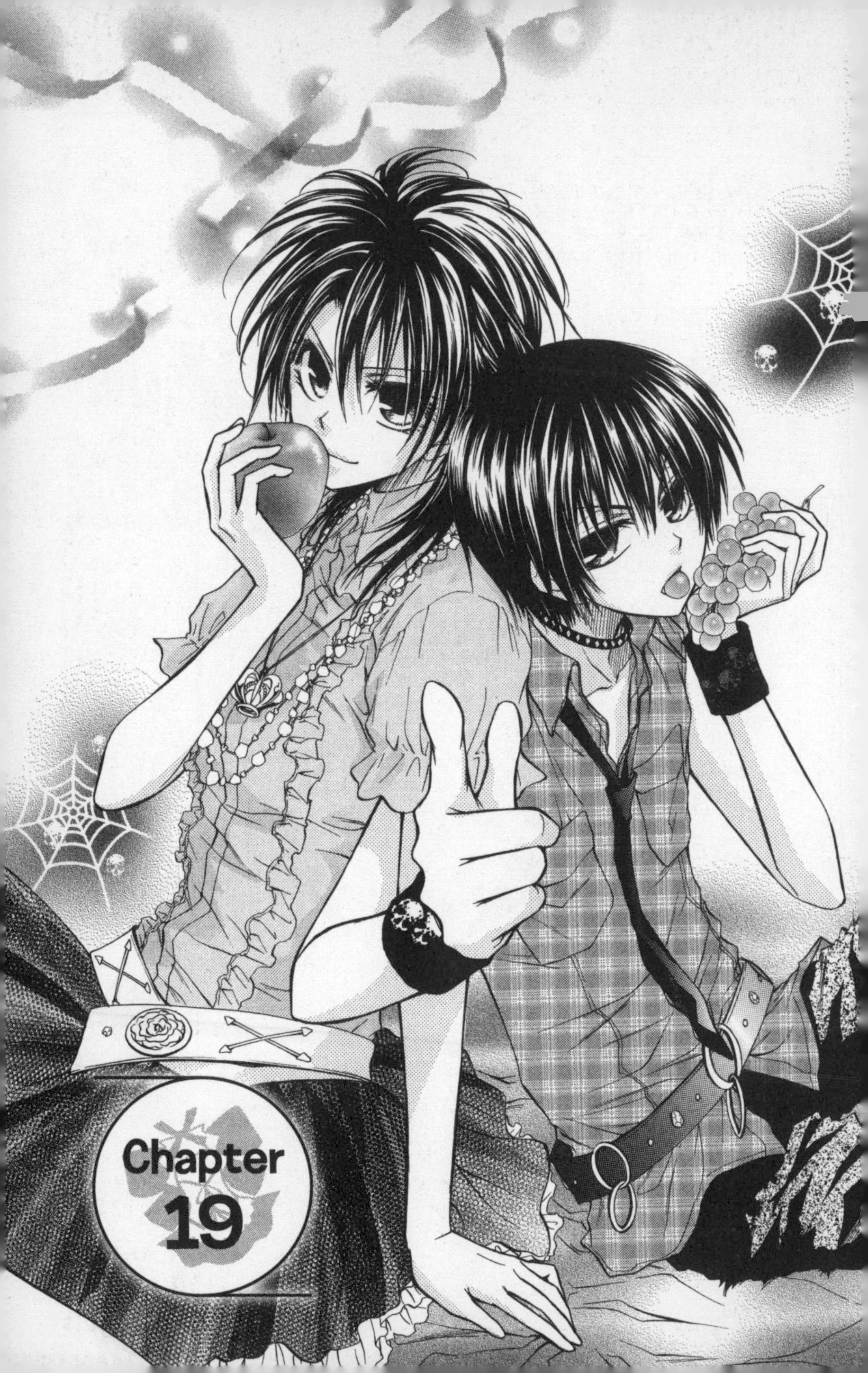
Chapter
19

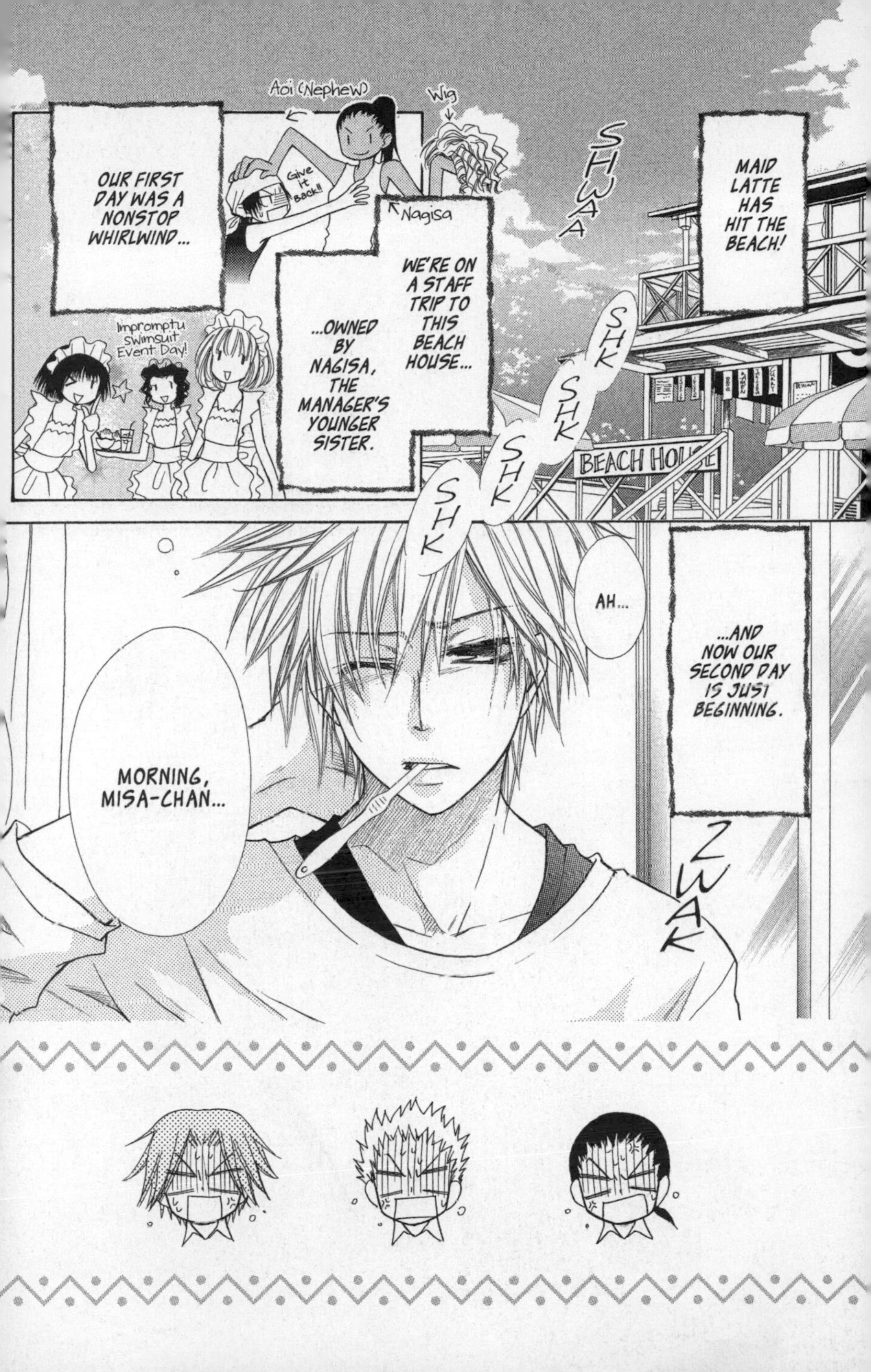
MAID LATTE HAS HIT THE BEACH!
SHWAA
WE'RE ON A STAFF TRIP TO THIS BEACH HOUSE...
...OWNED BY NAGISA, THE MANAGER'S YOUNGER SISTER.
Wig
Aoi (Nephew)
Nagisa
Give it Back!!
OUR FIRST DAY WAS A NONSTOP WHIRLWIND...
Impromptu Swimsuit Event Day!
BEACH HOUSE
SHK SHK SHK SHK SHK
...AND NOW OUR SECOND DAY IS JUST BEGINNING.
ZWAK
AH...
MORNING, MISA-CHAN...

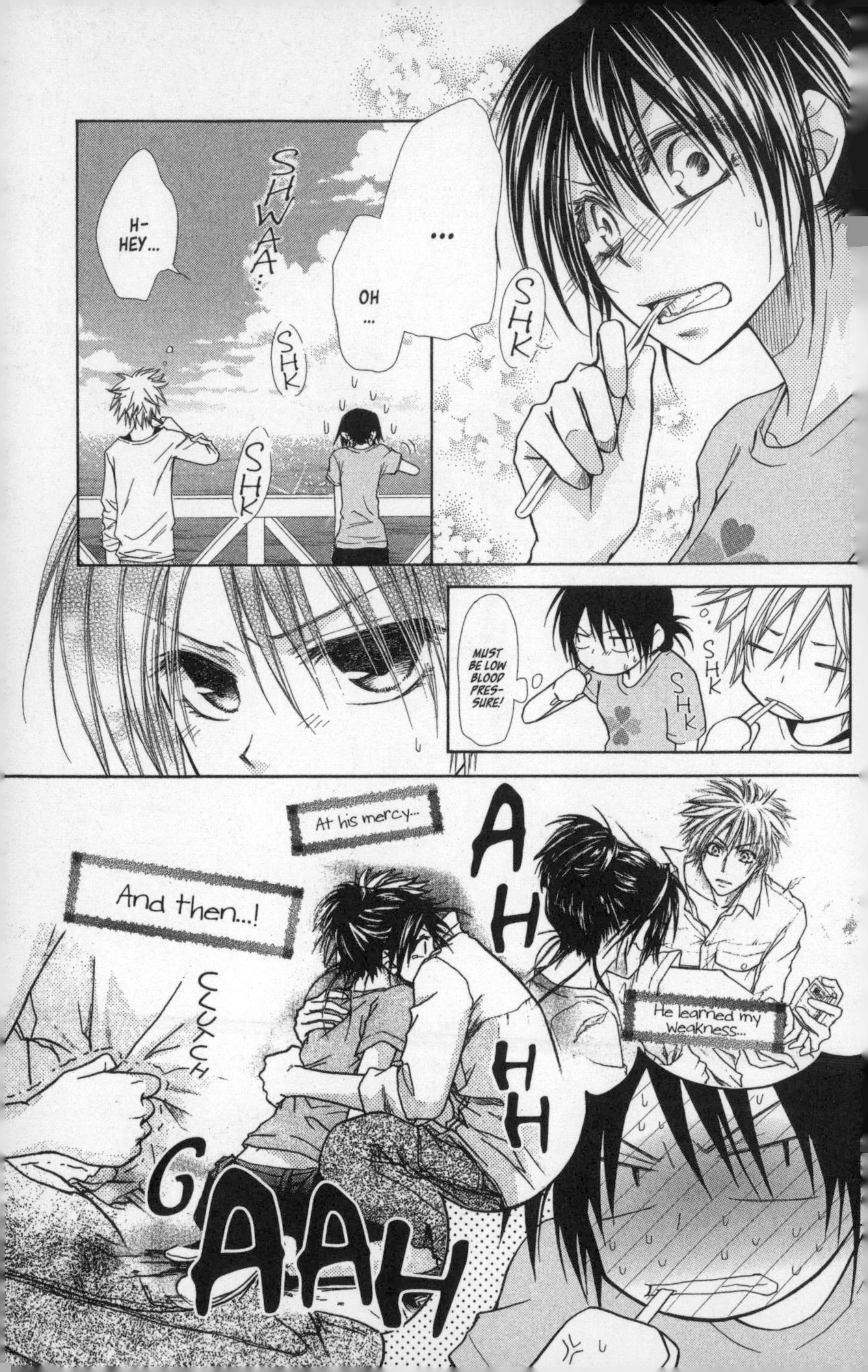
SHK
...
OH ...
SHWAA...
SHK
SHK
H- HEY...
SHK
SHK
MUST BE LOW BLOOD PRES-SURE!
At his mercy...
AHHHH
He learned my weakness...
And then...!
CLUTCH
GAAAH

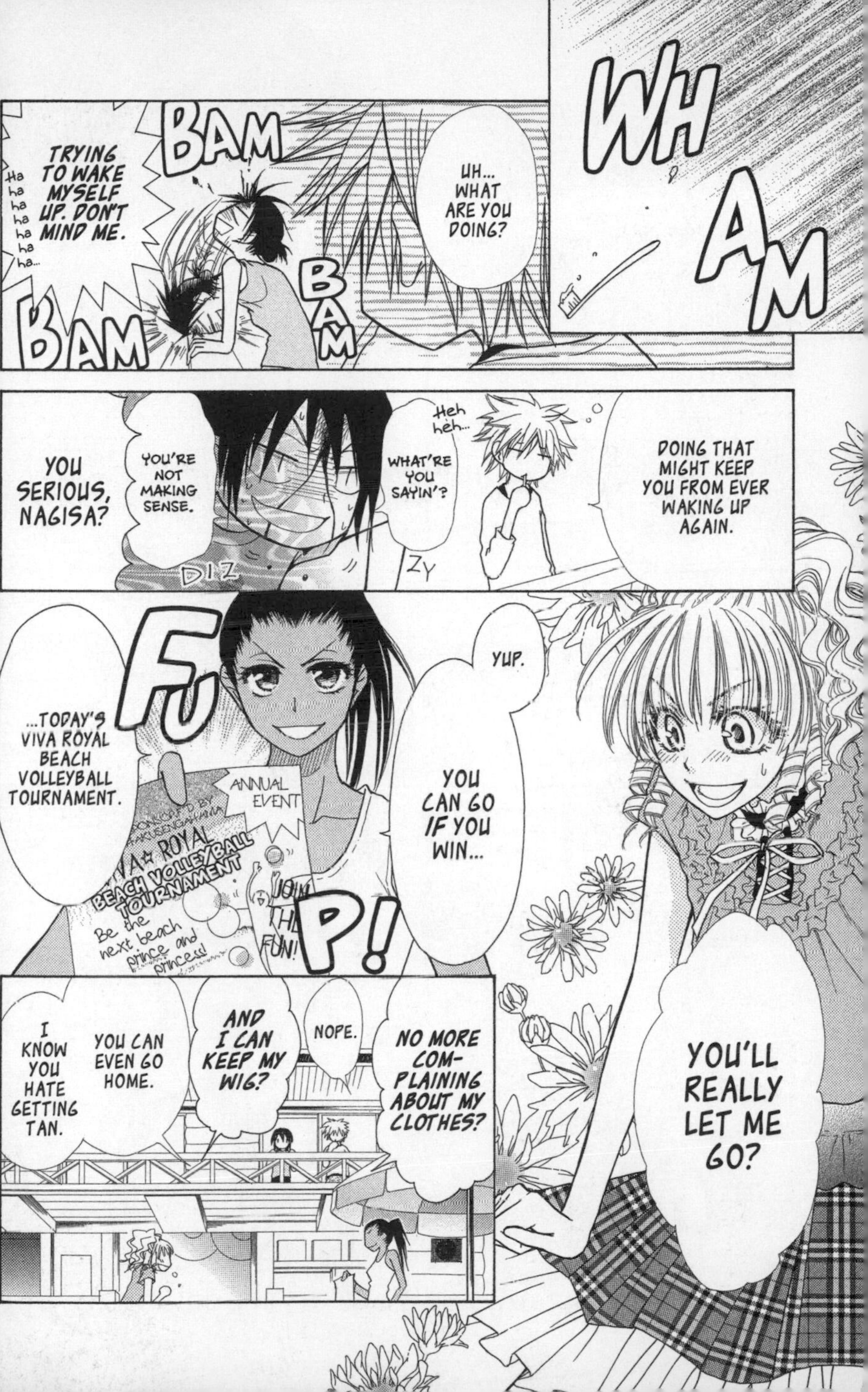
WHAM
UH... WHAT ARE YOU DOING?
BAM
TRYING TO WAKE MYSELF UP. DON'T MIND ME.
Ha ha ha ha ha ha ha...
BAM
BAM
DOING THAT MIGHT KEEP YOU FROM EVER WAKING UP AGAIN.
Heh heh...
WHAT'RE YOU SAYIN'?
YOU'RE NOT MAKING SENSE.
YOU SERIOUS, NAGISA?
DIZZY
YOU'LL REALLY LET ME GO?
YUP.
YOU CAN GO IF YOU WIN...
FUP!
...TODAY'S VIVA ROYAL BEACH VOLLEYBALL TOURNAMENT.
ANNUAL EVENT
VIVA☆ROYAL BEACH VOLLEYBALL TOURNAMENT
Be the next beach prince and princess!
JOIN THE FUN!
NO MORE COM-PLAINING ABOUT MY CLOTHES?
NOPE.
AND I CAN KEEP MY WIG?
YOU CAN EVEN GO HOME.
I KNOW YOU HATE GETTING TAN.

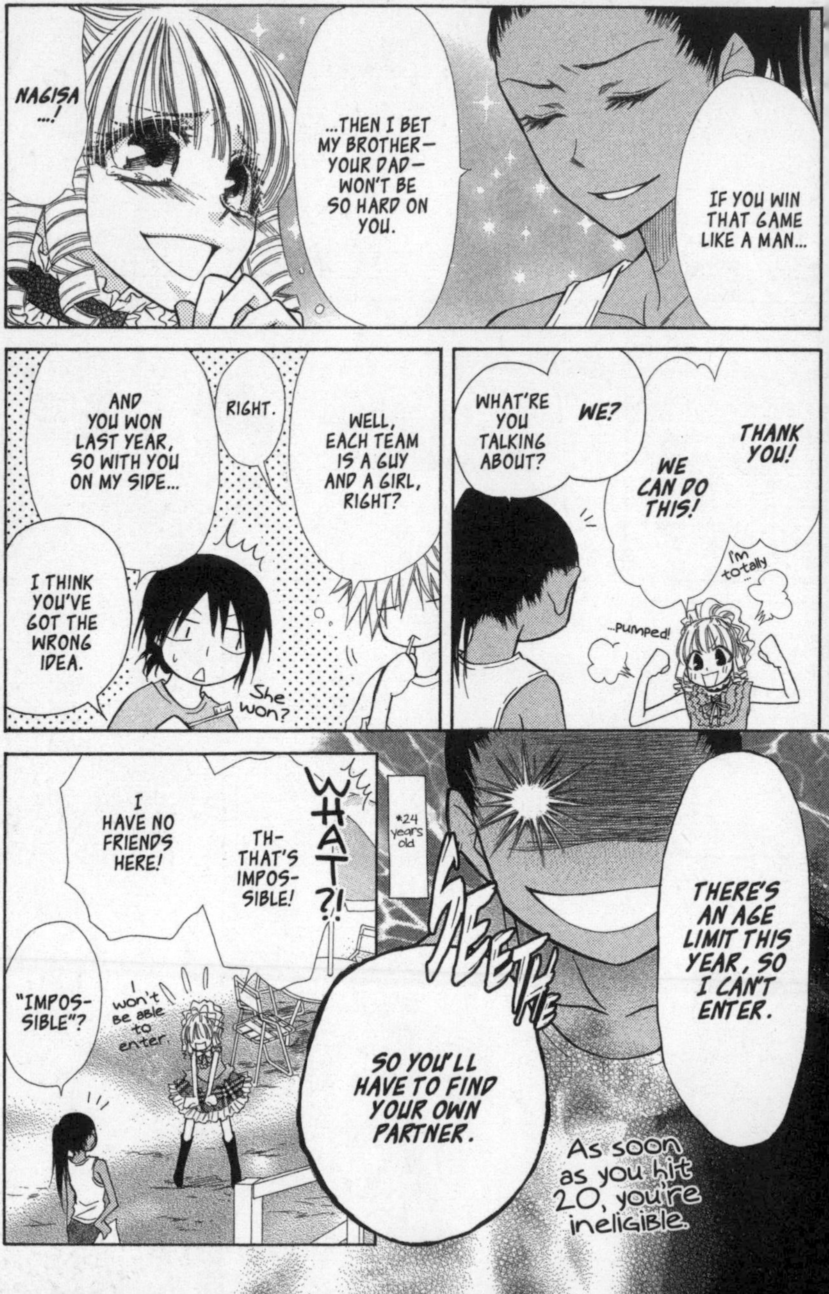
IF YOU WIN THAT GAME LIKE A MAN...
...THEN I BET MY BROTHER—YOUR DAD—WON'T BE SO HARD ON YOU.
NAGISA ...!
THANK YOU!
WE CAN DO THIS!
I'm totally ...
...pumped!
WE?
WHAT'RE YOU TALKING ABOUT?
WELL, EACH TEAM IS A GUY AND A GIRL, RIGHT?
RIGHT.
AND YOU WON LAST YEAR, SO WITH YOU ON MY SIDE...
She won?
I THINK YOU'VE GOT THE WRONG IDEA.
THERE'S AN AGE LIMIT THIS YEAR, SO I CAN'T ENTER.
SEETHE
*24 years old
SO YOU'LL HAVE TO FIND YOUR OWN PARTNER.
As soon as you hit 20, you're ineligible.
WHAT?!
TH-THAT'S IMPOSSIBLE!
I HAVE NO FRIENDS HERE!
I won't be able to enter
"IMPOSSIBLE"?

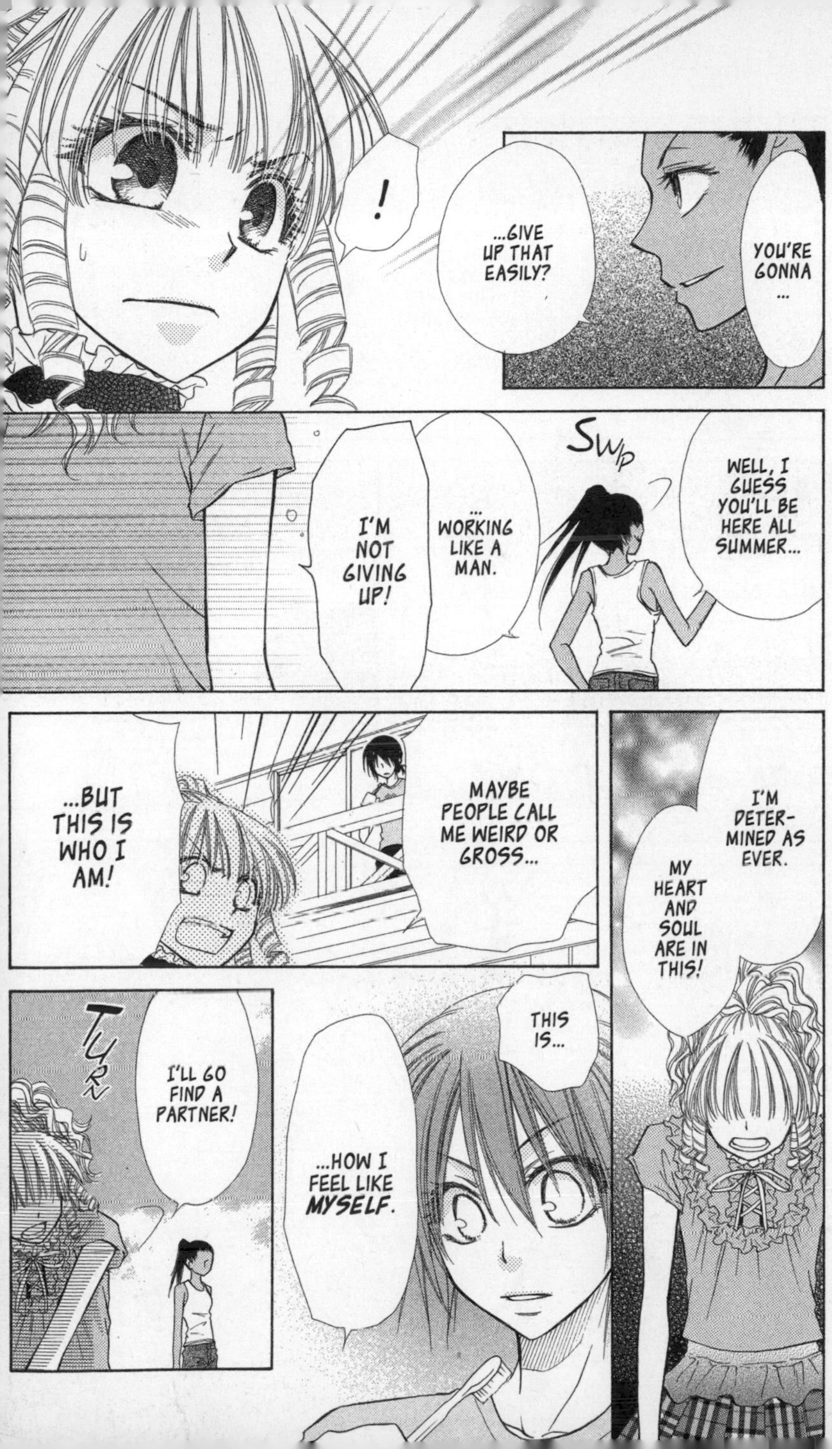
YOU'RE GONNA ...
...GIVE UP THAT EASILY?
!
SWP
WELL, I GUESS YOU'LL BE HERE ALL SUMMER...
... WORKING LIKE A MAN.
I'M NOT GIVING UP!
I'M DETER-MINED AS EVER.
MY HEART AND SOUL ARE IN THIS!
MAYBE PEOPLE CALL ME WEIRD OR GROSS...
...BUT THIS IS WHO I AM!
THIS IS...
...HOW I FEEL LIKE MYSELF.
TURN
I'LL GO FIND A PARTNER!

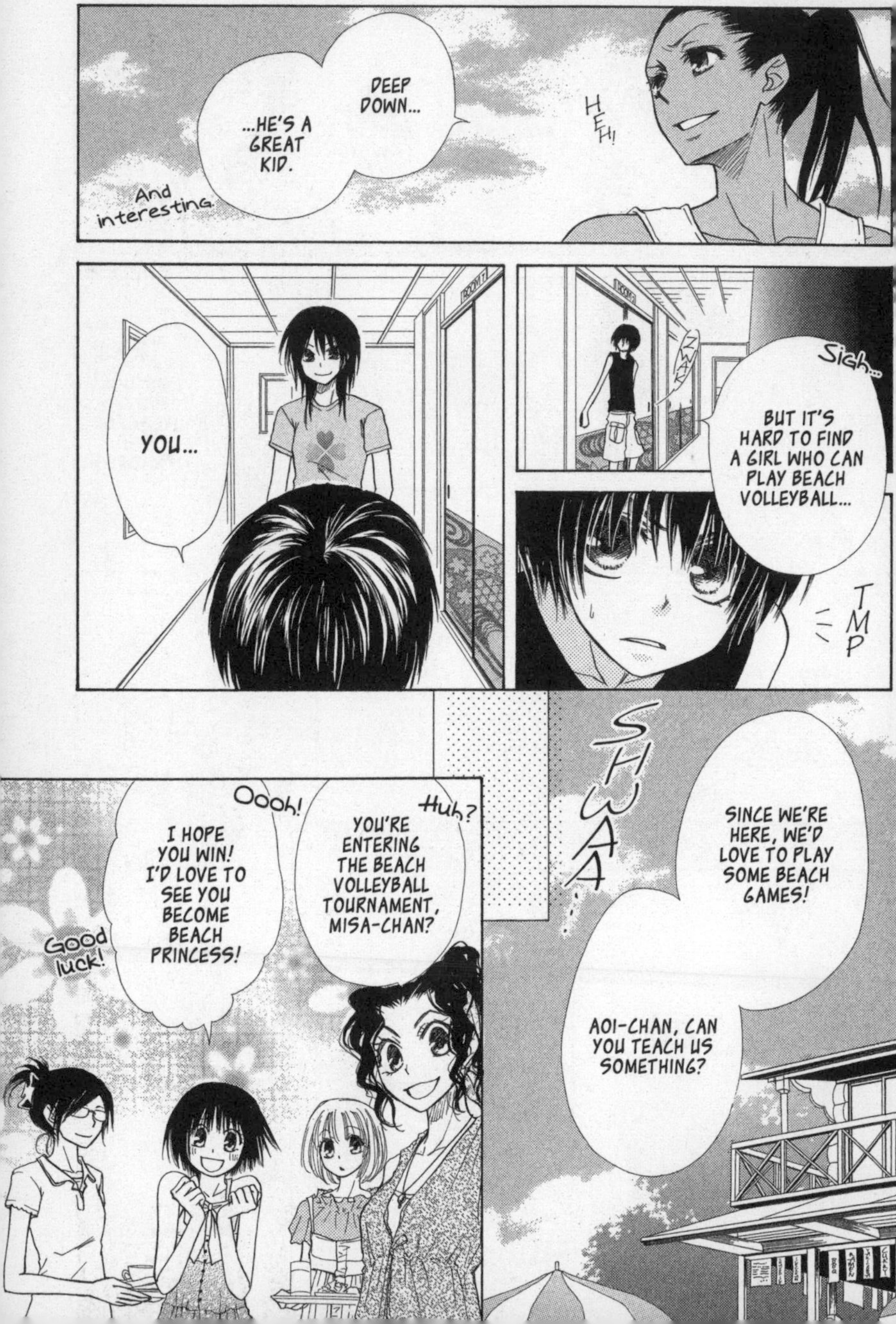
HEH!
DEEP DOWN...
...HE'S A GREAT KID.
And interesting.
Sigh...
BUT IT'S HARD TO FIND A GIRL WHO CAN PLAY BEACH VOLLEYBALL...
TMP
YOU...
SHWAA...
SINCE WE'RE HERE, WE'D LOVE TO PLAY SOME BEACH GAMES!
AOI-CHAN, CAN YOU TEACH US SOMETHING?
Huh?
YOU'RE ENTERING THE BEACH VOLLEYBALL TOURNAMENT, MISA-CHAN?
Oooh!
I HOPE YOU WIN! I'D LOVE TO SEE YOU BECOME BEACH PRINCESS!
Good luck!

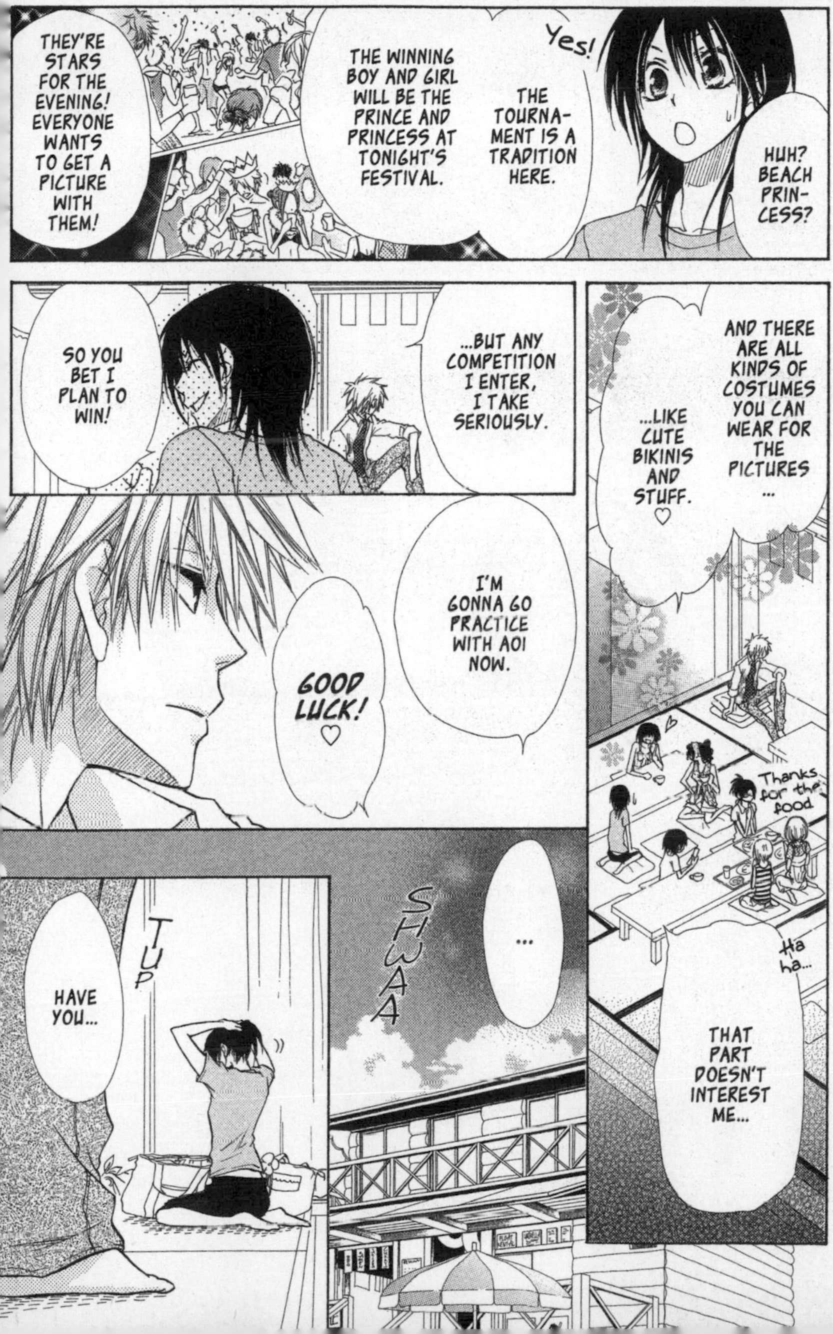
Yes!
HUH? BEACH PRIN-CESS?
THE TOURNA-MENT IS A TRADITION HERE.
THE WINNING BOY AND GIRL WILL BE THE PRINCE AND PRINCESS AT TONIGHT'S FESTIVAL.
THEY'RE STARS FOR THE EVENING! EVERYONE WANTS TO GET A PICTURE WITH THEM!
AND THERE ARE ALL KINDS OF COSTUMES YOU CAN WEAR FOR THE PICTURES ...
...LIKE CUTE BIKINIS AND STUFF. ♡
Thanks for the food
Ha ha...
THAT PART DOESN'T INTEREST ME...
...BUT ANY COMPETITION I ENTER, I TAKE SERIOUSLY.
SO YOU BET I PLAN TO WIN!
I'M GONNA GO PRACTICE WITH AOI NOW.
GOOD LUCK! ♡
SHWAA
...
TUP
HAVE YOU...

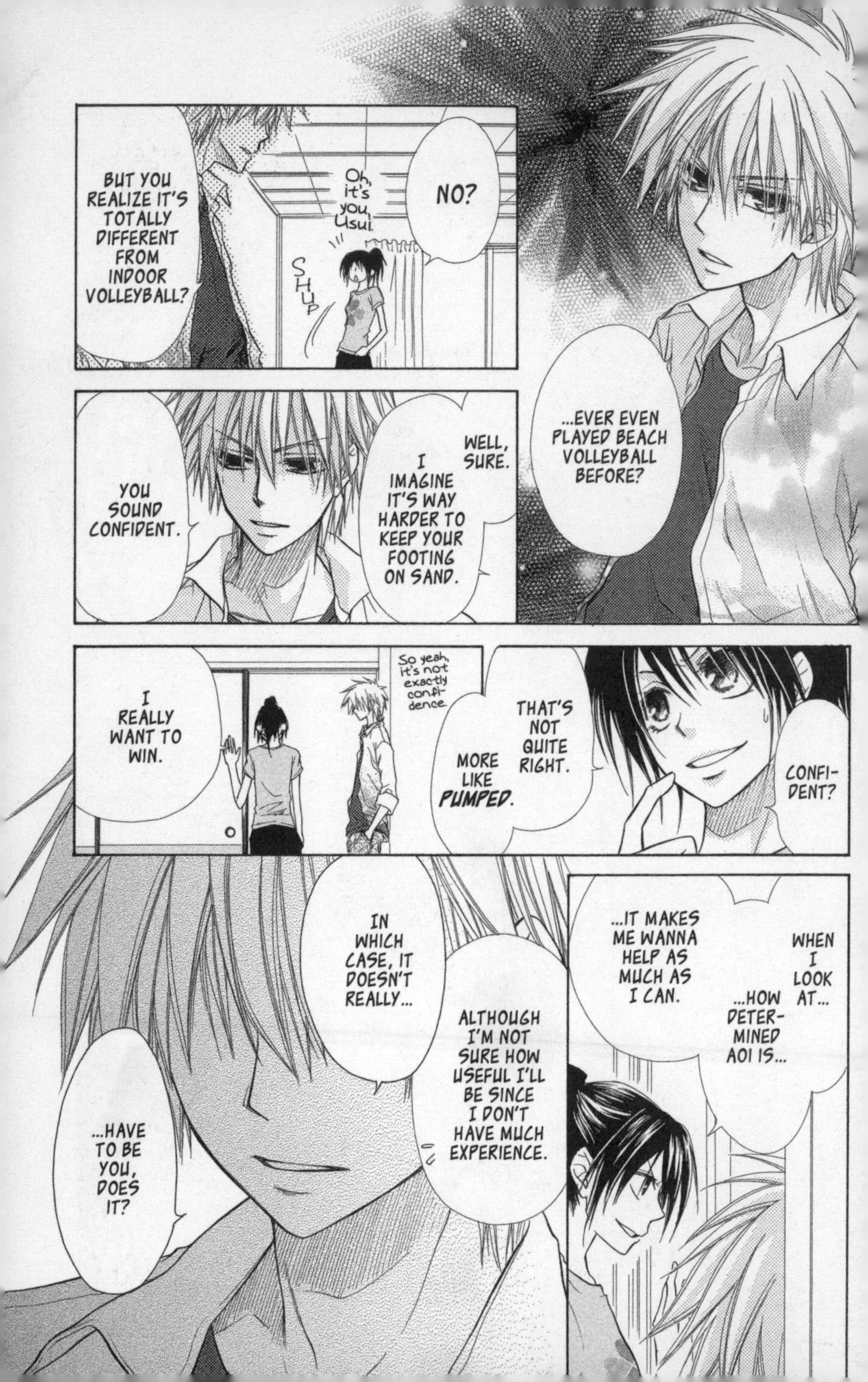
...EVER EVEN PLAYED BEACH VOLLEYBALL BEFORE?
NO?
Oh, it's you, Usui.
SHUP
BUT YOU REALIZE IT'S TOTALLY DIFFERENT FROM INDOOR VOLLEYBALL?
WELL, SURE.
I IMAGINE IT'S WAY HARDER TO KEEP YOUR FOOTING ON SAND.
YOU SOUND CONFIDENT.
CONFI-DENT?
THAT'S NOT QUITE RIGHT.
MORE LIKE *PUMPED*.
So yeah, it's not exactly confi-dence.
I REALLY WANT TO WIN.
WHEN I LOOK AT...
...HOW DETER-MINED AOI IS...
...IT MAKES ME WANNA HELP AS MUCH AS I CAN.
ALTHOUGH I'M NOT SURE HOW USEFUL I'LL BE SINCE I DON'T HAVE MUCH EXPERIENCE.
IN WHICH CASE, IT DOESN'T REALLY...
...HAVE TO BE YOU, DOES IT?

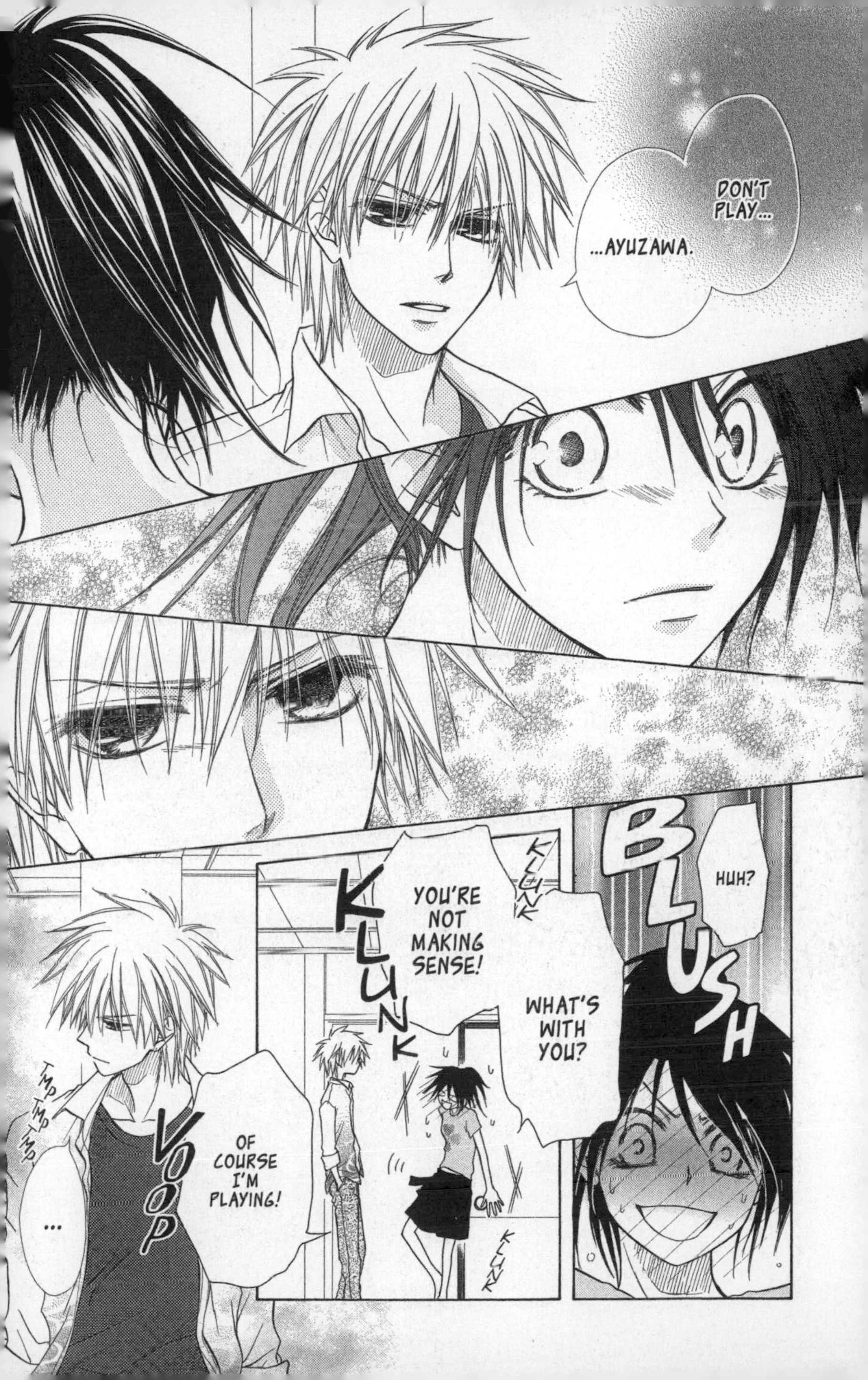
DON'T PLAY...
...AYUZAWA.
BLUSH
HUH?
KLUNK
YOU'RE NOT MAKING SENSE!
KLUNK
WHAT'S WITH YOU?
KLUNK
VOOP
OF COURSE I'M PLAYING!
TMP TMP TMP
...

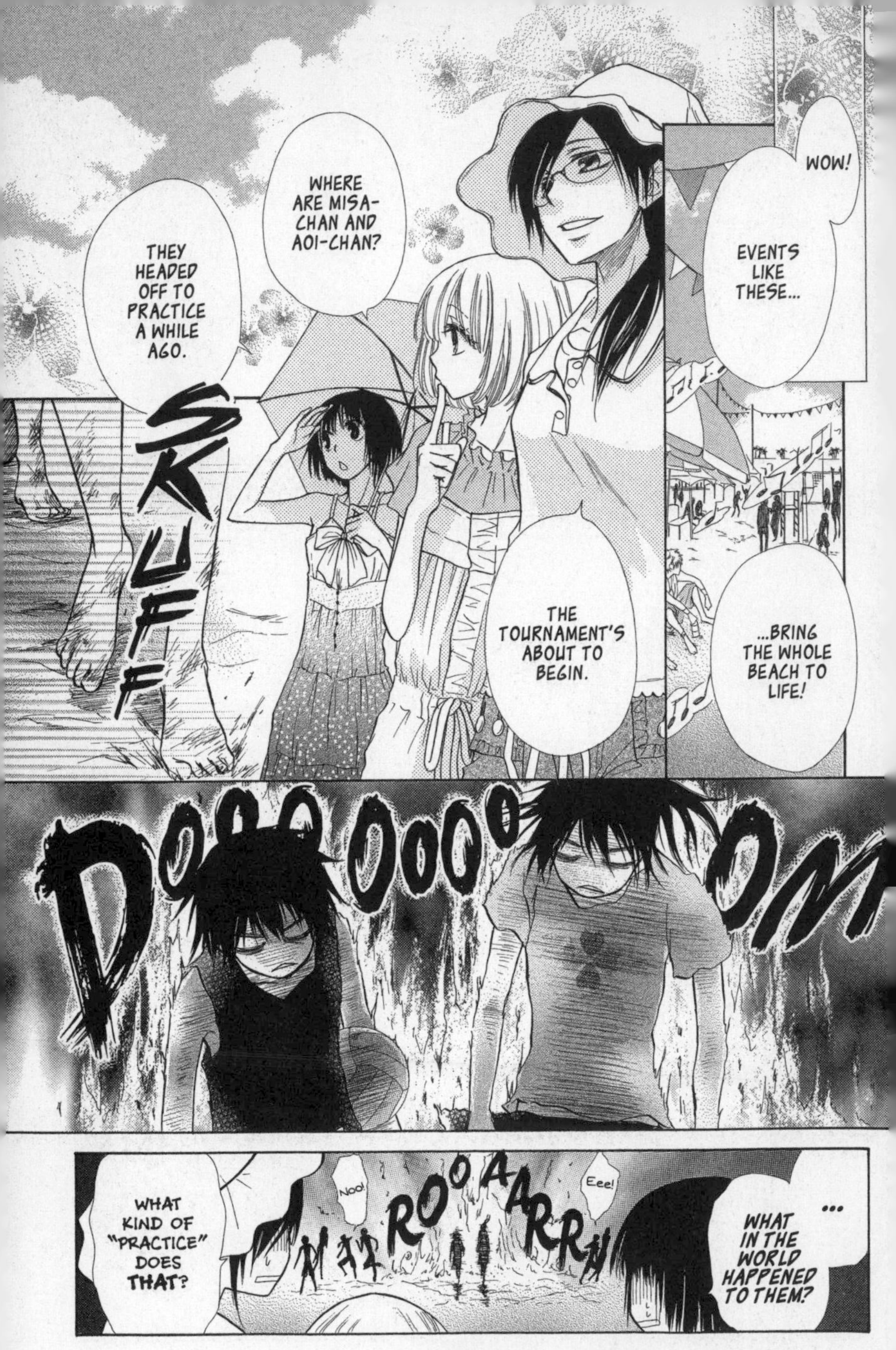

WOW!
EVENTS LIKE THESE...
...BRING THE WHOLE BEACH TO LIFE!
THE TOURNAMENT'S ABOUT TO BEGIN.
WHERE ARE MISA-CHAN AND AOI-CHAN?
THEY HEADED OFF TO PRACTICE A WHILE AGO.
SKUFF
DOOOOOOOOM
...
WHAT IN THE WORLD HAPPENED TO THEM?
Eee!
ROOAARR
Noo!
WHAT KIND OF "PRACTICE" DOES THAT?

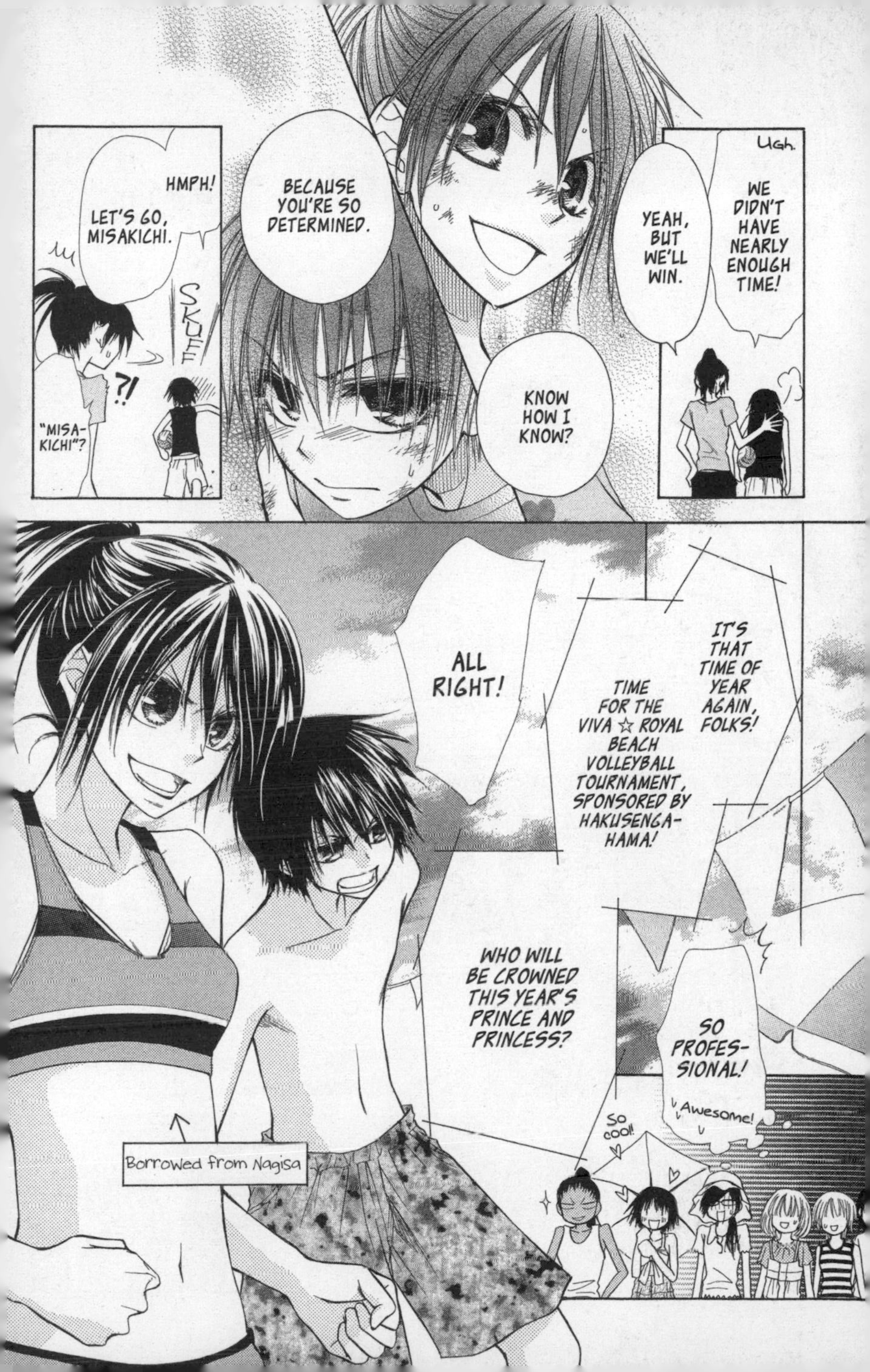
Ugh.
WE DIDN'T HAVE NEARLY ENOUGH TIME!
YEAH, BUT WE'LL WIN.
KNOW HOW I KNOW?
BECAUSE YOU'RE SO DETERMINED.
HMPH!
LET'S GO, MISAKICHI.
SKUFF
?!
"MISA-KICHI"?
IT'S THAT TIME OF YEAR AGAIN, FOLKS!
TIME FOR THE VIVA ☆ ROYAL BEACH VOLLEYBALL TOURNAMENT, SPONSORED BY HAKUSENGA-HAMA!
ALL RIGHT!
WHO WILL BE CROWNED THIS YEAR'S PRINCE AND PRINCESS?
SO PROFES-SIONAL!
Awesome!
So cool!!
Borrowed from Nagisa

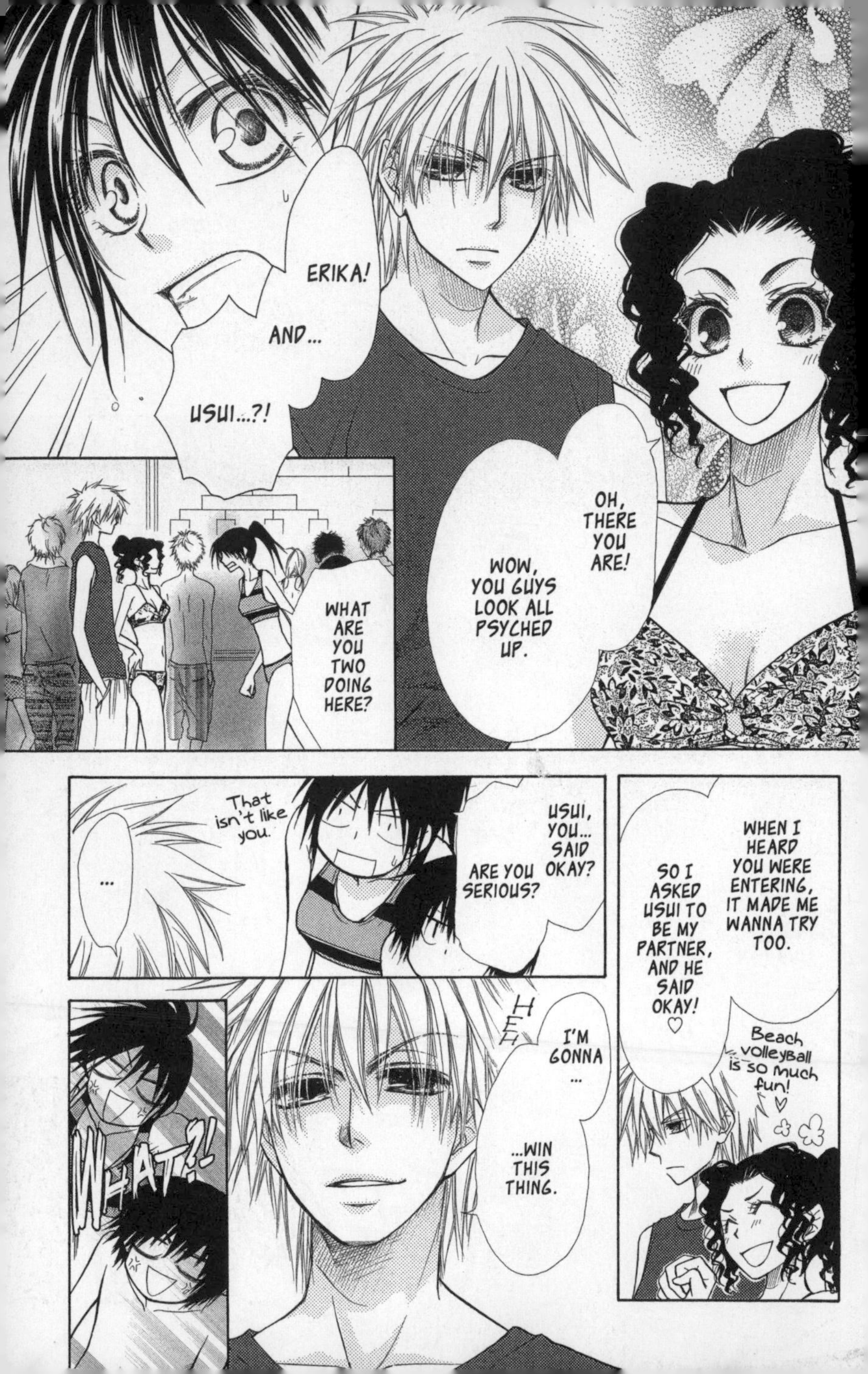
ERIKA!
AND...
USUI...?!
OH, THERE YOU ARE!
WOW, YOU GUYS LOOK ALL PSYCHED UP.
WHAT ARE YOU TWO DOING HERE?
WHEN I HEARD YOU WERE ENTERING, IT MADE ME WANNA TRY TOO.
SO I ASKED USUI TO BE MY PARTNER, AND HE SAID OKAY! ♡
Beach volleyball is so much fun! ♡
USUI, YOU... SAID OKAY?
ARE YOU SERIOUS?
That isn't like you.
...
HEH
I'M GONNA...
...WIN THIS THING.
WHAT?!

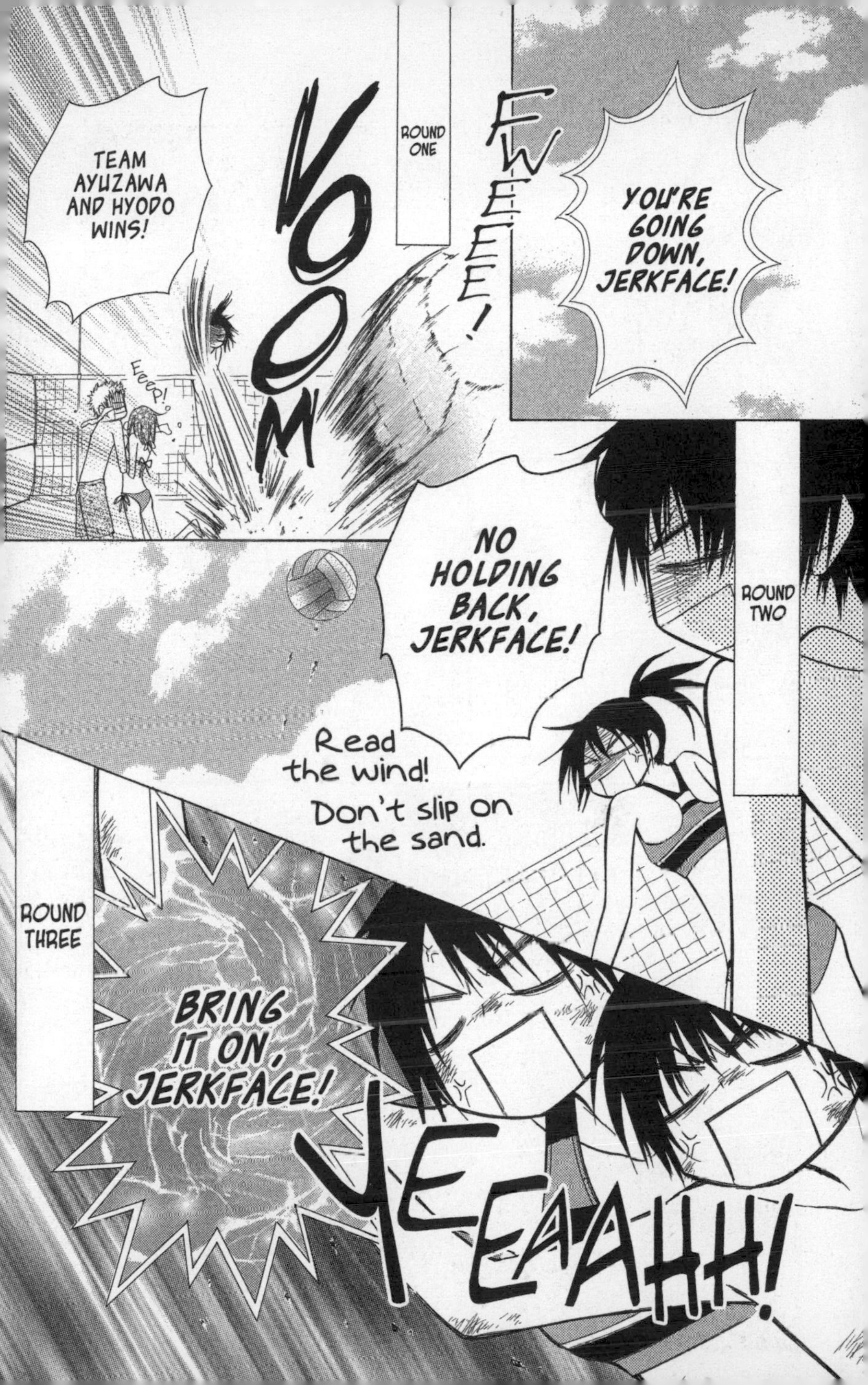
YOU'RE GOING DOWN, JERKFACE!
ROUND ONE
FWEEEE!
VOOM
TEAM AYUZAWA AND HYODO WINS!
Eeep!
ROUND TWO
NO HOLDING BACK, JERKFACE!
Read the wind!
Don't slip on the sand.
ROUND THREE
BRING IT ON, JERKFACE!
YEEAAHH!

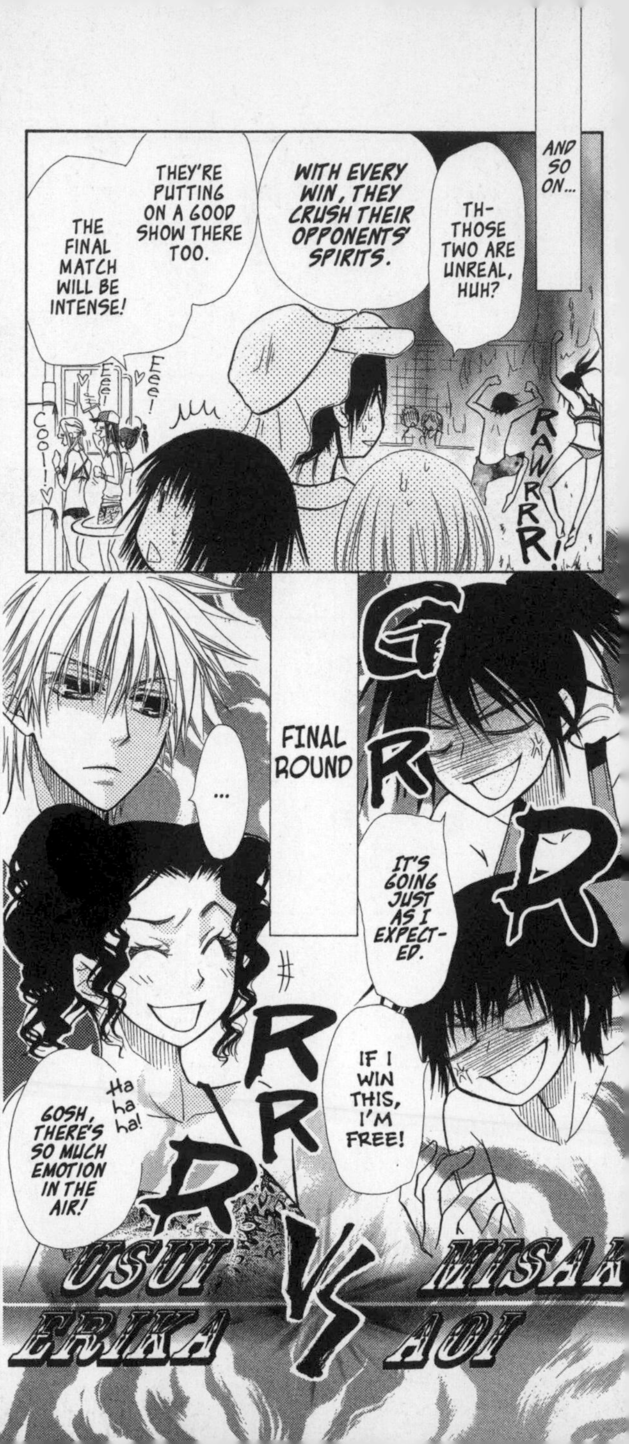
AND SO ON...
TH-THOSE TWO ARE UNREAL, HUH?
WITH EVERY WIN, THEY CRUSH THEIR OPPONENTS' SPIRITS.
THEY'RE PUTTING ON A GOOD SHOW THERE TOO.
THE FINAL MATCH WILL BE INTENSE!
Eee!
Eee!
COOL!
RAWRRR!
GRRR
IT'S GOING JUST AS I EXPECTED.
IF I WIN THIS, I'M FREE!
FINAL ROUND
...
Ha ha ha!
GOSH, THERE'S SO MUCH EMOTION IN THE AIR!
RRR
MISAK
AOI
VS
USUI
ERIKA

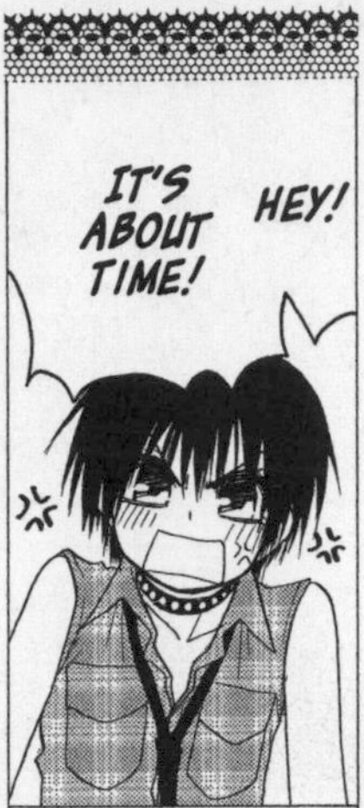
HEY!
IT'S ABOUT TIME!

NAME
AOI HYODO

AGE (CLASS)
14 YEARS OLD

BLOOD TYPE
B

HEIGHT
153 CM

WEIGHT
45 KG

SPECIAL SKILL
DRESSING LIKE A GIRL

FAVORITE THING
CUTE THINGS

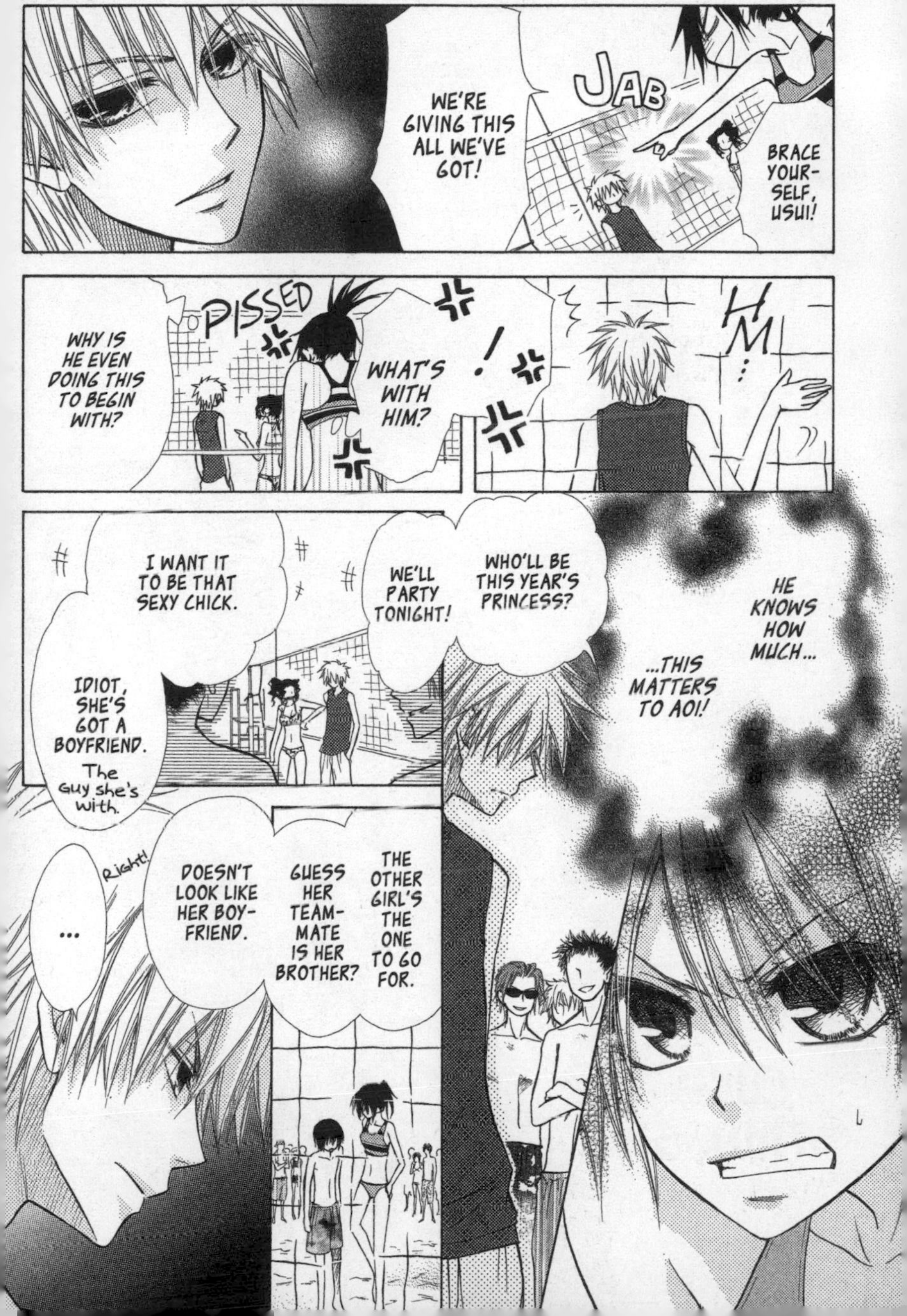

JAB
BRACE YOURSELF, USUI!
WE'RE GIVING THIS ALL WE'VE GOT!
HM...
!
WHAT'S WITH HIM?
PISSED
WHY IS HE EVEN DOING THIS TO BEGIN WITH?
HE KNOWS HOW MUCH...
...THIS MATTERS TO AOI!
WHO'LL BE THIS YEAR'S PRINCESS?
WE'LL PARTY TONIGHT!
I WANT IT TO BE THAT SEXY CHICK.
IDIOT, SHE'S GOT A BOYFRIEND.
The Guy she's with.
THE OTHER GIRL'S THE ONE TO GO FOR.
GUESS HER TEAMMATE IS HER BROTHER?
DOESN'T LOOK LIKE HER BOYFRIEND.
Right!
...

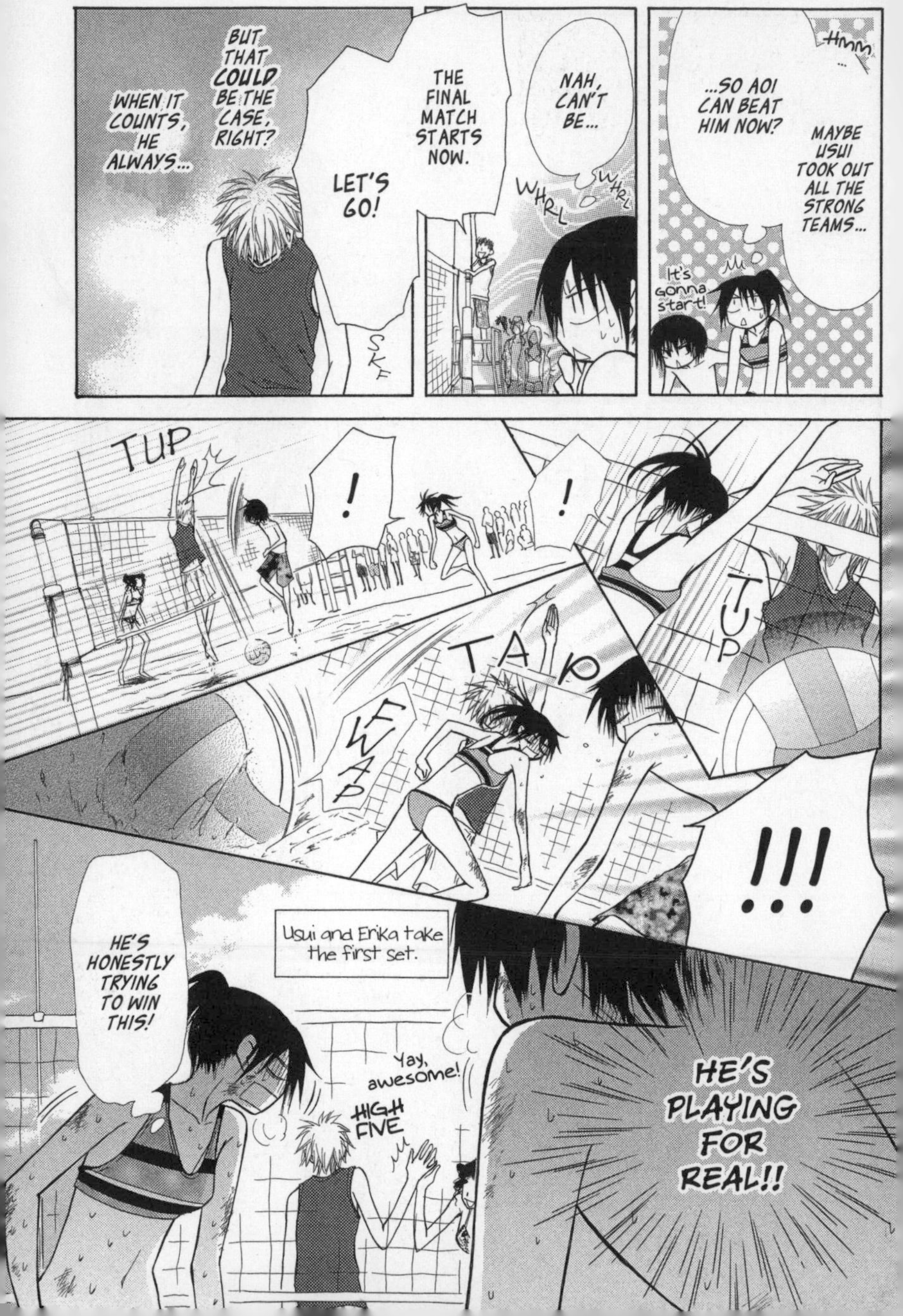
Hmm...
MAYBE USUI TOOK OUT ALL THE STRONG TEAMS...
...SO AOI CAN BEAT HIM NOW?
It's gonna start!
NAH, CAN'T BE...
WHRL WHRL
THE FINAL MATCH STARTS NOW.
LET'S GO!
BUT THAT COULD BE THE CASE, RIGHT?
WHEN IT COUNTS, HE ALWAYS...
SKF
!
TUP
TAP
FWAP
!!!
!
TUP
HE'S PLAYING FOR REAL!!
Usui and Erika take the first set.
Yay, awesome!
HIGH FIVE
HE'S HONESTLY TRYING TO WIN THIS!

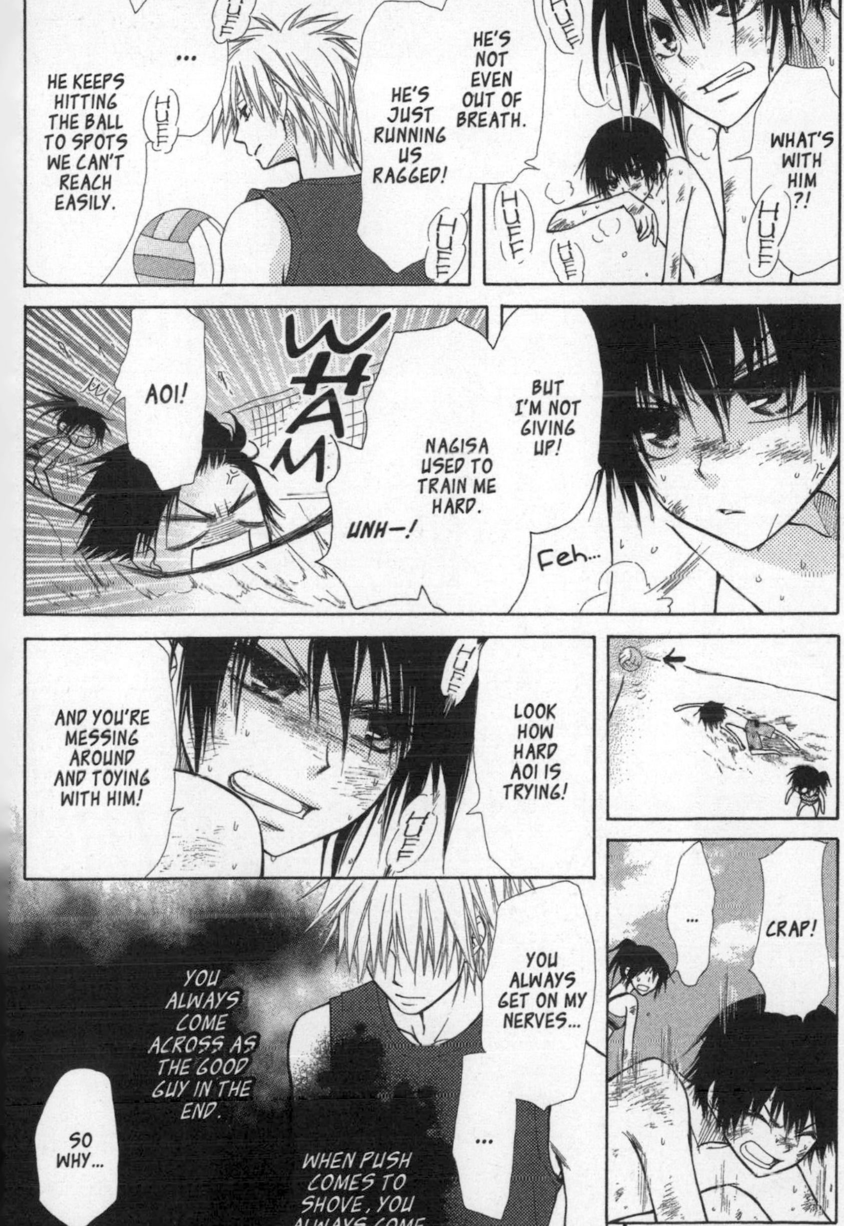
HUFF
WHAT'S WITH HIM ?!
HUFF
HUFF
HUFF
HUFF
HE'S NOT EVEN OUT OF BREATH.
HE'S JUST RUNNING US RAGGED!
HUFF
...
HE KEEPS HITTING THE BALL TO SPOTS WE CAN'T REACH EASILY.
HUFF
BUT I'M NOT GIVING UP!
NAGISA USED TO TRAIN ME HARD.
Feh...
WHAM
UNH—!
AOI!
LOOK HOW HARD AOI IS TRYING!
HUFF
HUFF
AND YOU'RE MESSING AROUND AND TOYING WITH HIM!
CRAP!
...
YOU ALWAYS GET ON MY NERVES...
...
YOU ALWAYS COME ACROSS AS THE GOOD GUY IN THE END.
WHEN PUSH COMES TO SHOVE, YOU ALWAYS COME HELP ME.
SO WHY...

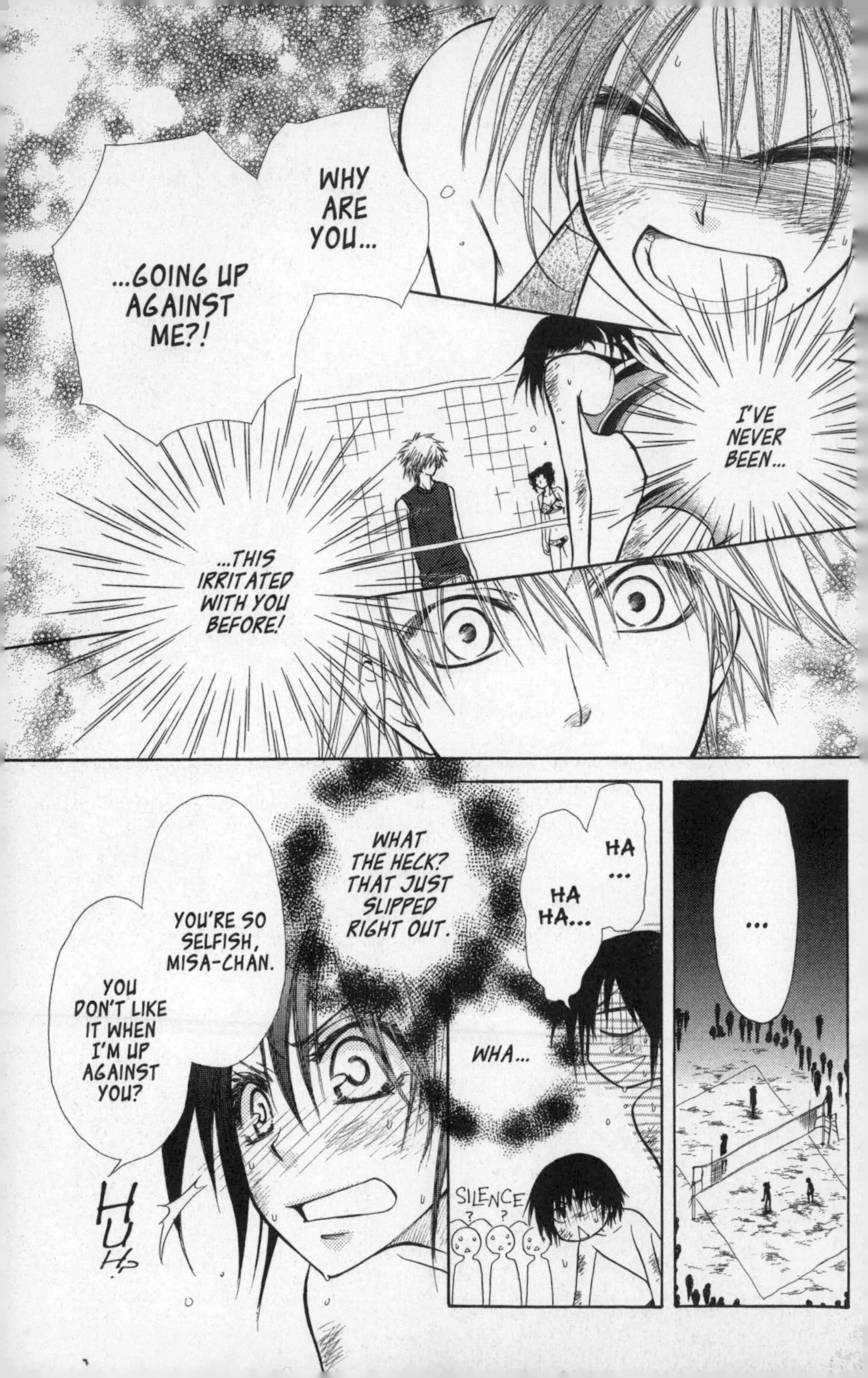
WHY ARE YOU...
...GOING UP AGAINST ME?!
I'VE NEVER BEEN...
...THIS IRRITATED WITH YOU BEFORE!
...
HA ... HA HA...
WHA...
SILENCE
? ?
WHAT THE HECK? THAT JUST SLIPPED RIGHT OUT.
YOU'RE SO SELFISH, MISA-CHAN.
YOU DON'T LIKE IT WHEN I'M UP AGAINST YOU?
HUH?

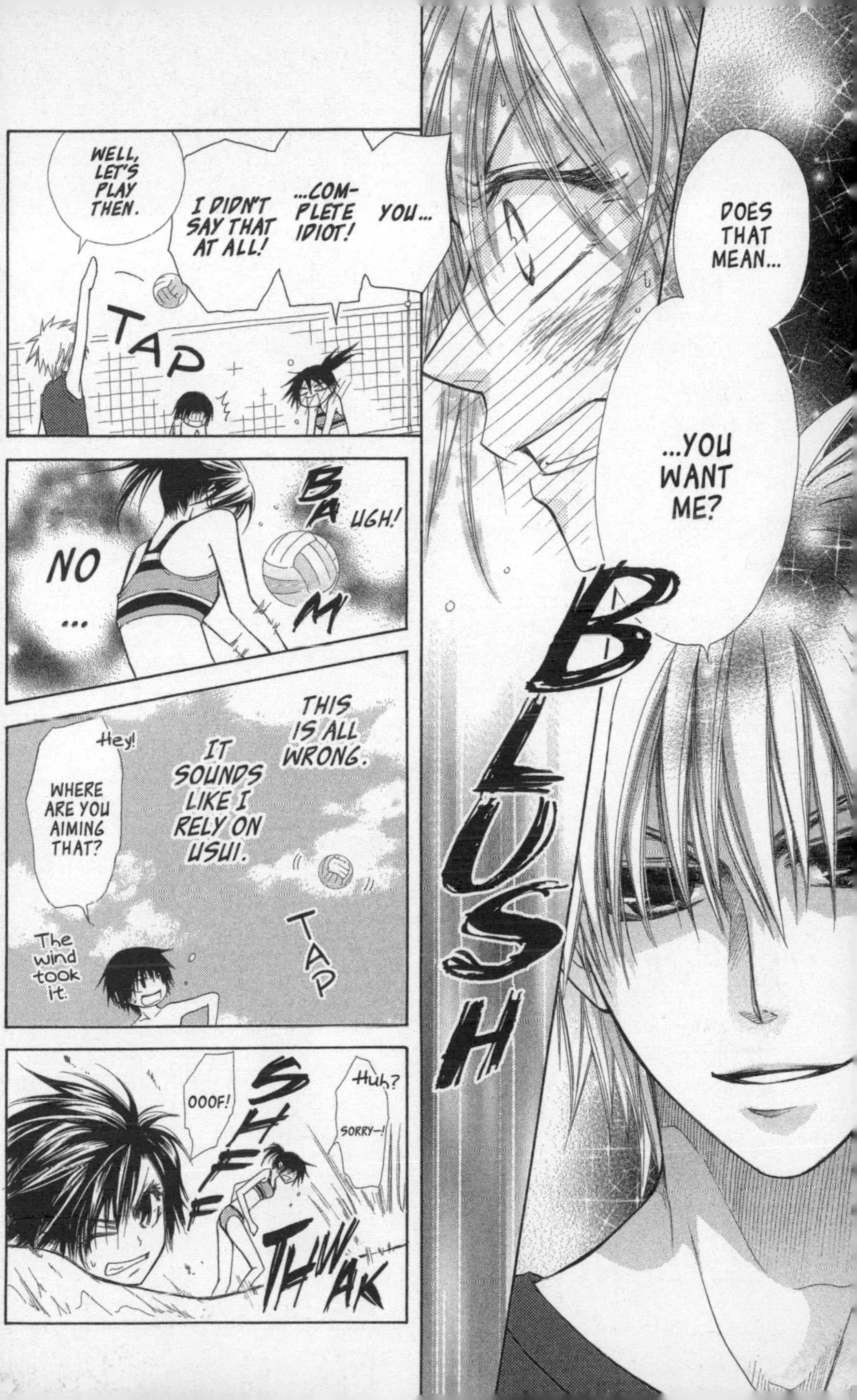
DOES THAT MEAN...
...YOU WANT ME?
BLUSH
YOU...
...COM-PLETE IDIOT!
I DIDN'T SAY THAT AT ALL!
WELL, LET'S PLAY THEN.
TAP
BAM
UGH!
NO...
THIS IS ALL WRONG.
IT SOUNDS LIKE I RELY ON USUI.
Hey!
WHERE ARE YOU AIMING THAT?
TAP
The wind took it.
Huh?
SORRY—!
SHFF
OOOF!
THWAK

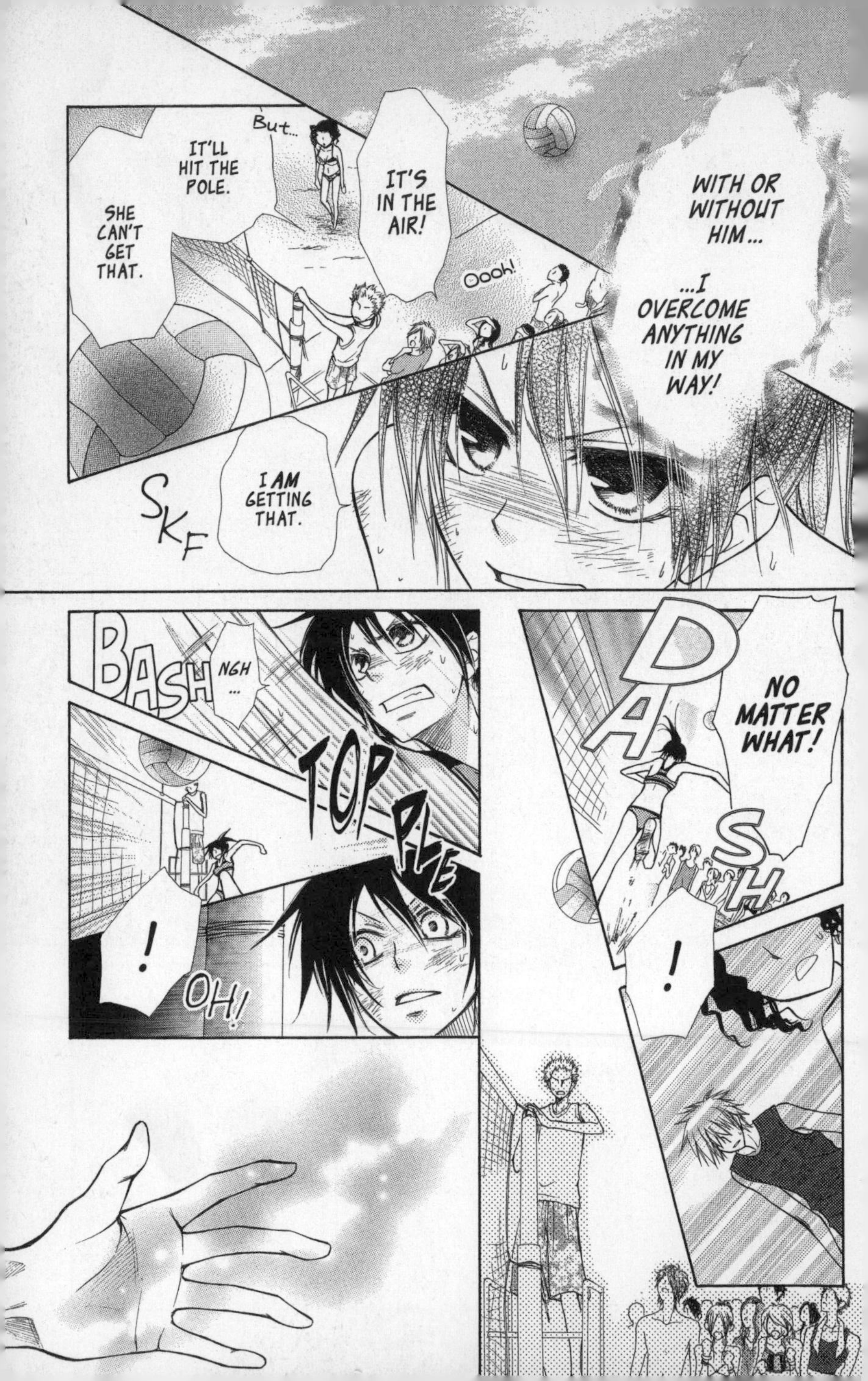
WITH OR WITHOUT HIM...
...I OVERCOME ANYTHING IN MY WAY!
IT'S IN THE AIR!
But...
IT'LL HIT THE POLE.
SHE CAN'T GET THAT.
Oooh!
I AM GETTING THAT.
SKF
NO MATTER WHAT!
DASH
BASH
NGH...
TOPPLE
!
OH!
!

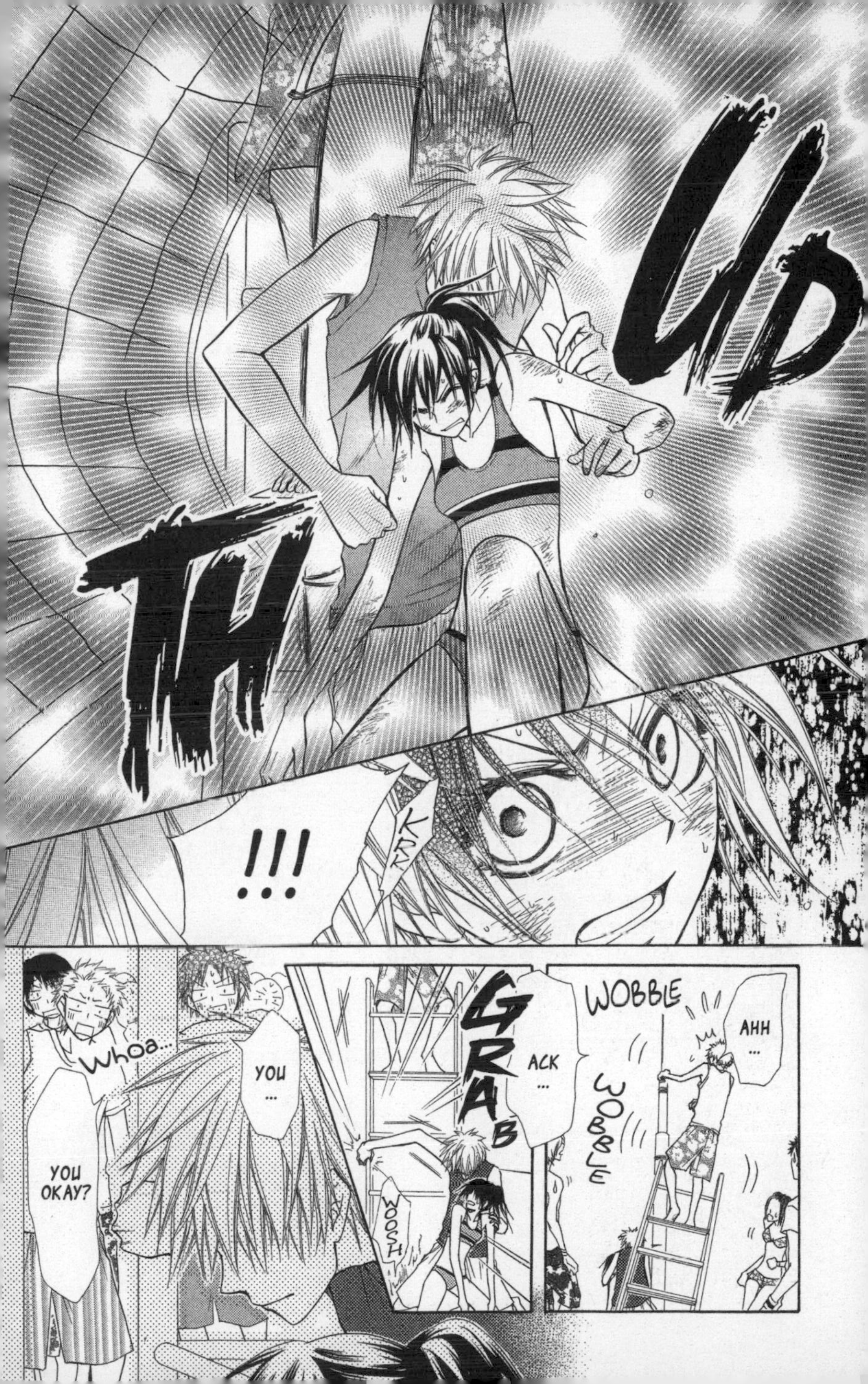

TH UD
KRK
!!!
WOBBLE
AHH ...
WOBBLE
GRAB
ACK ...
WOOSH
YOU ...
Whoa...
YOU OKAY?

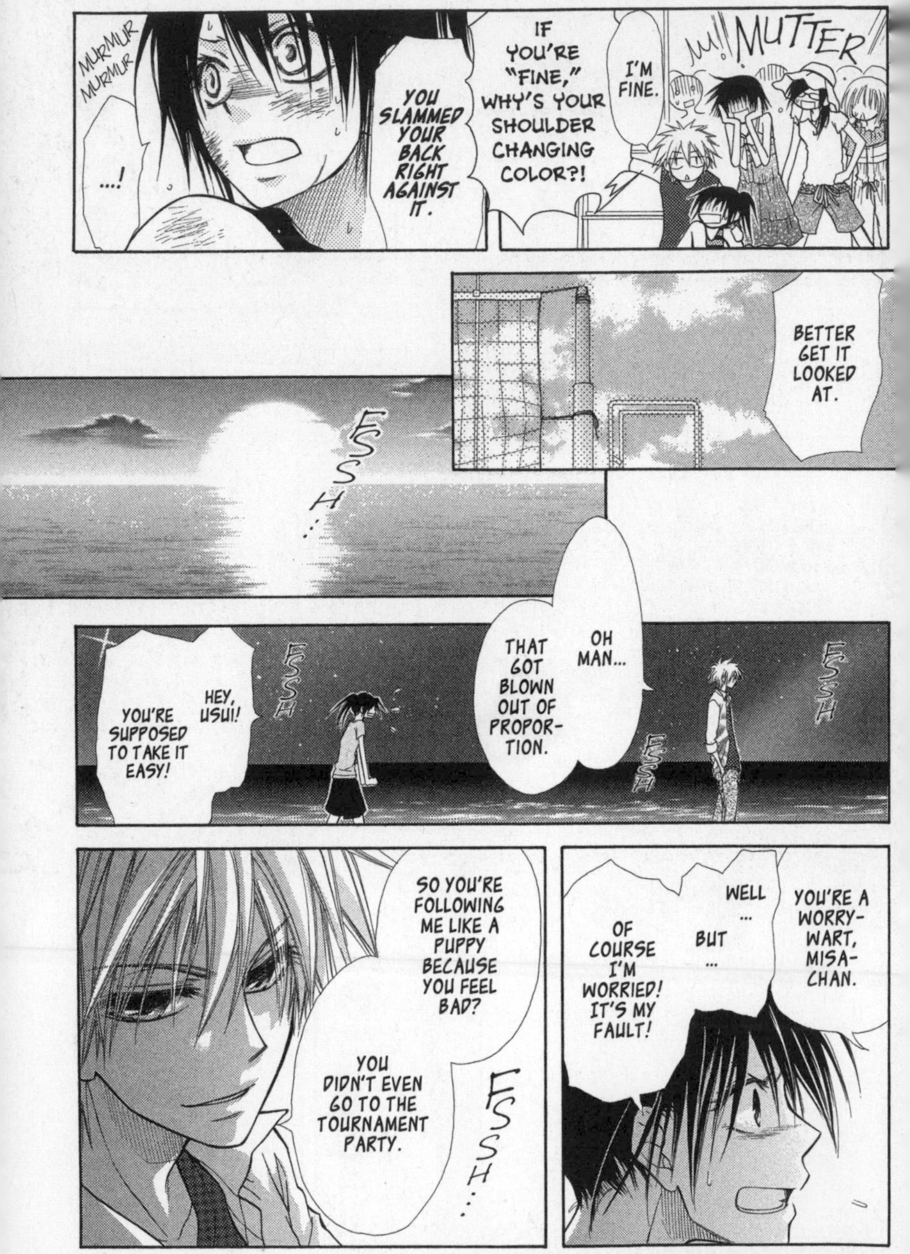
MU!! MUTTER
I'M FINE.
IF YOU'RE "FINE," WHY'S YOUR SHOULDER CHANGING COLOR?!
YOU SLAMMED YOUR BACK RIGHT AGAINST IT.
MURMUR MURMUR
...!
BETTER GET IT LOOKED AT.
FSSH...
OH MAN... THAT GOT BLOWN OUT OF PROPORTION.
FSSH
FSSH
HEY, USUI! YOU'RE SUPPOSED TO TAKE IT EASY!
FSSH
YOU'RE A WORRY-WART, MISA-CHAN.
WELL... BUT... OF COURSE I'M WORRIED! IT'S MY FAULT!
SO YOU'RE FOLLOWING ME LIKE A PUPPY BECAUSE YOU FEEL BAD?
YOU DIDN'T EVEN GO TO THE TOURNAMENT PARTY.
FSSH...

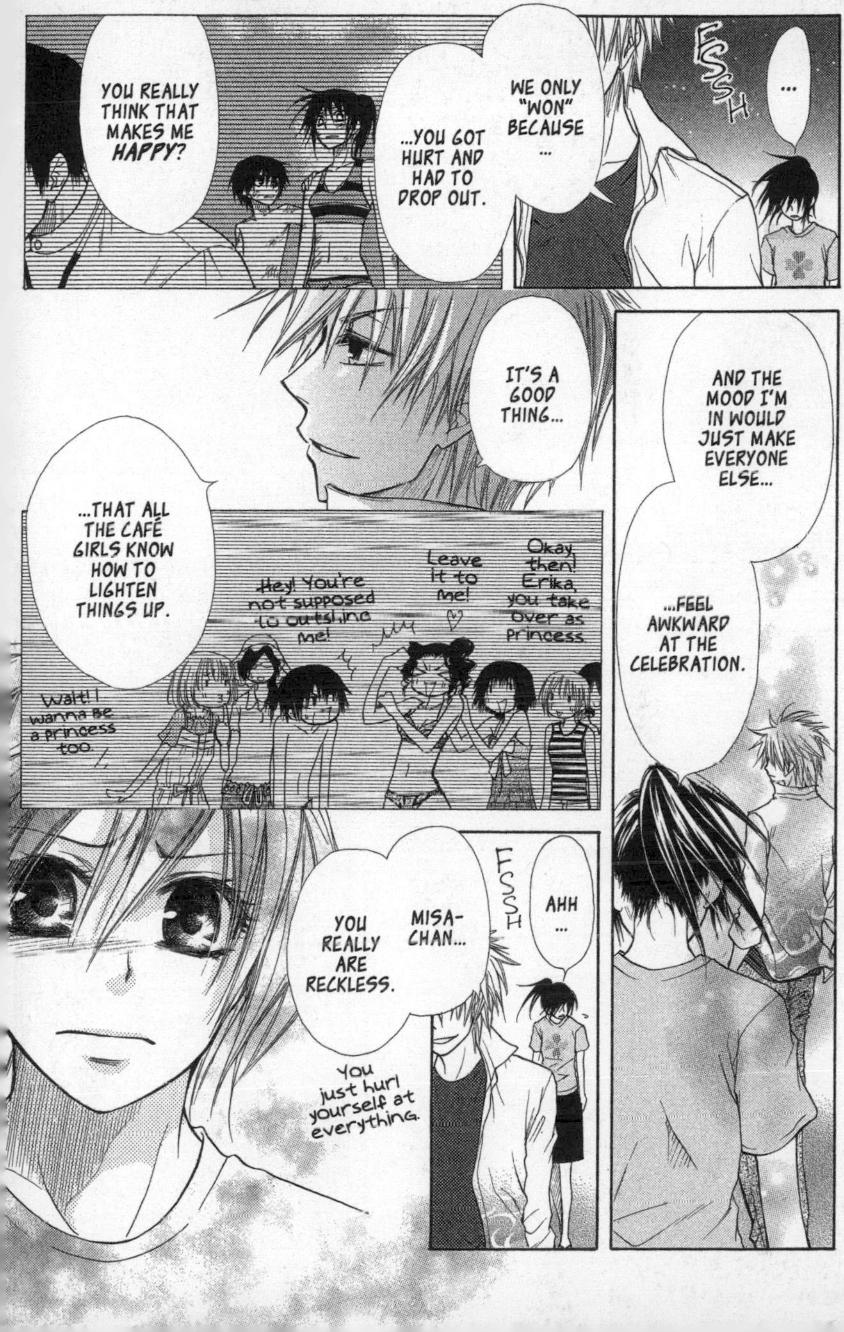
...
FSSH
WE ONLY "WON" BECAUSE ...
...YOU GOT HURT AND HAD TO DROP OUT.
YOU REALLY THINK THAT MAKES ME HAPPY?
AND THE MOOD I'M IN WOULD JUST MAKE EVERYONE ELSE...
...FEEL AWKWARD AT THE CELEBRATION.
IT'S A GOOD THING...
...THAT ALL THE CAFÉ GIRLS KNOW HOW TO LIGHTEN THINGS UP.
Okay, then! Erika, you take over as princess.
Leave it to me!
Hey! You're not supposed to outshine me!
Wait! I wanna be a princess too.
FSSH
AHH ...
MISA-CHAN...
YOU REALLY ARE RECKLESS.
You just hurl yourself at everything.

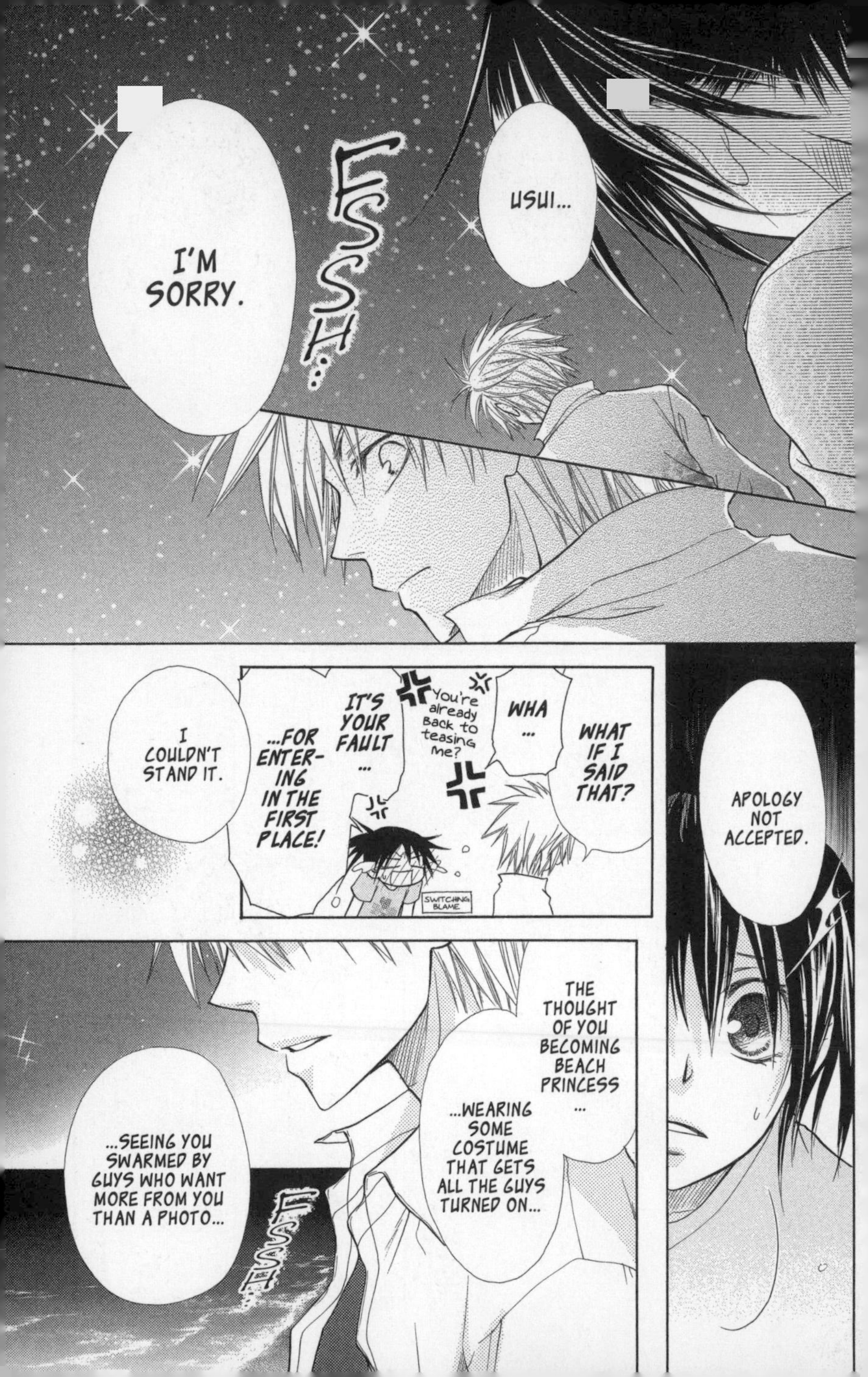
USUI...
FSSH...
I'M SORRY.
APOLOGY NOT ACCEPTED.
WHAT IF I SAID THAT?
WHA...
You're already Back to teasing me?
IT'S YOUR FAULT...
...FOR ENTERING IN THE FIRST PLACE!
SWITCHING BLAME
I COULDN'T STAND IT.
THE THOUGHT OF YOU BECOMING BEACH PRINCESS...
...WEARING SOME COSTUME THAT GETS ALL THE GUYS TURNED ON...
...SEEING YOU SWARMED BY GUYS WHO WANT MORE FROM YOU THAN A PHOTO...
FSSH...

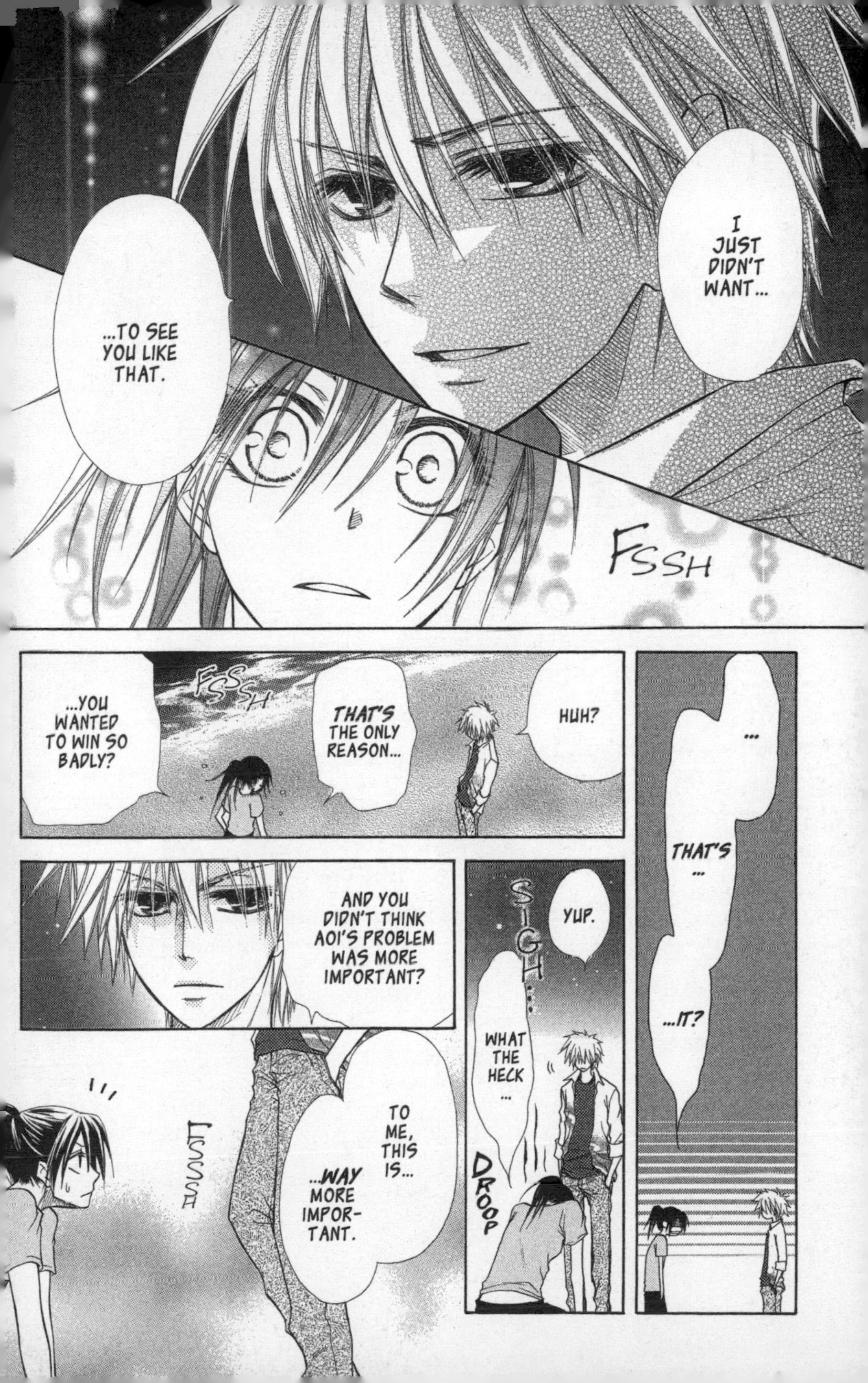
I JUST DIDN'T WANT...
...TO SEE YOU LIKE THAT.
FSSH
...
THAT'S ...
...IT?
HUH?
THAT'S THE ONLY REASON...
...YOU WANTED TO WIN SO BADLY?
FSSSH
YUP.
SIGH...
WHAT THE HECK ...
DROOP
AND YOU DIDN'T THINK AOI'S PROBLEM WAS MORE IMPORTANT?
TO ME, THIS IS...
...WAY MORE IMPORTANT.
FSSSH

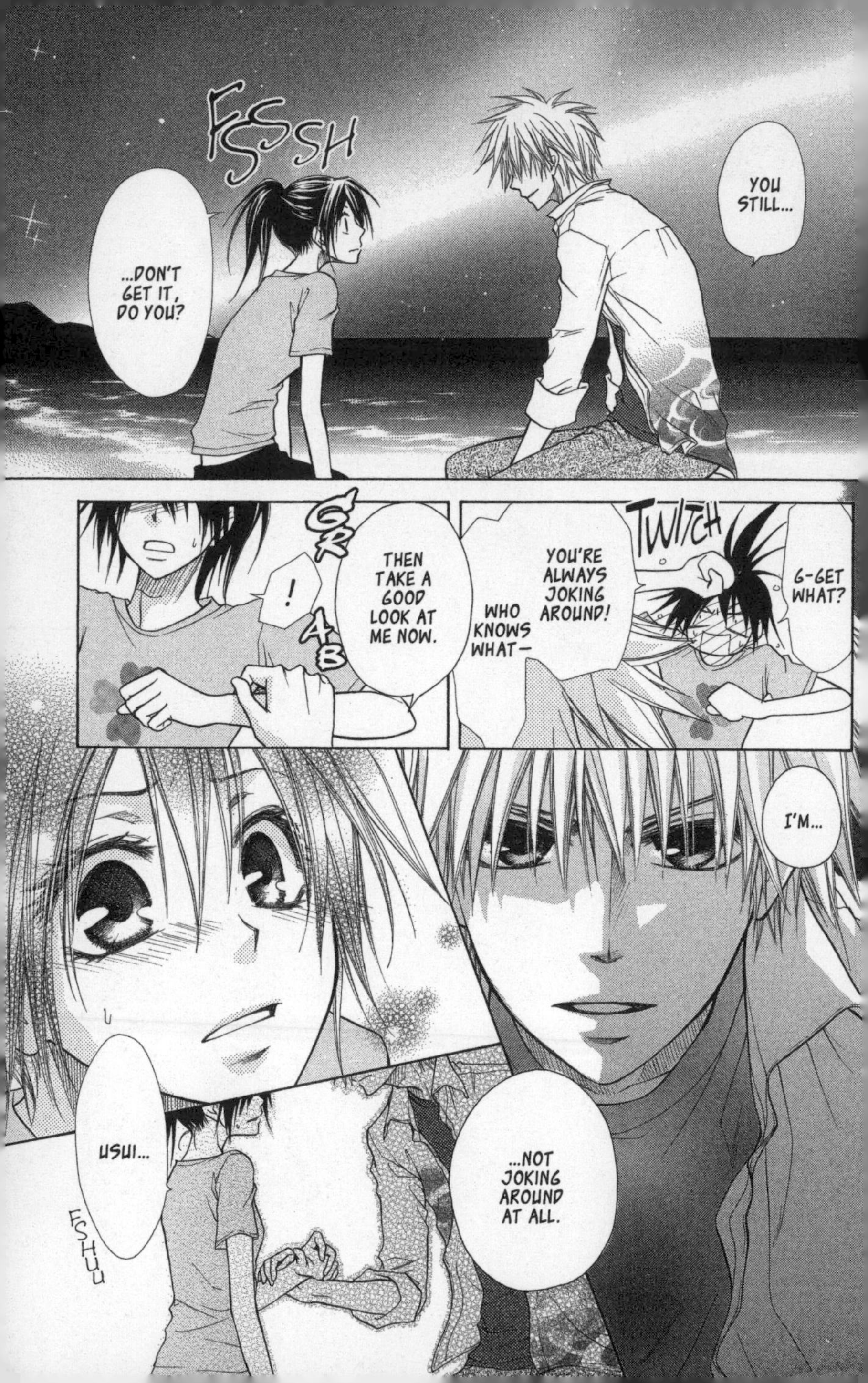
YOU STILL...
FSSSH
...DON'T GET IT, DO YOU?
G-GET WHAT?
TWITCH
YOU'RE ALWAYS JOKING AROUND!
WHO KNOWS WHAT—
GRAB
!
THEN TAKE A GOOD LOOK AT ME NOW.
I'M...
...NOT JOKING AROUND AT ALL.
USUI...
FSHUU

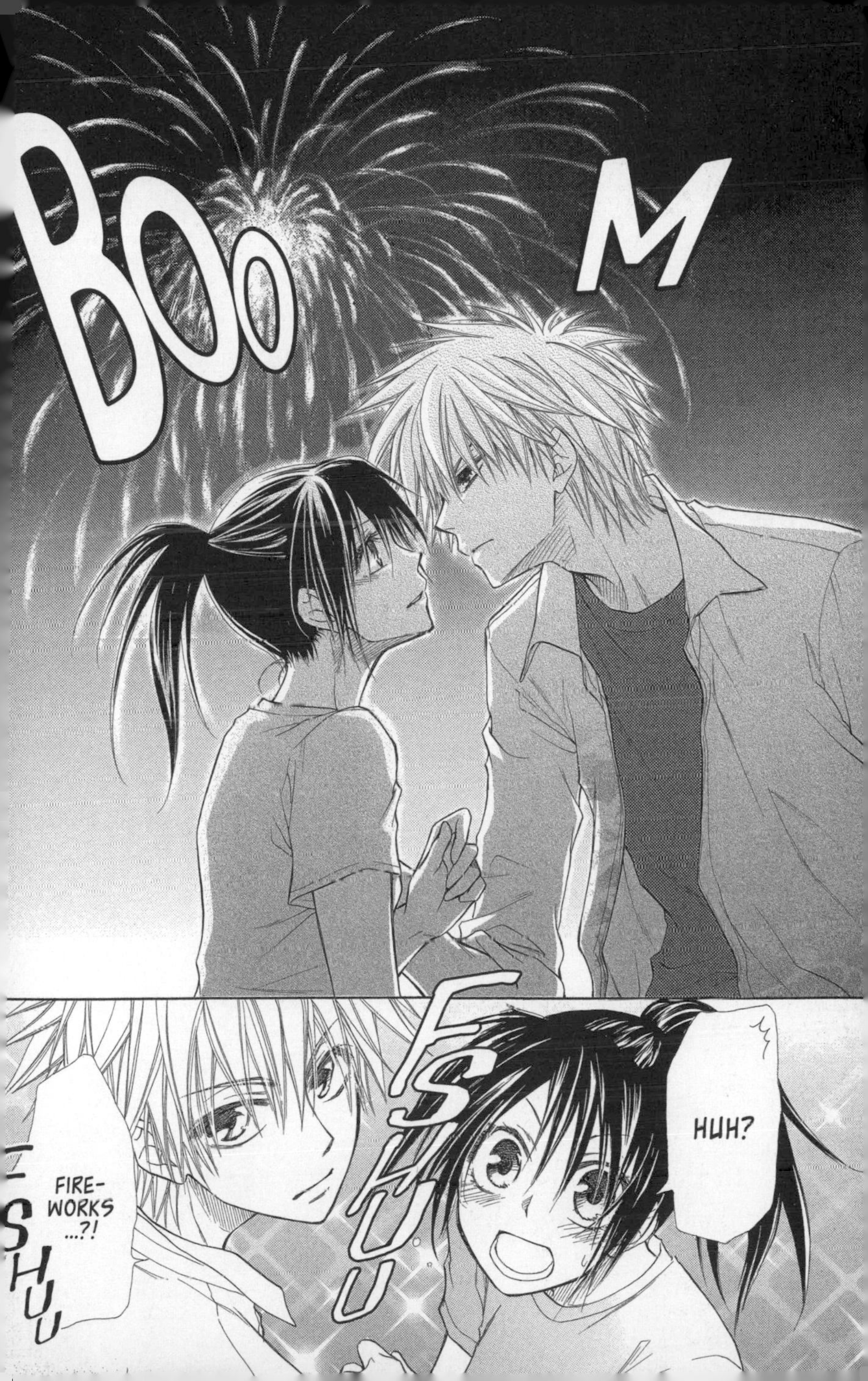
BOOM
HUH?
FSHUUU
FIRE-WORKS ...?!
SHUU

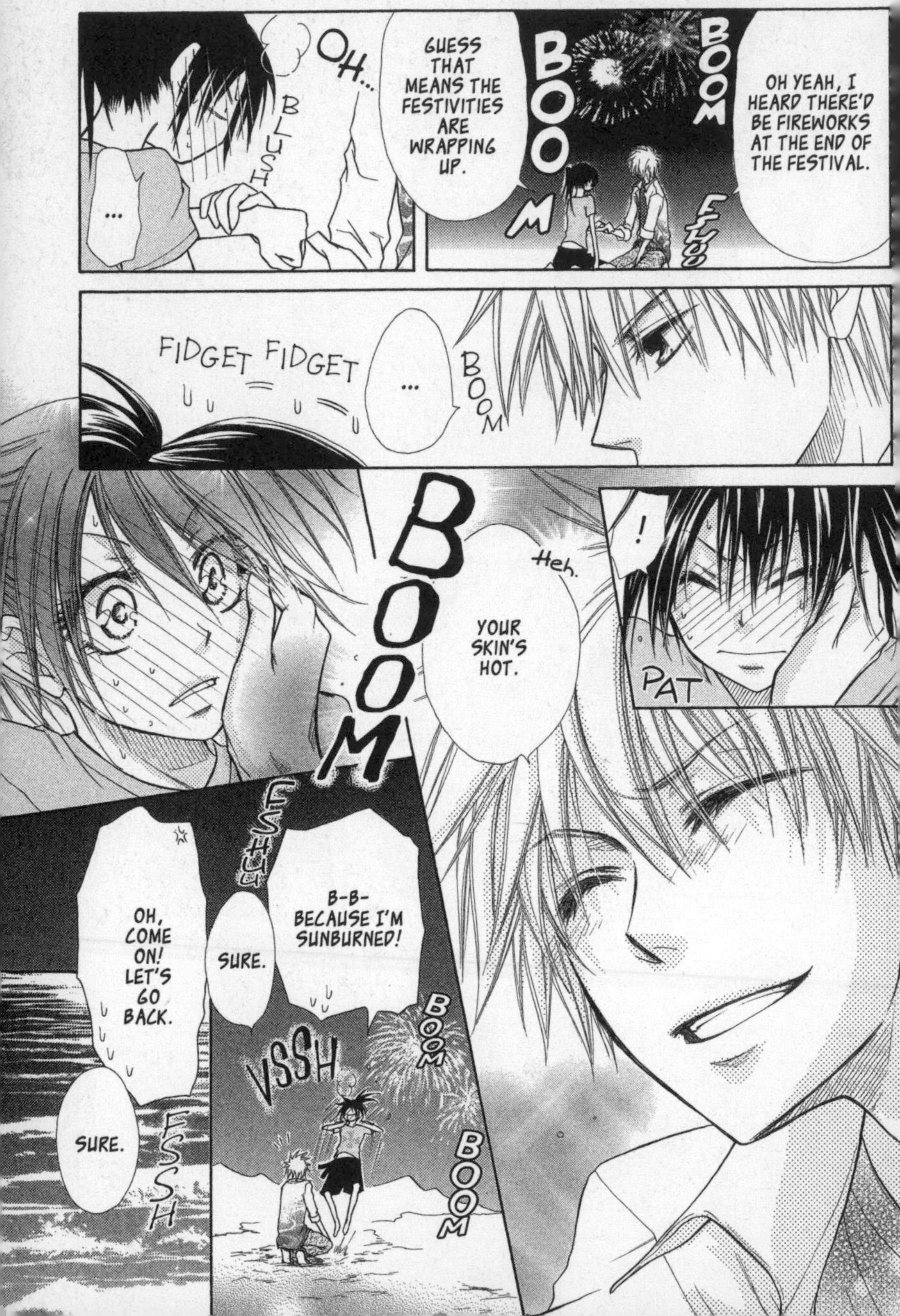
OH YEAH, I HEARD THERE'D BE FIREWORKS AT THE END OF THE FESTIVAL.
BOOM
BOOM
GUESS THAT MEANS THE FESTIVITIES ARE WRAPPING UP.
OH...
BLUSH
...
BOOM
...
FIDGET FIDGET
!
PAT
BOOM
Heh.
YOUR SKIN'S HOT.
B-B-BECAUSE I'M SUNBURNED!
SURE.
OH, COME ON! LET'S GO BACK.
SURE.
BOOM
VSSH
BOOM
FSSH

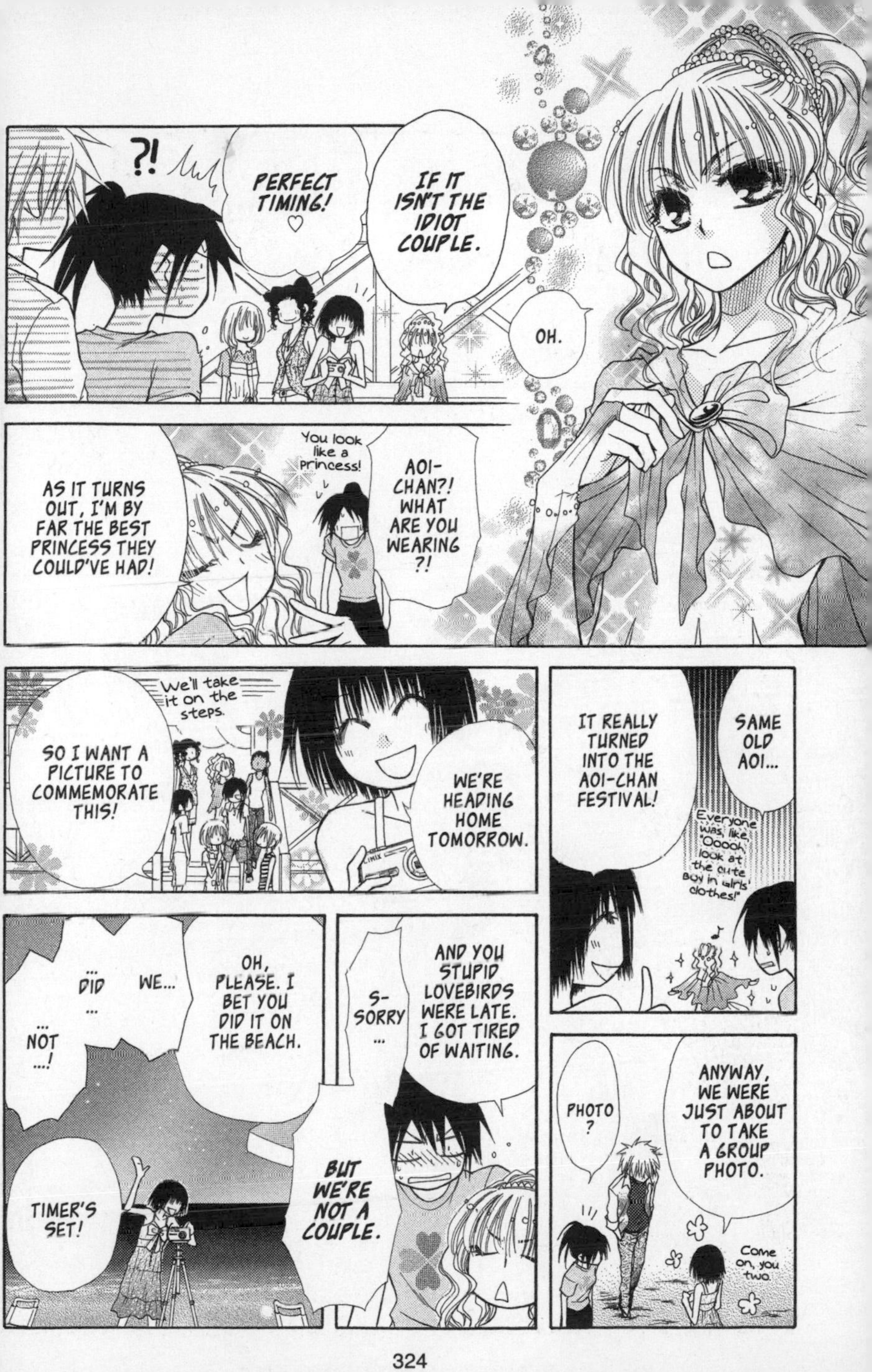
OH.
IF IT ISN'T THE IDIOT COUPLE.
PERFECT TIMING! ♡
?!
AOI-CHAN?! WHAT ARE YOU WEARING?!
You look like a princess!
AS IT TURNS OUT, I'M BY FAR THE BEST PRINCESS THEY COULD'VE HAD!
SAME OLD AOI...
IT REALLY TURNED INTO THE AOI-CHAN FESTIVAL!
Everyone was, like, "Ooooh, look at the cute boy in girls' clothes!"
ANYWAY, WE WERE JUST ABOUT TO TAKE A GROUP PHOTO.
PHOTO?
Come on, you two.
WE'RE HEADING HOME TOMORROW.
We'll take it on the steps.
SO I WANT A PICTURE TO COMMEMORATE THIS!
AND YOU STUPID LOVEBIRDS WERE LATE. I GOT TIRED OF WAITING.
S-SORRY...
BUT WE'RE NOT A COUPLE.
OH, PLEASE. I BET YOU DID IT ON THE BEACH.
WE...
...DID...
...NOT...!
TIMER'S SET!

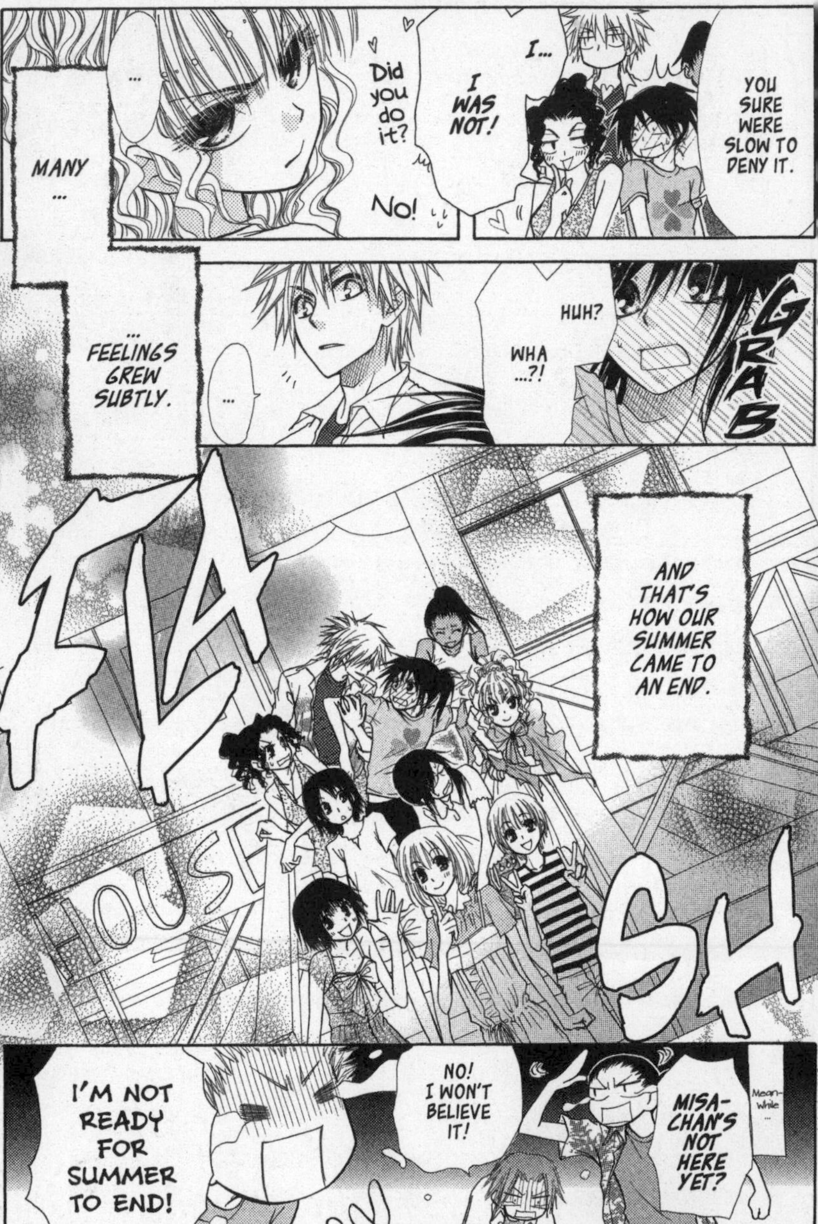
YOU SURE WERE SLOW TO DENY IT.
I... I WAS NOT!
Did you do it?
No!
...
MANY ...
GRAB
HUH?
WHA ...?!
...
... FEELINGS GREW SUBTLY.
AND THAT'S HOW OUR SUMMER CAME TO AN END.
FLA
SH
Mean-While ...
MISA-CHAN'S NOT HERE YET?
NO! I WON'T BELIEVE IT!
I'M NOT READY FOR SUMMER TO END!

MAID-SAMA! ④ / THE END

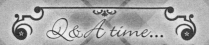

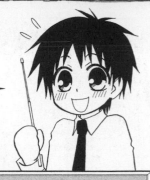

UM, HELLO! I'M SHOICHIRO YUKIMURA. SOMETIMES PEOPLE WRITE THE "YUKI" PART OF MY NAME USING THE KANJI CHARACTER FOR "SNOW," BUT IT'S ACTUALLY THE ONE FOR "HAPPY." SPEAKING OF WHICH, I'M HAPPY TO TRY TO ANSWER YOUR QUESTIONS!

 LET'S START WITH THIS LETTER.

QUESTION 16: "DO YOU THINK USUI'S HAIR IS GETTING THICKER? (IT'S FUNNY IF IT IS SINCE HIS NAME MEANS 'THIN'!)"

 ...!!! I...I HAVE TO ANSWER THIS? REALLY?

WELL, UH... LET'S SEE... I THINK IT MUST BE YOUR IMAGINATION, HONESTLY. I'M SURE IT IS. HA HA! WHAT WOULD GIVE YOU THAT IDEA?

 YEAH, 'CAUSE I'M WEARING A *WIG*.

 RIGHT! IT'S A WIG—HUH? USUI?

 YEAH, IT'S TOO MUCH HASSLE TO MAINTAIN.

 HUH? R-REALLY?

 HEY, USUI! STOP MAKING UP STORIES! YUKIMURA, DON'T BELIEVE EVERYTHING HE SAYS!

 HUH? OH, R-RIGHT! THANK GOODNESS.

 WERE YOU SERIOUSLY WORRIED ABOUT MY HAIR?

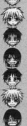 *JUST GO BALD OR SOMETHING!*

NEVER MIND HIM, YUKIMURA. JUST PRETEND HE'S NOT HERE, AND GO TO THE NEXT QUESTION.

WOW, ARE YOU GOING TO HELP ME ANSWER THEM, PRESIDENT? I FEEL A LOT BETTER NOW!

OKAY, ON TO THE NEXT QUESTION...

QUESTION 17: "WHICH DO YOU PREFER? AN UGLY BUT FUN PERSON OR A GOOD-LOOKING BUT BORING PERSON?"

 THAT'S...THE QUESTION...? UM...

 H-HEY, IS THIS QUESTION REALLY MEANT FOR US? IT DOESN'T SEEM APPROPRIATE.

 BEST WE CAN DO. IT'S PRETTY MUCH THE ONLY QUESTION LEFT THAT WE CAN PRINT.

 W-WHERE DO YOU GET THAT KIND OF INFORMATION?

Q&A time...

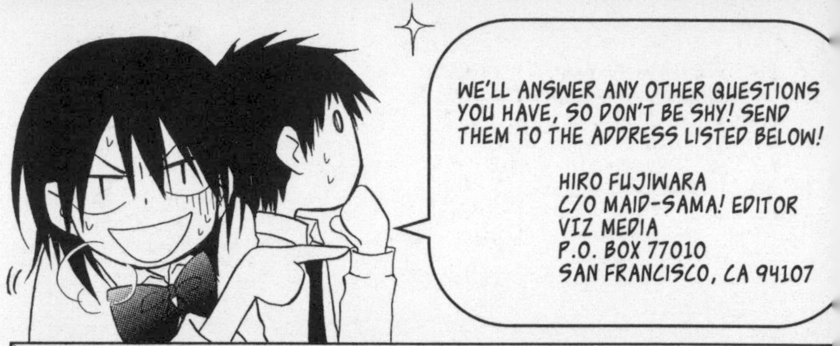
WE'LL ANSWER ANY OTHER QUESTIONS YOU HAVE, SO DON'T BE SHY! SEND THEM TO THE ADDRESS LISTED BELOW!
HIRO FUJIWARA
C/O MAID-SAMA! EDITOR
VIZ MEDIA
P.O. BOX 77010
SAN FRANCISCO, CA 94107

IF THAT'S TRUE, WE SHOULD'VE ANSWERED THE OTHER QUESTIONS MORE SERIOUSLY

YUKIMURA, HAVE YOU EVER HEARD THE SAYING "***IGNORANCE IS BLISS***"?

LIKE I SAID, WHO THE HECK ARE YOU? WAIT—OH, RIGHT. ***YOU'RE AN ALIEN.***

UM, WE'RE RUNNING OUT OF SPACE.

YOU'RE RIGHT. LET'S TAKE A STAB AT THAT QUESTION. UM...UGLY BUT FUN OR GOOD-LOOKING BUT BORING... HMM... THAT'S A TOUGH CALL.

I VOTE FOR CUTE AND FUN.

TH-THAT'S NOT ONE OF THE OPTIONS...

SOMEONE LIKE ***YOU***, YUKIMURA.

STOP IT, YOU PERVERT!

P-PRESIDENT...

BE STRONG, YUKIMURA! IGNORE USUI.

BUT NO ONE'S AS CUTE AND FUN AS YOU, PREZ. ♥

UGH! JUST GO BACK TO PLANET PHEROMONE!

OH, WE'RE ALMOST OUT OF ROOM.

THANKS TO THAT ALIEN, IT WASN'T MUCH OF A SEGMENT...

I-IS USUI OKAY? HE SURE WENT FLYING...

HE'S FINE. I'M SURE HE LANDED SAFELY BACK ON HIS WEIRDO PLANET.

O-OKAY...

ALL RIGHT, THEN! THAT FINISHES OUR QUESTION AND ANSWER SEGMENT. MAYBE WE'LL HAVE ANOTHER CHANCE TO ANSWER SOME QUESTIONS. ***BUT NEXT TIME WITHOU USUI, OKAY?***

SO PLEASE KEEP SENDING IN YOUR QUESTIONS!

YUP. DON'T BE SHY! ASK US ANYTHING YOU WANT.

WE LOOK FORWARD TO YOUR LETTERS!

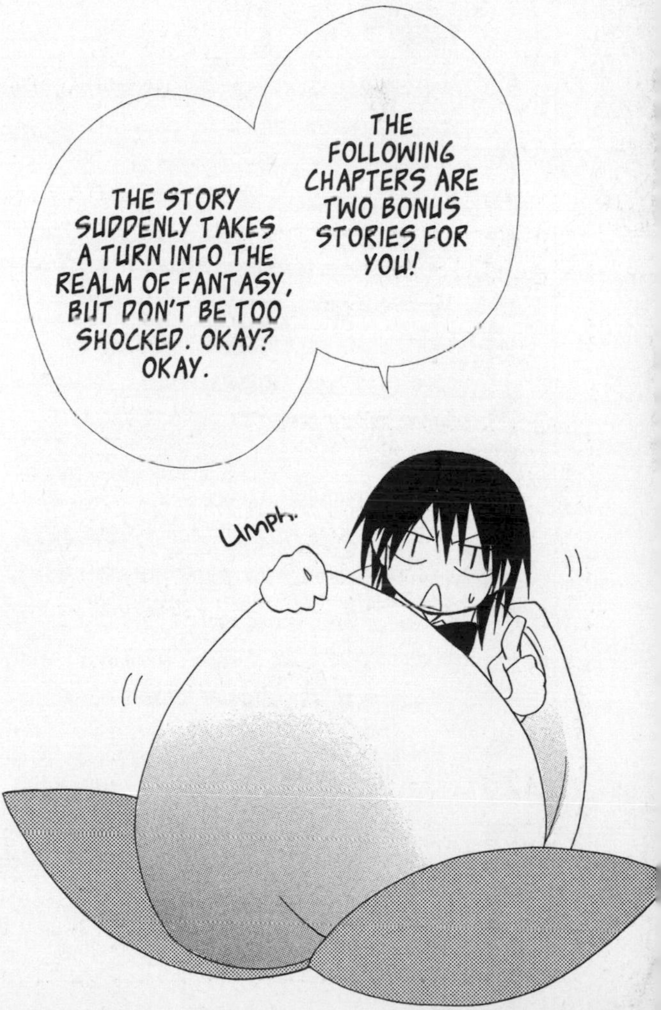
THE FOLLOWING CHAPTERS ARE TWO BONUS STORIES FOR YOU!
THE STORY SUDDENLY TAKES A TURN INTO THE REALM OF FANTASY, BUT DON'T BE TOO SHOCKED. OKAY? OKAY.
Umph.

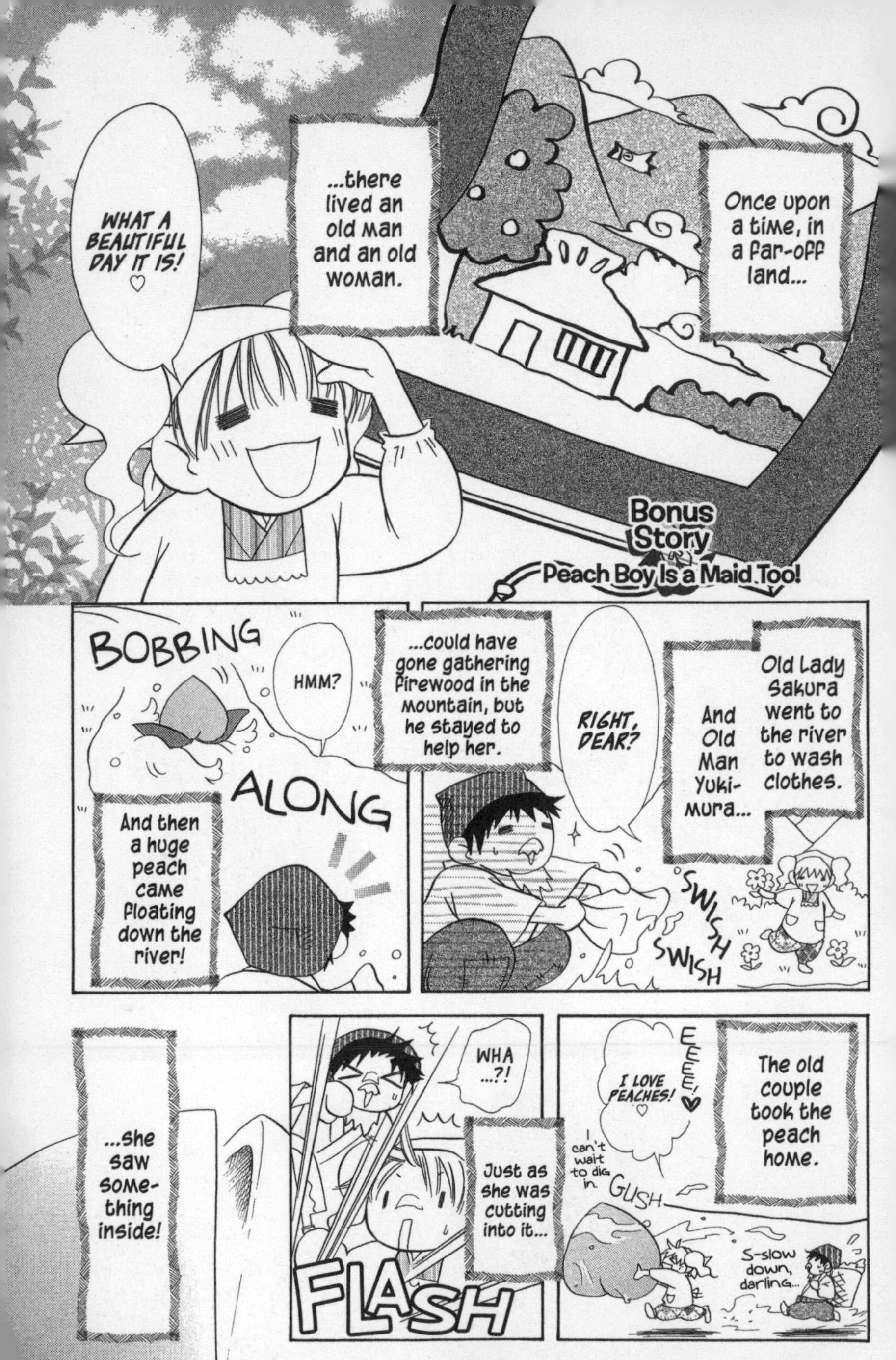
Once upon a time, in a far-off land...
...there lived an old man and an old woman.
WHAT A BEAUTIFUL DAY IT IS! ♡
Bonus Story
Peach Boy Is a Maid Too!
Old Lady Sakura went to the river to wash clothes.
And Old Man Yuki-mura...
...could have gone gathering firewood in the mountain, but he stayed to help her.
RIGHT, DEAR?
SWISH SWISH
HMM?
BOBBING ALONG
And then a huge peach came floating down the river!
The old couple took the peach home.
EEEE! ♥
I LOVE PEACHES! ♡
I can't wait to dig in.
GUSH
S-slow down, darling...
WHA ...?!
Just as she was cutting into it...
FLASH
...she saw some-thing inside!

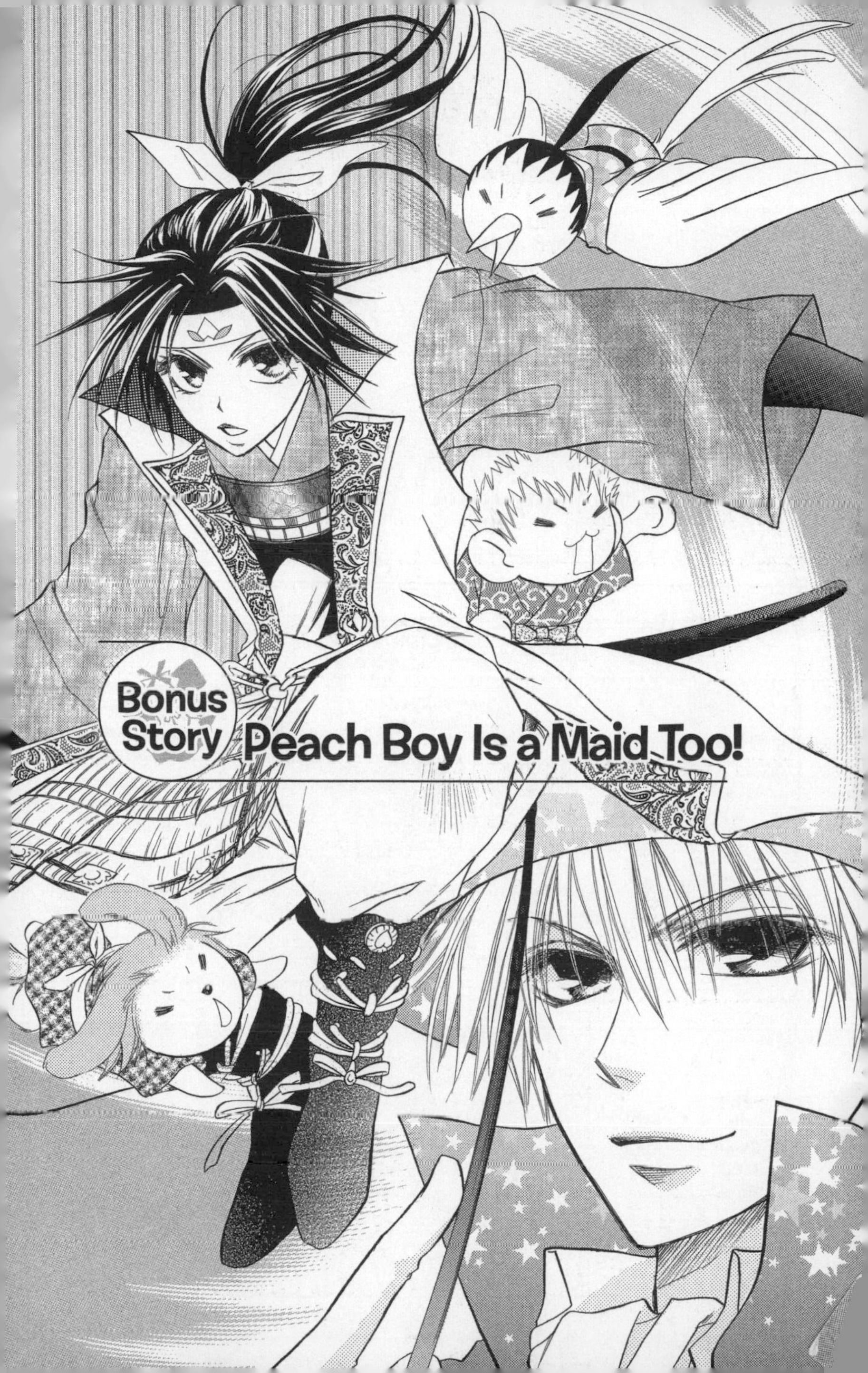
Bonus Story
Peach Boy Is a Maid Too!

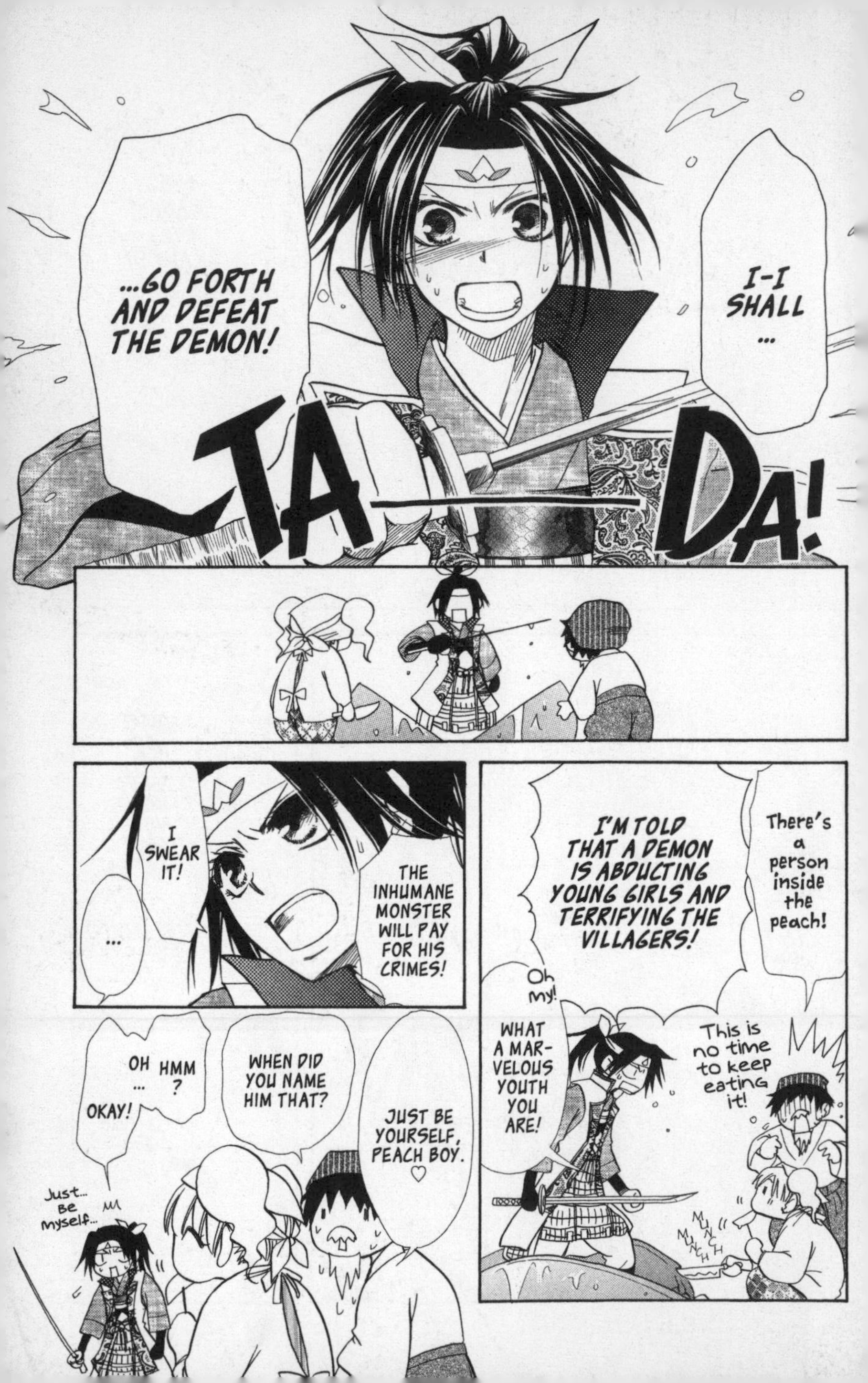
I-I SHALL ...
...GO FORTH AND DEFEAT THE DEMON!
TA—DA!
There's a person inside the peach!
I'M TOLD THAT A DEMON IS ABDUCTING YOUNG GIRLS AND TERRIFYING THE VILLAGERS!
Oh my!
WHAT A MAR-VELOUS YOUTH YOU ARE!
This is no time to keep eating it!
MUNCH MUNCH
THE INHUMANE MONSTER WILL PAY FOR HIS CRIMES!
I SWEAR IT!
...
JUST BE YOURSELF, PEACH BOY.
WHEN DID YOU NAME HIM THAT?
HMM?
OH ... OKAY!
Just... be myself...

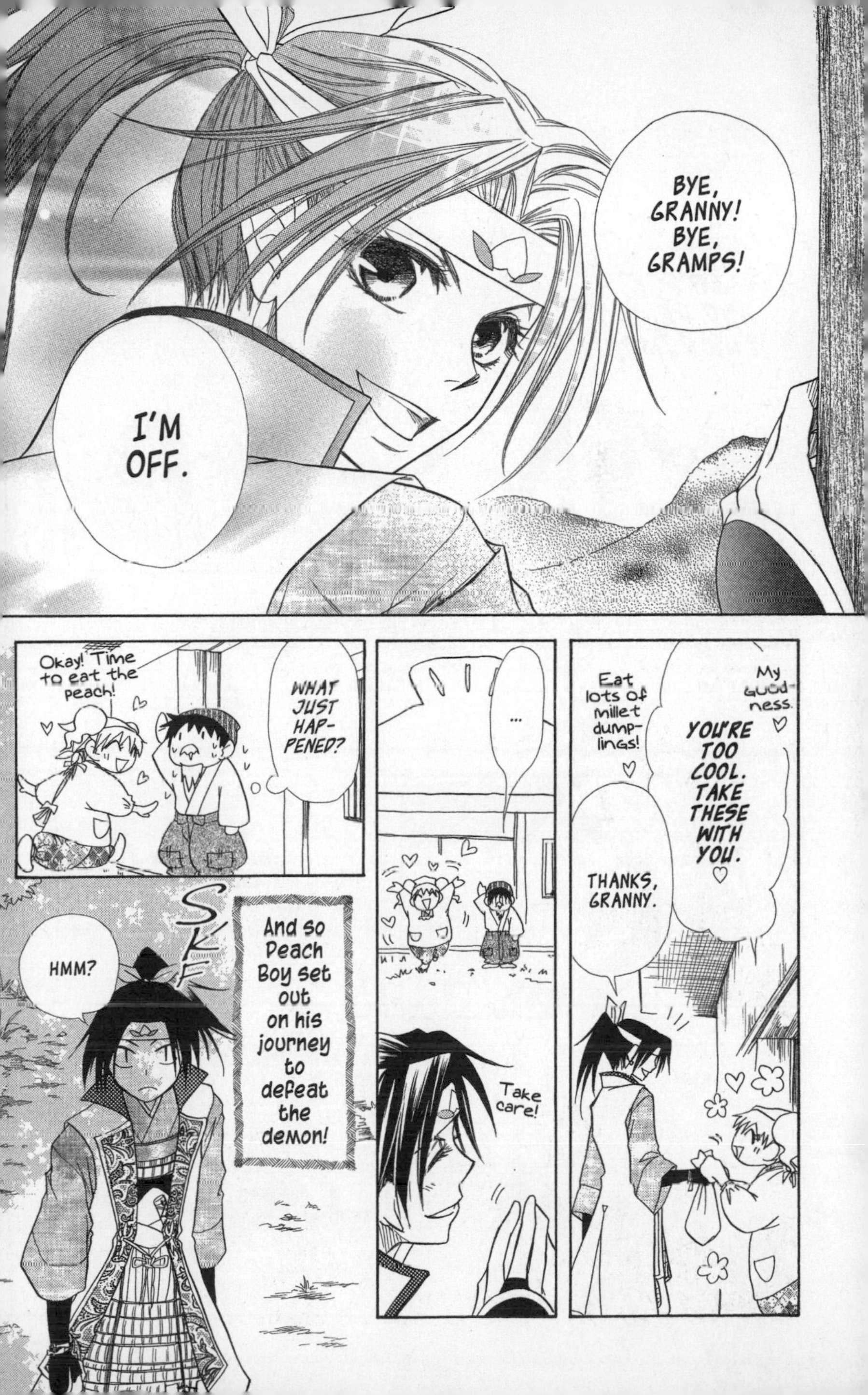
BYE, GRANNY! BYE, GRAMPS!
I'M OFF.
My goodness.
YOU'RE TOO COOL. TAKE THESE WITH YOU.
Eat lots of millet dumplings!
THANKS, GRANNY.
...
Take care!
WHAT JUST HAPPENED?
Okay! Time to eat the peach!
And so Peach Boy set out on his journey to defeat the demon!
SKF
HMM?

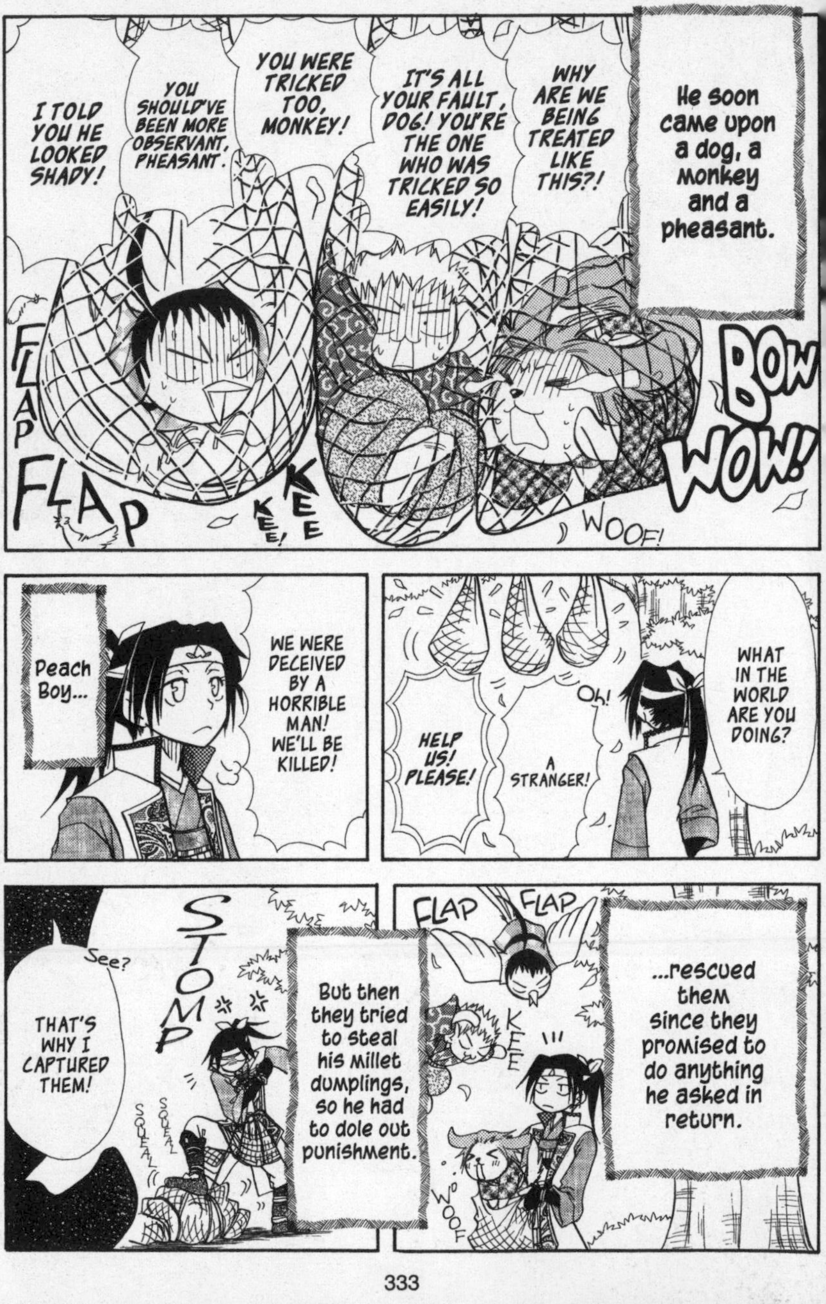
He soon came upon a dog, a monkey and a pheasant.
BOW WOW!
WHY ARE WE BEING TREATED LIKE THIS?!
IT'S ALL YOUR FAULT, DOG! YOU'RE THE ONE WHO WAS TRICKED SO EASILY!
YOU WERE TRICKED TOO, MONKEY!
YOU SHOULD'VE BEEN MORE OBSERVANT, PHEASANT.
I TOLD YOU HE LOOKED SHADY!
WOOF!
KEE KEE!
FLAP FLAP
WHAT IN THE WORLD ARE YOU DOING?
Oh!
A STRANGER!
HELP US! PLEASE!
WE WERE DECEIVED BY A HORRIBLE MAN! WE'LL BE KILLED!
Peach Boy...
...rescued them since they promised to do anything he asked in return.
FLAP FLAP
KEE
WOOF
But then they tried to steal his millet dumplings, so he had to dole out punishment.
STOMP
See?
THAT'S WHY I CAPTURED THEM!
SQUEAL SQUEAL

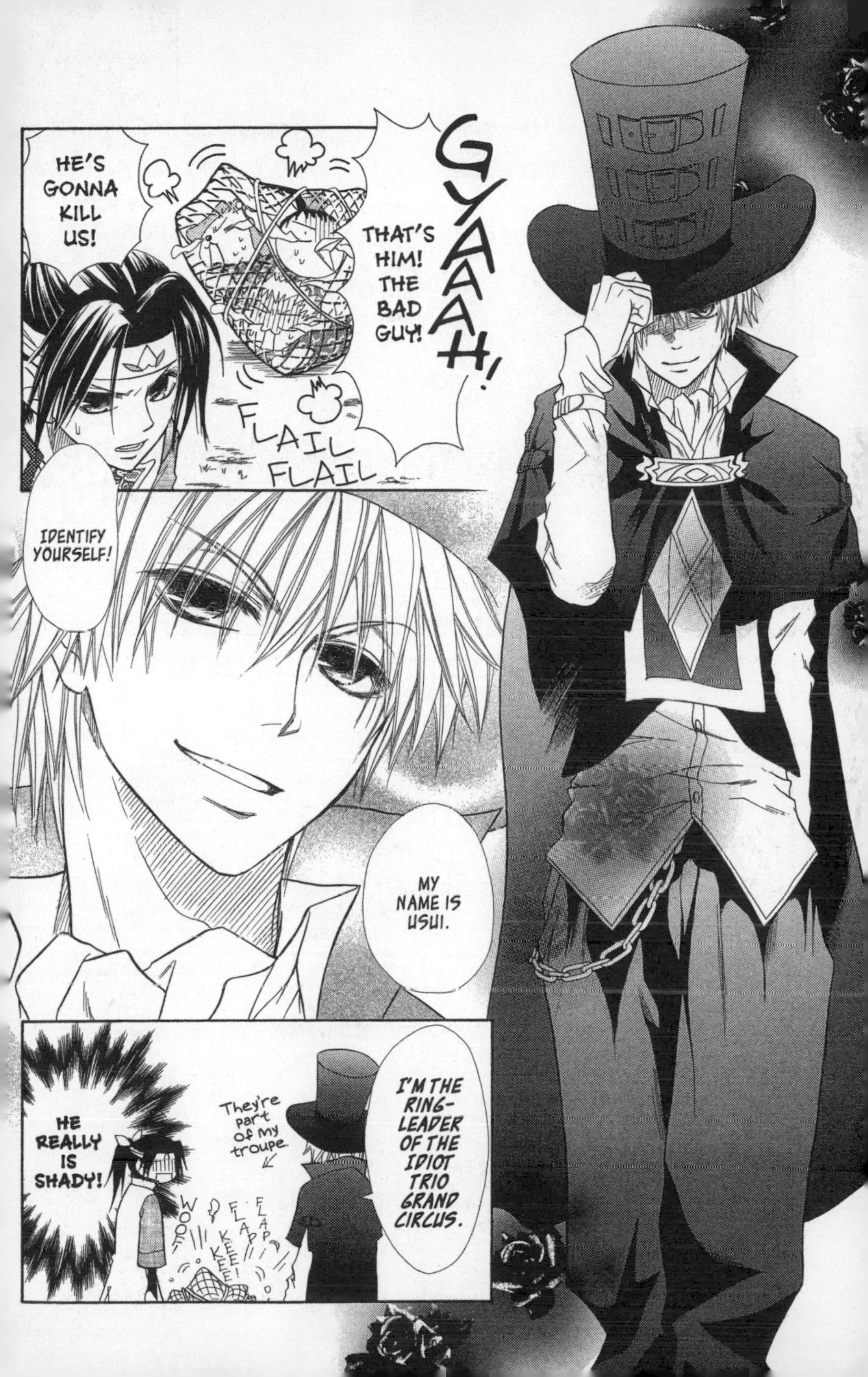
GYAAAH!
THAT'S HIM! THE BAD GUY!
HE'S GONNA KILL US!
FLAIL FLAIL
IDENTIFY YOURSELF!
MY NAME IS USUI.
I'M THE RING-LEADER OF THE IDIOT TRIO GRAND CIRCUS.
They're part of my troupe.
FLAP FLAP
KEE KEE!
WOOF!
HE REALLY IS SHADY!

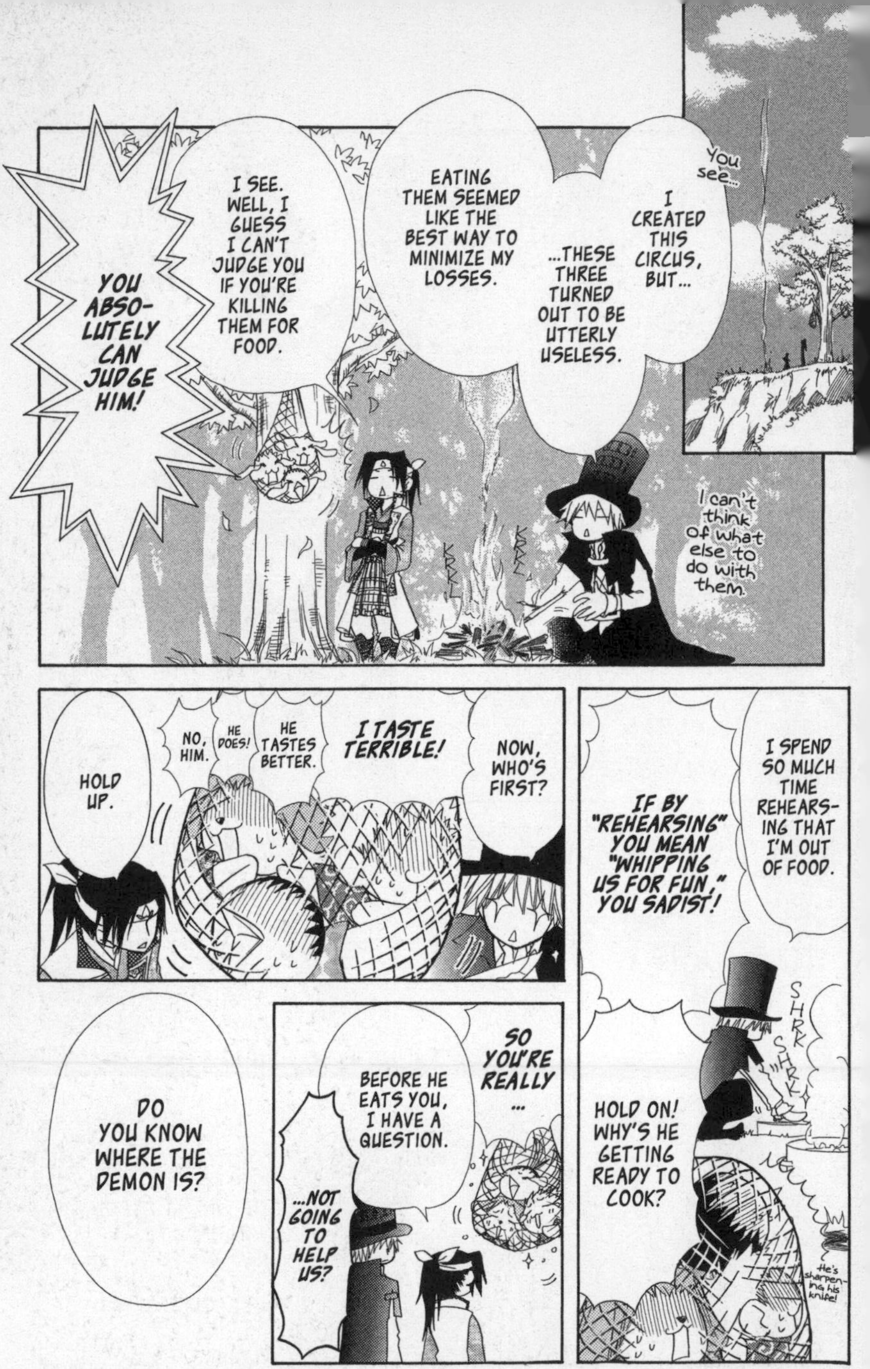
You see...
I CREATED THIS CIRCUS, BUT...
...THESE THREE TURNED OUT TO BE UTTERLY USELESS.
EATING THEM SEEMED LIKE THE BEST WAY TO MINIMIZE MY LOSSES.
I can't think of what else to do with them.
KRKL
KRKL
I SEE. WELL, I GUESS I CAN'T JUDGE YOU IF YOU'RE KILLING THEM FOR FOOD.
YOU ABSOLUTELY CAN JUDGE HIM!
I SPEND SO MUCH TIME REHEARSING THAT I'M OUT OF FOOD.
IF BY "REHEARSING" YOU MEAN "WHIPPING US FOR FUN," YOU SADIST!
SHRK
SHRK
HOLD ON! WHY'S HE GETTING READY TO COOK?
He's sharpening his knife!
NOW, WHO'S FIRST?
I TASTE TERRIBLE!
HE TASTES BETTER.
HE DOES!
NO, HIM.
HOLD UP.
SO YOU'RE REALLY ...
BEFORE HE EATS YOU, I HAVE A QUESTION.
...NOT GOING TO HELP US?
DO YOU KNOW WHERE THE DEMON IS?

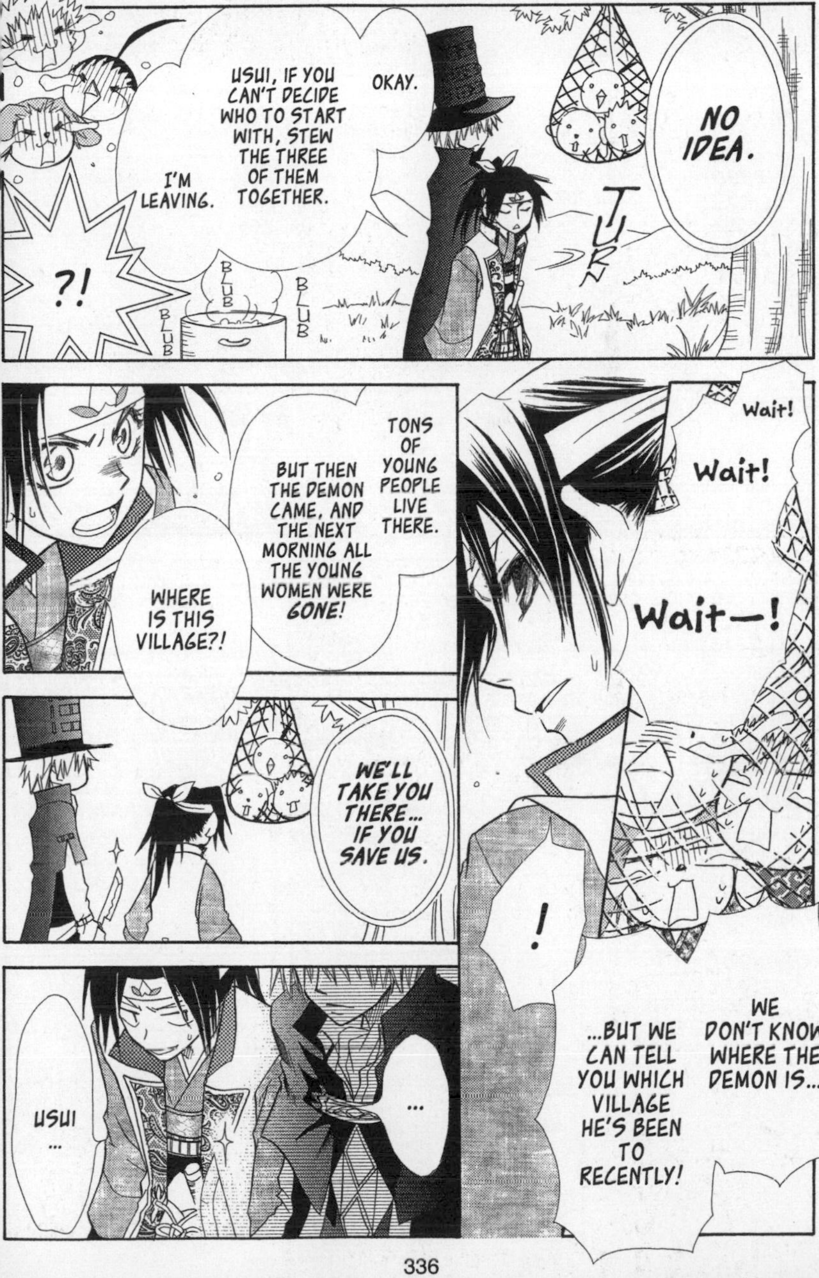
NO IDEA.
TURN
OKAY.
USUI, IF YOU CAN'T DECIDE WHO TO START WITH, STEW THE THREE OF THEM TOGETHER.
I'M LEAVING.
?!
BLUB BLUB
BLUB
BLUB
Wait!
Wait!
Wait—!
!
WE DON'T KNOW WHERE THE DEMON IS...
...BUT WE CAN TELL YOU WHICH VILLAGE HE'S BEEN TO RECENTLY!
TONS OF YOUNG PEOPLE LIVE THERE.
BUT THEN THE DEMON CAME, AND THE NEXT MORNING ALL THE YOUNG WOMEN WERE GONE!
WHERE IS THIS VILLAGE?!
WE'LL TAKE YOU THERE... IF YOU SAVE US.
...
USUI ...

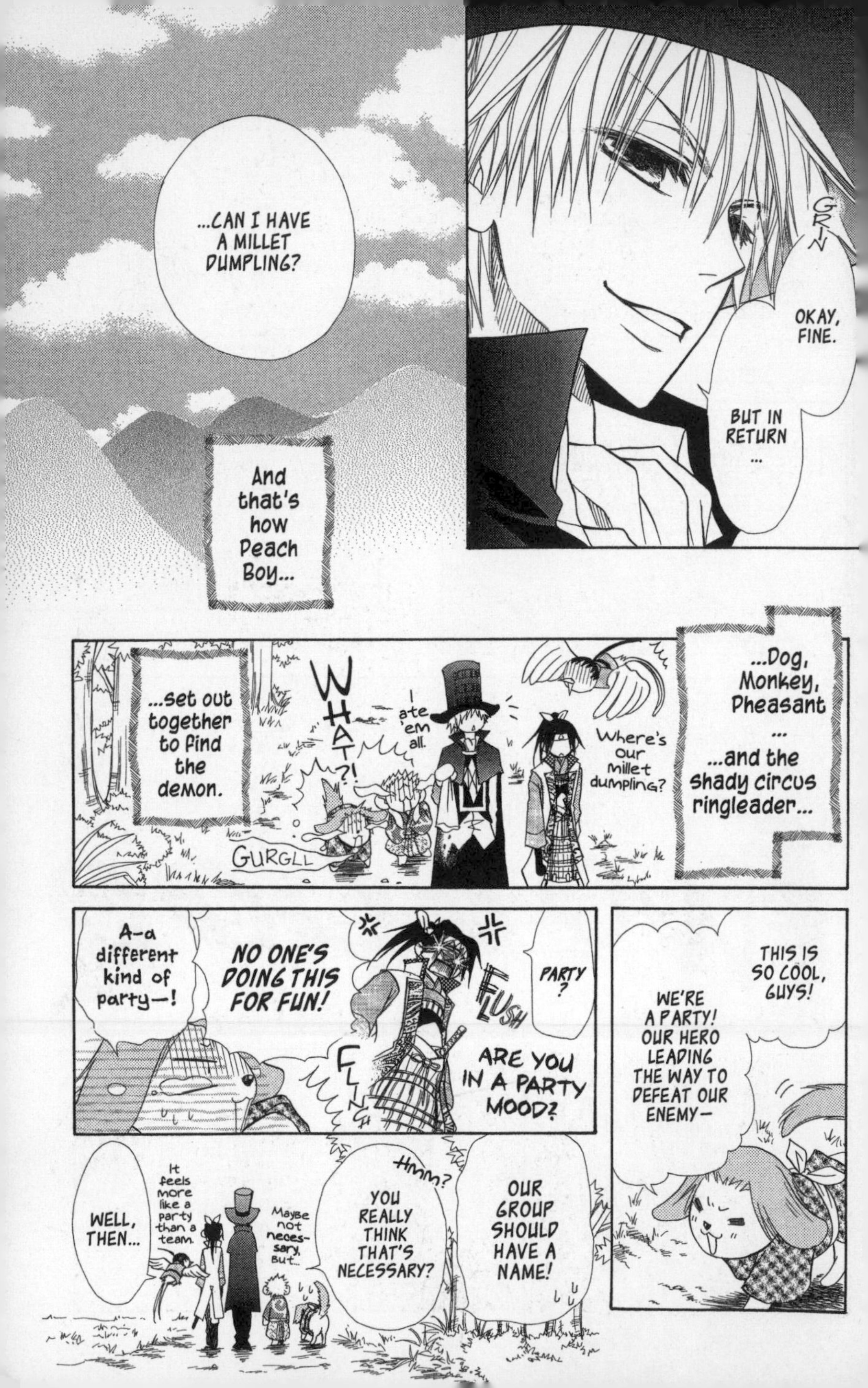
GRIN
OKAY, FINE.
BUT IN RETURN ...
...CAN I HAVE A MILLET DUMPLING?
And that's how Peach Boy...
...Dog, Monkey, Pheasant ...
...and the shady circus ringleader...
Where's our millet dumpling?
I ate 'em all.
WHAT?!
GURGLL
...set out together to find the demon.
THIS IS SO COOL, GUYS!
WE'RE A PARTY! OUR HERO LEADING THE WAY TO DEFEAT OUR ENEMY—
PARTY?
ARE YOU IN A PARTY MOOD?
FLUSH
NO ONE'S DOING THIS FOR FUN!
FLING
A-a different kind of party—!
OUR GROUP SHOULD HAVE A NAME!
Hmm?
YOU REALLY THINK THAT'S NECESSARY?
Maybe not neces-sary, but...
It feels more like a party than a team.
WELL, THEN...

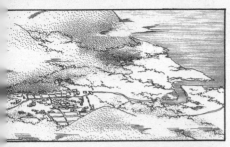

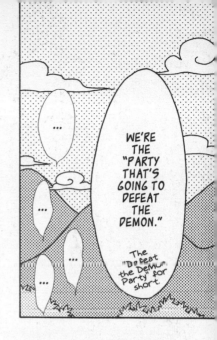

... ...

WE'RE THE "PARTY THAT'S GOING TO DEFEAT THE DEMON."

The "Defeat the Demon Party" for short.

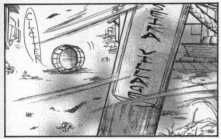

CLATTER

YULARA VILLAGE

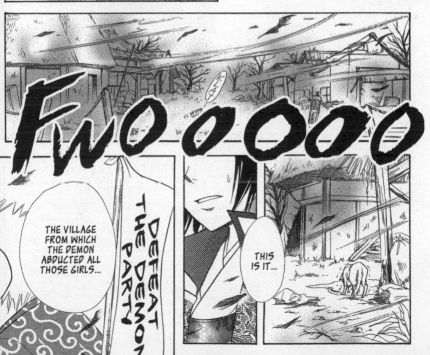

FWOOOOO

THE VILLAGE FROM WHICH THE DEMON ABDUCTED ALL THOSE GIRLS...

DEFEAT THE DEMON PARTY

THIS IS IT...

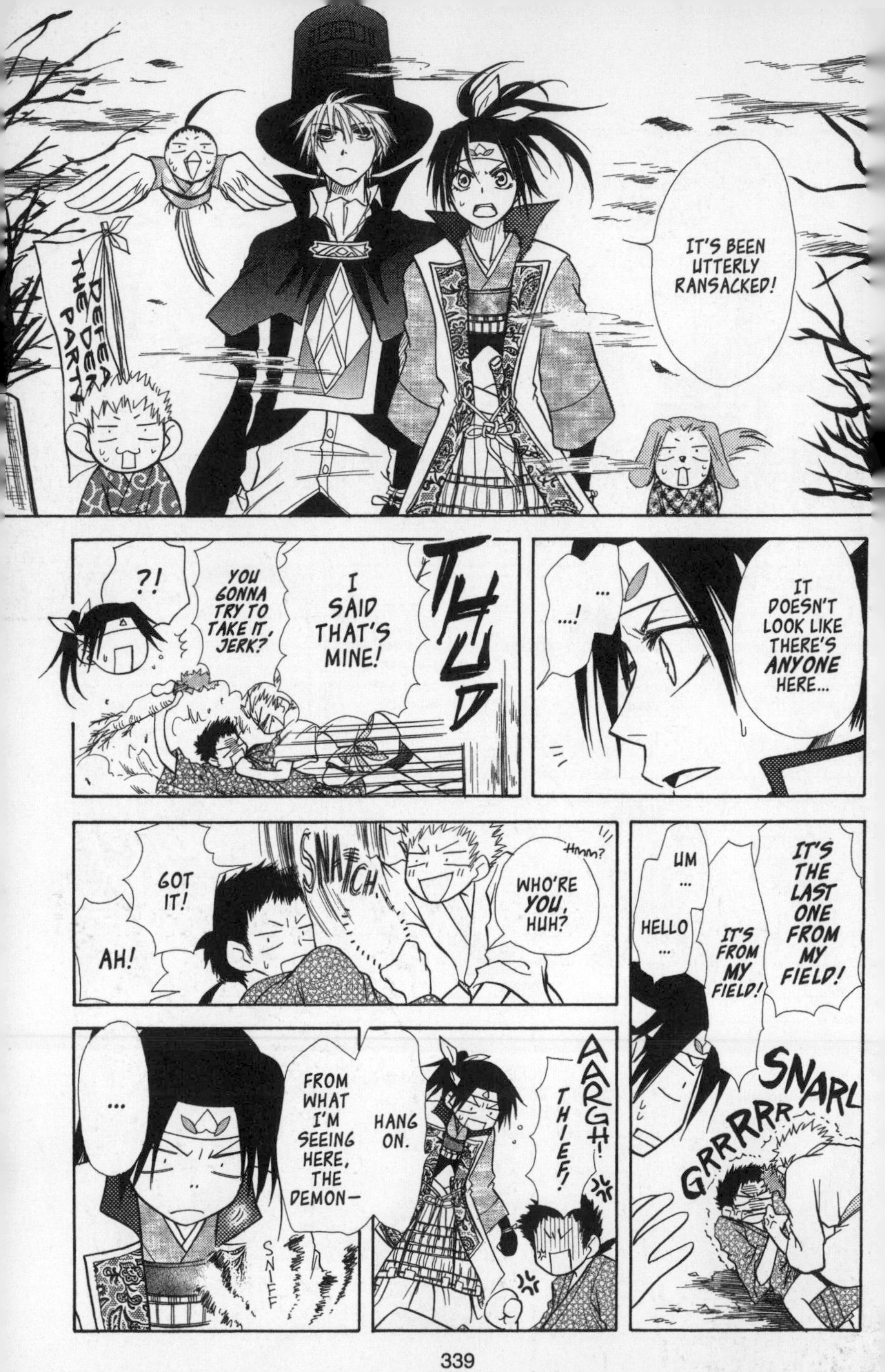
IT'S BEEN UTTERLY RANSACKED!
IT DOESN'T LOOK LIKE THERE'S ANYONE HERE...
... ...!
THUD
I SAID THAT'S MINE!
YOU GONNA TRY TO TAKE IT, JERK?
?!
IT'S THE LAST ONE FROM MY FIELD!
IT'S FROM MY FIELD!
UM ... HELLO ...
SNARL
GRRRRR
Hmm?
WHO'RE YOU, HUH?
SNATCH
GOT IT!
AH!
AARGH! THIEF!
HANG ON.
FROM WHAT I'M SEEING HERE, THE DEMON—
...
SNIFF

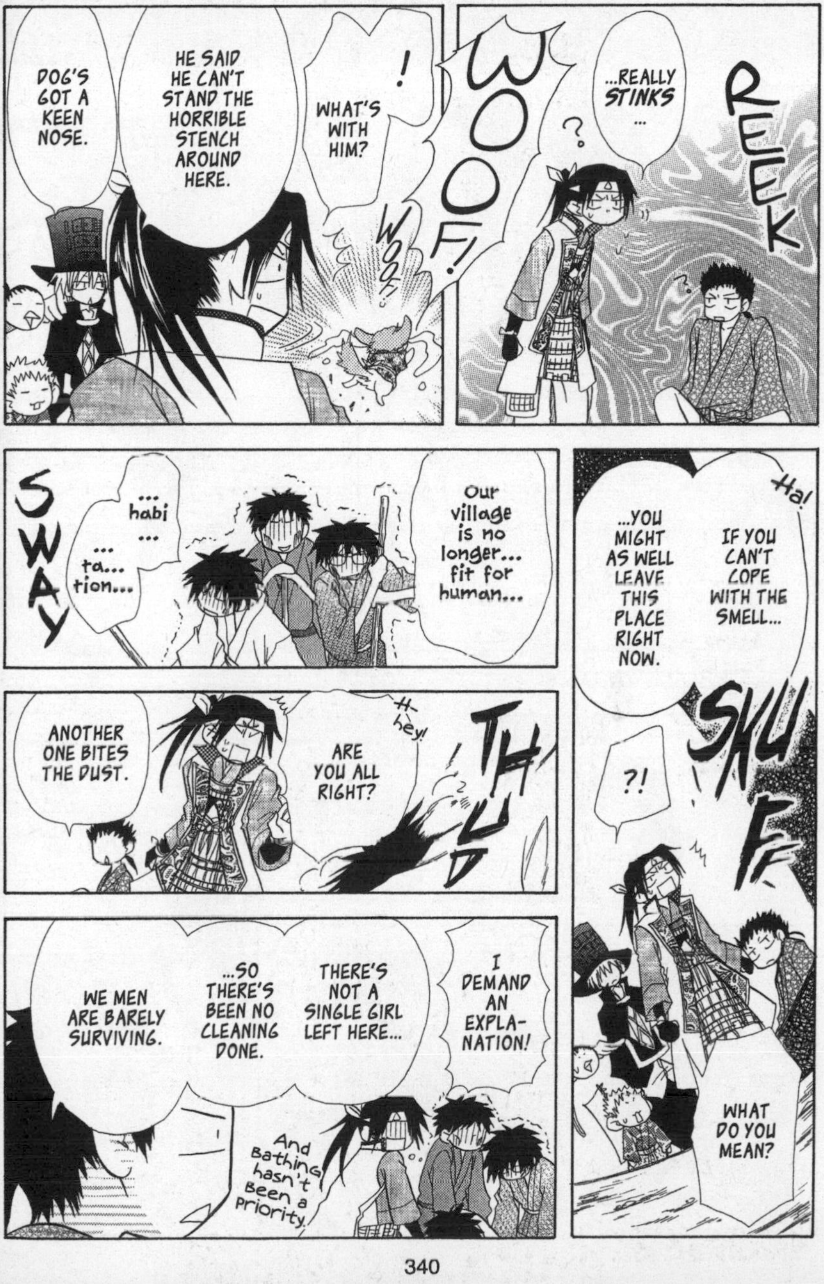
REEK
...REALLY STINKS...
?
WOOF!
WOOF!
!
WHAT'S WITH HIM?
HE SAID HE CAN'T STAND THE HORRIBLE STENCH AROUND HERE.
DOG'S GOT A KEEN NOSE.
Ha!
IF YOU CAN'T COPE WITH THE SMELL...
...YOU MIGHT AS WELL LEAVE THIS PLACE RIGHT NOW.
SKUFF
?!
WHAT DO YOU MEAN?
Our village is no longer... fit for human...
...habi...
...ta... tion...
SWAY
THUD
hey!
ARE YOU ALL RIGHT?
ANOTHER ONE BITES THE DUST.
I DEMAND AN EXPLANATION!
THERE'S NOT A SINGLE GIRL LEFT HERE...
...SO THERE'S BEEN NO CLEANING DONE.
WE MEN ARE BARELY SURVIVING.
And Bathing hasn't Been a priority.

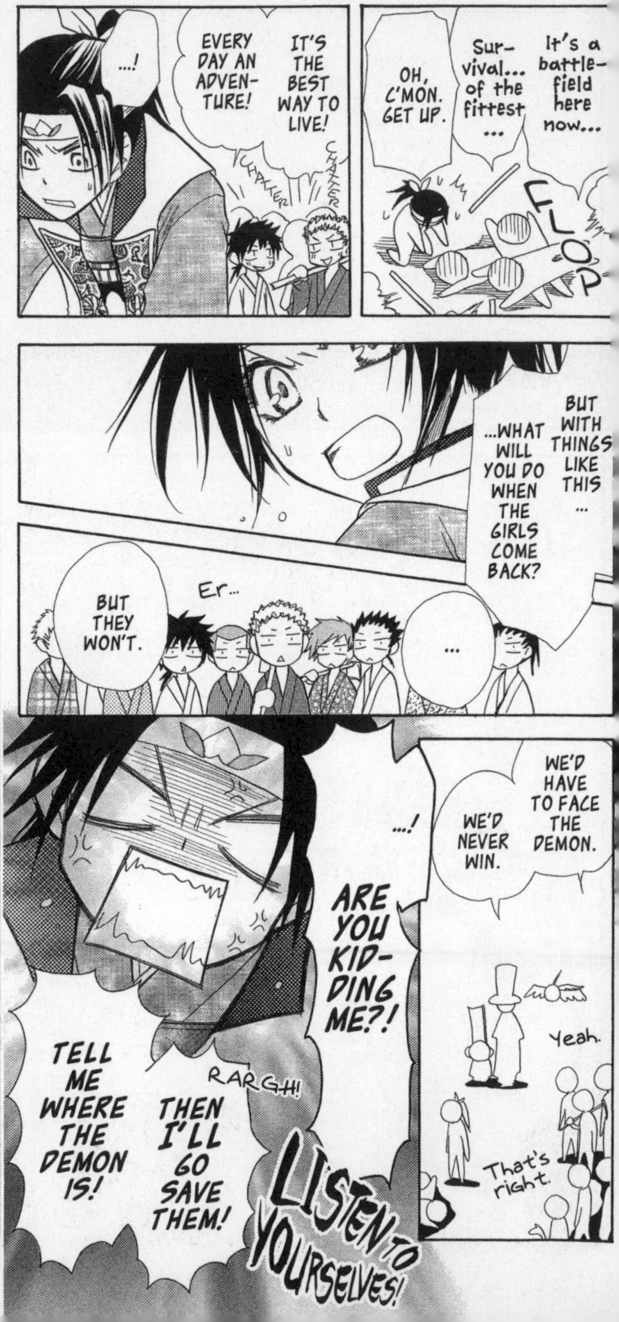
It's a battlefield here now...
Survival... of the fittest...
OH, C'MON. GET UP.
FLOP
IT'S THE BEST WAY TO LIVE!
EVERY DAY AN ADVENTURE!
...!
CHATTER
CHATTER
BUT WITH THINGS LIKE THIS...
...WHAT WILL YOU DO WHEN THE GIRLS COME BACK?
...
Er...
BUT THEY WON'T.
WE'D HAVE TO FACE THE DEMON.
WE'D NEVER WIN.
...!
Yeah.
That's right.
ARE YOU KIDDING ME?!
RARGH!
THEN I'LL GO SAVE THEM!
TELL ME WHERE THE DEMON IS!
LISTEN TO YOURSELVES!

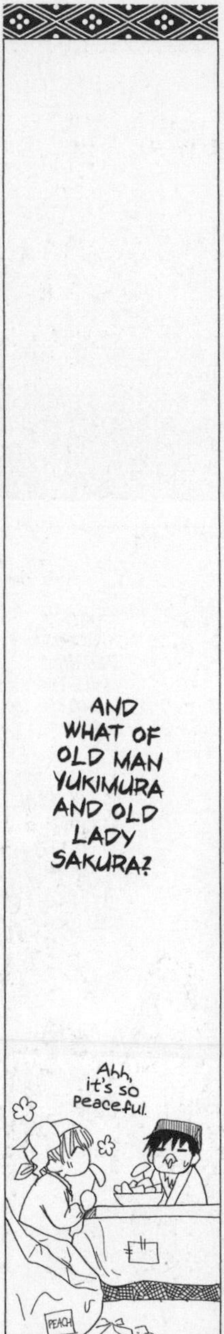
AND WHAT OF OLD MAN YUKIMURA AND OLD LADY SAKURA?
Ahh, it's so peaceful.
PEACH

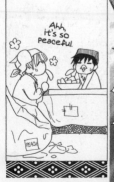

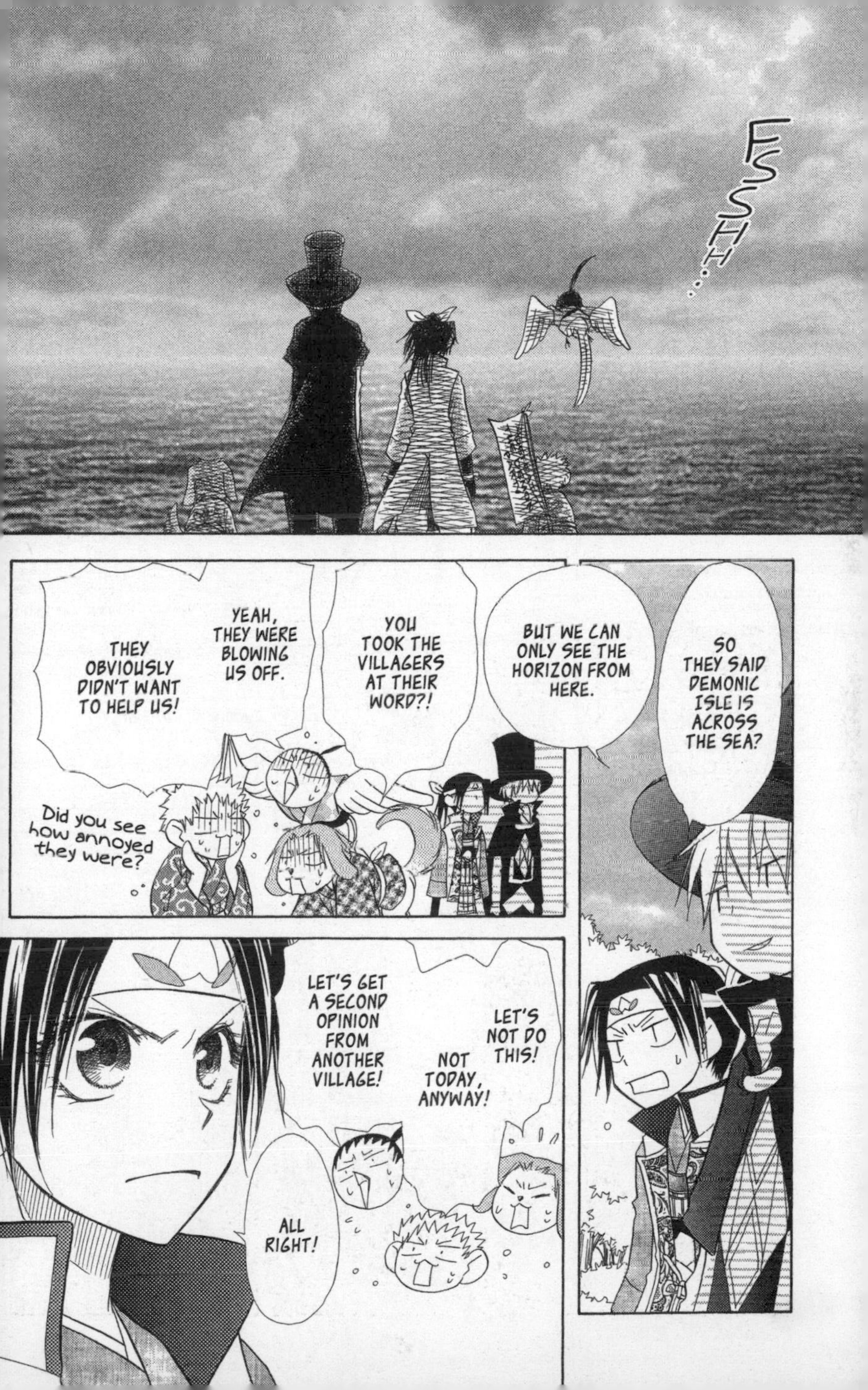

FSSHH...
SO THEY SAID DEMONIC ISLE IS ACROSS THE SEA?
BUT WE CAN ONLY SEE THE HORIZON FROM HERE.
YOU TOOK THE VILLAGERS AT THEIR WORD?!
YEAH, THEY WERE BLOWING US OFF.
THEY OBVIOUSLY DIDN'T WANT TO HELP US!
Did you see how annoyed they were?
LET'S GET A SECOND OPINION FROM ANOTHER VILLAGE!
LET'S NOT DO THIS!
NOT TODAY, ANYWAY!
ALL RIGHT!

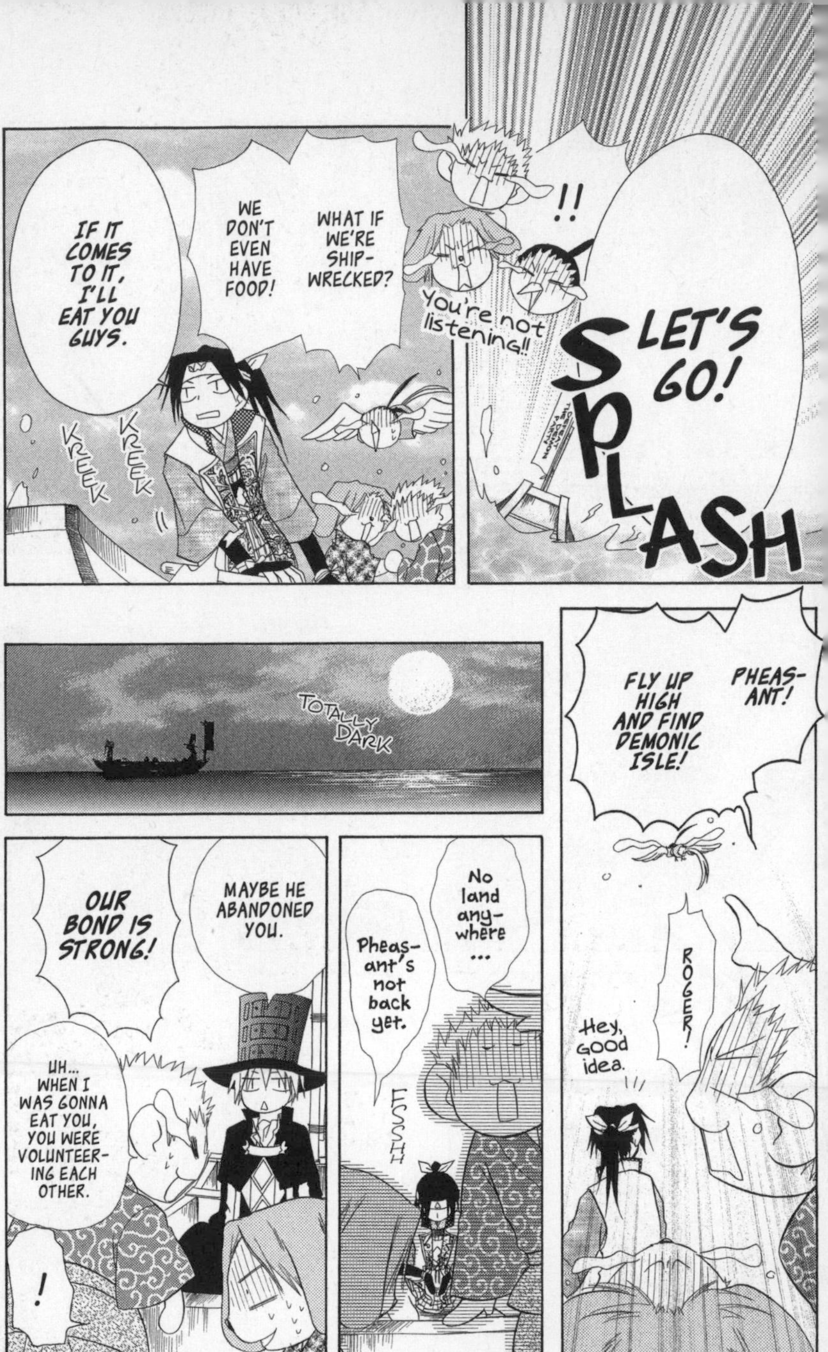
LET'S GO!
SPLASH
!!
You're not listening!!
WHAT IF WE'RE SHIP-WRECKED?
WE DON'T EVEN HAVE FOOD!
IF IT COMES TO IT, I'LL EAT YOU GUYS.
KREEK KREEK
PHEAS-ANT!
FLY UP HIGH AND FIND DEMONIC ISLE!
ROGER!
Hey, good idea.
TOTALLY DARK
No land any-where...
Pheas-ant's not back yet.
FSSSH
MAYBE HE ABANDONED YOU.
OUR BOND IS STRONG!
UH... WHEN I WAS GONNA EAT YOU, YOU WERE VOLUNTEER-ING EACH OTHER.
!

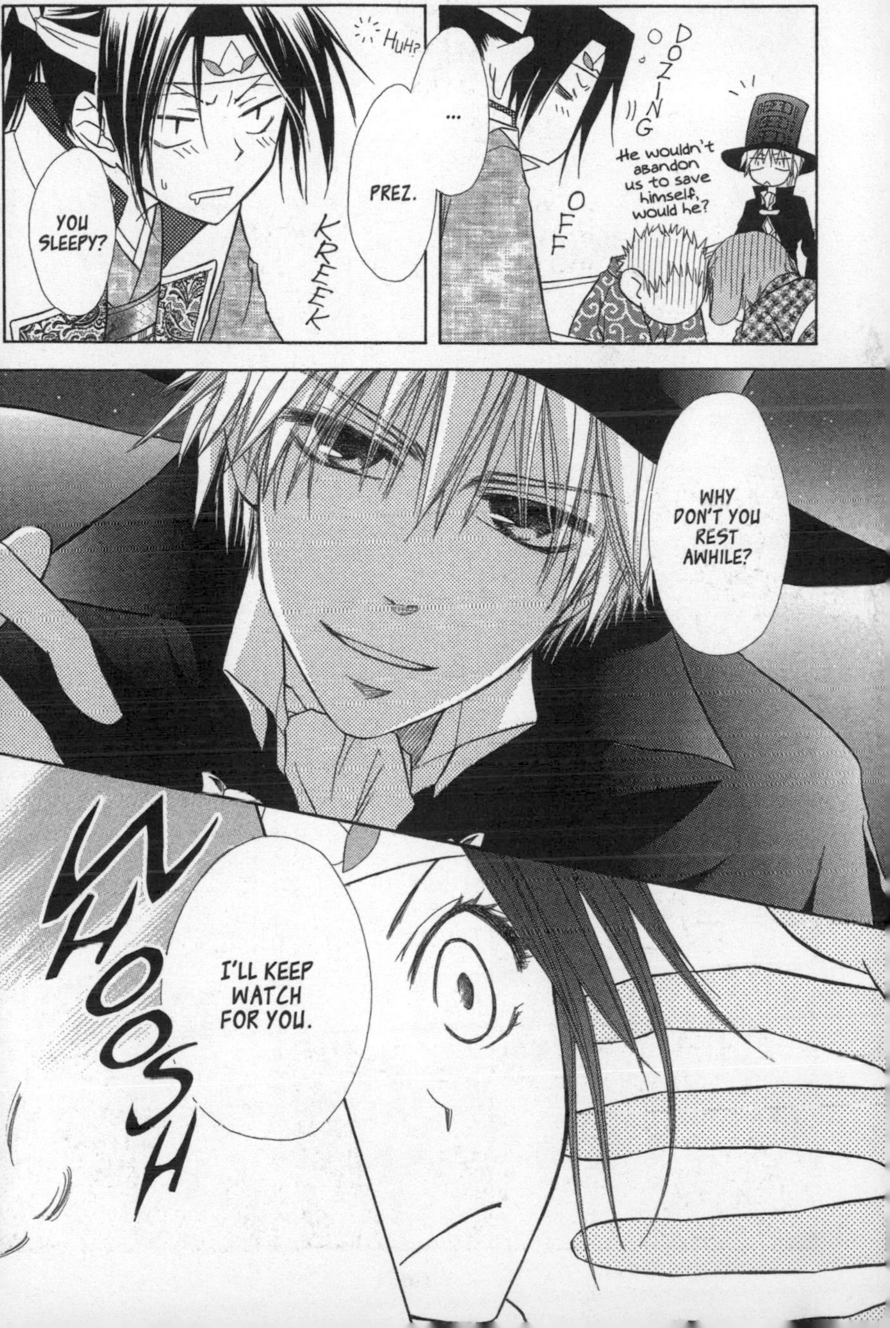
DOZING OFF
He wouldn't abandon us to save himself, would he?
HUH?
...
PREZ.
KREEK
YOU SLEEPY?
WHY DON'T YOU REST AWHILE?
I'LL KEEP WATCH FOR YOU.
WHOOSH

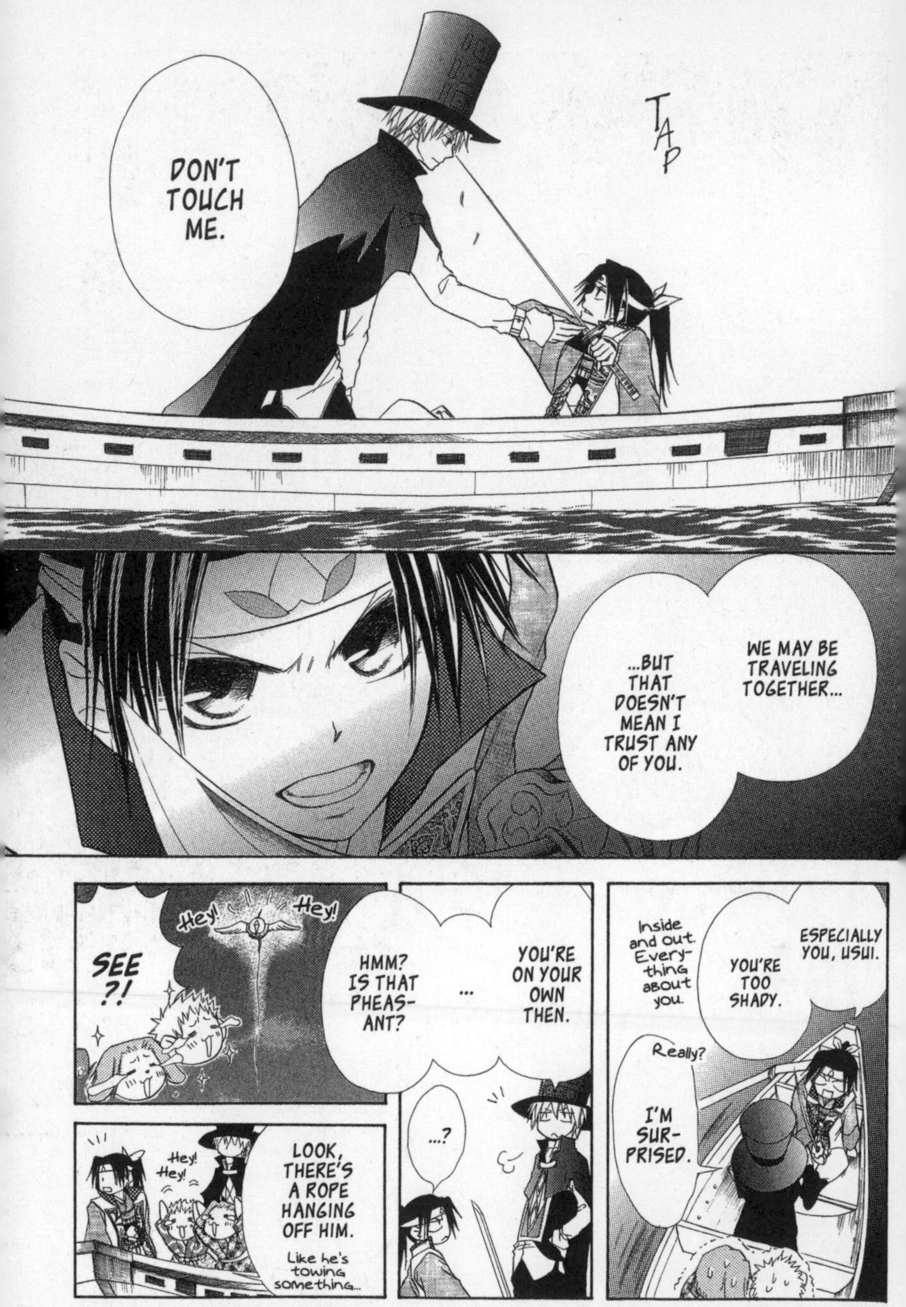
TAP
DON'T TOUCH ME.
WE MAY BE TRAVELING TOGETHER...
...BUT THAT DOESN'T MEAN I TRUST ANY OF YOU.
ESPECIALLY YOU, USUI.
YOU'RE TOO SHADY.
Inside and out. Everything about you.
Really?
I'M SURPRISED.
YOU'RE ON YOUR OWN THEN.
...
HMM? IS THAT PHEASANT?
...?
Hey! Hey!
SEE ?!
LOOK, THERE'S A ROPE HANGING OFF HIM.
Like he's towing something...
Hey! Hey!

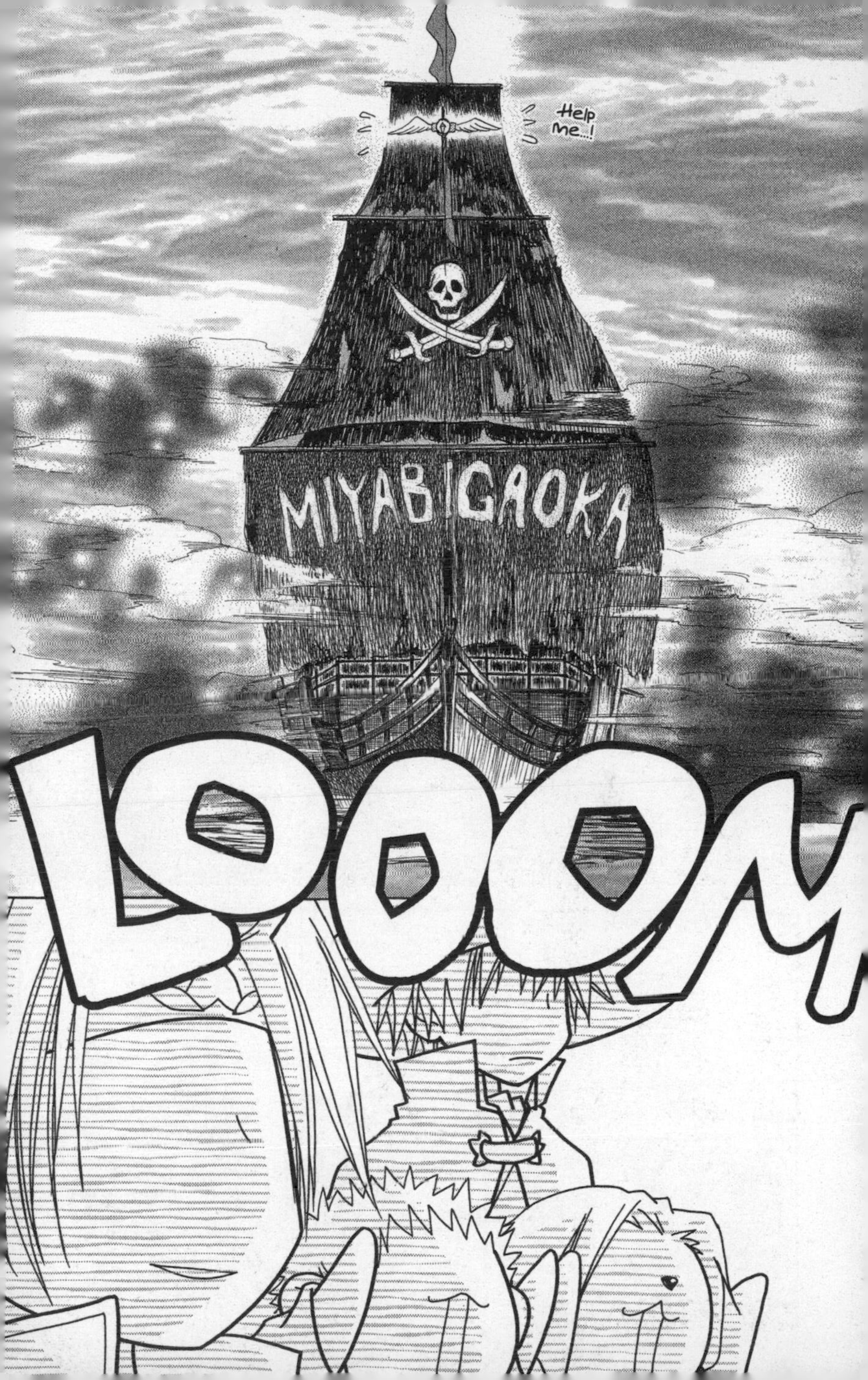
Help me...!
MIYABIGAOKA
LOOOM

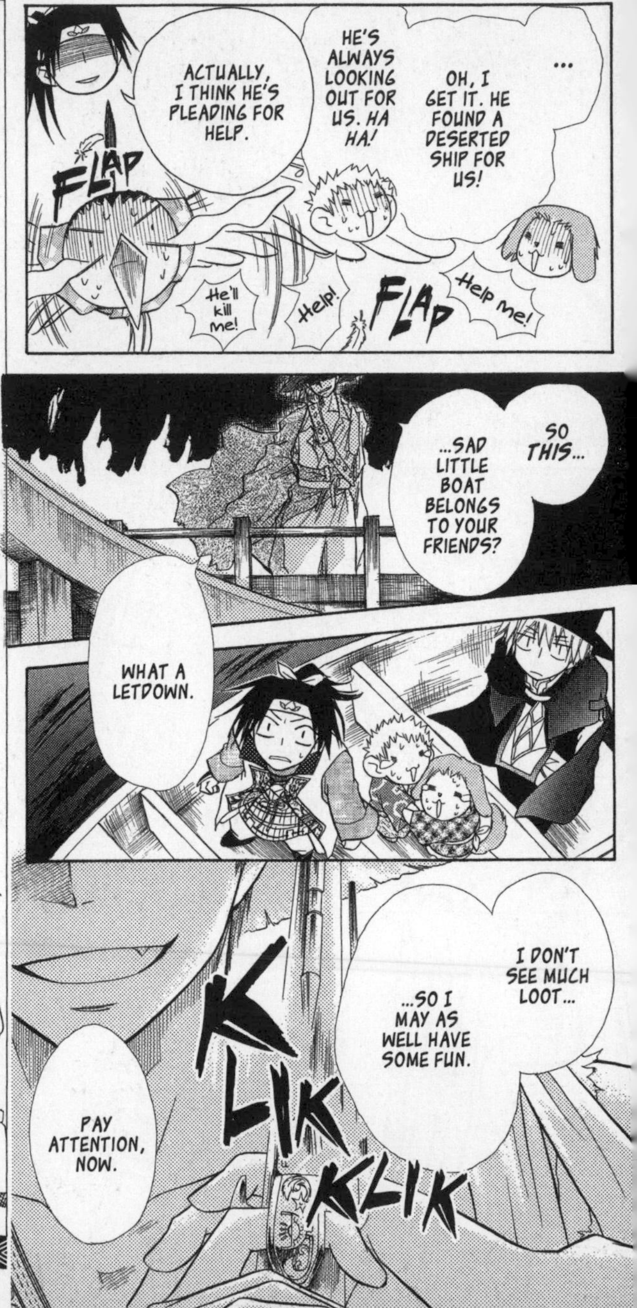
...
OH, I GET IT. HE FOUND A DESERTED SHIP FOR US!
HE'S ALWAYS LOOKING OUT FOR US. *HA HA!*
ACTUALLY, I THINK HE'S PLEADING FOR HELP.
FLAP
Help me!
FLAP
Help!
He'll kill me!
SO *THIS*...
...SAD LITTLE BOAT BELONGS TO YOUR FRIENDS?
WHAT A LETDOWN.
I DON'T SEE MUCH LOOT...
...SO I MAY AS WELL HAVE SOME FUN.
KLIK
KLIK
PAY ATTENTION, NOW.

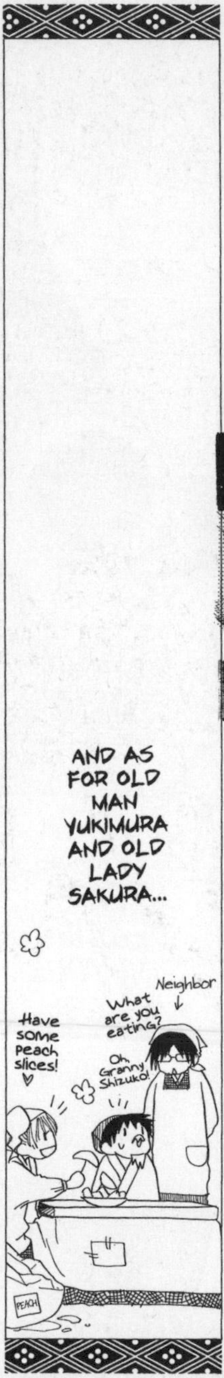
AND AS FOR OLD MAN YUKIMURA AND OLD LADY SAKURA...
Neighbor
What are you eating?
Have some peach slices!
Oh, Granny Shizuko!
PEACH

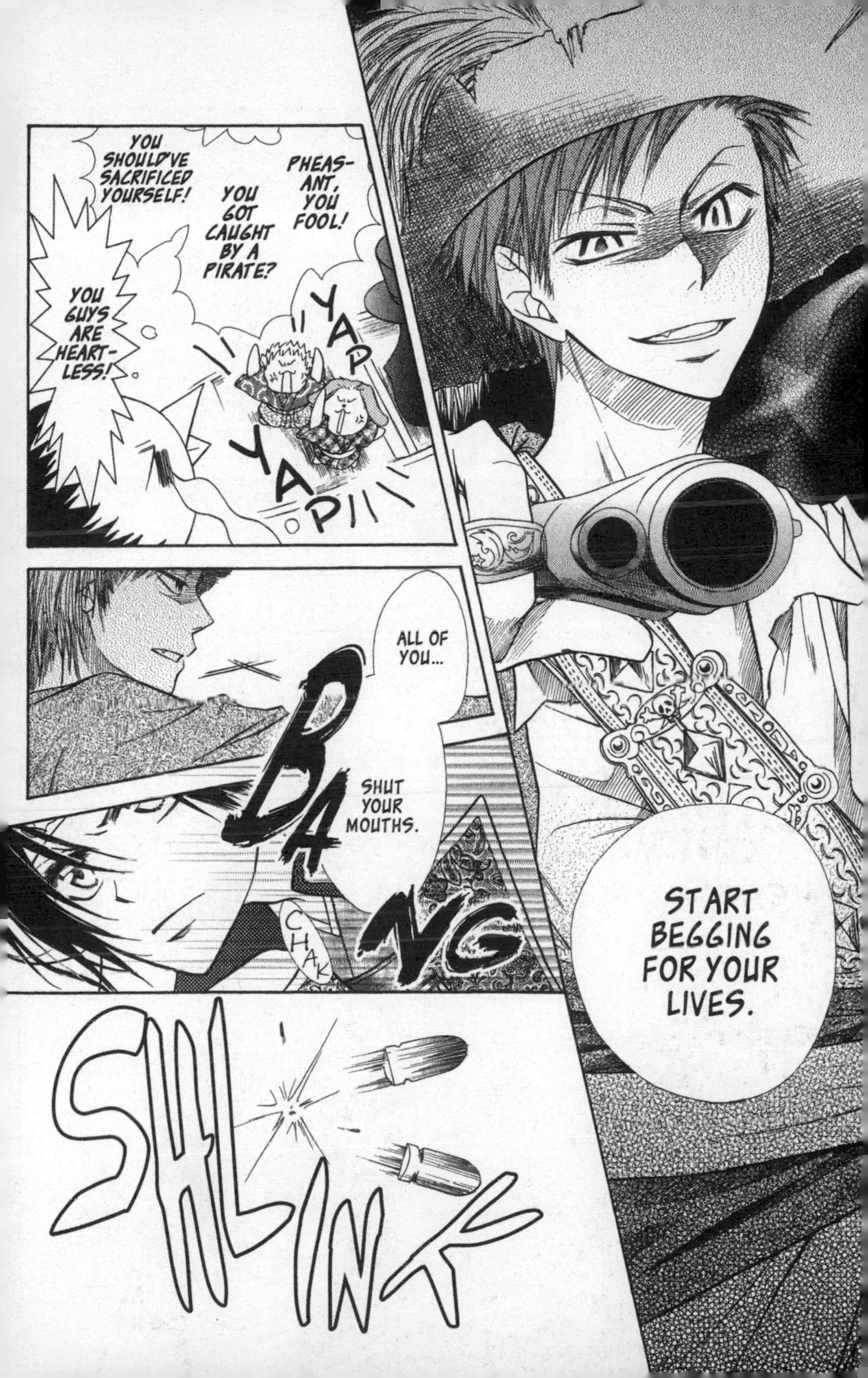
START BEGGING FOR YOUR LIVES.
PHEASANT, YOU FOOL!
YOU GOT CAUGHT BY A PIRATE?
YOU SHOULD'VE SACRIFICED YOURSELF!
YAP
YAP
YOU GUYS ARE HEARTLESS!
ALL OF YOU...
SHUT YOUR MOUTHS.
BANG
CHAK
SHLINK

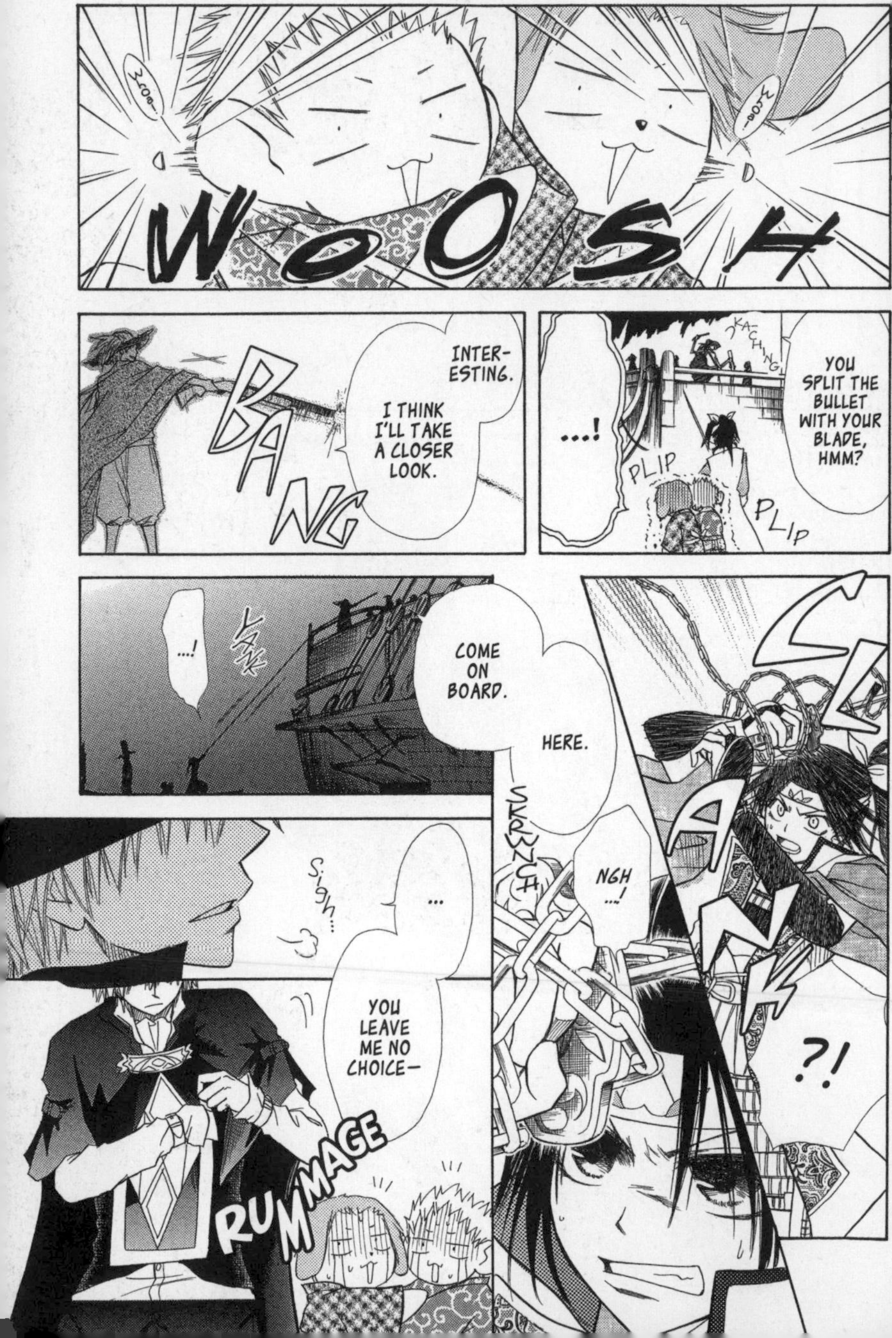
Wroo-
Wroo...
WOOSH
KA-CHING
YOU SPLIT THE BULLET WITH YOUR BLADE, HMM?
...!
PLIP
PLIP
INTER-ESTING.
I THINK I'LL TAKE A CLOSER LOOK.
BANG
CLANK
HERE.
SKRUNCH
NGH ...!
?!
COME ON BOARD.
YANK
...!
...
Sigh...
YOU LEAVE ME NO CHOICE—
RUMMAGE

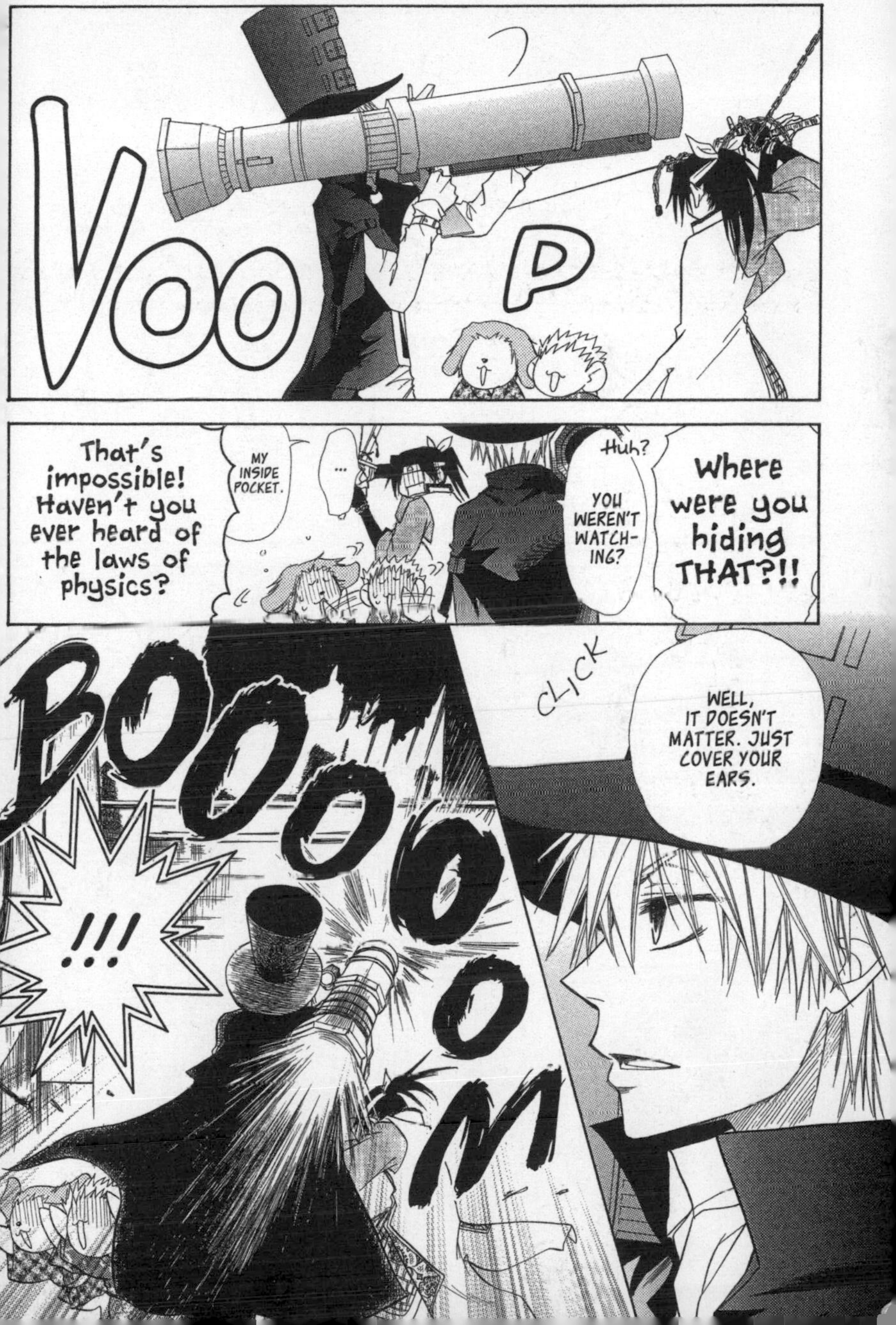
VOOP
Where were you hiding THAT?!!
Huh?
YOU WEREN'T WATCH-ING?
...
MY INSIDE POCKET.
That's impossible! Haven't you ever heard of the laws of physics?
CLICK
WELL, IT DOESN'T MATTER. JUST COVER YOUR EARS.
BOOOOOOM
!!!

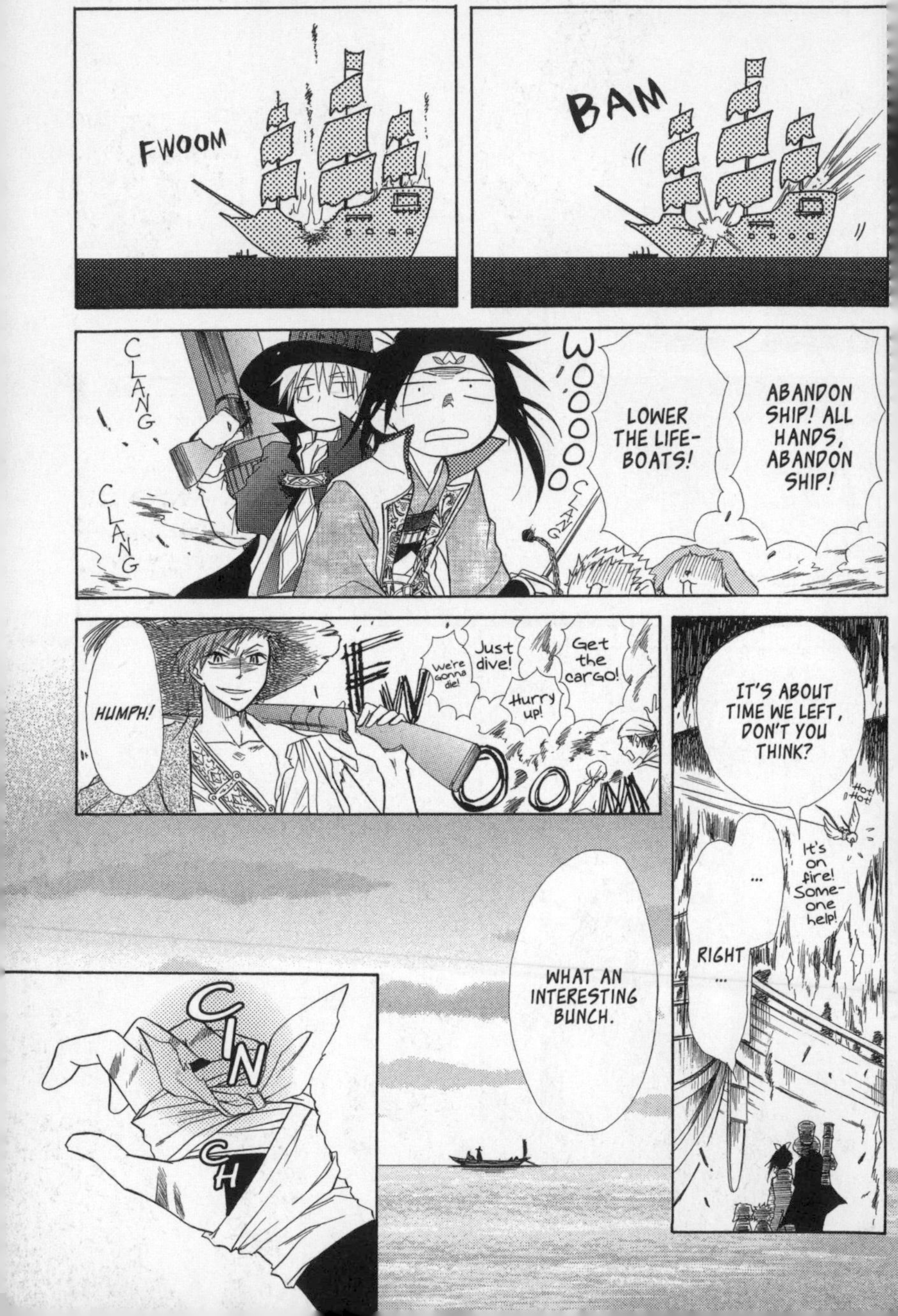
BAM
FWOOM
ABANDON SHIP! ALL HANDS, ABANDON SHIP!
LOWER THE LIFE-BOATS!
WOOOOO
CLANG
CLANG
CLANG
IT'S ABOUT TIME WE LEFT, DON'T YOU THINK?
Hot! Hot!
It's on fire! Someone help!
...
RIGHT ...
Get the cargo!
Just dive!
We're gonna die!
Hurry up!
FWOOOM
HUMPH!
WHAT AN INTERESTING BUNCH.
CINCH

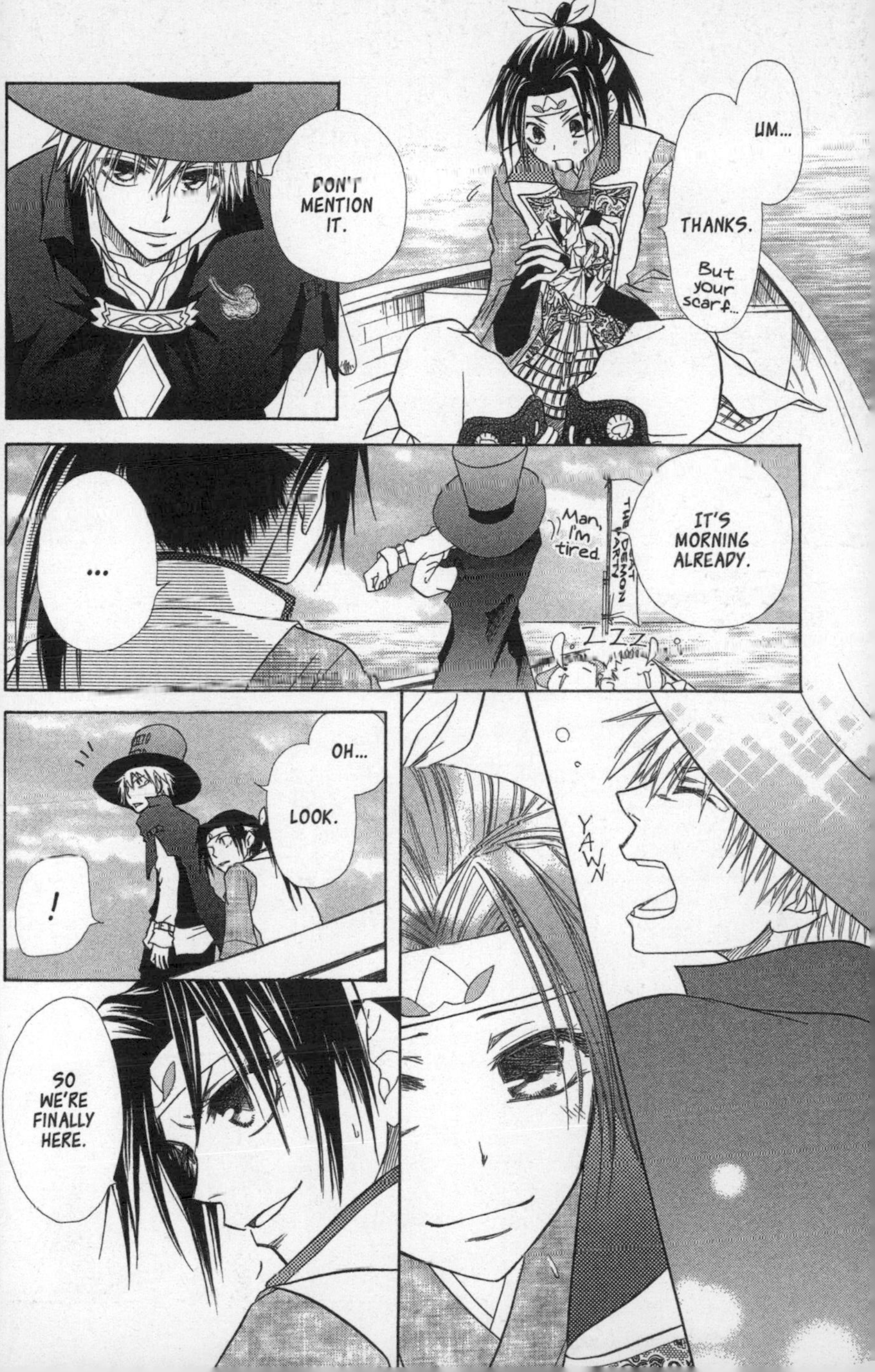
UM...
THANKS.
But your scarf...
DON'T MENTION IT.
IT'S MORNING ALREADY.
Man, I'm tired.
ZZZ
...
YAWN
OH...
LOOK.
!
SO WE'RE FINALLY HERE.

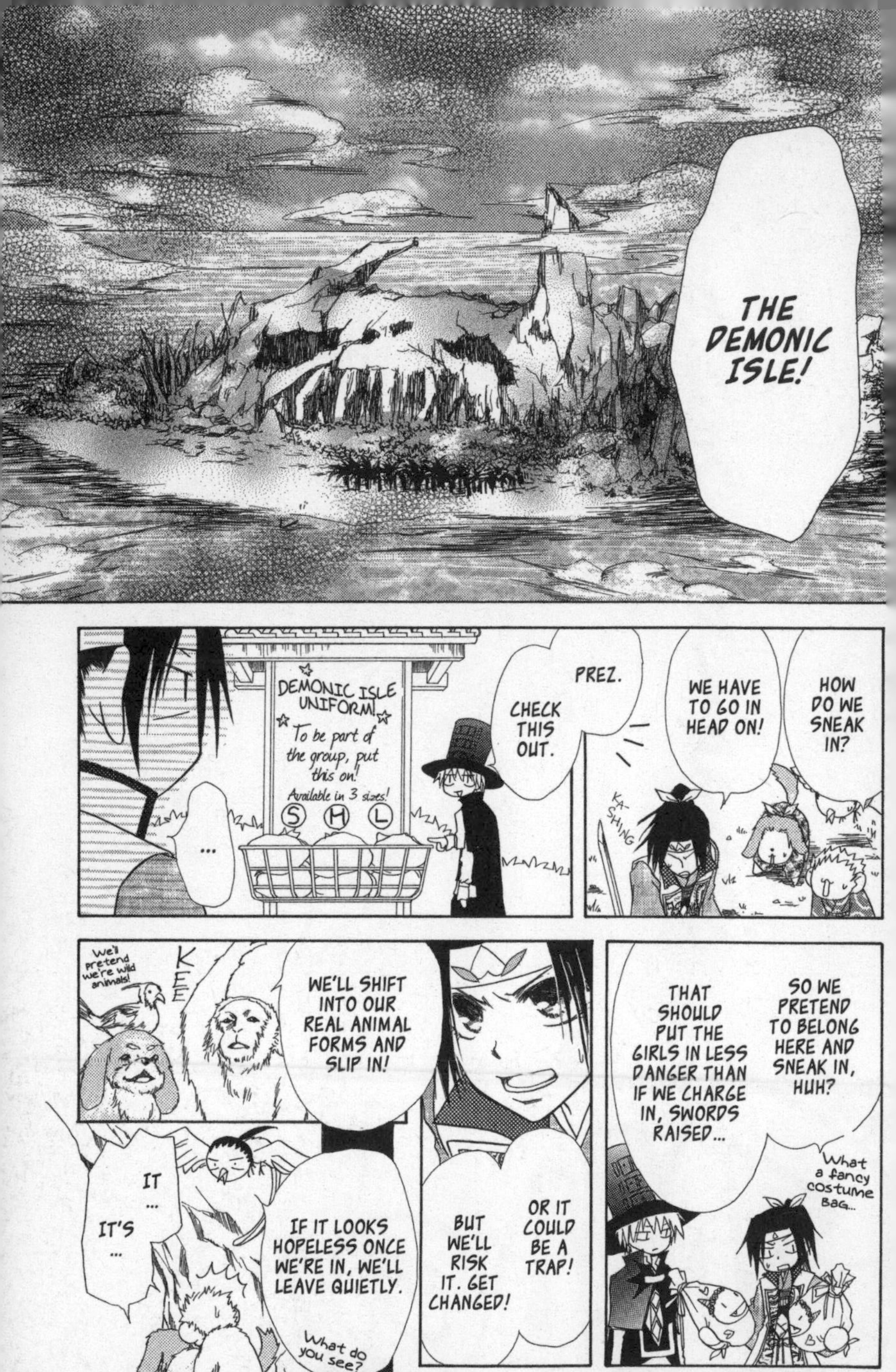
THE DEMONIC ISLE!
HOW DO WE SNEAK IN?
WE HAVE TO GO IN HEAD ON!
KA-SHING
PREZ.
CHECK THIS OUT.
DEMONIC ISLE UNIFORM!
To be part of the group, put this on!
Available in 3 sizes!
S H L
...
SO WE PRETEND TO BELONG HERE AND SNEAK IN, HUH?
THAT SHOULD PUT THE GIRLS IN LESS DANGER THAN IF WE CHARGE IN, SWORDS RAISED...
What a fancy costume bag...
OR IT COULD BE A TRAP!
BUT WE'LL RISK IT. GET CHANGED!
WE'LL SHIFT INTO OUR REAL ANIMAL FORMS AND SLIP IN!
We'll pretend we're wild animals!
KEE
IF IT LOOKS HOPELESS ONCE WE'RE IN, WE'LL LEAVE QUIETLY.
What do you see?
IT ...
IT'S ...

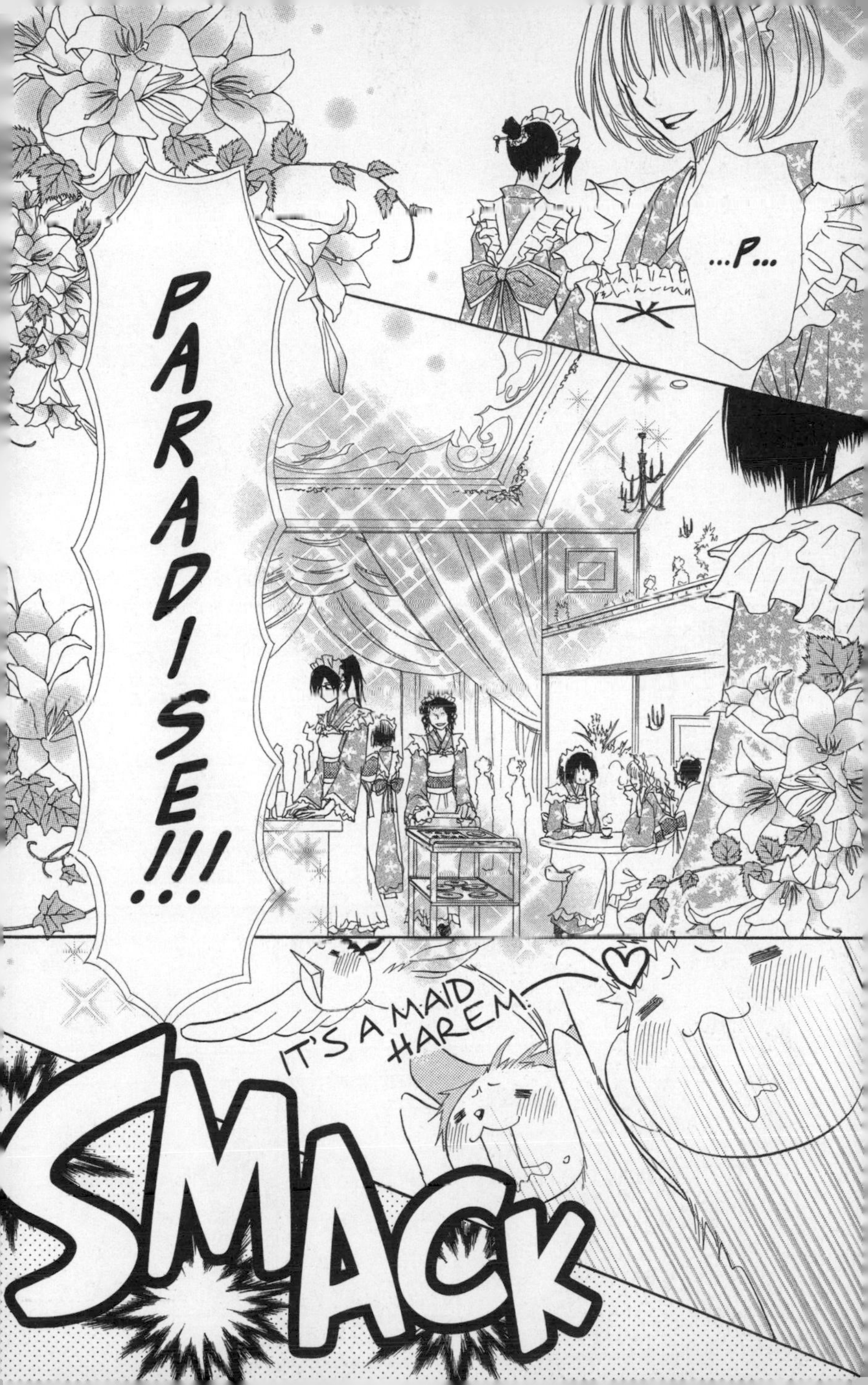
...P...
PARADISE!!!
IT'S A MAID HAREM!
SMACK

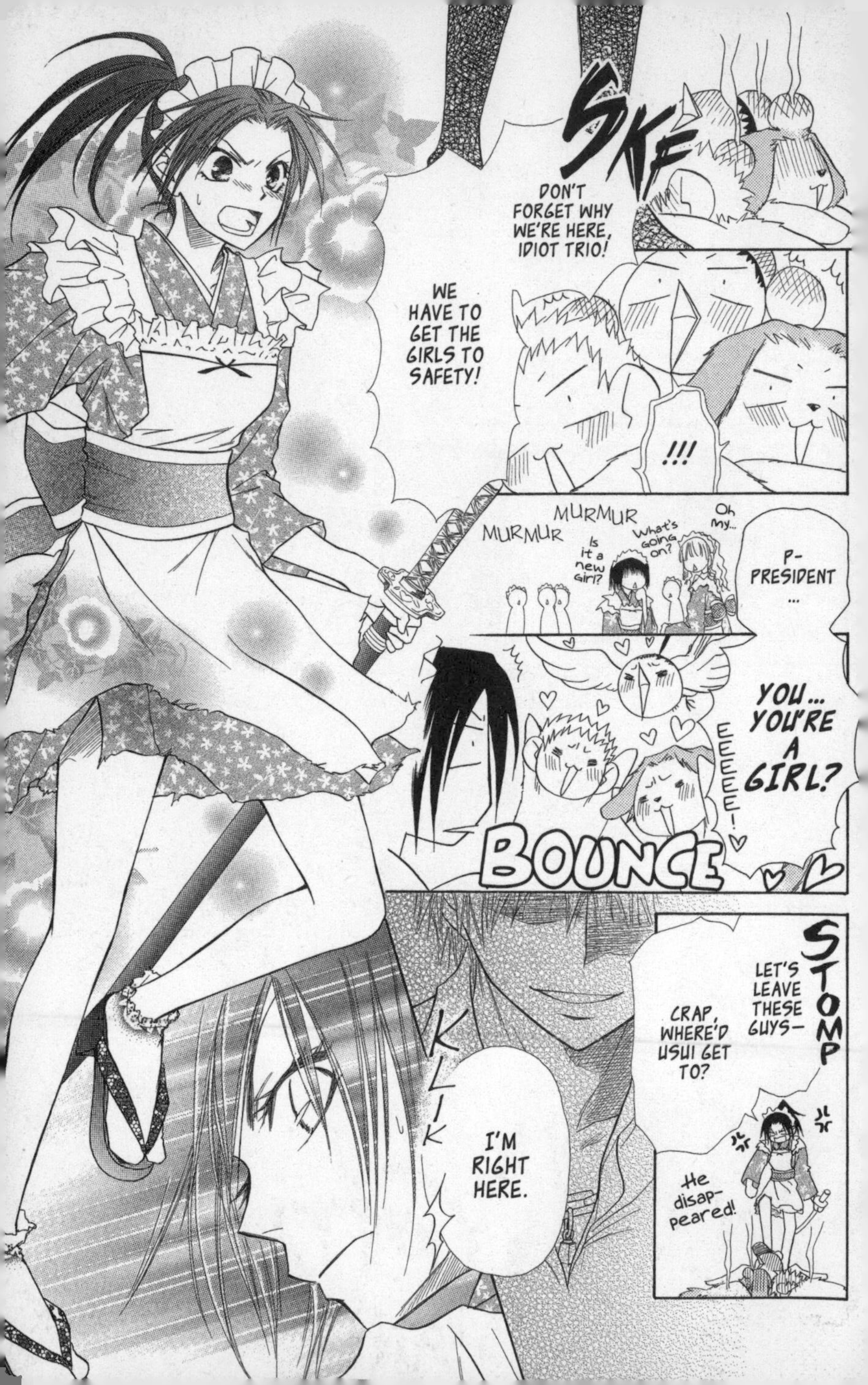
SKF
DON'T FORGET WHY WE'RE HERE, IDIOT TRIO!
WE HAVE TO GET THE GIRLS TO SAFETY!
!!!
P-PRESIDENT...
Oh my...
What's going on?
Is it a new girl?
MURMUR MURMUR
YOU... YOU'RE A GIRL?
EEEEE!
BOUNCE
STOMP
LET'S LEAVE THESE GUYS—
CRAP, WHERE'D USUI GET TO?
He disappeared!
KLIK
I'M RIGHT HERE.

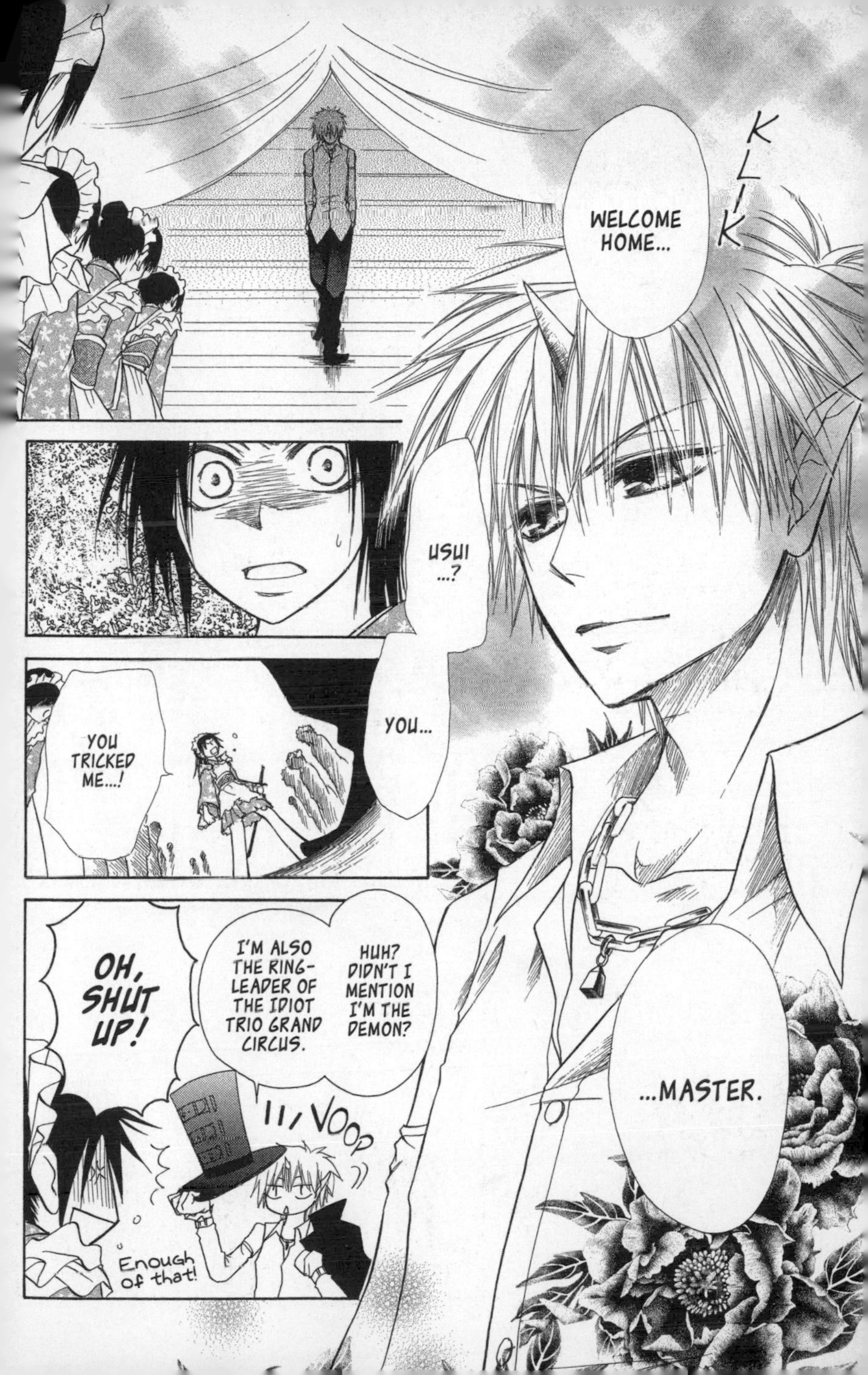
KLIK
WELCOME HOME...
...MASTER.
USUI ...?
YOU...
YOU TRICKED ME...!
HUH? DIDN'T I MENTION I'M THE DEMON?
I'M ALSO THE RING-LEADER OF THE IDIOT TRIO GRAND CIRCUS.
OH, SHUT UP!
VOOP
Enough of that!

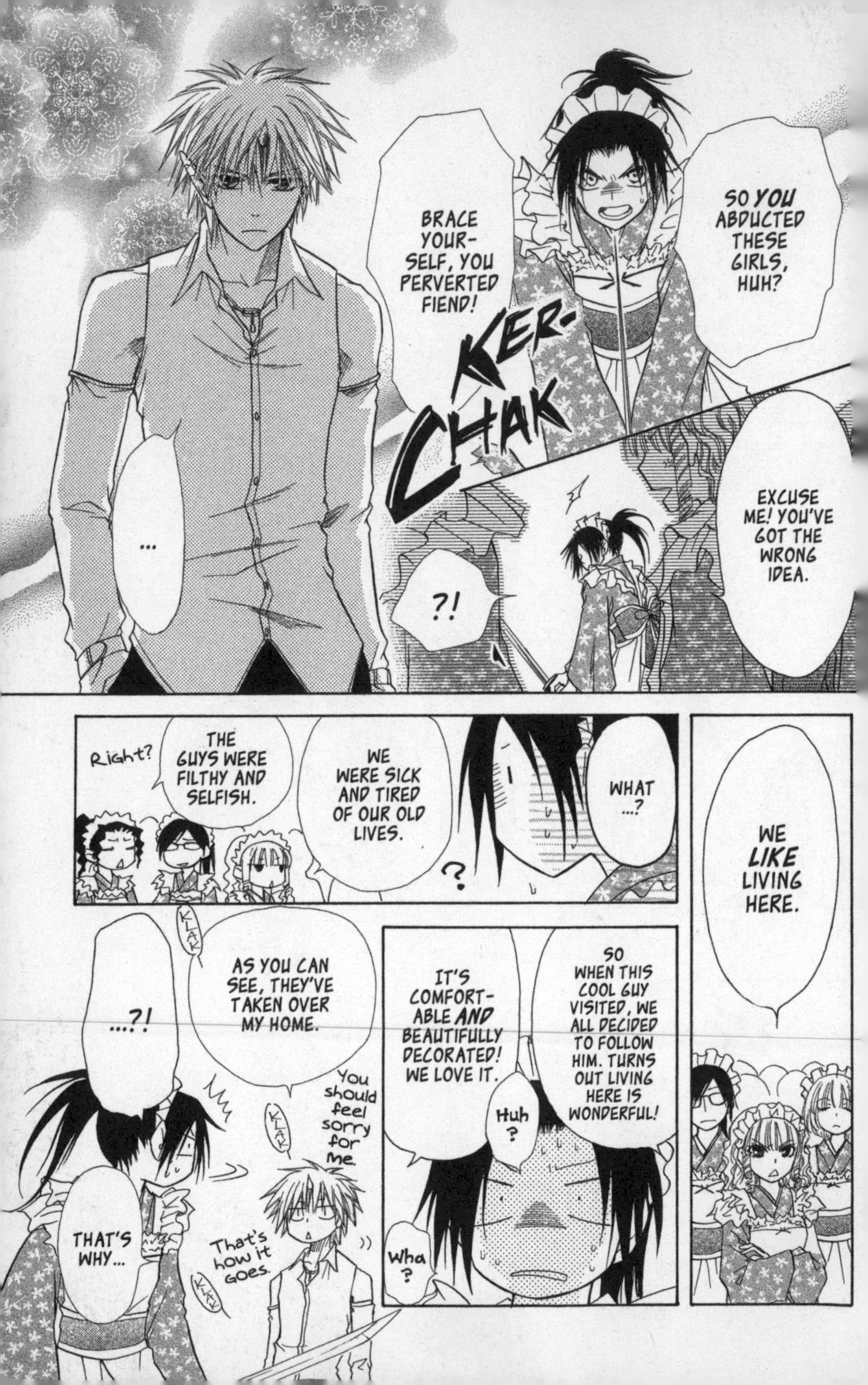
SO YOU ABDUCTED THESE GIRLS, HUH?
BRACE YOURSELF, YOU PERVERTED FIEND!
KER-CHAK
EXCUSE ME! YOU'VE GOT THE WRONG IDEA.
?!
...
WE LIKE LIVING HERE.
WHAT ...?
WE WERE SICK AND TIRED OF OUR OLD LIVES.
THE GUYS WERE FILTHY AND SELFISH.
Right?
?
SO WHEN THIS COOL GUY VISITED, WE ALL DECIDED TO FOLLOW HIM. TURNS OUT LIVING HERE IS WONDERFUL!
IT'S COMFORTABLE AND BEAUTIFULLY DECORATED! WE LOVE IT.
Huh?
Wha?
....?!
KLAK
AS YOU CAN SEE, THEY'VE TAKEN OVER MY HOME.
You should feel sorry for me.
KLAK
THAT'S WHY...
That's how it goes.
KLAK

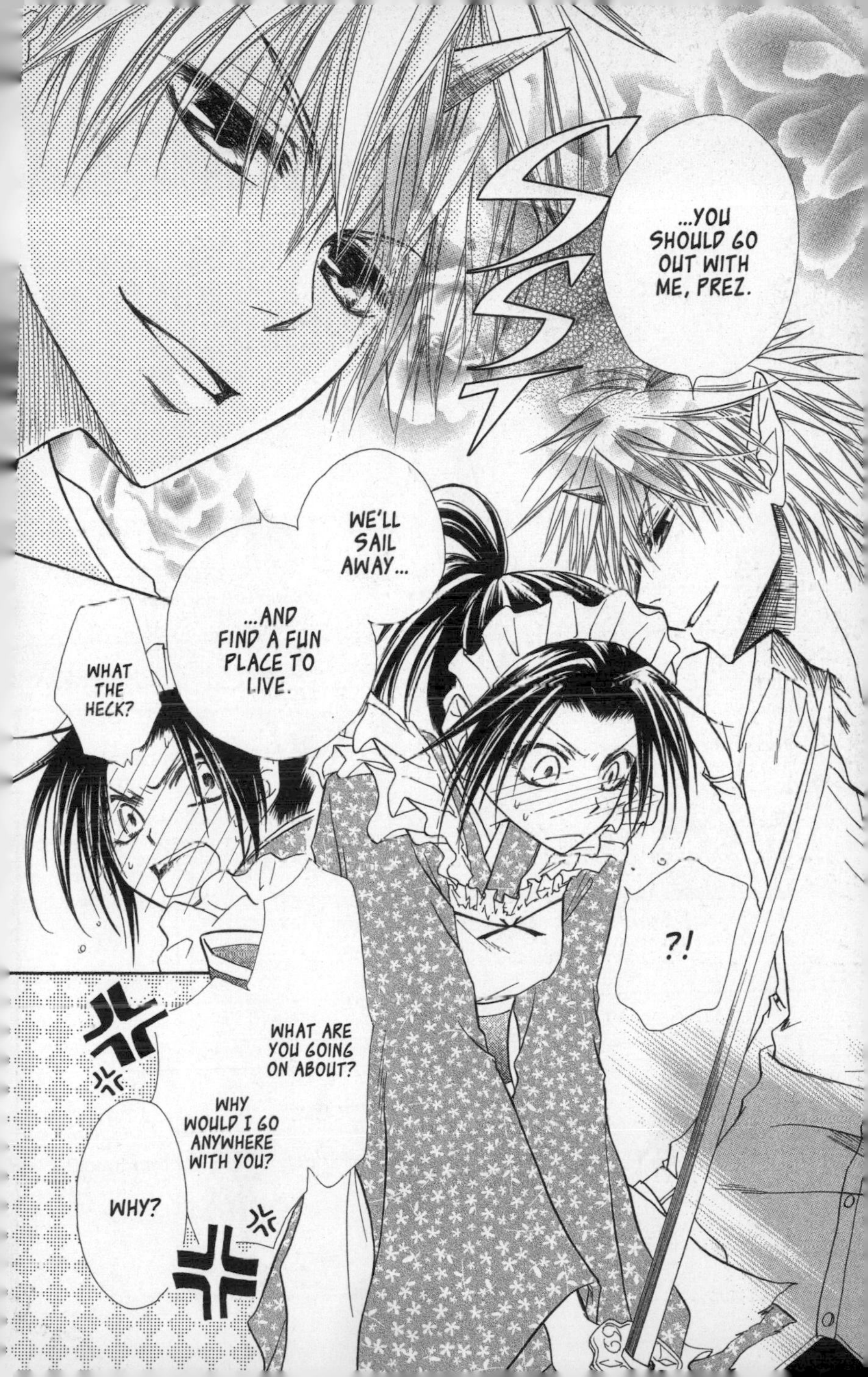
SST
...YOU SHOULD GO OUT WITH ME, PREZ.
WE'LL SAIL AWAY...
...AND FIND A FUN PLACE TO LIVE.
?!
WHAT THE HECK?
WHAT ARE YOU GOING ON ABOUT?
WHY WOULD I GO ANYWHERE WITH YOU?
WHY?

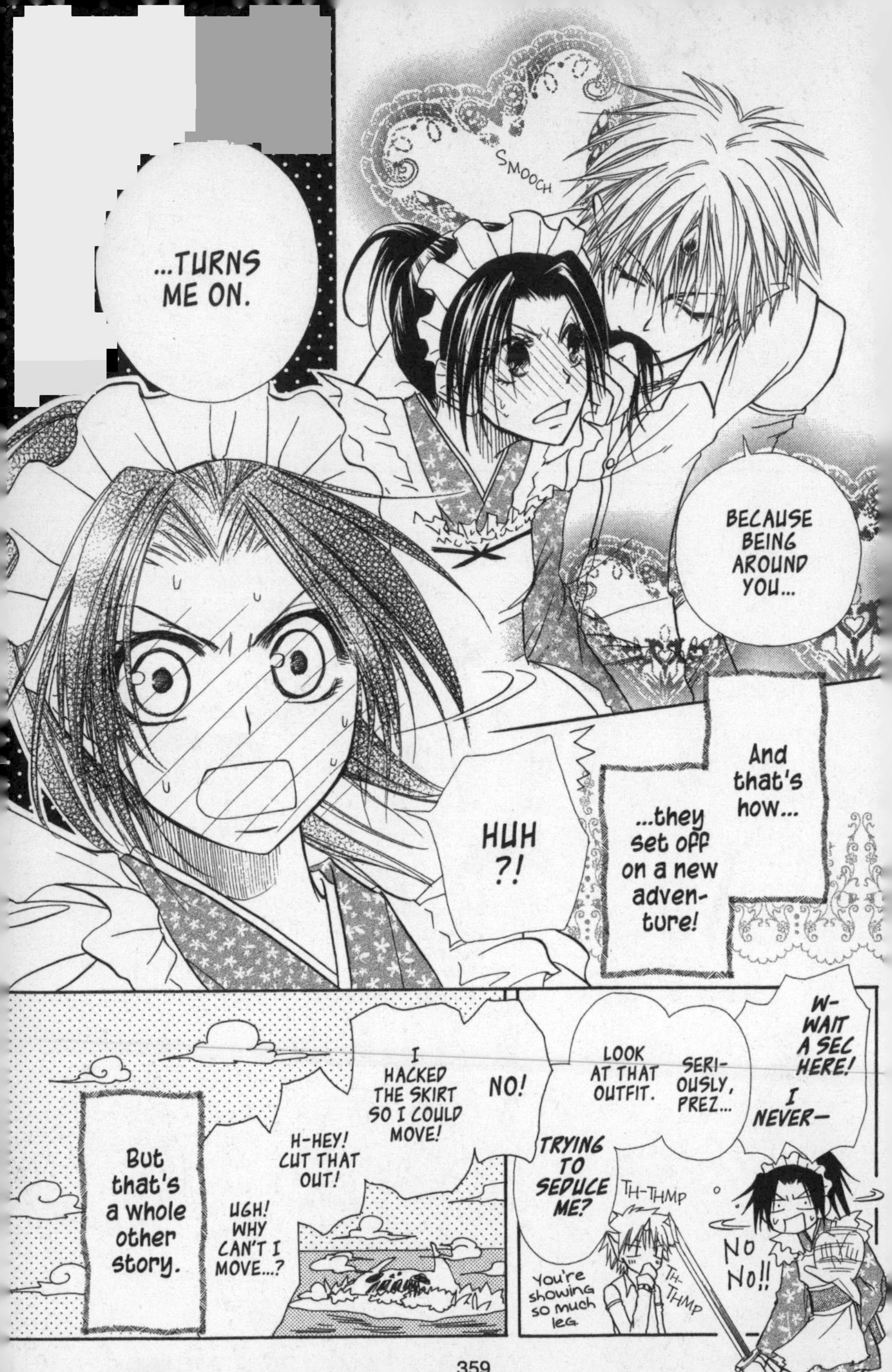
BECAUSE BEING AROUND YOU...
SMOOCH
...TURNS ME ON.
And that's how...
...they set off on a new adventure!
HUH ?!
W-WAIT A SEC HERE!
I NEVER—
SERI-OUSLY, PREZ...
LOOK AT THAT OUTFIT.
TRYING TO SEDUCE ME?
TH-THMP
TH THMP
No No!!
You're showing so much leg.
NO!
I HACKED THE SKIRT SO I COULD MOVE!
H-HEY! CUT THAT OUT!
UGH! WHY CAN'T I MOVE...?
But that's a whole other story.

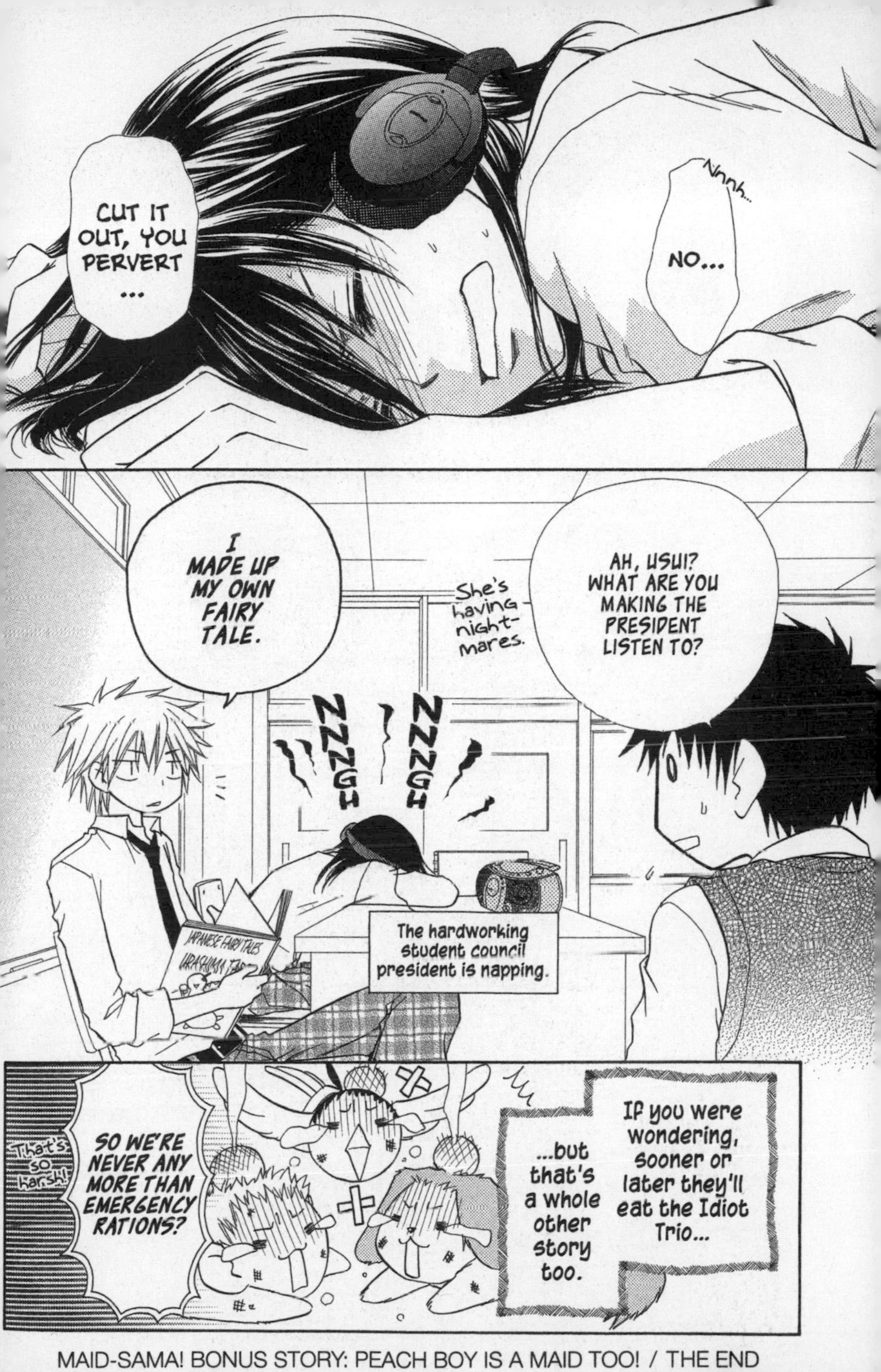
Nnnh...
NO...
CUT IT OUT, YOU PERVERT ...
AH, USUI? WHAT ARE YOU MAKING THE PRESIDENT LISTEN TO?
She's having night-mares.
I MADE UP MY OWN FAIRY TALE.
NNNGH
NNNGH
The hardworking student council president is napping.
JAPANESE FAIRY TALES
If you were wondering, sooner or later they'll eat the Idiot Trio...
...but that's a whole other story too.
SO WE'RE NEVER ANY MORE THAN EMERGENCY RATIONS?
That's so harsh!!

MAID-SAMA! BONUS STORY: PEACH BOY IS A MAID TOO! / THE END

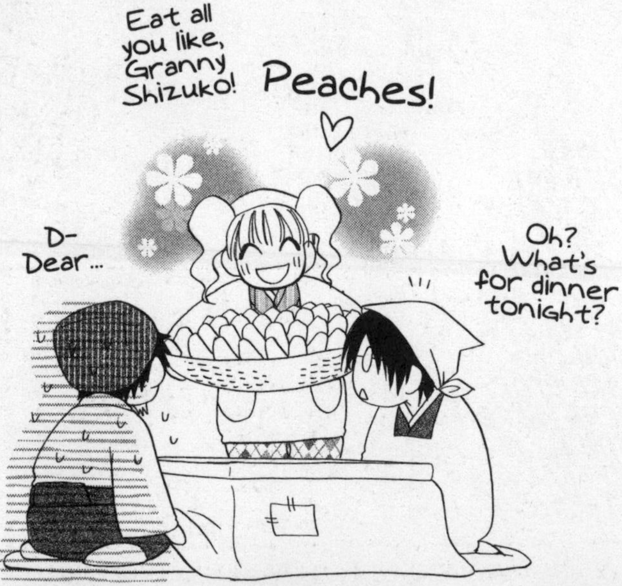
Eat all you like, Granny Shizuko!
Peaches!
Oh? What's for dinner tonight?
D- Dear...

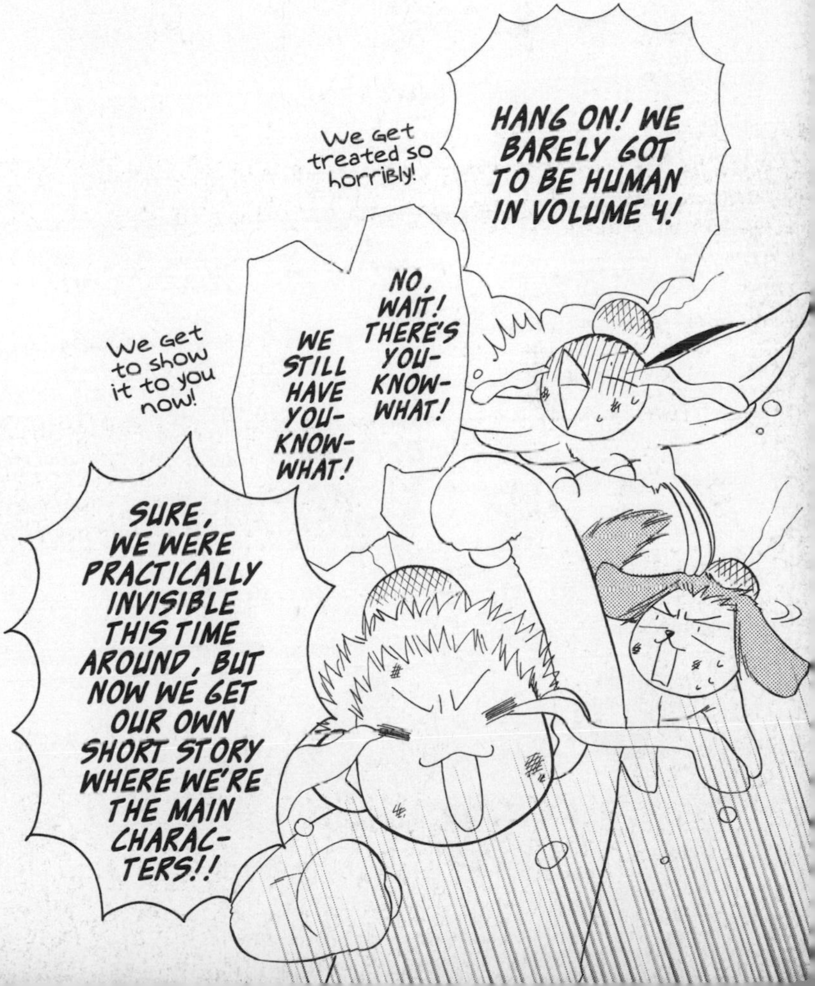
HANG ON! WE BARELY GOT TO BE HUMAN IN VOLUME 4!
We get treated so horribly!
NO, WAIT! THERE'S YOU-KNOW-WHAT!
WE STILL HAVE YOU-KNOW-WHAT!
We get to show it to you now!
SURE, WE WERE PRACTICALLY INVISIBLE THIS TIME AROUND, BUT NOW WE GET OUR OWN SHORT STORY WHERE WE'RE THE MAIN CHARAC-TERS!!

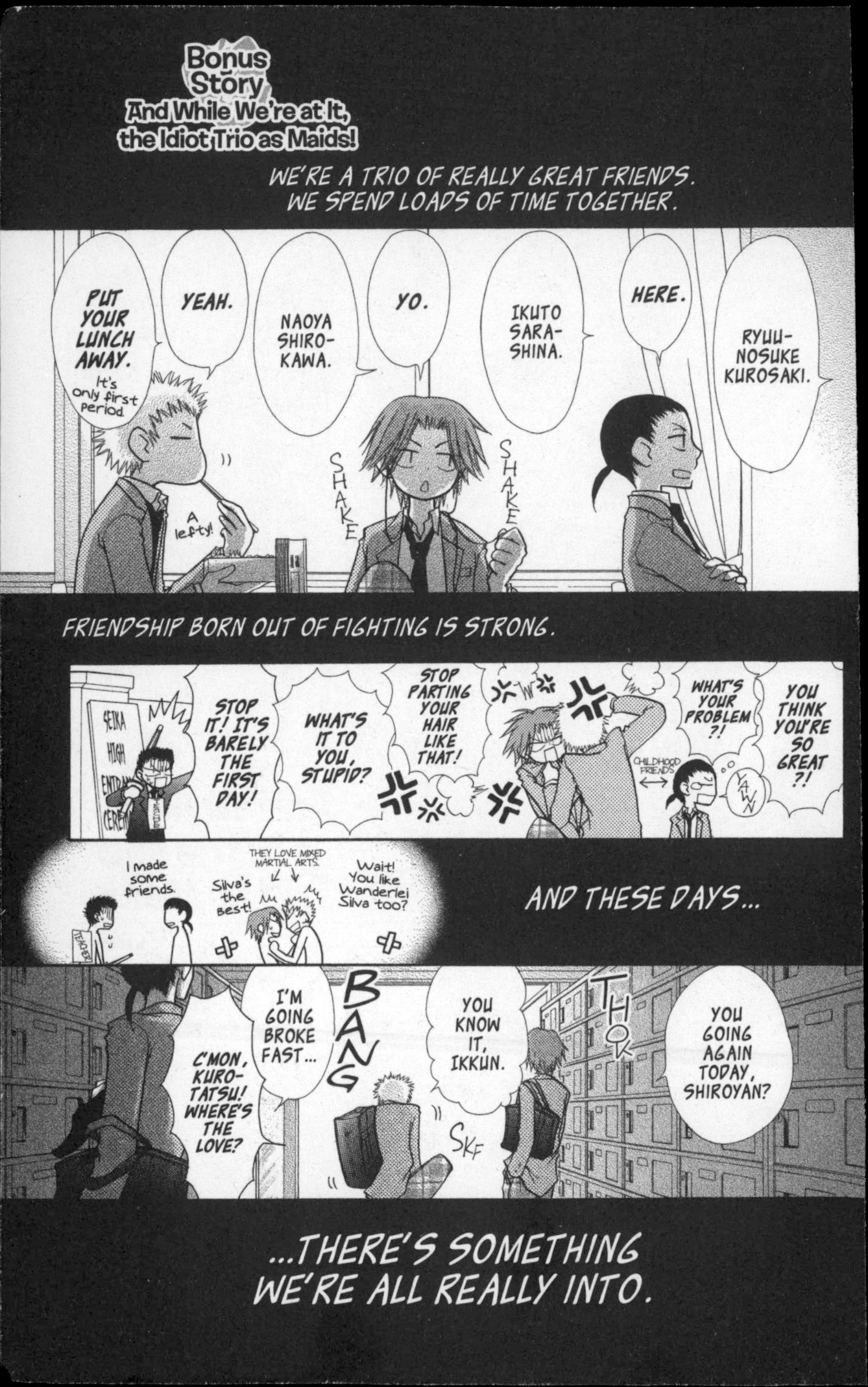
Bonus Story
And While We're at It, the Idiot Trio as Maids!
WE'RE A TRIO OF REALLY GREAT FRIENDS. WE SPEND LOADS OF TIME TOGETHER.
RYUU-NOSUKE KUROSAKI.
HERE.
IKUTO SARA-SHINA.
YO.
NAOYA SHIRO-KAWA.
YEAH.
PUT YOUR LUNCH AWAY.
It's only first period.
A lefty!
SHAKE
SHAKE
FRIENDSHIP BORN OUT OF FIGHTING IS STRONG.
YOU THINK YOU'RE SO GREAT?!
WHAT'S YOUR PROBLEM?!
CHILDHOOD FRIENDS
YAWN
STOP PARTING YOUR HAIR LIKE THAT!
WHAT'S IT TO YOU, STUPID?
STOP IT! IT'S BARELY THE FIRST DAY!
SEIKA HIGH
AND THESE DAYS...
Wait! You like Wanderlei Silva too?
THEY LOVE MIXED MARTIAL ARTS.
Silva's the best!
I made some friends.
TEACHER
YOU GOING AGAIN TODAY, SHIROYAN?
THOK
YOU KNOW IT, IKKUN.
SKF
BANG
I'M GOING BROKE FAST...
C'MON, KURO-TATSU! WHERE'S THE LOVE?
...THERE'S SOMETHING WE'RE ALL REALLY INTO.

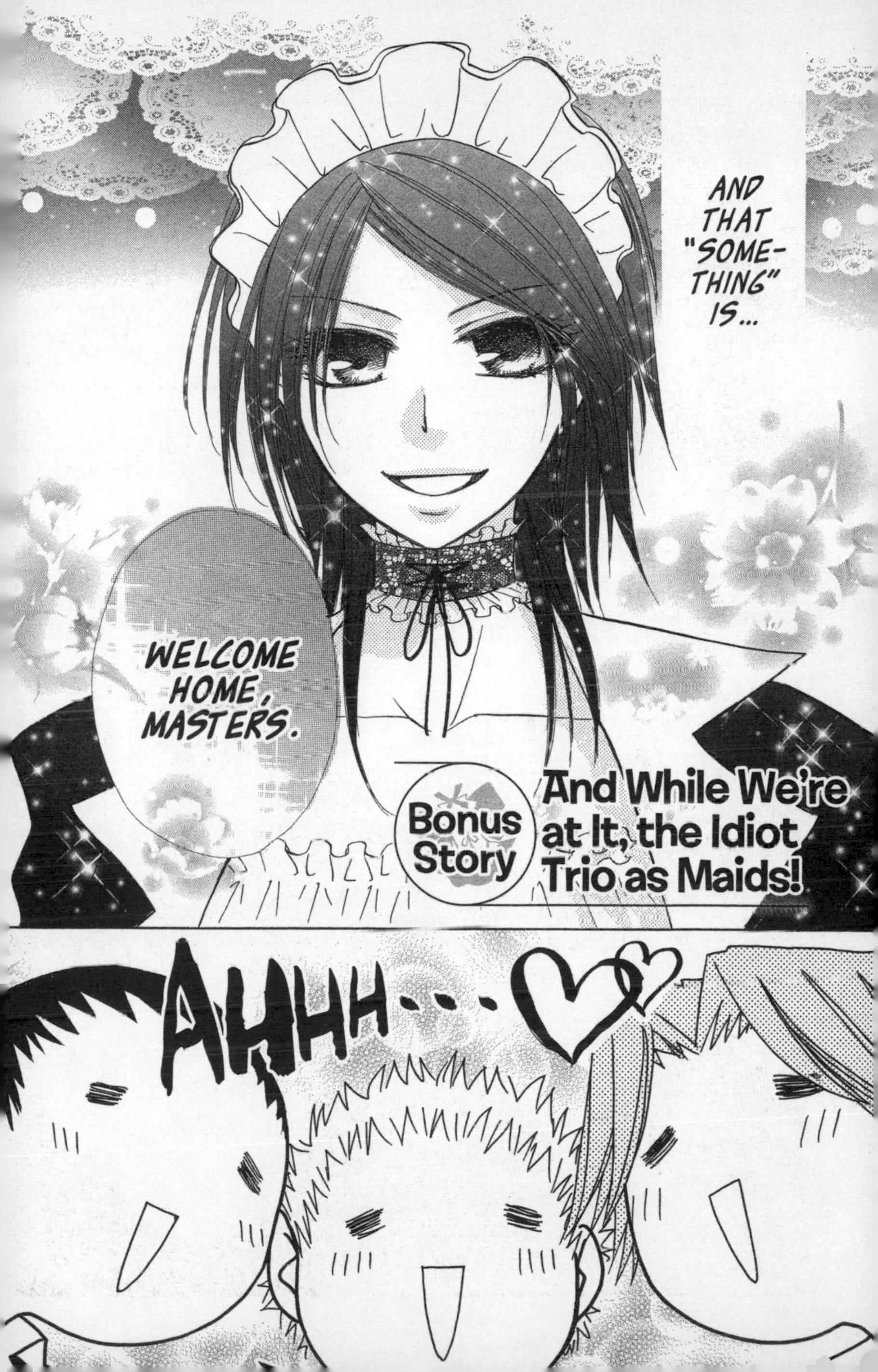
AND THAT "SOME-THING" IS...
WELCOME HOME, MASTERS.
Bonus Story
And While We're at It, the Idiot Trio as Maids!
AHHH...♡

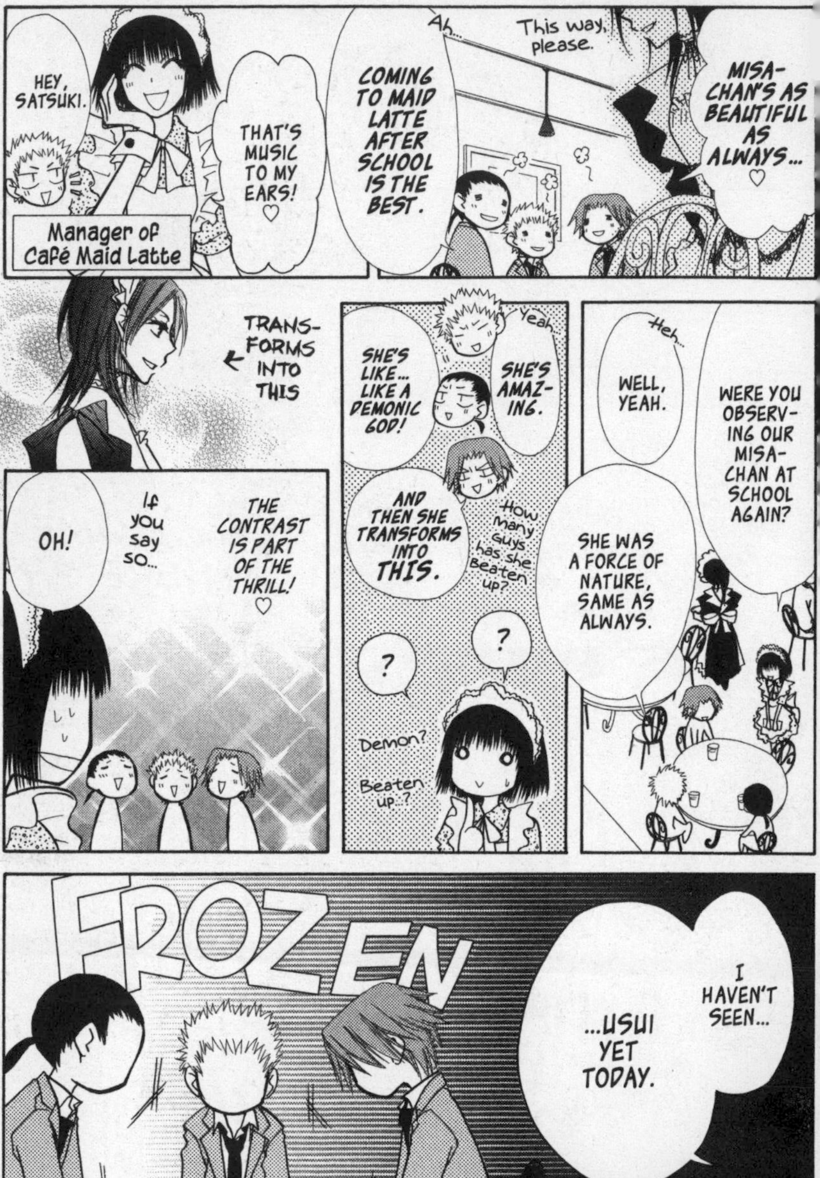
This way, please.
Ah...
MISA-CHAN'S AS BEAUTIFUL AS ALWAYS... ♡
COMING TO MAID LATTE AFTER SCHOOL IS THE BEST.
THAT'S MUSIC TO MY EARS! ♡
HEY, SATSUKI.
Manager of Café Maid Latte
Heh...
WERE YOU OBSERVING OUR MISA-CHAN AT SCHOOL AGAIN?
WELL, YEAH.
SHE WAS A FORCE OF NATURE, SAME AS ALWAYS.
Yeah.
SHE'S AMAZING.
SHE'S LIKE... LIKE A DEMONIC GOD!
How many guys has she beaten up?
AND THEN SHE TRANSFORMS INTO THIS.
?
?
Demon?
Beaten up..?
TRANSFORMS INTO THIS
THE CONTRAST IS PART OF THE THRILL! ♡
If you say so...
OH!
I HAVEN'T SEEN...
...USUI YET TODAY.
FROZEN

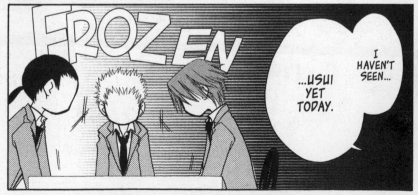

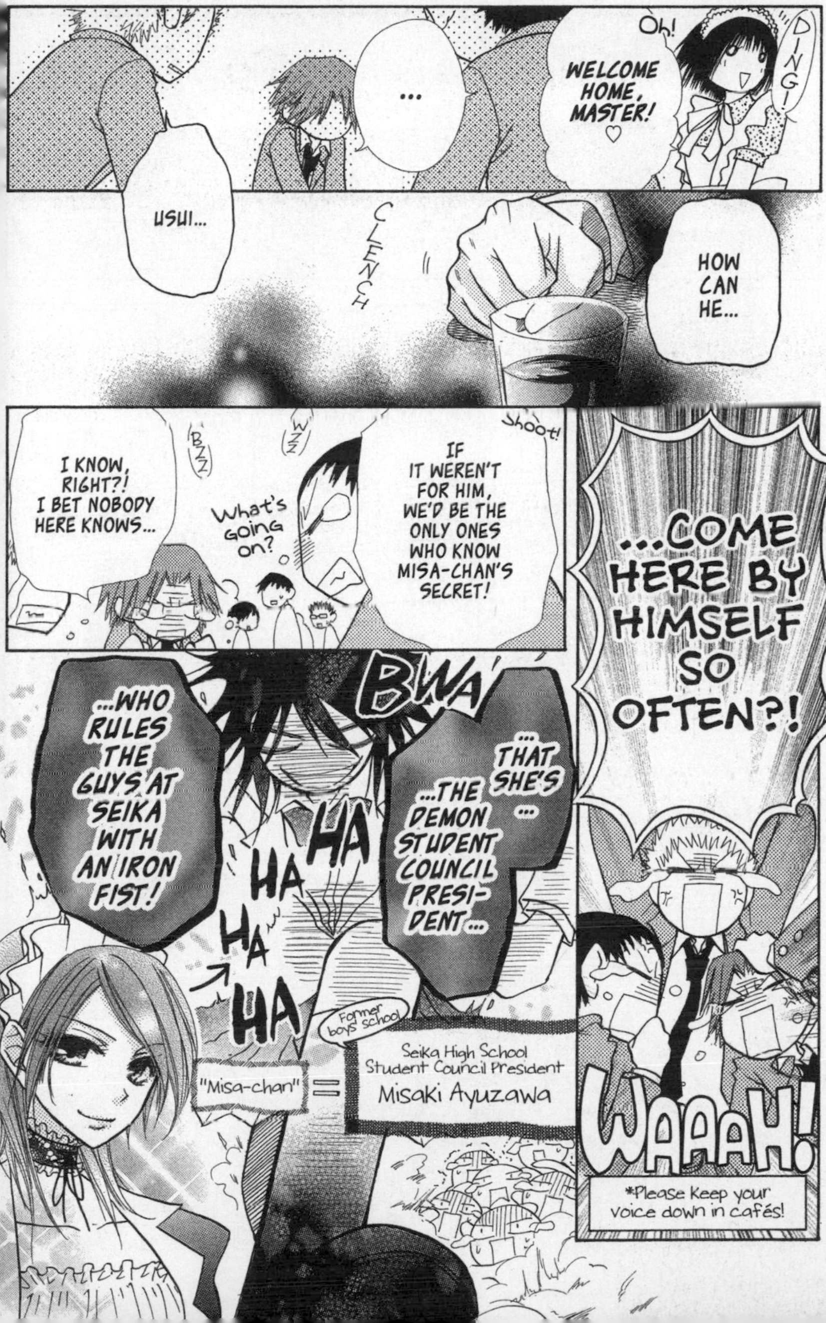
DING!
Oh!
WELCOME HOME, MASTER! ♡
...
USUI...
HOW CAN HE...
CLENCH
...COME HERE BY HIMSELF SO OFTEN?!
WAAAH!
*Please keep your voice down in cafés!
Shoot!
IF IT WEREN'T FOR HIM, WE'D BE THE ONLY ONES WHO KNOW MISA-CHAN'S SECRET!
WZZ
What's going on?
BZZ
I KNOW, RIGHT?! I BET NOBODY HERE KNOWS...
BWA
...THAT SHE'S...
...THE DEMON STUDENT COUNCIL PRESIDENT...
HA HA HA HA
...WHO RULES THE GUYS AT SEIKA WITH AN IRON FIST!
Former boys' school
Seika High School Student Council President Misaki Ayuzawa
"Misa-chan" =

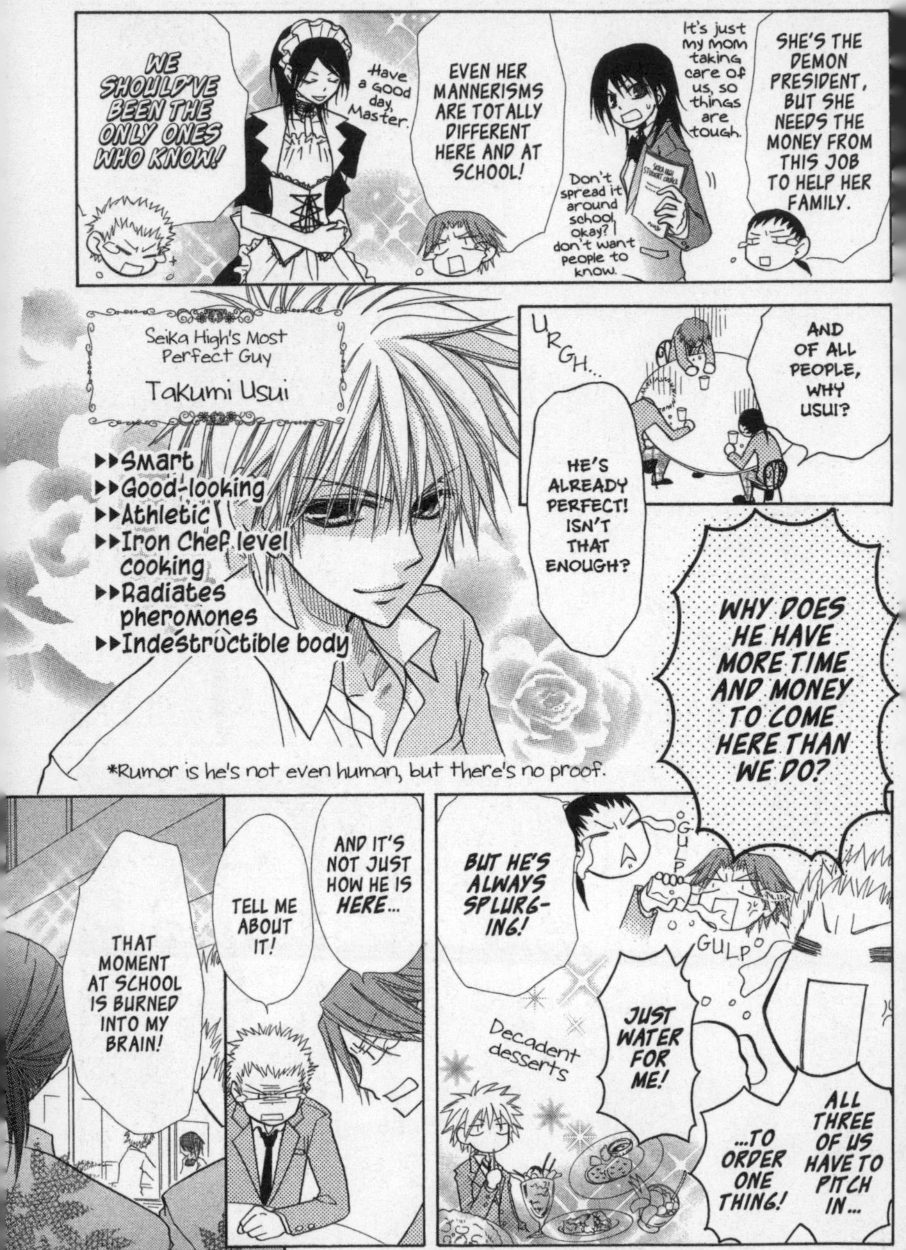
SHE'S THE DEMON PRESIDENT, BUT SHE NEEDS THE MONEY FROM THIS JOB TO HELP HER FAMILY.
It's just my mom taking care of us, so things are tough.
Don't spread it around school, okay? I don't want people to know.
EVEN HER MANNERISMS ARE TOTALLY DIFFERENT HERE AND AT SCHOOL!
Have a good day, Master.
WE SHOULD'VE BEEN THE ONLY ONES WHO KNOW!
AND OF ALL PEOPLE, WHY USUI?
URGH...
HE'S ALREADY PERFECT! ISN'T THAT ENOUGH?
WHY DOES HE HAVE MORE TIME AND MONEY TO COME HERE THAN WE DO?
Seika High's Most Perfect Guy
Takumi Usui
▸▸Smart
▸▸Good-looking
▸▸Athletic
▸▸Iron Chef level cooking
▸▸Radiates pheromones
▸▸Indestructible body
*Rumor is he's not even human, but there's no proof.
ALL THREE OF US HAVE TO PITCH IN...
...TO ORDER ONE THING!
JUST WATER FOR ME!
GULP
GULP
BUT HE'S ALWAYS SPLURGING!
Decadent desserts
AND IT'S NOT JUST HOW HE IS HERE...
TELL ME ABOUT IT!
THAT MOMENT AT SCHOOL IS BURNED INTO MY BRAIN!

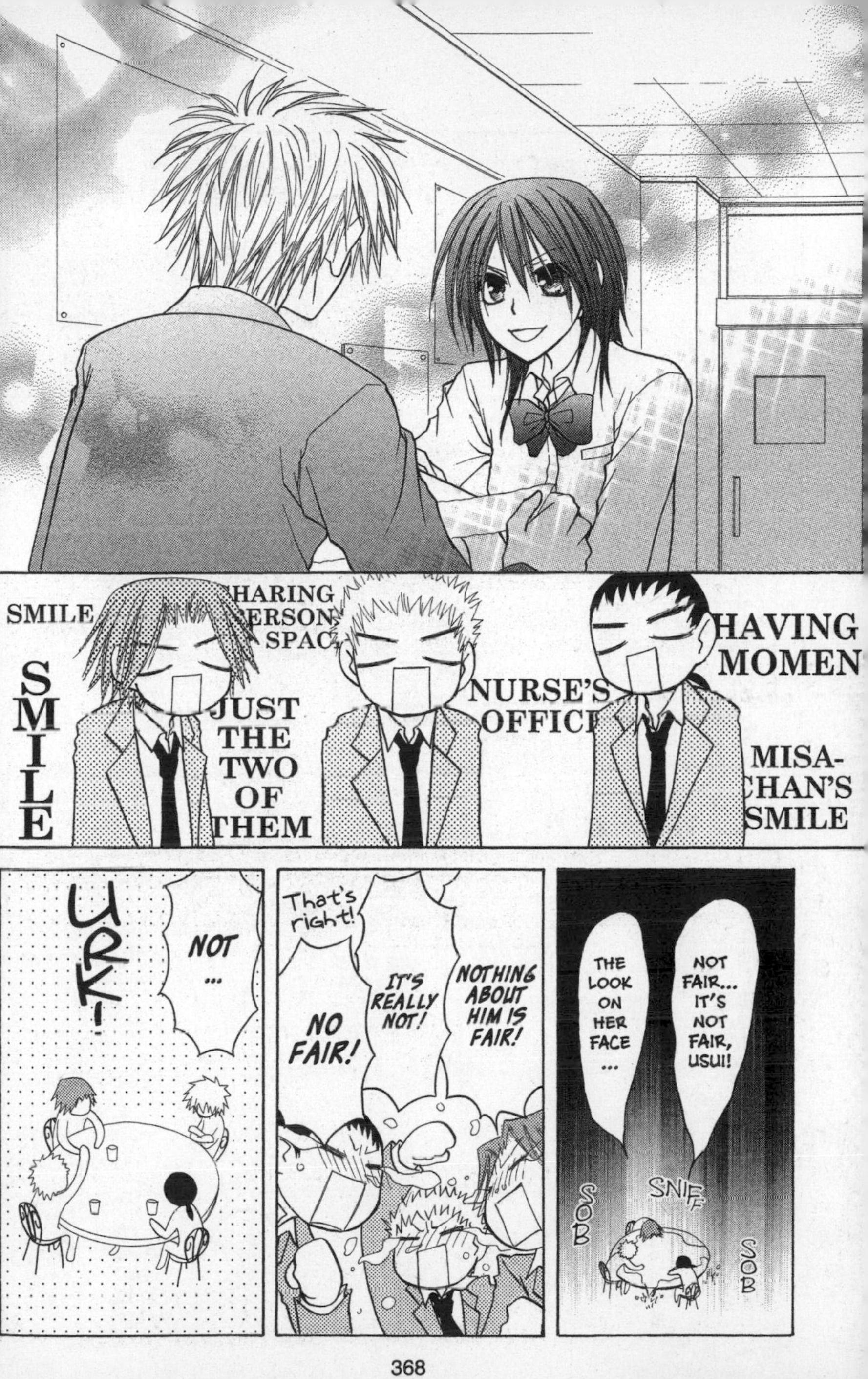
HAVING MOMEN
MISA-
CHAN'S
SMILE
NURSE'S
OFFIC
HARING
ERSON
SPAC
JUST THE TWO OF THEM
SMILE
SMILE
NOT FAIR... IT'S NOT FAIR, USUI!
THE LOOK ON HER FACE...
SNIFF
SOB
SOB
NOTHING ABOUT HIM IS FAIR!
IT'S REALLY NOT!
That's right!
NO FAIR!
NOT...
URK!

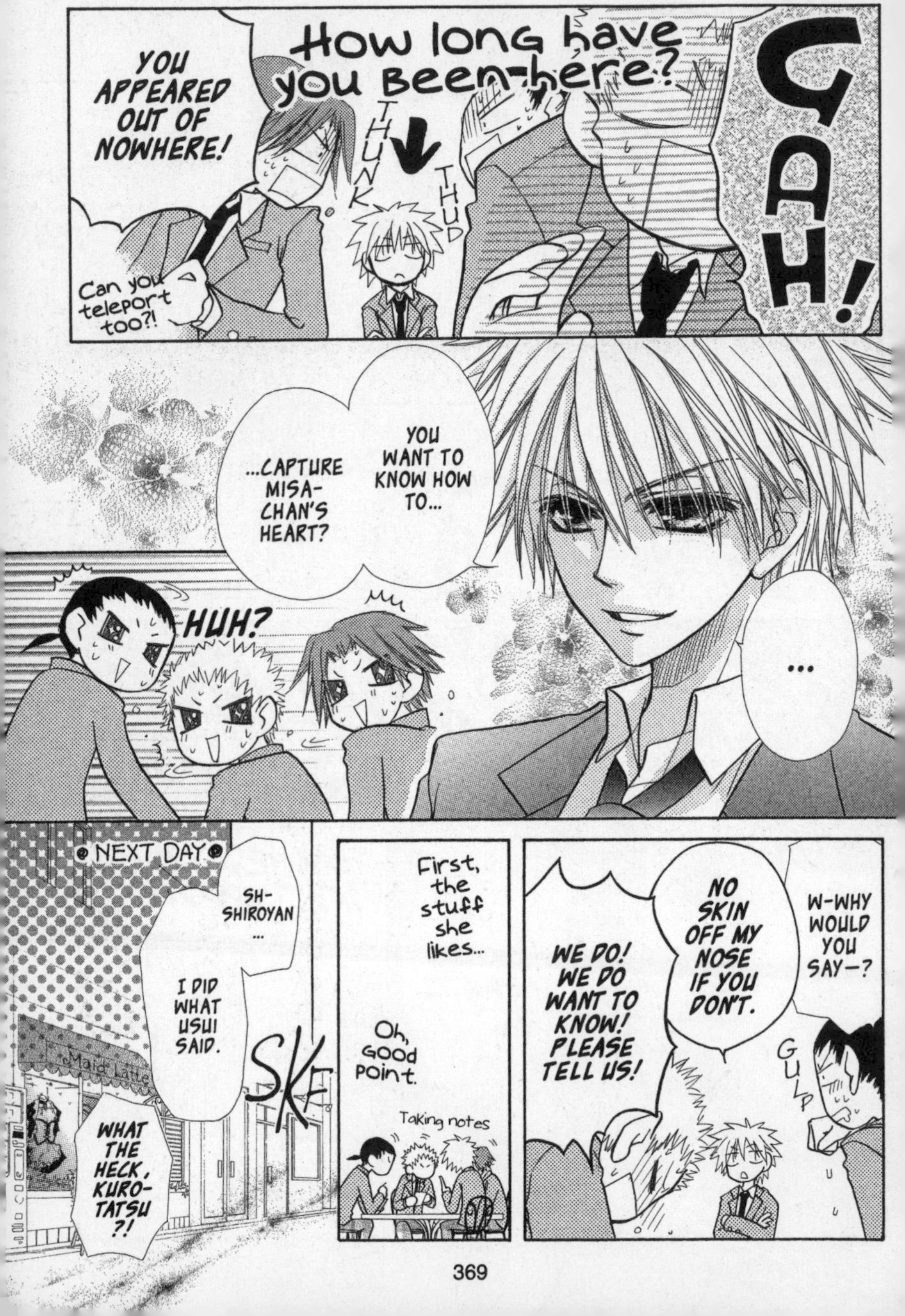
GAH!
How long have you been here?
THUD
THUNK
YOU APPEARED OUT OF NOWHERE!
Can you teleport too?!
YOU WANT TO KNOW HOW TO...
...CAPTURE MISA-CHAN'S HEART?
...
HUH?
W-WHY WOULD YOU SAY—?
GULP
NO SKIN OFF MY NOSE IF YOU DON'T.
WE DO! WE DO WANT TO KNOW! PLEASE TELL US!
First, the stuff she likes...
Oh, good point.
Taking notes
NEXT DAY
SH-SHIROYAN...
I DID WHAT USUI SAID.
SKF
Maid Latte
WHAT THE HECK, KURO-TATSU?!

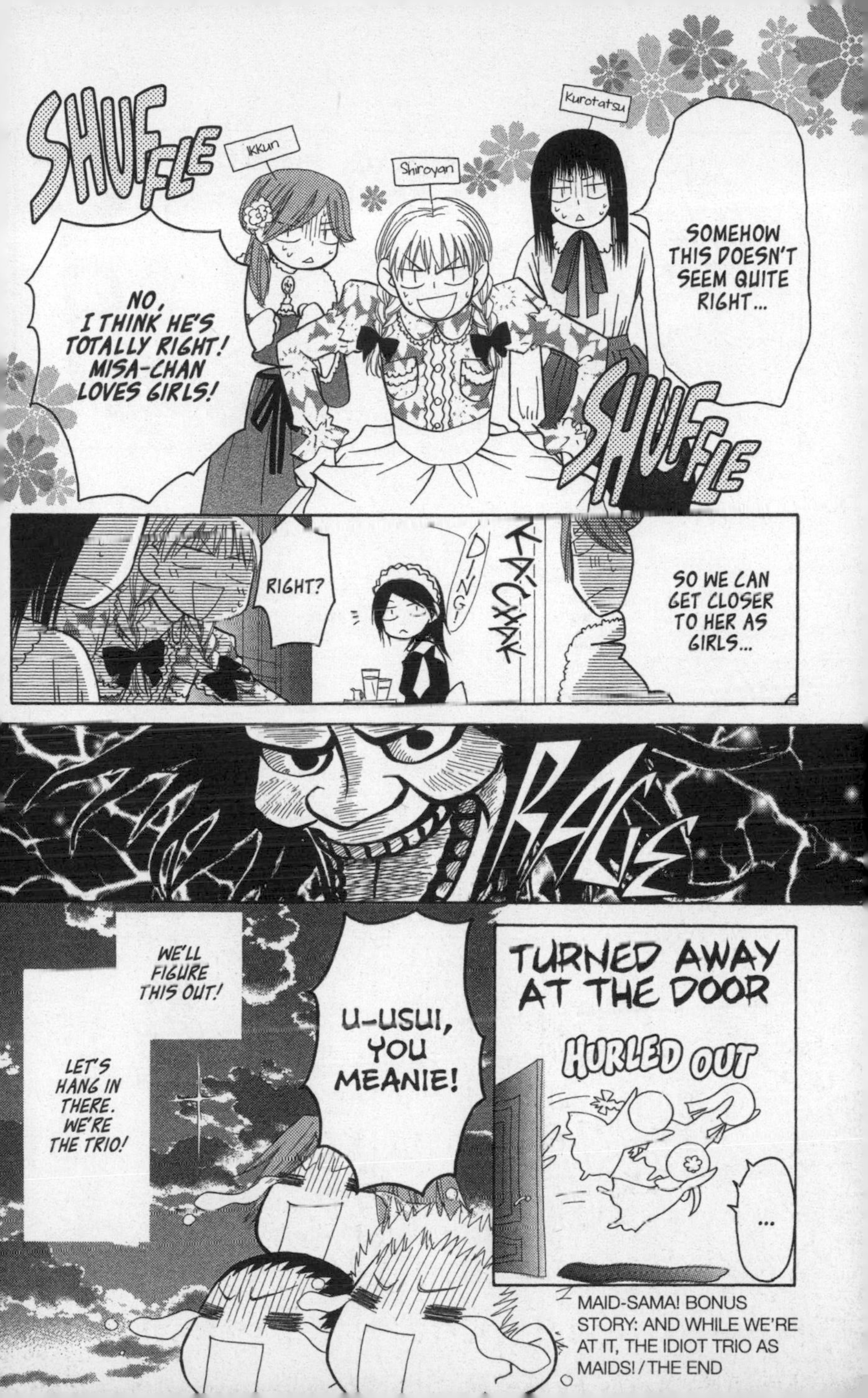
Kurotatsu
Shiroyan
Ikkun
SHUFFLE
SOMEHOW THIS DOESN'T SEEM QUITE RIGHT...
SHUFFLE
NO, I THINK HE'S TOTALLY RIGHT! MISA-CHAN LOVES GIRLS!
SO WE CAN GET CLOSER TO HER AS GIRLS...
KA-CHAK
DING!
RIGHT?
RAGE
TURNED AWAY AT THE DOOR
HURLED OUT
...
U-USUI, YOU MEANIE!
WE'LL FIGURE THIS OUT!
LET'S HANG IN THERE. WE'RE THE TRIO!

MAID-SAMA! BONUS STORY: AND WHILE WE'RE AT IT, THE IDIOT TRIO AS MAIDS! / THE END

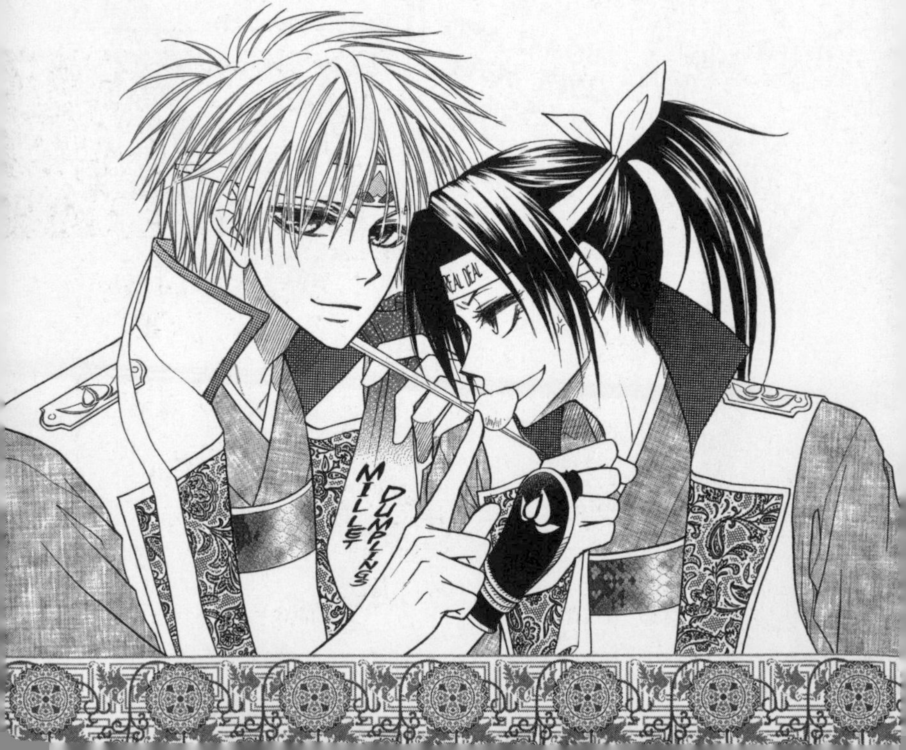
MILLET DUMPLINGS
REAL DEAL

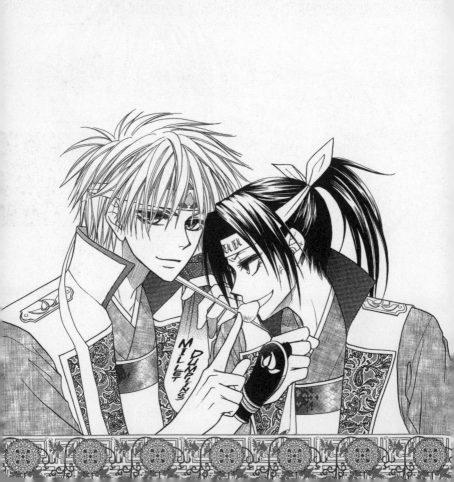

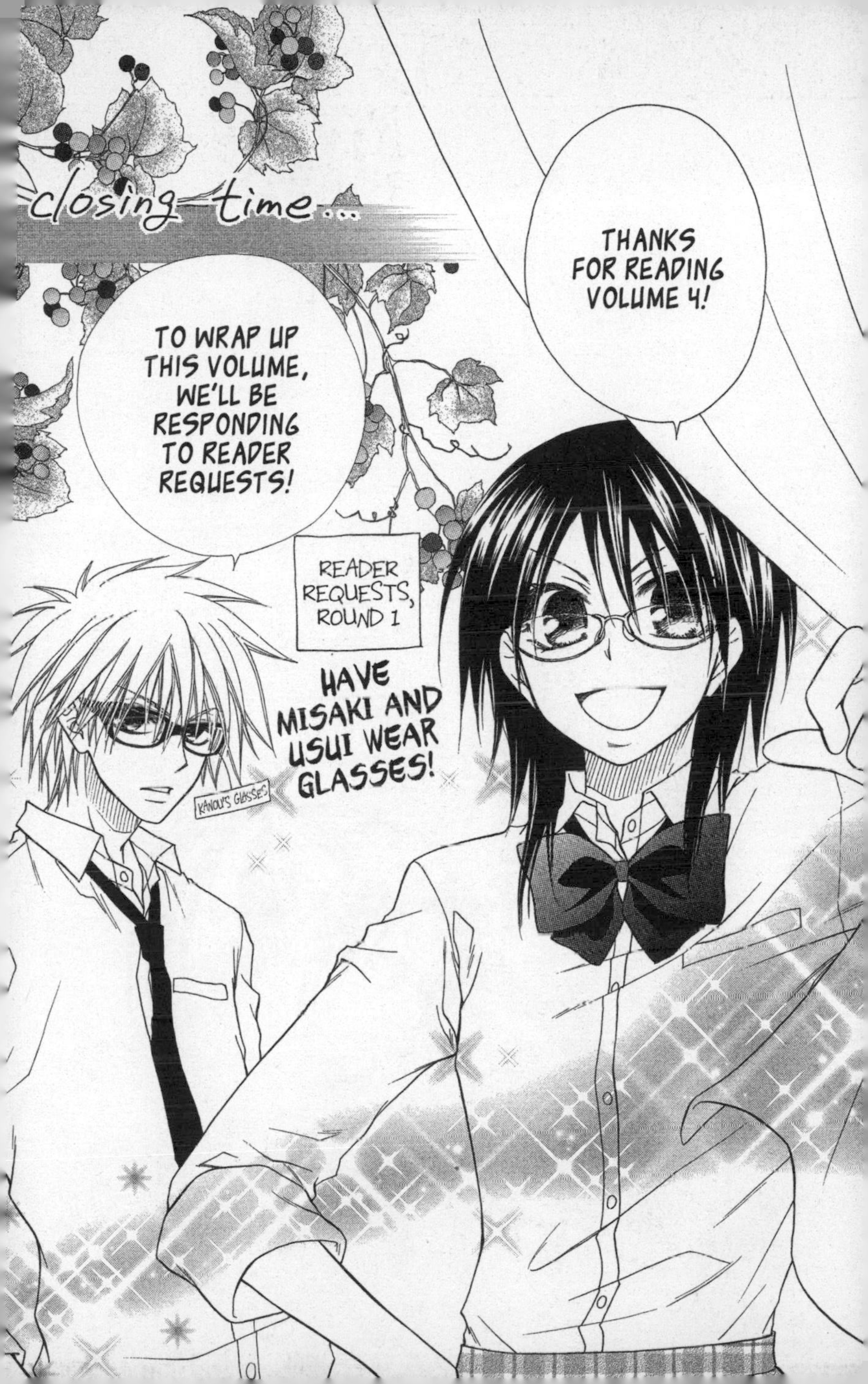
closing time...
THANKS FOR READING VOLUME 4!
TO WRAP UP THIS VOLUME, WE'LL BE RESPONDING TO READER REQUESTS!
READER REQUESTS, ROUND 1
HAVE MISAKI AND USUI WEAR GLASSES!
KANOU'S GLASSES

Requests corner

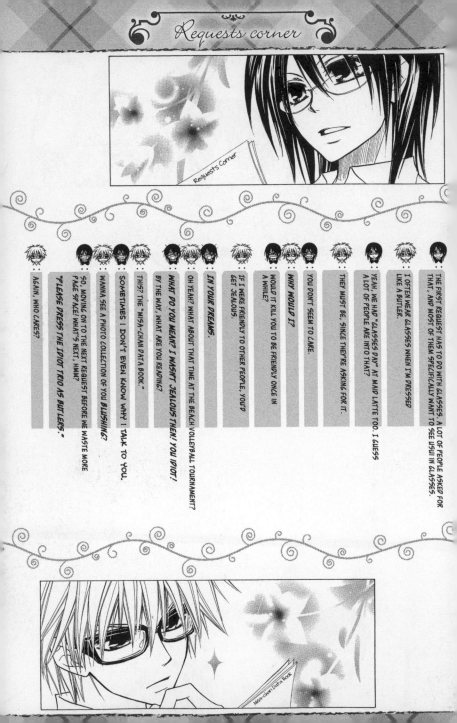

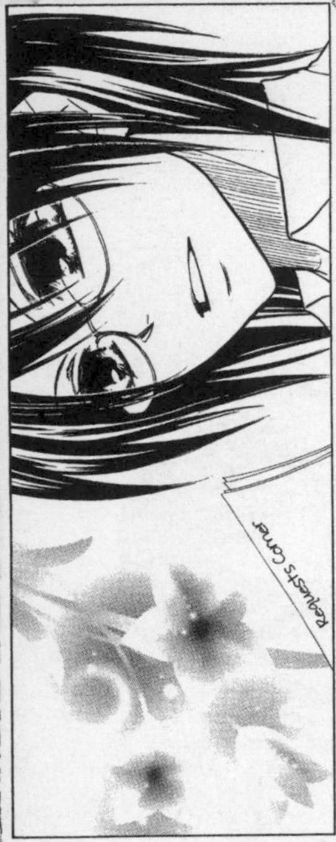
Requests Corner

: THE FIRST REQUEST HAS TO DO WITH GLASSES. A LOT OF PEOPLE ASKED FOR THAT, AND MOST OF THEM SPECIFICALLY WANT TO SEE USUI IN GLASSES.

: I OFTEN WEAR GLASSES WHEN I'M DRESSED LIKE A BUTLER.

: YEAH, WE HAD "GLASSES DAY" AT MAID LATTE TOO. I GUESS A LOT OF PEOPLE ARE INTO THAT?

: THEY MUST BE, SINCE THEY'RE ASKING FOR IT.

: YOU DON'T SEEM TO CARE.

: ***WHY WOULD I?***

: WOULD IT KILL YOU TO BE FRIENDLY ONCE IN A WHILE?

: IF I WERE FRIENDLY TO OTHER PEOPLE, YOU'D GET JEALOUS.

: ***IN YOUR DREAMS.***

: OH YEAH? WHAT ABOUT THAT TIME AT THE BEACH VOLLEYBALL TOURNAMENT?

: ***WHAT DO YOU MEAN? I WASN'T JEALOUS THEN! YOU IDIOT!***

BY THE WAY, WHAT ARE YOU READING?

: THIS? THE "MISA-CHAN DATA BOOK."

: SOMETIMES I DON'T EVEN KNOW WHY I TALK TO YOU.

: WANNA SEE A PHOTO COLLECTION OF YOU ***BLUSHING?***

: SO, MOVING ON TO THE NEXT REQUEST BEFORE WE WASTE MORE PAGE SPACE! WHAT'S NEXT, HMM?

"PLEASE DRESS THE IDIOT TRIO AS BUTLERS."

: AGAIN, WHO CARES?

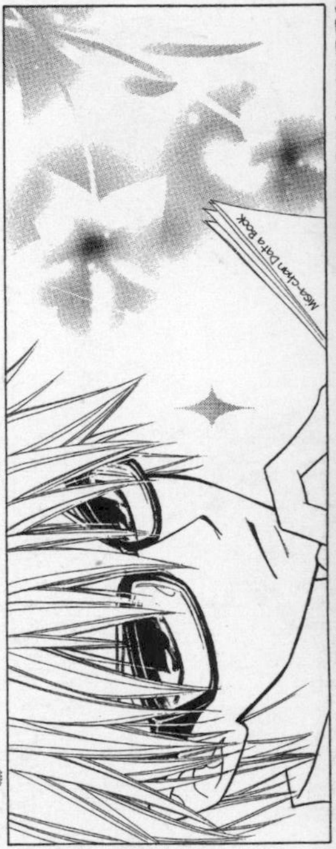
Misa-chan Data Book

Requests corner

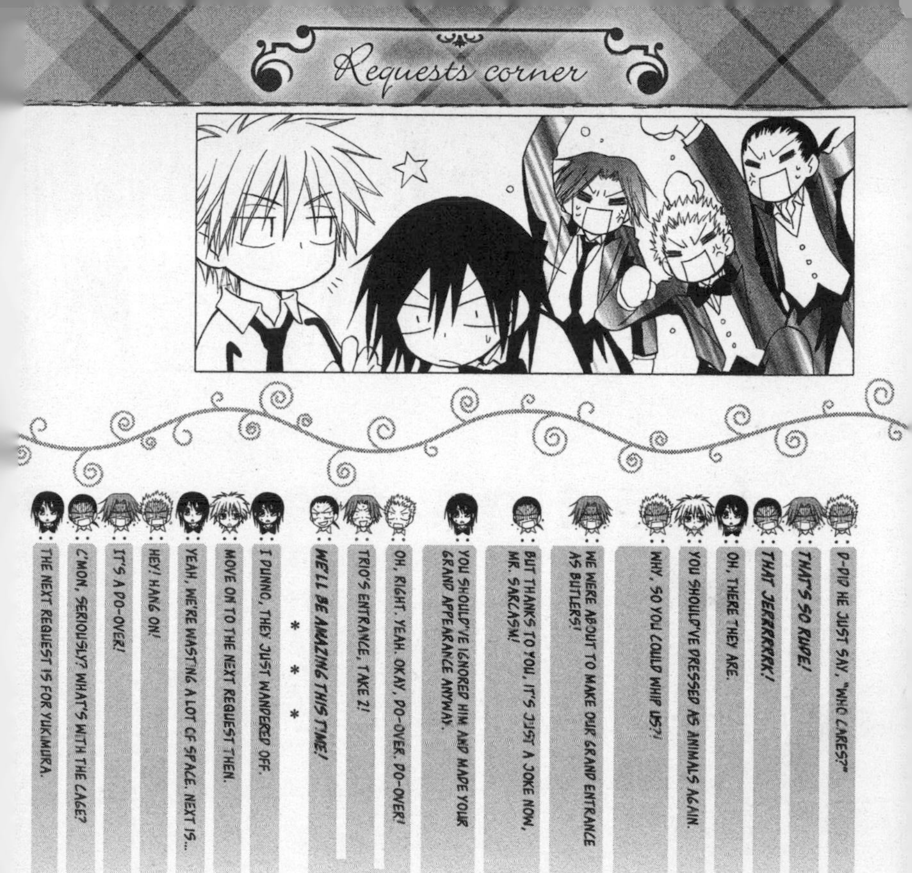

D-DID HE JUST SAY, "WHO CARES?"

THAT'S SO RUDE!

THAT JERRRRRRK!

OH, THERE THEY ARE.

YOU SHOULD'VE DRESSED AS ANIMALS AGAIN.

WHY, SO YOU COULD WHIP US?!

WE WERE ABOUT TO MAKE OUR GRAND ENTRANCE AS BUTLERS!

BUT THANKS TO YOU, IT'S JUST A JOKE NOW, MR. SARCASM!

YOU SHOULD'VE IGNORED HIM AND MADE YOUR GRAND APPEARANCE ANYWAY.

OH, RIGHT. YEAH. OKAY. DO-OVER. DO-OVER!

TRIO'S ENTRANCE, TAKE 2!

WE'LL BE AMAZING THIS TIME!

* * *

I DUNNO, THEY JUST WANDERED OFF.

MOVE ON TO THE NEXT REQUEST THEN.

YEAH, WE'RE WASTING A LOT OF SPACE. NEXT IS...

HEY! HANG ON!

IT'S A DO-OVER!

C'MON, SERIOUSLY? WHAT'S WITH THE CAGE?

THE NEXT REQUEST IS FOR YUKIMURA.

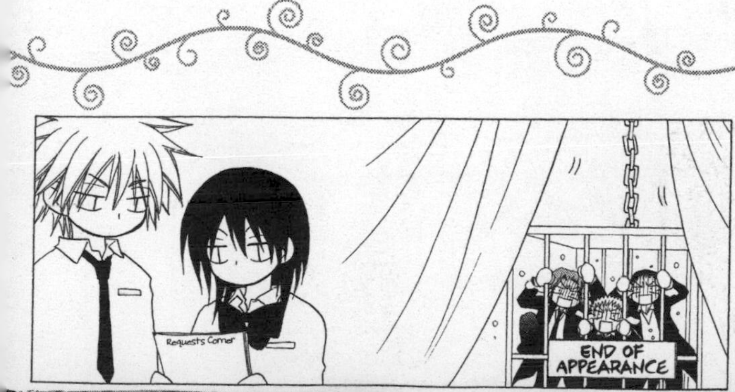
END OF APPEARANCE
Requests Corner

Requests corner

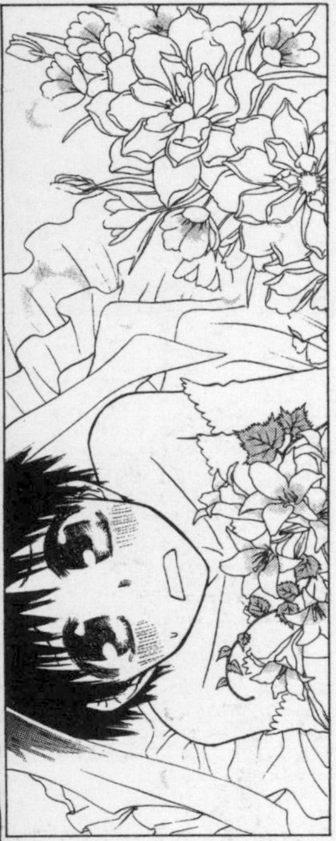

"I WANT YOUR SON AS MY BRIDE."

SURE THING. SEE YOU LATER!

WHAT...?!

WOW, YOU LOOK GREAT IN THAT, YUKIMURA. NO SURPRISE THERE.

W-WAIT A MINUTE. I-I'M A BOY! REMEMBER?

I CAN'T BE A BRIDE! ***THIS IS A WEDDING DRESS!***
SOMETHING'S WRONG!

REALLY?

WHAT DO YOU MEAN BY THAT? P-PRESIDENT! HELP ME!

BUT IT'S A REQUEST FROM OUR READERS...

DON'T WORRY. I'M SURE YOU'LL BE VERY HAPPY.

THAT'S NOT THE POINT.

THIS PROVES THAT PEOPLE LOVE YOU, YUKIMURA.

YEAH, SHOW SOME APPRECIATION.

M-M-ME?

I KNOW YOU'RE FLUSTERED, BUT JUST TRY TO GO WITH IT.

IF YOU WANT, I'LL ESCORT YOU MYSELF.

I WISH YOU ALL THE BEST, YUKIMURA.

P-PRESIDENT...!!

* * *

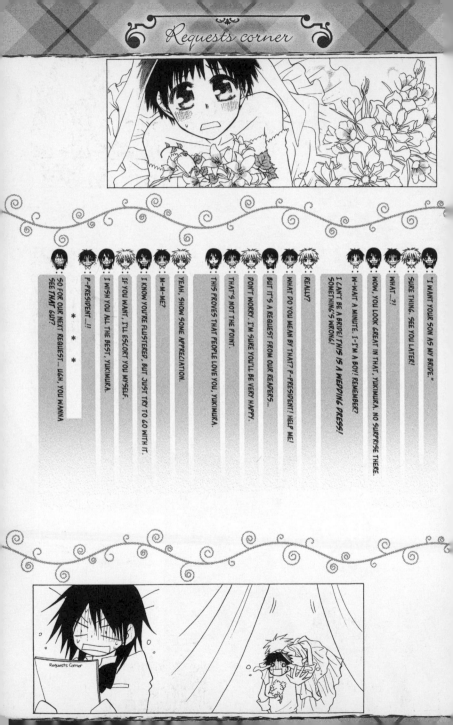

SO FOR OUR NEXT REQUEST... UGH, YOU WANNA SEE ***THAT*** GUY?

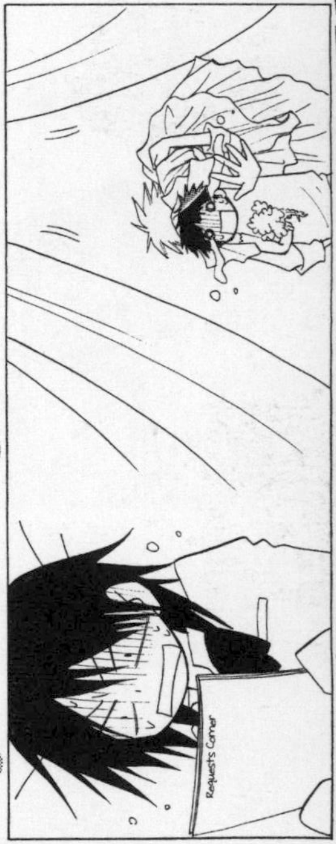
Requests Corner

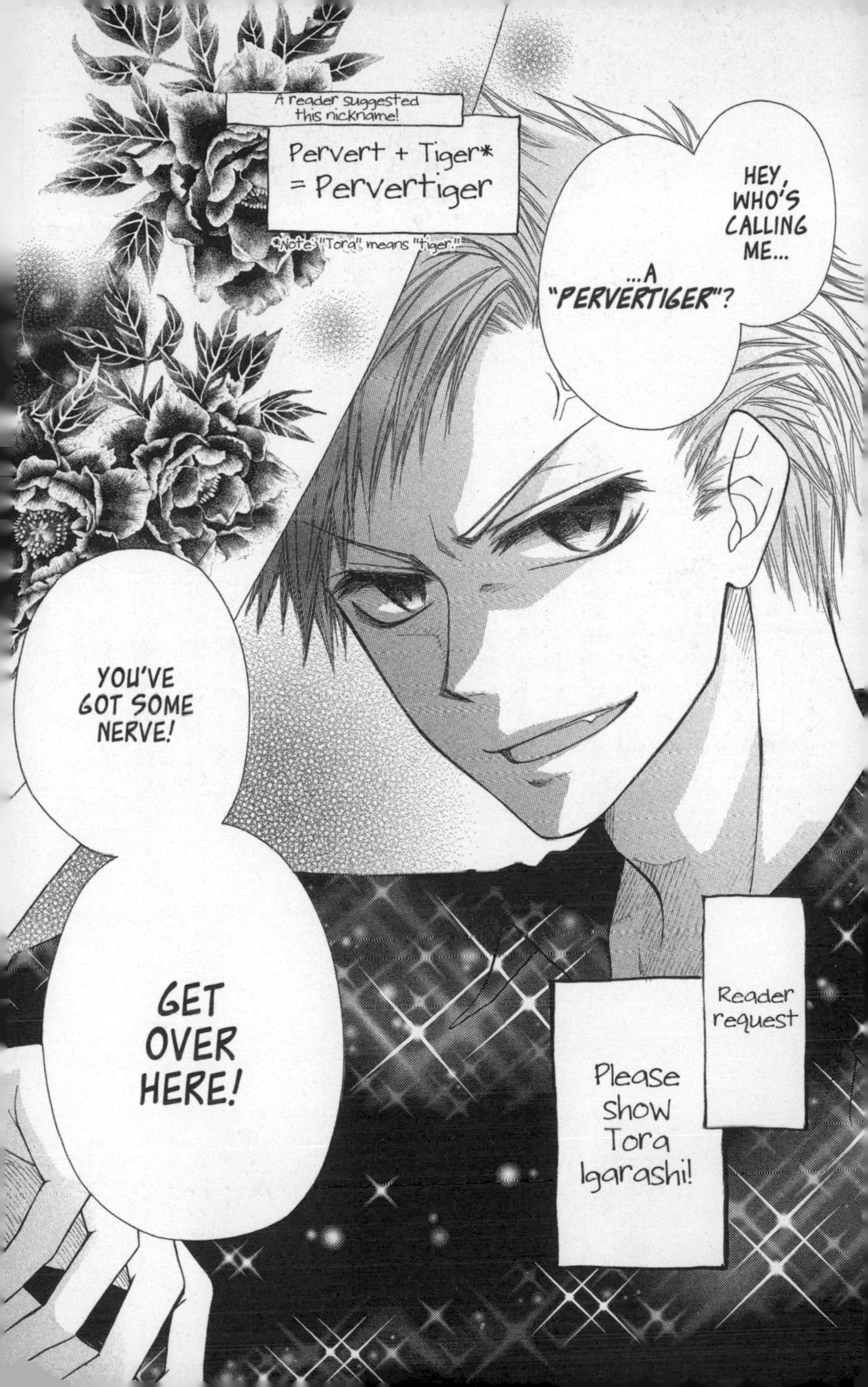
HEY, WHO'S CALLING ME...
...A "PERVERTIGER"?
A reader suggested this nickname!
Pervert + Tiger* = Pervertiger
*Note: "Tora" means "tiger."
YOU'VE GOT SOME NERVE!
GET OVER HERE!
Reader request
Please show Tora Igarashi!

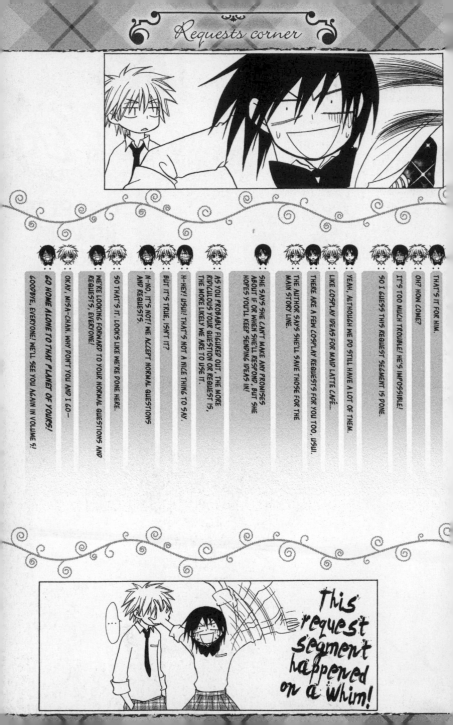

Requests corner

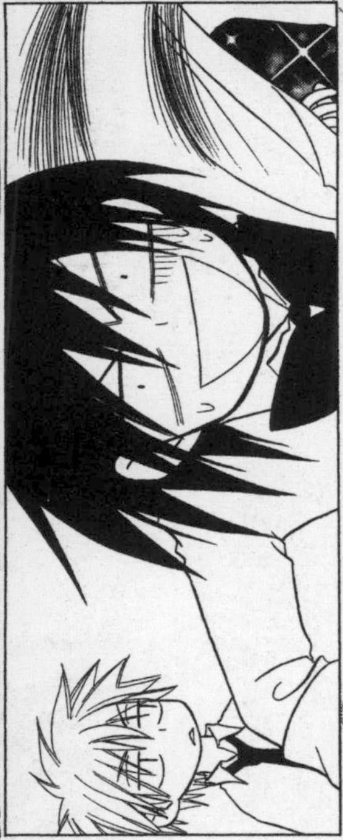

THAT'S IT FOR HIM.

OH? HOW COME?

IT'S TOO MUCH TROUBLE! HE'S IMPOSSIBLE!

SO I GUESS THIS REQUEST SEGMENT IS DONE.

YEAH, ALTHOUGH WE DO STILL HAVE A LOT OF THEM.

LIKE COSPLAY IDEAS FOR MAID LATTE CAFÉ...

THERE ARE A FEW COSPLAY REQUESTS FOR YOU TOO, USUI.

THE AUTHOR SAYS SHE'LL SAVE THOSE FOR THE MAIN STORY LINE.

SHE SAYS SHE CAN'T MAKE ANY PROMISES ABOUT IF OR WHEN SHE'LL RESPOND, BUT SHE HOPES YOU'LL KEEP SENDING IDEAS IN!

AS YOU PROBABLY FIGURED OUT, THE MORE RIDICULOUS YOUR QUESTION OR REQUEST IS, THE MORE LIKELY WE ARE TO USE IT.

H-HEY! USUI! THAT'S NOT A NICE THING TO SAY.

BUT IT'S TRUE, ISN'T IT?

N-NO, IT'S NOT! WE ACCEPT NORMAL QUESTIONS AND REQUESTS.

SO THAT'S IT. LOOKS LIKE WE'RE DONE HERE.

WE'RE LOOKING FORWARD TO YOUR NORMAL QUESTIONS AND REQUESTS, EVERYONE!

OKAY, MISA-CHAN. WHY DON'T YOU AND I GO—

GO HOME ALONE TO THAT PLANET OF YOURS!

GOODBYE, EVERYONE! WE'LL SEE YOU AGAIN IN VOLUME 5!

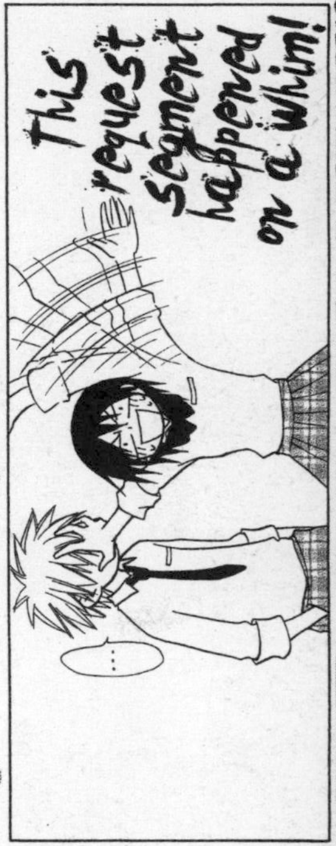
This request segment happened on a whim!
...

DISCOVERY!

*DESPITE HOW HE LOOKS, HE'S SUPPOSED TO BE 15 YEARS OLD.

Look, here are some sample sketches of Soutaro Kanou, the new character! I had such a hard time deciding what he looked like...

His hair was a last-minute decision.

~ Hairstyle Ideas ~

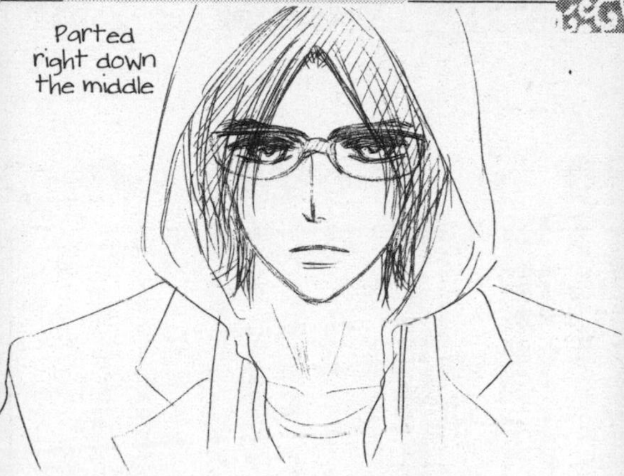

Parted right down the middle

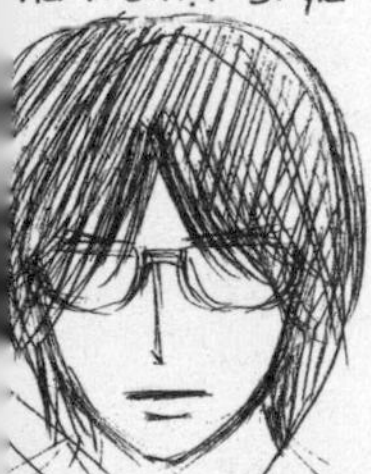

The "what era is he from?!" style

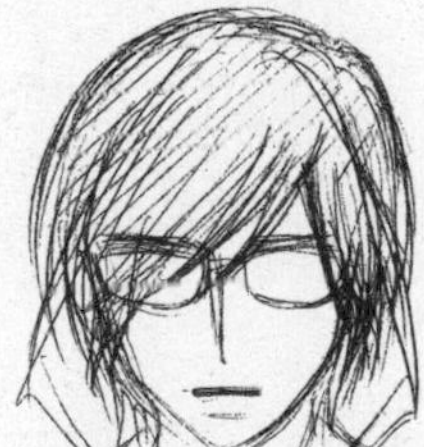

Parted to one side

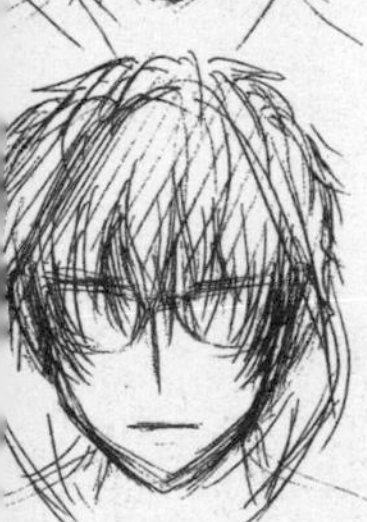

Short

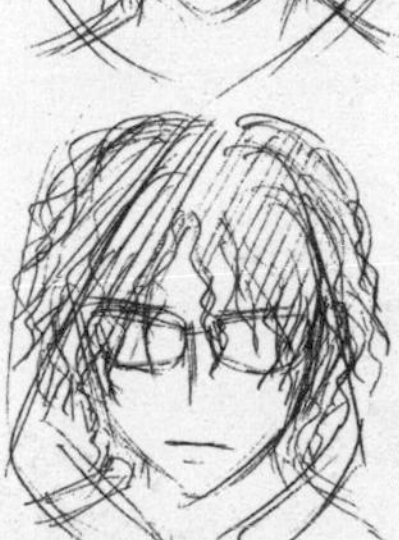

A totally different look

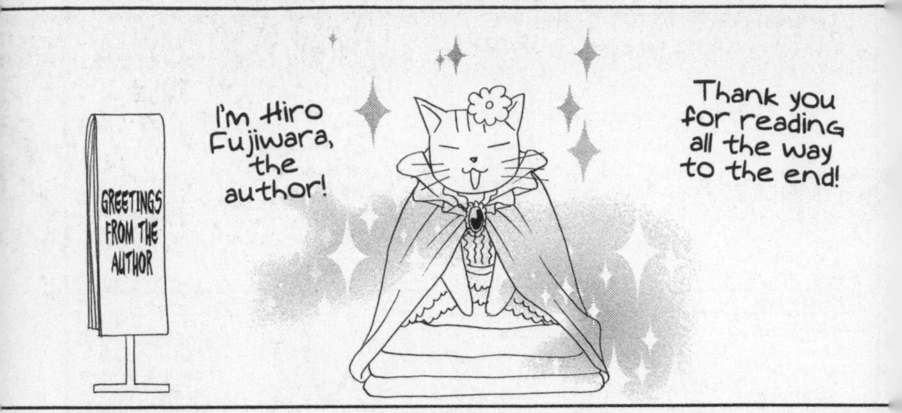
Thank you for reading all the way to the end!
I'm Hiro Fujiwara, the author!
GREETINGS FROM THE AUTHOR

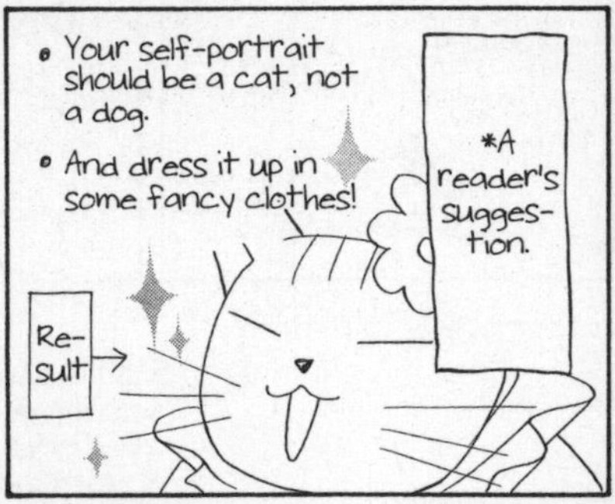
*A reader's sugges-tion.
• Your self-portrait should be a cat, not a dog.
• And dress it up in some fancy clothes!
Re-sult

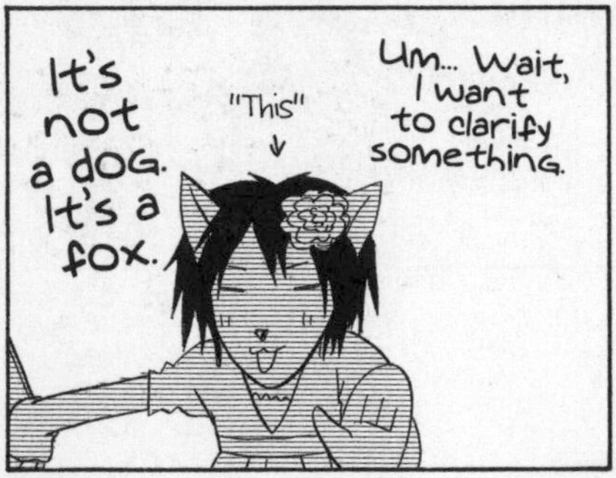
Um... Wait, I want to clarify something.
"This"
It's not a dog. It's a fox.

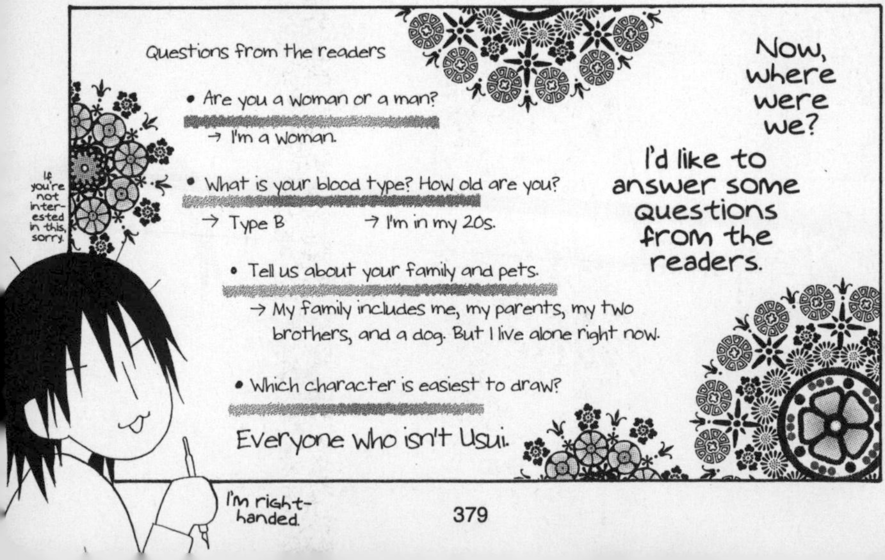
Now, where were we?
I'd like to answer some questions from the readers.
Questions from the readers
• Are you a woman or a man?
→ I'm a woman.
• What is your blood type? How old are you?
→ Type B → I'm in my 20s.
• Tell us about your family and pets.
→ My family includes me, my parents, my two brothers, and a dog. But I live alone right now.
• Which character is easiest to draw?
Everyone who isn't Usui.
If you're not inter-ested in this, sorry.
I'm right-handed.

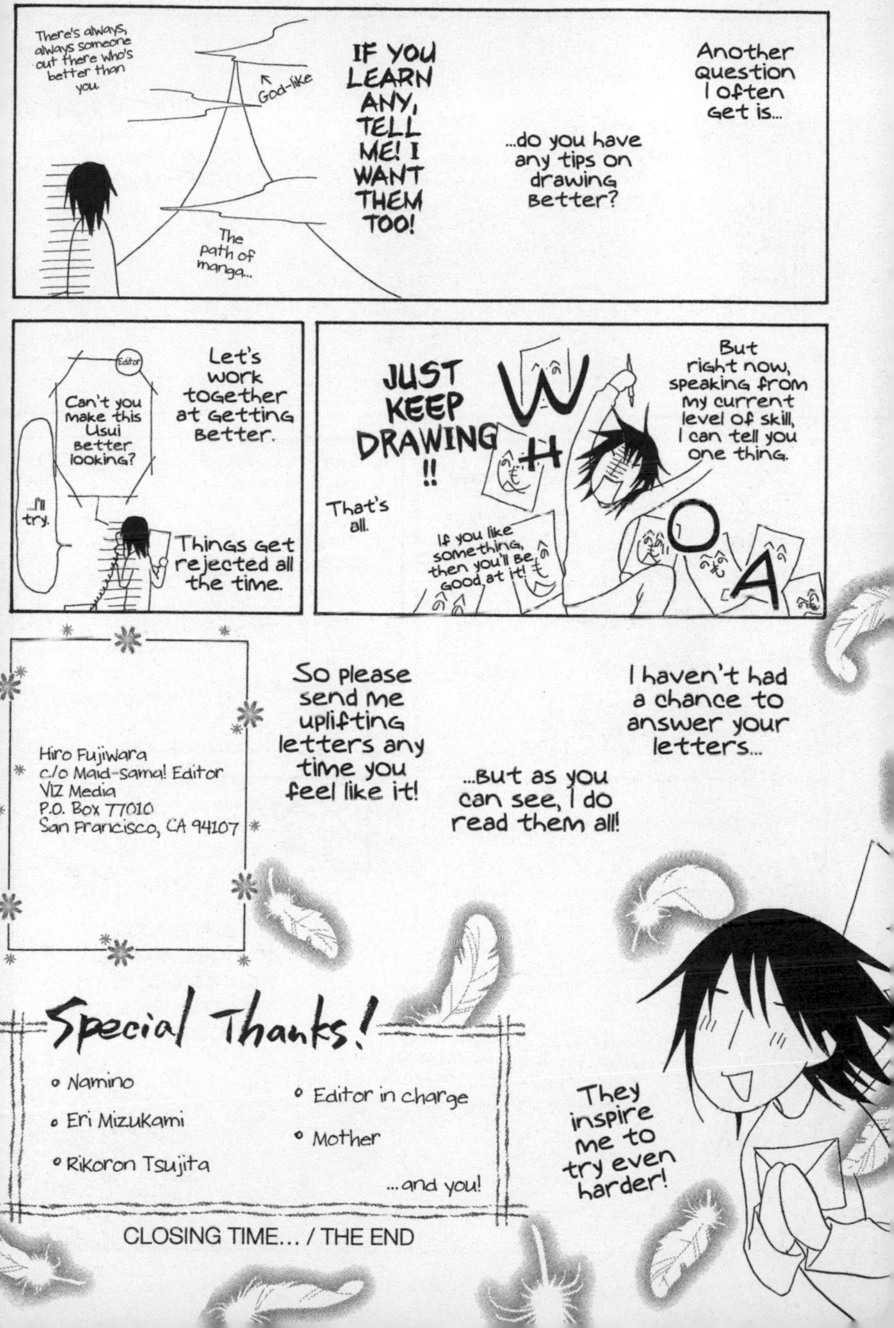
Another question I often get is...
...do you have any tips on drawing better?
IF YOU LEARN ANY, TELL ME! I WANT THEM TOO!
God-like
There's always, always someone out there who's better than you.
The path of manga...
But right now, speaking from my current level of skill, I can tell you one thing.
WHOA
JUST KEEP DRAWING!!
If you like something, then you'll be good at it!
That's all.
Let's work together at getting better.
Editor
Can't you make this Usui better looking?
...I'll try.
Things get rejected all the time.
I haven't had a chance to answer your letters...
...But as you can see, I do read them all!
So please send me uplifting letters any time you feel like it!
Hiro Fujiwara
c/o Maid-sama! Editor
VIZ Media
P.O. Box 77010
San Francisco, CA 94107
They inspire me to try even harder!
Special Thanks!
Namino
Eri Mizukami
Rikoron Tsujita
Editor in charge
Mother
...and you!

CLOSING TIME… / THE END

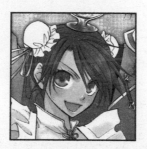

Hiro Fujiwara is from Hyogo Prefecture in Japan
and was born on December 23. *Maid-sama!*
(originally published as *Kaicho wa Maid Sama!*
in Hakusensha's *LaLa* magazine) is her first
long-running manga series and is available in
North America from VIZ Media.

MAID-SAMA!
2-in-1 Edition
Volume 2
A compilation of graphic novel volumes 3–4

STORY AND ART BY
HIRO FUJIWARA

English Adaptation/Ysabet Reinhardt MacFarlane
Translation/JN Productions
Touch-Up Art & Lettering/Annaliese Christman
Design/Yukiko Whitley
Editor/Amy Yu

Kaicho wa Maid Sama! by Hiro Fujiwara
© Hiro Fujiwara 2007
All rights reserved.
First published in Japan in 2007 by HAKUSENSHA, Inc., Tokyo.
English language translation rights arranged with HAKUSENSHA, Inc., Tokyo.

Printed in the U.S.A.

Published by VIZ Media, LLC
P.O. Box 77010
San Francisco, CA 94107

10 9 8 7 6 5 4 3 2 1
First printing, November 2015

www.viz.com

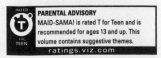
www.shojobeat.com

Surprise!

You may be reading the wrong way!

It's true: In keeping with the original Japanese comic format, this book reads from right to left—so action, sound effects and word balloons are completely reversed. This preserves the orientation of the original artwork—plus, it's fun! Check out the diagram shown here to get the hang of things, and then turn to the other side of the book to get started!

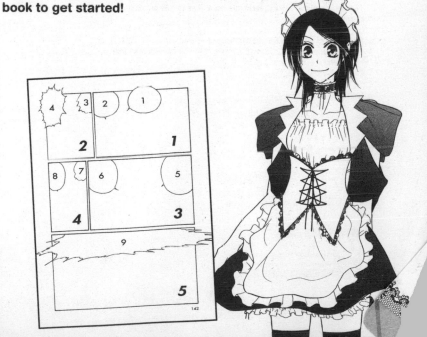